Houseman's Law of Life Assurance

Thirteenth edition

Houseman's Law of Life Assurance

Thirteenth edition

Robert Surridge
Chartered Insurer, Solicitor, Senior Legal Adviser AXA UK

Brian Murphy
Chartered Insurer, Senior Financial Planning Manager AXA UK

Noleen John
Consultant, Norton Rose

Tottel Publishing, Maxwelton House, 41–43 Boltro Road, Haywards Heath, West Sussex, RH16 1BJ

© Tottel Publishing Ltd 2007

A CIP Catalogue record for this book is available from the British Library.

ISBN   978 1 84592 242 9

Typeset by Phoenix Photosetting, Chatham, Kent
Printed and bound in Great Britain by CPI Antony Rowe, Chippenham, Wiltshire

Preface

As ever in producing this edition of Houseman we have tried to cover the areas we think a practitioner needs to be aware of in detail where possible and by signposting where that would be beyond the scope of this work. The book contains a number of new chapters on prudential regulation, with profits, insurance mediation, reinsurance and registered pension schemes. We have also taken the opportunity to reorganise the Financial Services and Markets Act 2000 related materials so that the Financial Promotion and Conduct of Business Rules are in one chapter and the overview of FSMA and authorisation issues are in another.

We find ourselves once again publishing this book at a time of change. From a regulatory perspective the FSA has decided to adopt INS PRU and GEN PRU in place of PRU and this is anticipated in the relevant chapters. It is also consulting on the implementation of MIFID (the successor to the Investment Services Directive) which is expected to result in a major overhaul of the FSA 's conduct of business rules. MIFID must be implemented by next November (ie 2007) and we anticipate that any tax changes will necessitate a new edition in the not too distant future. We await a slowing down in the pace of change!

We would like to thank all of those people whose patience and understanding has enabled this book to be rewritten including in particular AXA and Norton Rose. Robert would like to thank his colleagues in the Legal department of AXA UK for their helpful comments and suggestions and in particular his secretary Natalie King for her assistance on what appeared to be insurmountable IT issues! He would like to dedicate his contribution to his parents Marion and Richard. Brian would like to thank Colin Griffin of AXA for all his work on the sections of the book concerned with the new pensions regime and Brian Fisher of AXA and Tish Hanafan for their assistance with the long-term care section. In addition to a general thanks to her colleagues at Norton Rose, Noleen would like to thank in particular James Stonebridge for updating Chapter 12 and her secretary Coral Mendez who has done much to decipher incomprehensible instructions and changes.

This book is based on our understanding of the laws of England and Wales on 1 March 2007. Any views expressed by the editors are personal views and should not be regarded as views of our respective employers.

Robert Surridge
Brian Murphy
Noleen John
March 2007

Contents

ix

Table of Statutes

Table of Statutory Instruments

Table of Cases

Introduction

The authors feel that before launching into the more detailed areas concerning
the law relating to life assurance a basic overview of the way life companies and
life funds are taxed would be useful to the reader.

General Overview of the Taxation of Life Assurance Companies

Whilst a life company has a single corporation tax assessment, each class of
business it conducts has to be looked at separately as there are different tax rules
for each class. All of the company's income, gains and expenditure have to be
apportioned to each class in order to calculate the overall tax liability.

Unlike most companies which are taxed on their accounting profits life companies are largely taxed on the results in their annual FSA returns.

For a diagrammatic summary of life company taxation, and how it interacts
with the taxation of policyholders, see below.

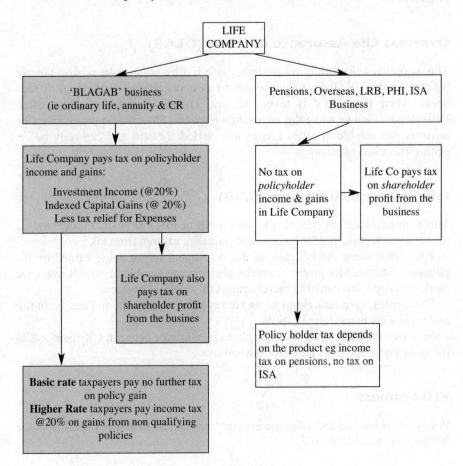

Definitions of each class of business and how they are taxed

Basic Life Assurance & General Annuity Business ('BLAGAB') – includes Capital Redemption Business

This is business that does not fall into any of the other classes below and is (generally) directly written life policies. It is taxed on the so called 'I-E' basis – that is investment income and capital gains less expenses and commission. Tax rate is currently 20%. The first slice of I-E profits equal to the shareholder profits from the business are taxed at an additional 10%.

Where there are excess expenses or capital losses, these are carried forward. Most of the world taxes life insurance only on the shareholder profits the so called 'gross roll up' or GRU system and this may be introduced into the UK.

Pension Business ('PB')

This is UK approved pensions policies (including reinsurance). Policyholder income and gains are exempt from tax. Shareholder profits from the business are taxable at 30%. Losses are carried forward and can only be set against this class of business.

Overseas Life Assurance Business (OLAB)

This is policies (including reinsurance) effected by policyholders who are not residing in the UK. It is subject to strict rules concerning certification of residence when the policy is taken out and changes in residence thereafter. Policyholder income and gains are exempt from tax. Shareholder profits from the business are taxable at 30%. Losses are carried forward and can only be set against this class of business.

Life Reinsurance Business (LRB)

This is reinsurance business that is not OLAB or PB. For business accepted (ie the reinsurer), policyholder income and gains are exempt from tax.

The cedant company is taxed on the investment return being earned by the reinsurer. Shareholder profits from the business are taxable at 30%. Losses are carried forward and can only be set against this class of business.

These rules were brought in as an anti avoidance measure and can be unfair and capricious in their application.

Note that the LRB rules do not apply to reinsurance between UK members of the same tax group or to pure risk business.

PHI business

Policyholder income and gains are exempt from tax. Shareholder profits from the business are taxable at 30%.

ISA business

Policyholder income and gains are exempt from tax. Until 5 April 2004, the 10% tax credits on UK dividends could be recovered. Shareholder profits from the business are taxable at 30%. Losses are carried forward and can only be set against this class of business.

TAXATION OF POLICYHOLDER FUNDS

Taxation of Life Funds

Life Funds (ie not pension business) are taxed on their investment income and gains as follows:

Income

Dividends from UK companies ('franked investment income') – no further tax on 'net' dividend received.

All other investment income (and sundry income such as underwriting commission) – 20%. Foreign tax suffered at source on overseas dividends can generally be offset against the UK tax liability on them.

Gains

Realised Capital Gains on equities and equity derivatives – 20% of the RPI indexed gain.

Realised *and Unrealised* gains on unit trusts/OIEC holdings – 20% but spread over seven years.

Realised *and Unrealised* gains on fixed interest securities and their derivatives – 20%.

The above rates are charged in the unit price. However, to preserve equity amongst policyholders, companies also make a deduction for tax on *unrealised* capital gains although this is at a rate lower than the full 20% to allow for the fact that the tax is not payable to HMRC until the investments are sold.

The life company gets tax relief on expenses and commission relating to Life Funds. Where these expenses relate to the acquisition of new business (as opposed to the administration of existing business), the tax relief is spread over seven years. For unit-linked business, the benefit of this tax relief is usually passed on through a lower management charge.

Taxation of Pension Business Funds

All investment income and gains belonging to policyholders are free of UK tax but it is not possible to reclaim the notional 10% tax credits arising from UK dividend income. Any foreign tax suffered at source on overseas dividends is deducted from the policyholder funds.

Shareholder profits on pension business are taxable.

CHAPTER 1

The contract of life assurance

SUMMARY

SECTION I   NATURE OF THE CONTRACT

1.1   A contract has been defined by Anson as 'an agreement enforceable at law made between two or more persons by which rights are acquired by one or more to certain acts or forbearance on the part of the other or others'. *Chitty* defines a contract as 'a promise or set of promises which the law will enforce'.

Contracts of insurance, like other contracts, satisfy these criteria but a more descriptive definition is required in order to more accurately describe the particular nature of a life assurance contract. The precise concept of an insurance contract itself has been difficult to ascertain as there is no statutory definition. An attempt at a definition of life assurance contracts was made in *Prudential Insurance Company v Inland Revenue Commissioners*[1] by Channel J. The funda-

---

1   [1904] 2 KB 658.

mental requirement for a contract of insurance is the payment of money (or another benefit) on the happening of an uncertain event. In addition, to be a life assurance contract the contingency insured against must relate to death or survival. Further examination of what constituted a life assurance contract occurred in *Fuji Finance Inc v Aetna Insurance Co*[1] where the fact that the amount payable on death was the same as that payable on surrender did not prevent the contract being one of life assurance. See **1.69** et seq for further consideration of this case.

1.2 A practical definition might be that a life assurance contract is one whereby one party (the insurer) undertakes for a consideration (the premium) to pay money (the sum assured) to or for the benefit of the other party (the assured) upon the happening of a specified event, where the object of the assured is to provide a sum for himself or others at some future date, or for others in the event of his death[2].

This is probably not comprehensive today because of the variety and complexity of products which are available. For example, it probably does not contemplate the fact that many life assurance policies are essentially wholly designed for investment purposes. It should, however, suffice as a working statement. The Regulated Activities Order[3] defines what constitutes 'long-term business'. 'Long-term business' is wider than just 'life assurance'. It includes pension fund management and capital redemption policies, even though there is no sum assured or amount payable on the death of the assured. In order to carry on these activities the requisite permission is required and very few (and in the case of capital redemption business it is believed no) UK authorised companies have this permission. (See further Chapter 3).

Other definitions relating to life assurance are set out in various statutes. For example, section 7 of the Policies of Assurance Act 1867 defines a 'policy of assurance' as 'any instrument by which the payment of moneys by or out of the funds of an assurance company on the happening of any contingency depending on the duration of human life is assured or secured'. Section 2 of the Life Assurance Companies (Payment into Court) Act 1896 defines 'life policy' as including 'any policy not foreign to the business of life assurance'. The FSA has avoided a definition of an insurance contract (although it has expressed its view on some of the borderline issues for non-life business (eg warranty cover)) but its rules do use the term 'life policy'. However, the definition in of limited usefulness because of the way the FSA distinguishes between investment and non-investment (eg protection) contracts. The result is that the definition in the FSA Handbook of a life policy excludes the most obvious and straightforward life

1 [1997] Ch 173.
2 See the definition in *Prudential Insurance Co v IRC* [1904] 2 KB 658 at 663–664, per Channel J, which was cited by Templeman J in *Dept of Trade and Industry v St Christopher Motorists Association Ltd* [1974] 1 All ER 395, although criticised by Buckley LJ in *Gould v Curtis* [1913] 3 KB 84 because of its failure to cover a life policy containing endowment provisions. See also *Medical Defence Union v Dept of Trade* [1980] Ch 82 in which it was held that one of the necessary elements of a contract of insurance is that the assured becomes entitled to money or its equivalent on the occurrence of some event.
3 SI 2001/544, Sch I, Part II.

assurance policies (ie pure protection). The definition is noteable because it includes personal pension schemes where the contribution is paid to a life office. For a UK authorised life company, any pension scheme it establishes and operates must[1] be incorporated into a life assurance contract, which must itself contain some element of insurance (eg provision of an annuity or benefits payable on death).

It is also important to note that life assurance contracts, unlike most other forms of insurance, are not essentially contracts of indemnity which means that unless the contract provides otherwise the amount payable is not limited to a loss suffered or incurred.

Although life assurance contracts have certain incidents peculiar to themselves, they are in most respects subject to the principles which apply to contracts generally. It is appropriate, therefore, to consider some general principles of the law of contract together with special reference to matters relating to life policies.

SECTION 2   FORMATION OF THE CONTRACT

A   Formation

1.3   There are three main elements in the formation of a valid contract. First, there must be an intention to contract. Second, there should be agreement, achieved through an offer and acceptance of mutually understood terms. Third, unless the contract is made in the form of a deed (for differing ways of execution see Section 6), there must be consideration.

In addition, in the formation of a contract, the parties must possess the capacity to enter into the contract and the object must not be illegal.

These various elements will now be considered.

I   Intention

1.4   There is no contract unless the parties intend to be bound. Intention to be bound, or the lack of it, may be inferred from the circumstances or the subject matter. Generally, in domestic or social situations, there would need to be evidence of clear intention to be bound before the courts would hold that a contract had been formed[2]. If, for example, two friends agree to dine together they would not normally regard such an agreement as legally binding. There is no contract between them.

On the other hand, in commercial agreements the parties will be presumed to have intended to enter into a contract. This presumption may, however, be rebutted and, indeed, the parties to an agreement may go further and expressly

---

1   See PRU 7.16.3 (INSPRU 1.5.13).
2   *Balfour v Balfour* [1919] 2 KB 571. However, the later cases of *Merritt v Merritt* [1970] 1 WLR 1211 and *Pettitt v Pettitt* [1970] AC 777 indicated possible limits to this doctrine.

state that they do not intend the agreement to be legally binding[1]. This is often encountered in respect of what are termed 'comfort letters' or in pre-contractual negotiations in what are sometimes referred to as 'heads of agreement'. There is generally little doubt in the business of life assurance whether or not the parties have intended to contract.

2 Offer and acceptance

1.5 An offer must be something more than a mere declaration of intention. It must consist of a definite promise to be bound provided that certain specified terms are accepted. The offeror must complete his part in the formation of the contract by declaring his willingness to undertake an obligation upon certain conditions. The offer may be expressed orally or in writing or by conduct.

An offer need not be made only to one person but may be made to the public at large.

Carlill v Carbolic Smoke Ball Co[2]

The defendants were the proprietors of a medical preparation called 'The Carbolic Smoke Ball' and they issued an advertisement offering to pay £100 to any person who succumbed to influenza after having used one of their smoke balls in accordance with certain directions. The advertisement stated that they had deposited a sum of £1,000 with their banks 'to show their sincerity'. The plaintiff, relying on the advertisement, bought and used the smoke ball as directed but caught influenza. She sued for the £100. It was held that there was a binding contract. It was possible for an offer to be made 'to all the world' with the contract being made with that limited portion of the public who come forward and accept the offer. In addition, the deposit of £1000 indicated an intention to be bound.

Carlill was followed in *Bowerman v Association of British Travel Agents Ltd*[3] where a package holiday was cancelled due to the insolvency of the tour operator, who was a member of the defendant association (ABTA). A notice in the tour operator's premises included the statement that in the event of the financial failure of an ABTA member before the beginning of the holiday, 'ABTA arranges for you to be reimbursed the money you have paid for your holiday'. A majority in the Court of Appeal held that these words constituted an offer as they would reasonably be regarded as such and so capable of being accepted by doing business with an ABTA member.

A distinction may be drawn between an offer and an 'invitation to treat'. The latter is an attempt to induce offers and is not normally an offer itself. For example, advertisements by way of circulars or catalogues of goods for sale would be regarded as merely invitations for someone to make an offer and not, as in the *Carlill* case, an offer to be accepted simply by replying.

1 *Rose & Frank Co v J R Crompton & Bros Ltd* [1925] AC 445.
2 [1893] 1 QB 256.
3 [1995] New LJ 1815.

This distinction could be relevant to life assurance business, as the use by an office of non-medical proposal or application forms would not, without more, it is contended, be regarded as an offer 'to all the world' but an invitation to treat, inducing proposers to make an offer. Therefore, whilst there might be commercial pressures on an office to accept such a 'simplified' proposal, the life office may still decline the offer. However, if the life office advertises (as is often the case for contracts sold by direct marketing) guaranteed acceptance if certain conditions are satisfied, then this would probably constitute an offer and not an invitation to treat. This is even more likely where the life office has personalised the 'offer'. In such circumstances, provided the prospective policyholder complies with the terms of the advert, he is entitled to accept the offer unless it is withdrawn, and that fact is communicated to him before acceptance. Acceptance in such cases would normally be by means of completion (and return) of an application form included in or with the advert which includes either a direct debit instruction or a promise to pay the premiums.

However, to avoid doubt, the life office should make clear its intention when wording proposal forms.

1.6   For an acceptance to be effective in law the parties must have agreed upon all the material terms of the contract they wish to make. It is not a requirement that absolutely every term be agreed upon. Sometimes the law may be able to imply a term but if this is not the case then a contract will not have arisen. There must be a 'consensus ad idem' (agreement as to the same thing) as to these terms (ie there must be either an express agreement or a reasonable inference from the circumstances that the parties had tacitly agreed). A qualified acceptance operates as a rejection of the offer, though it may itself constitute a counter-offer which the original offeror may then accept or reject[1].

Even if the offer is acceptable to the offeree, agreement between the parties is not complete until acceptance of the offer has been communicated to the offeror. The offer may be withdrawn at any time before acceptance is communicated. Withdrawal of the acceptance must reach the offeror before acceptance (normally when acceptance is communicated to the offeror but see 'postal rule' mentioned at **1.9**). The method of communication, unless prescribed in the offer, will depend upon the nature of the offer and the circumstances in which it is made[2]. Generally speaking, the prescribed method of acceptance must be adhered to[3] and the offeror is entitled to specify by what method the offeree is to signify and communicate acceptance.

(a)   Contractual process in establishing a life assurance policy

1.7   Clearly, the detail will differ between offices but the usual practice in the formation of a contract of life assurance is for the proposer to make an offer

1   *Lark v Outhwaite* [1991] 2 Lloyd's Rep 132, which found that a contract of insurance was created where there had been an unqualified acceptance by one party of an offer made by the other.
2   See *Entores Ltd v Miles Far East Corp* [1955] 2 QB 327 for a useful discussion on forms of communication.
3   *Beta Computers (Europe) v Adobe Systems Europe* [1996] SLT 604.

by completing a printed proposal (or application) form which will set out the amount of benefits required and the premium payable. The proposal form would usually only constitute an invitation to treat. It is advisable to state in the proposal form that the applicant is applying for a contract on the life office's standard terms and conditions. The life office will consider the proposal and, where relevant any medical reports and information. If the office is then prepared to issue a policy, it may send a letter, sometimes referred to as a 'letter of acceptance'. Whether this constitutes acceptance normally depends on whether it introduces any new terms or requirements (eg it could include a term that acceptance is dependent on payment of the first premium in which case the act of payment would constitute acceptance). As regular premiums are often now paid by direct debit it is not necessarily the case that acceptance would be deferred in this way.

If the letter from the life office states that it will grant a policy not on its standard terms but subject to additional requirements (eg additional premium or exclusion from cover) then the letter will in fact in most cases be a counter-offer, and the proposer would accept the counter-offer by complying with the conditions and, if so stated, by making payment of the first premium.

> *Canning v Farquhar*[1]
>
> C applied for life assurance on the usual type of proposal form. The office notified him that his proposal had been accepted at a stated premium, but that no insurance would take effect until the first premium was paid. Before he paid the premium C fell over a cliff and was seriously injured. The premium was then tendered, but refused and then C died. It was held by the Court of Appeal that the life office was not liable because (a) the proposal and the notification of 'acceptance' were not intended by the parties to constitute a binding contract, but were merely part of the preliminary negotiations; and (b) there would have been no binding contract, since the 'acceptance' contained a new term not previously mentioned (namely, the amount of the premiums) and therefore was in reality a counter-offer which could not be considered as continuing after the risk had changed, since the statements made in the proposal as to good health were no longer true.

The modern practice, particularly in relation to unit-linked investment contracts, is for acceptance to take place by issue of the policy (with or without a letter indicating the date risk is assumed by the life office). If there is no such letter the relevant details will be recorded in a schedule to the policy issued. It is important that this is clear for unit-linked contracts as the policy will specify the date premium received is allocated to units (ie notionally used to buy units in an underlying fund).

1.8 The negotiations which precede the issue of a life policy will vary greatly, depending upon the circumstances of each case, and can become quite protracted. Because of this, it is sometimes difficult to determine the precise point at which agreement is complete and a binding contract formed.

The offer and acceptance require a level of mutual agreement by the parties. However, the courts will not require the parties to reach separate agreement on

---

1   (1886) 16 QBD 727.

all the terms, provided there is agreement on essential ones such as the type of policy, assured and life assured, period of cover, sum assured, premium and mode of payment. Where there is no specific agreement on terms, the law may be able to imply a term into the contract. It will also normally be assumed that the proposer impliedly offers to contract on the life office's usual terms and conditions[1] and in many cases the proposal form contains express reference to this effect.

The case of *Rust v Abbey Life Assurance Co Ltd* held that the mere issuing of the policy constituted acceptance as the proposal stated that the policy issued was to be on the insurer's standard terms and conditions. The Statement of Long-Term Insurance Practice recommends[2] (and the FSA's conduct of business rules effectively require) that 'the proposal form (or a supporting document) should include a statement that a copy of the completed proposal form or of the completed proposal conditions is available on request'.

1.9   Mere communication of acceptance will not result in a binding contract unless it corresponds with the offer. This principle is important in cases where the proposer and the life office are at cross-purposes. In such cases there is no contract and the proposer may recover any premiums paid in the mistaken belief that a contract of insurance had been formed[3]. But where one party contends that they are not in agreement with the other, they may be prevented from arguing that they never meant to accept the terms put forward by the other party if, objectively, their conduct is that of one who accepts the terms offered to them and certain other conditions are satisfied. Where it is stipulated that the offer from the life office must be accepted by payment of the first premium, then acceptance is by the act of payment and no further communication to the life office is required in order to create a binding contract.

The moment of completion of a contract and the moment of commencement of the risk (which are not necessarily the same) are matters of intention to be ascertained from the documents used or from the conduct of the parties or from both. So, for example, the parties could have agreed a condition precedent that risk will not attack until payment of the first premium.

An offer may be withdrawn at any time before acceptance. It cannot be withdrawn after acceptance. Withdrawal does not take effect until notice of it reaches the offeree or his agent[4].

Note should be made of the postal rules, namely that a postal acceptance takes effect when the letter of acceptance is posted. Therefore, a postal acceptance prevails over a withdrawal of the offer which was posted before the acceptance but which has not yet reached the offeree when the acceptance was posted[5].

1   *General Accident Insurance Corp v Cronk* (1901) 17 TLR 233.
2   A statement of practice originally agreed between the Life Officers' Association, the Association of Scottish Life Offices and the Department of Trade for the conduct of life assurance business.
3   *Johnston v Prudential Assurance Co* [1946] IAC Rep 59, and *Batty v Pearl Assurance Co Ltd* [1937] IAC Rep 12.
4   *Byrne & Co v Leon Van Tienhoven & Co* (1880) 5 CPD 344.
5   *Adams v Lindsell* (1818) 1B & Ald 681.

The parties may, pending completion of the contract, enter into an interim contract in the form of a 'cover note'. Although this practice is quite common in the case of other forms of insurance, it is not so common amongst life offices. Many life offices do enter into interim cover arrangements, pending consideration of the proposal. Sometimes this is limited to fatal accident cover and is usually subject to relatively modest monetary limits. Very often the cover will be provided free of charge. If the office is not prepared to accept the proposal at ordinary rates, the interim contract comes to an end.

Rights to cancel life policies may arise for specified periods after they have been entered into under the cancellation rules in the FSA's Conduct of Business Sourcebooks[1].

3   Consideration

1.10   A promise not made by deed is not enforceable unless it is made for valuable consideration, which has been defined[2] as consisting:

> 'either in some right, interest, profit or benefit accruing to the one party or in some forbearance, detriment, loss or responsibility given, suffered or undertaken by the other'.

The promise it is sought to enforce must have been made in return for the doing, or forbearing from doing, something; or giving something (including a promise) of some value in the eyes of the law. Sir Frederick Pollock summarised the position in *Dunlop Pneumatic Tyre Co Ltd v Selfridge & Co Ltd*[3]:

> 'An act or forbearance of one party, or the promise thereof, is the price for which the promise of the other is bought, and the promise thus given for value is enforceable.'

In many modern contracts a bargain is struck by the exchange of promises. Thus, A orders goods on credit from B. From the moment of agreement both are bound, for where there are mutual promises the consideration for the promise by one party may consist of the promise of the other party.

In the case of life assurance policies the consideration which passes from the policyholder will be the premium(s) he pays, whilst the consideration given by the life office is the promise to pay the benefit stated in the policy on the happening of the event insured against.

Although consideration must be of some value, generally speaking the law is not concerned as to its adequacy[4]; this is a matter to be decided on by the parties themselves as part of the bargain. This principle is recognised and broadly pre-

---

1   See further Chapter 5.
2   *Currie v Misa* (1895) LR 10 Exch 153.
3   [1915] AC 847.
4   *Thomas v Thomas* (1842) 2 QB 851. It is also excluded from the scope of the Unfair Contract Terms Directive 93/13/EEC, see further Section 4.

served in the Unfair Terms in Consumer Contracts Regulations 1999[1]. The consideration must relate to the bargain, so that a promise by one party to do something which he is already under a general obligation, or an obligation to the other party, to do, is no consideration for a promise by the other party.

1.11   The general position is that a person claiming to enforce a contract must show that *he* has made some promise in consideration of the defendant's promise, or that some benefit or advantage has accrued to the other party *from him*, or that *he* has done, forborne or suffered something which was the consideration for the other's promise. 'Consideration must move from the promisee'[2], and an action to enforce a contract must be brought by the person from whom the consideration moved, and not a third party. This is subject to the possible effects of the Contracts (Rights of Third Parties) Act 1999. If its provisions have not been excluded a third party is not prevented from enforcing a term by the fact that no consideration has moved from him. The third party's right to enforce the promise has been described as a quasi exception to the rule that consideration must move from the promisor. If the Act is excluded, then if A contracts with B to pay money to C, C cannot sue on the promise, because he had not done or suffered anything in return for A's promise. In the case of *Price v Easton*, A was promised by the defendant that if A did certain work for him he would pay a sum of money to the plaintiff. A did the work but the defendant did not pay. The court held that the plaintiff could not sue. The contract between A and B is however enforceable, and A may sue B for damages. The damages will probably be nominal in most cases, however, and so A may prefer to bring an action for specific performance for the defendant to fulfil his contractual obligations to pay B[3].

There has been much discussion[4] about whether the inability of the third party to sue, in the circumstances outlined above, rests on the principle that consideration must move from the promisee or on the doctrine of privity of contract – which holds that only a party to a contract may bring an action on it (subject to the Contracts (Rights of Third Parties) Act 1999). The distinction, drawn by Lord Haldane in the *Dunlop* case, has been challenged by some learned authors as being no more than two sides of the same principle; and accepted by others as a true and important difference. In practice, the English courts have had no difficulty in reaching conclusions on the facts before them and it is likely that the debate is no more than academic.

In some cases the contract will create a trust in favour of C, in which case C can enforce the trust in equity, although not the contract as such.

4   Capacity to contract

1.12   The capacity of certain classes of persons to bind themselves by contract is restricted by law.

1   SI 1999/2083, reg 6(2)(b).
2   *Price v Easton* (1833) 4 B & Ad 433; *Tweddle v Atkinson* (1861) 1 B & S 393.
3   *Beswick v Beswick* [1968] AC 58.
4   See *Chitty on Contracts* (28th edn).

(a) Infants or minors

1.13 The general rule at common law was that a contract made by an infant or minor (these terms both mean a person under the age of 18 in English law)[1] was voidable at his option, although it is binding on the other party. However, 'voidable' had two meanings:

(i) some contracts were valid and binding on a minor unless repudiated by him before or within a reasonable time after attaining his majority;

(ii) others were not binding on the minor unless ratified by him when he attained his majority.

Two types of transaction were treated as exceptional; beneficial contracts of service, which were regarded as valid, and contracts for necessaries, which imposed liability on the minor.

These common law rules were affected in two important respects by the Infants' Relief Act 1874, which provided that:

(1) three kinds of contract should be absolutely void, namely contracts of loan, contracts for goods (other than necessaries) and accounts stated (an admission of a sum of money due from one person to another where neither is under a duty to account to the other); and

(2) it was no longer possible to ratify at majority those contracts which formerly were not binding on the infant unless he had ratified them.

The Infants' Relief Act 1874 was repealed by the Minors' Contracts Act 1987 and as such the 1874 Act will not apply to any contracts made after 9 June 1987. The effect of the repeal of the Infants' Relief Act 1874 is that contracts of loan, contracts for goods other than necessaries and contracts for accounts stated entered into by a minor made after 9 June 1987 will be subject to the common law rules. As regards ratification, the position now is that a minor, on attaining the age of majority, can ratify contracts that are unenforceable against him or voidable at his option.

1.14 An accident insurance policy has been held to be a contract beneficial to a minor[2]; moreover, it is possible to argue that, if a minor's financial and other social circumstances were appropriate, a life assurance or pension policy could be a 'necessary'. But the situations when either could arise are remote and, for minors, life assurance contracts will generally be voidable contracts (ie contracts of continuing obligation valid and binding on the infant unless he repudiates them during his minority or within a reasonable time of attaining his majority).

Thus, a minor may propose for and accept a policy of life assurance, which would be a contract voidable at his option[3]. This applies whatever the minor's

1 Family Law Reform Act 1969, ss 1 and 12.
2 *Clements v London and North-Western Rly* [1894] 2 QB 482.
3 *Ritchie v Salvation Army Assoc Soc Ltd* [1930] IAC Rep 31.

age but, in practice, most life offices will need to be satisfied that the child is old enough to know what he is doing – to render less likely the policy being avoided later and to counter accusations of improper selling.

When income tax relief was available on premiums payable towards qualifying life policies the Inland Revenue contended that no child of 'tender years' (which they interpreted as including a child of less than 12 years of age) was capable of 'making' a contract for the purposes of section 19(2) of the Income and Corporation Taxes Act 1970. As a result, many life offices were prepared to issue policies to children as young as 12 and take the risk of the contract being subsequently avoided by the minor. In view of the requirements for suitability and client understanding of risk as set out in the Conduct of Business Rules of the Financial Services Authority it must be unlikely that policies would now be issued to children of such a young age.

When minors propose for life assurance, it is sometimes suggested that a parent should complete and sign the proposal form for the infant, thereby, it is argued, making up for the want of capacity of the child. There is, however, no basis in law for this – signature by a parent does not validate the contract, as the parent is unable to authorise something which the infant cannot do himself. (The parent's signature may, of course, be of some significance in ensuring that the infant is not entering into a transaction beyond his means or if the form imposes obligations on the parent.)

1.15   In the context of voidable life policies issued to minors, two questions remain to be considered:

(1)   If the policy continues and premiums are paid, can the infant deal with the policy (eg by mortgage, sale, surrender or assignment) during his minority?

(2)   If the infant repudiates the contract during minority, or on attaining full age, can he claim a refund of premiums?

It is, generally, unsafe for the life office to deal with the infant in connection with the policy. The infant would not be able to give the office a valid discharge to a surrender or other payment until he had attained his majority. Although the point has never been judicially decided in this country so far as life policies are concerned, there is a line of cases on other types of contracts which supports the proposition that if the infant has derived any intermediate advantage from a voidable contract, he cannot get back what he has paid. The authority is *Steinberg v Scala (Leeds) Ltd*[1], and based on the principles enunciated in that case it is contended that if the infant has derived the benefit of life cover from the life policy then he should receive no return of premiums.

In S*teinberg* it was said that the right of recovery does not turn on whether the infant has derived *any* substantial benefit from the contract. As Younger LJ put

---

1   [1923] 2 Ch 452; a case involving the purchase of shares in which the minor could not recover the purchase moneys even though no dividends has been received. See also *Ritchie v Salvation Army Assurance* [1930] IAC Rep 31.

it: 'The question is not; Has the infant derived any real advantage? But: Has the consideration wholly failed?' Thus in *Steinberg*, the minor applied for and was allotted shares in a company and paid the amounts due on allotment and on first call, and subsequently repudiated whilst still under age. Since the infant had obtained the consideration for which she had bargained it was irrelevant that what she had obtained might be valueless.

On the basis of dicta in that case, it is likely that premiums would not be recoverable even under life policies which did not provide 'life cover' in the normal sense but merely expressed payment on death before the age of 16 or 18 as a return of the premiums paid. There is, however, still a risk in connection with unit-linked contracts, such as bonds or whole of life policies with a low sum assured/high investment content. For this reason many life offices, if they are prepared to deal with a minor in such circumstances, will allow investment in low volatility funds and will not permit dealings with the policy until the minor attains majority. However, it is likely that cases will need to be viewed on a case by case basis to prevent a challenge being upheld by the FOS.

By statute, an infant may be a member of a friendly society, whatever his age, but if he is under the age of 16 his parent or guardian should execute all instruments and other documents[1].

(b) Scotland

1.16   In Scotland the Age of Legal Capacity (Scotland) Act 1991 abolished the previous two-tiered system of pupils and minors. Now children aged 16 or over have full legal capacity. However, those aged under 18 have a period after attaining the age of majority in which to apply to the court for prejudicial transactions to be set aside. Prejudicial transactions being transactions which an adult exercising reasonable prudence would not have entered into in the circumstances and which has caused, or is likely to cause, substantial prejudice to that person. Furthermore, the Act introduced a procedure whereby the court can ratify transactions entered into by minors aged 16 and 17.

(c)   Married women

1.17   At common law a married woman could not contract for her own benefit, but under the Married Women's Property Act 1882 (and, in Scotland, under the Married Women's Property (Scotland) Act 1920) she was enabled to do so with regard to her separate property.

Under section 11 of the 1882 Act a married woman in England was specifically empowered to effect a policy on her own life or on the life of her husband for her own benefit. It was, however, not until 1980 that a similar power was given to married women in Scotland by the Married Women's Policies of Assurance (Scotland) (Amendment) Act 1980.

---

1   Friendly Societies Act 1974, s 60(1) and (2).

(d)   Aliens and enemy aliens

1.18   An alien can in England make a valid contract by English law and he may effect a life policy with an English insurer. However, he may be prevented by his own domestic law from effecting such a policy.

British subjects cannot, in ordinary circumstances, contract with enemy aliens. If before the outbreak of war an alien, who thereupon becomes an enemy alien, has already acquired an interest in an English life policy, his interest is not destroyed by the outbreak of war, but is merely suspended until peace is made; but in the cases of both the first and second world wars, there was special legislation and such interests were in most cases vested in the Custodian of Enemy Property. Similar restrictions applied also, for example, in the original Gulf War.

(e)   Mentally disordered persons

1.19   Generally speaking, a contract made by a person of unsound mind is binding upon him if his disability was not known to the person contracting with him. However, the contract is voidable if his disability was known to the other party[1]. The burden is on the disabled person to show that his disability prevented him from understanding the particular transaction, and that the other party knew of this. In certain cases the property and affairs of a mental patient are, following an application to the Court of Protection, placed under the management of the Court of Protection. The person has then no capacity to personally contract although he may still contract through a receiver provided the receiver has the requisite powers. Unlike most powers of attorney which contain a general power to act, a Court of Protection order specifically sets out what the receiver's powers are.

(f)   Corporations

1.20   A company or society which is incorporated is a legal person and has an existence distinct from its members.

The powers of a corporation to contract are to be ascertained as follows:

If incorporated by Royal charter	Generally speaking, they have absolute power as for an individual person
If incorporated by Special Act of Parliament	Powers defined or necessarily implied by the special Act
If incorporated under the Companies Acts	Powers within its memorandum of association and the Companies Acts

Power is implied to do all things incidental or reasonably conducive to the powers expressly conferred by the statute or memorandum, but contracts which are neither expressly nor impliedly authorised are ultra vires and void, subject to

---

1   *Imperial Loan Co Ltd v Stone* [1892] 1 QB 599.

what is stated below. In the case of a trading company it is probably impliedly within the company's powers to effect a policy on the life of a director, officer or employee to the extent of the company's insurable interest in his life. Nevertheless, some companies have express powers to do this in their memorandum.

Until the coming into force of the European Communities Act 1972, ultra vires acts were absolutely void. They were not binding on a company or enforceable by it, because parties dealing with a company were regarded as having notice of its public documents, ie all matters on the company file at Companies House, which includes its memorandum. However, the 1972 Act provided a somewhat uncertain protection for third parties dealing with companies in good faith. The provisions of the 1972 Act were subsequently amended by the Companies Act 1985 and further amended by the Companies Act 1989. The current position is covered by what is now section 35A of the Companies Act 1985 (as amended) which provides that:

> 'In favour of a person dealing with a company in good faith, the power of the board of directors to bind the company is deemed to be free of any limitation under the company's constitution.'

As a result, it is now very unlikely that a company will be able to avoid a transaction with a third party dealing in good faith, even if it is ultra vires the company's constitution. This is reinforced by the fact that a third party would be presumed to be acting in good faith and for this purpose will no longer be deemed to have notice of the company's public documents, for example its memorandum and articles of association filed at Companies House[1].

A company or corporation may contract in the same way as an individual; a company is only required to execute a document as a deed in those cases where an individual would also be required to do so (eg an enforceable gratuitous promise)[2]. A proposal for life assurance or a discharge for the policy moneys or a surrender may accordingly be signed on behalf of a company or corporation by any person acting under its authority, whether express or implied.

(g) Unincorporated associations

1.21   These are associations of persons which have not been incorporated but which are not partnerships as the members of such associations do not carry on a business or profession in common, with a view to profit.

As *Chitty* put it[3]:

> 'An unincorporated association is not a legal person and therefore cannot sue or be sued[4] unless such course is authorised by express or implied statutory provisions,

---

1   Companies Act 1985, s 711A.
2   Companies Act 1985, s 36A, introduced by the Companies Act 1989 and Corporate Bodies' Contracts Act 1960.
3   *Chitty on Contracts* (28th edn) Vol 1, 9–069.
4   *London Association for Protection of Trade v Greenlands Ltd* [1916] 2 AC 15; *Steele v Gourley* (1886) 3 TLR 118, 119; affirmed (1887) 3 TLR 772.

as in the case of a trade union[1]. . . . Nor can a contract be made so as to bind all persons who from time to time become members of such an association[2]. But a contract purportedly made by or with an incorporated association is not necessarily a nullity. If the person or persons who actually made the contract had no authority to contract on behalf of the members they may be held to have contracted personally[3]. On the other hand, if they had the authority, express or implied, of all or some of the members of the association to contract on their behalf, the contract can be enforced by or against those members as co-principals to the contract by the ordinary rules of agency'[4].

(h) Partners

1.22   Every partner normally has the capacity to contract for the partnership within the scope of the partnership business.

Where a firm takes out a life policy, it is preferable to issue the policy in the names of the individual partners, coupled if desired with the name of the firm (eg A, B and C trading as Z & Co), rather than it being effected by one partner on behalf of the partnership or simply in the name of the partnership as otherwise problems may arise when personnel leave or join the firm. A conventional partnership is not (in England) a legal entity and the title to a policy effected on behalf of a partnership could remain vested in the persons effecting the contract, unless and until the title is transferred to new owners by assignment or by operation of law. However, a great deal can depend on how the partnership is constituted and what mechanisms are in place when partners join, leave or die. Unless stated to the contrary in the partnership deed, a partnership comes to an end on the occurrence of one of these events. In Scotland a partnership is a legal entity but not normally a body corporate and theoretically a firm could take out a life policy simply in the name of the partnership.

Limited liability partnerships under the Limited Liability Partnerships Act 2000 are body corporates with separate legal personality. Their constitution will be governed by an incorporation document and not the general law of partnership.

5 Legality of object

1.23   A contract that is illegal is treated as if it had not been made at all. It is void ab initio and no remedy is available to either party.

A contract is illegal if it is prohibited at common law on grounds of public policy or if its formation is in contravention of a statute or opposed to its general interest. Thus, for example, if a company carries on the business of life assurance, without authorisation to do so, as currently required by the Financial Services and Markets Act 2000, then the policies it issues during the period it is unauthorised are illegal and void, as the object of the statute is to prohibit companies from

1   Trade Union and Labour Relations (Consolidation) Act 1992, s 10(1)(a).
2   See *Walker v Sur* [1914] 2 KB 930; *Jarrot v Ackerley* (1915) 85 LJ Ch 135.
3   *Bradely Egg Farm v Clifford* [1943] 2 All ER 378.
4   See further *Chitty on Contracts*.

doing business until authorised[1]. Similarly, the Life Assurance Act 1774 prohibits the making of insurances on lives without insurable interest, and policies made contrary to the provisions of the 1774 Act are therefore 'null and void'[2]. If an insurance contract is illegal, the general rule is that once it is entered into the insured can recover neither the policy moneys nor the premiums paid (but see further Chapter 2 in relation to cases where both parties are not at fault).

If a contract is on the face of it illegal then, if its illegality is not pleaded in defence to an action, it is the duty of the courts to take cognisance of it and refuse to enforce the contract[3]. Any bargain not to dispute a claim arising under a contract which is illegal and void is itself void.

However, the rule that there should be no benefit from a criminal act did not prevent the enforcement of a life insurance policy held by an assignee so far as it was necessary to protect the actual interest of the assignee. Such was the case in *Davitt v Titcumb*[4] where an endowment policy was taken out on the lives of two people and payable on the first death. The policy was subsequently assigned to the building society on the terms that if the policy paid out, then the proceeds would be used to pay off the mortgage. When one of the lives assured murdered the other, the building society were properly entitled to receive the proceeds of the policy. The murderer, the defendant, argued that he was entitled to a share in the proceeds of the house. However, because only the deceased's estate could force the building society to use the proceeds of the policy to pay off the mortgage, the defendant being unable to by reason of 'ex turpi causa non oritur actio' (a right of action does not arise out of an evil cause), it necessarily followed that the policy proceeds, as applied by the building society, belonged solely to the deceased's estate.

B   The proposal

I   The proposal form

1.24   A form of proposal is not a legally required preliminary to a contract of life assurance. However, in practice, where the contract in question contains more than a nominal amount of life cover, a prospective policyholder is usually required to give various details, such as his occupation, height, weight, medical and family history, whether he engages in hazardous pursuits and whether any

---

1   See *Bedford Insurance Co Ltd v Instituto de Resseguros do Brasil* [1984] 3 All ER 766 and *Phoenix General Insurance Co Greece SA v Administration Asiguraliror de Stat* [1987] 2 All ER 152, where the Court of Appeal held that the statutory prohibition on unauthorised insurance business is not limited to effecting contracts of insurance but extends to carrying out unauthorised insurance business (eg mere paying of claims may be caught). (It follows that although the prohibition is imposed unilaterally on unauthorised insurers, unauthorised insurance contracts are illegal and void and therefore unenforceable not just by the insurer but also by the insured).
2   *Harse v Pearl Assurance Co* [1904] 1 KB 558.
3   *Gedge v Royal Exchange Assurance Corp* [1900] 2 QB 214.
4   [1989] 3 All ER 417.

previous proposal for life assurance has been declined or accepted only at an increased premium. The completed proposal form is usually incorporated into the policy. Under the Statement of Long-Term Insurance Practice the life office is required to include specific questions in its proposal forms relating to any matter which it has commonly found to be material to risks of the relevant class of insurance.

The proposal form usually contains an authority to refer to any doctor who has attended the proposer. This aspect is governed by the Access to Medical Reports Act 1988, which lays down clear rules on when information can be released, inter alia, to life offices for insurance purposes. As such, a life office may have access to any medical report relating to a prospective policyholder (if he consents to such an application by the life office). The life office must inform the individual that he has the right to withhold consent and to have access to the report before it is supplied to the life office or within six months thereafter. It must also inform him that he has the right to withhold consent after he has had access to the report or to amend anything in it which he considers to be incorrect or misleading and that in certain circumstances (as described below) the doctor is not obliged to let the individual see the report (or any part of it).

The individual would normally give his consent in the proposal form, and he may request access to the completed report before it is supplied to the life office. If he does the life office must inform the doctor of that request and at the same time notify the individual that it has asked the doctor for a report. Both of these notifications must state that the doctor is not to give the report to the life office unless the individual has had access to it and consented to its being supplied, either as prepared, or as amended by the doctor. If the doctor refuses to amend the report the individual may attach a document setting out his objections. In addition the notification must include the information that if 21 days elapse from the life office application for the report without the individual having contacted the doctor in respect of it, the report may then be supplied.

On receipt of the life office application the doctor can then release the report to the life office, either once the individual has had access to it, or after 21 days from the making of the application if the individual has not contacted the doctor. Amendments to the report can be requested by the individual if he believes that parts are either untrue or misleading. The doctor may amend the report after such a request or, if he is not prepared to do so, the individual may ask the doctor to attach to the report a statement of the individual's views, which the doctor must do when sending it to the life office.

In the event that the individual does request to see the medical report before it is passed to the life office, the doctor may delete parts of the report if he believes that the report would be likely to cause serious harm to the physical or mental health of the individual or would indicate the intentions of the doctor in respect of the individual. The exemption also applies if it is likely to reveal information about another person or reveal the identity of another person who has supplied information to the doctor about that individual unless that person has consented or is a 'health professional'. If the doctor wishes to rely on these exemptions he must inform the individual of that fact and he is not to supply the report to the life office unless the individual consents. If the exemptions apply the individual would still be entitled to see the remainder of the report which is not affected.

Clearly, from a practical point of view, if the life office does not receive a report then it is very unlikely to be prepared to issue a policy.

(a) Joint life policies

1.25 Life assurance contracts may be issued to more than one person, normally but not necessarily on a joint life basis. Joint life policies can be specified to pay on either the first or last death. Some life offices may have recorded such policies as being issued jointly or alternatively if that were not the intention as tenants in common on a specified basis (such that no interest in the policy would pass by survivorship). Many merely state the policyholders/owners as the named individuals without an additional wording. The conventional thinking in respect of such policies was to regard them as jointly owned (as there is a presumption of a joint tenancy when no words of severance are used). This meant that on the death of the first policyholder their interest would pass to any surviving policyholder(s).

The law has been thrown into disarray somewhat in cases where the parties' intention has not been recorded by the case of *Murphy v Murphy*[1]. In that case a husband and wife had taken out a policy on a joint life death basis. The policy did not specify how the joint interest was to be held. The case concerned the right to make an order under the Inheritance (Provision for Family and Dependants Act) 1975. If the policy was held under a joint tenancy immediately before the first death the policy could have been the subject of such an order. The issue for the Court of Appeal was one of interpretation of the policy as to whether the policyholders had a joint interest or each held separate rights to the death benefit. The Court held that although there was no evidence in relation to the circumstances surrounding the policy, the plain inference was that it was to be held solely for the survivor and that each had a separate interest which was not defeasible by a notice of severance. The court came to this view by looking behind the policy itself and by analogy with other forms of insurance where policyholders have separate interests protected by the same policy. In the authors' view as a husband and wife each have an unlimited insurable interest in each other's lives it is not clear that this analogy is apt to cover this situation. Also, it is arguably not consistent with the fact that an assignment of the policy can only be made in relation to the whole policy and not just part (as here the death benefit).

The Court of Appeal did appear to accept that in the case of an endowment, it would ordinarily be intended that the benefit payable on maturity would be available for them jointly. This produces the very unsatisfactory position of the same policy wording, etc creating different types of interest dependent on the type of policy or the purposes for which it is used. From the life office's perspective this makes it very difficult to ascertain whether or not (as often happens on divorce) the owners can sever the joint tenancy on which they believe they have been holding the policy.

Following *Murphy v Murphy* it is not clear whether unit-linked policies should be treated as endowments (ie because there is some savings element). In any

1 [2004] 1 FCR 1.

event, to avoid confusion life offices may want to amend their policy schedules to make clear that the policy is issued to joint policyholders (and all rights under it are held by them) as joint tenants.

1.26   The proposal form may also include a declaration to the effect that the proposal, and sometimes statements made to the insurer's doctor (where, for instance, the individual has agreed to be consulted by the insurer's doctor as opposed to his own doctor), or by the proposer's medical attendant, shall be the basis of the contract. In the case of *Dawsons v Bonnin*[1] it was held that a warranty resulted from a statement in the policy that statements in the proposal form should be the basis of the contract. Such a statement is inconsistent with paragraph 1(b) of the Statement of Long-Term Insurance Practice that the proposal form must not contain any provision which converts any statement of fact, whether past or present, made by the proposer, into a warranty. There is an exception where the warranty relates to the life to be assured under a life of another contract, and there is also an exception which permits the life office to require specific warranties to be given about matters which are material to the risk to be insured. The Law Commission is considering amendments in this area to prevent basis of the contract clauses having such effect. The Law Commission is also looking[2] at the law on non-disclosure and this representation in insurance contracts (see Chapter 2).

The proposal form is customarily incorporated in the policy by reference.

The Statement of Long-Term Insurance Practice sets out certain matters which should be included in proposal forms. They should draw attention to the consequences of failure to disclose all material facts (ie that it could affect the payment of benefits) explaining that these are facts which an insurer would regard as likely to influence the assessment and acceptance of a proposal. Particular matters which have commonly been found to be material to particular risks should be the subject of clear questions in the proposal form, and life offices should avoid asking questions which would require knowledge beyond that which the proposer could reasonably be expected to possess and which would not be practicable for him to obtain. The proposal form or a supporting document should also include a statement that a copy of the completed proposal form and of the policy conditions is available on request.

In the case of a proposal for a sum assured which is large in relation to the life office's average sum assured per policy or the proposer's apparent circumstances, the office might ask for supporting 'financial' information (often termed 'financial underwriting') to ensure that the sum assured proposed:

(1)   is consistent with the insurable interest;

(2)   relates to the proposer's demonstrated needs; and

(3)   is within the means of the proposer to pay for it.

1   [1922] 2 AC 413.
2   Scoping paper, January 2006.

Furthermore, it is possible that proof of identity, required in accordance with money laundering obligations, may be requested in the proposal form (see Chapter 5 for further discussion on money laundering requirements).

1.27 Where a new policy is issued in substitution for a former one, the contract for the new policy should be based on a new proposal form, but if the life office waives full replies to the questions in the new proposal form, the new policy should be based on the declarations in the proposal forms for both old and new policies.

Where the proposal is for an assurance on the life of another person, the questions as to family and medical history are normally answered by the life to be assured, who is not a party to the contract, and the person effecting the assurance would normally declare that the answers are correct to the best of his knowledge and belief, although it would also be permissible with a life of another contract to require that the statements made shall form the basis of the contract. The proposer may also be required to declare that he has an insurable interest, and sometimes to give details. He may also be asked to provide consents relating to sensitive (eg information on health) and/or processing of information outside the EEA for the purposes of the Data Protection Act 1998.

Although an agent (for example, an attorney) may sign a form of proposal on behalf of the proposer, his signature will not ordinarily be acceptable to the life office in any case where information on the subject of health is required. Care should be taken that the person signing a proposal for a child's deferred assurance or any other policy on the life of the child, offered by a Friendly Society, is one who is in a position to know the state of health of the child.

Where the proposal form contains an agreement (expressly or impliedly) by the proposer to accept the usual form of policy of the life office, and in any particular case the life office wishes to vary that form, the life office must communicate this to the proposer. If, for example, the usual form of policy covers death from aviation, death from that cause cannot be excluded unless the life office has contracted on that basis by excluding that risk, such communication to the proposer being a counter-offer subject to acceptance by the policyholder.

In some instances the proposer may communicate information to the insurer other than via the proposal form. In *Ayrey v British Legal*[1] the proposer communicated orally to the company's agent and it was held that this was reasonable for the proposer to do. Life offices may therefore seek to include provisions in their proposal forms which deal with how material information is communicated to them (eg excluding communication to agents). (See also Chapter 4).

(b) Simplified proposal form

1.28 There is an increasing use by life offices of simplified proposal forms (ie which have fewer, or even no, medical or lifestyle questions) for certain classes of life assurance. As a result of relaxed underwriting standards many offices now use:

1 [1918] 1 KB 137.

(1) shortened proposal forms with fewer medical questions for direct-mail or 'off-the-page' selling and for those contracts where the sum assured is not high in relation to the premium;

(2) simplified proposal forms with no medical questions for:

  (a) endowment assurance policies which are to be used (subject to certain eligibility conditions) as collateral security for a mortgage loan for house purchase;

  (b) without-profit policies targeted at the older generation with relatively low premiums and sums assured.

(c) Annuity proposal form

1.29   A proposal form for an application to purchase an annuity should show the full name, address, description and date of birth of the life (or lives) on which the annuity is to depend and the type and amount of annuity and how it is payable. It should also show: (1) the identity of the person making the purchase; and (2) who is the person to whom the annuity is to be paid, and if this is jointly, to two or more persons, it should state how the annuity is to be divided or paid. Information as to the beneficial interest in the annuity is essential if the recipient wishes to take advantage of payment without deduction of income tax, as explained in Chapter 12.

(d) Capital redemption policy proposal form

1.30   The proposal form for a capital redemption policy is a simple document; nothing more is required than particulars of the guaranteed sum to be paid, term of years etc, and the name, address and (possibly) the occupation of the proposer.

2   Proof of age and name

1.31   It is desirable that proof of age should be furnished when a life assurance policy is effected. If there is any inaccuracy in the age stated, the terms of the contract can then be suitably amended (or the contract may not be proceeded with). In the case of an annuity, proof of age must be furnished before any payment of annuity is made.

If the assured misstates his age it is likely that the insurer will adjust the sum assured instead of avoiding the policy, but if he does neither and accepts further premiums after he has discovered the true age he will be fully liable under the policy[1].

Age is usually proved by production of a birth certificate (ie an official certified copy of an entry in an official register of births but not a photocopy). Under the Births and Deaths Registration Act 1953, a certified copy of any entry is admissible as evidence of the facts properly recorded therein. In cases where the

---

1   *Hemmings v Sceptre Life* [1905] 1 Ch 365.

birth is not registered or a birth certificate is not obtainable the best available evidence should be sought, supported, if thought necessary, by a statutory declaration.

Apart from setting the correct premium level, age can also be important in establishing the identity of the deceased as the life assured under the contract.

If there has been a change of name since registration of birth, it should be evidenced as follows:

(1) If a change on marriage, by a marriage certificate.

(2) If a change on adoption, by an adoption certificate. Where the adoption certificate contains a record of the date of birth it is itself also sufficient evidence of age[1].

(3) If a voluntary change, by deed poll, or by an office, copy of the deed poll where the original deed is enrolled at the Central Office of the Supreme Court.

A surname is, however, a name of repute, and any person may, without any deed poll or advertisement, assume any surname he pleases. In such a case the life office should require evidence of identity in the form of a certificate by a responsible person, supported, if thought necessary, by statutory declaration.

A company may change its name, and if it does so the change should be evidenced by production of the appropriate certificate issued by the Registrar of Companies.

C 'Cooling-off' and cancellation

1.32   The FSA's conduct of business rules provide cancellation rights which are a requirement of the Consolidated Life Directive and are generally 30 days for long-term insurance contracts. Whilst it is uncertain whether the existence of such rights prevents the contract from being formed from the outset, it is generally thought that the contract is in place but may terminate early in exercise of the right. Although the right is expressed to fully unwind the contract, it allows for investment shortfall and issue of the contract triggers other rights (eg in relation to distance contracts) (see further Chapter 5).

SECTION 3   E-COMMERCE

A   E-commerce and life assurance contracts

1.33   There are a number of relevant questions from an e-commerce perspective. The first is the ability of a provider to use the internet to sell online within the EU. The second is the law applicable to that operation and any resulting con-

---

1   Adoption Act 1958, s 20.

tract. The third is the legal disclosure and other requirements to the customer (eg both in relation to the provider and the process for contracting online). Finally providers need to consider the effect of digital signatures both in relation to their customers and intermediaries. This chapter deals with the issues relevant to contract formation (see Chapter 5 for marketing and sales-related issues). In order to do so it is necessary to give a brief overview of the relevant e-commerce regulation. There are two relevant EU Directives: the E Commerce Directive and the Electronic Signatures Directive. The E-Commerce Directive[1] was implemented by the Electronic Commerce (EC Directive) Regulations 2002[2]. Implementation of the directive in the UK by the Electronic Commerce Regulations is only part of the picture. For FSA regulated firms the directive was implemented via a new part of the FSA Handbook, the Electronic Commerce Sourcebook (ECO).

The directive is a harmonisation directive seeking to provide a basic framework of mutual recognition for businesses advertising online or providing goods and services online[3] within the EU[4]. Its aim was to enable online facilities established in one member state to have to comply only with the laws of their home state. This area of mutual recognition of laws is called the coordinated field. There are, however, a number of exclusions from the coordinated field, the most relevant ones being consumer protection measures established by the home state to comply with EU requirements, and the provisions of insurance[5]. The directive also does not affect the choice of law to govern the contract or issues of jurisdiction. However, subject to these exclusions and the requirements of existing EU single market directives, online providers should be able to operate from their home state in the same way as they do for their domestic customers. The directive requires disclosure of information (eg details of the provider) both generally to consumers and in relation to the process for contracting online.

The FSA's ECO cuts back the general freedom provided by the regulators (for both UK firms and other EEA firms doing business electronically) by specifying the FSA requirements under the consumer protection and insurance exemptions to the directive referred to above. ECO provides separately for incoming providers, outgoing UK providers and providers operating in the UK in the domestic market. So, for example, ECO 1.3.3 sets out the requirements in relation to EEA insurers carrying on business or advertising into the UK using their single market passport. Conversely, the provisions applying to EEA insurers are disapplied to UK insurers passporting out (as they will be subject to the host state rules). The rules for domestic providers within the UK are set out in ECO Annex 1(1) and (2) and apply in addition to COB. It should be noted that the insurance exemption applies only to insurers and not insurance intermediaries.

The Digital Signatures Directive (99/93/EC) was implemented in the UK by the Electronic Communications Act 2000 and the Electronic Signatures Regulations 2002[6]. They created an environment which enabled recognition of online contracts and the use of digital signatures.

---

1   2002/311/EC.
2   2002/13, 2002/1775, 2002/1776, 2002/2015 and 2002/2157.
3   Not merely by exchange of email.
4   The area is extended by a separate provision to the EFTA countries.
5   Tax, data protection and copyright issues are also excluded.
6   SI 2002/318.

B   Formation of e-commerce contracts

1.34   The question of how to categorise 'invitations to treat', offers, counter-offers and acceptance, in the area of life assurance may be more complicated where all or part of the transaction is concluded electronically or at a distance. A contract can be formed electronically, except where there are specific provisions requiring writing, etc (and even in such cases the position is arguable, see below).

From a contract formation perspective the first step in the e-commerce process is often a website. Websites are probably analogous to advertisements, price lists, circulars and displays of goods in supermarkets and constitute invitations to treat. Indeed most businesses will take steps to make it clear that their websites are invitations to treat. A popular method of reinforcing that websites are invitations to treat is for the business to state that they will not be bound until the customer's offer is accepted by the business, often by issue of an email confirmation.

To seek to avoid potential problems, the provider should clearly set out the procedure to be followed for a binding contract to come into existence so that customers have clear knowledge that the provider does not intend to be bound until that procedure is completed. The E-Commerce Directive (and, from a UK perspective, ECO[1]) require UK providers to provide an explanation of the different steps required for completing a contract electronically so that the parties can give their full and informed consent. Therefore, the provider should explain clearly how the contract comes into being by electronic means. All this must be provided before the contract comes into force. The provider must include information on the different stages involved in the contract, and, for example, whether the contract will be filed (not common in the UK), whether it will be accessible, etc. The procedure for correcting errors prior to placing the order must also be made clear. The terms and conditions of the contract must be made available in a way which allows the customer to store and reproduce them, for example, by enabling him to print out the relevant documentation.

Receipt of orders must be acknowledged without undue delay and by electronic means and providers must indicate any codes of conduct to which they are subject and information on how those codes can be consulted electronically.

Section 8 of the Electronic Communications Act 2000 gives powers for orders to be made by statutory instrument, to 'remove restrictions in other legislation which prevent the use of electronic communication in place of paper, and to enable the use of electronic communications to be regulated where it is already allowed'. It is not possible to make an order unless the Minister in question is satisfied that it will be possible to produce a record of anything that is done by virtue of the authorisation which is no less satisfactory than by any other means[2]. In addition, a person cannot be required to abandon paper-based transactions unless he has previously chosen to do so. The intention is that the Minister's powers should be used selectively to offer the alternative of electronic contracting to those who choose to contract in this manner.

---

1   See ECO 2.3 and 3.2.
2   See also section 8 authorising secondary legislation to remove legal obstacles.

C   Where is the contract formed

1.35   The place where the contract is formed can be crucial in e-commerce transactions. The provider and/or the customer may easily find themselves subject to different legal and taxation systems than they intended.

There is some doubt under English law as to which one of two approaches to contract formation applies to e-commerce. Receipt by the purchaser of the provider's acceptance is one test whereas the other is when the provider sends his acceptance (the so-called 'postal' rule which may have effect in an analogous way for e-commerce transactions). Generally speaking, the internet is a continuous communications medium so this would tend to indicate that the actual receipt of the acceptance is the important factor. This provides further arguments for the inclusion of clear statements in the terms and conditions as to how offer and acceptance is to be communicated, sent and received.

Under Article 11 of the E-Commerce Directive[1] the provider is obliged without undue delay to send the consumer acknowledgement of receipt of an order by electronic means. The order acknowledgement is deemed to be received when the party to whom it is addressed is able to access it. Unfortunately, the Directive does not state at what stage the contract is formed. Therefore, the place and time of contract formation will depend on national private international law provisions.

The place where the contract is formed will, in the absence of express provision, be likely to be where the purchaser is located. For life insurance contracts under the Consolidated Life Directive the law of the contract (which may determine issues of contract formation differently) are based on habitual residence of the policyholder. Ordinarily the law of the member state in which the policyholder has their habitual residence will be the law of the contract unless the policyholder chooses the law of the member state of which he is a national. Alternatively, member states may permit (and the UK has permitted) a free choice of law subject to mandatory rules of the member state of habitual residence. For non-insurance contracts the host state's consumer protection provisions may also include a mandatory choice of law.

D   Digital signatures

1.36   One particular risk which is brought into focus by the internet is that the 'purchaser' will seek to repudiate the contract by, for example, claiming that someone else was using his credit card number. A so-called 'digital signature' can offer protection to the provider in these circumstances.

The traditional function of a signature is to authenticate the document on which it appears. Except where the signature can be established to be a forgery, the signatory generally has an uphill struggle in subsequently denying the contract, or its provisions. Although it is rare for an actual signature to be a legal requirement on any type of contract, there is obviously a desire to seek to

1   See 2.3 and 3.2 of ECO.

replicate, so far as is possible, a verifiable alternative to the handwritten signature for online transactions. Such transactions are not normally amenable to the traditional concept of a written signature. The development of digital signature technology has been mainly driven by the banking sector, but it clearly also has potential applications to the life insurance industry.

1   Functions of digital signatures

1.37   A digital signature can establish the identity of the person entering into the contract.

An additional benefit is that a digital signature can definitively establish the time of such signature in a way which cannot be replicated by a 'physical' signature where a false date can be added or a date inserted at a different time to the time of the actual signature.

2   Technology underlying digital signatures

1.38   Although this book is not the place to examine the underlying technology, some reference to the basic concepts is useful. The ability to create digital signatures currently relies on the technology of cryptography and in particular the technology of public and private keys. A message which has been encrypted with the individual's or organisation's private key can be decrypted only with the public key which is appropriate to that private key.

3   Verification of identity

1.39   The two methods of authenticating 'signed' communications are either by the recipient directly or by third parties acting as referees/arbiters. The second method potentially overcomes the significant problem that the sending party could deliberately reveal its private key in circumstances where it wished to repudiate authorship of its own genuine digital signatures. Providers can incorporate as part of their digital signature scheme a 'trusted third party' who acts as an arbiter to settle disputes between senders and receivers. This person would therefore have some similarity with the functions undertaken by notaries.

4   Electronic Signature Directive

1.40   Although doubts exist with regard to the use of electronic signatures as a replacement for handwritten signatures on documents, this directive clearly envisages the recognition and use of 'electronic signatures' in the sphere of e-commerce in the EU for the purposes of data authentication. There is a distinction in the directive between simple 'electronic signatures' and 'advanced electronic signatures'. The latter are guaranteed under the directive to be legally effective and admissible in legal proceedings whereas the former only qualify for certain purposes and can be denied recognition on certain grounds.

'Advanced electronic signatures' must be created by a 'secure signature-creation device', as defined, and:

'(a) satisfy the legal requirements of a signature in relation to data in electronic form in the same manner as a handwritten signature satisfies those requirements in relation to paper-based data; and

(b) are admissible as evidence in legal proceedings'.

The essential features of an 'advanced electronic signature' are that it is uniquely linked to and capable of identifying the signatory. It must be created using means that the signatory can maintain under his sole control and is linked to the data to which it relates in such a manner that any subsequent change in data is detectable. Advanced electronic signatures must also be based on a 'qualified certificate' provided by a certification service provider. Article 5(2) provides, essentially, that a non-advanced electronic signature is not to be denied legal effectiveness or admissibility solely on the grounds that it does not meet any of the criteria for an advanced electronic signature.

5   UK implementation and the Electronic Signatures Regulations 2002

1.41   The Electronic Communications Act 2000 implemented the Electronic Signature Directive[1]. Section 7 of the Act makes it clear that all types of electronic signatures, whether or not approved providers are involved and irrespective of the jurisdiction where they were issued, will be legally admissible in court. Subsection 7(1) confirms the admissibility of electronic signatures where they are incorporated into the communication or logically associated with it. It will be for the court to decide in any individual case whether a signature has been used correctly and what weight should be given to it. Subsection 7(2) sets out what is meant by an electronic signature. Essentially this is 'anything in electronic form . . . for the purpose of being used in establishing the authenticity of the communication or data, the integrity of the communication or data, or both'. Essentially, therefore, it is something associated with an electronic document which performs similar functions to those of a manual signature, so it can be used to provide the recipient with confirmation that the communication really is from the person it purports to be from, or to provide confirmation that it has not been tampered with. Subsection (3) sets out how the electronic signatures are to be certified.

The development of secure e-commerce transactions clearly depends on the availability and development of cryptography services. Sections 1 to 6 of the Act concern the arrangements for registering providers of cryptography support services, such as electronic signature services and confidentiality services. Section 1 imposes a duty on the Secretary of State to establish and maintain a register of approved providers of 'cryptography support services'. Section 6(1) provides a definition of this term as any service provided to those sending or receiving

1   1999/93/EC.

electronic communications, or to those who store electronic data, and which is designed to facilitate the use of cryptographic techniques essentially for the purposes of ensuring that such communication or data can be accessed or put into an intelligible form only by certain persons, or for ensuring that the authenticity or integrity of such communication or data is capable of being ascertained. The regulations provide for the supervision of certification-service-providers, their liability and data protection requirements relating to them (eg consent of data subject and fair use of data).

E   Bringing contractual terms to the attention of the consumer

1.42   Providers in the world of e-commerce will generally wish to ensure that a set of standard terms and conditions apply to all transactions. A problem which is common to conventional providers but which is highlighted in online trading is how to bring standard terms to the attention of the consumer before the contract is concluded and to incorporate them into an online contract. Websites can be labyrinthine and it will not always be easy for a provider to prove that the consumer was aware of all relevant terms and conditions.

The approach which seems to be commonly adopted is to require the customer to read through the applicable terms and conditions and to signify his acceptance to them before proceeding. The provider will generally require that the customer 'clicks' on a relevant box to indicate his acceptance of terms. Of course, he may choose not to read them but proceed anyway (in much the same way as a conventionally concluded contract) but the provider must make reasonably sufficient efforts to bring terms to the attention of the customer and it is likely that this approach would satisfy this. This is not going so far as requiring the customer to attach his digital signature in each case which is likely to be viewed as being unduly burdensome.

Exclusion clauses and clauses limiting liability should in particular be highlighted and brought to the customer's attention. The E-Commerce Directive also requires that the customer be able to print out the required information together with the terms and conditions and the details of their order.

An alternative approach is to provide hypertext links to a page of 'legal information' but if it is possible to proceed to order or apply without this page necessarily appearing as part of the process then there must be an increased likelihood that this would not be construed by the courts as sufficient notice. However, it may be that for some products or services, especially those with a relatively low value (eg books or compact discs) that this is viewed as an acceptable risk.

E-commerce is by its nature best suited to standardised products and processes. In the area of life assurance complete e-trading has in the main been limited to protection type contracts where a case does not require individual underwriting. In such cases policy terms may also not be as complicated as for investment contracts and may therefore work better for this purpose (ie drawing the customer's attention to them).

F   The Distance Selling of Financial Services Directive

1.43   The distance selling of financial services to retail customers is now covered by rules adopted to implement the EU Directive on this subject[1]. As regards FSA-regulated financial services the rules are to be found in the conduct of business rules (see COB 1.10 and ICOB 1.7). The Treasury implemented other aspects in the Distance Marketing Regulations[2].

The purpose of the directive was to harmonise the basis on which contracts were sold at a distance to retail customers (ie without face-to-face contact at any stage of the process). It sets minimum standards for the provision of information before a contract is concluded, provides for cancellation rights, and includes provisions to protect consumers in relation to misuse of payment cards and unsolicited communications.

The FSA rules relating to the provision of information apply where a sale is conducted at a distance as part of an organised initiative and not under an 'initial' (in the sense of a framework) services agreement (see Chapter 5). The idea is to ensure that the consumer is fully informed before he is committed to the contract. In practice this means that a person contracting at a distance should have received very detailed contractual information 'in a durable' medium and had an opportunity to review it before he is bound.

SECTION 4   UNFAIR CONTRACT TERMS

A   The Unfair Contract Terms Directive

1.44   The Unfair Contract Terms Directive[3] was implemented into English law on 1 January 1995 by the Unfair Terms in Consumer Contracts Regulations 1994[4] (although the regulations did not commence and so did not apply to contracts concluded before 1 July 1995). The Directive's provisions should not be confused with the Unfair Contract Terms Act 1977 (UCTA), which applies only to exemption clauses. This directive potentially applies to *all* terms of a contract other than its core terms (eg description of subject matter and adequacy of price).

The DTI issued a consultative document on implementation of the directive in January 1994. In September 1994 a further consultative document and revised draft regulations were issued. The 1994 regulations were revoked and replaced in very similar terms by the Unfair Terms in Consumer Contracts Regulations 1999 which commenced in October 1999[5].

On 5 May 2005 the FSA issued a statement of good practice in relation to unfair terms in consumer contracts. This sets out the FSA's views in relation, in

1   2002/65/EC.
2   SI 2004/2095.
3   EC 93/13.
4   SI 1994/3159.
5   SI 1999/2083.

particular, to terms in a contract which allow the supplier of financial services to make changes. This statement refers to draft ABI guidance which was finalised and issued in May 2006. The ABI guidance is specifically directed at reviewable rate insurance contracts and it includes model wording for critical illness policies and key features documents. The ABI guidance also explains that the ABI had consulted with and achieved some buy-in from both the FSA and the FOS in relation to the approach adopted. Firms also need to bear in mind the need to treat their customers fairly and contract terms, including those not subject to the regulations, will need to be operated fairly in practice.

B Exclusions

1.45 Regulation 6(2)(a) and (b) effectively excludes from the requirement of fairness, terms which define the main subject matter of the contract or which relate to the question of adequacy of the price (also referred to as 'core terms') in so far as those terms are in plain, intelligible language. A recital to the directive also excludes terms in insurance contracts which define or circumscribe the risk. However, this was not adopted in the regulations as it is viewed as only one example of main subject matter exemption.

In the case of *Director General of Fair Trading v First National Bank plc*[1] the Court of Appeal took a restrictive interpretation of the exclusion of 'core terms' on the basis that otherwise 'almost any provision containing any part of the bargain would be capable of falling within the reach of regulation 3(2) [the equivalent regulation under the 1994 regulations]'. This case is discussed further at **1.47**.

The regulations also do not apply to:

(1) Contractual terms which are incorporated in order to comply with, or which reflect, mandatory statutory or regulatory provisions and the provisions or principles of international conventions to which member states or the community are a party.

(2) By implication, contracts which are not for the supply of goods or services.

C Unfair terms

1.46 The directive provides that:

> 'A contractual term which has not been individually negotiated shall be regarded as unfair if, contrary to the requirement of good faith, it causes a significant imbalance in the parties' rights and obligations arising under the contract, to the detriment of the consumer.'[2]

---

1   [2002] 1 All ER 97.
2   EC 93/13.

From this it is clear that the directive applies to terms (note it applies to individual terms rather than contracts in their entirety) which have not been individually negotiated, in contracts between a seller/supplier and a consumer. The regulations define consumer as 'a natural person who, in contracts covered by these Regulations, is acting for purposes which are outside his trade, business or profession[1]'. A seller or supplier, conversely, is someone acting in the course of his trade, business or profession. Clearly, insurance companies will be dealing in the course of their business. When a person is dealing as a consumer is straightforward in most cases but there are potentially difficult situations. For example, it is open to question how far someone is acting for purposes outside his business if he acts as a trustee of an occupational pension scheme, particularly if he is an employer representative of a small scheme.

The regulations specifically provide that a term shall always be regarded as not having been individually negotiated where it has been drafted in advance and the consumer has therefore not been able to influence its substance[2]. This would appear to apply to almost all insurance contracts where at least some, if not all, of the terms will be in a standard printed form and any negotiation will be likely to have been in relation to price.

1.47   It can be seen from the definition of unfair terms above that it appears to have three limbs:

(1)   It is contrary to the requirement of *good faith*.

(2)   It (the individual term) causes *a significant imbalance in the party's rights* and obligations arising under the contract.

(3)   It is to the *detriment of* the consumer.

The requirement of good faith in contracts is not something with which English lawyers, unlike many of their European counterparts, are familiar. There is, of course, the overriding obligation of utmost good faith (uberrima fides) in insurance contracts which is perhaps developing into a more general duty but is still predominantly concerned with pre-contractual disclosure of information material to the decision to accept business. There is a list of terms which may be regarded prima facie as unfair in Schedule 2 to the regulations. There is no longer a specific Schedule setting out guidance regarding factors relevant to an assessment of good faith as there was in the 1994 regulations. The essence of the matter, in most cases appears, therefore, to be fairness in relation to a consumer's interests. Hence, where a consumer takes out a contract to cover a particular loss, then it is presumably not dealing equitably with his legitimate interests for the insurer to include a term which results in the insurer avoiding paying at all, or paying less than the sum insured, whether as an abuse of stronger bargaining position or a technicality. Conversely, it is arguable, where powers in a contract exercisable at the discretion of the insurer are expressly subject to a requirement

1   Regulation 3.
2   Regulation 5(2).

31

of reasonableness, that the objectivity of the requirement of reasonableness is indicative of the insurer dealing fairly and equitably with the consumer's legitimate interests, particularly where such powers have been disclosed to the consumer before he became bound by the contract.

The second limb of the definition of unfair terms is difficult in insurance contracts with consumers where all inequality of bargaining power will almost always exist. That imbalance is not caused by the term, so presumably for the term to cause an imbalance to the detriment of the consumer it would need to produce an effect that is unreasonable (because the consumer would not expect a term of that nature and/or it was not disclosed to him prior to conclusion of the contract). The requirement of detriment to the consumer is also a somewhat uncertain requirement as the term is not defined in the directive or the regulations. The requirement of detriment is familiar in issues of contractual consideration or equitable estoppel, in the sense of a financial loss to the innocent party or arranging affairs in an irrevocable way. It is also possible that it would extend to loss of opportunity. It is particularly difficult to apply the concept of detriment where a term (eg price/rate review clause) may have either a positive or a negative impact. However, it would appear from the FSA's statement of good practice that it regards a potential detriment as sufficient to challenge a term. This is arguably supported by the *First National Bank*[1] case which did not appear to attach much significance to the requirement of detriment.

The *First National Bank* case concerned a clause providing for interest on a debt to continue to accrue after judgment in case of default. The court held that despite this term relating to the payment of interest, on a debt it is an ancillary, not a core term. It was therefore subject to the regulations. In fact having applied the regulations the court found the term to be fair. There is dicta in this case which is relied upon by the FSA to say that premium review clauses are not core terms and therefore are subject to the regulations. This point is not conceded in relation to premium review clauses in insurance contracts in the ABI guidance. From the point of view of the judgment it would not appear too difficult to distinguish a term applying only in the event of a potential future default from a term which provides that the price from the outset is variable, dependant on the effect of specified parameters. In reality much will turn on the circumstances of the case (eg whether the reviewable nature of a policy and the specified parameters are made sufficiently clear to the consumer).

However, although the Court of Appeal statements on core terms in the *First National Bank* case may therefore strictly be obiter as far as consideration of premium review clauses in insurance contracts are concerned, they are still worth reading. The case is also useful in explaining the concepts of good faith and significant imbalance in this context, as follows:

> 'The requirement of good faith in this context is one of fair and open dealing. Openness requires that the terms should be expressed fully, clearly and legibly, containing no concealed pitfalls or traps. Appropriate prominence should be given to terms which might operate disadvantageously to the customer. Fair dealing requires that a supplier should not whether deliberately or unconsciously

1   [2002] 1 All ER 97.

take advantage of the consumer's necessity, indigence, lack of experience, unfamiliarity with the subject matter of the contract, weak bargaining position or any other factor listed in or analogous to those listed in Schedule 2 of the regulations[1].'

D Potentially unfair terms

1.48 The definition of 'unfair terms' does not help to identify definitively or clearly terms which are unfair. Fortunately, the regulations provide an indicative, non-exhaustive list of terms which may be regarded as unfair[2].

Terms will be regarded as unfair which have the object or effect of:

(a) excluding or limiting the legal liability of a seller or supplier in the event of the death of a consumer or personal injury to the latter resulting from an act or omission of that seller or supplier;

(b) inappropriately excluding or limiting the legal rights of the consumer vis-à-vis the seller or supplier or another party in the event of total or partial non-performance or inadequate performance by the seller or supplier of any of the contractual obligations, including the option of offsetting a debt owed to the seller or supplier against any claim which the consumer may have against him;

(c) making an agreement binding on the consumer whereas the provision of services by the seller or supplier is subject to a condition whose realisation depends on his own will alone;

(d) permitting the seller or supplier to retain such sums paid by the consumer where the latter decides not to conclude or perform the contract without providing for the consumer to receive compensation of an equivalent amount from the seller or supplier, where the latter is the party cancelling the contract;

(e) requiring any consumer who fails to fulfil his obligations to pay a disproportionately high sum in compensation;

(f) authorising the seller or supplier to dissolve the contract on a discretionary basis where the same facility is not granted to the consumer or permitting the seller or supplier to retain the sums paid for services not yet supplied by him where it is the seller or supplier who himself dissolves the contract;

(g) enabling the seller or supplier to terminate a contract of indeterminate duration without reasonable notice except where there are serious grounds for doing so;

(h) automatically extending a contract of fixed duration where the consumer does not indicate otherwise, when the deadline fixed for the consumer to express this desire not to extend the contract is unreasonably early;

1   [2002] 1 All ER 97 at 108.
2   See art 3(3), the Annex and Sch 2 to the Regulations.

(i)   *irrevocably* binding the consumer to terms with which he had no real opportunity of becoming acquainted before the conclusion of the contract;

(j)   *enabling the seller or supplier to alter the terms of the contract unilaterally without a valid reason which is specified in the contract*;

(k)   *enabling the seller or supplier to alter unilaterally without a valid reason any characteristics of the product or services to be provided*;

(l)   providing for the price of goods to be determined at the time of delivery or allowing a seller of goods or supplier of services to increase their price without in both cases giving the consumer the corresponding right to cancel the contract if the final price is too high in relation to the price agreed when the contract was concluded;

(m)   giving the seller or supplier the right to determine whether the goods or services supplied are in conformity with the contract or *giving him the exclusive right to interpret any term of the contract*;

(n)   limiting the seller's or supplier's obligation to respect commitments undertaken by his agents *or making his commitments subject to compliance with a particular formality*;

(o)   obliging the consumer to fulfil all his obligations where the seller or supplier does not perform his;

(p)   giving the seller or supplier the possibility of transferring his rights and obligations under the contract where this may serve to reduce the guarantees for the consumer without the latter's agreement; or

(q)   excluding or hindering the consumer's right to take legal action or exercise any other legal remedy, particularly by requiring the consumer to take disputes *exclusively* to arbitration not covered by legal provision, unduly restricting the evidence available to him or imposing on him a burden of proof which according to the applicable law should lie with another party to the contract.

1.49   There are certain exceptions to paragraph (j) above, particularly the right to terminate a non-fixed term contract where reasonable notification is given to the consumer and where the consumer is free to dissolve the contract. In addition:

> '. . . terms under which a supplier of financial services reserves the right to alter the rate of interest payable by the consumer or due to the latter, or the amount of other *charges for financial services* without notice where there is a valid reason, provided that the supplier is required to inform the other contracting party or parties thereof at the earliest opportunity and that the latter are *free to dissolve* the contract immediately.'[1] (emphasis added).

This should permit variation for an undisclosed but valid reason even if it is not specified in the contract provided the conditions as to notice and cancellation of

---

1   Sch 2, para 2(b).

the contract are complied with. However, it is worth looking at the FSA's description of these provisions in its statement of practice. Rather than seeing them as exceptions, as stated, it treats them as factors making it 'less likely' that the terms will be unfair. It would appear that both the FSA and the FOS are keen for the reason and parameters around any ability to make changes to a contract to be specified in the contract itself. The exemption may therefore be limited in practice to force majeure type reasons or reasons which the parties could not have contemplated when the contract was taken out. In relation to the term 'free to dissolve the contract' the FSA statement confirms that a consumer is free to dissolve the contract even if that involves a loss of opportunity. Free to dissolve means without having to make a payment or give prior notice and that the issue of loss of opportunity may, however, fall within TCF issues (eg ability to get new cover, etc).

E   Clear disclosure

1.50   A recurrent theme running through these examples is that if the reason for a particular term is valid, is disclosed to the consumer at the earliest opportunity or the consumer has the right to dissolve the contract when they are notified of a change, then the term should generally be fair. This is coupled with, and to a certain extent exemplified by, the requirement in the directive and the regulations that all written terms be drafted in *plain, intelligible language*. Where there is doubt about the meaning of a term, the interpretation most favourable to the consumer shall prevail. It should be noted that the requirement of plain, intelligible language also applies to terms dealing with the main subject matter of the contract, as this is a condition of the core terms exemption.

The European aspect of this should also be noted. If a policyholder is resident in another member state and the law of that country applies (which it normally would) then, unless there was a choice of law available in that country, the requirement may well be for the terms to be in, for example, plain, intelligible Polish.

F   Relevance to life contracts

1.51   Clauses in life contracts that might be caught by the examples in Schedule 2 are:

(a)   terms excluding liability – limitation clauses or exemption clauses not related to the nature of the risk or arguably the main risk (ie not covered by the main subject matter exemption);

(b)   terms requiring payment of disproportionate amounts for failure to fulfil obligations – early surrender penalties;

(c)   clauses irrevocably binding the consumer to terms which were unavailable – this could apply to all terms of an insurer's standard contract which do not circumscribe the risk. It is arguable where cancellation rights exist and the policyholder receives the policy within that period that the consumer is not irrevocably bound until the end of the cancellation period. There is also an argument that the right to inspect a copy of the contract (which the Statement of Long-Term Insurance Practice requires to be made clear in the proposal form) is a real opportunity for the consumer to get a copy of the policy before he even completes the proposal form;

(d) power of unilateral variation – any power of alteration which is discretionary (subject to what has been said above in relation to altering rates of interest and charges in financial services contracts without notice for a valid reason);

(e) power to change charges – any terms allowing charges or fees to be increased without allowing the consumer a right to cancel – could be caught. However, there is an exemption in paragraph 2(d) of Schedule 2 which permits indexation of charges provided the basis is explicitly described;

(f) terms requiring formalities – imposing time limits (for example on claims), requirements of notification in a particular form (eg writing) without a valid reason.

The issue which has attracted the most attention to date is that of reviewable premium contracts. The FSA appears to accept that such contracts have a value in terms of affordability and flexibility in the marketplace and are not intrinsically unfair. The FSA's focus seems to be to ensure that there is a valid (ideally specified) reason for the clause permitting change and that the customer is given adequate notice and explanation so that any changes do not come as a nasty shock to them. This involves being very specific about why and how such changes are made. So, for example, a clause permitting the company to decide relevant factors at its discretion will not satisfy the requirements. Similarly, a non-exhaustive list of factors to be taken into account at the company's discretion will not, in the FSA's view, satisfy the requirement.

Generally, in assessing whether a reason is valid, the more the trigger for change is outside the control of the company, the more likely it is to be accepted (eg legal or regulatory changes). Contracts with third parties (eg reassurers) will not automatically benefit from being outside the company's control. The FSA indicates that the reasonableness of the reassurance contract itself would need to be reviewed. A term that only allows a change which is proportionate to the underlying reason for the change is also more likely to be fair than one where there is an element of subjective assessment.

In relation to reviewable contracts, the FSA states that a term should not allow a firm to recoup its investment losses prior to the review, to increase profitability, to loss lead or to increase premiums at all if its records do not enable it to prove the basis of the original premium. The FSA is also keen that review clauses do not give the company the discretion to decide when to carry out the review (or indeed not to carry one out).

The ABI guidance includes a statement from the FOS (1.2.5) about FOS's attitude. This states that the FOS will take both the FSA and ABI papers into account and will look at how fairly terms are applied in practice. The ABI paper is also useful because it contains model contract wordings for critical illness policies which all parties to the consultation have seen. The model approach is to explain why reviewable premiums are offered (eg affordability/potentially less than guaranteed rates) and why the premium might change, (eg because medical advances may affect the insurer's expectation of future claims). The trigger for the change is stated to be the company's view of the specified assumptions at the review date being different from that it took at the outset. The ABI example gives a de minimis change (x%) which will not lead to a change in premiums. It also states that the company will apply the method it uses to calculate premiums in a fair and reasonable way. It is worth noting that it does not seek to include a formula to actually calculate the increase. The ABI approach also makes clear (if it is true) that there is no maximum amount of increase. It had been suggested that specifying a maximum would be necessary to make such clauses fair but that is not the position adopted by the ABI.

G   Representative actions – function of Director General

1.52   In the original consultative document the DTI indicated that, based on the strict wording of the directive, it would not be implementing the provisions in the directive[1] allowing representative actions. However, consumers' representative bodies are understood to have complained and comments were also received from independent solicitors to the effect that action to implement Article 7 of the directive was required. It should also be borne in mind that, in relation to non-UK resident policyholders, other member states will have implemented this provision.

A compromise was suggested in the second consultative document. The result is found in Regulations 10 to 15, so that the Director General of Fair Trading is under a duty to consider complaints about unfair terms (unless they are frivolous or vexatious). If he finds them to be unfair, he may, if he considers it appropriate, then apply to the court for an injunction to restrict their use. The Director General must give reasons for his decision to apply or not to apply, as the case may be, for an injunction in relation to any complaint he is required to consider[2]. The court may grant an injunction on such terms as it sees fit, including prohibiting continued use of unfair terms in consumer contracts by sellers or suppliers or recommended by associations of sellers or suppliers[3]. Alternatively, a 'qualifying body' as set out in Schedule 1 may agree to consider a complaint that a contractual term is unfair in place of the Director General. This now includes the Financial Services Authority by virtue of the amending Regulations issued in 2001. These provisions should increase the likelihood of terms being challenged and, indeed, of their use being prevented. It should also increase the profile of the directive's provisions as the Director General is empowered to arrange for the

1   Article 7.
2   Regulation 10.
3   Regulation 12.

dissemination of information and advice to the public and all persons likely to be affected by the regulations.

The FSA also states that in deciding whether to take enforcement action (eg an injunction) it will consider any undertakings from the firm about the way the term is operated in practice. Whilst the courts are always the final arbiters, providers may be able to get a high level of certainty by giving the FSA such an undertaking. Undertakings are published by the FSA and can be useful in forming a view on similar terms.

H Blue pencil test?

1.53 Assuming that a term is found to be unfair, the effect is that the term in question is not binding on the consumer[1]. There is no power to rewrite or restrict the term and the remainder of the contract will continue to bind the parties 'if capable of continuing' without the unfair term(s). Thus the effect of the remaining terms of the contract may be entirely different without the offending term, but if they are capable of existence, even with that different meaning, they will continue. It remains to be seen how the courts will exercise this power in practice. It is suggested that clauses within a contract itself permitting changes to a contract to render a potentially unfair clause fair would not themselves be fair. Although arguable, this does not seem consistent with the intention of the parties or the need to interpret a contract in such a way as to make it workable. The FSA do not appear opposed to such variation clauses provided that they are narrowly drafted (ie the discretion of the provider is not too wide).

I Treating customers fairly

1.54 It is worth noting that although the directive does not apply to contracts made before 1 July 1995, insurers with such contracts are still subject to the FSA's Principles and in particular the need to treat customer's fairly. The FSA makes clear in its statement that even if terms (such as review clauses) were held to be core and therefore excluded from the regulations, they would still be subject to the need to apply the terms fairly, similarly for existing contracts.

J UCTA 1977

1.55 As has been seen, the directive's provisions are wider (ie applying to all terms and to insurance companies) than UCTA. The intention is, however, that for non-insurance contracts the regime will run alongside that of UCTA and will not qualify or restrict any rights under that Act. Insurance contracts remain exempt from the provisions of UCTA.

---

1   Regulation 8(1).

SECTION 5   LAW OF CONTRACT

1.56   The question of which law applies to a contract of life assurance is of practical importance in view of the increasingly international nature of much of the business transacted. Many life offices maintain branches or employ agents in a number of countries and issue policies to persons resident or carrying on business in the country in which the branch is situated or where the agent carries on business.

A contract of life assurance is governed by its proper law and many life policies will expressly state the country whose law governs the contract. The parties' choice of which system of law shall apply may depend upon where the proposer has his habitual residence, especially when selling in the EU.

The Second Life Directive harmonised the law applicable to life contracts in the EU. The general scheme of that harmonisation is that the law of the contract is the law of the member state in which the policyholder has his habitual residence or is a national, at the time the contract is effected, unless in that state a choice to the contrary can be and is made. This was implemented in the UK by changes to both the Insurance Companies Act 1982 and the Contracts (Applicable Law) Act 1990. The latter Act had incorporated the Rome Convention[1] into English law. The Insurance Companies Act 1982 provisions have been replaced by the Financial Services and Markets Act 2000 (Law Applicable to Contracts of Insurance) Regulations 2001[2]. These regulations leave the previous position unchanged. They do, however, provide that where there is more than one country within a member state each is treated as a separate state for these purposes. The Regulations now apply the 1990 Act to non-EEA situations and state that in determining freedom of choice of law in any part of the UK, the 1990 Act applies. The 1990 Act provides that there is freedom to choose the law of the contract except where the contract is only connected to one country and that country's law is not chosen, in which case the mandatory rules of that country would also apply.

The Second Life directive introduced the concept of 'Mandatory Rules' for insurance contracts, essentially rules which cannot be derogated from, irrespective of the law of the contract. They would, normally, therefore apply where the policyholder and the insurance company are in different member states. The two situations in which they can apply are:

(1)   where the law of the contract is not that of the member state of the commitment (ie where the policyholder is habitually resident) and the law of that member state provides for mandatory rules to apply where that member states law is not chosen as the law of the contract; and

(2)   where they are part of the law of the forum (ie the country in which a court case is being heard and that law is not the law of the contract.

1   Which excluded this issue.
2   SI 2001/2635.

The DTI published an extensive list of mandatory rules for UK purposes. The FSA's approach is to specify part of their rules that apply to EEA insurers but not to include in that list other provisions of the law applicable to insurers. EU insurers do not in practice seem to receive notice of the UK mandatory rules. It is therefore not clear whether the requirement of insurable interest would be a mandatory rule if the UK were the member state of commitment or if a case came before the English courts. This question has particular reference to the use of beneficiary clauses, a practice which is common in many other member states. The question was raised with the DTI whether UK insurers would be able to provide contracts which include a beneficiary clause to residents of other member states where such clauses are valid. The DTI's view was that where the law of the contract was English law, the provisions (section 1 of the Life Assurance Act 1774) would apply, but that where it was not they could only apply if the policyholder sued in the English courts. This would be on the basis that it is possible that the provisions would be held to be part of the procedural rules of the forum. In the authors' opinion it would seem odd if a contract with a foreign policyholder, which, according to the law of the contract could contain a beneficiary clause, could not be enforced in the English courts.

SECTION 6   THE POLICY

A   Form of the contract – the policy document

1   Policies in writing

1.57   It is important to distinguish the contract from its physical manifestation, the policy document. The policy document will not necessarily contain all the terms of the contract. Some may be contained in the proposal or other document and others may be implied by law.

The common law does not require a contract of insurance to be in any particular form or, indeed, to be in writing at all[1]. It was widely believed, however, that section 100 of the Stamp Act 1891 required a life assurance policy to be issued, as by that section any person who received or took the credit for any premium on any life insurance and did not within one month make out and execute a duly stamped policy of insurance incurred a penalty. It has been argued[2], on the other hand, that the Act does not require any such contract of insurance to be expressed in a policy as a condition precedent to the validity of the contract; it is concerned with the stamping of policies in being. However, section 100, which was concerned with the penalty for not making out a policy or making a policy not duly stamped, has been repealed by section 173(3) of the Finance Act 1989 and as such, section 173 abolishes stamp duty on policies of life insurance. In order for the policy to be a 'qualifying policy' for income tax purposes the contract must

---

1   *London Life Insurance Co v Wright* (1881) 5 SCR 466.
2   *MacGillvray on Insurance Law* (9th edn, 1997) p 111, paras 3–4, note 9.

be in writing. (See further Chapter 13.) In any event, it is now the general practice to issue policy documents.

Section 4 of the Policies of Assurance Act 1867[1] requires that the policy should specify the principal place or places of business at which notices of assignment may be given.

2   Form of policy and schedule

1.58   The policy is the document prepared by the life office to express the terms of the contract which has already been made, and with which it must conform. In earlier times the policy was usually prepared in advance so that it could be handed over in exchange for the first premium. Under modern practice, however, the proposer is very likely to pay the premium before the policy document is prepared and agrees expressly (in the proposal form) or impliedly to accept a policy on the life office's standard terms and conditions[2]. The life office must issue a policy which is in accordance with its marketing literature and the proposal form. The proposer need not otherwise accept it.

As it is drafted by the life office in case of any ambiguity the policy terms will be construed against the interests of the life office.

A life policy may be issued either under hand or under seal, but must be executed in accordance with the constitution or regulations of the life office. The general modern practice is to use two documents or one document which is in two parts, one document or part for terms of general application with a second document or part being a schedule for insertion of items specific to the assured. These latter items include the policy number, the name of the assured and the life assured, the nature and amount of the benefit, when and to whom it is payable, and the amounts of the premium and when they are payable. The general conditions and provisions attaching to the policy usually form part of the first document or part mentioned, and may include provisions as to payment of claims, days of grace for payment of premiums, protection against forfeiture, surrenders, loans (although if more than the possibility of obtaining a loan is expressed then the policy may then be subject to consumer credit legislation), conversions to paid up assurance and suicide (see Section B below for further information).

3   Segments

1.59   The advent of unit-linked life assurance business in the late 1970s led to the introduction of policies issued in 'clusters' or 'segments', so that when the assured proposes for a contract of assurance he receives, in return for a given premium, not one policy but a number of policies of equal value – each one issued in return for an equal fraction of the total premium payable. Life policies issued as 'clusters' offer opportunities for tax planning as it is possible to encash whole segments rather than make a partial surrender of the whole policy, the

---

1   See Appendix 2.
2   *General Accident Insurance Corp v Cronk* (1901) 17 TLR 233.

charging regime for partial surrenders being generally harsher. The general practice is for one document to be issued as the principal 'contract of assurance' together with a number of separate schedules of benefits which expressly incorporate the individual contracts by reference. This was originally achieved by having a separate piece of paper for each 'segment' which was rather artificial and probably unnecessary. As a consequence, the practice is dying out.

4 Group or master policies

1.60   Where a company contracts to grant assurances or annuities in respect of all (or defined categories of) employees of a particular employer, whether in connection with a pension scheme or otherwise, it is a common practice to issue a group master policy in respect of each employer. Such a group policy expresses the general terms applicable to all the assurances or annuities, and the individual benefits are usually recorded in duplicate, one copy being with the life office and the other with the employer.

The use of group policies is not confined to cases where the members of the group are bound together by common employment. They may, for instance, be members of an association, customers of a hire-purchase trader or parents of the pupils of a school.

B   Common terms and conditions of a life assurance policy

1.61   Although life assurance policies differ from office to office and from policy to policy, it may be useful to briefly describe some of the common terms and conditions found in life assurance policies. Obviously, not all of the following apply to all policies. Some policies such as term assurance policies will only have the basic provisions as described below (perhaps (i) to (viii)) whereas more sophisticated policies will have additional features. As mentioned above in Section A, specific personal details relating to the assured or life assured are often set out in a schedule although again for the simpler types of policy all the terms and conditions may well be in the same document. Example terms and provisions are set out below. It is likely that (i) to (viii) below will be in virtually all life policies.

(i)   Name of assured and of life assured[1].

(ii)   Policy date.

(iii)   Policy number.

(iv)   Sum assured – amount payable on death or maturity (as relevant).

(v)   Event upon which sum assured is payable – death of sole life assured, death of first life assured (joint lives (first death) contract), death of last

---

1   Life Assurance Act 1774, s 2.

life assured (joint lives (last survivor) contract) or survival to the maturity date (where relevant).

(vi)   Premium payments – amount, frequency, method of payment, consequences of non-payment.

(vii) Method of reinstating or reviving policies which have lapsed.

(viii) How notice is to be given to the life office including principal place of business of life office (for example, to give notice of assignment)[1].

(ix)   Details regarding surrender values (where relevant) and how this will be calculated (will differ considerably between unit-linked and with-profits policies).

(x)   Options to alter sum assured/premium/life assured.

(xi)   Options to convert policy into a different type, for example, from term assurance to endowment.

(xii) Options to effect further assurance with no further health evidence, for example, on the birth or adoption of a child.

(xiii) Option to issue replacement policy on, for example, surrender of, or reduction in, sum assured under, the original policy.

(xiv) Option to increase sum assured where an inheritance tax liability can be shown to have increased, for example as a result of a change in legislation or through an increase in the value of the estate.

(xv)   Option to increase sum assured on evidence of increase in value of assured's interest in a business.

(xvi) Waiver of contribution benefit (also known as premium waiver benefit). For an additional premium regular premiums may be suspended if the life assured is unable to pay them due to illness, etc.

(xvii) Accidental death benefit – sum assured is increased where death is due to an accident (as defined).

(xviii) Investment provisions/fund rules – as many life insurance products are almost wholly or at least partially investment-based there will be provisions relating to the underlying investment funds. This may well include the division of the fund into notional units, how units are valued, calculation of 'bid' and 'offer' prices, ability to close funds and make new funds available, where expenses are paid from, creation and cancellation of units, charges relating to investment management, rights to defer allocation or redemption of units, etc. In every case it should also be explained that the division of the fund into units is notional and the policyholder has no proprietary rights to the underlying investments.

1   Policies of Assurance Act 1867, s 1.

C The policy and extrinsic evidence

I General rules of construction

1.62 Where a contract is recorded in writing, the terms of the writing alone will normally be referred to in order to ascertain the rights and obligations of the parties: and the policy is the normal evidence of the contract of life assurance. The construction of policies is underpinned by certain basic rules which are outlined as follows: words are given their ordinary meanings (with reference to previous judicial authority as appropriate); a businesslike interpretation will be applied; unreasonable results should be avoided; ordinary meanings will be displaced if it can be established that they have a different technical legal meaning, the usage in that trade is different or the context requires a different meaning; the application of the 'ejusdem generis' rule whereby if certain words of a certain type are followed by general words, the general words are intended to describe only other things of the same type as those set out in the particular words[1].

Preliminary statements and documents, such as marketing literature, key features documents, quotations and proposal forms, which are part of the negotiations, form no part of the contract unless they are incorporated in the policy by reference or otherwise, in which case they are read as part of the policy. They cannot normally be referred to in construing the policy; although this rule is subject to many exceptions. A mere reference to the proposal in the policy is not in itself an incorporation of it in the contract. There must be something else to show that it is referred to as part of the contract and not merely by way of recital.

The statements made by a life office in any marketing literature or other advertisement will normally only be incorporated into the contract by express reference. If the statements are regarded as representations which induced the contract, they may afford grounds for rescission of the contract and return of premiums, but it would be rare for them to be read as part of the contract between the parties. The court may award damages under section 2(1) of the Misrepresentation Act 1967, which states that:

> 'Where a person has entered into a contract after a misrepresentation has been made to him by another party thereto and as a result thereof has suffered loss, then, if the person making the misrepresentation would be liable to damages in respect thereof had the misrepresentation been made fraudulently, that person shall be so liable notwithstanding that the misrepresentation was not made fraudulently, unless he proves that he had reasonable grounds to believe and did believe up to the time the contract was made, that the facts represented were true.'

Contrary to common law[2] but not equity[3], therefore, the life office will be liable for misrepresentations unless it can prove that it had reasonable grounds to believe, and did believe up to the time that the contract was made, that the facts represented were true. Companies are required by the FSA's rules relating to financial promotions to retain a record of the basis of any such statements. The

1 See further *MacGillivray on Insurance Law* (9th edn, 1997) p 264, 11–1 to 11–19.
2 *Anderson v Fitzgerald* (1853) 4 HL Cas 484.
3 Eg *Redgrave v Hurd* (1882) 20 Ch D 1.

life office will, furthermore, normally be liable for the representations made by
its agents.

2   Parol evidence

1.63   There is a presumption that the policy document contains all the terms
of the policy – the 'parol evidence' rule[1]. Also, where the words of the policy
possess a clear meaning then it is not required to look elsewhere for an alternative meaning[2]. For these two reasons the basic rule is that extrinsic evidence is
inadmissible.

Evidence extrinsic to the policy may, however, be admissible (in the absence
of an express stipulation to the contrary in the policy) and some more common
examples are set out below:

(1)   To show that the statements form part of the contract and that the policy
does not truly set out the full terms of the agreement between the parties.
The court will then need to refer to what passed during the preliminary
negotiations, including any relevant documents, and may order rectification
of the policy in order to represent the true contract between the parties.

Sun Life Assurance Co of Canada v Jervis[3]

The life office sent to J a proposal form with a document called an
'Illustration', showing how the suggested policy would apply in his case.
The 'Illustration' contained figures filled in by the agent. The wording of
the proposal form was such that it could be completed only by a person who
had read the 'Illustration'. Held, that the latter formed part of the contract
and the policy should be rectified accordingly.

(2)   To show the existence of a collateral agreement outside the terms of the
policy which does not vary those terms but which represents a supplementary part of the bargain[4]. This supplemental agreement must be strictly collateral to the policy contract; statements as to practice or probable benefits
to be derived from the insurance may be merely expressions of expectation
or belief and will not then be construed as promises forming part of the contract.

Thiselton v Commercial Union Assurance Co Ltd[5]

The assured effected a policy on the basis of a prospectus which contained
the following provision: 'Loans are granted upon security of the society's
policies at 4½%, except when the loan amounts to £200 or more when the
rate is only 4%'. Mr Thiselton sought to compel the society to lend to him

1   *Horncastle v Equitable Life Assurance Society* (1906) 22 TLR 735.
2   *Shore v Wilson* (1842) 9 Cl & F 355.
3   [1943] 2 All ER 425; see also *Anstey v British Natural Premium Life* (1908) TLR 871.
4   *Bowtle v Salvation Army Assurance Society* (1927) IAC Rep 47.
5   [1926] Ch 888.

at the rates quoted. Held, that although the existence of some agreement outside the policy could not be denied, such agreement must be strictly collateral and the *statement of practice* as to loans was not collateral.

(3) To explain words which may not be obvious, such as technical or foreign words or abbreviations or shorthand.

(4) To show the intention of the parties where there is a patent ambiguity in the policy or where there is, on investigation of the circumstances, a latent ambiguity.

Where there is ambiguity or inconsistency in the policy, the court may apply various principles in an attempt to give effect to the contractual intention of the parties. For example, an earlier clause would generally take priority over a later one, although great caution must be exercised in this respect as much will depend on the wording and structure of the policy. Also, written wordings would tend to be given precedence over the printed clause with which they were inconsistent. It would seem that where the parties have deleted printed provisions this should be a factor in the court deciding what the parties intended[1] and this may be enhanced by the parties in some way authenticating the deletion, for example by initialling. Also of relevance is the contra proferentum rule which means that the ambiguity in a policy is construed against the party which prepared it. In most cases this will be the insurer but could be the insured where, for example, the proposal form is incorporated into the policy and the ambiguity relates to the insured's answers. Note should also be made here of the Unfair Terms in Consumer Contracts Regulations 1999, which are considered in Section 4.

3 Rectification

1.64 If either party to the contract establishes that the policy document does not set out the full or correct terms of the agreement between them, then he is entitled to have the policy rectified so that it expresses their true agreement[2]. However, there is a presumption that a policy contains the complete and final contract between the parties and so a strong burden of proof lies on the party seeking rectification to show clearly that agreement was reached as to the terms of the contract to be set out in the policy and that the policy fails to record their agreement[3].

It is sometimes stated that mistake is not generally a ground for rectification of a policy unless the mistake is 'mutual'[4]. Such phraseology can be misleading in that for both parties to make the same mistake would not only be coincidental but an arbitrary basis for rectification. Perhaps a more accurate description is that both parties must have understood the agreement between them to be something

---

1 *Punjab National Bank v de Boinville* (1992) 1 WLR 1138.
2 *Collett v Morrison* (1851) 9 Hare 162.
3 *Parsons v Bignold* (1846) 15 LJ Ch 379.
4 *Slack v Hancock* (1912) 107 LT 14.

other than is mistakenly recorded in the policy issued by the life office[1]. The unilateral error of one party usually affords no grounds for rectification. Thus in *Royal Liver Friendly Society v Shearer*[2], a Friendly Society claimed rectification of its policy on the ground that in drafting the proposed form of policy the Society's officials had made a mistake in reading their own table of benefits set out in the Society's rules. Rectification was refused because there was no mistake on the part of the assured who got the policy he asked for.

In one case[3], not involving insurance, however, it was held that rectification would be allowed where there was a mistake on the part of one of the parties only. Rectification would be allowed in such cases provided it could be shown that: (1) one party erroneously believed that the document sought to be rectified contained a particular term or provision; (2) the other party was aware of the omission and that it was due to a mistake; (3) the other party had failed to draw the mistake to his attention; and (4) the mistake must be one calculated to benefit the other person. If those requirements were satisfied the court might regard it as inequitable to allow the other party to resist rectification to give effect to the mistaken party's intention on the ground that the mistake was not, at the time of the execution of the document, a mutual mistake.

It should be noted that under the Unfair Contract Terms Directive[4], and subsequent regulations implementing the Directive into UK law, a policyholder may argue that contractual terms which have not been individually negotiated shall be regarded as unfair and therefore deleted, if, contrary to the requirements of good faith, they cause a significant imbalance in the parties' rights and obligations arising under the contract to the detriment of the policyholder. For further discussion of this area, see Section 4.

D   Residence and occupation

1.65   Where a policy is intended to provide a significant level of cover there will normally be provisions relating to residence and hazardous occupations. Persons who at the time when they effect a policy have no intention of going abroad to live in a country where there is an undue health risk or risk of political disturbance are usually granted policies free from any restrictions as to residence. In other cases the policies may become free of such restriction after, say, five years provided the life assured has not been outside the 'free limits' during that period.

Where a policy free from restriction, on grounds of residence or occupation, cannot be granted at the ordinary rates of premium because:

(1)   the proposer is resident or is likely to reside in a country where there is an undue health risk or risk of political disturbance; or

---

1   *Fowler v Scottish Equitable Life Insurance Society and Ritchie* (1858) 28 LJ Ch 225.
2   [1930] 1 AC (NI) Rep 73.
3   *Thomas Bates & Son Ltd v Wyndham's (Lingerie) Ltd* [1981] 1 All ER 1077.
4   93/13/EEC.

(2) the proposer is, or is likely to be, engaged in some especially hazardous occupation;

the additional risk may be treated in one of the following ways:

(a) by provision that the policy shall be void if the additional risk shall be incurred unless covered by payment of an additional premium;

(b) by the issue of a policy free from restriction at an increased annual premium, to be paid whether the additional risk be in fact incurred or not; or

(c) by the exclusion from the cover under the policy of death from the additional risk.

Living in a country with undue health risks or engaging in a hazardous occupation may well affect the duration of life, even though death does not directly arise from it. The insertion in a policy of a condition equivalent to a warranty (method (a) above) is, however, very burdensome and the avoidance of a policy for breach of the condition may operate harshly, especially if the breach is trifling or due to some emergency. Method (c) is difficult to operate in practice and, if the circumstances permit, method (b) is to be preferred, as unrestricted policy being issued and a temporary or permanent extra premium being paid to cover the extra risk.

It is usual to cover, without extra premium, ordinary flying risk on recognised air routes, but extra premium is often required for flying personnel in the armed forces. For civilian lives, life offices normally cover war risks, but extra premium is sometimes required for members of the armed forces.

Where applications are received from persons resident or domiciled abroad, care needs to be exercised by the insurer. In some jurisdictions it is illegal to contract with foreign insurers. From the life office's viewpoint, the complicating factors relating to governing law, claims, position of agents and intermediaries has led many companies to conclude that such business if undertaken on an ad hoc basis is simply not worth the trouble.

E Stamps on policies

1.66 Stamp duty is no longer chargeable under the heading 'Policy of Life Insurance' in Schedule 1 to the Stamp Act 1891[1]. Furthermore, there is no stamp duty on annuity-certain policies (whether the policy is under hand or under seal ie executed by deed) or sinking fund or capital redemption policies.

F Glossary: some types of life policies and associated terminology

1.67 Life offices may be divided into:

---

1 Finance Act 1989, s 173(1)(a).

(1) *mutuals* – in which the effecting of a policy conveys membership of the company and the whole of whose distributable surplus or 'profit' belongs to the with-profit policyholders; and

(2) *proprietary companies* – which are limited by shares and which are established and carried on wholly or mainly for the purpose of providing profits for the shareholders (despite the fact that a major part of any distributable surplus is allocated in the form of bonuses to with-profit policyholders).

Contracts of great variety are now made. Set out below is a reference guide to the types of policies which are issued. The descriptions set out below are not necessarily mutually exclusive, so it is possible to have, for example, a whole life, last survivor policy.

Type of policy	*How or when the benefit is payable*
Whole life assurance	At death whenever it occurs. Premiums normally payable for whole life.
Endowment assurance	On survival to a specified date or on death before that date. (Often used as a mortgage repayment vehicle.)
Pure endowment	On survival to a specified date but not otherwise.
Temporary assurance (term assurance)	At death only if it occurs before a specified date. A surrender value would not be payable.
Convertible temporary assurance	At death only if it occurs before a specified date with an option to convert to a whole life or endowment assurance.
Joint life (first death) assurance	At the death of the first to die of two or more lives.
Joint lives (first death) endowment assurance	On survival of the lives assured to a specified date or at the earlier failure of the joint life of two or more lives.
Last survivor assurance	At the death of the last survivor of two or more lives.
Last survivor endowment assurance	On survival to a specified date or at the earlier death of the last survivor of two or more lives.
Contingent survivorship assurance	On failure of one life during the continuance of another.
Child's deferred assurance	At death after (usually) age 21 (or some are from 18 to 25) with options at the age chosen.

Type of policy	How or when the benefit is payable
Family income policy	On death if that should occur during a specified term from the issue of the policy – a fixed periodical instalment is payable until the end of that term.
Mortgage protection policy	A form of temporary assurance designed to cover the principal outstanding under a mortgage (usually decreasing in line with repayment of the capital sum).
With-profits policy	A contract (usually endowment assurance) entitled to participate in the profits made and distributed by the life office. (See below for further details.)
Without-profits policy	A contract which is not entitled to participate in the profits of the life office.
Accidental death policy	Benefits only payable if death occurs as a result of an accident and involving some external factor. May also be an additional feature under a whole life, endowment or term assurance and so would have the effect of an addition to the standard sum assured.
Unit-linked (or just 'linked') assurance	A contract where the benefits payable are determined by reference to the value of or income from, investment funds specifically designed for insurance policies unit trusts, open-ended investment companies, or by reference to fluctuations in, or in an index of, the value of any property. The policyholder receives, or is 'allocated', notional 'units' in return for his premium the underlying fund being divided up into units of equal value. The number of units depends on the value of those units at the time of allocation which will fluctuate in accordance with underlying investment values.
'Ten plus' policy (essentially a marketing name, so will be known by other names as well)	This is basically a ten-year endowment, or whole life policy under which premiums must be paid for a minimum of ten years (if there are to be no adverse income tax results). At the end of ten years the policyholder has the option:
	(1) to cease paying premiums and take the policy benefits; (2) to cease paying premiums and to let the capital sum continue to be invested in the insurance company's funds;

Type of policy	How or when the benefit is payable
	(3) to continue paying full premiums for a further selected period – usually ten years, and to withdraw part of the value of the policy each year as an 'income' which can be varied from year to year to suit the policyholder's requirements. This income will be free of tax in the hands of the policyholder.
Issue risk policy	An insurance effected by a person who, for example, holds a reversionary interest under a trust or who will suffer loss by the birth of a child or children, for example, to the life tenant. Sometimes effected as a contract of indemnity.
Whole of life dread disease/critical illness benefit	On death or on diagnosis of a disease or critical illness or disability specified within the policy document (possibly subject to conditions regarding survival after diagnosis).
Investment bonds (also known as single premium bonds)	Whole life policies which are almost entirely investment-oriented (see **1.69**).
Broker bonds	An investment bond where one of the unit-linked funds available to the policy is managed by an IFA, or their associate and generally branded with the IFA's name.
Life of another policy	Assured and life assured are different persons. Assured must have an insurable interest in the life assured. Benefits will be payable on the death of the life assured. Policy may be whole life, endowment or temporary.
Capital redemption assurance	Benefits payable at a specified date, not dependent on life, but still classified as long-term business.
Annuities	
Immediate annuity	Annuity payable during life commencing on completion of contract.
Deferred annuity	Annuity payable during life commencing at a future date. If the annuitant dies in the period prior to the vesting date the life office will normally refund the premiums paid.
Reversionary annuity	Annuity payable during life commencing at the death of a specified person.

Type of policy	*How or when the benefit is payable*
Guaranteed annuity	An annuity with a proviso that it shall continue for a stated number of years at least, irrespective of whether the annuitant dies in the meantime.
Joint lives and survivor annuity	Annuity payable during the joint lifetime and the life of the survivors or survivor of two or more lives.
Temporary annuity	Annuity payments cease at the end of a fixed term, or on the death of the annuitant, whichever happens first. May be on a joint first lives or last survivor or guaranteed basis.
Personal pensions	Replaced retirement annuity contracts are normally investment contracts offering the customer the option of an annuity when they take retirement benefits.
Stakeholder pensions	Similar to personal pensions but simplified and with restricted charges.

I With-profits

1.68 As future rates of mortality, interest and expense cannot be accurately forecast, it is not possible to fix a premium which on average will exactly cover the risk and therefore a margin is allowed by the life office. This margin should over time give rise to a surplus in the long-term business fund, which is revealed at the periodical valuations of the office's assets and liabilities. The long-term business fund may also be subdivided into several different funds. In the case of a proprietary company, a part of the surplus is available to pay dividends to shareholders; the balance of the surplus, or the whole of it in the case of a mutual office, can be allotted or distributed to the with-profit policyholders in the form of some benefit additional to the sum assured. The additional benefit usually takes the form of a 'reversionary bonus' payable with the sum assured, but may be in the form of a cash payment or of a reduction in the future premiums. In addition, on maturity of a policy (or on death) there may be a 'terminal bonus'. If there is a surrender of the policy before maturity or death an 'interim bonus' may be payable. The life office will not usually distribute the whole surplus but will retain some which is then carried forward for the purpose of 'smoothing' bonus levels over the investment period. The amount distributed is at the discretion of the life office in consultation with the actuary.

The management and operation of with-profits funds are now subject to very detailed FSA requirements. These are explained in Chapter 6.

2   'Bonds'

1.69   So-called 'bonds' offered by insurance companies are generally life assurances or capital redemption assurances (from non-UK companies) purchased with a single premium, the benefits under which are defined by reference to notional units. The underlying fund may consist of fixed interest investments, equities, real property, unit trusts, open-ended investment companies or a combination of some or more of these and the amount of additional life cover (in relation to the investment value if such a bond) is usually very modest. It is usually expressed as a percentage of the total value of units at the time of death. For example, 101% of the value of units.

Note should be made of the important decision in *Fuji Finance Inc v Aetna Life Insurance Ltd*[1] which raised some important issues for the life industry and which involved a consideration of the legal issues relating to bonds.

In 1986 Fuji, a Panamanian company, took out a single premium policy for a premium of £50,000. The life assured was an experienced investor and the central figure behind Fuji. Sums, which were calculated by reference to the amount and value of units allocated to the policy, were payable on the death of the life assured or the earlier surrender of the policy. The policy enabled the policyholder to switch units allocated to his policy between several funds effectively with the benefit of hindsight. As a result of such switching of the units, by June 1992 the policy was valued at over £1m. The insurance company, Aetna Life, then changed its switching procedures.

Fuji claimed this was repudiatory breach of contract and surrendered the policy. The surrender proceeds of £1,110,758 were paid. Fuji claimed damages for breach of contract. The insurance company denied committing any breach. One of its defences was that the policy as a life policy was null and void under section 1 of the Life Assurance Act 1774 (for lack of insurance interest). Another was that it was in breach of section 16(1) of the Insurance Companies Act 1982.

1.70   The policy could be surrendered at any time for a cash sum equal to the value of units held at surrender but if surrender occurred within the first five years, a modest discontinuance charge reduced the amount payable. The central decision at first instance was that a purported insurance contract where the same sum was payable on the death of the life assured as would be payable on demand before death was not a contract of insurance on the life of a person within section 1 of the Life Assurance Act 1774, and did not constitute insurance business for the purpose of section 16 of the Insurance Companies Act 1982 (section 16 required insurance companies to restrict their activities to insurance business or connected activities). Indeed, Sir Donald Nicholls V-C went on to say that it could not be that the presence of a minor and insignificant element of insurance sufficed to turn a contract otherwise of a different nature into a contract of insurance. Therefore, the 1774 Act did not apply to such contracts. If the policy was not a contract of insurance, it could not have been issued under section 16(1) of the Insurance Companies Act 1982, which restricted the business of an insurance

---

1   [1994] Ch 173; [1995] Ch 122; [1994] 4 All ER 1025.

company to insurance. However, he stated that Parliament did not, thereby, intend that a contract made by an insurance company in breach of section 16 should be unlawful and unenforceable. The intended remedy for a default lay in the powers of intervention conferred on the Secretary of State.

The conclusion which was reached from this decision, which was obviously of serious concern to the life assurance industry, was that single premium insurance bonds which offer little or no life cover were not insurance contracts. This raised the ominous issue of insurers having a considerable number of non-insurance contracts on their books. In most cases neither the insurer nor the policyholder would want the contract to cease. However, the public policy issues of permitting insurers to retain a large number of contracts which were not technically insurance contracts would have had to have been considered.

1.71   Another possible spectre related to taxation treatment. If such policies were not insurance policies, how would they be taxed? If they are not insurance policies they would appear to be unauthorised collective investment schemes. It would, however, be very rare for the Inland Revenue to act retrospectively. Historically, they have taken action from the date of pronouncement of any change of stance.

Fortunately for the life industry the Court of Appeal overruled the High Court decision. The contract was a life assurance policy under the 1774 Act and so Fuji was subject to the limitation set out in section 3. Morritt LJ did not consider that the fact that no greater sum was payable on death than on surrender was important provided that the event on which benefits were payable was sufficiently life or death related. In this case a benefit was payable on the death of the life assured. The timing of death was uncertain and it was this fact and the fact that the policyholder could not stop the policy paying out once death had occurred that rendered the policy one of life insurance. He also thought that the effect of the discontinuance charge (ie it did not apply on death only on surrender) could also have been relevant had he not already decided that the contract was a life assurance contract.

As a result the question whether the effect of section 16 of the Insurance Companies Act 1982 was that the contract was unenforceable against the insurance company no longer required consideration. It was a life assurance contract and hence within section 16. However, the Court of Appeal still considered the point, although of course, their comments are strictly 'obiter'. Morritt LJ agreed with the Vice Chancellor. The purpose of section 16 was only to limit the scope of an insurance company's undertakings and it was not a necessary implication that every contract entered into outside that scope was thereby invalidated. The fact that there were no criminal sanctions for breach of section 16 reinforced that view. Sir Ralph Gibson disagreed. His opinion was that such contracts were void and unenforceable.

The Court of Appeal decision was not ultimately appealed to the House of Lords. The position therefore seems to be that insurance contracts which offer little or no life cover in addition to the investment value of the contract can nevertheless be life assurance contracts. The consequences of any other conclusion would have had far-reaching effects for life offices, policyholders, the Inland Revenue and the DTI.

SECTION 7 THE PREMIUM

A First premium

1.72   The consideration required from the assured, in return for the life office's obligations under the contract of life insurance, is the premium or the promise to pay premiums. Premiums may be periodic or single. Periodic premiums may be annual or of greater frequency. Very often they are payable monthly. They may be payable throughout the life of the life assured, or may cease at the expiration of a fixed number of years or the death of the life assured, whichever occurs first. It is not unusual for whole life policies (ie providing cover for the whole of life) to provide for premiums to cease at the age of 85 or 90.

A policy may be effected at an annual premium payable by instalments, in which case any instalment for the year not already paid at the time of claim is deducted from the policy proceeds.

There is no principle of law which requires a premium to be paid before a contract of insurance is concluded. In circumstances where a policy is issued and cover commences prior to the payment of premium, it is probable that the life office would be able to deduct the first premium from any claim moneys which become payable. A contract cannot, however, be concluded unless there is agreement as to the amount of premium and the method of payment.

It is usual practice for the life office to provide that the cover will not commence until the premium has been paid. The policy will regulate how and where premiums are to be paid. However, premiums are usually paid by direct debit or by cheque. It should be noted that payment by cheque is merely conditional payment and policies often refer to payment or receipt of cleared funds.

Where the assured has engaged an intermediary to arrange the policy for him, payment of the premium to the intermediary (other than a tied agent) will not amount to payment to the life office[1]. Where payment of the premium has been made to the intermediary then the intermediary will hold that money subject to the FSA Client Money provisions under which the intermediary must in accordance with the regulations, inter alia:

(1)   keep client money separate from its own money in a client account with, in most cases, an approved bank;

(2)   pay the client money into the account as soon as is reasonably possible;

(3)   hold the client money as a fiduciary for the client; and

(4)   generally pay interest on the client money.

B Early cancellation of policies

1.73   For various reasons, someone buying a policy may not at the time appreciate fully the terms of the contract he is entering into. He may later find that the

1   See Chapter 4 for further discussion of the role of the intermediary and agent.

policy is not what he intended to buy and in some cases that it is not suited to his needs. Alternatively, he may have been subject to high pressure sales techniques. The right to cancel is now contained in the FSA's conduct of business Sourcebooks. These are considered in Chapter 5.

C Renewal premiums and days of grace

1.74 Where a life policy is issued at an annual or other periodic premium, the assured has a right to continue the policy from time to time on payment of the premium. Life assurance therefore differs from most classes of general insurance. There has been considerable judicial disagreement as to whether annual premium life policies are insurances for one year with an irrevocable order to renew upon payment of the agreed renewal premium or an insurance for the whole of the assured's life subject to defeasance upon non-payment of the renewal premium at the times stated[1]. It would appear that the latter view is probably the one which has the preponderance of judicial authority. In any event the precise terms of the policy may clarify the position. The question can be important in terms of ascertaining the effect of death during any days of grace.

As a general rule, days of grace are allowed for payment of the renewal premium. The position in the event of the death of the life assured during the days of grace and before payment of the premium must be ascertained from the policy and/or from the regulations of the life office. The life policy may expressly provide that cover continues during the days of grace even before payment of the premium, in which case the position is clear. Most policies for whole life assurance, endowment assurance and similar risks contain further provisions to define the position which arises if the renewal premium remains unpaid after the expiry of the days of grace.

The term of the days of grace and the conditions attached to them will be strictly construed. Time is of the essence in the matter and equity will give no relief against lapse for non-payment, for the assured and the life office are not on an equal footing. The assured has the right to renew but the life office cannot compel payment.

Rowan v Atlas Assurance Co Ltd [2]

S effected a policy at an annual premium with 30 days of grace. The renewal premium was not paid within the days of grace. The company voluntarily applied the cash value of the reversionary bonus attached to the policy so as to keep the policy alive for a fractional period. Held, that the calculation of that period by the company could not be questioned and no further days of grace would run from its expiry.

---

1 See *Pritchard v The Merchants' and Tradesmen's Mutual Life Assurance Society* (1858) 3 CB (NS) 622; *Stuart v Freeman* [1903] 1 KB 47.
2 (1928) 72 Sol Jo 285.

McKenna v City Life Assurance Co[1]

A policy was effected at a quarterly premium and contained the following condition: 'Any policy which has acquired a surrender value will not immediately lapse if a renewal premium be not paid within the days of grace, but will be kept in force for twelve calendar months from the date upon which the last premium became due'. Held that a tender of overdue premium must be made within 12 calendar months of the renewal date. A tender after that time, but within 12 calendar months of the expiry of the days of grace, was too late, and the policy had lapsed.

The assured is not entitled to rely on the receipt of a renewal notice or other reminder[2] as a warning that a premium is about to become due, and absence of such a notice is no excuse for non-payment.

1.75 Tender of payment without acceptance may suffice to keep the policy in force.

Farquharson v Pearl Assurance Co Ltd[3]

A policy allowed 30 days of grace for payment of premiums. It was mortgaged by the assured, and during the days of grace the mortgagee, being aware of financial difficulties of the assured, called at the district office of the company and offered to pay the premium. The offer was declined and the district manager said he was arranging for the assured to pay. The premium was not paid during the days of grace, and on the death of the assured the company denied liability on the ground that the policy had lapsed. Held, that the company could not be heard to say that the premium had not been tendered by a person authorised by the assured, since the mortgage deed signed by him contained a provision that the mortgagee might pay the premium. The company accordingly was liable.

The life office may extend the period during which payment of the premium may be made[4] or may waive any of the conditions precedent to the continuance of the risk, and although a policy has lapsed, the office may be held to have revived the assurance upon the same terms if they have led the assured to believe that they have reassumed the risk.

Stuart v Freeman[5]

An own-life policy allowed 30 days of grace for payment of the premium. The assured assigned the policy and the life office agreed orally with the assignee that if the assured did not pay the premium within the 30 days the assignee could pay it upon the following day. Held, that as between the life

1 [1919] 2 KB 491.
2 *Windus v Tredegar* (1866) 15 LT 108, HL.
3 [1937] 3 All ER 124.
4 This will normally be subject, where appropriate, to the rules for qualifying policies. See further Chapter 12.
5 [1903] 1 KB 47.

office and the assignee the policy must be read as if there were 31 days of grace.

I Non-forfeiture provisions

1.76 Policies often contain a provision intended to preserve the cover, or some part of it, in some cases for a limited period, if the premium is not paid by the end of the days of grace. The provisions vary with different offices, and reference should be made to the policy. The following are brief descriptions of some of these variations:

(1) The assurance is held in force so long as any surrender value exceeds the overdue premiums and any revival charges (an extra charge that would be made in the event of reinstatement), which are charged against the policy.

(2) The assurance is held in force for (say) one year and then converted to a paid-up policy of such a reduced amount as any surrender value will permit.

(3) The surrender value is used as a single premium for a temporary assurance for the full sum assured for such a period as it will cover.

(4) The assurance is converted at the end of the days of grace to the paid-up value of the policy at that date.

Of course, the policy could instead lapse without value and where the policy has no surrender value this would normally be the case. Non-payment of premium may not cause a policy to be forfeited if the requirement is waived by the life office. This may arise through a subsequent demand for, or acceptance of, the premium in circumstances which would lead the assured to believe the life office is treating the policy as subsisting. However, the mere acceptance of the premium after forfeiture is not in itself conclusive. It will depend essentially on the terms on which the waiver is given by the life office.

Some non-forfeiture conditions, it has been argued, may cause the policy to be regarded as a consumer credit agreement for the purposes of the Consumer Credit Act 1974. It is argued that these will not be deemed consumer credit agreements because the contract that the policyholder has with the life office has not, in the majority of cases, been taken out for the extension 'of credit or any other form of financial accommodation' (within the meaning of section 9(1) of the 1974 Act) and the 'credit' that arises is merely incidental to the parties' contractual arrangements. Therefore as the main purpose of the transaction is not the provision of credit, it being merely a part of the arrangements for reinstatement should premiums not be paid on time, it is argued that the contract is not subject to the 1974 Act[1].

In practice it does not appear that the contrary view, that the ambit of consumer credit agreements is sufficiently wide to catch such arrangements has been promulgated. In connection with the Consumer Credit Act 1974, the position of

---

1   *Pott's Executors v IRC* [1951] 1 All ER 76; *Re HPC Productions Ltd* [1962] 1 All ER 37.

premium payments by credit cards is increasingly common. Section 75 of the Act is noteworthy in that the insured will, where the section applies, have concurrent remedies against the credit card company for breach of contract or misrepresentation. Unless agreed otherwise, the credit card company is entitled to be indemnified by the insurer if it has to meet a claim by the insured[1].

2   Reinstatement and revival

1.77   When a policy has lapsed the life office may be prepared to reinstate it. Provision is usually made for revival of the policy within a specified time and the fulfilment of certain conditions. Technically, a new contract will be made as a result of reinstatement. The life office may require further health and lifestyle evidence and the premium level may have changed and/or an extra premium for reinstatement may be required. Some or all of these may be waived and prima facie would be waived by acceptance of the previously agreed premium after the expiry of the days of grace. The life office may also be prepared to reinstate the policy outside such time limits with or without imposing any further requirements. For qualification purposes HMRC will treat reinstatements as the continuation of the original policy provided it occurs within 13 months of the due date for payment of the last premium to be paid (see Chapter 13).

SECTION 8   DEEDS

1.78   For various reasons, deeds are relevant to, and frequently encountered in, the transaction of life assurance business. Knowledge of the basic features will, therefore, be helpful to the practitioner in the law of life assurance. This section provides a brief explanation of deeds generally.

A *deed* is (usually) an instrument whereby property is transferred or an obligation is undertaken, but its purpose may be merely declaratory (ie it sets out the rights, existing or future, of the parties mentioned in it). Under the Law of Property Act 1925 a deed was required to be a written document, signed, sealed and delivered. The law relating to deeds and their execution has been amended and is now contained within the Law of Property (Miscellaneous Provisions) Act 1989 (LP(MP)A). Prior to this Act, it was not necessary, even though it was usually the case, for the parties' signatures to be witnessed. The LP(MP)A now makes this a requirement of a properly executed deed[2]. The requirement of writing impliedly remains[3]. The requirement of sealing for the valid execution of a deed by an individual was abolished[4].

An *indenture* was formerly a deed executed in duplicate with both copies written on the same parchment or paper which was then cut in an irregular or

1   Section 75(2).
2   Section 1(3)(a).
3   Section 1(1)(a).
4   Section 1(1)(b).

tooth-like manner, so that the edges of each part were indented. The exact fit of the two parts was proof that the parts were genuine.

A *deed poll* was formerly a deed with a smooth or polled edge, not executed in duplicate.

The term *indenture* now simply denotes a deed to which there is more than one party and a *deed poll* is a deed to which there is only one party, though more persons than one may join in expressing the same intention.

The terms deed poll and indenture are not commonly used today (although the deed poll has made something of a comeback in the sphere of personal pension schemes not established by way of trust). A deed is now usually simply referred to as a deed or described by reference to the nature of transaction, eg a conveyance, settlement, assignment, mortgage, appointment of trustees, etc.

A   Parts of a deed

1.79   The customary parts of a deed are as outlined below.

1   The date

1.80   The date of the deed ought to be the date on which it becomes operative. Where, however, there are several parties in places distant from one another, the document may be executed by different parties on different dates. The deed should bear the date on which delivery is made to the person who takes an interest under it, or to his solicitor or other agent.

However, the deed will only be effective from the date of the last person to execute the deed unless the deed is completed in escrow, that is, that the deed is not to be delivered until a future date or until some condition has been fulfilled.

2   The parties

1.81   The names and addresses of the parties are given and where two or more persons are parties for the same purpose they are grouped together. For example, all the 'assignors' or all the 'continuing trustees'. All parties are presumed to be of full age until the contrary is proved[1].

3   The recitals

1.82   The recitals should give any necessary explanation as to the circumstances in which the deed is executed and its object. They 'set the scene' and describe the background and circumstances of the deed. They are not essential to the deed's validity.

1   Law of Property Act 1925, s 15.

4   The operative part

1.83   This is the part of the deed in which may be included some or all of the following.

(a)   The consideration

1.84   A deed is not void for lack of consideration. Where the consideration is the payment of money, it is the practice to state the amount, partly in order that any stamp duty may be ascertainable, and a receipt for the money should be embodied in the deed. Such a receipt is sufficient evidence to a subsequent purchaser of the payment, provided he has no notice that the money was not paid.

(b)   The covenants for title

1.85   Such covenants may include the following:

(1)   A covenant by the assignor that he is entitled to dispose of the property as he purports to.

(2)   Where the disposition is of leasehold land, a covenant by the assignor that the lease is subsisting at the time of the disposition and there is no breach of condition or obligation and nothing rendering the lease liable to forfeiture.

(3)   A covenant that the property is free from encumbrances other than those which the person does not and cannot reasonably be expected to know about.

(4)   A covenant by the person making the disposition that he has not, since the last disposition for value, charged or encumbered the property (and he is not aware of anyone else who has done so).

(5)   A covenant for further assurance, eg that the assignor will execute any further document to perfect the title of the assignee or do anything else that he reasonably can (at his own cost) to give the person to whom he disposes of the property the title he purports to give.

(The above is not an exhaustive list.)

Covenants for title need not be set out in the deed but are implied by the use of terms specified in the Law of Property (Miscellaneous Provisions) Act 1994 which, inter alia, provides for certain covenants for title to be implied on dispositions of property. Which covenants are implied depends essentially on whether the person making the disposition does so with 'full title guarantee' or with 'limited title guarantee'. Those at (1), (2) and (5) above apply whether or not the disposition is with full or limited title guarantee. The covenant at (3) only applies to those given with full title guarantee and (4) only applies to those given with limited title guarantee. The above covenants will be implied whether or not the disposition is for valuable consideration. Section 76 of the Law of Property Act 1925 is repealed.

(c) The parcels

1.86 The accurate description of the property is very important. It is often convenient to describe a life policy in a schedule and especially so where two or more policies are assigned by the same deed.

(d) The habendum

1.87 The habendum expresses the quantity of the estate or interest which the assignee is to take. It is the interest which the assignee is to *have*. It may be an absolute interest or qualified by being subject to some other interest (eg a mortgage).

B Execution

1.88 Section 1 of the Law of Property (Miscellaneous Provisions) Act 1989 (LP(MP)A) sets out the requirements for the execution of deeds:

(1) Section 1(2) of the LP(MP)A, which applies both to individuals and corporations, states that the instrument must make it clear on its face that it is intended to be a deed, and must be validly executed. Describing the instrument as a deed would satisfy this requirement as would expressing itself to be executed as a deed.

(2) Section 1(3)(a) of the LP(MP)A sets out the requirements for the execution of deeds specifically relating to individuals. The requirement of sealing has now gone and so deeds are validly executed by an individual if they are 'signed and delivered'.

l Companies

1.89 As a result of the Companies Act 1989 it is no longer necessary for companies to have a common seal[1]. However, it remains for the company to choose whether to execute a deed by affixing its common seal or to utilise the method as laid down in section 36A(4) of the Companies Act 1985 which provides:

> 'A document signed by a director and the secretary of a company, or by two directors of a company, and expressed (in whatever form of words) to be executed by the company has the same effect as if executed under the common seal of the company.'

It should also be noted that section 36A(6) of the 1985 Act provides that a document which purports to be signed by a director and the secretary or two directors shall, in favour of a purchaser in good faith, be regarded as duly executed by the company, no matter what is provided for in the company's articles and where it

1 Companies Act 1985, s 36A, as amended.

makes it clear on its face that it is intended by the person making it to be a deed it is deemed to be delivered on execution.

Where a company is in liquidation, the liquidator has power to do all acts and execute in the name of and on behalf of the company all deeds and other documents and for that purpose to use the company seal where necessary[1].

2   Attorneys

1.90   The donee of a power of attorney may execute a deed in and with his own name and signature but it is preferable that he should use the formula 'AB by his attorney CD'. Furthermore, Schedule 1, paragraph 6 of the LP(MP)A amends section 1 of the Powers of Attorney Act 1971 such that an instrument creating a power of attorney no longer needs to be 'signed and sealed', but now needs to be 'executed as a deed by' the donor of the power, if it is an ordinary power of attorney, and by the donor and the attorney if it is an enduring power of attorney. The standard form of enduring power of attorney requires execution as a deed (see also **1.94–1.97**).

3   The attestation of signatures

1.91   Section 1(3)(a) of the LP(MP)A makes it a requirement that the signature on a deed must be attested by a witness present at the time of signing. Furthermore, if the deed is not actually signed by a party it must be signed at his direction and in his presence with two witnesses attesting the signature. Circumstances where this may arise could be where the party is physically unable to sign the deed.

4   The delivery

1.92   A deed is binding on the maker of it if it has been signed, or possibly sealed in the case of a company, and delivered. Delivery does not mean handing over to the other side, it means an act done so as to evince an intention to be bound. When it has been fully executed but is awaiting the fulfilment of some condition it is called an *escrow*. After such fulfilment (and after delivery) it will become absolute.

5   Alterations in deeds

1.93   In the absence of evidence to the contrary, alterations in deeds are presumed to have been made before execution. Any material alteration should, however, be mentioned in the attestation clause and all alterations should be initialled by the parties.

---

1   Insolvency Act 1986, Sch 4, Part III.

SECTION 9 POWERS OF ATTORNEY

A Ordinary and enduring powers

1.94 A power of attorney is a deed by which one person (the donor or appointor) gives another person (the donee or attorney) authority to act for the donor either generally (which is the usual case) or only for specified matters. It is, therefore, a statutory species of agency arrangement. A power of attorney is often executed, for instance, when the donor is about to go abroad. The law regarding powers of attorney was altered and codified by the Powers of Attorney Act 1971 (which came into force on 1 October 1971) and the Enduring Powers of Attorney Act 1985 (which came into force on 10 March 1986). All powers of attorney must be made by deed. A donor who is unable to execute an enduring power of attorney because of some physical disability may direct another person to execute it on his behalf in the presence of two attesting witnesses. A person suffering from a mental disorder cannot confer a power of attorney. However, in such cases, an application can be made to the Court of Protection for the court to make an order giving directions as to how the affairs of that person should be carried out. Such directions will be specific and (unlike a general power of attorney) contain no general discretion on behalf of the 'receiver' to whom the powers will be given.

The contents of a power of attorney may be proved by production of the original document or by a photocopy. The copy must contain a certificate to the effect that the document or the page is a true and complete copy; the certificate must be signed by the donor, or by a solicitor or a member of the Stock Exchange. Photocopies of facsimiles are acceptable if certified.

A power of attorney expressed to be irrevocable and given to secure either a proprietary interest of the donee or the performance of an obligation owed to the donee cannot be revoked by the donor without the donee's consent so long as the donee has that interest or that obligation remains undischarged, and is not revoked by the donor's death, incapacity or bankruptcy, or by its winding up or dissolution where the donor is a company[1].

Powers not given as security may be revoked at any time by the appointor, and will be revoked by his death, unsoundness of mind, or bankruptcy. Section 5 of the Powers of Attorney Act 1971 gives protection to the attorney and to purchasers from him without notice of revocation. An attorney who acts in pursuance of a power without knowledge of its revocation incurs no liability to the donor or to any other person. A purchaser without notice of revocation will get as good title as if the power had not been revoked. If the purchase is made after the date (if any) on which the power is expressed to expire he will, of course, have notice of revocation. If the purchase is completed within 12 months of the date that the power came into force, the lack of knowledge of the purchaser will be conclusively presumed in favour of persons dealing with him. If the transaction is completed more than 12 months after the power comes into force, the purchaser can prove his lack of notice by making a statutory declaration that he did

---

1 Section 4, 1971 Act.

not at the material time know of the revocation. This declaration must be made before, or within three months after, the relevant purchase. 'Purchaser' and 'purchase' have the meanings assigned to them by section 205(1)(xxi) of the Law of Property Act 1925, so that a purchaser is one who acquires an interest for money or money's worth and includes a mortgagee.

1.95   The Powers of Attorney Act 1971 includes a short form of general power in Schedule 1 under which the authority extends to anything which can lawfully be done through an attorney[1]. This provision does not apply to any functions the donor may have as a trustee or personal representative[2]. The statutory form is as follows:

THIS GENERAL POWER OF ATTORNEY is made this

day of   *(year)* by   of

I appoint CD of

AB [*or* CD of   and EF of   jointly *or* [*jointly and severally*] to be my attorney[s] in accordance with section 10 of the Powers of Attorney Act 1971.

IN WITNESS etc.

If more than one attorney is appointed, their authority may be joint, or joint and several, as the deed may specify.

The attorney may execute documents with his own signature (and as a deed if required) by the authority of the appointor[3]. The execution should include a reference to the power.

Until the Enduring Powers of Attorney Act 1985 (EPA 1985) every power of attorney was automatically revoked if the donor became mentally incapable. An enduring power of attorney may continue even if the donor becomes mentally incapable[4]. The 1985 Act does not affect the position of ordinary powers of attorney and these can still be granted. However, whilst with an ordinary power of attorney the attorney may never know, or have consented, to his appointment, with an enduring power, the attorney is required to execute the deed as well as the donor. This, in effect, ensures that the attorney is aware and consents to his appointment.

Whilst the donor remains mentally capable the enduring power of attorney operates as an ordinary power of attorney. Once the attorney has reason to believe that the donor has become, or is becoming, mentally incapable he must make an application to the Court of Protection to register the power of attorney[5]. Until he does so all his powers are suspended[6] except as is set out in section 1(2).

1   Section 10(1), 1971 Act.
2   Section 10(2), 1971 Act.
3   Section 7(1), 1971 Act.
4   EPA 1985, s 1(1).
5   EPA 1985, s 4(2) and the Court of Protection (Enduring Powers of Attorney) Rules 2001.
6   Section 1(1)(b) and (c).

Once the court has registered the power, the attorney's powers are restored. Care should be taken by the life office to ensure that the attorney has the requisite powers to act for the donor.

The statutory form of enduring power of attorney is contained within the Enduring Powers of Attorney (Prescribed Form) Regulations 1990[1], and must be used. Failure to use the prescribed form will mean that the power of attorney will not take effect as an enduring power of attorney. The power may be effective as an ordinary power of attorney which would, in the ordinary way, be revoked in the event of the donor subsequently becoming mentally incapable. There is a case to support this view which held that an enduring power of attorney which was ineffective as such because of an inconsistency with section 11(1) was nevertheless capable of taking effect as an ordinary power[2].

B   Benefits and gifts

I   Ordinary powers of attorney

1.96   Unless expressly stated the attorney cannot make gifts to himself or to others. It is submitted that no such express provision exists with the short form of power in the 1971 Act.

2   Enduring powers of attorney

1.97   Section 3(4) of the Enduring Powers of Attorney Act 1985 provides that an attorney may provide for persons if the donor might be expected to provide for those persons' needs, and when benefitting those persons the attorney may do whatever the donor might be expected to do to meet the needs of those persons. The class of persons that may benefit includes the attorney.

There is also a limited power, by operation of section 3(5) of the 1985 Act, to make gifts under an enduring power of attorney, and the attorney can make gifts to himself, although this will be subject to any restrictions or conditions contained in the power of attorney. The Act allows gifts to be made 'of a seasonal nature or at a time, or on an anniversary, of a birth or marriage, to persons (including himself) who are related to or connected with the donor'[3], and 'to any charity to whom the donor made or might be expected to make gifts'[4].

When considering making gifts the attorney must consider whether or not it is of an unreasonable value taking into account all the circumstances and in particular the size of the donor's estate. A question which frequently arises in connection with life assurance transactions is whether an attorney can declare a trust of a life assurance policy. Although a universally agreed definition of a trust has been difficult to achieve it is clear that a trust is something more than a gift.

---

1   SI 1990/1376.
2   *X v (1)Y, (2) Z sub nom E* (2000) 1 FLR 882; [2000] 3 All ER 1004; (2000) 3 WLR 1974.
3   Section 3(5)(a).
4   Section 3(5)(b).

However, it should be noted that in *In Re the Estate of Marjorie Langdon Cameron Deceased*[1] it was held that a gift made by an attorney under a testator's enduring power of attorney superseded a bequest by will by the process of ademption. The gift involved an educational trust for the benefit of the son.

Where the attorney wishes to benefit either himself or others otherwise than in accordance with section 3(4) and (5) of the 1985 Act, he may apply to the Court of Protection, which has jurisdiction under section 8(2)(e) to authorise such benefits, subject to any restrictions contained within the power of attorney itself.

A life office dealing with the attorney must satisfy itself that the power is validly executed, that the time, if any, to which it is limited has not expired, and that the transaction with which the office is concerned is within the authority conferred by the deed. It will have to satisfy itself that: it has no notice of revocation; or, if it is dealing with a purchaser who derives title from an attorney, that the purchase was completed within 12 months of the power coming into operation; or, if it was not, that the original purchaser has made the prescribed statutory declaration or that the power had not been revoked; or, if it has, that the purchaser's lack of knowledge is proved by some other method.

SECTION 10   CUSTODY OF DOCUMENTS

1.98   On a claim, loan or surrender the life office may retain any documents of title which affect only the policy. It does not seem that the life office is entitled to insist on the practice, for the claimant might need the documents for other purposes, for example to defend a hostile claim against him. Objection is, however, seldom raised.

Where a document (1) affects property in addition to a policy, or (2) declares trusts, it should not be retained by the life office but, in the case of (2) especially it often is although in most cases the life office would take a copy, note it on its records and return the original. The life office normally retains a right to production of the original title documents in the event of a claim. Such documents include trusts, deeds appointing trustees, deeds of assignment, etc.

It is convenient in practice for a life office, during the currency of a policy, to accept custody of documents of title relating to transactions such as assignments or mortgages. The documents will in any event usually be required before payment under the policy is made, and if any transfer of title can be proved to the satisfaction of the life office, a step towards the ultimate full proof of title is taken to the advantage of all concerned. No life office can, however, be compelled to adopt the practice.

1   TLR 2/4/99; [1999] 2 All ER 924; (1999) 3 WLR 394.

CHAPTER 2

Insurance law issues

SUMMARY

Section 1   Insurable interest   **2.1**

Section 2   Utmost good faith and non-disclosure   **2.26**

SECTION I   INSURABLE INTEREST

A   Nature of insurable interest

I   General

2.1   A contract of insurance is a contract for the payment of a sum of money, or for some corresponding benefit, to become due on the happening of an uncertain event of a character adverse to the interest of the person effecting the insurance. Where a person makes a bet he hopes to make a profit, but where he makes an insurance, he seeks to cover a possible loss. This distinction is important in considering the law relating to insurable interest.

Under the common law of England, though not of Scotland, the courts would enforce a wager on the duration of a human life; and so insurance companies did not refuse to issue policies to persons who had no interest in the lives to be insured.

2   The Life Assurance Act 1774

2.2   It was found, however, that insurances on lives or other events, in which the assured had no interest, involved undesirable gambling, and by the Life Assurance Act 1774, commonly called the Gambling Act, which is still in force (see Appendix 2), it was provided:

(1)   That no life insurance should be made unless the person effecting the assurance had an interest in the life assured, and that any life insurance

69

made without such interest 'shall be null and void to all intents and purpose whatsoever'. Although not referred to as such in the Act itself, this has become known as the requirement for 'insurable interest'.

(2)   That there should be inserted in the policy the name of the person or persons interested in it.

(3)   That no greater sum should be recovered than the amount or value of the interest of the assured.

The Act, despite its title, does not apply only to life assurance contracts, but to all insurances other than those 'bona fide made . . . on ships, goods or merchandises'. However, by construction of the Act all forms of indemnity insurance fall outside its scope[1] so the Act is effectively limited to insurances which pay a specified sum on the happening of the insured event. It has also been held that the Act does not apply to buildings insurance.

3   Life assurance is not essentially a contract of indemnity

2.3   It is a well-known principle of marine, fire and other risks, that any claim must be by way of indemnity only (ie recovery is limited to the loss suffered).

In the case of life policies on the lives of third parties, it would be quite possible to transact life insurance by way of indemnity and, indeed, when the Life Assurance Act 1774 was passed life assurance was thought to be a contract of indemnity, like most other forms of insurance. It was not until 1854 that the courts decided that apart from by express agreement, life assurance was not a contract of indemnity; and that if there is a good insurable interest at the time of the contract, the policy remains valid although the insurable interest has ceased before the time of claim.

> *Dalby v India and London Life Assurance Co*[2]
>
> The Anchor Life Office, having issued policies to the Rev John Wright on the life of the Duke of Cambridge for £3,000, reassured £1,000 with the India and London Life Office. The principal policies were surrendered, but Anchor continued the reassurance. The reassuring office resisted a claim, made by Dalby as trustee for the Anchor Life, on the ground of lack of insurable interest. It was held that the Life Assurance Act 1774 required an interest only at the date of the contract and that the policy was valid.

The requirement for the interest only having to exist at the time of effecting the policy is also evident from the wording of section 1 itself which states that the policy 'shall be made' by a person having an insurable interest, ie there is no ongoing requirement for such an interest to subsist.

The Life Assurance Act 1774 did not define insurable interest, and its nature and extent must be ascertained principally from case law.

---

1   *Mark Rowlands Ltd v Berni Inns Ltd* [1985] QB 211.
2   (1854) 15 CB 365.

4   Nature of insurable interest

2.4   Most life assurances are made by persons on their own lives where the insurable interest is greater than a pecuniary interest and is not capable of valuation. Apart, however, from cases of insurances made by persons on their own lives[1], or on the life of a husband or wife, when insurable interest is presumed[2], and need not be proved, the insurable interest must be a pecuniary interest[3], capable of valuation in money, and must be founded on an obligation or liability[4] which will, or will be likely to, result from the death, or the loss or diminution of any right of property which would be recognised at law or in equity. A moral obligation or an expectation, however probable, is not sufficient.

In the absence of specific enquiry by the life office, it is not necessary to disclose the nature of the insurable interest, unless (exceptionally) it is a material fact. Some companies as a matter of practice require to know the nature of the interest; others content themselves with a declaration in the proposal that the person effecting the insurance has an insurable interest, and an increasing amount do not require even that.

5   Amount of interest

2.5   Section 3 of the Life Assurance Act 1774 provides that no greater sum shall be recovered from the insurer or insurers than the amount or value of the interest of the assured. The sum assured at the outset must be supported by an insurable interest of equivalent amount. Where the assured has effected more than one policy on the life, the total sum he can recover under all the policies will not be greater than the value of his interest at the time the policies were effected[5]. To this extent a life policy may include an element of indemnity.

A person has an unlimited insurable interest in his own life. A man has an unlimited interest in the life of his wife, and a woman in the life of her husband. In other cases the courts have not been inclined to limit the amount which may be recovered to the equivalent of an indemnity. Partly this is because the precise amount in many cases is virtually impossible in practice to ascertain. The realistic approach which appears to have been adopted is that provided the cover requested is not grossly out of proportion to the actual value of the interest then this will be permissible. Where, for example, a policy is effected by a creditor (and he pays the premiums) on the life of a debtor, the creditor may claim under the policy, and in addition obtain payment of the debt from the executors of the debtor. The rationale for this is that there has been a risk that his debt would not be paid.

1   *Gould v Curtis* [1913] 3 KB 84 and *Wainwright v Bland* (1835) 1 Mood & R 481.
2   *Griffiths v Fleming* [1909] 1 KB 805, *Reed v Royal Exchange* (1795) Peake Ad Cas 70 and the Married Women's Property Act 1882, s 11.
3   *Halford v Kymer* (1830) 10 B & C 724.
4   *Tidswell v Ankerstein* (1792) Peake NPC 151.
5   *Hebdon v West* (1863) 3 B & S 579.

6 Names of persons interested

2.6 Section 2 of the Life Assurance Act 1774 provides that there shall be inserted in the policy the name or names of the person or persons interested in the policy for whose use, or benefit, or on whose account, the insurance is effected. The court has been prepared to go behind the policy and, if satisfied that no interest exists, to declare the policy void where it is taken out on an own life basis for someone else.

> *Wainwright v Bland*[1]
>
> A policy had been effected by A on her own life at the suggestion of W with whom she lived. A paid the premiums with money provided by W. The jury decided that the policy was in reality effected by W, that he merely used A's name, providing the money himself and meaning to acquire the benefit of the policy for himself in some way and that W was someone who had no interest in A's life. It was held that W could not recover.

Payment of premiums towards a life policy by some person other than the assured is not conclusive to show that the policy was effected on behalf of that person, even though that person does in the event, obtain the benefit of the policy[2].

If the proposal is incorporated in the policy by reference, it is probably sufficient if the name of the person interested appears in the proposal. Also the words of section 2 have not, in practice, been construed too widely. Thus, they do not include all of those who are intended to benefit from the life policy by receiving the moneys payable. One of the main objects of life assurance is to enable a person, whenever death occurs, to have moneys to dispose of at death and a policy effected for this purpose is for the person's own benefit and account and not outside the Act, even though he intends to bequeath the moneys from the policy to others. The section has not been taken to mean, therefore, that, where a policy is payable to the life assured's executors or administrators, the names of the personal representatives, or the persons who will benefit under the will or intestacy, should be inserted in the policy.

Similarly, where a policy is effected by trustees, the names of the beneficiaries under the trust are not in practice specified (despite possible technical arguments to the contrary)[3]. Again, a policy may be effected in trust under the Married Women's Property Act 1882, although at the date of the policy the beneficiaries may not all be ascertained or even in existence.

During the 1960s concern arose that group life policies were illegal and voidable because they did not comply with section 2, in that the beneficiaries' names did not appear in them. Although this view was challenged by some, the matter was put beyond doubt by a change in the law in 1973. Section 50 of the Insurance Companies Amendment Act 1973 (which was not repealed by the Insurance Companies Acts of 1974, 1981 or 1982) provided that section 2 of the Life

---

1   (1835) 1 Mood & R 481.
2   *Shilling v Accidental Death Insurance Co* (1857) 2 H & N 42.
3   *Collett v Morrison* (1851) 9 Hare 162.

Assurance Act 1774 shall not invalidate a policy for the benefit of unnamed persons from time to time falling within a specified class or description, if the class or description is stated in the policy with sufficient particularity to make it possible to establish the identity of all persons who at any given time are entitled to benefit under the policy. The section applies to policies effected either before or after the passing of the Act[1].

7 Policy assigned immediately after issue

2.7   Any person may insure his own life provided the policy is bona fide and, at the time, for his benefit. There is nothing to prevent him from assigning the policy to someone else, even though at the time when he effected the policy he had the intention of doing so[2].

Where, for example, a proposer wishes to provide for another person, he can effect a policy and assign it to the beneficiary or to trustees for the benefit of a beneficiary. Where the beneficiary is only to be the wife or child of the proposer, the use of the Married Women's Property Act 1882 (see Chapter 9) to create a trust is simpler: and where the beneficiary is outside the class of persons within the Act it is of course still possible for the policy to be made subject to a trust (see Chapter 9).

An assignment cannot be used to defeat the statute where the insurance is really made by the beneficiary, for example, where there was a binding obligation to assign any policy which is issued to a person with no insurable interest. The court would go behind the wording of the policy to ascertain the true principal in the transaction[3].

Furthermore, in the *M'Farlane v Royal London Friendly Society* case it was stated that '. . . if ab initio the policy effected in the name of A is really and substantially intended for the benefit of B and B only' then this was 'within the evil and mischief intended to be met by the statute'. See, however, modern practice at **2.25**.

8 Spes successionis

2.8   A spes succession is the hope or expectation of succeeding to property. It may be a most likely event as in the case of one of the next of kin succeeding by intestacy to the estate of a mentally disordered person who has not made a will and is most unlikely ever to have the capacity to do so. A spes is not, however, an interest known to the law and is not a ground of insurable interest[4]. For this reason a person who expects to be the residuary legatee under a will has no

---

1   *Siu Yin Kwan v Eastern Insurance Co Ltd* [1994] 1 All ER 213, where it was held that the fact that the principal's name had not been inserted in the contract did not make the policy unlawful by virtue of the Life Assurance Act 1774, s 2.
2   *M'Farlane v Royal London Friendly Society* (1886) 2 TLR 755.
3   *Shilling v Accidental Death Insurance Co* (1857) 2 H & N 42.
4   A spes confers no interest at all, either vested or contingent, but only an expectation of an interest: *Clowes v Hilliard* (1816) 4 Ch D 413 at 416.

insurable interest to effect an insurance on the life of the testator to cover the probable amount of inheritance tax which will be payable out of his legacy. The recipient of a gift inter vivos (during lifetime) has, however, an interest known to the law and may protect himself by effecting a policy against any amount of inheritance tax payable on the death within seven years of the person who made the gift[1].

Similarly, a person with a contingent right would also have an insurable interest. For example, in *Law v London Indisputable Life Policy Co*[2] a son received a legacy contingent on attaining age 30. This interest was purchased by his father and it was held that the father thereby had an insurable interest in the life of his son. If the son had died before reaching 30, the value of the father's interest would have been nil.

B   Particular cases of insurable interest

1   A man and his own life

2.9   Although a person has an unlimited insurable interest in his or her own life, for the purposes of establishing insurable interest, a life office might, however, refuse to issue a policy where the cover/premium is out of proportion to the means of the proposer. Such a policy involves a consideration quite distinct from the ordinary mortality risk and has a bearing on what is known as 'moral hazard'. If, for example, an individual with little or no capital and low income were to propose for, say, £500,000 of life cover, being a high amount of cover in relation to his income, then the life office should satisfy itself of the need and/or the ability to pay for a policy of that amount.

2   Husband and wife, civil partners

2.10   The interest of a husband in the life of his wife is presumed and it is not necessary to give any evidence as to the amount[3].

It was established as long ago as 1795 that a wife has a similar insurable interest in the life of her husband to any amount.

> *Reed v Royal Exchange Assurance Co*[4]
>
> A wife insured the life of her husband. It was held that she was entitled to the sum assured and that it was not necessary to show an interest: per Lord Kenyon CJ: 'It must be presumed that every wife has an interest in the life of her husband'.

Civil partners will now have the same unlimited interest in each other's lives[5].

1   See generally Inheritance Tax Act 1984, s 3A.
2   (1855) 1 K&J 223.
3   *Griffiths v Fleming* [1909] 1 KB 805.
4   (1795) Peake Add Cas 70.
5   Civil Partnership Act 2006

3   Parent and child

2.11   A child, merely as such, has no insurable interest in the life of his parent. In Scotland because a parent used to have the right to be supported by his child[1] the parent had an insurable interest in the life of the child. This obligation was abolished by section 1(3) of the Family Law (Scotland) Act 1985.

> *Howard v Refuge Friendly Society*[2]
>
> A son insured the life of his father in which he had no pecuniary interest. Premiums were paid by the son for some time but then he gave notice to the Society that he would not pay any more and claimed a return of the premiums already paid. It was held that the son had no insurable interest in his father's life, the policies were 'wagering policies' and the premiums could not be recovered.

Similarly, a parent has, by relationship alone, no insurable interest in the life of his child.

> *Halford v Kymer*[3]
>
> A father effected a life policy in his own name on the life of his son in order to provide against the death of his son before he reached 21. It was held that, as the father had no pecuniary interest in the life assured on the event insured against, he had no insurable interest and the policy was void under the Life Assurance Act 1774.

The parent will have no insurable interest either in respect of money paid for education and maintenance or otherwise. He must by law provide for the child, and cannot recover money so spent.

Section 99 of the Friendly Societies Act 1992 provides that where a friendly society or registered branch or an industrial assurance company enters into a contract of insurance under which a benefit in excess of £800 is payable on the death of any person, and that person dies under the age of 10, then the obligation of the society, branch or company as to payment of benefit is only to pay £800 (without prejudice to any person's right to recover part of the premiums paid). However, where the benefit is payable to a person who otherwise has an independent insurable interest in the life of the person on whose death it is payable, then the £800 limit does not apply.

A person who fosters a child does not, by statute, have an insurable interest in the life of the child[4]. Under section 37(2) of the Adoption Act 1976, a person who maintains a 'protected child', within the meaning of section 32 of that Act (as amended), is deemed, for the purposes of the Life Assurance Act 1774, to have no interest in the life of the child. Accordingly, an insurance taken out on the life of a protected child by a person who maintains that child is void unless an independent insurable interest exists.

---

1   *Carmichael v Carmichael's Executrix* (1919) SC (Ct of Sess) 636.
2   (1886) 54 LT 644.
3   (1830) 10 B & C 724.
4   Children Act 1989, s 66(5), Sch 8, para 11.

4 Debtor and creditor

2.12 A creditor or a surety has an insurable interest in the life of the debtor[1] to the extent of the debt and accrued interest, but if the debt is statute-barred when the policy is effected it is not thought that insurable interest would exist at that time. The position is clearly different if the debt is not statute barred at the time of effecting the policy on the principle established in *Dalby v India and London Life Assurance Co*. However, future interest and other costs of servicing the debt could not be included in setting the sum assured as at the time of insurance these would be mere expectancies. If the debt is to be paid by two or more persons jointly, it will support a good insurable interest for a policy on the life of each of them for the whole amount. Co-sureties and joint debtors also have an insurable interest in each other's lives[2]. A debtor has, however, no insurable interest in the life of the creditor as he would suffer no loss on the death of the creditor even though the creditor may have made a voluntary promise that the debt shall not be enforced during his life. On the other hand a binding promise not to enforce a debt during the life of the creditor would therefore give the debtor a legal interest in the creditor's life[3].

5 Employer and employee

2.13 Strictly speaking an employer has an insurable interest in the life of his employee, but only to the extent of the value of services agreed to be rendered. An employee has an insurable interest in the life of his employer (if an individual), but only to the extent of his remuneration for the agreed period of service, if his contract is to serve the employer for a fixed term, or the agreed period of notice in other cases. However, in practice this may not accurately represent the employer's or employee's interest. In law, the additional amount of interest beyond the notice period is based on an expectancy and not a legal right and probably cannot therefore be technically supported[4]. Nevertheless, the concept of 'key man' insurance has evolved and this is considered at **2.14**.

> *Simcock v Scottish Imperial Co*[5]
>
> An employer insured the life of his employee by two policies for £250 each. A claim under one policy was paid, but under the other it was defended on the ground of lack of insurable interest. Held that the limit of insurable interest was the value of service for the period of notice and so the employer could only recover under the one policy.

1 *Von Lindenau v Desborough* (1828) 3 C & P 353.
2 *Branford v Saunders* (1877) 25 WLR 650.
3 *Hebdon v West* (1863) 3 B & S 579.
4 However, see the case of *Marcel Beller Ltd v Hayden* [1978] QB 694 at 697 where such an interest was accepted without questions.
5 (1902) 10 SLT 286.

Hebdon v West[1]

H became indebted to a bank of which P was the managing director. P agreed verbally with H that the bank would employ H for seven years at a salary of £600 per annum; and that the debt would not be enforced during P's lifetime. H insured P's life. Held, that H had an interest under the agreement to the extent of the salary for the remaining term of employment, although an oral agreement for service for seven years was not then enforceable by reason of the Statute of Frauds. Held further, however, that H had no interest in respect of P's promise not to enforce the debt due to the bank. The promise was without consideration and the mere expectation of the debt being allowed to remain outstanding during P's lifetime did not create an insurable interest.

6   Key man insurance – company or other employer on life of director or manager

2.14   The case of *Simcock* possibly suggested that a company has an insurable interest in the lives of 'key-men', ie directors or principal executives, the loss of any of whose special services would involve the company in reduced profit and the cost of finding a suitable successor and that this extended beyond the strict confines of the contract of service[2]. In such cases, the extent of the insurable interest would be the anticipated loss of profit, not the amount of remuneration, as in the case of employer and employee discussed above. A company has no insurable interest in the life of a director merely by virtue of his office. However, it may well be that there are technical objections to key man insurance in that that there is not necessarily a loss of profit, etc, so the insurance is therefore based merely on an expectancy. In practice life offices are nevertheless generally prepared to issue key man insurance subject to receiving satisfactory evidence of projected loss of profits and any costs and expenses which would be incurred as a result of the death.

7   Pension scheme trustees and employee

2.15   Where an employee has an enforceable right to death benefits provided by the employer under a pension scheme, the required funds may be provided by a policy of life assurance effected in the name of the trustees. Insurable interest arises from the legal obligation to make the payment under the pension scheme.

8   Partners and co-directors

2.16   The relationship of partner or director does not of itself give rise, inter se, to an insurable interest. However, partners would have an insurable interest in the life of a co-partner if the partnership deed provided that, on his death, they shall purchase from his personal representatives his share of the goodwill or other partnership assets. In many such cases it is doubtful whether the survivors would suffer a pecuniary loss merely on account of that obligation, except to the

1   (1863) 3 B & S 579.
2   See also Chapter 16 for more detail on this subject.

extent of the expense incurred in raising the sum required. However, most life offices are in practice prepared to issue policies to the full amount of any such partnership obligation.

Similar principles apply to co-directors of a private limited company where a 'buy and sell' agreement (see Chapter 16) is included in the Articles of Association or has been entered into subsequently by the directors, requiring the shares of a deceased or retiring director to be purchased, by the remaining directors. If appropriately worded, such agreement or arrangement creates the pecuniary liability, as between the directors, upon which the insurable interest would be based. As an alternative to a binding 'buy and sell' agreement the parties may enter into a 'cross option' (or 'double option') agreement. It should be noted that such an option arrangement would not create a legal obligation upon which an insurable interest must be based (albeit that this is the most efficient type of arrangement for inheritance tax purposes and is therefore often used in practice).

9 Trustees

2.17 Trustees of a settlement do not as such have an insurable interest in the life of any beneficiary, but in many cases inheritance tax will be payable on the death of a beneficiary who had an interest in possession in the settlement. In that case the trustees, who are accountable for the tax, have an insurable interest in the life of the beneficiary up to the probable amount of the tax, and may effect a life policy to cover this liability. Trustees of a voluntary settlement have an insurable interest in the life of the settlor during the seven years following the date of the settlement up to the amount of any inheritance tax for which they will be accountable on his death.

Another proposition which has been advanced is that the trustees may be viewed as agents of the beneficiaries. Trustees do not benefit personally (as trustees) from the insurance (although they may benefit as beneficiaries). However, the question remains that if there are a number of beneficiaries, some beneficiaries will not necessarily have an insurable interest in the life of the beneficiary whose life is being insured. Conversely the proposition is much stronger in the case of an absolute trust for a single beneficiary.

Whatever the strict legal position many life offices are prepared to issue policies to trustees, even where an insurable interest may not strictly exist, often on the basis of a declaration of insurable interest. This is especially the case for investment orientated policies with nominal life cover.

10 Mortgagees

2.18 A policy to provide security for a mortgage may be effected by the mortgagor and assigned to the mortgagee. Here no question of insurable interest arises. But the mortgagee, like any other creditor, has an interest in the life of the mortgagor and can effect a policy on his life and pay the premiums himself. If he does so he is entitled both to the policy and the mortgage debt. Where, however, the premiums are paid by the borrower or charged to him, the lender must account to the borrower for any money received under the policy.

11   Engaged couples/cohabitees

2.19   Unlike the position with civil partnerships, no insurable interest exists purely as a result of these relationships, although the position was different for engaged couples when breach of promise to marry was actionable. This was abolished by the Law Reform (Miscellaneous Provisions) Act 1970. However, frequently the persons in such a relationship will be jointly liable to, for example, a bank or building society for borrowings. In such cases the death of one may well result in a liability falling on the survivor as a result of which an insurable interest can arise.

In practice, many life offices are nevertheless prepared to issue policies even where no such joint liability exists. In respect of cohabitees the Scottish Law Commission have recommended that cohabiting couples have an interest in each other's lives[1].

12   Divorcees

2.20   Although the marriage no longer exists and so the unlimited insurable interest has thereby ceased it is very likely that there will be other pecuniary rights and liabilities which arise as a result of financial claims arising out of the divorce or associated court orders. The most common example is the obligation on a husband to pay maintenance. The ex-wife may wish to protect her position by insuring her ex-husband's life. Such an interest will, of course, be limited by, for example, the amount of the maintenance payments and life expectancies.

C   Policies unsupported by a good insurable interest

1   Effect of policy

2.21   Section 1 of the Life Assurance Act 1774 provides that a policy effected without insurable interest shall from the outset be 'null and void to all intents and purposes whatsoever'. Section 2 provides that failure to insert the names of interested parties in the policy renders it illegal.

The Act does not impose any punishment and the making of such an insurance is not a statutory crime. The fact that the insurance company is not obliged to pay out was possibly thought to be sufficient deterrent.

Lack of insurable interest is a defence which the life office may plead in resisting a claim. If it does not plead the lack of insurable interest but relies on some other defence, it is the duty of the court to take cognisance of the illegality of the policy and refuse to enforce the contract[2]. A practice note issued in connection with *Mercantile Credit Co Ltd v Hamblin*[3], reads as follows:

---

1   Scottish Law Commission (No 1350, Report on Family Law, para 16.41).
2   *Gedge v Royal Exchange Insurance Corp* [1900] 2 QB 214.
3   [1964] 1 All ER 680n.

> 'Where it occurs to counsel, however belatedly, that an agreement may be void for illegality, it is his duty, however embarrassing, to invite the court's attention to the matter and prevent the court from enforcing an illegal transaction.'

The court, however, will always lean in favour of an insurable interest, for after the company has received the premium the objection is usually technical and has no real merit between the company and the assured[1].

Where the life office waives the defence of lack of insurable interest and pays the policy moneys, the rights of property in those moneys will be determined irrespective of the statute. In the Australian case of *Carter Bros v Renouf*[2] it was held that section 2 of the Life Assurance Act 1774 does no more than make the policy void between the insurance company and the insured, and that, if the company does not choose to rely on the defence that the contract does not comply with section 2, and pays under the policy, the question 'who is entitled to the money?' must be decided as if the statute did not exist. The Australian court followed the English case of *Worthington v Curtis*[3] in which a father effected (for his own benefit under a separate agreement) a policy on the life of, and in the name of, his son, in whose life he had no insurable interest. It was thus illegal, under section 1 of the Act, and also under section 2 because the father's name did not appear on the policy. The son died intestate and the father took out letters of administration. The insurers paid the sum to him as the son's personal representative. The son's creditors claimed that the sum paid was part of the son's estate. It was held by the Court of Appeal that the defence of want of insurable interest was available only to the insurance company and since they had waived it and had paid the policy moneys to the father he was entitled to apply the money to his own use. A similar view was taken by the Court of Appeal in another case[4] where a father effected in his own name without insurable interest a policy on the life of his son and the insurance company paid the sum assured to the father's assignees, in effect as an ex gratia payment. A similar rule apparently applies in Scotland[5]. However, this view is not universally accepted. *Worthington v Curtis* has been criticised[6]. The reason for such criticism is mainly based on the fact that this would appear not to be recognising the illegality of the contract. A more modern example of the effect of lack of insurable interest is the case of *Fuji Finance v Aetna* which is examined in more detail at **1.69**. Essentially, the policy in issue, in that case a life assurance bond, offered no greater benefits on death than on surrender. It was decided that this did not prevent the policy from being a contract of insurance within section 1 of the Life Assurance Act 1774. As a result, as Fuji Finance had no insurable interest in the life assured, the policy was technically 'null and void' under that Act which prevented Fuji Finance from pursuing a breach of contract claim resulting from changes made to the policy. In

1   *Stock v Inglis* (1882) 12 QBD 564, per Brett MR.
2   (1962) 36 ALJR 67.
3   (1875) 1 Ch D 419.
4   *A-G v Murray* [1904] 1 KB 165.
5   *Hadden v Bryden* (1899) 1 F (Ct of Sess) 710; 36 SLR 524.
6   *Fitzsimmons v City of Glasgow FS* [1933] IAC Rep 24 and *McMeaken v Prudential Assurance Co* [1936] IAC Rep 21.

that case the life company had complied with the policy terms up to the point at which the changes were made and did not seek to merely return premiums paid.

2   Admission of insurable interest

2.22   A life office is sometimes requested to endorse a policy with an admission that it is satisfied that a good insurable interest has been shown. The parties cannot contract out of the statute and it does not appear that such an endorsement would bind the life office[1].

3   Deferred assurances

2.23   If a parent has effected a deferred assurance on the life of a child, and does not vest the policy in the child as soon as the life risk commences, it would seem that the policy is technically unenforceable for lack of insurable interest.

4   Consequences of lack of insurable interest

2.24   The 1774 Act does not prescribe any penalties for its infringement and the generally held view is that such contracts are voidable. Money paid under an illegal contract cannot generally be recovered. Therefore, technically it would appear that neither the sum assured nor the premiums paid will be recoverable. However, this may not be the position where the parties are not equally at fault in relation to the illegality (in 'pari delicto'). In such circumstances, if the person seeking to recover under an illegal contract was unaware of the illegality, he is entitled to recover the money provided he has not got what he bargained for.

> *Harse v Pearl Life Assurance Co*[2]
>
> H effected policies which were void for lack of insurable interest. He relied on the representation of the agent (of the company) that the policies were valid. Held, that as the agent had acted innocently, the parties were equally to blame and that the proposer could not recover the premiums.

This was an (innocent) misrepresentation of the law by the agent. It has been postulated that the decision would have been different had it been a misrepresentation of fact. Now that the long held principle that monies paid under a mistake of law cannot be recovered has been eroded by the case of *Kleinwort Benson Ltd v Lincoln City Council*[3], it may be that *Harse* would be decided differently today.

Where the life office has acted in such a way that its conduct can be said to have 'introduced the element of fraud, duress, oppression, or difference in the position of the parties which created a fiduciary relationship so as to make it inequitable for [it] to insist on the bargain' (Collins MR in *Harse v Pearl Life*

1   *Anctil v Manufacturers' Life Insurance Co* [1899] AC 604.
2   [1904] 1 KB 558.
3   TLR 30/10/98; ILR 4/11/98; (1998) 4 All ER 513; (1998) 3 WLR 1095; (1998) Lloyd's Rep Bank 387; (1999) LGR 1.

Assurance Co at 563) the assured will not be in pari delicto and recovery of premiums will be possible (eg where the assured was induced to enter into the contract by fraudulent misrepresentation as to the legality of the policy made by the company's agent).

Hughes v Liverpool Victoria Legal Friendly Society[1]

T effected five policies on the lives of others, but subsequently allowed them to lapse and burnt them. Later, an agent of the company persuaded H to pay overdue premiums and keep up the policies, giving her duplicate policies for the purpose, and fraudulently representing that they would be valid. She had no insurable interest. Held, that the premiums could be recovered.

British Workman's and General Assurance Co Ltd v Cunliffe[2]

The respondent insured the life of his brother-in-law in which he had no insurable interest. The policy was effected through the insurer's agent who fraudulently represented to the respondent that the policy would be valid. The respondent subsequently discovered that the contract was invalid and demanded the return of the premiums. As the representation was made by someone knowledgeable in insurance matters to a person ignorant of the true position, the premiums could be recovered.

D   Modern practice

2.25   This book is concerned with the law of life assurance and its practical application and not speculation about what the law ought to be. But a section on insurable interest would, in the authors' opinion, be incomplete if there were not some reference to the way in which the subject is viewed and approached in practice by life offices today.

The Life Assurance Act 1774 was introduced to curb the scandal of 'a mischievous kind of gaming' which had developed by way of the indiscriminate effecting of insurance policies on the lives of public figures, or the chances of public events. It is not clear whether the Act was passed to protect life insurers, their shareholders, policyholders or the general public from these abuses. But it has been suggested that whilst a statute such as this might have been essential in the commercial and social conditions prevailing in the eighteenth century, it is inappropriate more than two hundred years on, as it must be extremely unlikely that, if the Act were repealed, life offices would be willing to issue 'gaming' contracts now.

Moreover, the argument runs, not only is the 1774 Act unnecessary today, it is indeed a constraint on the business which life offices could write, as many insurers find the provisions of the statute and the case law which has developed around it most unsatisfactory as a framework for the transaction of life assurance in modern conditions and the demands made for life assurance cover in contemporary society. The law of insurable interest is therefore often viewed as a

---

1   [1916] 2 KB 482.
2   (1902) 18 TLR 502 CA; see also *Tofts v Pearl Life Ass Co* [1915] 1 KB 189.

technical prohibition preventing the issue of policies in circumstances in which life offices would be willing, subject to safeguards, to grant policies which in no sense could be regarded as 'gaming'. At the time of writing the Law Commission is looking at the need to retain the requirement and it is to be hoped that it might recommend either abolition or provide for a more flexible approach.

In terms of the way insurable interest is approached in practice, although insurers may not contract out of the 1774 Act they are sometimes prepared to issue policies where the assured has no insurable interest recognised by the law in the life to be assured, provided that the office is satisfied that there is a good reason for the proposed life cover and all parties signify their awareness of the nature of the transaction and the sum to be assured. Alternatively, and presumably in order to avoid any claim of having induced third parties into an illegal contract (which might enable them to seek a return of premiums), life offices rely upon an undertaking or statement in the proposal form that such interest exists.

Such policies are, however, strictly, 'null and void' or more accurately voidable. It would hardly be sound business practice in these cases for the life office to resist a claim on the grounds of lack of insurable interest (although *Fuji v Aetna* is a partial exception), but the fact that the practices of issuing such policies has developed is perhaps some comment on a statute that (at least in its current form) has outlived its usefulness.

There are other considerations for a life office in conducting business where an insurable interest does not exist. If it is openly permitting such business then it is potentially acting in breach of PRU 7.6.13 (INSPRU 1.5.13) (restriction of business to insurance and activities directly arising). In addition, if such business is not insurance business then it raises a question concerning the taxation status of such business.

These issues were discussed in connection with lack of insurable interest in *Fuji v Aetna*. See **1.69** et seq.

SECTION 2   UTMOST GOOD FAITH AND NON-DISCLOSURE

A   Uberrima fides

2.26   The general rule in contract law is that the parties to a contract need not furnish each other with information which if known might possibly influence their judgment. The rule does not justify misrepresentation but mere silence is not misrepresentation[1]. Failure to disclose a material fact which might influence the mind of the other party does not give a right to avoid the contract[2]. Subject to the growing body of consumer protection law the maxim 'caveat emptor' applies to contracts generally. The buyer must make such enquiries as he may think prudent.

However, a number of important exceptions to this general rule have been established for various classes of contract in order to redress what has been regarded by the courts and Parliament as an imbalance in the relative bargaining

---

1   *Hands v Simpson, Fawcett & Co Ltd* (1928) 44 TLR 295.
2   *Keates v Cadogan* (1851) 10 CB 591; *Fletcher v Krell* (1872) 42 LJQB 55.

positions of the parties. One such exception applies to all contracts of insurance, for here the party seeking to cover the risk has information as to the nature of the risk with which the insurer is not and cannot be acquainted, unless it is disclosed. The law will not allow the proposer, by non-disclosure of material information, to lead the insurer to make a bargain which the insurer would not entertain in the light of fuller knowledge of the risk. Each contracting party must, therefore, observe the utmost good faith. There must on both sides be what is known as uberrima fides[1].

In *Carter v Boehm*, Lord Mansfield said:

'Insurance is a contract of speculation. The special facts, upon which the contingent chance is to be computed, lie most commonly in the knowledge of the assured only; the underwriter trusts to his representation, and proceeds upon confidence that he does not keep back any circumstances in his knowledge, to mislead the underwriter into a belief that the circumstance does not exist. The keeping back such circumstance is a fraud, and therefore the policy is void. Although the suppression should happen through mistake, without any fraudulent intention, yet still the underwriter is deceived and the policy is void; because the risque run is really different from the risque understood and intended to be run at the time of the agreement. . . . Good faith forbids either party, by concealing what he privately knows, to draw the other into a bargain from his ignorance of the fact, and his believing the contrary.'

Over a hundred years later the Court of Appeal reiterated[2] the substance of this justification of the doctrine and emphasised that it would be inequitable for the insured to demand a competitive premium while he has the 'means of knowledge as to the risk, and the insurer has not the means or the same means'.

B   The duty to disclose and materiality

2.27   It is the duty of the proposer voluntarily to disclose without misrepresentation all material facts known to him or which he ought to have known if he had made reasonable enquiries. As the proposer will often not appreciate what is a material fact this is a very onerous obligation.

In *Rozanes v Bowen*[3] it was said:

'It has been for centuries in England the law in connection with insurance of all sorts, marine, fire, life . . . that, as the underwriter knows nothing and the man who comes to him to insure knows everything, it is the duty of the assured . . . to make a full disclosure to the underwriters *without being asked* for all the material circumstances.' (Emphasis added)

2.28   All facts and circumstances which are material to the risk must be disclosed by the proposer to the insurer. The proposer cannot withhold material

---

1   *Carter v Boehm* (1766) 3 Burr 1905. See also *London Assurance v Mansel* (1879) 11 Ch D 363, which made it clear that the principle applied to all classes of insurance.
2   *Seaton v Burnand* [1899] 1 QB 782.
3   (1928) 32 Ll L Rep 98.

information merely because no specific question on the point is asked in the proposal form or in the medical examination. But he may be justified in inferring from the fact that the question is not asked that the information withheld was not regarded by the office as material[1]. Where, for example, the proposer is required to state whether his parents or grandparents have suffered from certain illnesses, the proposer will know that the life office regards this information as material, but he may well be justified in assuming that to the life office it is immaterial whether or not brothers or sisters have suffered from those illnesses. But generally, it is no excuse for non-disclosure of a material fact, for the proposer to say that he omitted to disclose it through carelessness or mistake, or that he did not regard it as material[2].

In some cases the proposer will, for various reasons, omit to answer a question. It cannot be said that the insurer did not regard this information as material but if the insurer does not then reject the proposal the insurer is likely to be viewed as having waived such information.

Provisions contained in the proposal form are clearly also relevant here. The questions in the proposal form may either expand or restrict the proposer's duty of disclosure. It is common for proposal forms to contain (in what is often termed the 'Declaration') an indication as to whether the proposer is being asked to disclose information, even if not specifically covered by the actual questions contained in the proposal form. *Hair v The Prudential Assurance Co Ltd*[3] is an example of a case where such a declaration was deemed not to require the disclosure of material information beyond that specifically asked for. However, in many cases proposal forms will end with a general question requesting any other material information.

In order for a policy to be repudiated on the ground of non-disclosure, an inaccurate statement must be one of fact and not of opinion. Statements of opinion which in the event turn out not to be well-founded are not actionable if the opinion was given in good faith[4]. As a general rule, however, unless otherwise stated, an answer to a question in a proposal form will be construed as relating to the facts themselves and not to the proposer's knowledge or opinion of them[5].

The material facts which the proposer is required to disclose are all those circumstances which would influence a prudent insurer[6] in determining whether it will take the risk, at what premium and on what conditions. Other statements of the test of materiality refer to a 'reasonable insurer' but there is probably little significance in this difference[7]. The test is therefore an objective one. What an individual insurer thinks is not relevant.

2.29   The question as to what is and what is not a material fact was considered in the case of *Pan Atlantic Insurance Co Ltd v Pine Top Insurance Co Ltd*[8]; see

1   *Schoolman v Hall* [1951] 1 Lloyd's Rep 139; *Roberts v Plaisted* [1989] 2 Lloyd's Rep 341.
2   *Bates v Hewitt* (1867) LR 2 QB 595.
3   [1983] Lloyd's Rep 667.
4   *Anderson v Pacific Fire and Marine Insurance Co* (1872) LR7 CP 65.
5   *Zurich General Accident and Liability Insurance Co v Leven* 1940 SC 406.
6   *Lambert v Co-operative Insurance Society Ltd* [1975] 2 Lloyd's Rep 485.
7   *Mutual Life Insurance of New York v Ontario Metal Products Co* [1925] AC 344.
8   [1995] 1 AC 501 HL.

also *St Paul Fire and Marine Ins Co v McConnell Dowell*[1], which although concerned with marine insurance was considered to be equally applicable to non-marine cases. Essentially, it was decided that it was sufficient for a fact to be material if it had an influence on the mind of the insurer. It did not have to be a decisive influence. This has been criticised by some commentators essentially on the basis that this represented a very low level of influence on the 'hypothetical prudent insurer'. However, as the House of Lords decided that the non-disclosure must also have induced the particular insurer to accept the risk the overall position in practice, particularly for consumer contracts which do not normally contain warranties (see **2.36**), is probably not that different to there being a requirement that there must be a decisive influence on a hypothetical prudent insurer.

It is irrelevant that the proposer does not consider that a particular fact or set of facts is material; if it is material it must be disclosed despite his opinion.

> *Godfrey v Brittanic Assurance Co Ltd*[2]
>
> Clause 5 of the proposal form read 'Have you suffered from any illness or accident or received medical advice or treatment with or without an operation? If so give particulars and state name of medical attendant and the date, nature and duration of the illness for which he was consulted'. The insured disclosed that he had had an accident to his hand but not that he had been sent by his own doctor to a hospital for a suspected kidney ailment nor that he had suffered from pharyngitis. He died of nephritis. Held, that he knew he had been sent to hospital for a check on his kidneys and that his health had been generally bad for two years. It was conceded that he had honestly thought these details not material. Nevertheless he was under a duty to disclose to the company every material circumstance known to him, not only of which he had actual knowledge but of which he ought to have known. Every circumstance was material which would influence the judgment of a prudent underwriter; the opinion of the insured whether a fact was material was irrelevant. The company was entitled to repudiate the contract.

> *British Equitable Insurance Co v Great Western Railway*[3]
>
> The proposer consulted a specialist who informed him that he had a dangerous kidney condition. This was not disclosed in a life assurance proposal on the basis that his general practitioner had told him that the specialist was wrong. The Court of Appeal held that he should have disclosed the specialist's prognosis which was ultimately shown to be correct.

It is for the court to rule as a matter of law whether a particular fact is capable of being material and to give directions as to the test to be applied, but the decision ultimately is one of fact, depending on the circumstances.

2.30 The Statement of Long-Term Insurance Practice provides, for instance, that if the proposal form calls for the disclosure of material facts, a statement

1 [1995] 2 Lloyd's Rep 116.
2 [1963] 2 Lloyd's Rep 515.
3 (1869) 20 LT 422.

should be included in the declaration, or prominently displayed elsewhere on the form or in the document of which it forms part:

'(a)   drawing attention to the consequences of failure to disclose all material facts and explaining that these are facts that an insurer would regard as likely to influence the assessment and acceptance of a proposal ; and

(b)   warning that if the signatory is in doubt about whether certain facts are material, these facts should be disclosed.'

The Statement goes on to provide that those matters which insurers have commonly found to be material should be the subject of clear questions in proposal forms, and that insurers should avoid asking questions which would require knowledge beyond that which the signatory could reasonably be expected to possess.

2.31   The law also provides that a proposer cannot disclose what he does not know, and he cannot be expected to disclose matters, immaterial in themselves, which if further examined might lead to information which is material. As Fletcher Moulton LJ stated in *Joel v Law Union and Crown Insurance Co*[1]:

'The duty is a duty to disclose and you cannot disclose what you do not know. The obligation to disclose, therefore, necessarily depends upon the knowledge you possess.'

It is interesting in this context to consider the effects, if any, of the Data Protection Acts of 1984 and 1998 and of the Access to Medical Reports Act 1988, under which the proposer now has more extensive rights to information about his health than was hitherto the case. However, it is not clear that as a result he will be deemed to know the information in question. Also, such information (eg medical details) may still not be revealed to the proposer on the basis that its revelation could prove harmful to him. Although concerned with household contents insurance the case of *Economides v Commercial Union Assurance Co plc*[2] indicates that the proposer is under no duty to make further detailed enquiries.

The standard to be displayed by the proposer in considering whether a fact should be disclosed is the objective one of that of the reasonable man. So, for example, in *Fowkes v Manchester & London Life Assurance and Loan Association*[3] the fact that the proposer had gout (which might have been ascertainable to an experienced medical practitioner) this knowledge could not reasonably be inferred to a reasonable man. This can be contrasted with the case of *Godfrey* above where the proposer should have appreciated that he was possessed of knowledge which he should have disclosed.

It is also clear from *Carter v Boehm* that the proposer need not mention what the insurer already knows or what he ought to know or what he waives being informed about. For example, in *Ayrey v British Legal & United Provident Assurance Co Ltd*[4], the proposal form contained an agreement that if information which should have been disclosed was withheld then the contract would be void.

1   [1908] 2 KB 863.
2   [1997] 3 WLR 1066.
3   (1862) 3 F & F 440.
4   [1918] 1 KB 136.

The proposer did not disclose in the proposal form that he was in the Royal Navy Reserve, although he had told the district manager of the insurer. Premiums were paid to and accepted by the district manager. It was held that the district manager's knowledge was equivalent to knowledge by the insurer and acceptance of premiums amounted to a waiver of the breach of agreement in the proposal form. The contract was therefore valid. This case should be contrasted with *Malhi* at **2.34**.

In practice, if a proposer is in any doubt about disclosing information the best course of action would be to do so. Indeed, as stated at **2.30**, insurers are required to include this instruction in proposal forms under the Statement of Long-Term Insurance Practice.

2.32   The duty to disclose extends beyond the time of proposal and 'acceptance' of the proposal by the company until the contract is binding on both parties[1]. It is common in life assurance to include a statement in the proposal which provides that the life office shall not become bound until receipt of the first premium, and to include a continuing condition that the information supplied is still accurate at the time the policy is issued. It is therefore clear that the period during which disclosure is required extends up until a legally binding contract comes into existence so that any new or changed material facts affecting the terms upon which the policy is issued must be communicated to the office right up to the moment of receipt of the premium. However, it is crucial to examine the proposal/policy wordings in each case.

> *Looker v Law Union and Rock Insurance Co*[2]
>
> L made a proposal for a policy on his life and received a 'letter of acceptance' stating that the policy would be issued on the payment of the first premium, if the health of the life assured remained meanwhile unaffected, and reserving the right to alter or withdraw the acceptance. Before payment of the premium he became ill. A friend posted L's cheque for the premium but L died from the illness. Held, that the representatives of L could not recover as there was a duty to inform the insurers of any material change in the nature of the risk.

It is possible for a policy to lapse and for the assured to request that it is reinstated. In this case the duty of full disclosure revives. In practice the life office will ask the proposer to complete either a further full proposal form or an abridged version.

C   Inducement and avoidance

2.33   To avoid a contract for non-disclosure of a material fact, the life office has to show that it has been *induced* by the non-disclosure to enter into the policy

1   *Banque Financière de la Cité SA v Westgate Insurance Co Ltd* [1990] 2 All ER 947, where is was held that an insurer is under a pre-contractual duty of disclosure to his insured but only in respect of matters which are material to the risk or to the recoverability of the claim. Breach of such a duty could not sound in damages, whether in contract or tort, but merely lead to the return of premiums.
2   [1928] 1 KB 554.

on the relevant terms[1]. This is assuming that the fact in question is *material*. In cases of doubt it is possible for expert evidence to be admitted[2].

Avoidance results in the office being able to recover any sums paid by it as moneys paid out under a mistake of fact – for if the life office had known of the non-disclosure at the time, no benefits need have been paid. Similarly, premiums paid are returnable on the principle that there has been a failure of consideration. However, if there has been wilful or fraudulent non-disclosure there is no obligation to return the premiums[3]. But if the life office continues to accept premiums in respect of the policy with knowledge of the true facts, it cannot afterwards repudiate liability on the ground of non-disclosure.

The onus of proving on a balance of probabilities that there has been non-disclosure of a material fact is on the insurer. The insurer will therefore have to show that the material information existed at the time of contract, that it was known to the insured and that this information was not disclosed.

Joel v Law Union and Crown Insurance Co[4]

It was alleged by the office that the assured had not disclosed the facts that she had suffered from nervous depression after 'flu and had been attended by a specialist. The office adduced as supporting evidence the printed form containing questions which the medical examiner had put to her 'with any necessary explanation'. The answers given by the assured were filled in and a declaration that they were true was signed by her. In answer to the question 'What medical men have you consulted?', two doctors' names were entered but not that of the specialist. The medical examiner that had put the questions was not called as a witness. Held, that there was no evidence of non-disclosure. The printed form did not prove non-disclosure because it was not clear what questions or explanations had been put by the medical examiner. The insured therefore received the benefit of the doubt in this case.

The duty of good faith requires that representations made by the insurer as well as by the proposer as to all matters relevant to the contract shall be accurate.

2.34   Knowledge gained by a life office concerning a policyholder may be imputed to the life office in respect of other policies taken out by the policyholder, however, it is necessary to look at the circumstances in which the information is received by the life office and as such imputed knowledge may not arise unless the information is received by a person authorised and able to appreciate its significance. So it was held by the majority in:

Malhi v Abbey Life Assurance Co Ltd[5]

Mr Malhi (the deceased) and M took out a joint lives first death policy in May 1984 which lapsed and was reinstated in October 1985. On reinstating the policy the company relied upon the earlier declaration of health. Subsequently in 1986 a joint application for an endowment policy was made and declined by the

1   *Pan Atlantic Insurance Co Ltd v Pine Top Insurance Co Ltd* [1995] 1 AC 501 HL.
2   *Reynolds v Phoenix Assurance Co Ltd* [1978] 2 Lloyd's Rep 440.
3   *Feise v Parkinson* (1812) 4 Taunt 640.
4   [1908] 2 KB 863.
5   [1996] LRLR 237.

company's underwriters following a report detailing the deceased's alcoholism. The first policy was disclaimed on the deceased's death on grounds of non-disclosure, the deceased having been suffering from alcoholism prior to April 1984 and having contracted malaria prior to October 1985. It was established, inter alia, that it was impracticable for the underwriters, and there was no duty on them, to check earlier applications/policies. The majority of the Court of Appeal held that the information received in 1986 concerning the deceased was not received by a person authorised and able to appreciate its significance and therefore there was no imputed knowledge to the company to establish a waiver by election of its right to forfeit for non-disclosure.

The case has been criticised as being unduly lenient to the life office and there must be some doubt as to whether the decision in *Malhi* will continue to represent the law in the future taking into account the huge growth in information retrieval systems so that not only information in an insurer's own records may be imputed to him, but information generally available such as the Association of British Insurers database of proposals and claims.

D   Indisputable policies

2.35   If a policy is expressed to be 'indisputable', the life office cannot raise any question of non-disclosure, except where the policy was procured by fraud on the part of the contracting party; this is so even if there is no express exception of fraud in the policy[1]. An 'indisputable' clause would not prevent the insurer from raising the question of illegality, eg for lack of insurable interest[2]. It has also been held that it does not prevent an insurer from avoiding liability for negligent misrepresentation unless negligence is expressly mentioned in the exclusion clause or the clause does not otherwise make sense[3].

E   Warranty

2.36   A contract of insurance can be made on the understanding that it shall be enforceable only if certain facts have been truly stated. Such a contract is based on a warranty (or more correctly a condition), and it is not necessary for the insurer to show whether the matter warranted is or is not material to the risk, for the object of making it the subject of a warranty is to provide that the contract shall stand or fall by it. The insurer is therefore relieved from having to prove the materiality of statements made by the proposer.

If, for example, it is warranted that the assured has not suffered from a certain disease, and he has in fact suffered from it, although he did not know its nature, the policy is voidable at the option of the life office. If it is a condition that the assured shall not reside in a certain country or undertake a certain occupation, breach of the

1   *Anstey v British Natural Premium Life* (1908) 24 TLR 871.
2   *Anctil v Manufacturers' Life Insurance Co* [1899] AC 604.
3   *Toomey v Eagle Star (No 2)* [1995] 2 Lloyd's Rep 88.

condition will entitle the life office to void the policy, quite irrespective of the question whether the residence or occupation had any effect on the risk.

Where the proposal form includes a provision to the effect that the truth of the answers shall form the basis of the contract (known as a 'basis clause'), this means that the proposer warrants the accuracy of his answers and if it transpires that any of these are false, this will be a breach of warranty entitling the office to rescind the policy even though the statements were made in good faith and even if they are not material[1]. This also has the slightly odd effect of a crucial policy term being found outside the provisions of the policy document. Such provisions have been criticised both judicially and by academics. They are also contrary to the ABI Statement of Long-Term Insurance Practice which prohibits a life office from using a proposal form or issuing a policy if that document contains: 'any provision converting the statements as to past or present fact in the proposal form into warranties except where the warranty relates to a statement of fact concerning the life to be assured under a life of another policy' (eg 'basis of the contract'). However, a life office is still able to require specific warranties to be given about matters which are material to the risk to be insured.

Modern life office practice tends towards the use of a form of proposal where the proposer is asked to give replies to the best of his knowledge and belief. In such circumstances it is not always clear exactly what (if anything) is warranted, and it will be for the court to decide if necessary. If the proposer only warrants that his answers were in accordance with his knowledge and honest belief, then if he gives replies which are not in fact accurate, but so far as he knew and believed were correct, the policy will stand. It will not be voidable unless it can be shown that the proposer did not know or hold such a belief at all. The same applies if the proposer himself qualifies his replies by saying that they are given to the best of his knowledge and belief. Courts are generally reluctant to construe answers given by the assured as anything other than the belief of the assured[2] unless the proposal is clearly to this effect. However, if the proposal is not clear the proposer would be well advised to qualify his answers to this effect[3].

Anstey v British Natural Premium Life Association Ltd[4]

The proposer, who had had a miscarriage some 10 years before making the proposal, answered questions as follows: Q. 'Have you had any local or other disease, personal injury, illness or infirmity?' A. 'No'. Q. 'If you have had any illness or infirmity, have you fully recovered from it?' A. 'Had none'. The Court of Appeal considered that the answers were not untrue, since the miscarriage was not an illness or infirmity.

Kumar v Life Assurance Co of India[5]

K gave birth to a child by Caesarian section in February 1966, at a hospital. She was advised against becoming pregnant again for the next two years. She there-

1   The use of such warranties in relation to non-material facts is contrary to The Statement of
     Long-Term Insurance Practice.
2   *Delahaye v British Empire Mutual* (1897) 13 TLR 245.
3   *Wheelton v Hardisty* (1857) 8 E & B 232.
4   [1908] 24 TLR 871.
5   (1973) 117 Sol Jo 833.

fore consulted a doctor at a family planning clinic and was prescribed an oral contraceptive. The doctor asked her if she had ever had an operation. She answered 'No', but later mentioned the Caesarian section. In October 1966 K took out a life policy. The questions and answers in her proposal form included: Q. Have you consulted a medical practitioner within the last 5 years? A. No. Q. Did you ever have any operation, accident or injury? If so, give details. A. No. Q. Have you ever been in any hospital, asylum, or sanatorium for a check up, observation, treatment or an operation? If so, give details. A. No (only delivery).

The proposal form contained a declaration that her answers were true in every particular and that she had not withheld any information and that she agreed that the declaration and proposal should form the basis of the contract.

K took an oral contraceptive but she became pregnant and died in June 1968 after an operation for a ruptured ectopic pregnancy. The insurance company contended that K's answers were not true in every particular in that she had had a Caesarian section and had consulted a doctor at the family planning clinic, and that they were entitled to rescind the policy.

Held, that for the visit to the doctor at the family planning clinic to be a consultation within the meaning of the question the visit must be shown to be for a purpose material to the effecting of a life policy. 'Going on the pill' without any pre-existing health factor being involved was irrelevant. But there was here a pre-existing health factor and some risk, in the event of further pregnancy. The question about consulting a doctor was therefore answered incorrectly. The doctor had said in evidence that women from the East often did not consider a Caesarian section an operation but merely as part and parcel of having a baby. Nevertheless, her answer to the question about operations was held to be incorrect. The insurance company was entitled to avoid the policy.

2.37   If the answers to the questions in the proposal form are inconsistent or otherwise unsatisfactory the insurers must make further enquiries; otherwise they will be deemed to have waived their rights. If the space for the answer is left blank, there is no misrepresentation or breach of warranty, unless the circumstances indicate that leaving the space blank implies a negative answer to the question. There may, however, be non-disclosure of material information[1].

Where the proposer is medically examined by the life office's medical officer, or other doctor appointed by them, his replies to the doctor's questions must be correct to the best of his knowledge and belief. However, if they are, like the answers in the proposal form, made the basis of the contract and therefore a warranty, the policy will be voidable by the insurers if they are not accurate, even if they are honestly believed by the proposer to be true. However, it should be noted that basis (of the contract) clauses are not permitted under the AB1 Statement of Long-Term Insurance Practice.

The replies of private friends and medical referees are not usually, under modern practice, made the subject of warranty, so that the policy will not be voided by inaccurate replies by them unless there is an element of collusive fraud.

In the case of a life-of-another policy the non-disclosure or misrepresentation

1   *Roberts v Avon Insurance Co Ltd* [1956] 2 Lloyd's Rep 240.

of the life to be assured does not render the policy voidable unless: (a) the life assured is acting as agent of the assured; or (b) the truth of the life assured's statements are warranted or made the basis of the contract[1]. That said, however, it is the usual practice today for the proposer and life assured of a life-of-another policy to give answers 'to the best of their knowledge and belief' so it will be for the court to decide what might have been warranted.

A warranty can therefore operate very harshly against a proposer who answers a question which turns out to be irrelevant to future loss inaccurately. However, the effects of warranties are limited by the effect of the Statement of Long-Term Insurance Practice and the view of the Financial Ombudsman Service.

F   Waiver of breach of warranty

2.38   Subject to the above, if there is a breach of warranty or condition then, once the life office has knowledge of the breach, or sufficient knowledge to put it on enquiry, it may treat the policy as void or elect to waive the breach and treat the policy as valid.

Waiver of breach may be by express election to affirm the contract. Alternatively, it could be by conduct indicating an intention not to repudiate. Thus, for example, continuing to accept renewal premiums after knowledge of the breach[2] could amount to a waiver if the assured was genuinely led to believe that acceptance of his premium indicated clearly an intention to treat the policy as valid. This would not be so if the life office accepted the premium whilst reserving its position.

It is possible that delay which prejudices the assured or the rights of third parties would also amount to waiver of a breach.

G   Misrepresentation

2.39   A breach by the assured of the duty of disclosure may also amount to a positive misrepresentation of existing fact. This is likely to be the case where the breach consists of giving inaccurate information in answer to a material question in the proposal.

The circumstances in which a proposer supplies information to the life office may be such as to fall within the rules governing fraudulent misrepresentation. The office might, in such cases, pursue the proposer for fraud. Fraud renders the policy voidable at the option of the life office which may rescind the contract and recover anything paid[3]. It could also recover damages which would include all expenditure reasonably and properly incurred arising from the deceit. There is even authority for the proposition that if the policy is avoided for fraud then the office is not obliged to return the premium[4].

---

1   *Wheelton v Hardisty* (1857) 8 E & B 232.
2   *Holdsworth v Lancashire and Yorkshire Rly* (1907) 23 TLR 521.
3   *London Assurance v Clare* (1937) 57 Ll L Rep 254.
4   *Anderson v Fitzgerald* (1853) 4 HL Cas 484.

An innocent misrepresentation is, essentially, any misrepresentation which does not amount to fraud. Within the ambit of innocent misrepresentation two types can be distinguished. Misstatements which are a result of negligence or carelessness and those as a result of pure error made under a misapprehension not amounting to negligence. For an innocent misrepresentation to be actionable it must be a statement of fact and not of opinion or law. (It may be that statements relating to law are now actionable since *Kleinwort Benson Ltd v Lincoln City Council*.) It must be untrue or inaccurate; it must be material to the life office's acceptance of the proposal; it must be a statement as to present fact and must have induced the life office to accept the proposal on the terms upon which it did so.

Innocent misrepresentation is ground for avoiding the policy and rescinding the contract provided that the office restores the consideration received (ie the premiums which have been paid) and the recission is not inequitable to the assured.

H   Effect of non-disclosure or misrepresentation

2.40   As stated above, normally non-disclosure or misrepresentation by one party enables the other party to avoid the contract and this avoidance would take effect ab initio (ie from the beginning and not merely for the future). In seeking to rescind, the application must be made without undue delay after discovery of the truth[1] and the ability to rescind is lost if the person entitled to rescind has conducted himself in such a way as to give the impression that he has waived his right to rescind and intends to affirm the contract[2]. Rescission must be total, not partial[3].

In *Pan Atlantic Insurance Co Ltd v Pine Top Insurance Co Ltd*[4] the House of Lords decided that an insurer cannot rely upon the misrepresentation or non-disclosure of a material fact to avoid the contract if that misrepresentation or non-disclosure did not in fact induce the making of the contract on the terms accepted. The mere fact that a fact is established to be material does not necessarily mean that it induced the insurer to enter into the contract. The case of *St Paul Fire and Marine Co (UK) Ltd v McConnel Dowell Constructors Ltd*[5] supported the conclusions arrived at in *Pan Atlantic*.

In rare cases the materiality and inducement may be 'obvious' but in others the insurer must prove that he was induced. Generally, the standard of the prudent underwriter will be applied to see if he would have refused cover or changed its terms. As an alternative the underwriting practice of the particular office may be considered.

Under section 2(2) of the Misrepresentation Act 1967, it is possible that the

---

1   *Foster v Mutual Reserve Life* (1904) 20 TLR 715.
2   *Cleary v Prudential Ass Co* [1927] 1 AC Rep 29.
3   *Urquhart v Macpherson* (1897) 2 App Cas 831.
4   [1995] 1 AC 50.
5   [1995] 2 Lloyd's Rep 116 (CA).

court may award damages instead of recission to the innocent party where non-disclosure or misrepresentation comes to the notice of the insurer who then seeks to avoid the contract. Damages may be recoverable in the event of fraud or deliberate misrepresentation under section 2(1) of the Misrepresentation Act 1967 or even if not made fraudulently unless he had reasonable ground to believe and did believe the facts were true. Another alternative is that for negligent misrepresentation the insured may have a cause of action in tort[1].

I   Action on discovery of misrepresentation or non-disclosure

2.41   The aggrieved party has an election whether or not to avoid the contract as it is voidable, not void. When all the facts are ascertained, the other party should be informed within a reasonable time if the intention is to avoid the contract, otherwise the other party may be led to conclude that the contract is being affirmed, for example, where premiums are received after discovery of the facts this will be evidence of waiver[2]. It is clear, however, that the aggrieved party must actually have knowledge of all the relevant facts and of his right to avoid. Constructive knowledge or being put on notice is probably not sufficient.

In *Malhi v Abbey Life Assurance Co Ltd*[3], it was argued that a life office had waived its right to avoid a contract on the basis that the information in question was in the life office's records (there had been a previous application). This was rejected. There was no duty on the underwriters dealing with this case to search the office's files for previous disclosures.

J   Criminal sanctions

2.42   Under section 16 of the Theft Act 1968, a person who by any deception dishonestly obtains for himself or another any pecuniary advantage commits a criminal offence. A pecuniary advantage is to be regarded as obtained where he is allowed to take out any policy of insurance or annuity contract, or obtain an improvement of terms, as a result of his deception. 'Deception' is defined in section 15[4]. There is also a provision in the Financial Services and Markets Act 2000, which makes it a criminal offence to deliberately or recklessly make misleading statements and practices or to dishonestly conceal material facts[5]. However, the wording of the section seems to be designed to regulate the behaviour of insurers (and other investment providers) and does not apply to representations made by the insured.

---

1   *Hedley Byrne v Heller and Partners Ltd* [1964] AC 465.
2   *Hemmings v Sceptre Life* [1905] 1 Ch 365.
3   (1994) Times 2 June.
4   See *Norwich Union Life Insurance Society v Qureshi* [1998] CLC 1605, *Aldrich v Norwich Union Life Insurance Co Ltd* [1998] CLC 1621 and *R v Manning* [1999] 2 WLR 430.
5   Section 397.

K Unfair contract terms

2.43 Insurance companies were exempted from the provisions of the Unfair Contract Terms Act 1977 relating to contractual exemption clauses. The reason for this exemption was the acceptance of the industry's argument about the potential detrimental effects and the standing of the London market, and the agreement to adhere to a non-statutory code of good practice. This for life insurers code is contained in the Association of British Insurers (ABI) Statements of General and Long-Term Insurance Practice. This does much to redress the balance between the parties in consumer cases and the codes have effectively been enforced by the Insurance/PIA Ombudsman and now the Financial Ombudsman Service.

Also, the Unfair Contract Terms Directive[1], which came into force in this country on 1 July 1995, does apply to insurance contracts. The directive introduced for the first time the concept of good faith and allows policyholders to challenge terms in contracts which do not describe the risk covered by the contract. For further discussion of this area see Chapter 1.

L Statement of Long-Term Insurance Practice

2.44 The ABI Statement of Long-Term Insurance Practice observed by members of the Association of British Insurers. In connection with non-disclosure and misrepresentation, paragraph 3(a) provides that insurers will not unreasonably reject claims and will not repudiate liability for non-disclosure of a material fact which the policyholder could not reasonably be expected to have disclosed, or for misrepresentation unless it is deliberate or negligent. In addition, proposers must be warned on proposal forms of the requirement to disclose material facts and the consequences of failure to do so. Insurers are expected to ask clear questions about facts generally found to be material and refrain from asking questions outside of the proposer's knowledge. It is important to note that although the Statement of Long-Term Insurance Practice lacks the force of law in the consumer arena it has been reinforced by regulators' rules and the jurisdiction of various ombudsmen.

M Law Commission

2.45 At the time of writing the Law Commissions of England and Scotland are in the process reviewing the law in this area. There is also the possibility of a harmonisation of European Insurance law which could introduce proportionally (ie a reduction in payout to reflect the proportion represented by the unpaid premium) into these issues.

It is hoped that the issues which have been well explored, including by the Law Commission on a previous occasion, and the matters covered by the ABI statements can now lead to a modernisation of the law in this area.

---

1   93/13/EEC.

CHAPTER 3

FSMA and the Life Office

SUMMARY

SECTION I   INTRODUCTION TO THE FSMA AND THE FSA HANDBOOK

3.1   What follows is not a comprehensive review of the Financial Services and Markets Act 2000 (FSMA) or of the regulatory system in general. This is fully covered in standard works on the subject. The following commentary attempts to give an overview of the FSMA regime including the FSA's Handbook of rules and guidance and, in particular, to identify those provisions which are likely to be of most relevance to life assurance practitioners. Issues relating to insurance mediation (eg introductions, advice, sales and arranging insurance contracts) are covered in Chapter 4.

A   Background to the FSMA

3.2   By the beginning of the 1980s it was generally accepted that the system of regulation embodied in the Prevention of Fraud (Investments) Act 1958 was largely inadequate to deal with the considerable changes which had taken place in the financial services sector in that time period. Increased public awareness of the securities and financial markets, increasing competition and increasing complexity of financial products led to calls for the regulatory system to be over-hauled and investor protection to be increased. The Gower Report was commis-sioned in 1981 and the Financial Services Act 1986 owed its existence largely to the Report's recommendations. However, there was an increasing feeling that the 1986 Act was no longer adequate to cope with the challenges posed to regu-lators by increasingly intertwined financial markets. After the 1997 election it was announced that, in future, one authority would take on the responsibility for the regulation of the whole of the UK's financial services sector. A report was commissioned and was prepared by Sir Andrew Large. This led to the Securities and Investments Board (SIB) being renamed the Financial Services Authority (FSA) in October 1997. In June 1998 the FSA took over the Bank of England's responsibilities for banking supervision. The FSA also took over the regulatory and registration functions of a number of bodies, the most relevant to life assur-ance being the Insurance Directorate of HM Treasury and the Self Regulatory Organisation responsible for life insurance, Personal Investment Authority (PIA). The Financial Services and Markets Bill had a long and laborious journey onto the statute book. It received Royal Assent on 14 June 2000 but did not come into effect until 1 December 2001 ('N2').

B   Overview of FSMA

I   *Statutory objectives*

3.3   The FSMA provides a framework for detailed rules to be made by regula-tion. Under the FSMA the FSA are required to have regard to a set of statutory objectives set out in Part I. These are as follows: confidence in the financial system; public awareness; the protection of consumers and the reduction of financial crime. With regard to protection of consumers, section 5 refers to 'the appropriate degree of protection' so acknowledging that different consumers require different degrees of protection[1]. Section 2(3) requires the FSA to pursue these objectives having regard to the effective use of its resources; the responsi-bilities of senior management (which consequently places a significant onus on the management of authorised persons); the application of cost benefit analysis to the imposition of rules and regulations; the need for innovation in regulated markets; the international character of financial services markets and the desir-ability of maintaining the competitive position of the United Kingdom; and not distorting or impeding competition unnecessarily.

Initial concerns about the FSA's lack of accountability resulted in changes to the Bill so that the FSMA requires the governing body of the FSA to have a majority of non-executive members[2]. In addition, the FSA is required to set up a committee comprised solely of non-executive members which keeps under review various aspects of the FSA's activities. This is also contained in Part I.

1   Sections 3 to 6.
2   Schedule 1, para 3(1)(a).

2   Other obligations

3.4   Schedule 1 imposes further overarching obligations on the FSA. It is required to provide for the independent investigation of complaints[1]. It must make an annual report to the Treasury[2]. An annual public meeting is also required to enable this report to be considered[3]. The FSA is required to maintain arrangements to monitor and enforce compliance with the requirements of the FSMA[4]. Although the FSA may delegate the performance of these functions to a competent body or person who need not be regulated, it cannot delegate its duty in this respect. The FSA cannot fund its activities by levying fines. Fines are to be for the benefit of authorised persons but not in terms of reducing fees[5]. The FSA (including staff) has immunity from civil actions except in the case of bad faith or where the claim arises under the Human Rights Act 1998[6].

3   Consultation

3.5   The FSA has a duty to consult practitioners and consumers on policies and practices[7] and must create a Practitioner Panel and a Consumer Panel[8]. The Treasury may appoint an independent person to conduct a review of how the FSA is carrying out its functions[9]. The Treasury can also arrange independent inquiries where there appears to be a serious risk to the financial system or significant damage (or risk thereof) to the interests of consumers. The situation must also have occurred as a result of a serious failure of the regulatory system and such an inquiry must be in the public interest. This was designed to give a statutory basis to inquiries such as Barings (1995) and Bank of Credit & Commerce International (1991)[10].

4   General prohibition

3.6   Part I of the FSMA also sets out one of its core provisions namely 'the general prohibition' **that no person should carry on a regulated activity unless that person is authorised or exempt**[11]. The offences and consequences of breach are also set out[12]. Contravention of the general prohibition is a criminal offence and agreements made will generally be voidable and the customer can

1 Paragraphs 7 and 8.
2 Paragraph 10.
3 Paragraph 11.
4 Paragraph 6.
5 Paragraphs 16 and 17.
6 Paragraph 19.
7 Section 8.
8 Sections 9 and 10.
9 Section 12.
10 Section 14 to 18.
11 Section 19.
12 Section 23.

claim compensation for any loss[1]. There are limited exceptions when the courts may allow agreements to be upheld[2].

5 Regulated activities

3.7 Part II of the Act and Schedule 2 contain an indication of the activities which are regulated but the specific details are set out by Order. The Regulated Activities Order sets out the activities and investments which are in fact regulated[3]. The activities unsurprisingly include dealing, arranging deals in, and managing investments and investment advice. They also include effecting and carrying out contracts of insurance, deposit taking, custody, establishing collective investment schemes and using computer-based systems for giving investment instructions[4]. The definition of investments includes 'contracts of insurance' amongst a long list[5].

6 Financial promotion

3.8 Section 21 sets out the framework of restrictions on financial promotion. One of the aims in updating the legislation in this area was to bring together the two regimes relating to advertisements and unsolicited (or solicited) calls. One of the side effects of this is to create criminal sanctions for 'real-time' communications. Previously only a breach of section 57 of the Financial Services Act 1986 relating to 'investment advertisements' created a criminal offence. Financial promotions may only be communicated by authorised persons (or the communication may be approved by an authorised person) and where originating outside the UK the restrictions only apply where it is capable of having an effect in the UK (unless an exemption is available). This is clearly largely intended to have an application to internet communications. (See Chapter 5 for detailed coverage of financial promotions.)

7 Authorisation and exemption

3.9 The relevant requirements are set out in Part III. In order to obtain authorisation there would normally be an application for permission under Part IV. However, other methods are possible, namely by 'passporting' under the single market directives (such as the Consolidated Life Assurance Directive[6]); by the use of rights under the Treaty of Rome (where a 'passport' cannot be obtained via the single market provisions, provided the relevant Home State protections

1 Sections 21 to 27.
2 Section 28.
3 SI 2001/544.
4 Paragraphs 2 to 9 of Sch 2.
5 Paragraphs 11 to 24 of Sch 2.
6 Directive 2002/83/EC.

are equivalent to those of the Host State); and persons who are otherwise authorised under the FSMA[1].

The persons who may be exempted are set out by Order. The regime for exemption of 'Appointed Representatives' (previously under section 44 of the 1986 Act) is established under section 39. However, there were changes as a result of the creation of a single regulator, so that banks and building societies which could previously operate as appointed representatives of other product providers (and hence gain exemption) now have to be regulated directly for this business (or not do it at all). This is because it is not possible for an authorised person to be exempt for some activities and authorised for others. The implications for, for example, banks and building societies which previously operated as Appointed Representatives of other providers of life assurance and investment products is that they now have to be regulated directly for that business. In practice the banks or building societies involved have achieved much the same result via a subsidiary company being the Appointed Representative rather than the bank or building society itself. This is explained further in Chapter 4.

8   Permissions

3.10   The requirements relating to applications for permissions to carry on one or more regulated activities are set out in Part IV[2]. By obtaining the appropriate permission the applicant will become an authorised person. Permission is only granted once so if an authorised person wishes to carry on additional activities then they need to vary their permission[3]. This is supported by Schedule 6 which sets out the 'Threshold Conditions' which an applicant must meet before permission can be granted. These are: requisite legal status of applicant (insurance companies must generally be corporate bodies although not limited liability partnerships); requirement for Registered Office and Head Office to both be in the United Kingdom where constituted under the law of any part of the United Kingdom; provisions relating to the structure of the applicant's group and any 'close links' not inhibiting regulatory supervision; adequate resources including effective means to manage risks and that the applicant is 'fit and proper'. Interestingly, under section 42(7) the FSA may specify a *wider* description of regulated activity than that to which the application relates and give permission for the carrying on of a regulated activity which is not included in the relevant application. The FSA has power to place restrictions on the level of that activity[4]. Section 43 relates to the imposition of requirements by the FSA and subsection (3) is of particular interest as it enables the FSA to extend its requirements to 'activities which are not regulated activities'. This is extended even further by subsection (4) under which requirements may be imposed by reference to the person's relationship with his group or other members of his group.

1   Section 31.
2   Sections 40 to 55.
3   Sections 42 and 44.
4   Section 42(7)(a).

The FSA can vary or cancel permissions in certain cases at the request of the authorised person[1] and can also restrict or vary permissions or impose limitations on its own initiative[2]. Variations of permissions can also take place where control over an authorised person changes[3]. The FSA has six months in which to determine an application[4]. Incomplete applications may be refused but if not the FSA must decide on the application within 12 months of the initial receipt of the application[5].

9 Approved persons

3.11 Part V of the Act relates to the performance of regulated activities by such persons as employees and other office holders. This requires approval by the FSA for specified types of functions, known as 'controlled functions'. Such persons will attain 'approved person' status[6]. This status has a wide application. 'Controlled functions' are not set out in the FSMA but in SUP 10.5.4R. At the time of writing there are 29 controlled functions, which consist of 22 'significant influence functions' and 7 'customer functions'. The former are those functions which enable a person to significantly influence the conduct of an authorised person (eg a director) and the latter are functions which involve dealing directly with customers or dealing with a customer's property (such as stockbrokers or financial advisers). The FSA has the power to prohibit an individual from performing specific function(s)[7]. Further detailed provisions are contained in the FSA Handbook mainly in 'APER' (Statements of Principle and Codes of Practice for Approved Persons), FIT (the Fit and Proper Test for Approved Persons) and AUTH 6 (Approved Persons).

The FSA has power to issue statements of principle and codes of conduct for approved persons[8] although it is made clear that breach of these will not (in themselves) give a person grounds for action[9]. The FSA has confirmed that it intends to reduce the number of controlled functions.

10 Part VII transfers

3.12 Part VI and Part VIII relate to Official Listing and Market Abuse respectively and so do not have any particular relevance to life assurance.

Part VII relates to business transfers and its provisions replace section 49 and Schedule 2C of the Insurance Companies Act 1982. Further detail about the process is set out in regulations. The provisions are essentially the same but there

1   Section 44.
2   Section 45.
3   Section 46.
4   Section 52(1).
5   Section 52(2).
6   Section 59.
7   Section 56.
8   Sections 64 and 65.
9   Section 64(8).

are wider powers to modify the rights of both policyholders and third parties (see further Section 7 below).

11   Financial Services and Markets Tribunal

3.13   Part IX requires the establishment of the Financial Services and Markets Tribunal[1]. Where the FSA makes a decision which a party does not agree with he can appeal to this tribunal. Decisions of the Tribunal can also be appealed in the courts but only on a point of law[2], the Tribunal being treated as a Court of First Instance (ie appeal is to the Court of Appeal). The staffing, constitution and procedure of the Tribunal is set out in Schedule 13. A President and a panel of Chairmen must be appointed together with a panel of lay members. The President and Chairmen must possess an appropriate legal qualification. Experts may also be appointed to provide assistance to members of the panel. The Tribunal can award costs against a party to the appeal. The Financial Services and Markets Tribunal Rules 2001[3] sets out details of the procedure.

12   Rules and guidance

3.14   The power to make rules and issue guidance applicable to authorised persons in carrying out regulated activities is set out in Part X, and in particular section 138. In practical terms the provisions of this part of the Act enable the FSA to issue and update its Handbook and underlying Sourcebooks. Section 141 is of specific relevance in that it enables the FSA to make rules ('Insurance business rules'), for example, prohibiting insurers from carrying on a specific activity which may include activities which are not regulated. This section specifically makes reference to rules concerning linked benefits. It is partially pursuant to this section that the insurance aspects of the Integrated Prudential Sourcebook have been issued. Section 155 requires the FSA to consult on proposed rule changes. The FSA has the power to make rules in connection with the prevention and detection of money laundering under section 146. Section 157 enables the FSA to issue guidance where considered appropriate to do so in relation to certain specified circumstances.

In Part XI of the FSMA the FSA is given wide powers to gather information and documents[4]. The FSA also has investigative powers including powers to appoint competent ('skilled') persons to conduct investigations where the FSA has reasonable grounds to do so[5]. Sections 170 to 175 deal with the powers of persons appointed by the FSA to carry out investigations and the use of information arising from such investigations. Section 176 sets out the powers which the FSA has to enter and search premises.

1   Section 132.
2   Section 137.
3   SI 2001/2476.
4   Section 165.
5   Section 167.

Part XII requires persons who propose to acquire control over certain authorised persons to notify and obtain approval from the FSA. Part XIII confers powers on the FSA to intervene in the activities of authorised persons from other member states who are authorised pursuant to rights under the Treaty of Rome and EU Directives. It sets out the grounds on which the powers are exercisable and the procedures for exercising them.

The disciplinary measures available to the FSA are set out in Part XIV. The FSA can publish statements about how authorised persons have contravened certain specific requirements[1]. The FSA can also impose fines on authorised persons who have contravened the rules[2]. It is under an obligation to publish a statement of its policy in respect of the imposition and level of such fines[3].

13 The Financial Services and Markets Compensation Scheme

3.15 Under this scheme compensation will be payable to customers who suffer financial loss as a result of the inability of an authorised person to meet its liabilities. It derives its statutory basis from Part XV of the FSMA. It replaced five pre-existing schemes and, interestingly from a life assurance perspective, it replaced the Policyholders Protection Acts. The FSA is under a duty to establish a company to manage the new Scheme. The Board must be appointed by but be independent of the FSA. The Board is required to report at least annually to the FSA on the discharge of its functions[4]. Section 214 sets out the broad requirements of the Scheme. The detailed provisions are set out in rules[5] and are considered further in Section 6 below.

14 Financial Services Ombudsman

3.16 The relevant provisions are set out in Part XVI. The FSA is required to establish a single, compulsory ombudsman scheme for speedy and informal resolution of disputes between members of the public and authorised persons. The jurisdiction of the Ombudsman (the FOS) extends to certain small businesses which, in the insurance sector, was a new feature. Section 226 provides for a compulsory jurisdiction which applies to regulated activities. The Ombudsman will also have a voluntary jurisdiction for certain other types of dispute[6]. The Financial Services Ombudsman replaced eight existing schemes including,

1   Section 205.
2   Section 206.
3   Section 210.
4   Section 218.
5   See Consultation Paper 58, Consultation Paper 86 and the policy statement 'Financial Services Compensation Scheme Funding Rules' (September 2001). Also, the Financial Services and Markets Act 2000 (Compensation Scheme: Electing Participants) Regulations 2001, SI 2001/1783, as amended by SI 2003/1476, SI 2003/2066, and modified by SI 2001/3084.
6   Section 227.

amongst others, the PIA Ombudsman and the Insurance Ombudsman, although the Pensions Ombudsman remains as a separate statutory scheme. A motivating factor for the creation of one single scheme was the reduced potential for confusion and overlap which existed with numerous schemes. Schedule 17 sets out the constitution and other aspects of the scheme. Central to this is the creation of a separate limited company. The board is appointed by the FSA but must be independent in its operation. Annual reports to the FSA are required. As stated, a voluntary element is also provided for whereby it may be agreed that unregulated activities be bound by the scheme rules in relation to certain activities of a financial services nature[1]. The ombudsman has power to require specified information and documents under section 231. The disputes it deals with include mis-selling, unsuitable advice, unfair treatment, maladministration, misleading advertising, delay and poor service in relation to products or services provided by insurers and other financial services firms. The Ombudsman is not required to decide cases on ordinary legal principles and may impose a result it considers fair. This introduces great uncertainty into the scheme, makes the scheme difficult to assess for consistency and inevitably leads to a real lack of accountability. In practice the costs of the Scheme are borne by the industry and the service is generally free to the complainant.

Part XXII concerns the appointment of auditors and actuaries by authorised persons and their responsibilities. Part XXIII requires the FSA to maintain a public record of authorised (and certain other) persons, and makes provision regarding the purpose for which confidential information may be disclosed by and to the FSA. See also SUP 4 which deals with the appointment of actuaries by life companies.

The procedures which the FSA must follow when giving notices of proposed actions under various provisions of the FSMA are set out in Part XXVI. This includes such things as decisions not to give permission or to refuse applications for approvals and decisions to take regulatory action, such as imposing penalties and making public statements. The FSA must issue a warning notice in accordance with certain prescribed requirements[2]. Such a notice must be in writing and set out the reasons for the issuing of the notice. The FSA must give the person in receipt of the warning notice at least 28 days in which to make representations in respect of the notice. Following a warning notice there may be a decision notice[3]. This will set out in writing the FSA's decision and the reasons for that decision. The FSA is also required to explain any right the person receiving the decision notice has to refer the case to the Financial Services and Markets Tribunal.

Part XXVII creates certain offences, including making misleading statements and supplying false information to the FSA. This aspect of the FSMA is clearly of particular relevance in connection with financial promotions. Section 397 makes it an offence for a person to deliberately make a misleading statement with a view to influencing another person's decisions.

1   Section 227.
2   Section 387.
3   Section 388.

Part XXIX is an interpretation section and Part XXX contains certain supplemental provisions.

15 Professional firms

3.17 Under the regime of the 1986 Act another means of obtaining authorisation was certification by a recognised professional body (RPB) such as the Law Society, the Institute of Chartered Accountants and the Institute of Actuaries. However, the position changed under the FSMA and some firms previously regulated by such bodies now need to be authorised directly by the FSA. Where the activities undertaken by the professional firm which might otherwise necessitate authorisation are merely 'incidental' to the firm's professional services such activities will be 'exempt regulated activities'. Provided further that certain detailed conditions are met they will be able to carry on exempt regulated activities under the supervision and regulation of their professional bodies ('designated professional bodies') and will not need direct FSA authorisation. The FSA is under a duty to keep itself informed about the way in which designated professional bodies supervise and regulate the carrying on of exempt regulated activities by exempt professional firms and the way in which exempt professional firms carry on exempt regulated activities[1]. The relevant statutory provisions are set out in Part XX of the FSMA[2].

C The FSA Handbook

I Content and interpretation

3.18 The FSA's rules are contained in its Handbook. The FSA Handbook is made under Part X of the FSMA. The Handbook runs to thousands of pages and can be difficult to navigate if you are not familiar with it. The FSA has issued a Reader's Guide which, whilst not formally guidance, is a very useful starting point in trying to get to grips with the Handbook.

The first point to make about the Handbook is that the definitive version of it is in the statutory instruments effecting changes, the rule making instruments. In practice, as the FSA consolidates the web version of the Handbook on a daily basis, the web version is likely to be the most up-to-date version and is the version used most in practice.

Sections of the Handbook are known as sourcebooks or manuals. The FSA's guide makes clear that all of these sourcebooks and manuals (modules) fall into seven blocks. In addition there are sector specific tailored handbooks for small firms aimed at specific industry sectors.

1   PROF 3.1.1G.
2   Sections 325 to 333.

Block 1 of the Handbook deals with overarching requirements for all authorised persons and approved persons. This block includes the 11 FSA principles and the rules relating to the conditions for authorisation and the systems and controls requirement.

Block 2 sets out the Prudential requirements for insurers. This is currently IPRU (INS) and PRU (which became GENPRU and INSPRU on 31 December 2006).

Block 3 contains most of the requirements that apply to firms in conducting their day-to-day business. For insurers, predominantly COB and ICOB but including CASS (relating to client assets).

Block 4 consists of modules describing the operation of the FSA's authorisation, supervisory and disciplinary functions. These include the provisions on enforcement action by the FSA.

Block 5 deals with complaints and compensation.

Block 6 are specialist sourcebooks including the one for collective investment schemes.

Block 7 provides the sourcebooks relating to the UK official list (eg including the listing rules).

In addition, in order to reduce the size of the Handbook, the FSA has removed some guidance from the Handbook and issued regulatory guides. The main one is PERG – the Perimeter Guidance Manual which gives guidance in relation to the need for authorisation.

Each module of the FSA Handbook is divided into chapters. A chapter is divided into sections and each section is divided into paragraphs. Generally each module, or in some cases each chapter or section, will specify who it applies to.

The FSA Handbook contains three kinds of provisions: rules, evidential provisions and guidance. A rule clearly indicates a binding duty on the firm and is generally issued under section 138. If a firm complies with an evidential provision it will tend to establish a firm's compliance with the rule in question[1]. However, it is still possible for the firm to show that it has achieved compliance with the rule to which it is linked by some other means. Guidance[2], although not binding, may be used to flesh out a particular rule. Sometimes a specific example will be cited. However, it does not create an expectation that a firm must follow the guidance to ensure compliance and the burden of proof is not put onto the firm. However, where a firm has followed current guidance on a particular subject, then the firm will usually have the benefit of a 'safe harbour' from disciplinary action provided this is in the circumstances contemplated by that guidance. In the text itself the three kinds of provision are referred to by the identification letters 'R', 'E' and 'G' and each has its own specific typographic design. Where certain words or phrases have particular meanings which are defined in the Glossary part of the Handbook, they are set out in italics in the text.

1   Section 149.
2   Section 157.

107

2 FSA Principles for business

3.19

Table 1: The Principles

1 Integrity	A firm must conduct its business with integrity.
2 Skill, care and diligence	A firm must conduct its business with due skill, care and diligence.
3 Management and control	A firm must take reasonable care to organise and control its affairs responsibly and effectively, with adequate risk management systems.
4 Financial prudence	A firm must maintain adequate financial resources.
5 Market conduct	A firm must observe proper standards of market conduct.
6 Customers' interests	A firm must pay due regard to the interests of its customers and treat them fairly.
7 Communications with clients	A firm must pay due regard to the information needs of its clients and communicate information to them in a way which is clear, fair and not misleading.
8 Conflicts of interest	A firm must manage conflicts of interest fairly, both between itself and its customers and between a customer and another client.
9 Customers: relationships of trust	A firm must take reasonable care to ensure the suitability of its advice and discretionary decisions for any customer who is entitled to rely upon its judgment.
10 Clients' assets	A firm must arrange adequate protection for clients' assets when it is responsible for them.
11 Relations with regulators	A firm must deal with its regulators in an open and cooperative way, and must disclose to the FSA appropriately anything relating to the firm of which the FSA would reasonably expect notice.

The FSA has stated that it intends to move more towards principles-based regulation. Whilst in one sense this provides flexibility in another it will provide uncertainty. Principles-based regulation will not be used in areas like prudential regulation and conduct of business to the extent that matters are governed by EU directives (eg the Market in Financial Instruments Directive (MiFID)).

The FSA has already taken one of its principles, Principle 6, and developed the concept of applying a broad, and it has to be said, changing requirement, that of treating customers fairly. It has advanced a long way since the FSA's original paper on the subject. It is now clear that firms must embed the principle of 'treating customers fairly' (TCF) into their business. It requires an end-to-end process or, as it is often described, looking at the complete customer journey. In practice, it requires firms to analyse their products design against their target markets and against complaints. In relation to complaints, it will also mean that customers in the same situation need to be treated consistently. Making one-off ex gratia payments is becoming a thing of the past which can be difficult and appears harsh in cases where firms would (eg on compassionate grounds) have been prepared to make such a payment. The concept is evolving, as is that of principles-based regulation generally, but it needs to be very carefully monitored by all firms.

3   Conduct of Business Sourcebook (COB)

3.20   In practical terms the parts of the FSA Handbook which have most impact on an ongoing basis on life companies are the Prudential rules (currently in PRU but moving to GENPRU and INSPRU from 31 December 2006) and the conduct of business rules (COB and ICOB). The most relevant sourcebook for the day-to-day business of life offices is COB which applies to the marketing of all life contracts other than pure protection (eg term assurance) products.

The sale of 'non-investment' life contracts ('pure protection contracts') is covered by the Insurance: Conduct of Business Sourcebook (ICOB), which applies primarily to general insurance.

COB effectively continues the regulatory regime in place since 1988 under the Financial Services Act 1986, but which since 2001 has been significantly revised to reflect the ending of polarisation, the implementation of the Distance Marketing Directive and the Insurance Mediation Directive.

When an adviser and a potential customer first meet, COB requires that the adviser disclose his or her status (that is, whether advice is given on the whole of the relevant market, from a limited range of providers or on the products of a single product provider). They must also set out the basis upon which charges are made. This disclosure must be in a form prescribed by COB known as the IDD and Menu. Only firms offering advice on a whole of market basis and offering clients the option to pay fees can refer to themselves as independent advisers. This is dealt with in more detail in Chapter 4.

COB also contains the rules governing financial promotions. Different regulations apply to real time promotions (face-to-face meetings (solicited or unsolicited and telephone calls), non-real time promotions (brochures, sales aids, emails, websites) and direct offer promotions (mailing packs or magazine and newspaper advertisements which can lead directly to a purchase). This is dealt with in more detail in Chapter 5.

Advisers must ascertain the personal and financial circumstances of their client to satisfy the 'know your customer' requirements. Based on this information, the adviser must select the most suitable product from the relevant range. Advisers must select the most suitable product from the range available to them or the whole of the market as the case may be. When a personal recommendation is made, the adviser must issue a 'demands and needs' statement to the client unless he has issued him with a 'suitability letter'.

Clients must be provided with a 'key features document' prior to conclusion of the contract which sets out the main features and risks of the product in question. The form and content is prescribed in COB Chapter 6 and is examined in Chapter 5. The client must also be told the amount of commission payable to the adviser if the transaction proceeds unless the adviser is being remunerated solely by payment of a fee from the client.

4 Insurance: Conduct of Business Sourcebook (ICOB)

3.21 'Term' or 'temporary' life assurance (written for a term of less than ten years or to age 70 and with no investment element eg surrender value) are governed by the ICOB sourcebook. Its provisions are mostly similar to the COB sourcebook although generally less prescriptive (eg there is no requirement to disclose commission to private customers). The sale of general insurance business (technically known as 'non-investment insurance contracts') became regulated with effect from 14 January 2005. ICOB was also used to implement the Insurance Mediation Directive. To seek to provide a level playing field for the various sectors of the industry the Treasury and the FSA also decided that it was necessary to regulate the sales activities of insurance companies even though insurers are not covered by the IMD. The ICOB Rules apply to insurers and intermediaries although insurers are predominantly regulated only in relation to sales to retail customers.

ICOB sets out the information required to be given to customers when first meeting with an intermediary through the issue of an 'initial disclosure document' (IDD) which details the services a firm can offer and the charges to be made. The intermediary must also prepare a 'statement of demands and needs' which analyses the customer's requirements and sets out the proposed solution together with the intermediary's reasons for selecting the particular policy. ICOB also details the documentation to be provided to the customer before completion of the contract and the documentation to be issued upon completion of the contract. See Chapters 4 and 5 for more details.

5 Other relevant parts of the FSA Handbook

3.22 The Authorisation manual (AUTH) gives guidance about the circumstances in which authorisation is required, or exempt person status is available. Much of this is now in PERG. Other information in AUTH was transferred to other parts of the Handbook from 1 January 2007.

The Supervision manual (SUP) governs the ongoing relationship between the FSA and the authorised person. The FSA has stated that it will take a 'risk-based approach' to supervision and has emphasised, partly as a result of fears expressed by the industry, that the cost burden on firms should be proportionate to the benefits. More specifically, this manual deals with supervisory provisions relating to approved persons, auditors, waivers, individual guidance, notifications (eg of problems) and reporting. The Statements of Principle and Code of Practice for Approved Persons (APER) and the Fit and Proper Test for Approved Persons (FIT) set out standards in this area. The general reporting requirement is in SUP 15.3.

The Enforcement manual (ENF) describes the FSA's enforcement powers under the Act and sets out its policies for using those powers. Schedule 1 to the Act requires the FSA to 'maintain arrangements for enforcing the provisions of, or made under, this Act'[1]. In the guidance the FSA emphasises the need for an open and cooperative relationship between the FSA and those it regulates. The FSA states that it will seek to exercise its enforcement powers in a transparent, proportionate and consistent manner and that it seeks to ensure fair treatment when exercising its enforcement powers.

The Decision Making manual (DEC) is mainly concerned with, and sets out, the FSA's decision-making procedures involving the issue of statutory notices and the exercise of certain other powers. The governing section of the Act is section 395. The statutory notices are warning notices[2], decision notices and further decision notices[3], notices of discontinuance[4], final notices[5] and supervisory notices[6].

Senior Management Arrangements, Systems and Controls (SYSC) provides an obligation on firms to apportion responsibility and in particular in relation to controlled functions of senior management. It also requires and gives guidance in relation to the firm's systems and controls. A firm must take reasonable care to establish systems and controls which are appropriate to its business[7]. What is appropriate will depend on the nature, scale and complexity of the business. The firm is required by SYSC to assess its systems and controls. Guidance on the areas likely to be covered is set out in SYSC 3.2 and includes delegation, financial crime, the need for a risk assessment function and the provision of management information to the governing body, suitability of employees and agents, on audit committee and internal audit. With effect from 1 January 2007, SYSC will also include much of the specific rules and guidance contained in PRU in relation to risk management (SYSC 11–17).

It is recommended[8] that firms have appropriate arrangements for business continuity to ensure that they can meet their regulatory obligations in the event of a disaster or other unforeseen interruption. These arrangements should be updated regularly and tested to ensure their effectiveness. Fundamental to good systems and controls is the keeping of adequate records and adequate security arrangements in relation to them. There is a specific section of SYSC dealing with the systems and controls advisable to manage operational risk[9]. This includes, in particular, requirements relating to outsourcing.

6 FSA Outsourcing Rules

3.23 Material outsourcing is defined as outsourcing services of such importance that weakness or failure of the service would cast serious doubt on the firm's compliance with the FSA's Principles or the threshold conditions. SUP

1 Paragraph 6(3) of Sch 1.
2 Section 387.
3 Section 388.
4 Section 389.
5 Section 390.
6 Section 395(13).
7 SYSC 3.1.1.
8 SYSC 3.2.19.
9 SYSC 3A.

15.3.8G(i)(e) requires a firm to notify the FSA when it intends to enter into or significantly change a material outsourcing arrangement.

SYSC 3.9A contains the FSA's guidelines on outsourcing including 'due diligence' requirements in relation to any proposed outsourcing supplier. This is to ensure that the supplier is suitably solvent and has the requisite expertise. The guidance also sets out issues to be considered and covered in the contract between the parties. The areas to be covered include the following:

(1) Need to allow firm to monitor and control provision of the service (eg service levels, reporting, escalation processes, key employees) including qualitatively and by independent assessment/benchmarking.

(2) Process for making changes to the services (eg change management, volume, type, adding new services).

(3) Right to terminate or change the agreement in the event of:

    (a) a change of control of the service provider;

    (b) a significant change in service provider's, business and operations; or

    (c) inadequate services that may lead to the firm being unable to meet its regulatory obligations.

(4) Adherence to the firm's policy(ies) particularly if the supplier's staff are on the premises (eg IT security).

(5) Information ownership rights and confidentiality agreements (ie ownership rights/escrow arrangements for third party software used in provision of the services).

(6) Adequacy of guarantees and indemnities.

(7) Business continuity.

(8) Exit management.

(9) Access rights to and cooperation with internal auditors, external auditors or actuaries and the FSA.

(10) Cooperation with new service provider.

(11) PI cover (level, obligation to maintain and to evidence).

A firm should notify the FSA of significant operational exposures, changes to its organisation infrastructure or the wider business environment. It should also advise the FSA if it needs to invoke its disaster recovery arrangements.

A firm cannot merely rely on the fact that the outsourced service provider is regulated or a member of its group although this may be a mitigating factor and normally reduces the amount of due diligence required.

D   Misleading statements and practices

3.24   Section 397 broadly replaced section 47 of the 1986 Act (which effectively replaced section 13 of the Prevention of Fraud (Investments) Act 1958). The FSMA makes it an offence (under section 397(2)) for any person to make a statement, promise or forecast which he knows to be misleading, false or deceptive in a material particular (or to recklessly, dishonestly or otherwise, do any of the above) or to dishonestly conceal any material facts for the purpose of inducing, or to be reckless as to whether it may induce, another person (whether or not the person to whom the statement, promise or forecast is made or from whom the facts are concealed) to enter or to offer to enter into, or to refrain from entering into, a 'relevant agreement' or to exercise, or refrain from exercising, any rights conferred by a 'relevant investment'. It is a defence for the person to show that the statement, promise or forecast was made in conformity with price stabilising rules or control of information rules.

It is also an offence under section 397(3) for a person to do an act or engage in a course of conduct which creates a false or misleading impression as to the market in or the price or value of any relevant investments if he does so for the purpose of creating that impression and thereby inducing another person to acquire, dispose of, subscribe for or underwrite those investments or to refrain from doing so or to exercise, or refrain from exercising, any rights conferred by those investments. It is a defence if the person 'reasonably believed' he was not creating a false or misleading impression or that the conduct was for the purpose of price stabilisation and in conformance with price stabilising rules or the conduct was in conformity with control of information rules[1].

The act complained of under section 397(2) must have been made in or from the UK and the intended recipient must be in the UK or the agreement is or would be entered into or the rights are or would be exercised in the UK. The act or the course of conduct under section 397(3) engaged in, must have been in the UK, and the false or misleading impression created there.

E   Actions for damages

3.25   By virtue of section 71(1), contravention of certain sections of the FSMA[2] is actionable by a person who suffers loss as a result, subject to the defences and other incidents applying to actions for breach of statutory duty. Section 71(2) potentially extends this power to a person who is not a 'private person'. A person is not guilty of a criminal offence by virtue of section 71.

In addition, contravention of rules issued under the FSMA is actionable by a private person who suffers loss as a result of the contravention, subject to the defences applying to actions for breach of statutory duty[3]. In prescribed cases the provisions may be extended to non-private persons. In respect of certain rules no

---

1   Section 397(5).
2   Section 56(6) or 59(1) or (2).
3   Section 150.

actions for damages will lie, such as the financial resources rules and listing rules[1].

F   Permitted links

3.26   Linked contracts are:

'contracts under which the benefits payable to the policyholder are *wholly* or partly to be determined by reference to the value of, or the income from, property of any *description* (whether or not specified in the contract) or by reference to fluctuations in, or in an index of, the value of property of any description (whether or not so specified).'[2] (emphasis added)

The reference to wholly or partly in this definition is intended to catch contracts which are otherwise conventional policies but where, for example, benefits are linked to the value of an index, such as the retail prices index.

Rule 3.7 of IPRU INS provides, subject to specified exceptions, that linked contracts may only be linked to assets or indices specified in a list of 'permitted links' contained within Appendix 3.2 of Chapter 3 IPRU (INS). Permitted links are divided into those linked to the values of certain defined types of property (for example, via unit trusts, open-ended investment companies or an internal linked insurance fund) ('property linked') and those linked to the performance of certain defined indices ('indexed linked'). Appendix 3.2 sets out the full list of permitted links, it includes listed and unlisted securities which are readily realisable[3], units or other beneficial interests in a scheme falling within the UCITS Directive, or a collective investment fund where the fund holds property which itself is a permitted link. Further conditions apply to such units. They must be readily realisable and the price of units must be published regularly. Linked funds are not permitted to hold more than 10% of their benefits in unlisted securities. A similar percentage limit applies to holdings in collective investment schemes other than UCITS or those which have been marketed to the policyholder in accordance with the marketing rules which apply to that particular collective investment scheme[4]. Derivative contracts are permitted, subject to certain safeguards. Broadly they must be approved derivatives from the purposes of PRU 4.3 (INS PRU 3.2) and be based on or used in connection with assets which are themselves permitted links. Internal funds managed by the insurance company or by someone for whose acts and omissions the insurer is responsible (eg broker funds) are permitted. Where one insurer invests in the funds of another insurer in addition to accepting responsibility for it the arrangement would need to constitute reassurance and should be evidenced accordingly.

The permitted links rules also apply to business effected through a UK branch apparently even if the insurer is an EEA insurer. It is arguable, however, that

---

1   The Financial Services and Markets Act 2000 (Right of Action) Regulations 2001, SI 2001/2256.
2   IPRU (INS) 3.7.
3   Normally at 97.5% of their value within 7 days.
4   IPRU(INS) 3.7.

these rules constitute prudential requirements and that EEA insurers would be able to show that this is a matter reserved to its home state regulator.

SECTION 2   THE FSMA AND THE CONDUCT OF LIFE ASSURANCE BUSINESS

A   Life policies treated as investments under the FSMA

3.27   Insurance contracts, including life assurance contracts, whether or not they are investment orientated, will fall within the definition of 'investments' by virtue of Schedule 2, Part II, paragraph 20 of the FSMA. This refers to 'contracts of insurance'. This term is divided into 'contracts of general insurance' and 'contracts of long-term insurance' by the Regulated Activities Order[1] which sets out (in Part II of Schedule 1) the various 'contracts of long-term insurance'. This essentially replicates the previous Schedule 1 of the Insurance Companies Act 1982. The ambit of 'long-term insurance' includes life and annuity, linked long-term, permanent health insurance, capital redemption contracts and pension fund management. Life companies are also able to conduct class I or II general insurance (accident and sickness) on a supplementary basis[2]. The categories of long-term business are as follows:

I Life and annuity	Contracts of insurance on human life or contracts to pay annuities on human life, but excluding (in each case) contracts within paragraph III.	
II Marriage and birth	Contracts of insurance to provide a sum on marriage or the formation of a civil partnership or on the birth of a child, being contracts expressed to be in effect for a period of more than one year.	
III Linked long term	Contracts of insurance on human life or contracts to pay annuities on human life where the benefits are wholly or party to be determined by references to the value of, or the income from, property of any description (whether or not specified in the contracts) or by reference to fluctuations in, or in an index of, the value of property of any description (whether or not so specified).	
IV Permanent health	Contracts of insurance providing specified benefits against risks of persons becoming incapacitated in consequence of sustaining injury as a result of an accident or of an accident of a specified class or of sickness or infirmity, being contracts that—	
	(a)	are expressed to be in effect for a period of not less than five years, or until the normal retirement age for the persons concerned, or without limit of time; and

1   SI 2001/544.
2   IPRU (INS) 11.6(b).

	(b)	either are not expressed to be terminable by the insurer, or are expressed to be so terminable only in special circumstances mentioned in the contract.
V Tontines	Tontines.	
VI Capital redemption contracts	Capital redemption contracts, where effected or carried out by a person who does not carry on a banking business, and otherwise carries on a regulated activity of the kind specified by article 10(1) or (2).	
VII Pension fund management	(a)	Pension fund management contracts; and
	(b)	pension fund management contracts which are combined with contracts of insurance covering either conservation of capital or payment of a minimum interest
	where effected or carried out by a person who does not carry on a banking business, and otherwise carries on a regulated activity of the kind specified by article 10(1) or (2).	
VIII Collective insurance, etc	Contracts of a kind referred to in article 1(2)(e) of the first life insurance directive.	
IX Social insurance	Contracts of a kind referred to in article 1(3) of the first life insurance directive.	

3.28 The categories of insurance business are known by their class names so, for example, life business is generally class I or class III. Conventional life business (eg where a fixed premium is agreed for a specified benefit with or without profit) is much less common these days as an investment vehicle and is normally used for protection business. Class III (unit linked business) is more common for investment contracts. The idea behind unit-linked business is that the customer pays their money into an investment fund. The charges for benefits (eg life or sickness cover) are variable and are charged to this fund. The approach was much more attractive than conventional business whilst inflation and investment growth were high and mortality and morbidity charges were lower. At the time of writing because of the certainty and simplicity of conventional whole or life of term life and sickness contracts they have become popular again. Class II business is conversely not popular. Class IV business includes income protection or health insurance contract designed to provide a fixed sum when a person is incapacitated and cannot work due to injury or sickness. Class IV business is notable as it also forms part of the definition of class 2 general business, the two being mutually exclusive. It is also the only class of long-term business which is required to be a long-term contract. Income protection or permanent health insurance (PHI) will be long-term business where it is expressed to be in place for at least five years, to retirement, or it is whole of life (ie no limit is expressed) and the contract only allows the insurer to terminate it in special circumstances set out in the contract. The insured can be free to terminate at any time. In other cases (eg because the contract is expressed to be annual) it may instead by classified as class 2 general insurance. Class VII business is not very common these days. It enables insurers to manage pension funds. This business is normally conducted as class III business. Tontines (Class V) and Capital Redemption (Class VI) are not classes of business known to UK insurers although offshore insurance companies (eg in the Isle of Man) may be authorised to write them. These types of business are not consistent with the UK requirement for insurance interest. Tontines are basically a last man standing type contract. Capital redemption contracts provide a guaranteed amount at the end of a specified term. Both concepts are also used by other European insurers.

As has already been stated class 1 and class 2 general insurance benefits may be added to a life contract (class I or III) on a supplementary basis. These benefits are as follows:

1 Accident		Contracts of insurance providing fixed pecuniary benefits or benefits in the nature of indemnity (or a combination of both) against risks of the person insured or, in the case of a contract made by virtue of section 140, 140A or 140B of the Local Government Act 1972 (or, in Scotland, section 86(1) of the Local Government (Scotland) Act 1973), a person for whose benefit the contract is made—
	(a)	sustaining injury as the result of an accident or of an accident of a specified class; or
	(b)	dying as a result of an accident or of an accident of a specified class; or
	(c)	becoming incapacitated in consequence of disease or of disease of a specified class,
		including contracts relating to industrial injury and occupational disease but excluding contracts falling within paragraph 2 of Part I of, or paragraph IV of Part II of, this Schedule.
2 Sickness		Contracts of insurance providing fixed pecuniary benefits or benefits in the nature of indemnity (or a combination of both) against risks of loss to the persons insured attributable to sickness or infirmity but excluding contracts falling within paragraph IV of Part II of this Schedule.

It should be noted that there is no equivalent provision for general insurers to write any life business other than accidental death benefit falling within class 1 general insurance. They may write 'ancillary' risks only within other classes of general insurance.

3.29   It is notable that the classes of insurance business do not include 'pensions' business other than in relation to class VII pension fund management. Pension contracts, whether insured occupational schemes, personal pension contracts, or older retirement annuity products, are normally actually contracts to provide an annuity. Effectively their terms provide for investment (normally on a unit-linked basis) until such time as pensions benefits become payable. At that time the contract will provide for an annuity on the life office's then current terms and conditions.

In personal pension schemes the policyholder will have an open market option which means that whilst the insurer is bound to offer the annuity, the policyholder is not bound to accept it. The insurance risk on the annuity may therefore never materialise but it is the trigger for treating the contract as insurance business. Reinsurance in this area also normally utilises the obligation to provide an annuity on current terms to transfer insurance risk. As tax rules change (eg deferring the need to buy an annuity) this link starts to look a little tenuous. Thus begs the question whether insurers may instead seek to offer pensions contracts as life contracts, especially now that the decision in *Fuji v Aetna* (see **1.69**) appears to permit unit-linked contracts without any additional life cover. The counter argument based on the *Fuji* case is that this scenario is not sufficiently related to death of the relevant individual (eg because the intention is to take pension benefits with the bulk of the policy monies).

As has already been stated in Chapter 1, the FSA Glossary contains a definition of life policy which includes personal pensions contracts where the contributions are paid to the life office; the apparent purpose of this being to apply the relevant COB rules to such a contract. Personal pension schemes offered by UK insurance companies are incorporated into a contract of insurance. Otherwise insurance companies would not be able to sell them because of the restriction to insurance business in PRU 7.6.13 9 (INS PRU 1.5.13).

B Ambit of investment business

3.30 Having established that a life policy is an investment within the ambit of the FSMA, it is then necessary to ascertain whether the activity in question constitutes a 'regulated activity'[1]. The relevant 'regulated activities' are:

(1) effecting and carrying out contracts of insurance (Article 10);

(2) dealing in investments as agent (Article 21);

(3) arranging deals in investments (Article 25(1));

(4) arrangements with a view to bringing about an investment (Article 25(2));

(5) assisting in the administration and performance of a contract of insurance (Article 39A);

(6) managing investments (Article 37);

(7) investment advice (including basic advice in relation to a stakeholder product) (Article 53);

(8) establishing, operating and winding up a stakeholder pension scheme (Article 52) and from April 2007 any personal pension scheme including SIPPS.

1   Schedule 2, Part 1 and the RAO.

Effecting a contract of insurance broadly encompasses the negotiation and conclusion/issue of the contract whereas carrying it out means administering it and dealing with changes and claims. There is no statutory definition of these terms but the issues have been considered in case law[1] under the provisions formerly contained in the Insurance Companies Act 1982 relating to 'carrying on insurance business'. Carrying on insurance business encompassed both the effecting (issuing) of contracts and carrying them out (eg claims management) and it is submitted that the cases are therefore still relevant to the FSMA defined activities .The cases make clear that a non-UK insurance company may be able to cover UK risks without carrying on insurance business in the UK. In order to do so it will need to ensure that no insurance activities are carried on in the UK. It is not possible to be definitive about what these encompass but broadly it is likely to mean that neither the insurance company nor any intermediary acting on its behalf in the UK should:

(1)   accept risk or negotiate in relation to underwriting issues (acceptance of risk or price);

(2)   issue policies or receive premiums;

(3)   negotiate/manage or agree claims on the insurer's policies;

(4)   negotiate or agree terms under other insurance contracts (eg reinsurance).

Although the main regulated activity for an insurance company is effecting and carrying out contracts of insurance, because of the FSA's permission regime other activities conducted as part of an insurer's business of effecting and carrying out insurance contracts also need the requisite permission. So, for example, arrangements in connection with the effecting of a contract of insurance may require the insurer to have a permission which includes arranging deals in investments. The FSA seems to accept that an insurer managing its own investments is not doing so by way of business and does not require permission to manage investments.

Article 52 of the Regulated Activities Order requires the person establishing, operating or winding up a stakeholder pension scheme to be authorised. From April 2007, the same activities in relation to a personal pension scheme, including self-invested schemes ('SIPPs') will require authorisation. Life companies establishing such schemes should do so by way of an insurance contract. If they are the 'product provider' (eg they contract with the member to admit them to the scheme), then even if they outsource the administration to another company they are likely to still be the person operating the scheme. Conversely, in non-insurance situations, the scheme administrator would normally be the person operating the scheme[2].

The activity of assisting in the administration and performance of an insurance contract will by definition (ie assisting) be carried on by someone other than the

1   See *Bedford Insurance Co Ltd v Instituto de Resseguros do Brasil* [1985] QB966 and *Phoenix General Insurance Co Greece SA v Administration Asiguraliror de Stat* [1988] QB 216.
2   See CP 06/05 and PS 06/07.

insurer. In any event exemptions exist for an insurance company's own management of claims and claims management undertaken on behalf of an insurer on a
professional basis. Similarly, loss adjustment and expert appraisal of claims are
not regulated activities. Intermediaries or claims managers assisting claimants in
relation to claims will, however, constitute regulated activities.

The activities of life assurance salesmen or independent intermediaries
would clearly fall within the ambit of 'investment advice'[1] and 'arranging
deals in investments'[2]. The heading 'managing investments' would include, for
example, the management of what are generally known as 'private funds'.
These are a specified part of the life unit-linked life funds where independent
intermediaries or investment managers manage the investments held in the
insurers funds. The investment advisory activities and those of arranging or
introducing are covered by the Insurance Mediation Directive and are
explained further in Chapter 4.

SECTION 3 THE NEED TO BE AUTHORISED OR EXEMPT UNDER THE FSMA

A The general prohibition

3.31 Section 2 above and Chapter 4 explain which activities constitute regulated activities in relation to insurance contracts and in particular how effecting
and carrying out such contracts constitute regulated activities. Section 19 of the
FSMA prevents a person from carrying on regulated activities by way of business in the UK unless it is either authorised or exempt ('the general prohibition').
A person who contravenes this provision is guilty of a criminal offence. By
virtue of section 23, it would be a defence to prove that all reasonable precautions were taken and due diligence was exercised to avoid the commission of the
offence. Where a person who is authorised nevertheless carries on a regulated
activity otherwise than in accordance with his permission, this is not an offence.
The transaction is neither void nor unenforceable nor gives rise to an action for
breach of statutory duty. In prescribed cases any person who suffers loss as a
result of the contravention may bring an action subject to the usual provisions
applying to breaches of statutory duty[3]. Section 26 provides that an agreement
made in contravention of the general prohibition is unenforceable against the
other party and the investor is entitled to recover any money or other property
paid or transferred together with compensation for any loss sustained as a result
of having parted with it. Section 380 of the FSMA enables the court to grant
injunctions and make restitution orders in respect of actual or likely contravention of a 'relevant requirement' (essentially a requirement under the FSMA and
certain other provisions).

---

1   Article 53 RAO.
2   Article 25 RAO.
3   Section 20.

B   Financial promotions

3.32   Section 21 of the FSMA prevents a person from 'communicating an offer or inducement to engage in an activity specified by the FSA as a controlled activity' ('the financial promotion restriction'). This is explained further in Chapter 5 but includes marketing materials and brochures.

Life offices may be divided into:

C   How is authorisation obtained?

3.33   The way in which authorisation is obtained for a UK insurance company or branch of a non-EU company is set out mainly in Part IV of the FSMA. Authorisation will be achieved by a successful application for a permission[1]. It is not possible to apply for a permission if there is one already in force for that person. In this case there would have to be an application for a variation. It is also necessary to satisfy the 'threshold conditions'[2] which are set out in Schedule 6. Effecting or carrying out contracts of insurance requires the authorised person to be a body corporate, a registered friendly society or a member of Lloyd's. UK insurers must have their head office and registered office in the UK. The insurer's close link (connected companies) must not prevent effective supervision by the FSA. The insurer must have adequate resources and be suitable (essentially 'fit and proper').

An insurer will need to appoint people to carry on the appropriate controlled functions. There are currently 27 such functions but those of Chief Executive, the actuarial functions, the finance functions and the compliance oversight functions are likely to be closely scrutinised by the FSA for the appropriate knowledge and experience before approval of the appointment would be given. A new insurer may also wish to utilise outsourcing providers and the FSA is also likely to be keen to understand such arrangements and how the risks of outsourcing are to be managed. The management of risk more generally will be assessed as part of the suitability and resource requirements and in particular the insurer's assessment of the amount of capital it requires.

Alternatively, a person may be 'exempted', and the statutory provisions relating to this are set out in section 38 and particularly section 39. This is considered further in Chapter 4. Authorisation for insurance companies established in other EEA states by exercising 'passport' or 'Treaty' rights[3] is described in Section 4.

Existing insurers and friendly societies were 'grandfathered' at N2 with the appropriate permission.

1   Section 31.
2   Section 41.
3   Schedules 3 and 4.

SECTION 4   EU PASSPORTING

A   Background

3.34 The main sources of EU law are the EC Treaty signed in Rome (as extended by the Treaty of European Union 1993), legislation made under that Treaty (which may take the form of regulations, directives and decisions), and the case law of the European Court of Justice.

Upon their entry into force, Treaty provisions, regulations and decisions (in so far as the persons to whom they are addressed are concerned) become law and need no further enactment. Where the provisions of the Treaty are clear, precise and unconditional and intended to give individual rights, they are directly effective and may be relied upon by nationals in the national courts of member states. All directly effective community law overrides conflicting national legislation.

Directives are addressed to member states and leave to member states the choice of form and method for achieving the requirements of the directive[1]. If the terms of a directive are clear, precise and unconditional, namely without discretions to be exercised by member states, and if the date for implementation has passed, then it can be used by an individual in spite of conflicting national laws (see *Becker v Finanzamt Munster-Innenstadt*[2]).

EU law can also impact on national law in interpreting domestic legislation. In the *Marleasing* case[3] the ECJ held that national courts must interpret national legislation which is ambiguous in a manner which is as far as possible consistent with the relevant EC directive even where national law predated the directive.

The right to freedom of establishment and freedom to provide services within the EU are enshrined in the Treaty of Rome[4]. Most of the EU Single Passport directives were part of the European Communities' Single Market programme and latterly the Financial Services Action Plan, the aim of which was to harmonise parts of the laws of member states to achieve the main aims of the EU, namely freedom of movement of persons, services and goods and capital. The Financial Services Action Plan saw the introduction of a streamlined process for adopting EU Legislation (the Lamfalussy process) (based on the recommendations of the committee chaired by Baron Lamfalussy). This involves high level EU legislation with detail being agreed by committees with appropriate expertise. There are four levels to the process. The first stage is that the directives and regulation are drafted in higher level terms. The second stage is technical implementing measures determined by reference to relevant supervisory bodies. The third stage involves interpretative documents, guidelines and standards designed to produce consistency, particularly in relation to options or discretions in the directives/regulations. The fourth stage is a check by the Commission. The directives adopted using the process to date have been implemented in a much shorter timeframe than might otherwise have been the case. The process applies in

1   Article 249 of EC Treaty.
2   Case 8/81, *Becker and Finanzamt Munster-Innenstadt* [1982] ECR 53, [1982] 1 CMLR 499.
3   *Marleasing SA v La Comercial Internacional de Alimentacion SA* [1990] ECR I-4135, [1992] 1 CMLR 305.
4   Articles 43 and 49.

relation to securities, banking, insurance and pensions. The Solvency II directive (on insurance company solvency) should be adopted using this process. The relevant committee of supervisors for insurance is called the Committee of European Insurance and Occupational Pensions Supervisors (CEIOPS). The committee has input at level 2 by recommending legislation to be adopted and by conducting consultations in support of its level 3 activities.

The European Economic Area (EEA) includes, in addition to the member states of the European Union, Iceland, Liechtenstein and Norway (the EFTA countries)[1].

B   The First, Second and Third Life Directives

3.35   Previous editions of this book chart the history and implementation of these directives in some detail. For present purposes only a very high level summary is provided here. It should also be noted that the directives have been consolidated and the relevant provisions are now contained in the Consolidated Life Directive. The First Life Directive, known as the 'Establishment Directive', permitted insurance companies incorporated anywhere in the EEC (as it was then called) to establish a head office, branches or agencies in respect of their long-term business in other EEC countries, subject to the obtaining of a licence (or 'official authorisation')[2]. The directive also provided for a harmonised definition of long-term insurance business[3] which includes capital redemption business[4]. As a result of the directive, companies were required to maintain specified reserves and a margin of solvency calculated in accordance with the directive. They were also required to limit their activities to the business of insurance and operations arising directly therefrom[5]. Additionally, insurers were required to manage their life and general business separately and there was a prohibition on the authorisation of new composites. It was also necessary for future EEC life operations of a UK composite to be via a subsidiary and not a branch[6].

The Second Life Directive built on the right of establishment provided by the First Life Directive by providing the right for EC insurance companies to accept business from policyholders in other member states. The limited ability the directive provided to accept such business was superseded by the implementation of the Third Life Directive. However, it should be noted that the provisions of the Second Life Directive regarding the law of the contract and cancellation continue to apply and are dealt with in other chapters of this book[7].

What the Second Life Directive did, essentially, was to allow an insurer without a licence in that country, to accept unsolicited (called 'own initiative') business from residents of other EC states. Although the directive defined own

1   Separate provisions apply in relation to Switzerland.
2   Article 6.
3   Article 1.
4   This was implemented in the UK by the Insurance Companies Act 1982, Sch 1.
5   Section 16, ICA 1982.
6   Article 13.
7   Chapters 1 and 5.

initiative business as including unsolicited intermediary business, it contained an option which allowed own initiative business to be restricted further by member states to situations where there had been no contact at all with the prospective policyholder.

3.36 The Third Life Directive[1] was implemented in the UK from 1 July 1994. It provided a single licence (or 'single passport') for insurance companies to offer their products within the EU subject to a notification procedure. An insurance company authorised in the UK may now carry on insurance business from a sales or full insurance branch or via brokers, in any other member state, without having to be authorised itself or have its policy terms, conditions and premiums authorised in that other member state.

The directive introduced the concept of home state authorisation (namely the state where the insurance company is established), subject to compliance with the notification requirements. The host state still has power to require the notification of the technical basis for calculating scales of premium and technical provisions, but not prior to marketing. The directive itself provided for the co-ordination of the way technical provisions are calculated by laying down a basis of actuarial principles[2].

The single licence is, however, subject to the power of the host state to prohibit the sale of an insurance contract by an insurer if it conflicts with the host state's legal provisions protecting the 'general good'. There was also a specific requirement that overseas insurers comply with the rules of the host country regarding the form and content of advertisements adopted in the interest of the 'general good' (Article 41). The concept of 'general good' is a matter of EU law and applies throughout the EU. From existing cases of the ECJ and recital 20 of the directive, it appears that such restrictions will only be upheld if they are objectively necessary, in proportion to their objective, non-discriminatory and do not repeat any safeguards in the home (ie insurer's in this case) state. These requirements may be in addition to the mandatory rules of law applicable if the host states law does not govern the contract.

Other changes included changes to the assets which can be used to cover technical provisions (ie amount of future insurance liabilities), a requirement of localisation of assets anywhere in the EU and changes to the rules on valuation of assets and determination of liabilities. Specific requirements on the information to be provided to policyholders, both pre-contract and where a contract is varied, and the right for existing composites to establish life branches were also included. The directive also provided rules relating to the transfer of insurance portfolios and the obligation to monitor the suitability of anyone wishing to acquire qualifying holdings in an insurer (broadly, holdings of 10% or more of the capital or voting rights).

The directive required in Annex II that prior to a contract being entered into (or varied), the prospective policyholder be provided with certain details which are specified in the directive. Further, these should be provided in writing, in an

---

1   Which was also known as the 'framework directive'.
2   Articles 17 to 25.

official language of the member state of habitual residence, unless the policy-holder requests otherwise. The matters to be included are set out in COB 5 and ICOB. Generally they will be covered by key features document requirements apart from:

(1) The arrangements for handling complaints concerning contracts by policy-holders, lives assured or beneficiaries under contracts including, where appropriate, the existence of a complaints body, without prejudice to the right to take legal proceedings.

(2) The law applicable to the contract where the parties do not have a free choice or, where the parties are free to choose the law applicable, the law the assurer proposes to choose.

There is also a requirement to notify policyholders during the existence of the contract of changes in the details of the insurance company and to provide information every year on the state of bonuses.

C Using the single passport

I Introduction

3.37 The branch and services notification obligations are set out below. Broadly, insurance services can be undertaken on one month's notice and an insurance branch established on five months' notice. The passported activities would be subject to rules applied by the host state regulator 'in the general good'. The rules of the host state applicable to marketing products would also be applied on the same basis. Similarly, the host state may specify that any contracts covering risk in their territory or with policyholders habitually resident in their country must be governed by a law of that country. Alternatively, if a choice of law is permitted by the host state then 'mandatory rules' of that jurisdiction may also be applied if another law governs the contract. This will ordinarily necessitate advice from lawyers in each EEA host country.

The provision of financial services in the UK or by UK companies pursuant to a passporting right is governed by the FSMA. UK regulation is undertaken in relation to 'regulated activities' which include effecting and carrying out contracts of insurance ('insurance'). Section 418 of the FSMA extends the FSA's jurisdiction outside of the UK to allow it to regulate passported activities. The provisions of the single market directives have been incorporated into FSMA (Part III of Schedule 3); and in the FSA Passporting Regulations (the 'Passporting Regulations'). There is also relevant guidance in Chapter 13 of the FSA Supervision Manual (SUP). These provide that a UK authorised insurance firm needs to notify the FSA, as home state regulator, of its intention to use its passporting rights. The FSA then provides the appropriate certificates to the host state regulator. The process is described in more detail at **3.39**. However, in order to comply with the relevant notification requirements, it will be important to accurately identify whether the particular activities which the company wishes to pursue fall within the right of establishment or the freedom to provide services. The notification procedures for insurance business differ in terms of content and timing depending upon which passporting right is used.

A UK insurance company will have a separate 'permission' from the FSA to conduct insurance mediation activities (eg advising on, arranging or assisting in the performance of a contract of insurance). However, if it wishes to sell its products itself in another EEA country it will do so under the Consolidated Life Directive as the Insurance Mediation Directive (IMD) does not cover insurers. Insurance intermediaries would passport under the IMD.

There will also normally be taxation implications of establishing a permanent establishment in another EEA country, in that this is likely to expose the profits attributable to that permanent establishment to the corporate income tax of that country. Accordingly, establishing a permanent establishment in a high-tax jurisdiction may increase the UK insurance company's effective rate of tax and it is advisable to seek appropriate tax advice.

2 Distinction between 'establishment' and 'services'

3.38 In practice it is often difficult to distinguish between what constitutes an establishment and what constitutes the provision of services, and therefore which notification procedure should apply. The distinction can have taxation implications, as an establishment in an EEA country is more likely to give rise to liability to pay corporate income taxes in that country. This distinction is especially difficult in the case of insurance intermediation type activities.

The concept of provision of services is basically distinguished from that of establishment by its 'temporary character', to be assessed in the light of duration, regularity and continuity. This distinction caused problems following implementation of the Third Life Directive. The Commission therefore issued an interpretative document to provide guidance[1]. This states that a firm operating on a services basis may equip itself with necessary infrastructure: despite the temporary nature of its activities. This may cover both 'upstream and downstream support activities' (eg use of risk assessment services, receipt of notices of claim and evaluation of local damage). However, it is clear this cannot extend to performing insurance activities which would require a branch (eg accepting new proposals/agreeing claims).

The guidance also makes clear that use of an independent intermediary should not constitute a branch of the insurer unless that intermediary is:

(1) subject to the direction and control of the insurer;

(2) able to commit the insurer; and

(3) has a permanent brief.

This means that if the insurer were to use an 'independent person' (eg independent intermediary) as its agent in another EEA country, if such intermediary has

---

1 OJ CO43 16/2/2000.

permanent authority to commit and is subject to the direction and control of the insurer, the insurer would need to passport on an establishment basis in respect of that intermediary.

3   Procedure to establish a branch for insurance activities

3.39   The insurer should notify the FSA of its intention to passport its authorisation into the relevant EEA host state on an establishment basis. It would do this by completing and submitting to the FSA the FSA's pro-forma 'notice of intention' which identifies the activities and classes of business which it seeks to carry on through that branch and includes other specified information (in relation to, for example, its authorised agents in the host state); its organisational structure; its reinsurance arrangements; how its solvency requirements will be met.

The FSA has three months from the date of receipt of the 'notice of intention' to consider the proposal. If it does not object to the 'notice of intention', the FSA will give a 'consent notice' to the host state regulator; and give notice to the insurer that it has given such consent to the host state regulator (a 'written notice').

The FSA has discretion to refuse to send a 'consent notice' to the host state regulator only if it has reason to doubt the adequacy of the insurer's resources or its administrative structure in relation to business which it is proposed be written through the branch; or to question the reputation, qualifications or experience of the directors or managers of the insurer or its proposed authorised agent in relation to the business that it intends to conduct through the branch.

Whilst it is possible, therefore, that the FSA may ask the insurer for more information or require a report from a skilled person before giving its 'consent notice' to the host state regulator, provided that the 'notice of intention' is completed in sufficient detail the consent notice should be forthcoming. In the unlikely event that the FSA were to propose to refuse its consent, it would need to issue a warning notice to the insurer. Subsequently, if the FSA decided to actually refuse to give a 'consent notice' it would need to give the insurer a 'decision notice' to that effect within three months of receipt of the 'notice of intention'. The insurer could then appeal the FSA's decision to the Financial Services and Markets Tribunal.

The insurer can establish its branch in the host state either when the host state regulator notifies the FSA (and the FSA notifies the insurer) of any 'applicable provisions' (ie local rules with which the insurer will be required to comply with when conducting business through a branch in the host state; see Part III of Schedule 3 to FSMA); or two months have elapsed from the date of the written notice.

The insurer must notify the FSA and the host state regulator of any change to the relevant details of its branch (provided in the notice of intention), including, the address of the branch and the name of its authorised agent; the classes of business carried on and the nature of the risks covered; the details of the structural organisation of the branch; the guiding principles as to reinsurance of business carried on, or to be carried on; the estimated costs of installing administrative services; and for each of the first three years following the establishment of the branch, the estimate of the firms' margin of solvency, the margin of solvency required and the method of calculation.

Unless the change results from circumstances outside the insurer's control, the process to approve the change may take up to two months (one month for the FSA and one month's notice to the host stage regulator).

4 Insurance services

3.40 The procedure for establishing a 'services' authorisation for insurance (and for intermediaries if relevant the IMD) activities are much more straightforward. The insurer provides a notice of intention in the same way but the amount of detail required and the timings are different. The information required in relation to the activities to be carried out on a services basis is limited to details of the proposed host EEA country and the nature of the risks to be covered. As regards timing, the insurer may commence the activities unless it is notified that there is an issue within one month.

Similar provisions to those for a branch apply in respect of changes in the details notified in respect of services business and the FSA has a month to consider the effect of the proposed change.

5 EU providers passporting in

3.41 Under the Consolidated Life Directive EU providers can passport into the UK by going through the process specified by their host state. Somewhat strangely the FSA appear to seek, via the EEA Passporting Regulations, to impose additional notification requirements (to notify the FSA in addition to the home state regulator) in relation to changes to details of an EEA insurer.

In order to be able to exercise a passporting right an EEA insurer must be an EEA firm. A firm is an EEA firm if it is a direct insurer (or an insurance intermediary authorised under the Insurance Mediation Directive). An EEA firm becomes FSMA authorised by satisfying the establishment conditions in Schedule 3 of FSMA, broadly by notifying its regulator and the regulator providing an appropriate certificate to the FSA. The certificate from the home state regulator should specify the activities which the EEA insurer is authorised to carry on. An EEA insurer cannot apply for permission for these activities[1], it should automatically be given the appropriate permission by the FSA. It can apply for top-up permissions in respect of activities it would not be able to carry on under its EEA right. As non-UK insurers will normally be authorised in their own state to conduct activities which in the UK would constitute insurance mediation activities, it is arguable that their permission should also include limited insurance mediation permission (ie in relation to their own business). This does not appear to happen in practice.

EEA firms once authorised should be advised of relevant UK provisions applicable to them. The FSA has set out in SUP an extensive list of which

---

1 Section 40(3).

provisions apply to EEA firms but provides that they only apply to the extent that the matters concerned are not reserved to the firm's home state by the Consolidated Life Directive (eg prudential issues). The list distinguishes between UK and non-UK establishments broadly applying much more of the FSA's rules to a UK establishment. For example, a UK establishment will be subject to the Principles for business, parts of the approved person regime, the COB and ICOB provisions in full and the FOS and FSCS. Selling without a UK establishment still requires compliance with large sections of COB in particular and to a lesser extent, where relevant, ICOB. Firms writing with-profits business have to produce something similar to the Principles and Practices of Financial Management required for UK with-profits firms by COB 6.10. They will also need to comply with the permitted links rules for business effected by a branch in the UK. EEA firms are likely to find the quantity of material with which they have to comply quite daunting.

It is not clear which if any other provisions of the law of the relevant part of the UK would apply if the law of the contract were to be other than the law of that part of the UK (ie what the UK mandatory rules are).

SECTION 5   SUPERVISION AND INTERVENTION

A   Supervision

3.42   The FSA supervises UK authorised firms on many different levels. Because of its statutory objectives and the need to be proportionate it aims to focus its efforts on those areas where the risk to the consumer or orderly financial markets is perceived to be greatest. In practical terms the lifecycle of regulation starts with the application process and the need to satisfy the threshold conditions including the need to be fit and proper. The appropriateness of the firm's key personnel and those dealing with customers is assessed. On an ongoing basis those people need to adhere to standards of conduct or be potentially held personally liable or ultimately disqualified. Once a firm is up and running there are the overriding obligations imposed by the FSA's Principles. The emphasis also shifts primarily to prudential risk which now of course involves having adequate systems and arrangements in accordance with SYSC to manage risk. Conduct of business rules also start to feature prominently as does the need to report annually to the FSA on the basis set out in IPRU INS Rule 9, the Accounts and Statements Rules. At this point the FSA may decide it would like to come for a visit as part of its ARROW process. This involves individual interviews and the provision of information followed by a risk mitigation programme to sort out any issues arising.

Although there are many FSA requirements operating at different levels, it is probably fair to say that the emphasis on an ongoing basis is on risk management (and the effect on capital requirements). The FSA's supervisory tool ARROW was introduced as a means of adopting a risk-based approach to supervision and thereby complying with its statutory objectives (See Section 1 above). The process is based on thematic reviews and individual assessments, both desk-based reviews and on-site visits. The aim being to identify the large ticket items and the systemic or control failures in a business. Treating customers fairly is still an important issue for life companies being reviewed. The end product is a risk map which leads to a risk rating based on impact and probability of the risks concerned. This leads to a risk mitigation programme which the firm is expected to follow.

The ARROW process has been reviewed and at the time of writing the FSA is planning to replace it with ARROW II. This has a revised risk model, a process for seeking the firm's views on draft ARROW letters and will involve additional training for the FSA's staff. The FSA have described their risk categorisation process as aligned to their statutory objectives but their impact assessment (the potential harm that could be caused) is still in part the supervisor's subjective assessment against the risk model. There are plans to develop the process further and to fully integrate with capital requirements. It is to be hoped that as firms' risk management practices and procedures become more embedded the process may become a less daunting prospect.

B   Own initiative and powers to vary permissions

3.43   The FSA's own-initiative powers enable the FSA to vary, cancel or restrict a permission. Similar powers are also set out in Part IV[1]. In dealing with an application for permission the FSA may incorporate in the description of regulated activity such limitations (for example, as to the circumstances in which the activity may or may not be carried on) as it considers appropriate[2]. Similarly, a permission may include such requirement as the FSA considers appropriate[3]. The examples given being to require or prohibit certain specified action in relation to regulated activities. Section 45 of the FSMA sets out the own-initiative power. It authorises the FSA, on its own initiative, to vary a Part IV permission to remove a regulated activity, vary a requirement applicable to the permission or to cancel it, if it appears that an authorised person is not complying with the threshold conditions, is not carrying on regulated activities or it is desirable to do so to protect the interests of consumers or potential consumers. This last basis is very wide. However, ENF 3.5 makes clear that the FSA will normally seek to agree with the firm those steps it must take to address the FSA's concerns. Section 53 sets out when the variation would take effect. It can take effect immediately if the FSA reasonably considers it necessary. Normally, it will be on a specified date or when the matter to which the notice relates is no longer open to review. Notice to the authorised person should specify the period for representations to the FSA about it and inform the authorised person of their right to refer the matter to the Tribunal.

---

1   See sections 42 to 45.
2   Section 42.
3   Section 43.

C   Enforcement related powers

3.44   The Enforcement Manual sets out the enforcement related powers of the FSA and its policy on using them. It is worth bearing in mind the role of the Tribunal in reviewing decisions of the FSA. The Tribunal is independent of the FSA and is chaired by a legally qualified person. Its decisions are treated as decisions of a First Instance Court and may be appealed on questions of law but not fact. The appeal process is, however, a very public one which it is perceived puts some people off.

Although the FSA states in ENF that it will seek to exercise its enforcement powers in a transparent, proportionate manner which is consistent with its publicly stated policies and will ensure 'fair treatment' when exercising its enforcement powers[1], that is not necessarily the experience of those who have been through the process already. There have been a number of fairly high-profile cases, predominantly in relation to endowment mis-selling, which have led to significant fines (eg in excess of £750k). In some cases the firm has co-operated in order to lessen the ultimate fine and in others they have sought more robustly to defend themselves.

The FSA's powers of investigation are set out in Part XI of the FSMA and include the power to require information, send in investigators and in some cases apply for a warrant to search premises[2]. One important point in relation to such investigations is the effect of section 413 which enables a party to retain legally privileged documents (or documents which are enclosed with or referred to in such documents[3]). The FSA will often ask for such documents to be disclosed under Principle 11 but the firm cannot be required to do so unless the documents are held with the intention of furthering a criminal purpose. If a firm does decide to disclose such information to the FSA then it should seek to limit the purpose for which it can be used and make clear that privilege is not being waived.

The power to obtain documents from a firm (or a connected party) on request applies to such information and documents as are reasonably required in connection with the exercise by the FSA of its functions under FSMA. It can be a very burdensome obligation as the FSA may specify such format as it reasonably requires. Also, if the information is historical, there may be logistical problems of retrieval. If these cause anything other than delay then the firm will need to be careful to show that it has adequate systems in this area.

3.45   One option open to the FSA when it is investigating a firm is to require the firm to obtain a skilled person report from an appropriately skilled (expert) person approved by the FSA[4]. In some of the enforcement actions to date firms have themselves decided to commission such reports in order, it is assumed, to give themselves greater control over the scope of the report and the terms of reference.

---

1   ENF 1.3.
2   See section 176.
3   Section 413(2)(c).
4   Section 166.

The power to appoint investigators is set out in section 167 and may be exercised either by the FSA or the Secretary of State. The scope of the investigation is the nature, conduct or state of the business of the firm or its Appointed Representative, a particular aspect of that business or the ownership or control of an authorised person. The investigation can also be extended to group companies[1]. Section 168 enables investigations in particular cases (eg where it appears there may have been market abuse). There are three criminal offences in section 177 relating to non-cooperation with FSA investigators. Not surprisingly these cover providing false or misleading information but they can also cover destroying or otherwise disposing of documents that the person knows or suspects would be relevant to the investigation.

The FSA may also exercise certain powers at the request of an overseas regulator (eg power to investigate section 165). Conversely, the FSA's powers may be restricted in relation to EEA companies because of matters reserved to the home state regulator[2].

D Sanctions

3.46 The FSA sets out in ENF 11.4 factors which may be relevant to its decision as to whether to actually take enforcement action against a firm. These include breaches which reveal serious or systemic weaknesses of the management systems or internal controls relating to all or part of a firm's business. In addition, there may be additional capital consequences whilst such risks subsist. Other factors include the scale of the issue (amount gained or risk of loss to customers) and whether any financial crime is involved.

Having decided to take disciplinary action, often the most powerful regulatory sanction is a public statement followed closely by a large fine. Withdrawing, cancelling or imposing a requirement on a permission can also be effective too. Under section 205, if the FSA consider that an authorised person has contravened a requirement imposed on him by or under the FSMA it may publish a statement to that effect. On a similar basis the FSA has the power, in relation to a firm whose permission is not being withdrawn under section 33, to impose a fine of such amount as it considers appropriate[3]. The FSA has to give the firm a warning notice that it proposes to impose a fine or make a public statement setting out the fine and/or the statement as appropriate. If the FSA decides to go ahead with the planned action it must issue a decision notice. The firm may then refer the matter to the Tribunal.

The FSA also has powers to sanction approved persons and to make disqualification orders.

1 Section 167(2).
2 Section 199.
3 Section 206.

SECTION 6   FINANCIAL SERVICES COMPENSATION SCHEME

A   **Structure of the Scheme**

3.47   As a result of public criticism following the collapse of insurance companies, increased safeguards were introduced for the protection of policyholders.
One such measure was the Policyholders Protection Act 1975 (PPA) which initiated a compensation scheme to assist policyholders of an insurance company
which had been wound up. The compensation scheme was brought into force by
the Act and was administered by the Policyholders Protection Board. The
scheme was designed to protect 90% of the benefits payable under life policies.
The scheme was replaced from N2 by the Financial Services Compensation
Scheme (FSCS).

One of the objects of the FSCS was to merge all the previous compensation
schemes applicable to retail investments and to provide a single point of contact
for consumers in the event of a firm being unable to pay claims against it.
However, that merger did not mean harmonisation of the levels of cover. For
protected investment business there is a limit of £48,000 (100% of the first
£30,000 and 90% of the next £20,000 up to £48,000). This limit does not apply
to life insurers where the limit for eligible claimants is 100% of the first £2,000
and still 90% of the remainder without limit.

The functions under Part XV of the FSMA are undertaken by the scheme
manager. The Financial Services Compensation Scheme Limited, appointed by
the FSA for this purpose, is independent of the FSA but accountable to it. FSMA
sets out the required constitution and essential provisions of the scheme[1] and provides for the FSA to be able to make rules relating to the scheme and also provides for the scheme manager to be able to impose levies[2]. Outline provisions for
the Scheme are provided for in section 214. The rights which the compensation
scheme has in the event of the insolvency of an institution covered by the scheme
are covered by section 215. Of particular relevance to life insurers are sections
216 and 217 which relate to the continuity of long-term policies and the provisions relating to insurers in financial difficulties respectively.

3.48   The scheme manager is required to report to the FSA on the discharge of
its functions[3] and has power to require specified information or documentation to
be provided or produced[4]. The scheme manager may also inspect information
held by receivers, administrators, liquidators, etc, but not where such person is
the Official Receiver and certain others[5], which requirement can be enforced by
the court[6]. The scheme manager and various officials also enjoy a degree of statutory immunity[7].

---

1   Section 212.
2   Section 213.
3   Section 218.
4   Section 219.
5   Section 220.
6   Section 221.
7   Section 222.

The scheme rules require FSCS Limited to manage, hold and apply the funds held by the scheme in accordance with the rules. The rules set out the details relating to the annual report as required by section 218. A three-monthly report on the business conducted by the scheme and other information requested by the FSA is also required. FSCS Limited must also advise on certain other events such as the appointment of a chief executive, secretary or a change in auditors. Further, FSCS Limited must keep records of the scheme's transactions for at least six years. FSCS Limited must take steps to inform potential claimants that claims may be made for compensation where a firm is declared 'in default'. Effective procedures and service standards must be put in place for dealing with complaints about the scheme.

When an authorised insurer which provides long-term insurance cover is declared in default, FSCS Limited must try to arrange to continue cover with another insurer if this is more cost effective than paying compensation[1]. If FSCS Limited determines that an authorised insurer is in financial difficulties, it must try to arrange for the transfer of the business to another authorised person or give financial assistance to the insurer in difficulty to enable it to continue. Such action must only be taken if it is more cost effective than paying compensation. 'Financial difficulties' encompasses provisional liquidation; inability to pay debts under formal insolvency proceedings or where an application has been made to court to secure a voluntary creditors' arrangement, but the firm is not yet in liquidation or being wound up.

B Eligible claims

3.49 Protection offered by the scheme is aimed at ordinary retail consumers. The FSCS may pay compensation to an eligible claimant in respect of claims under a protected insurance contract where the insurer is in default. An eligible claimant is a person entitled to bring a claim under COMP 4.2.1R. Essentially, all long-term policyholders will continue to be protected (even if they are large companies) unless they are connected with the insurance company in some way[2].

The claim must be in respect of a 'protected contract of insurance'[3]. Contracts will only be protected where the establishment of the relevant person is in the UK, another EEA state, the Channel Islands or the Isle of Man. The complainant must also be habitually resident in one of these territories at the time the policy is entered into[4]. Similarly EEA insurers issuing contracts through a UK establishment to people habitually resident in the UK are covered.

---

1   Rule 3.4.
2   COMP 4.4.2R.
3   See COMP 5.4.
4   COMP 5.5.4.4(a).

I   The circumstances in which a relevant person is in default

3.50   Examples include insolvency or bankruptcy. If compensation is offered the claimant may be required to transfer to FSCS Limited his rights to claim against other parties. The reasoning behind this is to maximise recoveries by FSCS Limited and prevent the affected consumer from taking action against the party(ies) in default[1]. Comp 8 contains provisions relating to the rejection of applications where the claimant has omitted material information or his claim contains inaccuracies (unless FSCS Limited considers the information was provided in good faith). Offers may be withdrawn if disputed or not accepted within 90 days. Offers may be reissued or varied. COMP 9 sets out time limits for payment of compensation. Payments in respect of life policies are to be made directly to the claimant or on his instructions. Partial payments or payments on account are also permitted where there may be some uncertainty about paying the full amount. Interest may also be payable on compensation payments at the discretion of FSCS Limited. The rate of interest may be no higher than the clearing bank base rate[2].

SECTION 7   PART VII PORTFOLIO TRANSFERS

A   Transfer of insurance business between companies

3.51   Firms seeking to reorganise or sell part of their insurance business would ordinarily need the agreement of their policyholders to change the insurance provider. The Consolidated Life Directive provides for portfolio transfers in relation to all or part of an insurer's book of business.

The provisions governing such transfers are set out in Part VII, sections 104–117, Schedule 12 of FSMA and the Control of Business Transfer Regulations[3]. Essentially the process requires an application to court. The insurance company has to put together a scheme setting out in detail how the transfer of funds is to take place and comment on the effect of the transfer on all different classes of policyholder. The firm's actuary then has to produce a report to the Board on the scheme stating that in his opinion the scheme should proceed and that no class of policyholder will be disadvantaged by the scheme. The report sets out how the scheme would work and the benefits of the transfer. An independent actuary (acting as an expert) must also produce a report. The appointment is a personal one but in order to satisfy the requirement of independence the position of any firm the actuary works for should also be considered. The independent actuary (the independent expert) must have no interest in either party to the transfer which would prejudice his status in the eyes of the court. If the independent expert's firm were, for example, the only firm used by either party recently, it would probably struggle to show the required level of independence,

1   COMP 7.
2   COMP 11.
3   SI 2001/3625

even if the individual actuary had not personally been involved. The FSA needs to approve the independent expert's appointment. (See also the provisions relating to reattribution schemes in Chapter 6 where the scheme involves the inherited estate of a with-profits fund).

B   The Scheme Report

3.52   The independent expert must produce a report in a form approved by the FSA. The principal purpose of the Scheme Report is to inform the court of the likely effects of the Part VII transfer on all relevant classes of policyholder. Accordingly, the independent expert producing the report is under a duty to the court and must comply with the rules on expert evidence set out in Part 35 of the Civil Procedure Rules.

The Scheme Report should cover:

(1)   information relating to the independent expert, including his qualifications, any circumstances which might prejudice his independence and the person or persons who appointed him;

(2)   the purpose of the Part VII transfer and a summary of its terms;

(3)   the documents, reports and other information considered in producing the Part VII report, including whether any requested information has not been provided;

(4)   the extent to which the independent expert has relied on information provided by or the opinion of others; any steps taken to verify such information or opinion; and why he believes such reliance to be reasonable;

(5)   the Independent Expert's opinion on the likely effects of the Part VII transfer on the security and reasonable expectation of:

    (a)   the transferring policyholders;

    (b)   the remaining policyholders of the transferor (if any); and

    (c)   the transferee's existing policyholders; and

(6)   any matters not taken into account that may be relevant.

C   Issues

3.53   Although the consent of the FSA is not formally part of the process the Scheme is almost certainly going to fail if it is opposed by the FSA. In practice this means that the FSA is involved (as they should be in accordance with Principle II) in a scheme's planning from an early stage.

The practical issues likely to arise in relation to a proposed scheme are the time required when there are overseas risks, the notice requirements for different classes of policyholder and the effect of the scheme on non-UK assets or contracts not subject to a law of the United Kingdom.

Where a risk to be transferred is situated in another EEA state the FSA is required to consult with the host state regulator(s) concerned. As the regulators may take three months to respond before deemed consent will apply, the FSA may need to wait three months before it can issue a certificate as to long-term business. If the transferee is not UK authorised, the FSA must also seek a certificate from the EEA home state regulator that the transferee will meet relevant solvency margin requirements after the transfer (certificate as to margin of solvency).

The portfolio transfer process is designed to work within the EEA and will not necessarily work in other jurisdictions.

Although notice of an application to transfer an insurance should be circulated to all known policyholders of the transferor and the transferee, the FSA may waive part of this requirement if it is satisfied that the policyholders not receiving notice will not be adversely affected. This is a welcome relaxation as there are cases where it is either impractical and/or more confusing for distinct classes of policyholder who cannot be affected by the transfer. The FSA expects policyholders to be provided with a summary of the scheme (including the scheme report). (This summary and the full report itself must be made available free of charge on request.)

As regards non-UK assets or contracts governed by a law of a country outside the UK it is possible for the court order effecting the transfer not to have the required effect. The relevant provisions of section 112(2) of the FSMA permit the UK court to transfer 'other property or liabilities'. This provision has been held to be wide enough to enable contracts to be transferred without the consent of the other contracting party[1] (eg reinsurers whose consent was required under the reinsurance agreement). In practice companies may obtain the consent of such third parties (even where the court could make an order without consent). Significant practical issues can arise where, for example, a treaty is to be split between the transferor and transferee and ideally these should be resolved in advance so as not to prejudice the feasibility of the scheme.

D   The process

3.54   The court process itself is commenced by submission of a claim form with supporting witness statements. A 'hearing for directions' will then be requested by application notice accompanied by the Scheme Report. At the hearing for directions the court will establish the timetable for the process.

The court is likely to rely on the evidence of the independent expert that the respective policyholders are not likely to be prejudiced by the transfer. It is also likely to have regard to the FSA's view of the proposals. It seems inconceivable that a transfer opposed by the FSA could be approved. The FSA, and any person affected by the transfer, have the right to attend and speak at the court hearing. In the AXA Equity & Law Life Assurance Society and AXA Sun Life plc[2]

---

1   *Carter Insurance Co Ltd v WASA International Insurance Co Ltd* EWHC 2698 (Ch).
2   [2001] All ER (Comm) 1010.

reattribution scheme (under the predecessor legislation) the Consumers Association appeared on behalf of a representative policyholder.

The court must normally be satisfied that the transferee company will be able to carry on the classes of business transferred under the scheme and that the appropriate certificates have been provided.

Although the court may sanction a scheme where all the required certificates have not been provided it is unlikely in practice to do so. The court cannot sanction any scheme until at least 21 days after the FSA is given the documents relating to the scheme. The transferee must deposit the court order with the FSA within ten days of it being made.

CHAPTER 4

Intermediation and distribution

SUMMARY

SECTION I   INTRODUCTION AND THE IMD

A   Overview

4.1   The current UK regulatory regime applicable to insurance intermediary and other distribution businesses is to a large extent the result of historical provisions (many of which, eg polarisation, have now been removed) and the EU Single Passport Directive in this area, the Insurance Mediation Directive ('IMD'). The activity of arranging or introducing a client to an authorised person in relation to the potential sale of an insurance contract is now more tightly regulated than similar activities carried on in relation to other regulated products.

B   Depolarisation

4.2   One of the original aims of the Financial Services Act 1986 was to try to make it clear who intermediaries were acting for. The legal position in the UK for insurance brokers (see Section 7 below) is that insurance brokers, other than Appointed Representatives ('ARs'), are generally regarded as the agent of the client. At the time of writing this is an area of law which is still causing problems in the wider insurance market. The Law Commission are currently looking at whether the existing law should in effect be reversed to make the broker the agent of the person paying them (eg normally the insurer).

The rule, known as polarisation, included in the original rules of the relevant Self Regulatory Organisation LAUTRO (rather than the 1986 Act) required brokers to be either independent (selling based on the whole of the market), or tied to only one product provider (or their group companies) and to disclose their status to potential clients[1]. For many years it therefore provided clarity in this area. As a result of a report by the Office of Fair Trading in 1999 into the anti-competitive nature of the polarisation rule, the FSA announced its intention to remove it[2]. The FSA issued a series of consultation papers[3]. The earlier consultation papers provide a good summary of the polarisation regime and the issues involved in making changes to it. The FSA also started diluting the rule by not applying it to stakeholder pension schemes and direct offer financial promotions. Much of the focus in the latter stages of the FSA's consultation was on the precise mechanism for disclosing to clients the intermediary's status and commission levels (ie the content of the new Initial Disclosure Document and the Menu). Removal of the polarisation rule[4], full depolarisation took effect from 14 January 2005, allows a firm to operate on a whole of market or more limited basis provided it discloses its 'scope' to its customer. A firm that advises on a whole of market basis can offer customers a more limited range initially and then widen its range if that becomes appropriate. Even firms restricted to a number of providers (or to just one) have the ability, on a one-off basis, to gap fill or sell products which are outside of their range. Firms can also offer different ranges to different customers and increase their range during the course of a sale to a particular customer. Controls still apply to the use of the term 'independent' by firms operating on a whole of market basis. Its use depends on whether the customer is given the option to pay by way of fee rather than commission. Changes were also made by removing the 'better than best' rule which effectively prevented many sales of products of connected providers.

The only extent to which the polarisation rule now applies is in respect of ARs who may have only one principal for investment purpose (but this may extend to product providers in the same group). In practice, if that one principal is a distribution company (eg authorised in its own right to sell), then the limitation will create a whole of market or multi-tie situation (ie acting for a limited number of providers). It remains to be seen whether this improved customer choice will come at the cost of increased charges.

C   The IMD

4.3   The Insurance Mediation Directive ('IMD') was adopted by the EU in 2002. Insurance mediation activities are the activities of introducing, proposing

---

1   In relation to packaged products.
2   July 2000.
3   CP 80, 121, and 04/03.
4   With effect from 2005.

or carrying out other work preparatory to the conclusion of a contract of insurance or of concluding such contracts, or of assisting in the administration and performance of such contracts, in particular in the event of a claim[1]. The IMD also provides that these activities when undertaken by an insurance undertaking or an employee of an insurance undertaking, who is acting under the responsibility of the insurance undertaking, shall not be considered as insurance mediation. In implementing the directive the Treasury and the FSA decided to extend the relevant provisions to insurance companies in relation to their authorised activities (ie the permission they need) and in their dealings with private customers (COB/ICOB). This has the bizarre effect of requiring UK insurers to have permission to arrange their own contracts. The IMD requires member states to authorise and keep a register of authorised intermediaries carrying on insurance mediation. Only appropriately authorised individuals can be involved in the sales process[2]. Intermediaries must be of good character, satisfy minimum training and experience requirements and maintain appropriate capital assets. Authorised intermediaries must disclose information to customers, including providing a statement of demands and needs, and a policy summary.

I Exclusions

4.4   The IMD provides an exclusion for insurance mediation in connection with short-term[3] non-life contracts with an annual premium of 500 euros or less which are 'complementary' to a product or service ('connected contracts'). The requirements of this exclusion are that the insurance covers risk of breakdown, loss of baggage and other risks related to travel booked with the provider[4]. This travel cover may include life and liability risk (which are otherwise excluded) provided they are ancillary to the travel-related risk. It is further a requirement of this exclusion that the principal professional activity of the intermediary is not insurance mediation and that the intermediary is not required to have knowledge of other types of insurance contract in order to provide its services in relation to the contract.

The IMD does not apply if the activity undertaken is limited to the provision of information as part of another professional activity and provided the provision of information was on an incidental basis. Further exclusions apply in relation to the activity of assisting in the administration or performance of a contract of insurance in respect of an insurance company's own management of claims and management undertaken on its behalf on a professional basis. Similarly, loss adjusting and expert appraisal of claims do not constitute insurance mediation. However, it is worth noting that the provisions of the Directive do apply to insurance mediation activities in connection with reinsurance business.

The IMD was implemented in the UK on 14 January 2005 ('NGI')[5] at the same time as the regulation of general insurance. It was implemented in the main by

1   Article 2.
2   PRU 9.
3   Five years or less.
4   Article 1, para 2.
5   Except in relation to long-term care insurance which was regulated from 31 October 2004.

changes to the Regulated Activities Order[1] (RAO) and the Appointed Representatives Regulations. Unfortunately, it was not also implemented in other EU countries which led to an overlay of some UK conduct of business requirements for UK companies operating in other EU jurisdictions (the Gap Rules).

SECTION 2   THE NEED FOR AUTHORISATION

A   Overview

4.5   IMD activities include both the obvious advising, dealing as agent and arranging in relation to insurance contracts and the much less obvious activities of introducing to authorised or exempt persons, assisting in the administration of contracts and agreeing to carry on any of these now regulated activities. The scheme of FSMA 2000 is that the Regulated Activities Order ('RAO') sets out the detail of the instruments (investments) and the activities in relation to investments which are regulated. In implementing the IMD (and to provide for the regulation of general insurance contracts) by extending the investments and activities covered by FSMA 2000, the FSA had to deal separately with ARs and their 'representative'[2] staff who are also covered by the Directive[3].

B   Implementation of the IMD

4.6   The FSA only needed to introduce two new regulated activities as IMD activities were, subject to existing exemptions, already covered by the RAO. These exemptions may not now apply where they relate to contracts of insurance. This will affect preliminary or introductory activities which could lead to the sale of an insurance contract, particularly where the intermediary is remunerated on the basis of the number of insurance contracts sold. The FSA has included fairly detailed guidance in PERG (the Perimeter Guidance Manual) in relation to activities which constitute IMD activities.

The changes to the 'investments' covered by the RAO extend from 31 October 2004 to long-term care insurance and from 14 January 2005 to general insurance and pure protection (mainly term assurance) life contracts. The first new activity is assisting in the administration and performance of a contract of insurance[4]. Consistent with the IMD this does not include claims management and loss adjusting on behalf of an authorised insurer or expert appraisal carried on in the course of any profession or business[5]. The second activity is in Article 25(2), making arrangements 'with a view' to a person buying an insurance contract (eg

---

1   SI 2001/544.
2   Glossary definition representative.
3   Appointed Representatives Regulations SI 2001/1217.
4   Article 39A.
5   Article 39B.

introducing them to someone else for that purpose). The dividing line for this activity and the exemption in Article 72C (allowing the provision of information on an 'incidental' basis) is a fine one. PERG 5 makes clear that the exemption in Article 72C could allow a dentist to provide information about dental (but not pet insurance) but it would not permit the dentist to assist in the completion of any forms.

The question of how the dentist is remunerated may also be relevant. Another important requirement emphasised in the FSA guidance is the need to carry on the activities by way of business (as required by section 22 of FSMA 2000)[1]. In relation to insurance mediation, the FSA says there are two questions. First does the person receive remuneration (in its widest sense), and second, if so, does he pursue the activities by way of business? This is obviously slightly circular but will not usually cover activities undertaken on a one-off basis. Normally an activity (eg introduction in exchange for a fee) will be a critical element. A flat fee for the provision of information on an incidental basis[2] may not be caught whereas a volume-related payment could be. PERG 5.4.8 G contains a table that summarises the main issues surrounding the business test and draws out the difference between a 'reward' for insurance mediation activities and remuneration which is not specifically identified as such by the parties involved. This is perhaps the most difficult area of this FSA guidance to follow.

It is worth looking in detail at the guidance in PERG which takes you, the reader, through most of the issues relating to who should be authorised for IMD purposes. In PERG 5.15.2 G the FSA has included a flowchart to assist with the question of whether authorisation is required. PERG 5.2.8 summarises the regulated activities that may potentially apply in relation to a contract of insurance as follows:

(1)   Article 21   Dealing as agent.

(2)   Article 25(1)   Arranging (bringing about) deals.

(3)   Article 25(2)   Arrangements 'with a view' to bringing about (eg introducing).

(4)   Article 39A   Assisting in administration and performance of.

(5)   Article 53   Advising.

(6)   Article 64   Agreeing to carry on any regulated activities.

Whilst the RAO relies in the main on its own categorisation of 'investments' and activities, whether certain exemptions will continue to apply is determined by reference to the IMD itself. The relevant provisions of the IMD are included in Schedule 4 of the RAO[3].

---

1   PERG 5.4.2 and the Business Order.
2   Article 72C.
3   In relation to Articles 39, 66 and 67. Article 4A of the RAO.

1 Arranging

4.7   In relation to the other potential triggers for authorisation for insurance mediation purposes, the guidance makes clear[1] that in the FSA's view, Article 25(1) (arranging) extends to a person whose involvement in the chain of events leading to the contract of insurance is so important that without it there would be no policy. Somewhat surprisingly it then goes on to include in this category the insurance company issuing the policy. This means that in order to 'effect' a contract of insurance a UK authorised insurer must have permission to arrange it. The FSA's stance in applying the IMD provisions to insurers is at odds with the previous nature of the authorisation given to insurers which exempts them from other requirements (eg in relation to deposits and activities undertaken as part of the investment of their assets) in carrying on insurance business and with the provisions of the Consolidated Life Directive.

2 Introducing

4.8   Arrangements 'with a view' to bringing about a potential transaction generally take the form of introductions. Article 33 provides an exemption for specified introductions which was previously relied upon in relation to insurance contracts. As a result of the IMD, this exemption may not now apply in relation to activities in respect of potential insurance contracts. Article 33 can still, however, apply where the introduction is for independent advice on investments[2]. The FSA emphasises that to require authorisation for the purposes of introducing the person must first satisfy the 'by way of business' test. Part of this test is likely to be whether the person introducing receives a pecuniary reward linked to the volume of insurance business done as a result of his introductions. The FSA guidance also makes clear that one-off introductions not part of a pre-existing arrangement between introducer and introducee will not be caught by Article 25(2). A table in PERG 5.6.21 contains examples of the application of Article 33. A further exclusion is set out in Article 32 in relation to introductions in relation to the provision of finance to fund the acquisition of the contract of insurance.

The exclusion in Article 72C is also relevant. This exclusion applies[3] to information provided to potential or actual policyholders. It must be provided by a person carrying on any profession or business which does not otherwise consist of regulated activities. The FSA emphasises that the business may involve carrying on regulated activities (eg exempt professional firms) but those activities must not be the main focus of the business. The provision of information must also be capable of being reasonably regarded as 'incidental' (in the sense of being complementary to that profession or business (eg the dentist providing information related to dental but not pet insurance)).

---

1   PERG 5.6.2G.
2   PERG 5.6.19.
3   In relation to arranging and assisting in the administration and performance of a contract of insurance.

Further exclusions to Article 25(2) apply in respect of communication companies[1] and where the arranger is the policyholder but not the insurer[2].

3   Advice

4.9   In relation to the regulated activity of providing advice the FSA makes the point[3] that the advice must relate to a particular contract of insurance (eg a particular insurer or contract but not just life insurance). Generic or general advice will not therefore be caught by this. Further guidance is included in the table in PERG 5.8.5. Article 54 contains an exclusion from Article 53 in relation to advice given in periodical publications, regularly updated news and information services and broadcasts provided the principal purpose of the publication is not to provide advice.

4   Assisting in administration or performance

4.10   Exclusions also apply to the new regulated activity of assisting in the administration and performance of a contract of insurance in relation to claims management and loss adjustment on behalf of an authorised insurer. Similar activities undertaken on the policyholder's behalf, particularly where they involve the person dealing with the insurer (eg notifying and/or settling claims) or helping the policyholder to complete a claims form are likely to require authorisation[4].

5   Agreeing to carry on

4.11   In relation to Article 64 (agreeing to carry on other regulated activities) the FSA emphasises that merely making an offer to do so is not enough. A legally binding agreement is required. Also exclusions applicable to the underlying regulated activity itself will also apply in relation to agreeing to carry on the activity.

6   Other exclusions

4.12   Generally available exclusions, including Article 67 (activities as part of a profession or non-investment business), Article 72B (connected contracts) and Article 72 (large risks outside the EEA) also apply to IMD activities.

Article 67 permits professional firms, such as solicitors, to continue to provide insurance mediation activities (subject to the relevant individuals' names being kept on the register of their designated professional body (eg by the Law Society)): Connected contracts are the contracts referred to at **4.4** and cover breakdown of non-motor goods and travel insurance provided on an incidental

1   Article 27 providing the means of communication.
2   Article 28.
3   In PERG 5.8.4.
4   PERG 5.7.7.

basis. Other exclusion are specifically stated not to be available in connection with contracts of insurance (eg Article 29, arranging deals with or through an authorised person and Article 69, activities provided within a group or joint enterprise). These were both previously important exemptions. In relation to groups, the FSA points out that the group company (eg normally a service company) has to be providing the relevant service by way of business to be caught which should mean it would be providing services to third parties (and hence the need for authorisation). This could happen if a service company helps a policyholder to fill in an application form (eg arranging)[1].

7   Territorial scope

4.13   PERG 5.15.8G contains a flowchart to help answer the question of whether regulated activities are carried on in the UK. Consideration should be given to section 418 of FSMA 2000 which extends territorial scope (eg in relation to UK authorised companies using passporting rights) and the availability of the overseas person exemption (Article 72 – where there is no UK place of business). The FSA notes that the activity of arranging will usually be considered to be carried on where those activities take place[2]. In relation to advice it will generally be carried on where the advice is received. PERG 5.2.17 reminds firms that services provided by electronic means will, despite the E-Commerce Directive, be required to comply with IMD requirements (eg registration in country of origin).

8   Appointed Representatives

4.14   An AR can only carry on the activities specified in the Appointed Representatives Regulations[3]. These include the IMD activities set out in the table in PERG 5.3.4. For life policies they are arranging, introducing, advising and assisting in administration and performance of a contract of insurance and agreeing to carry on those activities. SUP 12.4 sets out what a firm must do when it appoints an AR. SUP 12.5 sets out detailed requirements relating to the content of the contract making the appointment. An AR will not be able to provide insurance mediation activity until he is included on the FSA register for such activities. It is worth remembering that the principal will need to be authorised for insurance mediation activities.

SECTION 3   APPOINTED REPRESENTATIVES

A   Exempt status

4.15   Section 39 of FSMA 2000 allows an authorised person to appoint others (ARs) for specified purposes that are treated as 'exempt' for the purpose of

---

1   PERG 5.11.G.
2   PERG 5.12.8.
3   Financial Services and Markets Act 2000 (Appointed Representatives) Regulations 2001, SI 2001/1217.

FSMA 2000. This does not mean that their activities are not regulated; they are but normally through the authorised person, their principal. The principal will have to accept responsibility for any such activities undertaken by the AR[1]. One of the changes under FSMA 2000 from the 1986 Act is that a person can no longer be an authorised person for one regulated activity and an AR for others[2]. The activities that can be undertaken by an AR are set out in a statutory instrument (the Appointed Representatives Regulations). These regulations also deal with the provisions to be covered by the contract between an AR and their principal. Even in the post-depolarisation world ARs selling packaged products (eg life products other than pure protection) are required to sell only the products of one principal (or relevant companies in their group). It is common for ARs appointed in relation to life investment contracts to also sell mortgages and general insurance. This means that they will have other principals (in the case of general insurance there may be more than one principal for different classes of such business). The contract is required to deal with this (see **4.19**).

SUP 12 contains rules and guidance relating to ARs. SUP 10 contains provisions in relation to Approved Persons which are also relevant.

It is implicit in the rules (and the FSA states it to be the case in SUP 12.4.1A) that regulated activities covered by an AR agreement need to fall within the scope of the principal's own permission or be excluded by Article 28 (arranging transactions to which the arranger is a party). This means UK authorised insurers also need a permission to cover these activities. This approach creates some uncertainty when it is applied to EEA insurers passporting into the UK whose own home authorisation includes such activities. As there is no passporting right under the IMD for insurers, their single licence is derived from their home state under the Consolidated Life Directive which enables them to both sell into and set up branches in the UK. Also, in their home state they will normally be able to appoint agents to do what they themselves can do. It is submitted that such authorisation should apply throughout the EEA and in particular should enable them to sell through a UK agency arrangement by satisfying the branch requirements for passporting (see Chapter 3). However, passporting companies do not apply for permission (unless they are top-up permissions to cover activities not covered by their passport right). Appropriate permission is granted by the FSA once the EU Passporting procedure has been completed. In practice, passporting insurers do not seem to be granted IMD status automatically. This has led some people to suggest that such passporting insurers cannot appoint ARs. It is not clear why this should be the case. If the EU insurer could have done so under their home licence, then provided such agency is limited to the sale of the insurer's own products, there does not seem any reason why an AR could not be appointed in the UK.

4.16 Before looking at the Appointed Representatives Regulations and the provisions of SUP 12, it is worth setting out the meaning of some of the terms used in this area (eg Adviser AR, Representative, Introducer, Introducer AR Network).

1 They will have responsibilities as Approved Persons.
2 FSMA 2000, s 39(1).

Adviser: an individual who is: a representative; or an appointed representative.

Appointed Representative: (in accordance with section 39 of the Act (other than an authorised person)):

(a) is a party to a contract with an authorised person (his principal) which:

  (i) permits or requires him to carry on business of a description prescribed in the Appointed Representatives Regulations; and

  (ii) complies with such requirements as are prescribed in those Regulations; and

(b) is someone for whose activities in carrying on the whole or part of that business his principal has accepted responsibility in writing;

and who is therefore an exempt person in relation to any regulated activity comprised in the carrying on of that business for which his principal has accepted responsibility.

Introducer: an individual appointed by a firm, or by an Appointed Representative, to carry out in the course of designated investment business either or both of the following activities:

(a) effecting introductions;

(b) distributing non-real time financial promotions.

Representative: an individual who:

(a) is appointed by a firm, or by an appointed representative of a firm, to carry on any of the following activities:

  (i) advising on investments;

  (ii) [not applicable to life assurance];

  (iii) arranging (bringing about) deals in investments;

  (iv) dealing in investments; or,

(b) although not appointed to do so, carries on any of the activities in (i) to (iii) on behalf of a firm or its appointed representative.

An AR may be a company, a partnership or an individual. Where the AR is an individual they may also be a 'representative' for the purposes of regulation.

B Prescribed activities and the AR contract

4.17 The prescribed activities an AR can be appointed to perform are:

(1) Article 21: Dealing in investments as agent.

(2)   Article 25(1) and 25A(2): Arranging (bringing about) deals in investments or regulated mortgages.

(3)   Article 25(2) and 25A(2): Arrangements 'with a view to' a transaction in investments or regulated mortgages.

(4)   Article 39A: Assisting in the administration and performance of a contract of insurance.

(5)   Article 40: Arranging safeguarding and administration of assets.

(6)   Article 52B: Basic advice on stakeholder products.

(7)   Article 53 and 53A: Advising on investments or regulated mortgages.

(8)   Article 64: Agreeing to carry on any of the above regulated activities.

4.18   A firm therefore needs to satisfy itself that the terms of the AR contract enable it to ensure that the AR's activities fall within both the prescribed activities and the scope of the principal's own permission. The contract must also require the AR to co-operate with the FSA and allow it access to premises[1]. It must provide access rights for the firm's auditors specified in section 341 of the FSMA 2000[2].

The AR must be required by the contract to advise the firm when it is 'seeking' appointment as an AR of another firm[3]. It must also be required to advise the firm as soon as possible of changes to or termination of such appointments. This will only be relevant where the principal has not prohibited such appointments. The AR agreement must allow the principal to prohibit or restrict such appointments in the future[4]. Where the AR is carrying on IMD activities other than introducing, there must be a provision to the effect that he is not permitted to carry on such business unless he is included in the FSA register for IMD purposes[5]. The AR contract must also provide for compliance with relevant requirements (including the FSA Rules) by contractors or employees of an AR firm. In relation to the AR's activities on behalf of the firm, the firm must also be able to terminate the contract unless it has reasonable grounds to believe that the AR is suitable (see below), that the firm has adequate control over the activities for which it is responsible and that the firm is able to and is organised to comply with requirements of SUP 12.

C   Approved Person status

4.19   The AR, its senior management (governing functions) and any representatives dealing with customers will need to become Approved Persons. In addition to the application to the FSA for 'approval', the firm will need to

---

1   SUP 14.5.3. See also SUP 2.3.4G and 2.3.5G(2).
2   See SUP 3.6.6.G
3   SUP 12.5.5.
4   SI 2001/1217, reg 3(1)–(3); SUP 12.5.6A.
5   SUP 12.5.2(3).

comply with other rules before appointing an AR. In relation to a full AR (as opposed to an introducer AR) the firm must establish on reasonable grounds that the AR is suitable to act as its AR. This includes a requirement that the AR is solvent and has no 'close links' (eg connected parties) likely to prevent the effective supervision of the AR by the firm. In considering suitability the firm should have regard to SUP 12 Annex 2G. The process includes reviewing the character, competence and financial resources of the AR. The firm must also ensure that the appointment does not prevent it from continuing to satisfy the threshold conditions[1]. In particular it must have adequate control of the AR's activities and be organised and able to comply with SUP 12.

Where the AR has already been appointed as the AR of another authorised person, the firm should enter into a multiple principal agreement with the other principals before it appoints the AR. The main purpose of the multiple principal agreement is to provide clarity to consumers (eg in relation to a single principal to manage complaints)[2]. The requirements include arrangements for approving financial promotions, training and competence, co-operation and sharing of information between the principals. The firm to whom the consumer complains is known as the 'lead principal'[3].

D Introducer Appointed Representatives

4.20 The requirements are slightly different in relation to Introducer ARs. Although the firm still has to check that the person is of good repute and otherwise fit, it does not have to carry out the more extensive due diligence required for the appointment of an AR under SUP 12.4.2.R. Introducer AR contracts are also not included for the purpose of the requirement to enter into multiple principal agreements or the Approved Persons regime[4].

E Continuing requirements

4.21 The continuing obligations of the firm in relation to ARs are set out in SUP 12.6. These require the firm to take immediate remedial action and/or terminate the AR contract if appropriate. ARs holding client money must be required to comply with CASS (the client money rules). Firms should also ensure that the AR does not overstep its authority or hold itself out as being able to do so[5] and complies with the required terms of the AR contract[6]. Notification to the FSA of the appointment of an AR and any changes are required in accordance with SUP 12.7. SUP 12.8 requires firms to make and retain records in relation to its dealings and agreements with ARs[7].

1   SUP 12.4.2.
2   SUP 12.4.5B and C.
3   SUP 12.4–5D.
4   SUP 10.4.1R.
5   SUP 12.6.6.
6   SUP 12.6.11A.
7   SUP 12.9.1.

Training and competence requirements are a major part of the practical requirements in respect of ARs. Training and Competence. T&C is the relevant part of the FSA Handbook. It sets out requirements for advisers in relation to recruitment, training and competence including the need to be assessed and pass relevant exams before being authorised to advise customers.

SECTION 4   THE COB REQUIREMENTS – CLIENT CLASSIFICATION, KNOW YOUR CUSTOMER AND SUITABILITY

A   Overview

4.22   The Conduct of Business Sourcebook includes many of the provisions implementing depolarisation. One of the consequences of the liberalisation permitted by depolarisation is the obligation to provide disclosure of the intermediary's status and its charges (eg the required Initial Disclosure Document ('IDD') and the fees and commission statement ('Menu')) which must be provided before a firm can start to charge for its services in relation to packaged products (eg life contracts other than pure protection contracts). Many of those obligations also satisfy the requirements[1] of the IMD (eg relating to the customer and their requirements).

At the time of writing significant changes are expected in this area due to the implementation of the Markets in Financial Instruments Directive (MIFID) due to be implemented by November 2007.

B   Classifying the customer

4.23   The first obligation in COB 4 is to classify the client for regulatory purposes. Much of the protection provided by COB relates only to private customers but this is expanded (particularly in relation to product disclosure to cover information provided for example in relation to pension schemes and life policies sold by intermediaries to other customers). 'Private customer' is a defined term but will generally cover private individuals (eg acting outside the course of their ordinary business) and small businesses (eg annual turnover £5m) acting on a similar or mixed purpose basis. The obligation on a firm to classify the client is therefore vital to establish the way an intermediary firm should deal with that client. It should also enable particularly sophisticated customers to opt out of regulatory protection at least in part. At the other end of the investment spectrum a range of simplified stakeholder products can be sold with very limited basic advice (see Section G below).

COB 4.1 provides that before conducting designated investment business with or for any client a firm must take reasonable steps to establish whether that client is a private customer, an intermediate customer or market counterparty. COB 4.1.1 makes clear that it does not apply in relation to any customer where the firm intends to provide basic advice on stakeholder products.

1   Similar provisions existed pre-NG1.

1   Private customer

4.24   The definitions are a little circular in that a private customer is a customer who does not fall into either of the other two classifications (ie market counterparty or intermediate customer). A market counterparty is a body corporate (including an LLP) whose holding companies or subsidiaries have a called up share capital of at least £10m, or who satisfy two of the following criteria: a balance sheet total of 12.5m euros, a net turnover of 25m euros or an average number of employees during the year of 250: a local or public authority, a partnership with at least £10m, a trustee of a trust with assets of that amount or a trustee of a large occupational pension scheme[1].

2   An intermediate customer

4.25   A firm may classify a client who would otherwise be a private customer as an intermediate customer if, having taken reasonable care in its determination, it decides that the client has sufficient experience and understanding to be classified as an intermediate customer. The firm must also give a written warning to the client of the regulatory protections he will lose, give the client sufficient time to consider the implications of that and obtain either the client's written consent or be able to demonstrate that informed consent has been given. The client will lose the benefit of the following protections:

(1)   COB 3 Financial promotions.

(2)   COB 4.3 Disclosure about services fees and commission.

(3)   COB 5.1 Advising on packaged products.

(4)   COB 5.4 Customer's understanding of risk.

(5)   COB 5.7 Disclosure of charges remuneration and commission.

(6)   COB 6.2 Disclosure.

(7)   COB 8.2 Periodic statements.

(8)   COB 9.3 Client money (modified).

The firm will need to warn the client that its expertise will be taken into account in the way the firm communicates with the client. The client will also lose the right to complain to the Financial Ombudsman Service.

C   Terms of business, the IDD and the Menu

1   Generally

4.26   Having categorised a customer as a private customer a firm is required to provide its terms of business to potential private customers with or for whom

1   Which at any time during the previous two years/may also be market counterparties with at least 50 members and assets under management of not less than £10m.

it may conduct designated investment business[1]. This requirement does not apply to insurance companies in relation to the issue of their own policies[2]. In practice, because firms are required to provide the IDD and Menu and are permitted[3] to add additional items to the IDD instead of issuing terms of business, they may not in fact issue terms of business.

When the firm first makes contact with a private customer with a view to arranging, dealing or giving advice in relation to a life contract (other than a pure protection contract) its representative should provide the IDD and Menu to the customer[4]. The information to be included in both documents should be that which the firm reasonably considers will be appropriate for the customer. If the firm may also act in relation to other insurance contracts (eg pure protection or general insurance) or regulated mortgage (or lifetime mortgage) contracts it may provide a combined initial disclosure document. (CIDD) The obligation to provide an IDD also applies if the activities are carried on in relation to a variation of a life policy.

Exemptions which are summarised later apply to the requirement to provide the IDD and Menu. The main exemptions are for execution only and telephone sales.

The obligations also apply to firms other than insurers in relation to the same activities carried on for an intermediate customer or market counterparty in relation to a life policy.

2   Form of the IDD and Menu

4.27   COB 4.3.9 sets out the requirements for an IDD. The details are in COB 4 Annex 4R and notes forming part of it. As with key features, the document must contain the key facts logo and heading and text in the order shown in the Annex. CIDDs must comply with COB 4 Annex 5R. The requirements for the Menu are in COB 4 Annex 6R. Depending on its business model a firm may have different versions of the Menu (eg based on whether it charges a fee and/or receives commission). Keeping those statements up to date can be an onerous requirement if a firm has a number of different versions. It also has to maintain a record of each particular Menu provided to a private customer (other than merely in response to a request)[5]. Where a firm alters its services (eg expands its range of products) it has to provide an updated Menu and get the customer's consent if the basis on which it will be remunerated changes[6].

In order to understand the nature of the IDD and the Menu it is advisable to look at the examples in the Annexes. The notes which do not form part of the IDD are also very useful. The purpose of the IDD is to explain the range of services provided by the firm and the nature of the services (eg whether advice is

1   COB 4.2.5 in good time before the business is conducted.
2   4.3.17.
3   4.3.
4   COB 4.3.3.
5   COB 4.3.11(4).
6   COB 4.3.13(3).

being provided). It also provides details about the regulation of the firm and, if relevant, its ARs including the process for complaints and details about the Financial Services Compensation Scheme (FSCS). Firms are required to disclose any links with other regulated firms (eg shareholdings and loans). Where an AR is involved this will cover loans made by or to that AR. A firm must explain any direct or indirect shareholding of more than 10% in the capital of the firm which is held by a product provider or its parent. Similarly, where the firm has such a holding in the provider of a packaged product (whether held directly or indirectly) that should also be explained. Where credit exceeding 10% of a firm's share and loan capital is provided by a product provider or any undertaking in its immediate group (other than in relation to indemnity commission) a short description of such credit must also be included.

The Menu is designed to explain how much a firm charges and to provide comparative commission information. This information shows maximum costs in relation to different products, providers and a market average cost (calculated by the FSA). There are also prescribed statements where a firm may charge fees, including a statement of the amount or rate of its fees (eg hourly or other rate or percentage of funds under management). Where fees and commission may be payable a firm must ensure that the total of both fees and commission does not exceed the maximum shown. COB 4 Annex 7R shows how a firm calculates the maximum rate of commission. Annex 8G shows a worked example.

3 Exemptions to the IDD and Menu requirement

4.28 Firms are not required to provide the IDD and Menu where:

(1) The appropriate information has already been given to the customer on a previous occasion and it is still likely to be accurate and appropriate.

(2) Where initial conduct is made by telephone and COB 4.3.16 applies.

(3) Execution only transactions.

(4) Non-advised sales by an insurer.

Where a firm's initial contact with the private customer is by telephone then COB 4.3.18 sets out information which must be provided and requirements satisfied by the firm. This includes details of the firm, the range of its service, whether it will provide advice and the firm's basis for remuneration. This information must subsequently be provided in writing. If a contract is to be concluded by telephone the firm must comply with 4.2.5 (the requirement to provide terms of business or the IDD and Menu if appropriate) immediately after conclusion of the contract. The firm must also comply with COB 4 Annex 1 which extends the information to be provided to include details about cancellation and to require the customer's explicit consent to receiving limited information[1].

---

1 In relation to packaged products the obligation to provide terms of business may be satisfied by providing a suitably amended IDD and Menu.

(a)   Execution only[1]

4.29   An execution only transaction is one where a transaction is performed (or a third party is instructed to execute) the transaction under the specific instructions of the client and the firm does not give advice on investments relating to the merits of the transaction. An example could be where the client knows what they want to buy (eg a Distribution Band from a particular provider) and merely asks the firm to execute (ie pass the application to the life office) which can be beneficial financially to the customer.

4   Intermediate customer

4.30   A firm conducting IMD activities for an intermediate customer or market counterparty in relation to a life policy must also make specified disclosures[2]. These are more limited and are similar to the policy summary required by ICOB. The information to be disclosed is set out in a table in 4.3.21. It includes details of any AR involved and shareholdings and credit provided by a product provider to the firm. The information must be provided in English if it relates to activities of a UK establishment or in an official language of the relevant EEA State if it relates to activities of an EEA branch[3]. The information must be provided in a durable medium at any time before conclusion of the contract (ie not necessarily in good time before) and, if necessary, (unless an exemption applies) on amendment or renewal of the contract. A firm may instead provide an IDD or combined IDD to satisfy this obligation. It may use the key facts logo if the IDD is unamended but if it is amended then the logo may not be used.

A firm must also maintain an up-to-date list of the insurers it deals with in relation to each type of life policy. A customer may request a copy of this information in a durable medium.

Different rules apply to introducers who are only required to provide information about the firm including where relevant its ARs and its statutory status (eg GEN 4 Annex 1 requirement). This must be provided when the introducer makes initial contact with the client and the information may be supplied orally if a copy is provided in a durable medium immediately after the initial contact with the client.

5   GPP disclosure

4.31   There are also rules providing for disclosure to employees where the firm makes contact with them to promote their employer's GPP or stakeholder pension scheme. This is designed to make it clear whether advice is provided, whether it is limited to the pension scheme and the amount and nature of fees and commission payable by the employee for the advice.

---

1   This option is of course open to abuse but firms will always need to be able to prove no advice was given if challenged.
2   COB 4.3.20–25.
3   4.3.22(2).

D Depolarisation

1 Overview

4.32   The rules in COB 5 build on the requirements of COB 4, in particular the IDD and the Menu. COB 5 applies to firms which give advice on packaged products to a private customer. The full advice regime does not apply to basic advice on stakeholder products for which there is a simplified but obligatory process (see Section G below). The IDD requires firms to disclose their status (ie whole of market, limited number of providers or single company (or group)). The customer is also 'invited' to ask for details of the range of packaged products available to the firm. COB 5 sets out rules which limit the ability of a firm providing advice to alter the range of products. The requirements in relation to advised sales are that firms know their customer (fact-find), give best advice and explain why a recommended product is suitable to that customer. Firms also need to ensure that their advisers only advise on products in relation to which they are technically competent and that they refer the client on appropriately or, if necessary, do not sell any product to that client. This could happen where the products available to a sales representative do not form best advice to the customer.

2 The range of products

4.33   COB 5.1.6A requires firms to take reasonable steps to ensure that the scope of the advice it gives to private customers on packaged products is based on:

(a)   the whole (or a specified sector) of the market;

(b)   a limited number of product providers; or

(c)   a single company or single group of companies.

As explained above, the FSA's new regime now allows firms much greater latitude than previously. Broadly, they can increase their range of products in particular cases (but they cannot decrease it), they can go off panel or refer to someone else. Having made the scope of its advice clear to the customer, if the firm does extend its scope or the range of products, there may be an impact on its remuneration. If as a result the firm could be paid more then it will need the customer's prior consent to the change[1]. In some cases (eg where the change in remuneration results from the product sold having a longer term and the increase is proportionate to the difference in the term) this requirement does not apply[2]. COB 5.1.6A(3) provides that in any case where the basis of a firm's remuneration is materially altered the firm must provide a new Menu.

The main issues arising from depolarisation are the practical ones of how the firm makes its variable scope clear to its customers and how it ensures that its

1   4.3.7(1).
2   4.3(4).

representatives are qualified to the appropriate level in each case. This is particularly the case for firms offering a whole of market option (ie those who can call themselves independent if they offer a fee option – see **4.34**). In practice the FSA accepts[1] that a firm may cover the whole of a market by the use of appropriate panels of product providers provided it reviews the panel on a regular basis. Similarly, the FSA accepts that some firms will operate only in niche markets (eg pension transfers)[2]. As previously stated, although firms should ensure that they stay within their scope and within the particular range on which advice is offered to individual customers[3], they are permitted to go 'out of range'[4]. This should cover one-off situations where there is a 'gap' in the range (eg a limited or single tie situation) or where the firm does not wish to change the scope or range of the advice that it offers to a particular customer.

Firms have fairly onerous obligations to keep records in relation to the scope and range offered to each customer and in relation to their own ARs. COB 5.1.6E provides that a firm must keep records for six years of the scope of its advice, its range and ranges of associates and each of its ARs (if different from the firm). This will include details of each product provider and their products where anything less than whole of market is offered to customers.

3   Independent financial advice

4.34   One of the debates which ensued from the depolarisation changes related to whether, and in what circumstances, intermediaries would be able to call themselves 'independent'. The issue is of course complicated by the fact that intermediaries may be operating in a number of other markets (eg non-package product insurance and mortgages). An intermediary may be independent in one sector but not in another. COB 5.1.11A specifies the basis on which a firm can hold itself out as acting independently. First, it must give advice in relation to the whole of the market and second it must offer its customer the opportunity to pay a fee for its services (rather than the firm receiving commission)[5]. If payment by fee is an option firms may as an alternative offer a choice of fee or commission. Where a fee is agreed the firm must obtain the customer agreement to the fee level before acting for the customer. Any commission then received should be used to reduce the fee, increase the investment or refunded direct to the customer. The firm may, however, retain renewal commission up to an amount each year specified in the agreement and in practice which is too small to be returned or rebated[6].

4   Appointed Representatives

4.35   Pre-depolarisation ARs normally had to be able to advise in relation to the whole of the principal's product range. Now each representative may have a

1   5.1.6.B(4).
2   5.1.6.B(5)
3   5.1.7.
4   5.3.8A.
5   Unless offering a SPP under COB 4.3.27.
6   COB 4.3.6.

different scope based on their technical understanding and experience of the products in the firm's range. COB 5.1.6C sets out the requirement to record the scope of advice of each AR. COB 5.1.12 allows a representative not to advise in relation to whole range (ie if not sufficiently competent) and requires the representative to be competent enough to understand when it should refer the client to another representative of the firm.

COB 5.1.13 also includes provisions supplementing COB 2.1 (see Section 5) and imposing a duty on firms to structure their representatives' remuneration to provide suitable advice. The requirement is that the representative is not likely to be influenced by the structure of the remuneration to give unsuitable advice to a private customer or to refer private customers to another firm in circumstances which would amount to the provision of an inducement under COB 2.2.3.

E   Know your customer

4.36   Advising a client in relation to a financial product can be a very complicated business. The advice given can be completely unsuitable if relevant information is not made available to the adviser. Similarly, a client cannot realistically be expected to understand the interdependence between products and the impact of their own circumstances. COB therefore contains a requirement on firms giving advice to a private customer in relation to packaged products to 'know their customer'. The requirements do not apply in relation to basic advice on stakeholder products. They are, however, applicable to arranging pension opt-outs or pension transfers from an occupational scheme and are extended to intermediate customers and market counterparties.

The firm must take reasonable steps to ensure that it has such personal and financial information about the customer as is relevant to the services that the firm is to provide[1]. Where advice is given on a continuing basis the firm should keep its information about the customer under regular review. If only occasional advice is given, the firm should undertake a review at the point of the most recent instruction[2]. If, however, a customer declines to give such information a firm should not provide any services without promptly advising the customer (and ideally confirming in writing) that the lack of such information is likely to adversely affect the quality of services[3]. The precise type of information required and enquiries to be made vary depending on the type of customer concerned. The process is commonly referred to as a 'fact-finding'. Guidance is given in table 5.2.11G regarding the collection of relevant information.

The information collected must be recorded in writing, the document often being called a fact-find[4]. Unless the personal recommendation is not proceeded with, the record of the customer's circumstances must be kept for a minimum period after the information is obtained. For life policies this is six years.

1   COB 5.2.5.
2   COB 5.2.6.G.
3   5.2.7G.
4   COB 5.2.9.

Information relating to a pension transfer, opt-out or free-standing additional voluntary contribution (FSAVC) must be kept indefinitely.

A statement of demands and needs must be given to the customer unless a suitability letter or explanation of a personal recommendation in accordance with COB 5.3 is provided to him.

F   Suitability – best advice

I   Overview

4.37   A firm which makes a personal recommendation to a private customer to buy or sell a packaged product or which promotes a pension scheme[1] must take reasonable steps to ensure that it is the most suitable one from the relevant range (in accordance with COB 5.1.7R) having regard to the facts disclosed by the private customer and any other relevant facts of which the firm is or should reasonably be aware[2]. The suitability rules expand the high level requirement set out in Principle 9 (Customers: relationships of trust) which requires firms to take reasonable care to ensure the suitability of advice and discretionary decisions. Suitability should be assessed by reference to the client's needs, priorities and attitude to risk, income and expenditure and to any likely changes in these[3]. The same requirement applies in respect of a recommendation provided by a firm (other than an insurer) to an intermediate customer or market counterparty to take out a life policy. If there is no product in the firm's relevant range which is suitable for the client, no recommendation should be made.

If the firm reasonably concludes that there are several products in the relevant range which would satisfy the test in COB 5.3.5R(2), it is able to recommend only one of those products. If a client does not wish to proceed in accordance with a recommendation, a firm may nonetheless make further recommendations providing they are suitable for the client. Pre-depolarisation, where a product was issued by a connected person, the firm could only recommend it if it was 'better' than any other packaged product which was generally available. This provision, known as the better than best rule, has now been deleted[4].

One issue which has given rise to problems in this area in the past is churning. 'Churning' means entering into transactions with unnecessary frequency having regard to the customer and the agreed investment strategy. The FSA refer to 'switching' in relation to packaged products rather than churning. A firm should not switch a private customer within or between packaged products (such as life policies) unnecessarily, having regard to suitability for that customer.

The importance of ensuring the suitability of adviser's recommendations was highlighted in April 2006 when the FSA imposed a fine of £550,000[5] in relation to the sale of with-profits policies. Essentially the policies were sold as general

---

1   Personal pension or stakeholder.
2   5.3.1 does not apply to basic advice on a stakeholder product.
3   COB 5.3.5R.
4   COB 5.3.9R (now deleted).
5   On Liverpool Victoria.

savings vehicles to significant numbers of the firm's older customers who had no demonstrable need for the life cover sold.

4.38 A firm must keep a record of the suitability letter or other document relied on to satisfy the suitability letter requirements. Such records shall be kept for such period as specified, which in the case of life policies is six years[1]. Records need to be keep indefinitely when they relate to a pension transfer opt out or FSAVC.

2 Suitability of packaged products out of range recommendation

4.39 A non-whole of market firm may recommend a product outside the range of products on which it provides advice to a client if it is suitable for the client and if, had it been in its range, it would have been at least as suitable as the most suitable packaged product in that range. A firm must also take reasonable steps to ensure that its ARs only act in this way with its explicit written permission, either generally or in relation to the specific recommendation[2]. This enables firms to go 'out-of-range' with their advice on a one-off basis without the firm needing to change its scope or range of the advice on investments which the client is expecting to receive[3].

3 Suitability: whole-of-market advisers

4.40 A firm giving whole-of-market advice (or advice from the whole of a sector) must not give any personal recommendation unless it has carried out a reasonable analysis of a sufficiently large number of packaged products generally available from the market (or that sector). That analysis must be conducted using criteria which reflect adequate knowledge of the products generally available from the whole market (or from the relevant sector). The firm must satisfy COB 5.3.5R(2) by taking reasonable steps to ensure that a personal recommendation is in accordance with the analysis and is therefore the most suitable one to meet the customer's needs[4]. Firms giving personal recommendations to intermediate customers or market counterparties on life policies from the whole market (or from a relevant sector) need to comply with the provisions of COB 5.3.10BR.

4 Requirement for a suitability letter

4.41 A firm giving a personal recommendation, in relation to a life policy, to a policyholder or a prospective policyholder must provide a suitability letter before the conclusion of the contract, unless one of the exceptions in COB 5.3.19R applies[5]. The suitability letter must explain why the firm has concluded

---

1 5.3.19A.
2 COB 5.3.8AR.
3 COB 5.3.8B.
4 COB 5.3.10AR but see also COB 5.1.6. B(4) on the use of panels.
5 COB 5.3.14R.

that the policy is suitable for the customer, having regard to his personal and financial circumstances. It must contain a summary of the main consequences and any possible disadvantages of the transaction[1]. The letter must also identify the individual authorised by the firm to advise on the product that has been recommended. If that product is from a provider identified in section 6 of the firm's IDD or CIDD[2] (or if relevant, an undertaking in the same 'immediate group' as that provider). It must include the information given in section 6 of that document (eg loans and shareholdings). In the case of an out-of-range recommendation it must explain why it has recommended such a packaged product, including why it is suitable for the customer.

5   Suitability letter: exceptions

4.42   COB 5.3.19R sets out the exceptions from the requirement to provide a suitability letter. The following are relevant to life assurance. The requirement does not apply:

(i)   if the customer is habitually resident in another EEA State at the time of acknowledging consent to the proposal form to which the personal recommendation relates (subject to certain e-commerce exceptions);

(ii)   if the customer is habitually resident outside the EEA and the customer is not present in the UK (expanded to EEA for certain e-commerce activities) at the time of acknowledging consent to the proposal form to which the personal recommendation relates;

(iii)   to any personal recommendation by a friendly society for a life policy sold by it with a premium not exceeding £50 a year or, if payable weekly, £1 a week;

(iv)   to any personal recommendation to increase a regular premium on an existing contract; and

(v)   to any personal recommendation to invest additional single premiums to an existing packaged product to which a single premium has previously been paid.

6   COB 5.3.30G: guidance on the content of suitability letters

4.43   Although commonly referred to as the 'suitability' or 'reason why' letter, it need not be in the form of a letter. It could, for example, form part of a financial report to the customer provided it is prominent; or a fact-find document (a copy of the whole fact-find or just the recommendation section being given to the client). If a copy of the fact-find or the recommendation section is used, the copy should be of sufficient quality to be clearly legible.

1   COB 5.3.16R.
2   Given in accordance with COB 4.3.3R(1).

A successful suitability letter explains simply and clearly why the recommendation is viewed as suitable having regard to the customer's personal and financial circumstances, needs and priorities, as identified in the fact-find and attitude to risk in the relevant area. The style and presentation is mainly left for firms to decide so that they can design a document which works best for their particular market. However, the FSA do give certain pointers. The more personalised the suitability letter, the more effective it is likely to be. The language used should be plain English. If technical terms need to be used and the customer is unlikely to understand them they should be explained in brief terms. Ideally each suitability letter will be different, reflecting the approach of the representative, the customer's profile, subjects discussed and the considerations on which the advice was based. The FSA recommends that any standardisation of the letter is best limited to the description of the most common needs and the products which will satisfy those needs; the firm should clearly link the customer's own needs, priorities and attitude to risk to the product recommended rather than just setting out stock motives that may apply to all customers. Tick box, pre-printed forms should rarely be used, and if they are, only in the simplest and most straightforward advice situations.

The letter should explain why the customer's needs, priorities, attitude to risk and financial situation all combine to make the product suitable for the customer. It should not merely state the product being recommended with no link to the customer's personal circumstances. Other needs discussed during the fact-find process which the customer does not wish to consider do not need to be included (although they should be recorded in the fact-find). They should be included if they assist in demonstrating why the product is considered suitable. Alternative products which were recommended but rejected by the customer should be mentioned; only the available options under a contract which have been recommended, whether accepted or rejected, need be mentioned. Where the range of products from which advice has been given derive from more than one provider in respect of the same type of product, the letter needs to explain why a particular provider has been recommended. Reasons may include product features not available elsewhere, price, service levels, performance track record, investment prospects, medical evidence terms, reputation and financial strength. Each suitability letter should be signed by a person authorised by the firm to advise on the type of product being recommended. Ideally this will be the representative who gave the advice but, if not, both the signatory and the representative should accept responsibility for the letter and the recommendation.

Suitability letters should be issued at the time the recommendation is made or as soon as possible afterwards, to allow as much time as possible for the customer to consider the recommendation before any cancellation period ends. In any event the letter should be issued no later than the issue of the cancellation notice or where none will be issued, before the life policy is concluded.

7   Suitability: pensions and other specific requirements

4.44   A specific regime applies to pension transfers and opt-outs which requires use of suitable staff (preferably a pension transfer specialist) and completion of a transfer value analysis[1] prior to a recommendation. COB 5.3.29G contains guidance in relation to the specific basis on which such advice is provided which includes the initial assumption that to opt or transfer out of a defined benefit scheme would not be suitable. The table in COB 5.3.29G also contains guidance relevant to the sale of personal pensions, FSAVC or hybrid products (eg product combinations investment/annuity), borrowing to invest and contracting out of SERPs.

The guidance also deals with advice in relation to income withdrawals (including elections to take income withdrawals on existing products which are also covered by suitability requirements[2]) and short-term annuities. The guidance makes clear the need to highlight the significance of the risk inherent in purchasing a drawdown rather than an annuity and that the maximum income available after age 75 is significantly less than available before age 75.

8   Direct offer personal pensions

4.45   COB 5.3.28 sets out rules applicable to the sale by direct offer of a personal pension scheme to a group of employees of a third party. The firm must record why it thinks the promotion is justified as likely to be at least as suitable for the majority of employees as a stakeholder pension scheme. The firm is required to be satisfied 'on reasonable grounds' that this is so. The firm must retain the record for a minimum period of six years after the financial promotion is last communicated.

9   Broker funds

4.46   Special rules apply in relation to broker funds (eg where the firm is the investment adviser of a fund recommended by the firm or the investment adviser is connected to the firm). Historically there have been issues with the long-term performance and charges of such funds. Firms are therefore required to disclose the connection and charges and to make a comparison with other non-broker funds available. COB 5.3.20 provides that a firm acting as a broker fund adviser for a private customer must take account of the characteristics (eg including charges) of the fund when assessing suitability. In addition, post sale, the firm has to monitor continued suitability and make a recommendation on an annual basis to the client whether or not to remain invested in the fund and if not to recommend an alternative. Firms must also ensure that the customer is advised of significant changes proposed to the fund's investment strategy before they take place[3] and is provided with confirmation that the fund remains suitable or if not, receives an alternative recommendation.

---

1   In accordance with COB 6.6.87–93.
2   5.3.14.2(b).
3   Unless the fund is unaware of it.

G Basic advice on stakeholder products

4.47 In response to concerns about the cost of advice and the need to encourage saving and pension provision the government introduced the Stakeholder Pension Scheme in 2001. The concept is a simple product with low (initially 1%) charges. Employers not offering a pension scheme were required to offer a stakeholder scheme. The problem was that they were not required to contribute to it. It has not as yet proved to be a success. However, the concept and the idea of basic advice have been extended to other types of stakeholder product.

Establishing, operating or winding up a stakeholder pension scheme is a regulated activity[1] as is providing basic advice to a retail consumer on any stakeholder product[2]. Basic advice is a curtailed form of assessment of the customer's needs in relation to a limited range of products[3]. A person provides basic advice when with the customer's agreement he assesses whether a stakeholder product is appropriate to the customer based on the information provided by the customer. Stakeholder products in addition to pensions (and other deposit-based products) are Child Trust Funds and units in collective investment schemes or linked long-term contracts (other than smoothed products) which satisfy the stakeholder criteria[4]. These include cautious/balanced investment criteria and requirements as to and costs and expenses.

COB 5A sets out the requirement to provide an IDD to show the scope and range of advice and if requested to explain the basis on which the firm has chosen products on which to offer basic advice. Basic advice cannot be given on a whole of market or independent basis. The firm's range can also only include one stakeholder collective investment scheme/linked life policy product, one stakeholder pension scheme and one stakeholder Child Trust Fund[5]. The advice should not extend to fund choices under the products or contribution levels needed to achieve a specific income in retirement. The advice must be provided through a process which incorporates pre-scripted questions. The customer should be given or sent a copy in a durable medium of the completed scripted questions and answers[6]. The adviser must describe the product to the customer and make a recommendation.

The rest of the basic advice process involves explaining the 'aims', 'risks' and commitment sections of the key features document and providing a summary sheet specific to the customer for each product recommended, which sets out the amount the customer wishes to pay and the reasons (taking into account the information provided by the customer) for the recommendation. Customers must also be advised that any complaints to the Financial Ombudsman Service may take the limited nature of the advice process into account. Further provisions apply to conducting basic advice by telephone[7]. The customer has to indicate that they have understood the description of the product and the adviser's recommendation.

1   Article 52 RAO.
2   Article 52B.
3   Someone acting outside the course of a business carried on by him.
4   See Article 7, Financial Services and Markets Act 2000 (Stakeholder Products) Regulations 2004, SI 2004/2738.
5   COB 5A.3.1(2).
6   COB 5.4.4.1(2).
7   COB 54.4.9 and 5A.2.5–6.

Similar rules to those applicable to non-basic advice (eg record-keeping) apply[1]. As do rules on the structure of remuneration and white labelling[2]. Also, whilst basic advice should stay within the appropriate range[3], it is possible, provided the customer is advised that this is what is happening, to 'depart' from the process[4].

H   Information about the firm

4.48   A firm must take reasonable steps to ensure that it gives its private customers adequate information about the firm (and any relevant agent of the firm); the identity and status, or relationship with the firm, of employees and other agents with whom the customer may have contact and the firm's statutory status (in accordance with GEN 4 Annex 1 (Statutory status disclosure)) unless the private customer has been given information on a previous occasion which is still up to date. The type of information which would satisfy COB 5.5.3R is set out in Table 5.5.5E. On all business stationery (written communications including stationery, business cards) published by the firm or used by its employees, agents, representatives, or introducers the following information should be included:

(1)   name, business address and telephone number of the firm to which the firm belongs, or of the branch or office of the firm from which the communication originates;

(2)   the name and status or relationship with the firm of the individual from whom the communication originates;

(3)   a statement of the firm's statutory status (in accordance with GEN 4 Annex 1 (Statutory status disclosure));

(4)   if the communication is by or relates to an introducer, a statement of the introducer's capacity.

Additional disclosure is required for overseas business for UK customers. Therefore, a firm must provide a written statement making it clear that in some or all respects the regulatory regime applying (including compensation arrangements) will be different from that in the UK. However, it may indicate the protections or compensation available under another system of regulation.

1   COB 5A.3.4 and 5A.3.6.
2   COB 5A.3.7.
3   COB 5A.3.8.
4   COB 5A.3.1(5).

SECTION 5 REMUNERATION – CONFLICT, DISCLOSURE AND THE IDD

A Overview

4.49 COB 2 contains provisions designed to prevent allegations that intermediaries have directed business to product providers on the basis of a benefit to the intermediary rather than the best interests of the client. These provisions supplement Principles 1 (integrity) and 6 (customers' interests). Although in a different format, these provisions have a long history. One of the original aims of the regulation under the Financial Services Act 1986 was to harmonise the level of permissible commission payable to intermediaries. This was to prevent any apparent consideration of commission levels as a factor in the decision-making process. Unfortunately this very laudable and practical aim was to be prevented by competition considerations. The current rules therefore seek to achieve the same aim but arguably in a more convoluted fashion. In practice, the LAUTRO maximum commission rules are also still in use as a means of defining commission (eg 120% LAUTRO).

At a high level the FSA rules aim to prevent a firm or its associates giving or receiving 'inducements' in placing business (eg agreeing to channel business to a provider in return for a benefit to the firm). The main focus of the rule against inducements (other than in respect of payment of commission) is directed at holdings in intermediary companies or loans provided by a product provider. The rules are supplemented by some permitted exceptions (mainly relating to the provision of marketing literature and training). These exceptions are known as the 'indirect benefit rules'. All of the rules are drafted widely to catch group companies carrying on the specified activity but are generally disapplied where all parties are in a group. Similarly, they do not apply to a firm's own appointed representative but do apply to other distributors including multi ties (ie firms selling products of a limited number of providers). If strictly applied the rules could create issues for 'multi ties or distributor companies' particularly new companies in need of capital. In practice the FSA may agree that there is no conflict of interest if there is disclosure to the client of payments made or accommodation afforded in such a situation.

B COB 2.3 inducements

4.50 The Rules provide that a firm must take reasonable steps to ensure that any person acting on its behalf (eg including an unregulated associate) does not offer, solicit or accept an inducement and that business is not directed or preferred to another person if in either case it is 'likely to conflict to a material extent' with the duty owed to the firm's customers in connection with such designated investment business[1]. FSA guidance indicates that a firm may be able to demonstrate that it could not reasonably have knowledge of an associate giving or receiving an inducement.

---

1 2.2.3.

1   COB 2.2.3: Giving or receiving 'inducements'

4.51   There is a detailed evidential provision relating to the meaning of inducement. This relates to the holding of an interest (eg in the capital or voting rights) in an intermediary firm (or related companies) and the provision of credit to such companies. These are not permitted unless the interest is acquired on commercial terms. This means that the terms should be such that an independent person, unconnected to the product provider, would be prepared in all the circumstances to acquire the interest or offer the credit or accommodation. This fact must be supported by 'reliable written evidence'. There are further conditions relating to the channelling of business. There must be no arrangements relating directly to the channelling of business and the product provider (and its associates) must not actually be able to exercise any influence over the advice given in relation to packaged products because of the arrangement. The rules relating to inducements also apply to arrangements between authorised intermediaries and unauthorised packaged product providers (eg insurance firms or the operator of a regulated collective investment scheme outside of the UK) or investment trusts[1].

2   Indirect benefits

4.52   In addition to interests in and credit provided to intermediaries, COB 2.2.6(G) makes clear that indirect benefits can constitute an inducement. The most obvious being gifts and hospitality, but extending to possible business benefits like use or provision of software to help the intermediary improve their business offering. It can also limit compensatory payments made to intermediaries involved in sorting out problems caused by a life office. This is one of the areas where the contrast with a product provider's own representatives is most marked as these provisions do not apply (but see rules on Commission Equivalent). A list of benefits that may be provided to intermediaries without constituting an inducement are set out in a table forming part of COB 2.2.7. Strictly, this table is indicative guidance but it is extensively relied upon in practice. There is a fine line between assistance given to an intermediary which does not conflict with its duty to its clients and that which does. COB 2.2.6(2) makes clear that a product provider may assist an intermediary to promote its packaged products so that the quality of its service to customers is enhanced but this may not extend to the provision of software (see the specific exemption of software in COB 6.10 9BR(3)(a) (ii).

The list of permitted indirect benefits includes joint marketing exercises but provides rules about the use of generic materials and the costs which the product provider is permitted to bear. This includes distribution costs (postage, freepost envelopes which are made available generally to intermediaries). It may also provide a generally available freephone link. Literature may include the name of the intermediary but, in line with the FSA's view on white labelling, it must be less prominent than the product provider and it must be clear who the product provider is. It also generally excludes the use of such literature for broker funds. More product specific literature may also be provided (eg key features) on a

---

1   2.2.5A.

similar basis (ie prominence of product provider and not used to promote broker funds).

There are a number of other exemptions covering financial promotions paid for at a market rate (eg adverts in the client magazine of an intermediary), participation in seminars and conferences (where the participation is for a genuine business purpose, any contribution to costs is proportionate to the active involvement of the provider's staff at the seminar and, if it is a third party seminar, access is open to other firms generally) and training provided by the product provider (if made generally available to firms which might advise on its packaged products). A product provider may also provide technical information in writing either generally or to niche areas of the market. A product provider may reimburse some reasonable travel and accommodation expenses of another firm in specified circumstances including to attend training provided or visits to the product provider's office to receive information about administrative systems or client meetings[1].

3   IT support

4.53   In this day and age where much business is done at least in part online, the provision of software or contribution toward the cost of software used (eg by a multi tie company and its 'principals') is an important issue. The rules state that product providers may give access to software that provides information about their packaged products or 'where appropriate' (the example given being for use in a scheme for review of past business or for producing projections or technical product information). However, a product provider may only pay cash or give assistance to another firm for the development of software or other facilities 'necessary' to operate software it supplies and then only to the extent that by doing so it will generate an 'equivalent cost saving to itself or consumers'. Product providers are, however, permitted to provide access to data processing facilities or to data and to third party electronic dealing or quotation systems that relate to the product provider's business.

If a broker fund adviser cannot produce its periodic statements then the product provider may supply them. Quotations and projections provided on a general basis may also be supplied in relation to broker funds.

C   Commission payments

4.54   Perhaps the easiest way in which a product provider could pass a benefit to intermediaries is in the terms on which it pays commission. Restrictions apply in those cases where commission is required to be disclosed to the client purchasing a packaged product (eg such as a life investment contract)[2]. These rules seek to prevent arrangements like volume overrides which the FSA views as intrinsically in conflict with the interests of customers. They also prevent

1   2.2.7(12).
2   Evidential provision in 2.2.5.

commission being paid unless the firm has been involved in the sale or has passed on its rights to another firm. Another firm may become entitled to commission if it has given advice on investments to the same customer after the sale. Note this need not be in relation to the product paying the commission. Commission may also be paid in respect of direct marketing (eg by a product provider to an intermediary's clients)[1].

To those unfamiliar with the sale of insurance products the arrangements under which commission is paid are strikingly one sided. For regular premium contracts a couple of years' commission (depending on the initial period) can be paid upfront discounted slightly to reflect early payment. If all of the customers' premiums are not paid then clawback of the 'unearned' commission is triggered. This is called indemnity commission. It is not prohibited by the FSA rules but the rules provide that the terms on which indemnity commission is paid/clawed back must not permit an additional financial benefit to the intermediary in the event of the commission becoming repayable[2]. This will mean that such debts should attract interest and be pursued in a commercial manner.

Commission must also not be increased beyond the level disclosed to the customer unless the increase is as a result of an increase in premium[3]. As a separate and overriding requirement commission must also not be 'excessive'.

SECTION 6   ICOB

A   Overview

4.55   As has already been stated the COB rules set out detailed requirements relating to the sale of packaged products. Life companies may also sell 'pure protection' contracts (eg term assurance). A pure protection contract is a contract in respect of death or incapacity, written for a maximum term of ten years or to age 70 and which has either no surrender value or, for single premium contracts, the surrender value is not more than the premium paid. The FSA is currently looking at changing the age 70 restriction. The IMD also applies to these contracts. As part of the regulation of general insurance and implementation of the IMD, the FSA introduced a new section of the Handbook, the 'Insurance Conduct of Business' section, known as ICOB. ICOB is similar to COB in high level terms but generally much less detailed. The FSA has deliberately adopted a lighter approach than in COB.

This section provides a brief summary of the ICOB provisions relevant to insurance mediation or the product provider of a life contract which is not an investment contract. The product disclosure requirements (eg policy summary) are dealt with in Chapter 5.

ICOB only applies to direct insurers and intermediaries (reinsurers are not caught by ICOB unless acting as intermediaries), but only to the extent that the

1   2.2.5(1)(d)(iii).
2   2.2.5(1)(9c).
3   2.2.5(1)(b).

party has direct contact with the customer or is the product provider. All chapters of ICOB apply to any firm that deals with a retail customer (an individual acting outside the course of his trade, business or profession). Some chapters, however, will only apply in part or not at all if a firm is dealing with a commercial customer (ie all other customers). The provisions of ICOB 4 relating to advising and selling[1] apply only to IMD intermediation activities (ie including those carried on by an insurer or reinsurer). Intermediaries are subject to requirements in relation to both retail and commercial customers. Insurers are not subject to the status disclosure, statement of demands and needs (unless a recommendation is made and even then the customer may consent to forgo the statement) or commission disclosure rules when dealing with a commercial customer[2]. Certain requirements do, however, apply to the insurer where there is no authorised intermediary[3].

B   ICOB 2: Unfair inducements

4.56   The firm must take reasonable steps to ensure that it, and any person acting on its behalf, does not offer, give, solicit or accept an inducement; or direct or refer any actual or potential business in relation to any insurance mediation activity to another person on its own initiative or on the instructions of an associate, if it is likely to conflict to a material extent with the firms' duty to treat its customers fairly. An 'inducement' is a benefit offered to a firm, or any person acting on its behalf, with a view to that firm, or that person, adopting a particular course of action.

There may be circumstances where a firm is able to demonstrate that it could not reasonably have knowledge of an associate giving or receiving an inducement[4]. The FSA's guidance[5] makes clear that inducements that operate at a distance from the sales process may not be unfair if they do not have an effect on the sales person. The rule on inducements is therefore less detailed than the equivalent COB provision which specifically prohibits certain shareholdings in and loans to intermediaries. Whilst some such arrangements may still in principle be capable of having the effect of an inducement that fact would need to be proved (unlike the position in COB).

C   ICOB 4: Advising and selling

I   *Commission disclosure*

4.57   The most noticeable difference between the COB and ICOB regimes for retail customers is in relation to commission disclosure. Under ICOB fees are

---

1   Except ICOB 4.7.
2   4.1.4.
3   1.2.7 (eg where connected contracts are sold).
4   2.3.3.
5   2.3.8.

disclosed but currently commission is not, unless requested by a commercial customer[1].

2 Disclosure of status and fees

4.58 An insurance intermediary (including an insurer carrying on insurance mediation activities) must make disclosure of its status to a retail customer before conclusion of the insurance contract. As in COB, exemptions exist for telephone sales. An exemption also exists if the customer requests an oral disclosure or requires immediate cover[2]. Where either exemption is relied upon, the disclosure must be provided immediately after the conclusion of the contract. The disclosure must be in a durable medium and must include the information set out in the table in ICOB 4.2.8. It is quite like the information in the COB IDD and may be satisfied by use of the IDD (in ICOB 4 Annex 1G) or where relevant the CIDD (in ICOB 4 Annex 2G). The information includes details of shareholdings by the intermediary in an insurer (if more than 10%) and similar interests held by an insurer (or its parent) in the intermediary. This latter provision does not apply if the intermediary is an insurer. There is no disclosure in relation to credit provided. As with COB the key facts logo can only be used on IDDs if they are provided unchanged[3]. ICOB 4.2.6 sets out requirements in relation to the use of the logo.

The terminology in relation to scope of the intermediary's services is different to COB. An intermediary may advise on the basis of a 'fair analysis'. It must disclose whether or not it is contractually obliged to limit its scope in this way. The intermediary must maintain a list to be provided to customers on request of the insurers it selects or deals with in relation to the contract to be provided. To provide services on the basis of 'fair analysis', a firm must consider a sufficiently large number of contracts from the relevant market and be knowledgeable enough to make the assessment. An intermediary may satisfy this requirement by operating an appropriate panel. The panel needs to be reviewed on a regular basis[4]. Selection of products should also be based on the product features, etc and not solely on the benefit that the insurer offers to the intermediary.

Where the intermediary is introducing to another person or an insurer a more limited disclosure is required[5]. This includes details of the firm and its regulatory status, details of fees and whether the introduction is between members of the same group.

An insurance intermediary may have a different scope of advice for different types of non-investment insurance[6]. An insurance intermediary must also provide customers with information on fees (or their basis of calculation) before the earlier of the customer incurring the liability to pay the fee, or conclusion of the relevant contract. This information may be provided orally before the

---

1 4.6.11.
2 ICOB 42(2).
3 ICOB 4.2.5.
4 4.2.12.
5 ICOB 4.2.7.
6 42.13.

contract is concluded but it must be provided in a durable medium immediately after the conclusion of the contract. Disclosure to UK retail customer by overseas intermediaries must satisfy the requirement of ICOB 4.2.19(2) making any loss of regulatory protection, including complaints and compensation rights clear.

3 Suitability

4.59 The rules on suitability in ICOB are slightly more relaxed than those in COB, particularly in relation to the extent to which the intermediary is required to know their customer or to not make a recommendation if the products in their range are not the most suitable. The suitability requirement in ICOB is simply that the recommended product is 'suitable to the customer's demand and needs[1] and consistent with the intermediary's disclosed scope[2]. However, if there is not a contract within that scope which meets all of those needs, provided the needs that will not be met are pointed out to the customer, a recommendation may still be made.

Unlike the 'know your customer' requirements in COB, an intermediary need only seek such information as might reasonably be expected to be relevant to the customer's current requirement. This should include existing insurances but if such information is not provided it does not necessarily prevent the intermediary making a recommendation[3]. The intermediary can either not make a recommendation or make clear that any recommendation made may not be suitable because he has been unable to take those details into account[4]. However, if such information is readily available or accessible to the intermediary, then it should be taken into account. One aspect of the ICOB process which is not really applicable in the COB is the need to explain the duty of non-disclosure. ICOB 4.3.2(3) requires the intermediary to explain to the customer the need to disclose all circumstances material to the insurance and the consequences of failing to do so. The intermediary must also take account of any such information disclosed by a customer. ICOB 3.3(G) provides the intermediary should make clear the type of information that needs to be disclosed in relation to the particular contract proposed. Suitability also includes consideration of exclusions and limitations[5].

Where an intermediary arranges for a customer to enter into a contract (and on renewal of an existing contract), it needs to provide a statement of demands and needs. This statement should set out the customer's demands and needs, confirm whether a contract has been personally recommended and, if so, why it has. The statement should be provided in a durable medium unless the customer requests otherwise or immediate cover is required. In either case it must be provided in a durable medium immediately after the contract is concluded. Similar provisions permit telesales to be concluded orally but with a statement provided afterwards.

Insurers need to provide a statement of demands and needs to commercial customers they have advised to take out a contract unless the customer consents (and

1 ICOB 4.3.1(i).
2 ICOB 4.3.1(ii).
3 ICOB 4.3.5.
4 ICOB 4.3.5.
5 ICOB 4.3.6(2).

before the consent is given the insurer has explained the consequences of giving such consent[1]) not to receive the statement. The insurer must still retain a record, in a durable medium, of the reason for the recommendation. If an insurer does not make a recommendation to a commercial customer it need not provide the statement of demands and needs.

The content of the statement can vary depending on whether a recommendation has been made. If it has the guidance in ICOB 4.4.6 applies. Whilst there is no prescribed format, firms need to bear in mind that the statement will be used to demonstrate the suitability of the advice given and must be retained for three years[2]. The guidance recommends that the link to the customer's needs is clear and that where an insurer has been chosen, the reason for that choice is recorded. The statement can be incorporated into another document such as an application form[3]. Statements where no recommendation is given also need to be retained for three years but they can more easily be incorporated in product documentation[4] and can be more standardised[5].

4   Prohibitions

4.60   As in COB, ICOB contains a prohibition, in this case limited to retail customers, on excessive charges. ICOB 4.7 prohibits unsolicited services, in relation to distance contracts, for which the firm will charge. This provision does not apply to tacit renewal of a distance contract.

5   The gap rules

4.61   ICOB 1.3.10 provides what are known as the gap rules. These apply where a UK firm is passporting IMD activities into a member state that has not implemented Articles 12 and 13 of the IMD. ICOB 1.3.11 sets out the relevant provisions.

SECTION 7   AGENCY AND LIFE ASSURANCE

A   Introduction

4.62   This sections seeks to deal with the legal consequences applicable (under the general law of agency) to an agency relationship and, in particular, in relation to FSA authorised intermediaries. The requirements apply in addition to any FSMA-related requirements.

As has already been stated, one of the objectives of the 1986 Act was to make clear whether an intermediary was an agent of the client or the product provider.

1   ICOB 4.4.2.(B).
2   ICOB 4.4.7(2).
3   ICOB 4.4.3.
4   ICOB 4.4.4(G)(2).
5   ICOB 4.4.4(G)(1).

Post-depolarisation the position has become slightly blurred. It is not clear whether a multi-tie distribution company is merely the agent for a number of providers or is the agent of the client. The law in this area predates this change but it is submitted that it is likely the distribution company, authorised in its own right and subject in the main to the same FSA rules as a whole of market adviser (eg inducements), would be treated as the agent of the client. This can have far-reaching consequences as the law in this area is harsh (eg disclosure to such an intermediary would not satisfy the requirement to disclose to the insurer). The Law Commission issued a scoping paper in January 2006 in relation to insurance law. One of the issues it identified is the difficulty of insurance brokers being remunerated by the insurer but categorised as the agent of the client. One proposal to remedy this is to switch the relationship around so that the broker acts for the person paying them. In the life sector this will not necessarily solve the problem as status could then depend on whether the client pays a fee. For the avoidance of doubt this section deals with the current law in relation to insurance brokers (which for these purposes are referred to as Financial Advisers) not those acting as agent of the life office.

B General principles

I Nature of agent

4.63   In simple terms an agent is any person who has authority (ie actual authority) to act on behalf of another, known as a 'principal'. In this wide sense the term may include an employee, because a company or corporation (including an insurance company) can only act through an agent. The agent, through whom the principal organisation acts, may therefore be a director, the chief executive or other employee.

Actual authority (ie within the specific terms of the agency appointment) also encompasses implied authority. Implied authority relates to those acts which an agent with actual authority needs to do in order to exercise his actual authority and those acts which are incidental to the exercise of actual authority. Ostensible or apparent authority arises from the position or office in which the agent is placed or the credentials which he has been permitted to hold. This is the authority which the law regards as having been conferred on the agent by the words or conduct of the principal. The effect may be to create an agency where none previously existed or extend the scope of existing actual authority. A person dealing with the agent is entitled to assume that the agent's actual authority is equal to his apparent/ostensible authority unless there is reason to suspect otherwise[1]. However, it is not possible for an agent to confer ostensible authority upon

---

1   *Willis, Faber & Co v Joyce* (1911) 27 TLR 388; *Eagle Star Insurance Co Ltd v Spratt* [1971] 2 Lloyd's Rep 116. See, however, the case of *British Bank of the Middle East v Sun Life Assurance Co of Canada (UK)* [1983] 2 Lloyd's Rep 9, HL, in which it was held that neither the life office's salesman nor branch manager had actual or ostensible authority to give undertakings to a bank despite a statement by the branch manager that the salesman was so empowered.

himself[1]. It has been said that ostensible authority is based on an estoppel such that the principal is estopped by his conduct from denying that the agent had the requisite authority to bind the principal. A third party affected in this way and claiming against the principal must show that the principal by his words or conduct or even by silence and acquiescence[2] held out the agent as having the alleged authority, which he relied upon and that he acted to his detriment in so doing. In some cases the agent will claim to have authority when he does not. In this case the third party who is thereby affected will have a claim for any loss suffered against the agent personally on the basis of breach of warranty of authority. In practice the third party will generally not want this result as the principal will in most cases be the party worth suing. Another possible scenario is where the third party is put on enquiry or he ought to have asked questions which would have established the true position. In such a case he will not be entitled to rely on the ostensible authority to bind the principal. Furthermore, even if the agent acted outside the scope of his authority, the principal may ratify his unauthorised act provided that it is within its own powers[3].

There are significant differences, in practice, between the positions of agents acting in relation to life insurance when compared to those of general insurers. For example, general insurance agents often have the power to conclude contracts. The position of Financial Advisers is in many respects a basic agency in that such 'agents' do not have such authority from the life office and will generally only recommend and suggest actions to the client. Only rarely will the Financial Adviser be in a position to conclude life contracts on behalf of the client.

2   Duties of the agent

4.64   It is the duty of the Financial Adviser, as agent, to deal honestly with his principal who will generally be a member of the public with little or no specialist knowledge[4]. One aspect of this relationship is the fiduciary duty owed by the agent to his principal. Therefore, a Financial Adviser employed by a proposer to effect an insurance contract must not secretly take a commission from the life office[5], or if he does he must account to the proposer for what he receives[6]. Under the general law of agency there is no objection to his retaining such commission where the principal is aware he is receiving it, or where he might reasonably have inferred that the agent was to have commission, even though he may not know

1   See *Freeman & Lockyer v Buckhurst Park Properties (Mangal) Ltd* [1964] 2 QB 480, where Diplock LJ summarised the position and also considered the additional layer of complication created by a corporate body purported giving such ostensible authority. In such circumstances the official of the company must himself have actual authority. These principles were applied in *British Bank of the Middle East v Sun Life Assurance Co of Canada (UK)* [1983] 2 Lloyd's Rep 9.
2   *Eagle Star Insurance Co Ltd v Spratt* [1971] 2 Lloyd's Rep.
3   *Re Phoenix Life Assurance Co* (1862) 2 John & H 441.
4   *Connecticut Fire Insurance Co v Kavanagh* [1892] AC 473, PC.
5   *Leete v Wallace* (1888) 58 LT 577.
6   *Re Lord Berwick, Lord Berwick v Lane* (1900) 81 LT 797, CA.

the actual amount (although for all practical purposes this if governed by COBS disclosure of commission will be made either in the Key Facts document or separately).

In addition to commission payments as understood, payments which may be covered by these general principles include claims by agents against life offices for additional work undertaken as a result of administrative errors and oversights by the life office. If a claim is made in connection with a particular client's business, the agent remains the agent of that client, unless he has agreed with the life office to act as their agent and has disclosed this agency to his first principal and that principal has assented. If he fails to account to his principal (the client) for the receipt of such payments, it would appear that this amounts to a secret profit. The life office might also expose itself to a claim from the client for payment of the same amount on the basis of having facilitated such payment.

In general terms, it is the duty of the agent to carry out the transaction which he is employed to carry out, or, if it is impossible for him to do so, to inform the principal promptly in order to prevent the principal from suffering loss through relying upon the unsuccessful completion of the transaction by the agent. Financial Advisers acting for clients in connection with life assurance (and other financial products such as pensions and unit trusts) consider which contracts would best meet identified needs of the client and advise accordingly. In view of the number of broadly similar contracts available on the market, this is a potentially onerous undertaking. Assuming the client is happy to proceed with the Financial Adviser's recommendation an application is then made for a policy. The Financial Adviser is likely to assist with the application process. He may even suggest answers to certain questions but care must be exercised by the Financial Adviser in this respect. As agent of the client if his advice in some way disadvantages his client, for example non-disclosure of a material fact, the Financial Adviser could be liable to his client. It is quite common to find in proposal forms a statement to the effect that in signing the proposal the client confirms his agreement to anything which is not in his own handwriting, which offers a degree of protection to the life office for anything written by the Financial Adviser.

The agent has a duty to obey his instructions and to act strictly in accordance with the terms of his authority[1] or, as regards matters on which they are silent, the usual course of business. In the exercise of the authority entrusted to him, the agent must act with reasonable and proper care, skill and diligence. If he is a professional agent, such as a Financial Adviser, the standard by which the duty is measured is the standard of skill and care which is normally possessed by persons in that profession, otherwise he is to be judged by what an ordinary person might, given the particular circumstances, be expected to do. The test is not whether the Financial Adviser was correct in arriving at the advice in question but whether 'he did or did not exercise reasonable and proper care, skill and judgment'[2]. This is to be judged by the standard of other Financial Advisers.

---

1 *Barron v Fitzgerald* (1840) 6 Bing NC 201.
2 *Chapman v Walton* (1833) 10 Bing 57.

3 Authority

4.65 An agent is responsible to his principal and can bind the principal only to the extent of his express, implied or ostensible authority. The terms of the express authority are to be found in the agreement between the agent and his principal. The implied authority arises from the further power to do all things necessary in the ordinary course of business for the efficient and proper performance by the agent of his duties. If a person contracts with an agent where the contract is not one usually within the scope of an agent's authority, the contracting party should ascertain that the agent has in fact express authority.

4 Payment

4.66 Unusually for the position of an agent, in most cases Financial Advisers are paid by the life office rather than by their principal (ie the client). The fact that Financial Advisers receive commission from life offices is one of the factors which tend to cause confusion in ascertaining whose agent the Financial Adviser is. In most other cases the agent is paid by the client. There are a growing number of Financial Advisers who are paid on a fee basis by the client. In such cases it is normal for the Financial Adviser to rebate any commission to the client thus enhancing the value of (or reducing the cost of) the life assurance policy (or other product) to the client. Furthermore, this method of remuneration of Financial Advisers has the advantage that there should be no temptation for the Financial Adviser to seek to recommend a product merely for the purpose of generating a commission in breach of his duties as an agent. As mentioned, the Financial Adviser is required to disclose the amount of commission payable to him[1] in respect of packaged products.

Commission is paid under an agreement between the Financial Adviser and the life office (often termed a 'Terms of Business letter' or, misleadingly, an 'Agency Agreement'). Amongst other things, this will set out the details relating to commission payable to the Financial Adviser and how this is to be calculated. It will also deal with other methods regarding commission such as the 'claw back' of commission on early termination of contracts before the commission has been fully earned. This certainly muddies the water as to whose agent the Financial Adviser is. However, the law indicates that he is the agent of the client. Even an agent of the Insurer acting outside his authority has been held to be the agent of the client in some circumstances.

5 Whose agent?

4.67 In *Newsholme Bros v Road Transport and General Insurance Ltd*[2] an agent of the insurance company filled in the proposal form (for motor insurance) at the request of the proposer as a result of which it was decided that for those

1 COBS 5.7.5R.
2 [1929] 2 KB 356.

purposes he became the agent of the proposer[1] because he was not authorised by the company to do so. The majority of the cases on this point relate to general business a Lloyd's underwriters but the principle is the same. The rule that an insurance broker is the agent of the client was upheld in *Roberts v Plaisted*[2], where it was held that full and frank disclosure by a proposer to an Financial Adviser was not effective against the insurer. However, it is worth considering part of the judgment of Purchas LJ (which has been quoted by the Insurance Ombudsman in the past):

'To the person unacquainted with the insurance industry it may seem a remarkable state of the law that someone who describes himself as a Lloyd's broker, who is remunerated by the insurance industry and who presents proposal forms and suggested policies on their behalf should not be the safe recipient of full disclosure but that is undoubtedly the position in law as it stands at the moment. Perhaps it is a matter which might attract the attention at an appropriate moment of the Law Commission.'[3]

As stated above this is now likely to be reviewed by the Law Commission.

More recently, in the case of *Winter v Irish Life Assurance plc*[4] it was asserted that an Independent Financial Adviser was the agent of the life office. This was rejected and the appropriate question was stated to be: 'who has asked or authorised the intermediary to perform the particular service, is it the insurer or the assured?'. In this case the evidence was clearly that the proposers had constituted the Financial Adviser as their agent.

It is worth noting that the Insurance Ombudsman Bureau has stated that he was prepared to hold insurers liable for the default of intermediaries in what, he considered, were appropriate cases[5]. It is to be presumed that the Financial Ombudsman (FOS), which is not bound by the strict legal position, may do the same.

6 Knowledge of agent

4.68 As a general rule, the knowledge of an agent will bind the principal, so that the life office will ordinarily be bound by knowledge of its tied agents (ARs) or their employees. Conversely, a life office will not normally be bound by knowledge of Financial Advisers acting on behalf of a client.

Questions sometimes arise as to how far information given to an intermediary will bind the life office in respect of the completion of proposal forms and the various other dealings between the proposer, intermediary and life office at the

---

1   See also *Facer v Vehicle and General Insurance Co Ltd* [1965] 1 Lloyd's Rep 113 and *Bigger v Rock Life Assurance Co* [1902] 1 KB 516.
2   [1989] 2 Lloyd's Rep 341.
3   [1989] 2 Lloyd's Rep 345.
4   [1995] 2 Lloyd's Rep 274. See also *Searle v Hayes & Co* [1996] LRLR 68 for further support for the 'classical' position.
5   Insurance Ombudsman's Bureau Annual Report 1989, para 2.14. Although in his 1992 Report this view seems to have been contradicted. He referred to '. . . any intermediary or other person for whom the insurer has no responsibility'.

time of effecting the life policy. Although there is conflicting authority on the point, it is suggested that the line taken in *Newsholme Bros v Road Transport and General Insurance Co Ltd*[1] above is supported by the later cases.

The following case also illustrates the difficulties which may arise (in individual circumstances) in this area of the law[2]:

> *Bawden v London, Edinburgh and Glasgow Assurance Co*[3]
>
> B effected a policy against accidental injury, under which total incapacity included loss of both eyes. The proposal had been obtained by an agent, Q, who saw that B had only one eye. B could neither read nor write, although he could sign his name. Q completed the proposal form at B's dictation and B signed it, but Q did not mention the previous loss of one eye. B subsequently lost the sight of his other eye in an accident. Held, that Q was the agent of the company and his tasks included putting proposals into shape. Consequently, his knowledge must be imputed to the company and therefore the company was liable.

This case was distinguished by the Court of Appeal in the *Newsholme* case as not being applicable to a case where the agent is requested by the proposer to fill in the answers in accordance with information supplied by the proposer. *Bawden* has been followed in other cases and was approved by the Court of Appeal in *Stone v Reliance Mutual Insurance Society Ltd*[4].

4.69   Summary of other cases:

> *Biggar v Rock Life Assurance Co*[5]
>
> B effected a policy against accident through the agency of C, who deliberately filled in the proposal form falsely. B signed the proposal without reading it. Held, that the agent may be the agent of the company with the responsibility to ensure that the form was properly completed, but he was not at liberty to invent answers. To the extent that he did so, he was agent not of the company but of the proposer and the company was not therefore liable.

> *Facer v Vehicles and General Insurance Co*[6]
>
> B was the agent of an insurance company and A was one of his employees. F proposed for a policy and disclosed to A that he only had one eye. A filled in the proposal form and included a statement that F did not suffer from defective vision or from physical infirmity. The form included the statement 'If this proposal is written by another it shall be deemed he shall be my agent and not an agent of the [company]'. F signed the proposal form and a policy was issued. Held, that F was not entitled to a declaration that the company were liable to indemnify him under the policy. A was F's agent, not the company's.

---

1   [1929] 2 KB 356.
2   It should be noted that these cases were decided at a time when it was possible for an independent intermediary, given the activities that he could conduct on behalf of the life office, to be the agent of the life office. This will now only be the case in the rarest of circumstances.
3   [1892] 2 QBD 534.
4   [1972] 1 Lloyd's Rep 469.
5   [1902] 1 KB 516.
6   [1965] 1 Lloyd's Rep 113.

Stone v Reliance Mutual Insurance Society Ltd[1]

S insured his home. Following a fire the policy lapsed. The company's inspector, O (ie as agent of the company), called on S to persuade him to revive the lapsed policy and to effect new ones. He saw Mrs S, produced fire and burglary proposal forms, and filled them in himself. Mrs S signed them as 'proposer' without reading them. The question as to lapsed policies and claims were both incorrectly answered with 'None'. The printed form contained a declaration that if any part of it was not written by the proposer, the person writing did so as the proposer's agent. The company rejected a claim for loss by burglary. It was shown that it was the company's policy that O should put the questions to the client and write down the answers and that the answers were put in by mistake, which was O's. It was his duty, owed to his employers, to take care in writing the answers. The mistake was not a misstatement by the insured which avoided the contract, but one induced by the company's employee, and the company could not rely on it to avoid the policy.

Lord Denning MR described the case as quite different from the *Newsholme* case (above), because there the agent was merely amanuensis to the proposer. It was far more like *Bawden*'s case (above), where the agent could see for himself that the proposer had lost an eye, and that knowledge was the company's knowledge. In *Stone* Mrs S assumed (justifiably) that the agent would have knowledge of the previous policy. The Company were not assisted by the declaration in the proposal that the answers were true and that where answers were not written by the proposers, the person who did write them did so as the proposer's agent.

4.70 It seems, therefore, that where a proposer signs a proposal containing a statement which is untrue or incomplete, but the agent had knowledge of the true facts (which were acquired by him *as agent of the company* and in the course of the transaction) the company is liable.

This point was reaffirmed in the following case:

Woolcott v Excess Insurance Co Ltd[2]

In April 1974, T, who were brokers, insured W's house with the defendant insurance company, E. In August 1974, the house was destroyed by fire. E denied liability because of W's non-disclosure of his criminal record, which W admitted but claimed that T knew about. Held, that (1) W ought to have disclosed his criminal past; (2) T, in the ordinary course of business as brokers and agents of E, had acquired some knowledge of W's past; (3) on these facts W had no duty to disclose his past to T; (4) therefore E could not avoid the policy, but was entitled to be indemnified by T, who were plainly under a duty to disclose their knowledge to E.

Again, *Newsholme* was distinguished because in *Woolcott*, rather than acting as the proposer's amanuensis, the broker had authority to issue policies on behalf of the insurers. He knew all the material facts and in the light of that issued the policy. All the knowledge which the intermediary had was therefore rightly imputed to the insurer. In practice the *Woolcott* scenario is very unlikely to arise in the context of life assurance and it is much more likely that Financial Advisers will be held to be the agent of the client.

1   [1972] 1 Lloyd's Rep 469.
2   [1978] 1 Lloyd's Rep 633.

CHAPTER 5

Financial promotion and product disclosure

SUMMARY

Section 1   Financial promotion **5.1**

Section 2   Product disclosure and Conduct of Business Sourcebook ('COBS') **5.63**

Section 3   Cancellation **5.91**

Section 4   Anti money laundering provisions **5.98**

Section 5   Insurance Conduct of Business ('ICOB') **5.102**

SECTION I FINANCIAL PROMOTION

A Introduction

5.1   Advertising is probably the most high-profile aspect of a life office's activities and the promotion of its products, whether in writing, television, radio, the internet, telephone or text message is a substantial undertaking for the majority of life offices which generally retain large marketing departments. In addition, direct marketing by, eg 'off the page' advertising, is a substantial part of some life offices' business and is accompanied by its own particular issues partly at least as result of the customer not receiving any personal advice and its target audience.

The Financial Services and Markets Act 2000 ('FSMA') contains restrictions on and provisions relating to investment advertising, or more precisely 'financial promotion', which are built on in considerable detail in Chapter 3 of the Conduct of Business Sourcebook Rules ('COBS'). Guidance in this area is provided in COBS itself and now also in the 'Perimeter Guidance' (see PERG 8 in the FSMA Handbook). 'Financial promotion' is wider than what might generally be understood to be 'advertising' and also encompasses provisions relating to unsolicited calls which used to be dealt with separately under the Financial Services Act 1986. The COBS Rules relating to financial promotion essentially amplify the FSA Principles relating to 'customers' interests' and 'treating customers fairly' (see **5.47–5.49** for further information on 'Treating Customers Fairly' (TCF)) set out in Principle 6 and also Principle 7 which relates to 'Communications with clients'.

By virtue of section 21 of the FSMA a person must not, in the course of business, communicate an invitation or inducement to engage in investment activity unless the person is an authorised person or its contents have been approved by an authorised person, the purpose being that there is an authorised person involved and responsible for ensuring that the relevant rules are met. There are exclusions for 'exempt' financial promotions set out in the Financial Services and Markets Act 2000 (Financial Promotion Order) 2005[1] (the 'FPO') (and other amending orders).

A person who contravenes section 21 is guilty of a criminal offence which is punishable with a maximum of two years' imprisonment or a fine, or both. However, it is a defence for the accused to show that he believed on reasonable grounds that the communication was prepared, or approved for the purposes of section 21, by an authorised person or that he took all reasonable precautions and exercised all due diligence to avoid committing the offence[2].

5.2   Section 21 does not itself refer to the term 'financial promotion' except in the heading and in a reference to subordinate legislation and so 'financial promotion' is shorthand for the reference in section 21(1) to the communication of an invitation or inducement to engage in investment activity.

In the case of a communication originating outside the UK section 21 only applies if the communication is capable of having an effect in the UK. This section would include internet advertisements. This appears to give a broad territorial scope to section 21 and would seem to catch all relevant communications originating from overseas capable of having an effect in the UK. However, the exemption for communications to overseas recipients in article 12 of the FPO prevents section 21 from applying to communications which are not directed at persons in the UK[3]. For communications made by persons in other EEA States account must be taken of the relevant EU directives, such as the E-Commerce Directive, to prevent the UK from imposing restrictions on incoming financial promotions.

COB 3.3.3R sets out the 'Exceptions to territorial scope: rules without territorial limitation' which, in broad terms, set out the more high level and general requirements relating to financial promotions such as 'clear, fair and not misleading'.

The meaning of 'communicated to a person . . . outside the United Kingdom' is that it is made to a person who receives it outside the UK or is directed only at persons outside the UK[4]. The meaning of 'directed only at persons outside the United Kingdom' is set out in COB 3.3.6R.

1   SI 2005/1529.
2   Section 25.
3   See COB 3.3.1R and PERG 8.8.3G for further details and guidance.
4   COB 3.3.5R.

B   Firms subject to financial promotion rules

5.3   Subject to COB 3.2 ('what?') and COB 3.3 ('where'?) the financial promotion rules apply to every firm (with an exception not relevant to life offices)
which communicates or approves a financial promotion[1]. Under section 39(3) of
the FSMA a firm is responsible for financial promotions communicated by its
appointed representatives when acting as such[2]. There is an exemption in article
36 of the FPO in relation to nationals of EEA States (other than the UK) where
the financial promotion is communicated by such a person in the course of a controlled activity lawfully carried on by him in that State.

A 'controlled agreement' (such as a life policy) entered into pursuant to an
'unlawful communication' is not enforceable, and a policyholder would be entitled to recover any money paid or other property transferred by him under that
agreement together with compensation for any loss resulting from having parted
with it. The compensation would be such as the parties may agree or as the court
may determine (on application by either party).

The court may allow an agreement to stand or money or property transferred
to be retained, if it is satisfied that it is just and equitable in the circumstances of
the case. Where a person elects not to perform an unenforceable agreement or
obligation he must repay any money and return any property received by him
under the agreement. If a person recovers money paid or property transferred by
him he must likewise repay any money or return any other property received
under the agreement or as a result of exercising the rights in question[3].

Exemptions are set out in the FPO[4] (which revoked and re-enacted, with
certain amendments, the 2001 Order), and in COBS itself and explained further
in the 'Perimeter Guidance' contained in the FSA handbook[5]. In practice, UK life
offices marketing to UK residents in the UK do not always seek to take advantage of exemptions for its financial promotions even where they may be available. The benefits to be gained from doing so are not usually that significant and
as it usually represents an exception to most life offices systems and controls it
can actually prove to be more trouble than it's worth.

As mentioned above, the term 'financial promotion' is wider than 'advertisements' and also includes personal visits and telephone calls. One of the effects of
this part of COBS is therefore to bring the old regime relating to solicited and
unsolicited calls under the same provisions as those relating to advertisements.

C   What constitutes a financial promotion?

5.4   Section 21 of the Act provides that 'A person ('A') must not, in the
course of business, communicate an invitation or inducement to engage in
investment activity' unless A is an authorised person or the content of the

1   COB 3.1.1R.
2   COB 3.1.3G.
3   Section 30.
4   SI 2005/1529.
5   PERG 8.12 to 8.15 and PERG 8.21.

communication is approved for the purposes of this section by an authorised person.

There is no restriction on the media of communication to which COB 3 applies. Guidance on the meaning of 'communicate', 'invitation or inducement' and 'engage in investment activity', which together make up the essential elements, is contained in PERG 8.6, PERG 8.4 and PERG 8.7.

I *'Invitation or inducement'*

5.5   There is no definition of these terms in the Act or in COBS. Guidance is contained in PERG 8.4. Only communications containing a degree of 'incitement' amount to 'inducements'. Purely factual statements would not ordinarily constitute an inducement although they could be presented in such a way that they did[1]. There must be some promotional element[2]. Objectively, there must be an intention to persuade or incite the recipient to engage in investment activity[3]. An 'invitation' is something which directly invites a person to take a step which will result in him engaging in investment activity. An example of this would be a direct offer financial promotion[4]. Merely asking a person if he wishes to enter into an agreement with no element of persuasion or incitement will not be an invitation[5].

In PERG 8.4.9G to PERG 8.4.34G the FSA set out at some length the application of the principles in PERG 8.4.4G to PERG 8.4.7G. From a life assurance perspective the following are of relevance:

(a)   *Directory listings* will not normally be inducements but could be depending on how they are presented.

(b)   *'Tombstone' advertisements* (announcements of a firm's past achievements) would not be inducements unless they contained some additional promotional material.

(c)   *Website links* will depend very much on their precise wording.

(d)   *Banner advertisements* will almost certainly be inducements.

(e)   *Publication or broadcast of investment prices* (historic or live) are probably not inducements without some additional promotional material.

(f)   *Journalists* may publish inducements although they are likely to be covered by the exemption in article 20 of the FPO.

(g)   *Investment performance tables* would not be inducements in their own right.

(h)   *Image advertisements* are almost certainly not an inducement or invitation.

1   PERG 8.4.2G.
2   PERG 8.4.3G.
3   PERG 8.4.4G.
4   PERG 8.4.5G.
5   PERG 8.4.6G.

(i)   Advertisements which invite contact with the advertiser are likely to be inducements.

(j)   'Introductions' as described in this part of PERG do not seem to be the same as the activity of 'introducing' as described in the Glossary and in COBS but rather mean 'an offer to make an introduction or action taken in response to an unsolicited request'. Introductions in this context may be inducements, but very much depends on the particular circumstances of each case.

(k)   Distributors of financial promotions which have been issued or approved by an authorised person are likely to be covered by the 'mere conduit' exemption in article 18 or article 18A of the FPO but will not be covered if they go further.

(l)   *Invitations to attend meetings or to receive telephone calls* will clearly be invitations or inducements. Whether this will be to engage in investment activity will depend on their purpose and content.

(m)   *Explanations of terms*, without more, will not be an invitation or inducement.

(n)   *Enquiries about a person's status* (eg whether or not they are a certified high net worth individual) or intentions (eg what they intend to do in respect of a takeover offer) will not in themselves be inducements to engage in investment activity.

(o)   *Solicited or accompanying material* which does not contain any invitation or inducement to engage in investment activity will not in itself be a financial promotion.

(p)   *Telephone services* will be inducements where a person seeks to persuade or incite the prospective customer to receive investment literature or a personal call or visit from a representative. However, if the services are purely reactive and contain no element of persuasion or incitement then they will not be financial promotions.

(q)   *Personal illustrations* on their own would not be an invitation or inducement.

(r)   *Instructions or guidance on how to invest* will not, in themselves, be inducements.

(s)   *Communications by employers to their employees* arises more often in the context of personal pensions and stakeholder schemes and these are covered by specific exemptions under the FPO. In the context of life assurance the employer will have to be careful that material produced by the authorised person is merely referred to by the employer in, for example, a covering letter which does not seek to persuade or incite employees into action. Otherwise it will need to be approved by an authorised person.

2 'In the course of business'

5.6   Under section 21(4) of the FSMA the Treasury has the power to specify the circumstances in which a person is viewed as 'acting in the course of business' or not as the case may be for financial promotion purposes. To date this power has not been exercised so it bears its ordinary or natural meaning[1].

'In the course of business' requires a commercial interest on the part of the communicator. The interest does not have to be direct nor does the communicator need to be carrying on regulated activities. It does not need to be part of the communicator's business. Nor does the communication need to be in the course of carrying on activities as a business in their own right. For individuals the position is slightly less clear although it is designed to exclude such things as conversations in the pub, letters or emails between family members, internet chat-rooms or bulletin boards for personal reasons. Persons who carry on a business which is not a regulated activity need to be particularly careful when making communications which may amount to financial promotions. Examples include financial promotions regarding employee share schemes, group-wide insurance arrangements and stakeholder pensions schemes although many will be covered by exemptions. If not so covered, approval by an authorised person is required.

3 'Communicate'

5.7   This is extended to include causing a communication to be made[2]. A person is communicating where he gives material to the recipient or where, in certain circumstances, he is responsible for transmitting the material on behalf of another person. The distinction between 'communicators' and 'causers' is not usually of great significance (both are subject to section 21). The important and more difficult point is whether a person is or is not causing a communication to be made by another. Primary responsibility rests with the originator. This person is responsible for its overall contents. Where a person other than the originator (such as a newspaper publisher) transmits a communication on the originator's behalf he is communicating it and the originator is causing the communication[3].

The FSA have indicated certain persons who they do not consider to be communicating or causing the communication as follows: (1) advertising and design agencies; (2) printers or producers of material; (3) professional advisers; (4) persons responsible for securing the placing of the advertisement[4]. In order to communicate a person must take an active step to make the communication. The FPO contains an exemption for 'mere conduits' in article 18. This will include (1) postal services providers; (2) telecommunication services providers; (3) broadcasting services providers; (4) courier services providers; (5) persons employed simply to hand out or disseminate communications; (6) newsagents

1   PERG 8.5.1G.
2   FSMA 2000, s 21(13).
3   PERG 8.6.1G.
4   PERG 8.6.3G.

selling newspapers and journals containing financial promotions[1]. Website operators providing links to other sites are not usually regarded as communicating the contents of those other sites[2]. An exemption will apply equally to a person causing a communication to be made as it does to the person communicating it[3]. Guidance on 'made to', 'directed at' and 'recipient' are set out in PERG 8.6.9G.

4   Exemptions

5.8   There are certain exemptions set out in the FPO *and* summarised in Table 3.2.5R and Annex 1G to COBS 3. Guidance on certain exemptions is also contained in PERG 8 (Financial Promotion and related activities).

Exemptions include:

(1)   Certain 'one-off' communications. This is largely (but not exclusively) aimed at correspondence which is specifically written to a particular individual, so mass mailshots would not be exempted. However, if a personal recommendation is made it will then be subject to other obligations such as know your customer and suitability requirements[4].

(2)   Personal quotations or illustrations[5].

(3)   'Image' advertising or advertising which is very general and which only contains one or more of the following: (a) name of the firm; (b) name of the investment; (c) a contact point (address (including email address), telephone or facsimile number); (d) a logo; (e) a brief factual description of the firm's activities, for example, 'life and pensions' and 'life assurance and pensions business'[6]; (f) a brief factual description of the firm's fees; (g) a brief factual description of the firm's investment products; (h) the price or yields of investments and the charges.

(4)   Communications such as Companies' report and accounts[7].

(5)   Financial promotions in newspapers, etc printed and published overseas which may be brought into the UK, provided that the financial promotion is not communicated to persons in the UK[8].

(6)   Financial promotions communicated only to 'market counterparties' or to 'intermediate customers'[9]. The firm must have taken reasonable steps to establish that the recipients fall into these categories or where the financial

---

1   PERG 8.6.5G.
2   PERG 8.6.6G.
3   PERG 8.6.7G.
4   COB 5.2 and COB 5.3, FPO articles 28 and 28A, COB 3.2.5R(4). See also the very detailed guidance in PERG 8.14.3–13G.
5   COB 3.2.5R(6).
6   COB 3.2.5R(5).
7   COB 3.2.5R(2) and COB 3.2.7G(4).
8   See also COB 3.3 and PERG 8.12.2G.
9   COB 3.2.5R(1).

promotion may reasonably be regarded as directed at such recipients. When a person is classified as an intermediate customer on the basis that he is an 'expert private customer'[1] the exemption only applies in respect of the designated investments or designated investment business for which he has been so classified[2]. With regard to 'sophisticated investors' for exemption under article 50 of the FPO the recipient of the financial promotion must have a current certificate from an authorised person stating that he has enough knowledge to understand the risks associated with the investment in question. The recipient must also have signed a statement in the terms of article 50(1)(b). Unsurprisingly, the financial promotion must not invite or induce the recipient to engage in investment activity with the person who has signed the certificate but, perhaps more surprisingly, this does not preclude associates or group members. Certain warnings must be given to the investor.

The second exemption in article 50A relates to financial promotions (non-real time and solicited real time) made to a person who the communicator believes on reasonable grounds to be a self-certified sophisticated investor (see PERG 8.14.28B). The exemption is extended to apply to associations of sophisticated investors by article 51.

(7) Communications to persons in the business of placing promotional material[3].

(8) Promotions in connection with listing applications, particulars and prospectuses[4].

(9) Certain financial promotions from outside of the UK[5].

(10) Financial promotions subject to the Takeover Code (or exempted from complying) or the requirements relating to takeovers or related operations in another EEA State[6].

(11) Decision trees for stakeholder pension schemes[7].

(12) Communications in connection with joint enterprises[8].

(13) Communications in respect of group personal pension schemes and stakeholder schemes offered by employers (article 72).

(14) Financial promotions made by a person in the course of his duties in an advice centre are exempted by article 73.

1 COB 4.1.9R.
2 COB 3.2.5R(1).
3 FPO article 38.
4 FPO articles 70–74.
5 COB 3.2.5R(3), FPO articles 30–33 and 36.
6 COB 3.2.5R(7).
7 COB 3.2.5R(8).
8 FPO article 39, PERG 8.14.19G.

D   Medium of financial promotions

5.9   Guidance[1] makes it clear that there is no restriction on what medium a financial promotion may appear in, so it includes printed advertising, personal visits, telephone calls, emails, the internet, pictures, films, radio or television programmes and other forms of electronic media such as digital and other forms of interactive television and media. Examples of financial promotions include product brochures; advertising in magazines, newspapers, radio and television programmes and websites; telemarketing activities; written correspondence, telephone calls and face-to-face discussions; sales aids; presentations, etc.

For the purposes of compliance approval prior to the communication of the financial promotion, a distinction is drawn between 'real time communications' and other types of communication. The former essentially refers to invitations or inducements made in the course of a personal visit, telephone calls or other interactive dialogue. 'Non-real time communications' includes financial promotions '… made by letter, email or contained in a newspaper, journal, magazine, other periodical publication, website, television or radio programme, or teletext service'[2]. Clearly 'includes' means that there could be other media.

E   Obligations of firms

5.10   Before a firm communicates or approves a non-real time financial promotion it must meet the requirements of the financial promotion rules[3].

If a firm becomes aware that the promotion no longer satisfies the financial promotion rules it must ensure that it is withdrawn as soon as reasonably practicable[4].

Confirmation that a financial promotion is compliant must be made by an individual with appropriate expertise, which can vary with the complexity of the financial promotion in question. This may even be undertaken by a third party but the responsibility remains with the firm[5].

Firms should monitor financial promotions so that they continue to be compliant, perhaps using 'review dates'. If found not to be compliant it should be withdrawn. If a firm becomes aware that a private customer may have been misled it should consider contacting them with a view to explaining the position and offering redress where appropriate[6].

Where another firm has confirmed compliance the firm communicating the promotion must take reasonable care to establish that the other firm has already confirmed such compliance. The communicating firm must take care to only communicate the promotion to the recipients it was intended for. The communicating firm must also be aware (or reasonably be aware) that the financial pro-

---

1   3.2.2G(1).
2   COB 3.5.5R.
3   3.6.1R.
4   3.6.3R.
5   COB 3.6.1R.
6   COB 3.6.4G.

189

motion has not ceased to be clear, fair and not misleading and that confirmation of compliance has not been withdrawn[1].

A firm must make an adequate record of each non-real time promotion which it has confirmed as complying with the financial promotion rules. In respect of life policies such record must be retained for at least six years[2]. Adequate records are likely to include information regarding the individual confirming compliance; date of confirmation (and approval where relevant); details of the medium and evidence supporting any material factual statement[3]. A firm should also retain a copy of the financial promotion as finally published or, if not practicable, then monitor the published version to ensure it is in substantially the same format as the complying version[4]. A record for the purposes of COB 3.7.4R may be in any form provided it is readily accessible for inspection by the FSA[5]. Records may be kept in such form as the firm chooses, eg hard copy, disk, tape. If the promotion is not in writing it should represent the actual financial promotion as accurately as possible. A record is 'readily accessible' if it is available for inspection within 48 hours of the request[6].

F Rules applying to the content of all non-real time communications

5.11 The name of the firm must be included (whether the firm communicates or approves the financial promotion). An address, or a contact point from which an address is available, must also be provided[7]. The name may be a trading name or shortened version of the legal name of the firm[8]. The 'contact point' may simply be the address or it may be an email address or telephone or facsimile number through which the customer can find out the address. Clearly, other legislation such as the Companies Act will also be relevant here (see further below at **4.28–4.36**).

It is not a requirement that financial promotions (except direct offer financial promotions) name the FSA as the regulator but if the firm chooses to do so and the financial promotion relates to matters which are not regulated by the FSA this fact must be made clear[9]. Under the 1986 regime details relating to the regulator were required on all except Category A advertisements.

The broad requirement of Rule 3.8.4R is that the promotion should be clear, fair and not misleading and these are concepts which permeate the whole of the FSA Handbook in respect of any form of customer communication. The firm must have taken reasonable steps to ensure this.

1 COB 3.6.5R.
2 COB 3.7.1R.
3 COB 3.7.2G.
4 COB 3.7.3G.
5 COB 3.7.4R.
6 COB 3.7.5G.
7 3.8.2R.
8 3.8.3G(1).
9 3.8.3G(3).

COB 3.8.4(2) is specifically concerned with comparisons or contrasts, so it is only possible to compare investments which meet the same needs or are intended for the same purpose. This can pose some difficulty of interpretation. Some people may, for example, use an instant access building society account for long-term savings and others may use it as a home for day-to-day income and expenditure. Generally, however, the more disparate the types of investment being compared the more difficult it probably is to justify the comparison. Comparisons must be objective and must not confuse the firm with other firms or with other firms' intellectual property or products or services. Comparisons must not discredit or denigrate competitors or take unfair advantage of another firm's reputation. Investments or services must not be presented as imitations or replicas of a competitor's investments or services. Where a comparison refers to a special offer then all the pertinent terms of that special offer must be mentioned.

If information relating to protection under the Financial Services Compensation Scheme or any other compensation scheme is mentioned this must be restricted to factual references[1].

G   Evidential provision

5.12   3.8.5E(1) requires accuracy in general, with specific reference to aspects which have been identified as of particular concern. It provides that the non-real time financial promotion:

(1)   does not disguise or misrepresent its promotional purpose (some advertisements, for example, appear to be part of the normal text of the publication in which they appear – known colloquially as 'advertorials');

(2)   does not contain any statement of fact, promise or prediction which is not clear, not fair or misleading and any relevant assumptions are disclosed;

(3)   does not contain a statement of opinion ('testimonial') held by any person which is not the honestly held opinion of that person and, unless consent is impracticable, it must be given with that person's consent;

(4)   must provide that the facts on which any comparison or contrast is made are verified, or that relevant assumptions are disclosed and that comparison or contrast is presented in a fair and balanced way, which is not misleading and includes all factors relevant to the comparison or contrast;

(5)   does not contain any false indication, in particular as to the firm's independence, the scarcity of any investment or service (for example, incorrectly representing that the investment is available in limited quantities or for a limited time) or the scale of activities or the resources available to the firm. For example, some firms have not always sufficiently differentiated the assets of the firm with the funds it has under management which are clearly two entirely different things.

---

1   COB 3.8.4R(3).

(6) The content, design or format of a promotion must not in any way disguise, obscure or diminish the significance of any statement, warning or other matter required to be included in it. For example, risk warnings should not be 'counterbalanced' by text which detracts from the impact of risk warnings or be hidden in 'small print'. Generally, risk warnings must be sufficiently prominent. Risk warnings should be appropriately placed in context and in a typeface comparable with the statements which they are intended to balance. An example of counterbalancing would be a statement such as 'past performance is not a guide to the future, but it is usually the best measure you have of a fund's likelihood of achieving its objectives (or similar)'.

The question of 'balance' is a constant source of difficulty for marketing departments. It can be a very subjective issue which in practice is not assisted by the competing commercial and compliance pressures. Where benefits or positive features of products are stated then, in general, this should be followed reasonably closely by relevant risks.

(7) Promotions must not contain any statement or implication that the promotion is approved by the FSA or any government body unless such approval has been obtained in writing from the FSA or that body[1].

(8) The financial promotion must also not omit matters which no longer render it clear, fair and not misleading.

(9) The accuracy of all statements of fact must be capable of substantiation.

5.13   COB 3.8.7G contains guidance on the important 'clear, fair and not misleading' requirement. 3.8.7G(1) explains that recipients will not necessarily have an understanding of the investment being promoted and so the use of ambiguous terms or the targeting of an audience which is unlikely to understand the promotion are relevant factors in deciding whether the promotion is 'clear, fair and not misleading'. The firm must make it clear if it is directing a promotion at a specific collection of individuals who are reasonably believed to have relevant specialist knowledge.

Also, where an investment is described as being 'guaranteed' the general rule (and indeed the strict legal meaning) is that this term may only be used if there is a legally enforceable arrangement with a third party to meet the customer's claim in full. However, this provision is specifically excluded in the case of life policies providing guaranteed benefits[2]. This represents a relaxation for life policies but questions still arise in view of the fact that 'guaranteed' in connection with life policy benefits is not defined. Presumably, it is intended to mean 'fixed' or 'definite'.

A useful list of examples is set out at 3.8.7G(3) which suggest that a financial promotion does not meet the general requirement of being clear, fair and not misleading. So far as life assurance is concerned these are as follows:

1   3.8.5E(1)(g).
2   3.8.7G(2).

(i)   a statement such as 'no initial charges' or 'no entry or redemption charges' where, for unit-linked policies, the 'bid' and 'offer' (selling and buying) prices of units are different;

(ii)   a statement of a company's assets without also stating its liabilities or a statement of its total costs, or income or turnover, without making it clear the period to which the statement relates;

(iii)   an implication that the assets of the whole group can be drawn on by a subsidiary when this is not the case;

(iv)   a statement of the amount of authorised share capital of a company without the amount of the issued share capital.

In direct marketing in particular the use of quotes or testimonials in support of the firm's products is quite common. Therefore, a promotion must not quote anything said or written by anyone, unless:

(1)   where only part of the opinion is quoted, it should still be a fair representation;

(2)   any relevant connection of the holder of the opinion to the firm is made clear.

Also, the 'return' on an investment is the gain or profit. The original capital invested is not included[1].

5.14   Some of the following examples will hopefully provide a flavour of the issues arising in deciding whether or not a financial promotion is 'clear, fair and not misleading':

(i)   Use of the term 'unique'. In order to be unique the subject must be 'without a like'. This is a demanding test which on a more thorough analysis is often not found to be the case.

(ii)   Sometimes the wording of promotions can be construed as advice or a 'personal recommendation'. Clearly, for an anonymous financial promotion wording of this nature should not be used.

(iii)   Use of the term 'free'. Some promotions state that the first premium is 'free'. In the sense that no payment is actually made at the time then this is correct. However, it may be that the loss to the life office in offering the first premium for free is recouped by a corresponding increase to subsequent premiums in which case the original statement may not now appear so correct.

(iv)   Use of term 'affordable' in relation to premiums. This can be difficult in that the financial circumstances of all recipients is not necessarily known. It may be that if the life office had conducted research into the premium

---

1   COB 3.8.7(5)G.

level(s) in question which had revealed that the premium level was thought to be affordable then this might be acceptable evidence to support such a statement.

(v)   Directive nature of promotions. Especially for more vulnerable customers language which urges action may go beyond what is reasonable especially if it appears in official sounding language.

(vi) Audience. Some promotions may be appropriate for advisers or experienced investors but would not be for less sophisticated readers.

(vii) Popularity rather than 'needs'. Some promotions focus on the fact that a product has been taken out by many other customers rather than the financial needs it meets for those customers. The fact that a product may be popular should not be a prime factor upon which it is marketed.

(viii) Use of false 'close-by' dates. Dates up to which a product is available should not be artificial (in order to encourage action) or there should at least be a warning that the offer may be repeated. There may, of course, be genuine reasons for close dates, eg, birthdays may pass (so premiums may increase) or mailing lists acquired from third parties may only be available for a certain time.

H   Rules applying to financial promotions which identify and promote specific investments ('specific non-real time financial promotion')

5.15   Rules 3.8.8 to 3.8.25 set out the provisions applying to advertisements which 'identify and promote' specific investments.

The mere mentioning of the name of the investment does not in itself constitute its promotion, and so is not covered by this section of the rules. The provisions of these rules are in addition to the requirements in Rules 3.8.1 to 3.8.7. A financial promotion which identifies and promotes a specific investment must include a fair and adequate description of the nature of the investment(s) and the financial commitment and risks involved[1]. Also, if the person issuing or approving the financial promotion is different, the name of the provider whose product or service is being promoted must also be included[2].

Guidance indicates that financial promotions should give a fair and balanced indication of the requirements outlined in the previous paragraph. The details of the financial commitment required will depend on the nature of the investment. Therefore, it could refer to the minimum amount to be invested and for regular payments the time over which such payments must be made. It may also refer to minimum or maximum periods of investment or, if relevant, that it could be some time before the customer may see a return on the investment. Firms should avoid emphasising the potential benefits of an investment without also fairly indicating the risks (ie the presentation must be 'balanced').

1   3.8.8R(1).
2   COB 3.8.8R(2).

Firms should describe the benefits under a policy which are not fixed. In addition, it should not draw attention to favourable tax treatment without mentioning that this might not continue. Past performance should not be over-emphasised and prominent headline rates of return should not be used where these are unrealistic or unlikely to be obtained by most investors[1].

Where there is a possibility of loss of initial capital invested this must be identified and disclosed as one of the main points of the promotion[2].

5.16   A financial promotion which gives information about past performance of an investment or of a firm must include[3]:

(1) Suitable text which states unambiguously and without reservation that past performance should not be seen as an indication of future performance. It must be specifically designed for that type of financial promotion and its target audience and must be presented legibly in the main text of the financial promotion.

(2) Information relating to a relevant and sufficient period of past performance to provide a fair and balanced indication of the performance.

The stated purpose of these provisions is to prevent an investment being promoted so as to induce a customer to believe that previous favourable performance will necessarily be repeated, especially where investment conditions have changed, and to encourage firms to draft warnings designed to be appropriate to both the financial promotion and the target audience. Risk warnings have been largely presented to date in a highly uniform manner so that it is feared that their impact has been reduced.

Despite indications that the FSA may ban past performance information completely around the time of the introduction of the FSMA 2000 this did not happen although there has been a considerable tightening up of the rules in this area.

3.8.12G(2) indicates that any of the following may mean that a financial promotion does not meet the 'clear, fair and not misleading' criteria:

(a) an unfair comparison of performance with other types of investments;

(b) the use of an inappropriate or irrelevant investment period;

(c) the use of an unreasonably short time period;

(d) the use of inconsistent time periods for a range of funds;

(e) if a comparison is made with bank or building society accounts, the fact that unlike a bank or building society account the capital value is not secure should be equally prominent. In addition, the ease of access of building society accounts should also be mentioned (where relevant).

1 3.8.9G(1) to (3).
2 COB 3.8.9(7)G.
3 3.8.11.

5.17 It is possible to give past performance information relating to a conventional with-profits contract in connection with a unitised with-profits contract but the differences between the two systems and factors reducing the relevance of the past performance, including differences in bonus policy and the level of charges and expenses, should be clearly explained[1]. The position on information relating to euro-based information is also touched upon with the need for firms to look carefully at how such information is presented[2].

Where past performance information is designed to be used over a period of time the following should be made clear:

(a) the period of time over which the information relates;

(b) the fact that the information may not be current (if relevant) and where information on up-to-date past performance information may be found (again if relevant)[3].

If past performance information is presented over several pages, for example, in a brochure or over the internet, the past performance warning required by COB 3.8.11R(1) must be included on every page on which past performance information is presented.

A firm may only use hypothetical past performance where actual past performance information does not exist and the result is clear, fair and not misleading. Past performance information based wholly on hypothetical past performance is only possible where it relates to a fund which has never been actively managed (such as 'tracker' funds) and where the actual existence of such a fund would not have influenced the prices on the relevant markets[4].

For a unit-linked life policy (but not a unitised with-profits life policy) where past performance is referred to there must also be 'standardised past performance information' presented in accordance with the Table at COB 3.8.13AR[5]. Single pricing should be used or, if unavailable, the bid to bid prices, unless the firm has reasonable grounds to be satisfied that another basis would better reflect the past performance[6].

5.18 If reference is made to an actual return, or a comparison of performance is made with other investments, the reference or comparison must be on an 'offer to bid' basis (ie what the investment was bought at compared to what it was sold at), or if a comparison is made with performance of an index (for example the FT-SE index) or with movements in the price of units, any of the 'offer to offer' or 'bid to bid' or 'offer to bid' bases may be used (the relevant basis should be stated) or, if appropriate, on a single pricing basis with allowance for charges[7].

1 3.8.12G(4).
2 3.8.12G(3).
3 COB 3.8.12(5)G.
4 COB 3.8.12(7), (8)G.
5 COB 3.8.13AR.
6 COB 3.8.13R(4).
7 COB 3.8.14G(1).

The standardised past performance information required by COB 3.8.13R(1) must be no less prominent than any other past performance information. Past performance information can only be used if such information exists for the previous 12 months (this includes where hypothetical past performance information is to be included)[1].

If the pricing policy of an investment has changed the prices used to comply with COB 3.8.13R should include all necessary adjustments to remove distortions resulting from the pricing method. In addition, where the performance relates to a different investment vehicle then any material differences should be stated[2].

Past performance information must not be presented to suggest that it is a projection of future investment values or that a similar return will be achieved in the future[3].

The FSA will take into account the way in which past performance information is presented, how it is positioned and the accompanying wording when determining whether COB 3.8.15R has been satisfied. Paragraph headings and the positioning of information can sometimes contribute to an overall impression that past performance and future prospects are linked[4].

I   COB 3 Annex 4: Additional guidance on particular types of financial promotion

5.19   Additional guidance which, so far as life assurance is concerned, relates to the following areas.

I   'High income' products

5.20   The regulator, whether this has been LAUTRO, PIA or the FSA, have on several occasions expressed concerns about the advertising of so-called 'high income' products. The crux of the problem is the fact that, with regard to single premium insurance bonds (or indeed any life assurance product), the 'income' in question is technically a withdrawal of capital, so that the capital sum represented by the investment is thereby eroded, the danger being that this could become worth less than the amount originally invested where investment performance does not compensate for such withdrawals.

For life assurance products (and in spite of the implications in much marketing material produced by life offices) it is not possible for an income to be produced in the established legal and taxation sense of the word. A life assurance policy is a non-income producing asset although it is possible for beneficiaries under a trust of such a policy to have an interest in possession for inheritance tax purposes on the basis that if it did produce income then it would have been payable to the beneficiary or beneficiaries in question (see Chapter 13).

1   COB 3.8.13R(2).
2   COB 3.8.14G(2), (3).
3   COB 3.8.15R(1), (2).
4   COB 3.8.16G.

The confusion has been exacerbated by virtue of the fact that some life office investments (eg so-called 'distribution bonds') have been structured so that they pay out the amount of income earned by the underlying fund investments. Nevertheless, these would still be capital payments from the policy.

The FSA have therefore stated in COB 3 Annex 4 that if the term 'income' is used, it will be difficult for the promotion to avoid being misleading unless it is used to indicate payments which are solely interest or dividend earnings (which, as mentioned, is not possible for life assurance policies but would be for unit trusts and open-ended investment companies) or 'income' is clearly defined at an early point as having a different meaning, and in particular specifies the risk to capital necessary to achieve the payment.

If the rate of income available is at some capital risk or at the expense of growth, or the income or some of it comprises a return of capital, this must be clearly explained.

Where an 'income' is guaranteed but the capital is not there should be a clear statement where the relevant benefits are not guaranteed, or no benefits are guaranteed.

2   With-profits bonds

5.21   LAUTRO Enforcement Bulletin No 15, amongst other matters, addressed the issue of the marketing of with-profits bonds. Concern was expressed in several areas, including failure to emphasise the fact that such bonds were not suitable for short-term investment; unclear statements as to the factors which determine the cash-in value of the bond; reserving the right to adjust the encashment value without adequately explaining the significance or likelihood of such a procedure (generally referred to now as the 'market value reduction' by life offices) and using a bonus rate implying that this rate will necessarily apply throughout the term of the investment.

The FSA have reiterated these concerns in COB 3 Annex 4. In particular they have pointed to the quotation of values based on existing bonus rates to lead customers to anticipate receiving such amounts as being a problem area. They have also pointed to references to building society accounts in comparison to such bonds without adequately explaining the difference between the two.

Quoting high initial bonus rates has historically been a commonly used marketing tool. However, the FSA have identified that such rates may only be available for customers who make a sizeable or early investment. In addition, bonus rate may be affected by a variety of charges and market value reduction factors so it should be made clear that such bonus rates may not actually be achievable.

3   'Hybrid bonds'

5.22   Concern was again originally expressed by LAUTRO in this connection in Enforcement Bulletin No 6 (and best advice considerations were addressed by the Personal Investment Authority in Regulatory Update 16 relating to the fact that there are two elements to such a product which may be better obtained from separate providers). Generally, hybrid bonds are lump sum life assurance arrangements which divide the investor's investment into two parts. The first is used to provide a high 'guaranteed income' for a limited period. This is achieved by means of an annuity.

The second part is invested, for example, in a unit-linked life investment bond with the objective of restoring over a similar period the total amount of capital originally invested. LAUTRO identified four interconnected problems:

(1)   The use of the word 'income' with regard to the annuity part is not entirely correct as the major part of the payment comprises a return of the capital itself.

(2)   Whilst 'income' may be guaranteed the original capital is not similarly guaranteed.

(3)   In order to seek to replace the first part over a reasonably short time span the second part is invested in investment vehicles with a considerable risk of loss.

(4)   Although most of the investor's capital is invested in the second part, the 'income' provided by the first part is given by far the greater prominence. This gives an unbalanced picture of the product and the balance of risk of the investment as a whole.

LAUTRO therefore issued guidance in respect of hybrid bonds or similar products which has been substantially reiterated in Annex 4 G I of COBS. In particular, the description of 'income' where this is provided out of capital and that capital is vulnerable to varying degrees of risk exposure needs careful attention. The presentation should not over-emphasise one component part of the plan as against another where this is disproportionate to the amount of investor's capital which goes into it.

The use, size and prominence of the word 'income', together with associated graphics, figures or the word 'guaranteed' must not distract from the overall makeup of the product and the overall risks. In this context the use of a product which uses the words 'guaranteed' or 'income' should be avoided. Unless payments are generally comprised of solely interest and/or dividend earnings, the use of the word 'income' to describe such payment should be avoided altogether – unless 'income' is specifically and clearly defined elsewhere in the advertisement.

4   'Stock market products'

5.23   Generally, in the context of life assurance such products are single premium investment bonds under which the investor is offered the growth potential of a stock market or other index. The guarantee is that some, or all, of the original capital sum invested will be protected against the volatility of the relevant market by a guaranteed minimum payment at the end of the specified term. Six interconnected issues were originally identified and these have been substantially reiterated and added to by COBS Annex 4G as follows:

(1) *Minimum amount payable at end of term*. The word 'guarantee' is usually used but this is at some cost to the investor and so it must be made clear what that cost is and when it is levied.

(2) *Growth potential*. Expressions such as 'stock market growth' or 'the growth of the FT-SE Index' are often used and may be misleading because the underlying investments do not wholly reflect the stocks which make up the index. Advertisements for products linked to growth in the FT-SE 100 Index should also make it clear that this index does not include an allowance for any return or reinvestment of dividend income.

(3) *Amount invested*. Advertisements which quote returns in excess of the percentage increase in the FT-SE 100 and which do not mention that there will not be a full 100% allocation of capital invested will be misleading unless there is a full explanation regarding the allocation rate (where less than 100%).

(4) *Gross returns and tax on underlying fund*. Advertisements showing guaranteed returns against the FT-SE 100 expressed in 'gross' terms are potentially misleading where the underlying funds are taxable and so a gross return is thus unavailable to the investor. Only advertisements showing the net position after tax has been levied should be shown.

(5) *Taxation of investors*. The tax treatment of the investment in the investor's hands should be made clear.

(6) *Early encashment*. The consequences need to be fully explained. Where there is a minimum return an appropriate risk warning should be included where the value of the investment can fall on early encashment.

(7) *Averaging*. Sometimes the value of the contract is based on an average level of the index over a certain time period. The FSA state that this will reduce the investment potential of the contract. Where the averaging covers more than six months then it should not be implied that averaging is to protect against falls at the end of the term. It should be made clear that investors only benefit from some of the performance of the index and that one effect of averaging is likely to constrain the final level of the index used to calculate benefits.

(8) *Maximum benefits*. These should not be promoted as a particular feature if the economic circumstances required to meet such benefits are in excess of the higher of the growth assumptions specified by the FSA.

5 *'Guaranteed or protected products'*

5.24 These are not specifically defined in COB 3 Annex 4 but in most cases it should be clear whether or not a life policy falls within the classification.

(a) Equal prominence should be given to both guaranteed and non-guaranteed benefits.

(b) Guaranteed income but not capital – (a) clear statement where relevant benefits are not guaranteed, (b) name of guarantor (if any), (c) an equivalent annualised rate of return should be quoted if the cash rate is quoted.

(c) If relevant the words 'guarantee', 'protected element' or similar may be used to describe the minimum amount payable at the end of the term. If there is a cost to the investor in doing this the amount of that cost and how it is imposed must be made clear.

(d) Explanation of any risk of counterparty failure.

J Overseas insurers' advertisements

5.25   There are specific provisions in the rules relating to financial promotions of non-UK authorised insurers. Certain statements are required depending on whether or not the insurer is named in the advertisement.

For all overseas life insurers (which do not have an establishment in the UK) it is necessary to state the full name, country of registration and, if different, where the head office of the insurer is situated. It is also necessary to give a prescribed warning about the Financial Services Compensation Scheme not applying. Also, where any trustee, investment manager or UK agent of the overseas life office is named which is not independent of the overseas life office, there must be a prominent statement of that fact[1].

In addition, where the overseas life insurer is authorised in Jersey, Guernsey, the Isle of Man, the Commonwealth of Pennsylvania or the State of Iowa it is additionally necessary to give the full name, principal address and registered office, if different, of any trustee of any property held by the overseas life office in respect of the promoted contracts or, if relevant, as the above-mentioned details regarding any external investment manager used in relation to such property. It is also necessary to give details of any UK agent of the overseas life insurer[2].

Where the insurer is not named in the financial promotion (which would only seem possible where the overseas life office has some sort of establishment in the United Kingdom[3]) then there is a required statement to make it clear that the advertisement relates to an insurance contract of a non-UK supervised insurer, which is not subject to the supervision of the Financial Services Authority and that the policies issued will not be protected by the Financial Services Compensation Scheme and that there is no right of complaint to the Financial Ombudsman Service[4].

The rules provide further that the above-mentioned statements must be prominent and must be stated immediately after or alongside the full name of the insurer or the most prominent mention (or if two or more mentions are equally prominent then the first mention) if the full name appears more than once[5].

1   3.13.2R.
2   3.13.3R.
3   See COB 3.13.2R which requires the full name of the insurer where no establishment in the UK.
4   3.13.4R.
5   COB 3.13.5G.

K Rules which apply to direct offer financial promotions: 'off the page' advertisements[1]

5.26 A direct offer financial promotion is defined as 'a non-real time financial promotion which contains:

(i) an offer by the firm to enter into a 'controlled agreement' with anyone who responds to the financial promotion; or

(ii) an invitation to anyone who responds to the financial promotion to make an offer to the firm to enter into a controlled agreement; and

(iii) specifies the manner of response or includes a form in which any response is to be made (for example, by providing a tear-off slip).

The provisions at 3.9 are additional to the provisions at 3.8.1 to 3.8.20AR.

Direct offer financial promotions for life policies must contain key features information[2] and this should generally be given in the same order and format as that required by 6.5[3] unless, for example, a rearrangement would assist customer understanding.

Where investments, or income distributions, can fluctuate in value, this must be made clear to the target audience[4] and set out with due prominence and in print size no smaller than that used in the main text[5]. This information should normally be set out in the main body of the promotion. If in a separate 'stand-alone' statement (which is likely to be a rare occurrence) firms should satisfy themselves on reasonable grounds that this is likely to offer the best prospect of it being seen and read and should record such reasons for the purposes of the record-keeping requirements set out in COB 3.7[6]. Some of the explanations relevant to life policies which could meet 3.9.15 are[7]:

(i) 'You are not certain to make a profit; you may lose money/make a loss';

(ii) 'You may not get back the full amount of your investment';

(iii) (for investment income): 'The income is not fixed – it can go up or down';

(iv) (for property funds): 'This fund invests in property and land. This can be difficult to sell – so you may not be able to sell/cash in this investment when you want to. We may have to delay acting on your instructions to sell your investment' and 'The value of property is generally a matter of valuer's opinion rather than fact';

1   COB 3.9.10R.
2   3.9.8R(1).
3   3.9.11G.
4   3.9.15R.
5   3.9.15(2).
6   3.9.16G.
7   3.9.17G.

(v) (for front end loaded contracts): 'We take most of our charges in the early years of this investment. This means that if you withdraw during this time you may lose money/get back less than you invested'. It is submitted that this particular guidance is not worded entirely satisfactorily as it could be implied that money will not be lost after this period on withdrawal which may not, of course, be the case;

(vi) (for with-profits policies): 'The value of this policy depends on how much profit we make and how we decide to distribute this profit'.

Direct offer financial promotions in respect of life policies must state which benefits (if any) are fixed, and what those amounts are, and which benefits are not fixed[1].

5.27 A summary of the taxation position of the investment and for investors is also required for direct offer financial promotions[2]. Specifically, this must include a warning that taxation levels, bases and (if relevant) reliefs can change; assumed rate of taxation; and (where taxation reliefs are mentioned) statements distinguishing between reliefs which apply directly to investors and those which apply to anyone else (for example, the underlying funds); that the reliefs are those which currently apply; that the value of the relief depends on the circumstances of the investor. For example, the fact that the proceeds on maturity of a qualifying endowment policy are tax-free for a higher rate taxpayer means that this is more valuable to him than to someone who is a non-taxpayer or who pays tax at the lower rate(s)[3].

Where the words 'free from tax liability' (or similar) are used then, if relevant, a statement with equal prominence is required that this only describes the benefits paid to the customer and there must be a statement of equal prominence that the benefits are payable out of a fund which has already paid income tax, capital gains tax or corporation tax (as relevant)[4].

L Other provisions relating to financial promotions

5.28 COBS itself recognises that firms may be subject to 'other regulations and guidelines'. The examples given in 3.5.3G which could be relevant to life assurance are the codes issued by the Advertising Standards Authority, Office of Communications ('OFCOM') (the independent regulator and competition authority for the UK communications industries); regulations of an overseas regulator and the Privacy and Electronic Communications (EC Directive) Regulations[5]. There are, of course many others and some of the provisions are considered below.

1   3.9.18R.
2   3.9.19R.
3   3.9.20.
4   3.9.20(4).
5   SI 2003/2426.

I   Advertising Standards Authority ('ASA')

5.29   The ASA Code applies to a wide range of advertising and advertising media and not just that relating to financial services or life assurance. The Codes do not have the force of law but are designed to work within and complement the legal controls which affect advertising. All advertisements are required by the code to be 'legal, decent, honest and truthful'.

In many cases the provisions of the ASA Code will be satisfied by adherence to the financial promotion rules issued by the FSA. However, it is still important to bear in mind the ASA Code when considering issuing advertisements. For example, 13.1 to 13.5 of the Code relates to 'Protection of privacy' so that advertisers should obtain written permission in advance if they refer to individuals or their identifiable possessions in any advertisement. Advertisers who have not obtained prior permission from those with a high public profile should ensure that they are not portrayed in an offensive or adverse way, and advertisements should not imply an endorsement where none exists. References to members of the royal family are not normally permitted.

The Committee of Advertising Practice (CAP) devises, reviews and amends the Code, gives advice and provides information. The purpose of the ASA is to provide independent scrutiny of the system, to identify and resolve problems and investigate complaints and to ensure that the system operates in the public interest. The ASA is a limited company, and independent of both the government and the advertising business. In the event of the ASA upholding a complaint it may ask that the advertisement be withdrawn or amended. Adjudications and editorial guidance are published in a monthly report which is distributed free of charge.

Complaints are also investigated free of charge. They should be in writing and accompanied by a copy of the advertisement or a note of where and when it appeared. Complainants are not identified by the ASA without permission (unless required to do so by a competent court) and complainants are encouraged to resolve differences with advertisers wherever possible. Complainants will be asked to assure the ASA that they have no commercial or other interest in registering a complaint. Complaints are not normally pursued where there is a simultaneous legal action. The Secretariat of the ASA and CAP will conduct a fact-finding investigation into those complaints which are pursued and will produce a recommendation to the ASA Council based on its findings. Such recommendations can be reviewed by the appropriate Review Panel. The final decision on complaints rests with the Council. Advertisers may be asked to take interim action. Appeals against ASA adjudications are made in writing to the ASA's chairman and they should be accompanied by new evidence or demonstrate a substantial flaw in the conclusion reached by the ASA Council.

5.30   The principle sanctions for breach of the codes are as follows:

(1)   the media may deny access to space;

(2)   adverse publicity may result;

(3)   trading sanctions may be imposed or recognition revoked by the advertiser's professional association;

(4)   financial incentives provided by trade, professional or media organisations may be withdrawn; and

(5)   under the Control of Misleading Advertisements Regulations 1988[1], if an advertisement continues to appear after the Council has ruled against it, the ASA can refer the matter to the Director General of Fair Trading which can ask for an undertaking that it will be discontinued. If not given or not honoured the Office of Fair Trading can seek an injunction. Any defaults may be a contempt of court and punishable accordingly.

Since November 2004, the ASA have also had responsibility for regulating broadcast advertising under a delegation arrangement with OFCOM.

2   Consumer Credit Act 1974 (as amended by Consumer Credit Act 2006)

5.31   The effects of this Act on marketing activities of life offices is very limited but may apply, for example, to advertising loans against the security of life policies.

3   Companies Acts

5.32   In connection with communications from life offices the provisions of these acts require certain basic details on all business letters, in all notices and other official publications and certain other items such as invoices, receipts, promissory notes and cheques[2]. 'Limited company' may be abbreviated to 'Ltd' and 'public limited company' may be shortened to 'plc'[3]. Every company must also have the following particulars in all business letters and order forms which, it could be argued, might also include proposal/application forms. These requirements are (so far as life offices are concerned) (a) company's place and number of registration; (b) the address of its registered office. The Companies (Registrar, Languages and Trading Disclosures) Regulations 2006[4], which came into force on 1 January 2007, extended these existing disclosure requirements to cover documents in electronic form and specifically extend to all of a company's websites.

4   Forgery and Counterfeiting Act 1981

5.33   In some financial promotions the advertiser wishes to represent bank notes for marketing purposes. Section 18(1) of this Act requires the prior consent of the Bank of England for the reproduction of bank notes. The Bank of England also owns the copyright in its notes. If the Bank gives permission it will restrict what type of images can be shown in advertising literature in terms of size and the angle from which the note is viewed. See also the Coinage Act 1971.

---

1   SI 1988/915.
2   Companies Act 1985, s 349(1).
3   Companies Act 1985, s 27(2).
4   SI 2006/3429.

5 Intellectual property rights

5.34   Life offices need to be aware of issues relating to 'passing off', copyright and trademarks. Regarding 'passing off' the life office must ensure that the product being advertised is sufficiently differentiated from others such that the public does not confuse the product with one issued by another provider[1]. The basis upon which a 'passing off' action is pursued is that the complainant party has lost the customer because the latter is misled by the representations of a competitor. Copyright is the right given against the copying of defined types of productions and it is feasible that this could extend to marketing literature. Generally, life office logos and emblems would also be registered as trademarks.

With regard to comparative advertising care needs to be exercised in connection with displaying other companies' logos as this will often involve displaying another advertiser's registered trademarks, although relief may be obtained via section 10(6) of the Trade Marks Act 1994.

6 Libel

5.35   Whilst reasonable comparison and criticism is possible the life office must ensure that it does not go too far and unfairly criticise other product providers (or any other person mentioned in advertising literature).

7 Gambling Act 2005 (replacing the Lotteries and Amusements Act 1976)

5.36   Life offices may seek to encourage greater response to advertisements by incorporating prize draws or competitions. It should be borne in mind that this area is subject to its own detailed regulation. As a general rule (and subject to certain other limited exceptions) prize draws will be illegal unless the entrant does not provide any consideration for the entry. What constitutes 'consideration' can be difficult to ascertain. Clearly, an entry fee would be consideration but the position regarding, for example, commercial information, such as an entrant's details, may not be so clear although Schedule 2 to the Gambling Act 2005 ('Definition of Payment to Enter') has clarified this to some extent.

8 Consumer pressure

5.37   Consumer pressure can come from various sources, such as the Consumers Association (publishers of Which? magazine), newspaper campaigns, from groups of disgruntled policyholders forming themselves in to action groups, etc. Life offices will often be affected in their decisions and activities in such cases although, of course, much will depend on the life office's own interpretation of the facts and events. The issues and problems arising from endowment mis-selling in the 1990s saw a proliferation of consumer pressure groups[2].

---

1   See *Reddaway v Banham* [1896] AC 199.
2   See 'Restoring confidence in long-term savings: Endowment mortgages' House of Commons Treasury Committee, 25 February 2004.

9   Consistency between policy and marketing literature

5.38   With the increasing complexity and volume of the literature which accompanies life policies (for example, brochures, sales aids, flyers, key features documents, etc) the chances of information in those documents being inconsistent with the policy document will invariably increase. Life offices should seek to ensure consistency. As well as being fair to customers this will tend to protect their own positions.

M   'Real time communications'

5.39   Essentially this relates to personal visits, telephone calls and other interactive dialogue and specifically to an 'invitation or inducement' communicated by an individual during such real time communication. They may be solicited or unsolicited. The former being where there is an 'express request' by the recipient or was initiated by the recipient. There is no such express invitation where the person has simply omitted to indicate that he does not wish to receive a communication or further communication or by reason of agreeing to standard terms that indicate such communications will be made. If a real time communication is solicited by one person it is treated as having been solicited by any other person to whom it is made at the same time if that person is a close relative or is expected to engage in any investment activity jointly with the person who initially solicited the communication[1].

Guidance on what constitutes a real time financial promotion is contained in PERG 8.10.1G to 7G and on what constitutes 'solicited' and 'unsolicited' real time financial promotions is contained in PERG 8.10.8G to 14G.

Firms are unable to communicate unsolicited real time communications other than in respect of 'controlled investments' which are 'readily realisable securities' (except warrants) or generally marketable non-geared packaged products (which includes life policies) or where there is an existing customer relationship where the customer envisages receiving unsolicited real time financial promotions[2].

5.40   Broadly, the requirements are that communications must be clear, fair and not misleading; claims must not be untrue; the purpose of the communication must be made clear at the outset and the caller must identify himself and the firm he represents. Unless the time and method of communication were previously agreed he must check that the customer wishes him to communicate and terminate the communication if the customer does not wish him to proceed (but he may ask for another appointment). He must recognise and respect (promptly) the customer's right to end the call at any time and to refuse a request for another appointment. The customer must be given a contact point. Communication with the customer is not permitted at an unsocial hour, unless previously agreed, and

---

1   COB 3.10.1R(4).
2   COB 3.10.3R.

is not permitted via an unlisted telephone number (unless previously agreed). The caller must act in conformity with any applicable status disclosure requirements. The above requirements do not prevent a call centre which has received a call from a customer at an unsocial hour, either responding to that call or asking during such a call if the customer would like details of other investment products[1]. An unsocial hour usually means on a Sunday or before 9am or after 9pm on any other day. It could mean other days if the firm knows that a recipient would not want to be called then, for example, because of religious faith or night shift working[2].

SYSC 3.2.20R (Records) requires a firm to take reasonable care regarding making and keeping records. For a telemarketing campaign those records should include copies of any scripts used[3].

I   Miscellaneous obligations regarding financial promotions

5.41   COB 3.6 sets out the requirements for confirmation of compliance of financial promotions before issue. A firm must arrange for the confirmation required by 3.6.2R(1) to be carried out by an individual with 'appropriate expertise'. This can involve different people of different levels of expertise depending on the complexity of the financial promotion and the product in question. A record of the complying financial promotion must be retained for six years in the case of a life policy[4]. This record must contain the name of the individual confirming the compliance, the date of such confirmation or approval, a copy of the final proof version (if applicable), details of the medium involved and evidence supporting any factual statements[5]. A firm should retain a copy of the promotion as finally published (if practicable) otherwise it must monitor the published version to verify that it is substantially in the same format which was confirmed as compliant. Such records may be kept in such form as the firm chooses (hard copy, disk or tape) provided it is readily accessible for inspection by the FSA. If the financial promotion is not in a written form the record should represent the actual financial promotion as accurately as possible[6].

A firm may approve a financial promotion for an overseas person who does not have permission provided it makes it clear which firm has confirmed it as compliant. The financial promotion must also make clear (as appropriate) the extent to which the customer protection rules apply, that the Financial Services Compensation Scheme may not be available or only available to an extent, although references to another protection or compensation scheme may be included. The firm must have no reason to doubt that the overseas person will not 'deal with customers in the UK in an honest and reliable way'[7].

1   3.8.24G(3).
2   COB 3.8.23G.
3   COB 3.8.25G.
4   3.7.1R.
5   3.7.2G.
6   3.7.3G.
7   3.12.1R.

2   Internet and electronic media

5.42   COBS recognises that the rapid recent emergence of 'e-commerce' raises its own issues in the area of financial promotion and has provided guidance in this respect.

N   The Financial Services and Markets Act 2000 (Financial Promotion) Order 2005 ('FPO')

5.43   This statutory instrument specifies the controlled activities and controlled investments for the purposes of section 21 of FSMA 2000. It revoked and re-enacted the eponymous Order of 2001 with a few relatively minor amendments. Much of the Order is concerned with setting out the provisions relating to exemptions from the restrictions on financial promotions. The FPO (of 2005) has itself been subject to numerous, mainly minor, amendment orders.

Schedule 1 sets out the controlled activities which include the following which are of particular relevance to life assurance: effecting and carrying out contracts of insurance; arranging deals in investments, advising on investments and managing investments. Controlled investments includes 'rights under a contract of insurance'.

Part IV of the Order sets out those exemptions which apply to communication relating to all types of controlled activity. Guidance in this respect is set out in PERG 8.12. These are as follows:

(i)   Article 12: Communications to overseas recipients, or which are directed only at persons outside the UK. (This is subject to certain conditions, for example, the financial promotion is not referred to in or directly accessible from another communication which is itself made or directed at persons in the UK by the overseas person who is directing it and there are proper systems and procedures in place to prevent recipients in the UK from engaging in the investment activity to which the financial promotion relates.) There is no definition of 'proper systems and procedures' essentially because it is recognised that these may take many different forms depending on the precise circumstances.

(ii)   Article 13: Communications from customers and potential customers (only relevant to corporate customers or others acting in the course of business. Other types of customer will not be subject to section 21 at all).

(iii)   Article 14: Certain follow up non-real time communications and solicited real time communications.

(iv)   Article 15: Certain introductions to authorised or exempt persons.

(v)   Article 16: Communications from exempt persons.

(vi)   Article 17: Generic promotions which do not identify (directly or indirectly) a person who provides the 'controlled investment' in question (or any person as a person who carries on a controlled activity in relation to that investment). An example would be 'Investment Bonds are wonderful' provided no particular investment bond is mentioned.

(vii) Articles 18 and 18A: 'Mere conduits', by which is meant such person only communicates it in respect of a course of business carried on by him the principal purpose of which is transmitting or receiving material provided to him by others, the communication is wholly devised by another person and he does not in any way edit the content of the communication (unless required to do so in certain circumstances). Examples are postal and internet service providers, courier companies and telecommunications companies.

(viii) Article 19: Communications to persons who are investment professionals.

(ix) Article 20: Communications by journalists contained in a qualifying publication.

(x) Article 20A: Promotions broadcast by a company director, etc. The main purpose of this exemption appears to be to guard against the possibility that during a broadcast interview or a live website presentation a financial promotion is made inadvertently by a director or employee of an organisation.

(xi) Article 20B: Incoming electronic commerce communications (exemption not available to EU authorised life offices).

Part V of the Order sets out exemptions to communications in respect of deposits and insurance contracts which are not a 'qualifying contract of insurance' as set out in the Regulated Activities Order[1]. This will not apply to life policies (but will apply to 'pure protection' contracts).

O Distance Marketing Directive ('DMD')

5.44 The Distance Marketing Directive (DMD)[2] was implemented in the UK largely in October 2004 mainly through the Distance Marketing Directive Instrument 2004 and the Distance Marketing Directive (Amendment) Instrument 2004. The DMD has particular effects on the rules relating to direct offer financial promotions which are set out at COB 3.9.6R and COB 3.9.7AR. The DMD applies to 'distance contracts' which, essentially, are those contracts which constitute regulated activities which are advertised, negotiated and completed without any face-to-face contact. Therefore, the DMD would not apply if the customer completes the contract in a meeting with the firm's representative, even if it is as a result of responding to a promotion that could have led to a contract being completed 'at a distance'.

COB 3.9.6R(1) requires the promotion to be in a 'durable medium'. It must contain sufficient information to enable the person to make an informed assessment of the product or service. In particular, it must contain the information set

1 SI 2001/544.
2 The Distance Marketing of Consumer Financial Services Directive (2002/65/EC).

out in COB App 1. Where no advice has been given (which is the normal position) there must be a prominent statement to this effect and that if the person has any doubts regarding suitability he should contact the firm for advice (or another appropriate firm if that firm does not offer advice)[1]. Commission and remuneration details must also be included[2].

A customer must be provided with all the contractual terms and conditions of the service in a durable medium in good time before he is bound. The phrase 'in good time' is not defined anywhere and would depend on the nature of the contract and the target customers. So a simple plan would require less time than a more sophisticated one. There are certain exemptions to this, for example, if the contract is concluded at the customer's request by a means of distance communication which does not enable provision of the contractual terms in a durable medium. In such cases the firm must provide the information in a durable medium immediately after the conclusion of the contract (for example, telephone sales)[3]. Other exemptions which are probably of less relevance to the selling of life policies relate to successive or separate operations.

P   Systems and controls in relation to financial promotions

5.45   This is an area which has recently come to much greater prominence. The FSA have emphasised that failures in the area of non-compliant financial promotions may also be indicative of failures in a firm's systems and controls in SYSC 3[4]. In one case which went to Enforcement (essentially the FSA's disciplinary division) a firm was held to be in breach of SYSC 3.2.6R as a result of a failure to establish and maintain effective systems and controls to enable it to comply with the applicable requirements relating to financial promotions as set out in COB 3.

Q   Markets in Financial Instruments Directive ('MiFID')[5]

5.46   When implemented this 'high level' Directive (which was adopted in April 2004) will affect the way certain types of investment business is sold, organised, administered and controlled. It will replace the Investment Services Directive. MiFID will not directly apply to life offices, but to ensure a level playing field and in the interests of consumers, business efficiency and competition the FSA will extend some of the MiFID requirements to insurance companies and apply some of the wholesale requirements to retail firms. Therefore, as a result of having to implement MiFID, the FSA will review and amend much of its current regime, even for firms which are not within MiFID's scope.

1   COB 3.9.6R(2)(b).
2   COB 3.9.6R(2)(c).
3   COB 3.9.7AR(2).
4   COB 3.2.8G(1).
5   2004/39/EC.

The FSA will also take the opportunity to take forward other initiatives which are dependent to some extent on its approach to MiFID. This includes the move towards principle-based regulation (as opposed to rules-based), to simplify its rule book and to review the financial promotions regime, disclosure and projections. The FSA has indicated that it would like to bring in all these changes at the same time. Implementation of MiFID is due on 1 November 2007.

Although much wider in its effects than just in relation to financial promotions, MiFID will clearly have a significant effect. Whilst the precise terms of MiFID and its application are not yet finalised the following are likely to be the areas which will be affected:

(a) Balance of positive and negative information.

(b) Additional customer information for direct offer promotions for suitability purposes. The financial promotion should be understood by the average member of the group at whom it is directed.

(c) Restrictions on hypothetical past performance.

(d) More onerous requirements for image advertisements.

(e) Reviews to Systems and Controls arrangements will have to be made to ensure any new requirements are satisfied.

In May 2006, HM Treasury and the FSA issued a joint implementation plan for MiFID. In particular, this emphasises the 'better regulation' principles arising out of the Hampton Review (March 2005). This focussed on proportionality, accountability and transparency. The FSA issued Consultation Paper CP 06/14 in July 2006 regarding implementation of MiFID. In January 2007 the FSA issued Policy Statement 07/2 ('Implementing the Markets in Financial Instruments Directive (MiFID)').

R   Treating Customers Fairly ('TCF')

5.47   In view of its potential effects on the financial promotion regime (although its effects permeate throughout the whole of regulated financial services) it is thought appropriate to include a brief description of the FSA's TCF initiative. TCF is a major part of the FSA's move towards principle-based regulation and away from the current, predominantly rules-based regime. Indeed, the FSA have stated that TCF will help it 'remove a significant number of detailed requirements'. Perhaps unsurprisingly the concept of TCF has met with some criticism from some quarters of the legal profession for potentially imposing legal liability on the basis of high-level principles.

I   Origins of TCF

5.48   In September 1998, the FSA issued Consultation Paper 13: 'The FSA's Principles for Business'. This set out an expanded version of Principle 6 which included additional aspects such as paying due regard to customer's information needs, communicating information in a way which is fair and not misleading and managing conflicts of interest fairly. The subsequent Policy Statement (October 1999) split out Principle 6 so that what remained of Principle 6 was 'A firm must pay due regard to the interests of its customers and treat them fairly'.

In December 2003 Consultation Paper 207 specifically addressed issues of TCF for with-profits policyholders, and led to the introduction of the PPFM document (Principles and Practices of Financial Management). In July 2004, the FSA published a more general report 'Treating customers fairly: progress and next steps'. In May 2005, the FSA published a statement of good practice on fair contract terms, highlighting particular concern on 'variation clauses' affecting premiums under some long-term insurance contracts. In July 2005, the FSA published a further general report 'Treating customers fairly: building on progress'. In July 2006 the FSA issued a further report entitled 'Treating Customers Fairly – Towards fair outcomes for consumers' setting out: (1) an explanation of the outcomes for consumers that the FSA are looking to achieve in the TCF initiative; (2) the progress made by firms based on their own assessments and the findings of the FSA's own supervisory work; and (3) those areas where further work is required and how the FSA plan to take this forward.

2   What is TCF?

5.49   The FSA have not defined TCF on the basis that it is not possible to do so in a way which is meaningful to all firms. However, the FSA have stated what they consider TCF does not mean:

(a)   being 'nice' to customers or creating satisfied customers;

(b)   all firms required to offer the same, or highest, levels of service;

(c)   inhibiting innovation in new products;

(d)   that a firm must design or market different products for individual consumers;

(e)   that the FSA will be arbiter of what products consumers want;

(f)   that consumers will not be expected to take responsibility for their decisions;

(g)   new rules or obligations for firms;

(h)   a continuous ratcheting up of standards;

(i)   FSA will determine pricing policies;

(j)   firms adopting the same or bureaucratic processes;

(k)   collecting large amounts of management information[1].

1   FSA July 2005 Paper – 'Treating Customers Fairly – building on progress'.

'Fairness' is not a term defined by the FSA or, indeed, by English law generally. The FSA have attempted to correlate fairness with established legal principles such as equity and natural justice, although it has at the same time emphasised that its meaning is not the same.

3 Potential consequences of breaching TCF

5.50 The FSA 'Principles' Sourcebook ('PRIN') states, at paragraph 1.1.7G, that breaching a Principle makes a firm liable to various disciplinary sanctions. Paragraph 1.1.8G goes on to state that the breach of a Principle will be relevant in the FSA considering whether or not to exercise its intervention powers and in extreme cases in varying or cancelling a firm's Part IV permission.

In an Enforcement action against Legal & General Assurance Society Limited the Financial Services and Markets Tribunal stated (January 2005) 'It may be harder to show a breach of general standards than of specific rules'. The approach of the FSA may therefore be to cite specific rule breaches, alongside general principles, such as Principle 6. PRIN 3.4.4R states that breach of a high-level Principle does not (in itself) give rise to an action for damages whereas a breach of a rule provides a private person who suffers loss as a result of a breach with a statutory cause of action[1].

4 FSA cluster reports and case studies

5.51 Although the FSA's intention is not to be prescriptive concerning the meaning of TCF it has recognised the need to develop a common understanding of what TCF means in practice. It has developed this in two main ways, namely cluster reports and case studies. Cluster reports have focussed on product design; staff remuneration; managing the interface between producers and distributors; role of management information; complaints management and strategic change. In terms of financial promotion the issues for firms to consider (under the 'Product Design' heading) include communication of product features and risks to customers and adequacy of supporting literature in explaining product features and risks.

5 Implementing a TCF strategy

5.52 Unsurprisingly, the FSA have emphasised that one size does not fit all and that firms will need to take into account their various activities, products and services when implementing TCF. The FSA will look for evidence of a structured approach which is likely to involve: defining what TCF means for the firm; assessing current performance to identify gaps; developing an action plan to close any gaps and embed TCF in strategy operations and culture; implementing change where necessary and monitoring effectiveness. The FSA continually emphasise the role of senior management and that they are in the frontline for

---

1 Section 150.

developing TCF. TCF should be reflected in a firm's business strategy and embedded throughout the business.

6   Risk mitigation and enforcement

5.53   The main supervisory tool which the FSA will use to assess whether the firm is complying with its TCF obligations is its risk-based assessment process known as 'ARROW' ('Advanced Risk Responsive Operating frameWork'). The FSA have stated that where its supervision work identifies failures in systems and controls it will take account of whether firms have carried out a proper TCF analysis and whether senior management have played the role it would expect. Where they have not the FSA have said that it is more likely to take enforcement action.

7   Criticism of TCF regime

5.54   The TCF regime, for all its undoubtedly laudable intentions, has not met with universal approval. In particular, some parts of the legal profession have expressed the view that TCF may be unpredictable, retrospective and potentially falls foul of its own standards of legitimacy. Predictability must be a fundamental requirement of a principle-based regime and it is argued that TCF principles may be unacceptably vague. One of the detrimental effects of this could be a reduction in innovation due to uncertainty that certain actions could be judged not to be in line with TCF.

S   'Financial Promotions: taking stock and moving forward' (February 2005)

5.55   This paper was issued by the FSA with a view to setting out how they had progressed against the objectives set out in their 2004/05 Business Plan and their current approach to regulating financial promotion. It also set out some of their major concerns about financial promotions and systems and controls. It described how the FSA will build on its work reviewing promotions, visiting firms and communicating with the industry. Of particular interest is the FSA statement that they do not wish to introduce more detailed rules and this is clearly consistent with (and indeed the FSA specifically make reference to) this forming part of the overarching theme of TCF.

The status of papers such as this is for information purposes. It is not guidance. 'General guidance' is set out in the Handbook and it is possible for firms to receive 'individual guidance' in particular circumstances.

The FSA emphasised that as part of TCF firms should, when preparing promotions, consider whether:

(a)   the material is clear, fair and not misleading;

(b)   it provides a balanced picture of the product;

215

(c)   the marketing matches the product;

(d)   they have identified and understood their target audience; and

(e)   the promotion will be easily understood by their customers.

This paper develops and adds to the April 2002 paper ('The FSA's regulatory approach to financial promotions').

The 2004/05 Business Plan intimated the setting up of a new department devoted exclusively to financial promotions. This was set up in April 2004. This has, for example, expanded the monitoring activities, focussed on direct offer materials and has resulted in visits to firms to assess their systems and controls. A hotline has also been set up so that consumers and regulated firms can report purportedly misleading financial promotions. One tool the FSA have used is the 'Dear CEO Letter' which highlights the issues and concerns which the FSA have in a particular area. Relevant information also appears on the FSA website. Financial promotions are monitored through a combination of proactive and reactive work. Proactive work tends to focus on areas of the highest risk to consumers.

I   Where the FSA consider that a financial promotion does not comply

5.56   Any action taken will be based on the seriousness of the breach and the likely risk to consumers. After initial communication with the firm involved there are a number of possible outcomes:

1   accept the firm's position;

2   ask the firm not to issue the promotion again;

3   ask the firm to amend the promotion or withdraw it (in the unlikely event that the firm does not agree to withdraw it then it can vary the firm's permission or seek an injunction to require it to withdraw the promotion);

4   if there has been actual customer detriment (or the customer has purchased on the basis of a non-compliant promotion) the FSA may ask the firm to offer remediation either by withdrawing from the product without penalty or by offering compensation;

5   refer the case to enforcement.

In enforcement actions concerning financial promotions the FSA have, for example, highlighted failures to provide sufficient information on how the product worked or the risks involved. Issues of balance have been raised where there was focus on the benefits (including the offer of free promotional gifts) but less prominence was given to key information about risks.

2   Systems and controls

5.57   The FSA visit firms to examine their strategies, policies and procedures for producing promotions and to establish how effective these procedures actually are. Interviews with staff and senior management will be held and 'walk through tests' of the firm's processes may be carried out. The firm's records may also be reviewed.

Issues which have been identified in visits include the following. Where firms do have good procedures, sometimes these are not followed by staff. Monitoring of adherence to procedures can be irregular. Senior management are not always fully involved and, in particular, do not have adequate management information. Some firms do not have adequate audit trails of how financial promotions are approved.

Other aspects to look out for include:

1   Ensuring systems and controls apply equally to electronic as well as paper financial promotions.

2   Ensuring adequate controls over appropriate staff issuing financial promotions.

3   Establishing clear accountabilities for design and approval of promotions.

4   Making sure the 'shelf life' of financial promotions is managed regularly.

5   Ensuring complaints are analysed and the findings applied.

Adequate training should also be given and positive steps should be taken to ensure that the approval system is operating properly.

3   General concerns

5.58   The FSA identified five particular recurring issues:

1   *Clarity of product*. A financial promotion should clearly indicate what the product or service is. Technical descriptions may not be relevant or meaningful to intended customers. Exposure to the ups and downs of the stock market should be made clear.

2   *Risk warnings*. There should obviously be a description of the risks associated. Financial promotions must present a balanced indication of the product but not every possible risk needs to be incorporated in a short advert. Risk warnings should have sufficient prominence and not be buried in small print and/or on the back page.

3   *Percentages and headline claims*. Unrealistic and misleading headline figures should be avoided.

4   *Misleading statements*. Statements should not mislead the customer into believing something that is not true, or highly unlikely.

5   *Charges and early redemption penalties*. Information about charges and early redemption penalties should be described appropriately with the relevant degree of prominence.

4   Issues arising from thematic work

5.59   The FSA looked at particular products, industry sectors or media in depth.

1   *Website promotions*. These may be financial promotions or even direct offer financial promotions. Specific concerns included: non-compliant past performance warnings (should be on every page mentioning past performance); use of the FSA logo on sites.

2   *Direct offer material*. Specific deficiencies identified included: balance (risk warnings should appear close to the relevant benefits and not just in, for example, the key features document); target audience (explanations should be tailored to the audience to which they are directed); media (communications should be adjusted depending on what media they appear in).

3   *Investments for children*. The issues here mainly involved lack of balance. In particular, comparisons with bank or building society savings accounts did not refer to the relevant differences such as risks to capital, certainty about growth and access.

4   *Capital secure structured products*. Also known as 'guaranteed equity bonds' or 'secure equity bonds'. Some promotions did not indicate that there were early encashment penalties or no access to capital until the end of the period. In view of the complexity of such products there should be an adequate explanation of all important features of the product.

5   'MiFID'

5.60   The paper concludes with a reference to the forthcoming effects of MiFID and the preference for a principle-based approach is emphasised moving away from a detailed, prescriptive approach. TCF and senior management responsibility is reiterated.

T   'Financial Promotions: progress update and future direction' (August 2006)

5.61   The February 2005 paper was followed relatively swiftly by a further paper in August 2006, indicating that financial promotions continue to be a priority of the FSA's as part of the TCF initiative, although the FSA did acknowledge that generally the standard of financial promotions had improved.

This paper provides updates on the FSA's work over the last two years and outlines the FSA's future including how the financial promotions work forms part of the wider move towards a more principles-based approach to regulation. It also details the specific areas on which the FSA intend to focus. The FSA will also focus on the 'outcome' of financial promotions rather than on compliance with detailed rules. This will be supported by the implementation of MiFID. Emphasised strongly again is the role of firms' senior management in taking a lead in ensuring effective systems and controls are in place around advertising and marketing and that they receive and act where necessary on accurate management information.

The FSA do specifically accept, however, that some important detailed rules will need to be retained perhaps accepting that a purely principles-based regime can be difficult to police.

U   'Financial Promotion and other Communications': Consultation Paper: October 2006 (06/20)

5.62   This consultation paper was issued at the same time as another FSA consultation paper 'Reforming Conduct of Business Regulation'. Together these consultation papers represent a significant step towards more principles-based regulation. They are also intended to implement the relevant parts of MiFID.

The proposed new rules are to be located in a new Conduct of Business Sourcebook known as NEWCOB. This contains in NEWCOB 4 the basic continuing requirement for all communications to be 'fair, clear and not misleading'. In addition, there are high level rules around the identity of the sender and accuracy of information; comparative information and performance information. In NEWCOB 5 it is proposed to include rules on the form and content of financial promotions; past performance; future performance; appropriate and proportionate use of performance information; identification of marketing communications; direct offer financial promotions (including increased flexibility over the timing of disclosure material and the removal of 'direct offer financial promotion' as a defined term).

SECTION 2   PRODUCT DISCLOSURE AND CONDUCT OF BUSINESS SOURCEBOOK ('COBS')

A   General

5.63   The rules relating to 'product disclosure' are concerned with seeking to ensure that the potential investor understands all the details relating to the contract he is considering purchasing prior to actual purchase.

The disclosure requirements as set out in COB 6.1 to 6.5 underpin Principle 7 (Communications with clients) which requires a firm to pay due regard to the information needs of its customers. In the case of packaged products such as life policies there is a special need to ensure that customers are supplied with information which will highlight product features. This needs to be achieved in a way which will optimise the customer's ability to make a comparison of different products. An additional aim of these requirements is compliance with the disclosure requirements contained in what is now the Consolidated Life Directive (previously contained in the Third Life Directive). When a firm sells or personally recommends or arranges the sale of a life policy (or other type of packaged product) to a private customer then prior to completing an application form he must be given details of:

(1) 'Key features' of the product about which he ought to be aware above all else[1]. Where a customer responds to a direct offer financial promotion, this must include an example 'key features'. There is no requirement to provide a further set of key features in respect of the same transaction[2].

(2) The basis or amount of charges (other than commission) for conducting the business in question and the nature and amount of any other income receivable by it (or by an associate) and attributable to that business[3]. This disclosure may be made in its terms of business, in a customer agreement or in a separate written statement. Disclosure should include any product-related charges that are deducted from the private customer's investment. In practice, for life policies, such disclosure will usually occur in the key features document[4]. The requirements set out in 5.6.3 regarding not making excessive charges must also be noted. Whether or not charges are excessive should be considered by comparing charges for similar products or services, the degree to which the charges abuse the trust which the customer has placed in the firm and the nature and extent of the disclosure of charges to the private customer[5].

(3) In cash terms: (a) any 'commission equivalent' payable by it to a representative or appointed representative; and (b) any commission or commission equivalent receivable by it, or by any of its associates in connection with the transaction unless an exception as set out in COB 5.7.9R or COB 5.7.10R applies. In (b) a firm is to be regarded as receiving commission equivalent if: (a) it is received from a product provider or an associate of that provider; and (b) either that provider or its associate is in the same immediate group as the firm; and (c) the value of the commission equivalent (as assessed in accordance with these rules) is greater than the amount of commission in cash terms. 'Cash terms' in relation to commission does not include the value of any indirect benefits which the firm may receive in accordance with COB 2.2.

5.64 An additional requirement for life policies is that when a private customer buys a life policy (or varies such a life policy such that cancellation rights arise) the life office must also send to such private customer a post sale confirmation[6]. This does not apply to life policies which are pure protection contracts.

The product provider has no obligation to provide key features where the life policy is sold by another firm (or appointed representative) operating from an establishment within the UK or another person operating from an establishment in an EEA State whose law obliges him to operate subject to relevant provisions of the Distance Marketing Directive (DMD)[7] although in practice the product provider will almost always provide such key features.

1 6.2.7R.
2 6.2.8G.
3 5.7.3R.
4 5.7.4G.
5 5.6.4G.
6 6.3.3R.
7 6.2.9R(1).

Where, before the proposal form is completed, the terms of the proposed life policy are varied, revised key features must be issued unless the alteration relates only to the amount of premium or the amount of commission or a rider benefit is added, removed or amended. (However, where this contract is a distance contract the DMD may require notification of the changes[1].) So, for example, a change in premium and sum assured under a policy designed to cover a mortgage (where the loan has to be increased before the sale is finalised) would not require revised key features[2]. Where key features have already been provided and the terms of the policy are materially altered or extended after completion of the proposal form or there are changes to the commission or charging structure details of the change must be provided as soon as practicable in a durable medium and revised key features offered. 'Materially altered' may not always be easy to define but one example given in the guidance is an increase of premium of more than 25%[3].

Where the policyholder applies to vary a post-1 January 1995 life policy (or is recommended to do so) and such variation would give rise to a right to cancel, then certain minimum information must be given. A complete set of new key features would, of course, satisfy this requirement and this may be easier to provide in practice[4]. For pre-1 January 1995 policies the firm must provide such information which it believes on reasonable grounds is sufficient for the policyholder to understand the variation[5]. The variation provisions set out in Rules 6.2.16R and 6.2.18R do not apply where the variation to the life policy is recommended or arranged by certain other persons[6]. The above information requirements do not apply where the personal recommendation or arrangements derive from another person operating from an establishment in an EEA State whose law imposes an obligation on the person to provide information about the variation in accordance with relevant provisions of the DMD[7].

B   Requirement to produce key features

5.65   6.1.4R requires a provider to produce key features which, in terms of design and content, comply with COBS 6.1, 6.2 and 6.5 for each packaged product that it offers for sale. A firm may produce key features in printed hard copy format or in an electronic format[8]. Key features must be produced and presented to at least the same quality and standard as the associated marketing material and generally they must be separate (or 'stand alone') from any other material[9].

1   6.2.12R(2).
2   6.2.12R.
3   6.2.14R, 6.2.15G.
4   6.2.16R, 6.2.17G.
5   6.2.18.
6   6.2.19R.
7   6.2.19R(2).
8   6.1.5R.
9   6.1.5R.

I   Content of key features and important information

5.66   COB 6.5 sets out the framework for production of the key features document. There will normally be one set of non client specific elements for each type of investment contract. It must be produced as a stand-alone document and so it must be separate from any other material, such as marketing or technical brochures. Firms may, however, provide other documents together with the key features document provided they are presented or given in such a way that they will not detract from the key features document. Market research initially conducted by LAUTRO indicated that investors are more attracted to documents which appear on no more than four sides of A4-sized paper. The normal style of technical product particulars and marketing material was generally found to be off-putting, purely because of its length. At the present time key features documents are frequently much longer than this and probably contain much more detail than was probably envisaged by LAUTRO when they were first introduced. The concern is that the purpose of key features documents is defeated where documents are of such length and detail.

Firms must ensure that any pre-printed parts of the key features document are designed and presented to a standard commensurate with that used in any related product brochures or leaflets. Style of print, presentation and use of colour should therefore be the same. For direct marketing packages the key features document should be equal in standard and quality to any other material which might be included in the same envelope. The required contents of a key features document are set out in COB 6.5.

As mentioned above, a firm which makes a recommendation to a customer must ensure that before he completes an application form or proposal, he is given the appropriate key features document. Whilst the provider is technically relieved of this responsibility in circumstances where the contract was recommended or arranged by another firm (for example an independent intermediary), in practice the provider will produce and provide the key features documentation.

C   Key features and important information

I   General

5.67   The obligation to provide key features documents is explained above[1]. The key features document must use prescribed sub-headings as set out in Table 6.5.11R[2]. A firm may amend the prescribed content and format but only where it can show that this is necessary to reflect the terms and nature of the product and that, in relation to a distance contract with a retail customer, in doing so it does not omit the contractual terms and conditions and information in COB App 1[3].

1   See **5.66**.
2   6.5.2R.
3   6.5.3R.

Ignoring provisions which are not relevant to life assurance, the key features document should be entitled or headed 'Key Features of the [Name of the Life Policy]'[1].

The policy must be described under certain sub-headings: 'its aims', 'your commitment or your investment' (whichever is more appropriate) and 'risk factors'[2].

The aim of the policy is quite simply what it will actually or potentially achieve for an investor. Therefore, the aim of an endowment mortgage policy would be to repay a mortgage on maturity or death.

The commitment for regular premium policies is that the investor must pay a certain amount as a regular monthly or yearly premium for a specified number of years. If relevant it should be pointed out that if the investor fails to maintain the commitment and, for example, stops the policy early there could be additional charges. For a single premium policy the heading which is probably more appropriate is 'your investment'. This will simply be a lump sum single premium. The risk factors are those matters which may have an adverse effect on performance or are otherwise material to the decision to invest[3]. The following are some examples given in the guidance which may be relevant to life policies:

(i)   whether the value of capital and any income from it might fluctuate;

(ii)   cancellation issues – for example, the fact that where notice of cancellation is given, a full refund of the original investment may not be provided if there has been a fall in investment values;

(iii)   extra degrees of risk concerned with certain types of investment, eg emerging markets funds where there may be dealing difficulties or settlement or custody issues; potential problems with investment in property in respect of liquidity, that the property may not be readily saleable, and that property valuation is a matter of the valuer's judgement;

(iv)   that certain funds carry special risks, such as high volatility;

(v)   special risks such as capital erosion or constraints on capital growth where charges are deducted from capital;

(vi)   possibility of 'market value adjustment' (or 'reduction') for with-profits policies which could reduce the benefits payable;

(vii)   the risk that current tax benefits (or other external factors) may be withdrawn;

(viii) if a customer does not maintain contributions he may not meet any projected target benefits and may lose any life cover;

(ix)   for new funds if assumed size is not achieved the proportion of charges and expenses may be higher and the value of the investment will consequently suffer;

1   6.5.12R.
2   6.5.13R.
3   6.5.13R(2).

(x) the fact that there is no guarantee (where this is the case) that a life policy will provide sufficient funds at the end of its term to repay a mortgage and the investor may need to increase payments;

(xi) that in the case of guaranteed products, there may be a capital shortfall at the end of the contract (where relevant);

(xii) where there is a fixed regular payment of income, the customer should be informed that such payments often involve a risk to capital (where relevant);

(xiii) the effect or potential effect of guarantees or other liabilities, whether they relate to the product which the customer is or may be acquiring; or to any of the provider's other products or the business activities of the provider or its associates (if they have or may have a material adverse effect on returns or are otherwise material to the decision to invest)[1].

These examples are not, however, exhaustive.

2   Projections in key features document

5.68   There is also a requirement to include a projection of how the principal terms of the transaction would apply to the customer[2]. This should take into account such factors as age and sex, the proposed sum assured, premium and any other relevant factors[3]. For single premium policies, or where the key features are part of a direct offer financial promotion, and for policies under which the total premiums do not exceed £120 per year (or £130 per year if premiums paid every four weeks) or premiums are less than £1,000 in total, the projection may, instead of being specific to that customer, be based on an example which typically represents the type of business which the firm conducts in relation to the life policy in question[4].

The benefit projections must be given at the three prescribed rates of growth for the policy in question, currently 4%, 6% and 8% for taxed life products and 5%, 7% and 9% for tax exempt products[5].

Rule 6.6.14R requires the prescribed statements as set out in Rules 6.6.16–6.6.18 R to be included in the document containing the projection. Where a firm reasonably believes that a statement is not wholly appropriate to the contract in question, they may be amended but the alteration must not reduce the significance or impact of the statement. Such statements must appear adjacent to the projected values and be in a type size no smaller or less prominent than that used for the projected values.

A further requirement is to set out in question and answer format a description of the principal terms of the policy and any other information necessary to enable

1   6.5.14G.
2   6.5.15R.
3   6.5.19R (and 6.6).
4   6.5.19R.
5   Table 6.6(50)R.

the customer to make an informed decision[1]. The content of these questions and answers is for the firm to decide having regard to their own policies although guidance is set out in 6.5.21G. For example, for a life policy which is being used to repay an interest-only mortgage, details should be set out of how and when the customer will be notified whether the policy is on target to repay the loan, and if not, what options he has. Also, the consequences of making the policy paid up or stopping contributions must also be set out. Also, for a with-profits policy, a cross-reference to the Customer Friendly PPFM (see COB 6.10.9GG(8)) is required.

5.69   A table is required for life policies which can acquire a surrender value (unless one of the exceptions in COB 6.5.28R applies[2]. This must set out potential surrender values for each of the first five years, contributions paid to date, the effect of deductions to date and what the customer might get back. Optionally, accumulated deductions to date may be included for each year. This must be set out under the heading 'The early years'. The following warning should be included (if appropriate), namely 'WARNING – if you cash in during the early years you could get back less than you have paid in'. Arguably, this is potentially misleading in that the customer may get back less than he has put in at any time – not just in the early years. The following wording must also appear: 'The last two columns assume that investments will grow at [insert the intermediate rate appropriate to the type of life policy set out in COB 6.6.50R] a year'.

The second part of the table must show longer-term values, at the tenth and at five-yearly intervals thereafter. This should appear under the heading 'The later years'. COB 6.5.25 R sets out what must be included. Note that a table is not required where life policies do not have a surrender value. In such cases the following warning must be given in place of the tables: 'WARNING – this policy has no cash-in value at any time'. The table must consist of either four or five columns.

First column	This shows the years where amounts are being disclosed. Projections are given for the tenth year and at five-yearly intervals thereafter. Where the figures would depart significantly from a steady trend, figures are also required for the intervening years. For a whole life policy, figures must be included for every tenth year and the final year, assuming that the life policy will continue (unless converted to a fixed term) until the insured life (or youngest insured life) reaches 75 or to a term of ten years if later. Or, if earlier, the year in which the projected fund reaches zero (the consequences of this must be brought to the customer's attention). In the case of a single premium policy with no fixed term, a term of ten years should be assumed although figures for a longer term may also be shown. For a ten-year life policy, the figures for the final year may be included in the 'early years' table. Such tables of values have been criticised as encouraging investors to believe that these are guaranteed encashment amounts.

1   6.5.20.
2   6.5.23R.

Second column	This shows total cumulative contributions assumed paid in to that date and should allow for automatic changes in premium where applicable.
Third column	'Total actual deductions to date' – this is an optional column of information.
Fourth column	This shows the cumulative effect of total deductions (charges and expenses) to date. These are defined in accordance with 6.6.23R. Also included are the costs of any protection benefits (ie life cover).
Fifth column	This should show the projections of surrender values calculated in accordance with 6.6.38R assuming the premium and any other relevant matters given for the purpose of 6.5.13R (Nature of Policy) and 6.5.15R (An Example). Where any surrender values are guaranteed they must be provided with a suitably adjusted heading and introductory text.
(Sixth column – where relevant)	Where a customer exercises the right to make partial surrenders, a column headed 'Withdrawals' must be included. The sum of planned withdrawals must be shown.

3 Required statements to accompany projections

5.70   The following statements as set out in 6.5.27R(1) to (3) and one of (4) or (5) should appear after the table. The accumulated deductions should be entered where indicated in the sentence required by the rules. This should be followed by a statement showing the reduction in investment growth, that amount is known as the 'reduction in yield'. This calculation may (in accordance with the terms of the policy) include the cost of life cover and/or sickness benefits (if any), commission/remuneration, expenses, charges, any surrender penalties and other adjustments. The following statements must appear beneath the information required by COB 6.5.23R, unless COB 6.5.28R (which relates to a small range of very limited types of life policy) applies: (1) 'What are the deductions for?', (2) 'The deductions include [the cost of life cover, sickness benefits,] [commissions/remuneration,] expenses, charges, any surrender penalties and other adjustments.', (3) 'The last line in the table shows that over the full term of the policy the effect of the total deductions could amount to £x.'

Subsequently, one of the following statements must appear:

(4)   'Putting it another way, leaving out the cost of life cover [and sickness benefits] this would have the same effect as bringing investment growth from x% a year down to y% a year.'

or

(5)   'Putting it another way, if the growth rate were to be x%, which is in no way guaranteed, this would have the effect of reducing it to y% a year.'

Information relating to 'Total actual reductions to date', 'Effect of deductions to date' and reduction in yield is not required for a without-profits policy if the benefits, except on surrender or variation, are guaranteed benefits, or for a life policy for five years or less or a life policy held within a Child Trust Fund[1].

The calculation method for 'effect of deductions to date' for life policies is set out in 6.5.29R.

Further, under the heading 'How much will the advice cost?' either the following prescribed statement should appear:

> 'Your adviser will give you details about the cost. The amount will depend on the size of the premium and the length of the policy term. It will be paid for out of the deductions[2]'

or an actual statement of the amount or value in cash terms of the commission or remuneration and an indication of the timing of these payments together with a statement that commission or equivalent is paid for out of the deductions (or charges if more appropriate) and, if applicable, that the amount will depend on the size of the premium/contribution and the length of the policy term[3].

4   Further information

5.71   6.5.40R sets out the further information which must be included in the key features, separately or as part of the information required by 6.5.2R(1). This consists of a clear indication, in one place, of the nature and amount or rate of charges or expenses and an explanation of how the investor may obtain further information about the policy and compensation arrangements. If charges or expenses are levied in the form of reduced investment, both the method and effect must be clearly explained. In the case of a single premium charge for mortality or morbidity under linked benefit policies it is sufficient to describe its nature and basis. Also required is the information that Annex III of the Consolidated Life Directive requires to be communicated to policyholders as specified in 6.5.49R[4].

5   Projections and surrender values

5.72   The provisions relating to projections and surrender values are designed to avoid the practice of using projection rates based on historically high rates of investment return which are almost certainly not sustainable, producing misleadingly high figures[5]. Projections are therefore carried out on the basis of uniform and consistent rates of investment return so that firms cannot compete on the basis of wholly speculative forecasts as to the potential value of future benefits. This should help ensure that customers purchasing a life policy receive information about possible future returns in a way which is fair and not misleading. Standard projection rates have been continually reduced to reflect the trend of lower investment returns and interest rates.

1   COB 6.5.28R.
2   6.5.39G.
3   6.5.38R.
4   6.5.40R.
5   6.6.2G.

A 'projection' is defined as a reference to 'the amount of any future benefit payable under a contract or policy, being a benefit the amount of which is not ascertainable under the terms of the contract or policy when the calculation is made'. It is, therefore, capable of quite a wide interpretation, which is probably intentional in view of the many ways in which future benefits can be shown.

The Glossary in the FSA Handbook sets out the definitions of 'projection date' and 'surrender value'. The definition of 'surrender value' makes it clear that 'amount' includes a nil amount.

Rule 6.6.4R provides that a firm may only issue a projection if calculated and presented in accordance with the rules in COB 6.6 subject to the exceptions set out in 6.6.5R. Projections in respect of what are known as higher volatility contracts are not permitted[1]. The rules in 6.6 do not apply, for example, where all the benefits are fixed and do not depend on an assumption of a future investment return or in respect of existing contracts where the date to which the benefit is being projected is no more than six months after the date on which the projection is given.

A document containing a projection must include the information contained in 6.5 (Key Features) under the headings 'An Example', 'Tables', 'Deductions Summary' and 'Commission and remuneration' unless the projection is in respect of existing contracts or 'financial promotions' (other than direct offer financial promotions)[2]. Except where the contract is not proceeded with, a record of the projection must be kept for at least six years by the life office in the case of life policies[3]. It is necessary to quote or make clear the total number or amounts of premiums or contributions paid over the term of the projection for regular premium contracts[4].

5.73 Where the projection makes allowance for premium increases the premium in the last year must be shown (or if the rate of future increases depends on growth in a salary or index, details of that salary or index must be included)[5].

A firm may provide a generic projection for illustrative purposes based on a single rate of investment return where this is within a financial promotion (other than a direct offer financial promotion) which comprises a table (or extracts from a table) published by a newspaper (or similar publication) or by the firm itself which compares projections from at least five product providers, or where the purpose is to indicate the likely cost of the proposed transaction, or to provide an estimate of the additional premium required to achieve a specified target[6].

Where a generic projection is issued a firm must ensure that (i) it does not relate solely to an existing contract, (ii) the rate of return used does not exceed the relevant higher projection rate, (iii) where the rate used exceeds the middle rate by more than 0.5% a statement is included stating why it is believed reasonable to assume such a high rate, (iv) where the charges and expenses of the

1 6.6.6.
2 6.6.8R(1) and (2).
3 6.6.19.
4 6.6.8R(3).
5 6.6.8R(4).
6 6.6.9R(1).

product provider are available, they are used, or an estimate is given based on the firm's knowledge of charges and expenses applicable to similar contracts, (v) it is accompanied by the written statements set out in COB 6.6.17R and (vi) appropriate key features are supplied if a recommendation is subsequently made[1].

Projections must be accompanied by certain prescribed statements[2]. Amendments are possible where the revised wordings are reasonably believed by the firm not to be wholly appropriate to the contract in question although the alteration must not reduce the significance or impact of the statement[3]. Such statements must appear adjacent to the projected values and be in a type size no smaller or less prominent than that used for the projected values[4].

Briefly, the statements required are as follows. Whenever benefits are not guaranteed there should be a statement that: 'These figures are only examples and are not guaranteed – they are not minimum or maximum amounts. What you get back depends on how your investment grows and on the tax treatment of the investment' and 'You could get back more or less than this'. Additionally, there must be a statement regarding the effects of inflation: 'Do not forget that inflation would reduce what you could buy in the future with the amounts shown'. A further required statement relates to growth rates: 'All firms use the same rates of growth for projections but their charges vary'. Other required statements relate to currency fluctuations for non-sterling investments.

For generic projections the first required statement is that 'These figures are only illustrative'. Also, that 'An assessment of your needs will be confirmed before a recommendation can be made' or 'Your needs will be confirmed before a recommendation can be made'. It must also be stated that a personalised key features will be provided if a recommendation for an investment is made[5].

The provisions relating to how projections are calculated are set out in COB 6.6.21 to 6.6.53. Being mainly of interest to actuaries they are not considered further here, nor are the provisions relating to calculation of the reduction in yield which are set out in COB 6.6.54 to 6.6.85.

6   Disclosure of commission or remuneration

5.74   Commission must be disclosed in the key features document under the heading: 'How much will the advice cost?' by stating the amount or value in cash terms of the commission or remuneration and an indication of the timing of these payments and that this is paid for out of the deductions (or charges) and, if relevant, that the amount will depend on the size of the premium and the length of the life policy. This information may include the name of the representative to whom the commission or equivalent is to be paid.

Alternatively the firm may include a statement to the effect that the adviser will give these details[6].

1   6.6.9R(2).
2   6.6.16R.
3   6.6.14R(2).
4   6.6.14R(3).
5   Table 6.6 17R.
6   6.5.38.

7 Post sale confirmation

5.75   A life office, having sold a policy or having effected a variation of it which gives rise to the issue of a cancellation notice, must send investors the prescribed information specified in COB 6.5.46. This information confirms the information given at the point of sale and also confirms any changes occurring between point of sale and acceptance. This information covers items such as the personal illustration, the table of surrender values and deductions and the commission or remuneration. Such information must be sent as soon as reasonably practicable after the contract is effected[1]. The purpose is that it serves as a useful reminder and checklist for the investor[2].

There are exceptions to the requirement to provide post sale confirmation. These include where the policy was purchased by an investment manager exercising discretion on behalf of the policyholder, by trustees of an occupational pension scheme, for variations where the life policy was issued before 1 January 1995, where at the time of the application the customer was habitually resident in an EEA State other than the UK or outside the UK and not present in the UK[3].

If a customer has approached the firm through electronic media or has responded by submitting his application through an electronic medium (such as e-mail or through the internet) the post sale confirmation may be provided through the same means instead of by a hard copy through the post. But this media may only be used where the private customer expects to deal in this way[4].

At the consultation stage thought was given to dispensing with the need for post sale confirmation on the basis that it merely duplicates information which the consumer should already have received and so could be confusing. It also entailed further administrative burden for firms and, in any event, the cancellation notice should be sufficient warning to the customer. Arguably, there would be no loss of consumer protection. Counter arguments were on the basis that customers were more likely to retain post sale documentation whereas pre-sale documentation would be more likely to be viewed as part of the decision-making process and consequently not retained. For the time being at least, the obligation to provide post sale information still exists.

With regard to the purchase of traded (or 'second-hand') policies, a firm responsible for a recommendation must supply the information specified in 6.5.49R. Such information must be supplied in writing before the customer is asked to complete any application form or authority giving effect to the purchase[5]. Additionally, if this constitutes a distance contract with a retail customer, all the contractual terms and conditions and the information in COB App 1 in place of key features (in accordance with COB 6.4.14R) must be provided[6].

1   COB 6.3.5R.
2   6.3.3R.
3   6.3.6(5).
4   COB 6.3.4G.
5   6.4.14R.
6   6.5.44R.

8   Principles and Practices of Financial Management (PPFM)

5.76   The PPFM requirements set out at **6.6** and **6.7** replace the previous requirements relating to with-profits guides. A firm which issues with-profits policies is required to produce a PPFM guide relating to its with-profits fund or funds and also a 'customer friendly' version (CFPPFM). There are also requirements relating to the provision of such information. These requirements are set out in more detail in Chapter 1.

D   Clear, fair and not misleading communication

5.77   There is a general requirement set out in COB 2.1.3R that all information be communicated in a way that is 'clear, fair and not misleading'. It includes all communications with customers such as 'client agreements, periodic statements, financial reports, telephone calls and any correspondence which is not a financial promotion'[1]. (The requirement for financial promotions to be 'clear, fair and not misleading' is set out in its own specific rule at COB 3.8.4R(1)). When considering these requirements the firm must take into account the customer's knowledge of the investment business to which the information relates[2].

1   Second-hand or 'traded' life policies

5.78   When the policy being recommended is a second-hand or traded policy, a firm may provide a customer with certain other prescribed information[3] (and in relation to a distance contract with a retail customer, all the contractual terms and conditions and the information in COB App 1) instead of key features.

2   Broker funds

5.79   Where the firm is a 'broker fund adviser', at the same time as providing the customer with a suitability letter (or before any change in investment objectives or strategies), the firm must inform the customer in writing of:

(i)   the investment objectives, and the policies and strategies which will be followed;

(ii)   the relevant published index or other indicator with which comparison of the performance of the fund may fairly be made. For life policies, where the life office has its own managed unit-linked fund, this will be the average performance of that fund. Alternatively it will be the average performance of one or more non-broker funds, into which the customer can switch,

---

1   2.1.5G.
2   COB 2.1.4G.
3   6.5.44R.

where the objectives do not conflict with those of the broker fund, or where there is no such fund, the sector average of general managed life funds;

(iii) a published index or sector average which the firm must identify as appropriate to the investment objectives and strategy of the fund under comparison; and

(iv) the name of any person providing advice under the arrangement.

3 Post sale confirmation

5.80   COB 6.5.46 sets out the information which must be given to investors once the customer buys a life policy. It also applies to variations of life policies which give rise to cancellation rights. It must be sent no later than the issue of the cancellation notice or if none is required then as soon as reasonably practicable after the contract is effected. The information given to the investor in the original key features document is confirmed (ie an example, tables and deductions summary and the commission/remuneration which has been paid). It is also necessary to confirm the adviser's status where the customer has been recommended to purchase the policy by a representative.

Post sale confirmation can be provided by printed hard copy and posted directly to the customer. If the customer has approached the firm or has submitted his application by email or internet, the post sale confirmation may be provided in the same way. However, electronic methods may only be used where the customer expects to communicate in this way, although it is not entirely clear how the firm is to establish the customer's expectations in this respect[1].

There is no requirement to provide post sale confirmation where the life office reasonably believes that the policy or variation has been purchased or effected on behalf of a customer by an investment manager exercising discretion, or a pre-1 January 1995 policy is being varied or at the time of signing the application for the policy or variation the customer was habitually resident in a member state other than the United Kingdom or outside the EEA, and the customer was not present in the United Kingdom[2].

4 Consolidated Life Directive

5.81   The requirements of the Consolidated Life Directive are set out in Table 6.5.49R. The firm must communicate in writing the information prescribed in this table to the potential policyholder, before the policy is concluded, in an official language of the EEA State of the commitment (which means, for an individual, the EEA State in which he resides). This information may be in another language if the potential policyholder so requests and the law of the EEA State so permits or the potential policyholder is free to choose the law applicable. Usually this would be achieved by inclusion of the required information in the key features document.

---

1 6.3.4G and 1.8 ('Application to electronic media').
2 6.3.6R.

E   Commission and remuneration disclosure

5.82   A firm is required to disclose to a customer the amount or value, in cash terms, of any commission equivalent payable by it to an appointed representative or representative or any commission receivable by it in connection with the transaction. This must be before effecting the transaction and at any time the customer subsequently requests[1].

Disclosure must be made in a way which is fair, clear and not misleading and which indicates the timing of such payments[2]. Disclosures should normally be made in writing, for example in the key features or a separate document given at the same time[3]. A firm must put a proper value on cash payments, benefits and services which it provides in connection with the transaction[4].

There are exceptions to the requirement to disclose commission or commission equivalent. In particular, where the customer is not present in the UK at the time the application form is signed (this provision only applies in respect of life policies); where the customer is habitually resident overseas and where the firm is acting as an investment manager[5]. Also, it does not apply where example key features are provided, but the firm must disclose the actual amount within five business days of effecting or arranging the transaction[6].

Guidance is set out in COB 5.7.11–14G regarding the content and wording of remuneration and commission disclosure. Table 5.7.16E sets out the basis on which the firm should determine the value of the commission equivalent (ie the total of the cash payments, benefits and services) to be disclosed under COB 5.7.5R(1). Benefits and services only need to be included where the value is such that they could not be provided as an indirect benefit under 2.2.6G and 2.2.7G. 'Cash payments' cover all payments by a firm to a representative and, broadly, consists of any monetary payments together with an amount to reflect the cost of benefits and services provided by the firm.

F   Calculating commission equivalent

5.83   Table 5.7.16E sets out how the commission equivalent is determined. This contains a lot of detail and the following is necessarily only a brief overview.

Part A: *Cash payments.* Where representatives, etc receive a straightforward payment on each sale, the first element is relatively simple. However, the precise rate of commission equivalent may not be known in advance. In such cases the firm must reasonably estimate the likely rate applicable.

Part B: *Benefits.* Such benefits include any item considered as a benefit or expense under the Income and Corporation Taxes Act 1988 (eg use of a car,

---

1   5.7.5R.
2   5.7.11G.
3   5.7.13G.
4   5.7.6R, 5.7.8E.
5   5.7.9R.
6   5.7.10R.

subsidised loans, attendance at conferences, contributions to pension schemes, value of share options, etc). Such items must be included whether or not the individual is liable to income tax on them and regardless of whether any such item is chargeable to tax.

Part C: *Services.* 'Services' for these purposes include those which cannot be provided under the indirect benefits rules[1].

Part D: *Calculation methodology.* This covers where estimating commission equivalent is appropriate and construction of commission equivalent scales.

5.84   If the firm pays commission equivalent to another firm in the same immediate group, or an appointed representative which is an associate of the firm, the commission equivalent may not be on a commercial basis. In such circumstances it is prescribed that the sum disclosed will be based on the higher of (a) all payments, benefits and services provided to the firm or its appointed representatives, from whatever source plus an additional allowance for profit of 15% unless the firm can demonstrate that this figure is inappropriate and can substitute a more realistic figure in its place; or (b) the cash payments actually paid by the firm, plus the value of services provided.

I   Content and wording of disclosure statements[2]

5.85   A statement of disclosable commission should state the essential features of amount and incidence as briefly as possible. Some of the more pertinent examples for life assurance purposes are set out below:

(1)   Intermediaries and Independent intermediaries (in a direct offer financial promotion or post sale information): 'For arranging this policy/contract XYZ Life Ltd will pay commission to IFA Ltd £. . .'

(2)   Representatives employed by an appointed representative: 'For arranging this policy/contract XYZ Life Ltd will pay remuneration and provide services to AR Ltd. worth £. . .'. At the point of sale or in a direct offer financial promotion an alternative could be: 'For arranging this policy/contract AR Ltd expects to receive remuneration and services from XYZ Ltd worth £. . .'

(3)   Representative employed directly by the firm (including self-employed sole trader appointed representatives): 'For arranging this policy/contract I expect to receive remuneration and services from XYZ Ltd worth £. . .' or 'for arranging this policy XYZ Ltd expect to incur sales costs of £. . .'. An acceptable alternative in a post sale situation is: 'For arranging this policy XYZ Ltd has provided remuneration and services to your adviser worth £ . . .'

---

1   2.2.6G and 2.2.7G.
2   5.7.17G.

Larger amounts of commission or remuneration may be rounded up to three significant figures. The example set out in COB 5.7.17G is '£122 instead of £122.35'.

The description of the monetary amount will vary according to the incidence and basis of the remuneration. Some examples are set out below:

(1)   Indemnity commission (on a monthly premium policy): '£X immediately and £Y each month from the Nth month to the end of the term'.

(2)   Level commission (on an annual premium whole life policy): '£X each year'. For a representative sale, the provision of benefits and services would probably require a statement such as '£X immediately and £Y each year thereafter'.

(3)   Fund-related basis: using the same rate of growth and the same periods as those in the key features document, the example will normally show the commission or remuneration in the first year in which it is paid and the tenth year; or for an investment of £P: 'For arranging this policy, XYZ Ltd will pay commission to IFA Ltd of £X, and half a percent of the fund value each year. For example, if your fund was worth £P, we would pay £X per year: if it was worth £2xP, we would pay £Z per year. Commission is paid every six months'.

(4)   Increasing premium policies: '£X immediately and a variable amount in each year thereafter, being, for example, £Y in the second year and increasing to £Z by the final year.'

G   Information about the firm

5.86   A firm must take reasonable steps to ensure that it gives to its private customers adequate information about the firm (and any relevant agent of the firm) and where relevant the identity and status, or relationship with the firm, of employees and other agents with whom the customer may have contact and the firm's statutory status (in accordance with GEN 4 Annex 1 (Statutory status disclosure) except where the private customer has been given information on a previous occasion which is still up to date[1]. The type of information which would satisfy 5.5.3R is set out in Table 5.5.5E. On all business stationery (written communications including stationery, business cards) published by the firm or used by its employees, agents, representatives, or introducers the following information should be included:

(1)   name, business address and telephone number of the firm to which the firm belongs, or of the branch or office of the firm from which the communication originates;

(2)   the name and status or relationship with the firm of the individual from whom the communication originates;

1   5.5.3R.

(3) a statement of the firm's statutory status (in accordance with GEN 4 Annex 1 (Statutory status disclosure));

(4) if the communication is by, or relates to, an introducer, a statement of the introducer's capacity.

The provisions of the Companies Acts should also be borne in mind where relevant (see **5.32**).

H Churning and switching

5.87 'Churning' means entering into transactions with unnecessary frequency having regard to the customer and the agreed investment strategy. In addition, a firm should not switch a private customer within or between packaged products (such as life policies) unnecessarily, having regard to suitability for that customer[1]. The FSA refer to 'switching' in relation to packaged products rather than churning although everyday language in the life industry tends to refer to 'churning' in both contexts. This is a specific example of the application of Principle 6 (Customers' interests) which requires a firm to pay due regard to the interests of its customers and treat them fairly.

I 'Know your customer'

5.88 This is one of the core requirements of COBS and of investor protection generally and seeks to ensure that the interest of the customer is paramount. A firm giving a personal recommendation concerning a designated investment to a private customer (or acting as an investment manager for a private customer)[2] must take reasonable steps to ensure that it has such personal and financial information about the customer as is relevant to the services that the firm is to provide[3]. Where advice is given on a continuing basis the firm should keep this information under regular review. If only occasional advice is given the firm should undertake a review at the point of the most recent instruction[4]. If, however, a customer declines to give such information a firm should not provide any services without promptly advising the customer (and ideally confirming in writing) that the lack of such information is likely to adversely affect the quality of services[5]. The precise type of information required and enquiries to be made varies depending on the type of customer concerned. Guidance is given in Table 5.2.11G regarding the collection of relevant information.

The analysis of the customer's personal and financial circumstances should lead to a clear identification of his needs and priorities so that, combined with his attitude to risk, a suitable investment can be recommended. Due regard should be

1   7.2.2G and 7.2.3R.
2   5.2.1R.
3   5.2.5R.
4   5.2.6G.
5   5.2.7G.

had to the customer's current level of income and expenditure and to any likely changes in this.

The 'fact-find' is the process which is undertaken in order to establish the investor's current financial position and his needs and requirements for the future. It is retained and recorded pursuant to COB 5.2.9R. Unless the personal recommendation is not proceeded with, a firm must make and retain a record of a customer's personal and financial circumstances that it has obtained in satisfying COB 5.2.5R for a minimum period after the information is obtained. For life policies this is six years.

The 'know your customer' requirements are an example of the operation of Principle 9 (Customers: relationships of trust) which requires firms to take reasonable care to ensure the suitability of its advice and discretionary decisions.

A statement of demands and needs must be given to the customer unless a suitability letter or explanation of a personal recommendation in accordance with COB 5.3 is provided to him. For telephone sales this may be provided immediately after the conclusion of the sale[1].

J   Calculation of charges and expenses and their effect

5.89   The effect of charges and expenses on investment returns is known as the 'reduction in yield'. The basic calculation methods for the reduction in yield are set out in 6.6.55 to 6.6.57.

'Charges and expenses' to be taken into account are set out in 6.6.23R (with regard to unit-inked policies). Charges and expenses are all explicit charges and expenses the customer will or may bear. This includes all other expenses and deductions such as those relating to the funds or units in which the assets are invested but not the dealing costs of the underlying portfolio. Sub-paragraph (ii) requires the deductions from the premium of charges and expenses which do not accrue for the benefit of the customer. In the case of with-profits contracts and unit-linked contracts where not all expenses are levied by means of explicit charges a list of items to be considered is set out in 6.6.23R which indicates what the firm is to have regard to, such as the principal terms of the contract, tax relief available to the firm, transfers to shareholders funds (or equivalent) but dealing costs are to be excluded. Firms would be expected to determine the charges and expenses after consultation with their appointed actuary and therefore account must be taken of guidance published by the Institute of Actuaries or Faculty of Actuaries.

The underlying rate of return is specified as the intermediate projection rate appropriate to the category of business as set out in the Tables in COB 6.6.50 to 6.6.52R, or the lower rate if COB 6.6.38R(1) applies (projections of surrender values and transfer values)[2]. Essentially where the firm reasonably expects this rate to overstate the potential rate a lower rate must be used and disclosed or where the customer specifically requests that a lower rate of return be used.

1   COB 5.2.12–5.2.14.
2   6.6.33R.

6.6.25 explains the 'contract period'. The various types of contract are set out in this section and the contract period may not be the most obvious one, for example, for a unit-linked 'endowment' written as a whole life contract to provide flexibility at the end of the initial premium term and also contracts where payment options contained in the contract are expected to be exercised.

K 'NEWCOB'

5.90   On October 31 2006 the FSA published a consultation paper which is likely to lead to changes in the Conduct of Business rules. This was entitled 'Reforming Conduct of Business Regulation (06/19)'. This reflects the move towards more principles-based regulation and away from prescriptive rules. The aim is to remove around one half of the existing COB Sourcebook and replace it with the substantially shorter new rulebook, NEWCOB. In addition, it would also partly implement MiFID. NEWCOB will replace the existing COB Sourcebook from 1 November 2007. Product disclosure issues are dealt with in Chapters 18 and 19. Whilst key features documents will be retained the requirement to provide an additional key features document for life policies after sale will be removed.

SECTION 3   CANCELLATION

A   Background

5.91   The underlying purpose of the cancellation rules coupled with the associated disclosure requirements is to give investors the opportunity to make considered and well informed investment decisions. Therefore the rules give the investor in appropriate circumstances a period for reflection. An ancillary purpose of these rules is to reduce the incentive to adopt 'hard sell' tactics.

The cancellation rules also give effect to requirements of the Consolidated Life Directive and are contained in COBS 6.7.

The rules are subject to the 'habitual residence' of the customer. Where a customer is habitually resident in an EEA State other than the UK at the time of signing the proposal or a state which is not an EEA State and the customer is not present in the UK at the time of signing the proposal the right to cancel does not apply. However for non-UK EEA State customers firms must apply cancellation in accordance with the rules of that member state (except in relation to certain e-commerce transactions)[1].

A right to cancel arises only for those contracts set out in the Table in COBS 6.7.15R and survives the exceptions set out in that Table. Exceptions include such contracts as life policies of six months or less, certain life policies effected by the trustees of occupational pension schemes or the employer, or the manager

1   6.7.16R, Note 4.

or trustees of a stakeholder pension scheme, traded life policies, life policies for defined benefits pension schemes, etc. Also, by virtue of COBS 6.7.23R agreements providing for increases in premium of more than 25% on existing contracts are regarded as deserving cancellation rights on the same basis as the original agreements. Note that this does not apply where the variation is as a result of a 'pre-selected option', eg index-linked premiums. The provisions of COB 6.7.19R provide for the alternative of a 'cancellation substitute' to be possible in some circumstances. These arrangements apply to pension transfers and annuities only.

B   Giving the investor notice of his right to cancel

5.92   In an agreement that can be cancelled under these rules the investor must be given clear and prominent notice of his right to cancel[1]. The notice must be sent no later than the end of the fourteenth day after the contract has been concluded. The notice must be given in writing or electronically where the customer can be demonstrated to wish to communicate in this manner[2]. If a firm does not give the customer information about his cancellation rights in accordance with COB App 1.1.1R(17), the contract remains cancellable and the customer will not be liable for any shortfall[3].

Where the customer is a trustee who is reasonably believed by the firm to be expected to act on the instructions of the individual beneficiary or purchaser of the policy the firm must send a copy of the cancellation notice to the trustee and the beneficiary or purchaser and must inform the beneficiary or the purchaser of the need to give instructions, within the specified cancellation period, to the trustee where the right to cancel is to be exercised[4].

C   Exercising the right to cancel

5.93   An investor who has the right to cancel may, without giving any reason, cancel the contract by serving notice on the firm, before the expiry of the relevant cancellation period either by post to the firm's last known address or in accordance with any other practical instructions for exercising that right provided to the customer in accordance with COB App 1.1.1R(17)(b) (which could be electronic if the firm has told customers that method is acceptable)[5]. If the firm voluntarily gives rights to cancel the contract must be treated as if it were cancellable in accordance with 6.7.7R(1)[6]. Notice of cancellation is valid where it is served in accordance with COB 6.7.42R[7]. Where the notice is in a durable

1   6.7.30R.
2   6.7.27G.
3   6.7.41G.
4   6.7.31R.
5   6.7.42R.
6   6.7.21R.
7   6.7.44R.

medium and served in accordance with COB 6.7.42, it must be treated as being served on the firm on the date it is despatched by the customer[1]. Notice is not valid if given outside the relevant period provided the firm has provided information on cancellation rights in accordance with COB App 1.1.1R(17)[2]. Where there are joint policyholders, cancellation by one of them (if he has a right) is as valid as cancellation by all[3].

D   Effect of cancellation

5.94   By exercising the right to cancel the customer withdraws from the contract which is thereby terminated. The firm must pay back to the customer any sums paid to the firm (including sums paid to any agents) in connection with the agreement. These sums must be paid without delay (with a limit of 30 days after having received the cancellation notice). The firm is entitled to receive back any sums paid by the firm or property which became the customer's under the agreement and the firm is also generally entitled to retain any shortfall[4].

E   Shortfall

5.95   Where the cancellation notice is sent back to the firm in the required time period and the price of the investment falls during the cancellation period, the firm is entitled to a charge on cancellation to make up for the market loss involved in the termination[5]. Table 6.7.58R explains how shortfall is calculated. Broadly speaking, it is the difference between the actual premium paid and what the premium would be for an equivalent agreement being taken out at the time of cancellation. In terms of life assurance it is only single premium policies which are subject to the shortfall provisions.

A firm cannot reclaim shortfall in certain circumstances: (i) where the firm has not given notice of cancellation rights as required, (ii) where the firm fails to make prominent mention of shortfall in the information about cancellation, (iii) on failure to send a reminder notice, (iv) where the customer has served the cancellation notice before the agreement is concluded[6].

F   Record-keeping

5.96   Where notice of cancellation has been validly served on the firm (or its appointed representative or agent) the firm must make and retain records (including a copy of any receipt of notice issued to the customer and the customer's

1 6.7.44R.
2 6.7.48R.
3 6.7.50R.
4 6.7.52R.
5 6.7.54R.
6 6.7.56R.

original notice instructions) for at least six years in the case of life policies and this period runs from the date when the firm first became aware that the notice of cancellation had been served[1].

SECTION 4   ANTI MONEY LAUNDERING PROVISIONS

5.97   It is necessary for persons involved in life assurance to have an understanding of money laundering issues and for life offices to implement the necessary regime in order to counter (so far as it is possible) the practice of money laundering with its links to organised crime and terrorism.

A   Relevant legislation

5.98   The Money Laundering Regulations 2003 were introduced on 28 November 2003 and came into force on 1 March 2004 (with certain exceptions) and implement in the UK the Second EC Money Laundering Directive (2001/97/EC). In the UK the authorities responsible for their enforcement are HM Treasury, the Financial Services Authority and HM Customs & Excise. The 2003 regulations revoked the Money Laundering Regulations 1993, the Money Laundering Regulations 2001 and the Financial Services and Markets Act 2000 (Regulations Relating to Money Laundering) Regulations 2001.

The Proceeds of Crime Act 2002 ('POCA') was enacted in July 2002 and was effective from 24 February 2003. The relevant sections are sections 327 to 340.

This piece of legislation has made the most significant impact on the money laundering legislation since 1994. It consolidates the previous legislation in respect of drugs (Drug Trafficking Act 1994) and serious crime (Criminal Justice Acts 1988 and 1993). The legislation relating to drugs and crime money laundering are encapsulated in POCA and the legislation relating to terrorist funding is encapsulated in the Terrorism Act 2000 and the Anti-terrorism Crime and Security Act 2001.

Money laundering offences have been created under Part 7 of POCA. The Act focuses on knowledge of the illegitimacy of funds being dealt with by persons. It introduces an objective test of 'knowledge or suspicion' in respect of offences of 'failing to report' under section 330. Sections 327 to 329 of the Act relate to the laundering of money or property that is or represents a benefit from criminal conduct. The 2002 Act has also extended the range of persons who are subject to money laundering provisions. In addition to firms which undertake investment business such as life offices it now extends to general professional activities, such as accountancy and legal services.

In ascertaining the application of money laundering provisions POCA refers to the 'regulated sector' and the Money Laundering Regulations 2003 (MLR) refer to 'relevant business'. The 'regulated sector' is defined in Schedule 9 and 'relevant business' is defined in MLR, Part I, para 2(2): Interpretation.

---

1   6.7.47R.

I What are the obligations?

5.99 Part II of the MLR sets out the 'obligations on persons who carry on relevant business'. These are:

(a) systems and training to prevent money laundering (reg 3);

(b) identification procedures (reg 4);

(c) record-keeping procedures (reg 6); and

(d) internal reporting procedures (reg 7).

They must also establish other procedures of internal control and communication for the purposes of forestalling and preventing money laundering.

B   Money Laundering Sourcebook

5.100 The FSA Handbook used to contain a dedicated Money Laundering Sourcebook but its provisions have now been amended and moved to the SYSC Handbook. The relevant provisions in the Senior Management, Systems and Controls Sourcebook (SYSC) are a less prescriptive approach and aim to put a clear focus on senior management responsibility for Anti Money Laundering systems and controls rather than simply treating Anti Money Laundering as complying with detailed requirements. Firms should benefit from having more flexibility to implement relevant systems and controls in the most appropriate way for them. It should also create a better fit between FSA requirements and money laundering legislation and industry guidance, so the overlaps are less.

C   Joint Money Laundering Steering Group's Guidance Notes for the Financial Sector

5.101 The Joint Money Laundering Steering Group ('JMLSG') is comprised of the leading UK trade associations in the financial services industry. Its aim is to promulgate good practice in countering money laundering and to give practical assistance in interpreting the UK Money Laundering Regulations. The primary tool used to achieve this is the publication of Guidance Notes.

The JMLSG has been producing Guidance Notes for the financial sector since 1990. The Guidance Notes have been regularly updated to reflect changing circumstances and developing good practice. The latest Guidance Notes were issued in January 2006.

The Guidance Notes are issued by the trade associations and not by the regulators and so their application is not mandatory. Failure to comply with the Guidance Notes does not mean that a financial sector firm has automatically breached the Regulations or the FSA rules. They do, however, provide an indication of what is expected of financial sector firms and in assessing compliance with SYSC, the FSA will have regard to these Notes. The specific sectoral guidance relating to life assurance is set out in Sector 7 of Part II of the Notes and it is specifically recognised that most of what might be described as the 'traditional' types of life assurance would not provide the functionality and flexibility to be the first choice for money launderers but others such as single premium investment bonds are more likely vehicles. Therefore, term assurance policies are generally categorised as 'reduced risk', endowment savings plans are 'intermediate risk' and single premium investment policies are 'increased risk'.

5   INSURANCE CONDUCT OF BUSINESS ('ICOB')

5.102   It is necessary for those involved in life assurance, or more specifically those involved in 'term' or 'temporary' life assurance, to now also be aware of the ICOB Sourcebook. Its provisions are mostly similar to the COB Sourcebook although there are differences.

Prior to FSMA 2000, and the creation of the FSA, there was little regulation of the way general insurance business was conducted. Insurance companies were subject to prudential regulation, first by the Department of Trade and Industry, then by the Treasury Insurance Directorate and latterly by the FSA. Insurance brokers were regulated by the Insurance Brokers Registration Council (IBRC), which was dissolved in April 2001. Intermediaries not regulated by the IBRC were subject to a voluntary code of practice issued by the Association of British Insurers and monitored by its members in conjunction with an accountancy firm. During 2001 the regulation of the conduct of general insurance business (whether by insurers or intermediaries) passed to a self-regulating body, the General Insurance Standards Council (GISC).

Before the adoption of the EU Insurance Mediation Directive[1], which required state regulation, it had been hoped by many in the industry that the existence of the GISC would be sufficient in terms of regulatory involvement in connection with the conduct of general insurance business. However, the requirement of state regulation meant that this attempt at self-regulation by the industry was superseded on 14 January 2005. The FSA assumed responsibility from that date for regulating the conduct of general business. The rules which came into force on that date implement the Insurance Mediation Directive and also the Distance Marketing Directive[2].

General insurance business (technically known as 'non-investment insurance contracts') became regulated with respect to both prudential and conduct of business issues with effect from 14 January 2005 although insurance companies have been prudentially regulated since 2001. Although falling within the definition of 'Contracts of Long-term Insurance' under Schedule 1, Part II of the Regulated Activities Order[3] contracts such as 'pure protection' life insurance (for example, term assurance) are currently governed by the ICOB as opposed to COB Sourcebook.

1   2002/92/EC.
2   2002/65/EC.
3   SI 2001/544.

The Insurance Mediation Directive is concerned with the regulation of all types of insurance intermediaries, including 'tied' insurance intermediaries. The Treasury and the FSA also decided that it was necessary to regulate the sales activities of insurance companies to seek to provide a level playing field for the various sectors of the industry. From 14 January 2005, the processes by which insurers and intermediaries alike sell policies must comply with the relevant FSA rules.

A   General approach

5.103   ICOB applies to firms who: (a) deal with general insurance business, term assurance or critical illness policies; and (b) hold an FSA permission to carry on one or more of the following regulated activities:

(a)   dealing as an agent;

(b)   arranging (bringing about) deals;

(c)   making arrangements with a view to transactions;

(d)   assisting in the administration and performance of a contract of insurance;

(e)   advising;

(f)   agreeing to carry on any of the above regulated activities.

ICOB sets out the information required to be given to customers when first meeting with an intermediary through the issue of an 'initial disclosure document' (IDD) which details the services a firm can offer and the charges to be made. The intermediary must also prepare a 'statement of demands and needs' which analyses the customer's requirements and sets out the proposed solution together with the intermediary's reasons for selecting the particular policy. ICOB also details the documentation to be provided to the customer before completion of the contract and the documentation to be issued upon completion of the contract.

B   Types of customers

5.104   ICOB distinguishes between retail customers (persons effecting a policy other than in a business or professional capacity) and commercial customers. The information requirements for commercial customers are significantly less than for retail customers, reflecting the basis of ICOB as the method of implementing the Distance Marketing Directive and the FSA's emphasis on consumer protection.

C   Distance contracts

5.105   Another distinction made in ICOB is with regard to the information to be provided to the customer where the policy is being arranged as a 'distance contract' and the information to be provided where the transaction is not a distance contract, and also the point at which information has to be provided. A distance contract is a transaction which is carried out by means of 'distance communication' (for example telephone, correspondence or internet) and where there is never any 'face-to-face' contact.

D   'Advised' and 'non-advised'

5.106   Another distinction made in ICOB relates to the responsibilities of the intermediary, depending on whether the sale of the policy is an 'advised' or a 'non-advised' sale (that is, whether the intermediary gave advice on the policy or the selection of insurer).

E   Conduct of Business Rules

5.107   These are not examined in detail here. In many respects they are very similar to the COB Rules for investment products. However, there are some important and interesting differences. For example, in connection with unfair inducements there is no prohibition on volume overrides in ICOB.

From March 2006 the requirements for insurers dealing direct with retail customers have been modified so that insurers do not have to issue IDDs and do not have to issue a statement of demands and needs where the sale is non-advised, provided that the documentation issued to the customer makes it clear that no personal recommendation has been made.

Under ICOB (unlike COB) there are currently no commission disclosure requirements applicable to retail customers.

If a personal recommendation is made (that is, the intermediary recommends a particular policy as meeting the customer's requirements) the recommendation must be suitable for the customer's demands and needs and within the scope of services offered according to the IDD. The demands and needs statement is the general business equivalent of the fact-find used in investment business as the insured must be asked sufficient questions to enable a full assessment of his or her requirements to be made. ICOB does not prescribe a format for a demands and needs statement but it must have the content set out in ICOB 4.4.6G. The statement must be provided in a durable medium before the conclusion of the contract unless the sale is taking place by telephone, when it can be provided immediately after conclusion of the contract.

ICOB 5 requires several categories of information to be provided to customers two of which have no direct 'equivalence' in COBS, namely provision of a policy document, which must be consistent with the policy summary (the latter being broadly equivalent to the key features document) and information about the claims-handling process.

F Particular requirements for distance contracts for retail customers

5.108 Prior to conclusion of the contract the customer must be provided with: policy summary; statement of price (premium and any other fees, charges and taxes); directive-required information; policy document; information about the claims-handling process; information about cancellation rights; information about compensation schemes.

In the case of telephone sales and other means of distance communication, it is possible to depart from these requirements at the request of the customer before the conclusion of the contract. However, such information must be provided in a durable medium immediately afterwards.

CHAPTER 6

With-profits funds

SUMMARY

Section 1   Introduction and the nature of with-profits   **6.1**

Section 2   Principles and Practices of Financial Management (PPFM)   **6.6**

Section 3   COB 6.12 – treating with-profits policyholders fairly   **6.18**

Section 4   COB 6.13 – process for reattribution of inherited estates   **6.29**

Section 5   Closed long-term funds   **6.32**

Section 6   Governance   **6.33**

SECTION 1   INTRODUCTION AND THE NATURE OF WITH-PROFITS

A   Introduction and background

6.1   Chapter 1[1] explained the difference between a mutual insurer and a proprietary company. The traditional model for mutual long-term insurers was as providers of with-profits funds. With-profits funds have also traditionally been provided by proprietary companies. Often the provision of with-profits investment is part of the constitution of such companies and policies may refer to an Act of Parliament and/or the Articles of the Company.

As its name suggests, with-profits business is a means by which 'investors' share in the profits generated by the company. One of the primary aims of with-profits investments is to provide a stable return. This is done by 'smoothing' the return, holding back in some years and supplementing in others.

The advent of unit-linked policies highlighted the discretionary nature of with-profits arrangements and led to a slightly more transparent version: the unitised with-profits contract. Whilst something of a hybrid, it is not a unit-linked con-

---

1   See **1.67**.

247

tract because of the discretion still exercised by the life office in setting bonus payments.

With-profits business is not as straightforward a concept as it might seem. This is due to the differing nature of assets held to back different types and generations of policies and the fact that not all offices operate their with-profits business in the same way. In addition commercial interests, particularly of proprietary companies, often have a bearing on the contracts offered, the bonuses payable and the source of such payments (eg from other resources of the insurer or 'inherited' estates).

Following the House of Lords judgment in *Equitable Life v Hyman*[1] in 2000, the sector attracted much criticism and ultimately a regulatory overhaul. This regulatory overhaul involved changes to key personnel (the introduction of the new with-profits actuary role), the requirement to produce Principles and Practices of Financial Management, and a host of new rules designed to ensure policyholders are treated fairly. Each of these is described in more detail in this chapter.

B The nature of with-profits contracts

6.2 With-profits as a concept has been the investment vehicle used to provide a guaranteed level of life cover with a potential investment upside. It worked well in high inflation/high growth environments but this led to a general investor expectation that the target amount desired (often as part of an endowment mortgage) would not only be achieved but would be exceeded. For a number of years in the late 1980s and 1990s it is probably fair to say that with-profits endowments were mis-sold because it was not anticipated that the prevailing favourable economic conditions would change[2]. As a result of the stock market falls in the first few years of the new millennium and the effect of the *Equitable Life* decision, many with-profits funds have had to adopt a much more cautious investment strategy. The likely level of return on a with-profits policy does not, at the time of writing, make it a very attractive proposition.

A conventional with-profits insurance contract will have a guaranteed maturity value to which bonuses can be added either annually (reversionary bonuses), when the investor surrenders (interim), or at maturity (terminal bonuses). From a strict contractual perspective the policyholder is only entitled to the guaranteed amount on maturity or death. Entitlement to bonuses already declared also only arises at that time (there is no contractual right to any future bonuses). Whilst there are a number of commercial variants, for example only part of the insured sum attracting bonuses, the general structure is normally the same.

A unitised with-profits contract is an arrangement whereby the assets are notionally allocated to establish the value of units. However, unlike a unit-linked fund where there is a direct link to the underlying assets, the process of valuation contains discretions enabling the value of units to be increased (or reduced) to

1 [2000] 3 All ER 961.
2 FSA Endowment Mis-selling Review.

reflect any past or potential future poor performance of the underlying assets (similar to bonus setting on conventional contracts with smoothing). The bonus is, however, added to the value of the existing contract, giving the policyholder a clearer view of how much their contract is currently worth and the amount available on surrender unless a Market Value Adjustment or Reduction (MVR) is applied by the life office to reduce that value.

6.3   The nature of with-profits has led to a number of practical issues. First is the dissatisfaction with the calculation of surrender values. Prior to 2005 there was little formal control of surrender values as contractual provisions gave huge discretion to the life office in determining the amount payable on surrender. It was therefore possible for a surrender value to be hugely discounted. Because of the difference in the surrender value and the market value of certain types of life policy, a market has established in second-hand endowment contracts, predominantly in relation to with-profits contracts. New rules in COB 6.12 relating to the calculation of surrender values may, however, restrict this market in the future.

A second major issue for with-profits contracts is the perception that even if policies are held to maturity that policyholders do not get their fair share of 'profits'. The *Equitable Life* decision (see **6.4**) is relevant here. Regulators have had a difficult task historically checking that policyholders are being treated fairly. In part this arises because of the vague nature of the bargain the policyholder struck (ie a share in some of the profits of the life office). Over time companies have held different assets to support different groups of with-profits policies, sharing in different types of profit. This has meant that different rates of bonus are awarded to such groups. This was facilitated by the creation of different bonus series', sometimes with different charges and participation in other business such as non-profit business. Unfortunately, life offices' practices in operating their funds varied quite significantly, which made the regulator's task difficult. The FSA has now mounted a multi-level attack on this area by imposing minimum standards and standardising some of the terminology and calculations. It has significantly increased the disclosure requirement in relation to each fund by replacing the With-Profits Guide with a much more detailed Principles and Practices of Financial Management ('PPFM'). A customer-friendly version of this document is also now required. (See **6.16**). In addition to providing transparency, these requirements also have the knock-on effect of requiring life offices to ensure that they have documented the processes referred to. Historically, many of the practices may not have been formally recorded even within the life office itself.

Another way in which with-profits policyholders may not get their fair share of profits is in relation to smoothing. Although a with-profits fund is designed to smooth out the peaks and troughs of investment performance, it is not an exact science. A life office's assumptions about future returns may be too cautious and the life office therefore retains reserves which arguably should be distributed to policies who participated in the relevant profits. Over time significant amounts of money can be built up. If this is not distributed to the policies responsible for creating it, it can become what is known as an inherited estate or 'orphan assets'. A certain amount of money in 'an estate' is required to run a fund efficiently and to provide flexibility. However, once this level is exceeded, and particularly where the excess has been passed from generation to generation of policyholder, it becomes difficult to establish who actually owns it. The FSA has introduced new rules as part of its treating with-profits customers fairly project (COB 6.12), which are designed to prevent such surpluses being built up in future. It has also introduced new requirements in relation to the process for reattributing existing inherited estates (COB 6.13).

There have also been a number of other issues which have caused the nature and use of with-profits funds assets to be called into question. These include the use of the with-profits fund to buy assets for strategic purposes (ie business reasons) and new business strategies which result in existing business being disadvantaged by the terms on which new business is accepted. The new rules in COB 6.12 and the PPFM requirements in COB 6.10 also seek to deal with these issues.

C   The *Equitable Life* decision

6.4   *Equitable Life Assurance Society v Hyman*[1] was something of a watershed in terms of with-profits business. The fallout from it and the Penrose report into the collapse of the Equitable played a large part in the FSA's treating with-profits customers fairly initiative which has led to a much more stringent form of regulation of with-profits business. The case was an application to the court for a declaration to enable the directors to make an allocation of bonus in accordance with asset share (which was the bonus philosophy of the fund and therefore the primary driver from the Equitable's perspective of achieving fairness between its policyholders). Interestingly, as will be seen later, it (ie distribution of asset share) has subsequently become the driver of the FSA's treating with-profits customers fairly initiative although now there are also requirements to communicate and explain it to customers. Mr Hyman was a representative policyholder who would lose out if the declaration were approved. He was expecting to get more than his asset share because the benefits under his contract could be taken in the form of an annuity at guaranteed rates. It is important to bear in mind that this annuity was an intrinsic part of the contract, as without the obligation on the life office to provide the annuity, it may not have been an insurance contract at all. It should arguably have been different if the annuity were a separate product to be purchased from the proceeds of the first contract.

To understand the case it is helpful to start from basics. All policyholders, whether or not their policy contained guaranteed rates on the ultimate annuity, bought a contract which guaranteed a maturity value which could be increased over-time by bonuses. These bonuses were normally allotted annually and on maturity, the amount, (if any), being allocated in accordance with the contract. The contract provided for allocation by the directors among the participating policies using 'such methods and principles as the directors may from time to time determine'. This meant that the directors had potentially a very wide discretion.

1 [2000] 3 All ER 961, HL and [2000] 2 All ER 331, CA.

The stated bonus policy of the Equitable was to aim for payment of asset share (broadly the amount the individual policy's premiums had earned less charges). The terms of the guarantee were an add-on to this and, it is fair to say, were something of a marketing gimmick as when originally included they were not necessarily of any value. However, over time they acquired value and the Equitable did not seek to impose any charges in relation to them, it would appear believing that as bonuses for individual policies should reflect asset share, the value could be dealt with in the amount allocated by way of terminal bonus. The directors made the adjustment by way of differential terminal bonuses because the contracts allowed the policyholder to decide to use the policy proceeds to buy an annuity with another provider. The bonus amount under the differential bonus was therefore always the asset share amount. If the option to buy an annuity from a third party was taken then the asset share was paid as a lump sum. If the option to take the annuity under the existing contract was taken then the annuity amount reflected the cost of the guarantee. Whilst this ensured that the policyholder got their asset share (and only that) irrespective of how they took their benefits, it had the effect in practice of negating the value of the guarantee.

As the contractual discretions included were very wide and as stated the aim was to return asset shares, it is arguable that the real mischief in such cases was the prominence given to the guaranteed rates in marketing the contracts to individuals. Such marketing should have made clear that the guaranteed rates would not increase the person's share of the amount distributed (either because a charge would be imposed or because a lower terminal bonus would be applied to that benefit) – not an ideal marketing message and certainly not the one conveyed. Also, marketing of these policies at that time tended to be high level relying on the policy terms. Although the court case did not deal with individual sales issues, it did clearly take into account the impression that had been created (in part by the guaranteed rates added to the policy) that the guaranteed rates were somehow additional to the main with-profits bargain and could result in the person getting more than their asset share.

6.5   The original application for the declaration in the High Court was successful and it is worth quoting from the reasoning of Sir Richard Scott VC which sets out the whole issue very succinctly:

> 'He [a policyholder taking an annuity at the guaranteed rate] is being allotted a lesser final bonus because a lesser final bonus is all that is needed to bring the value of the benefits he receives up to his asset share . . . to allot final bonus on . . . a basis that used assets share as a yardstick for the value of benefits taken rather than as a yardstick for the capital sum by reference to which the amount of the annuity taken was calculated, was in my judgment a decision well within their discretion.'

It is only a pity, in view of the consequences, that the case did not stop there but the rest, as they say, is history.

The House of Lords decision, which confirmed the Court of Appeal's majority decision, was that it was necessary to imply a term into the contract to prevent the directors acting as proposed and thereby cutting across the reasonable expectations of the relevant policyholders. The fact that the Equitable was a mutual without the means to satisfy the judgment and that the result of the decision would be to cut across the reasonable and contractual expectation of the non-guaranteed annuity option holders did not prevent such a term being implied. It was clearly a difficult situation because there was a conflict between the main terms of the contract and the way the guaranteed annuity rates had been added. In the authors' view it is clear (from the differential bonus scheme) that the Equitable did not intend to offer the guaranteed rates as a means of increasing one person's asset share at the expense of another and had the implied term which effectively permitted that to happen been suggested to them at the outset, they would not have agreed to it. Much of the mischief appears to have resulted from the fact that the guaranteed annuity options were marketed in a way which implied that they were additional to the with-profits bargain.

Arguably a fairer basis for the decision, in view of the consequences, would have been to accept that the contractual provision was wide enough to allow the directors to allocate differential bonuses and to treat the additional costs of the guaranteed annuity rates as a mis-selling cost that should, as it was a mutual, have been applied to all policies.

There is some unclear dicta between the two appellate court decisions relating to what has been known as the 'ring-fencing' issue. Waller LJ suggested in the Court of Appeal case that the Equitable could lawfully have declared different bonuses for classes of policies with guaranteed annuity options and for those without. This would in effect have reduced the bonuses to reflect asset share. Lord Steyen makes clear in the House of Lords judgment that he believes this would be precluded by the implied term described above. The House of Lords judgment leaves a number of questions unanswered such as the extent to which existing policyholders can be charged for the cost of benefits such as guarantees where life offices have not charged for them before. Some life offices have tried to deal with this issue in their PPFMs by specifying the basis on which such charges could be imposed in the future. It is difficult, in relation to existing policies, to be clear from a legal perspective whether over time such statements will be sufficient to prevent the creation of a reasonable expectation that such charges will not be imposed.

It is fair to say that the result of the House of Lords case was an unmitigated disaster. Although Equitable Life had brought most of the consequences on itself because of its own financial position, because it was a mutual, those consequences were borne by its members. The result was a 746 page report, the Penrose report, which highlighted failings in the management of Equitable Life. Apart from issues with specific individuals and an apparent failure to challenge the senior management, it appears that the company was over distributing and not reserving for significant downturns, which is supposed to be one of the features of with-profits business. The practice of relying on terminal bonus adjustment rather than reserving for the guaranteed annuity options (which started in 1994) should also have been picked by the regulator at the time but it appears it was not. Had Equitable Life been required to do so then either guaranteed annuity option policies or even all policies could at that stage and for the future have borne the cost of establishing the relevant reserves.

SECTION 2   PRINCIPLES AND PRACTICES OF FINANCIAL MANAGEMENT (PPFM)

6.6   COB 6.10 sets out the requirement to produce a PPFM for life offices conducting with-profits business. The detailed requirements apply to UK autho-rised life offices but EEA life offices are also required to provide equivalent information[1]. The PPFM is a very detailed record of the life office's relevant pro-cedures and practices. The idea seems to be to get insurers to disclose the infor-mation required to enable assessment of whether their funds are being operated as they should be – almost providing an external benchmark by which to judge it. Life offices are also required to produce a customer-friendly 'potted' version of the PPFM in language the customer would be able to understand.

   If a life office has more than one with-profits fund it may need to produce a PPFM for each fund unless they are, and have in the past, been operated in a similar way, in which case the relevant differences would need to be noted. Life offices are required to provide a copy of the PPFM free of charge to their with-profits policyholders and for a reasonable cost (to cover copying) to anyone else. The FSA's guidance advises that a life office may wish to publish its PPFM on its website. This is in contrast to the requirement[2] to prominently signpost the availability of its customer-friendly PPFM on its website.

   The required contents of the PPFM are set out in COB 6.10.22. Each topic is split between the high level principle which is not expected to change and prac-tices which may in certain circumstances be changed. The PPFM requirements can be categorised as follows:

A   Calculation of bonuses and smoothing (COB 6.10.26–6.10.29)

B   Investment strategy (COB 6.10.40–6.10.45)

C   Business risk (COB 6.10.46–6.10.51)

D   Charges and expenses (COB 6.10.52–6.10.55)

E   Management of the inherited estate (COB 6.10.56–6.10.58)

F   Controlling new business and closure to new business (COB 6.10.59)

G   Equity between the fund and shareholders (COB 6.10.62–6.10.64)

The rules work by setting out the actual requirement and then giving guidance to indicate what should be covered by the principles and what should be covered by the practices.

A   Calculation of bonuses and smoothing

6.7   The requirements in relation to the calculation of the amount due to with-profits policyholders (eg bonuses and smoothing) focus on the need to

---

1   COB 6.10.21B.
2   COB 6.10.9F.

record the methods used, the degree of approximation, how changes are made and where it is all recorded. The practices also need to specify the target ranges for maturity values (and therefore surrender values) and the factors a life office is likely to have regard to under COB 6.12.59 (ie the basis on which it holds additional monies in the fund to address 'matters relevant to the policyholders' interests or security other than amounts held to support insurance businesses or to maintain financial strength'). It is not really clear what these could be, but if there are any, and if they are to be taken account of in calculating excess surplus (see **6.23**), then they need to be specified in the PPFM. The practices should also make clear whether expenses are borne by the inherited estate or in some other way. There is a theme in the PPFM requirements which is to make transparent the extent to which external support is provided to the fund, the idea being to commit the provider of the support, either the inherited estate or the shareholder, to provide the specified level of support. (See also 6.10.41(2), 6.10.42(1) and 6.10.43). Following the *Equitable Life* decision, life offices are also required to describe in the practices how they bring items such as the cost of guarantees and charges for the use of capital into account[1].

The PPFM requires life offices to explain their approach to setting annual and final bonuses. The principles should specify constraints due to economic factors and indicate how the life office would determine 'the range or generations of policyholders' covered by a single bonus series. In relation to final bonuses, the significance of early surrender on the maturity value or application of a Market Value Reduction (MVR) (to reduce the value of unitised with-profits) should be described. The practices should also describe any limits applied in setting bonuses (eg maximum/minimum changes in bonus rates from one year to the next) and the life office's approach to setting interim bonuses.

The PPFM should also set out the life office's approach to smoothing and include matters specified in COB 12.47. This provides that a life office's PPFM must include details in relation to the smoothing policy applied to each type of with-profits policy, any limits to the total cost or excess amount to be smoothed and any limits applied to year on year maturity amounts for the purposes of consistency. The principles should also specify whether a life office considers that the cost of smoothing will be neutral over time and the time period over which it is expected to be neutral. This can be difficult in practice if in reality it is linked to the economic cycle, in that case the overall limit to the cost of smoothing the life office is prepared to tolerate must be specified[2]. A life office must also state in the practices whether or not it applies a single smoothing strategy to all generations of policyholder, and in particular how it deals with new entrants when the accumulated costs of smoothing are high. COB 6.10.39(16) states that life offices should go on to describe how accurately the life office applies MVR or surrender and transfer bases to give effect to smoothing. This seems slightly at odds with the provisions of COB 6.12, in particular in relation to the application of a MVR which should be limited to reduced asset value or liquidity issues (see **6.20**).

1   COB 6.10.30(15).
2   COB 6.10.39(2).

B   Investment strategy

6.8   By manipulating or simply changing its investment strategy a life office could significantly change the return on a with-profits policy. Changing the investment strategy is arguably currently of most concern in relation to closed life funds. COB 6.12 deals with a life office's ability to change its investment strategy. This is complemented by the requirement to describe in the PPFM the significant aspects of its strategy, including the degree of matching, the life office's approach to credit liquidity and market risk and the effect of and justification for holding strategic assets (ie assets that would not normally be traded because of their importance to the life office, such as head office premises). The principles should specify the investment strategy in some detail. The FSA states[1] that it should be in more detail than simply achieving the best return within the framework of the likely volatility of asset values. The principles should also set out the role of derivatives and the life office's counterparty limits, especially those relating to derivatives. Reliance on assets held outside the fund should be described.

The practices provide for the life office to describe the process by which assets relied upon to permit flexibility in investment would be transferred to the fund and recognised as an irretrievable transfer. In many demutualisation schemes arrangements exist to provide support to with-profits funds either when policyholders' expectations will not be met, or perhaps more drastically, to ensure solvency of the with-profits fund on a stand-alone basis. These schemes often provide contingent support which becomes permanent in specified circumstances. Other similar arrangements may exist more informally. Such arrangements should be explained in the PPFM.

C   Business risk

6.9   In relation to strategic assets the principles should describe why the assets are of use to the fund and how that is reviewed, any limits on such assets and whether holding them will impact the policyholders' pay out.

The PPFM must cover the life office's exposure to business risk, in particular how it decides which risks to take and how it allocates profits and loss. It is common for different classes of with-profits policyholder to be exposed to different business risks (eg in relation to non-profit business relating to their own age/sex). A life office should make clear how it considers business risk exposures before accepting them and how it assesses the risk/reward position. In its principles the life office should set out general limits on new risk and how it controls existing risk. In particular it should define where compensation costs from a business risk would be borne. The practices should describe the degree of smoothing of such risk and specify the extent to which different classes/generations of policyholder bear particular risks.

---

1   COB 6.10.41G/1.

D Charges and expenses

6.10 The PPFM must explain how a life office applies charges and allocates expenses including, if material, any interaction with connected life offices (eg service companies)[1]. The risk for with-profits policyholders is that the life office extracts additional profit from the fund which because of the lack of transparency in the fund is difficult to identify. Where service company arrangements exist they may have been set up to fix the amount the fund pays for a service but with a view to the service company making a profit by providing the service more efficiently. In practice, the FSA (and the DTI as its predecessor) has often exerted a substantial amount of control over the amount such service companies can charge. The requirement in the PPFM is to disclose to the policyholder, and anyone else reading the PPFM, how charges and expenses are borne. For conventional policies this will normally be an allocation of expenses. For unitised policies there will often be an explicit management charge but the fund will also bear expenses (eg dealing costs) so that the total cost is a mixture of charges and expenses. Where the fund invests in a collective investment scheme (either of an associated company or a third party) the costs and expenses of such investment must also be included. The principles should also set out the factors that would drive a change in the life office's practice.

The practices should describe the current charges and expenses apportioned to major classes of with-profits policies and the 'relationship' between the actual charges and expenses and those applied to the policy. Life offices also need to state the circumstances under which they charge expenses on a basis other than at cost and the reason for doing so. Furthermore, a life office should specify how often it reviews its outsourced services and how it can terminate such arrangements[2]. Finally, the PPFM should make clear the criteria the life office applies when it has to decide how to apply charges or apportion expenses between the fund and shareholders.

E Inherited estate

6.11 The PPFM must describe the life office's management of any inherited estate (ie excess assets built up over generations of policyholder) and the uses to which the life office may put that inherited estate[3]. The principles should indicate the amount of inherited estate the life office is aiming for, for example, by reference to the volume of its business or the risks borne by the life office's existing business. The principles should also describe any restrictions applying to inherited estate by virtue of a scheme or reattribution. The practices should specify the costs the inherited estate is currently meeting. They also need to describe the investment strategy of the estate and how the life office would deal with the estate if it were to become too big or too small.

1   COB 6.10.52.
2   COB 6.10.54(4).
3   COB 6.10.56.

F   New business

6.12   The value of with-profits funds can be affected both by business risk undertaken by the fund and by new with-profits business. In some cases it is better for the fund to accept business only into new bonus series' or not to accept such business at all. COB 6.12 contains rules to restrict the ability of a fund to enter into new arrangements. In its PPFM a life office which is still open to new business must describe its practice for reviewing limits on the quantity and type of new with-profits business and the actions that the life office would take if it ceased to take on new with-profits business of any significant amount[1]. The principles should describe how the life office would limit its exposure to new business and how it would deal with closing to significant new business, in particular how it would deal with the inherited estate[2]. The practices should also describe the level of new business required to keep the fund open.

G   Equity

6.13   One of the other major potential sources of concern for with-profit policyholders in a proprietary company is the inherent difficulty in situations where there might be a conflict of interests between the policyholders' interests and those of the shareholder. For this reason rules exist to prevent life offices manipulating the amount that can be distributed to shareholders. The PPFM has to describe the basis on which the shareholder's share in profits to be divided can be changed. It also has to deal with other means of passing value to shareholders (eg by the way tax is borne on the shareholder distribution or the effect of a change in the valuation basis[3]. The practices should also state whether the pricing of any policies are being written at the expense of the inherited estate.

H   Changes to the PPFM

6.14   When the requirement to produce PPFMs was first introduced life offices were able to make changes to the principles on three months' notice, changes to practices merely having to be notified. Now COB 6.12.13 provides that changes must, in the opinion of the governing body, be justified by the need to: respond to changes in the business or economic environment (including changes in the law); protect the interest of the policyholders; or, in respect of a change in the practices, better achieve the principles. Other changes are permitted to rectify errors, to improve clarity or presentation, or if they are immaterial (it is not clear what immaterial means for this purpose). In any event these requirements mean that life offices need to ensure the continued accuracy of their documents and be able to justify any changes made.

1   COB 6.10.59.
2   COB 6.10.60.
3   COB 6.10.64.

I EEA

6.15 COB 6.10.21A–K sets out the obligations for EEA insurers. 'Equivalent information', which must not be narrower in scope or less detailed in content than the equivalent PPFM (the full version not the customer-friendly one), has to be provided on request. The EEA insurer must also give three months' advanced notice to its UK habitually resident customers of changes to 'principle' equivalent information and give notice in relation to changes to 'practice' equivalent information.

J Customer-friendly version

6.16 COB 6.10.9B requires life offices to produce a consumer-friendly version of the PPFM. It must describe the most important information set out under each of the headings in the PPFM in language that can be easily understood by inexperienced policyholders. Life offices need to provide a copy of the customer-friendly PPFM with written notices proposing changes to the PPFM, annual statements sent to with-profits policyholders (unless there has been no material changes since last supplied) and with key features documents. The customer-friendly PPFM can be included in another document and must be provided free of charge.

K Annual report

6.17 COB 6.11 provides guidance to a life office in relation to the systems and controls in relation to with-profits business. It also requires a life office to make an annual report available to its with-profits policyholders. See further **6.33–6.34**.

SECTION 3   COB 6.12 – TREATING WITH-PROFITS POLICYHOLDERS FAIRLY

A   An overview of TCF and COB 6.12

6.18 The FSA needed to deal with the issues identified in **6.3** (the lack of transparency making it difficult to assess whether customers were getting a fair deal and the consequences of the *Equitable Life* decision). This coincided with the FSA's increased emphasis on the concept of treating customers fairly (TCF) which led to the issue of a number of consultation papers and a policy statement[1] directed at the fair treatment of with-profits policyholders. In high-level terms what the FSA has sought to do is to require detailed disclosure in PPFMs,

---

1   CP207, CP04 and PS05/1.

including disclosure of maturity and surrender value targets, supported by a need to manage the fund to achieve those targets. Restrictions are also now applied to the calculation of surrender values and Market Value Adjustments/Reductions (MVRs). To prevent the under distribution of profits life offices are required to assess the surplus held and, where there is an excess surplus, they would normally be expected to distribute it or do a reattribution. New rules also apply to the reattribution of inherited estates. A further myriad of rules seek to prevent the life office from changing its investment strategy or using its funds inappropriately and to control the basis on which it enters into significant new transactions.

In addition to the detailed rules, COB 6.12.11 requires life offices to consider both their strict contract with customers and their 'wider bargain'. It is assumed that this incorporates obligations that would reasonably be presumed from the course of dealings with the customer, but its extent is not clear. It should be noted that COB 6.12.11 also requires a life office to consider whether any discretion is being exercised 'for the purpose for which it was granted or reserved'. Then, as a catch all, life offices should consider any material factor that 'may' be relevant to the fair treatment of their with-profits policyholders[1].

COB 6.12 applies to all with-profits funds maintained and operated in the UK but as non-directive friendly societies are not required to produce PPFMs, it applies appropriately amended to such companies. COB 6.12 is designed to supplement the FSA Principles in particular Principle 6 (Treating Customers Fairly), Principle 7 (Communications with Clients) and Principle 8 (Conflicts of Interest).

6.19   COB 6.12 came into force on 30 June 2005 (apart from in relation to maturity and surrender targets, which came into force on 31 December 2006). It applies to EEA life offices carrying on with-profits business in the UK but only to the extent that a matter is not reserved to the home state regulator[2]. In broad terms it contains the following:

- Rules requiring life offices to set target maturity (and surrender values) for their contracts and to manage the fund with a view to achieving those targets in at least 90% of cases.

- Rules restricting a life office's ability to charge early surrender penalties or Market Value Reductions (for unitised contracts) where the amount involved is not directly related to the value of the underlying assets or their liquidity.

- Rules restricting a life office's ability to vary its investment strategy.

- Rules restricting a life office's ability to make changes to its PPFM.

- Rules preventing distribution (other than from surplus) and requiring an annual assessment of 'excess surplus' which should normally then be distributed or reattributed.

---

1   FN 6.12.11(5).
2   COB 6.12.2.

- Rules restricting the charging of expenses to a with-profits fund.

- Rules preventing the payment of compensation or redress (other than out of the inherited estate or shareholder funds) from a with-profits fund.

- Rules restricting the ability to write new business that might have a material adverse effect on existing with-profits policyholders.

- Rules preventing loans or guarantees to or for connected parties other than on commercial terms and for the benefit of the fund.

- Restriction on material transactions (eg bulk outwards or *any* inwards reinsurance or financial engineering transactions), unless the governing body is satisfied that they will not have a material adverse effect on the fund. A report from an appropriate adviser will be required to substantiate this.

- Notification and other rules relating to closing funds and run off.

Each of these is explained in more detail below except the rules on closed funds which are described at **6.32**.

B   Target maturity and surrender values

6.20   One of the ways in which the FSA has sought to provide greater transparency and consistency in with-profits funds is by introducing the concept of target maturity and surrender values. This is coupled with a requirement to manage the fund in a way which aims to achieve the target values. The obligation to specify a target range is expressed in relation to unsmoothed asset share (premiums paid plus investment return on them (net of charges)). To the non-actuarial mind it may come as something of a surprise to find that the term 'asset share' did not have a universally accepted meaning. Some life offices apparently calculated asset shares to include purely investment returns whereas others included a share of other businesses in which a policy or group of policies (or the estate) were participating. The FSA's rules define how it should be calculated. Having said that the FSA accepts that an unsmoothed asset share may not always be possible or appropriate in all circumstances[1]. In such cases a life office may use a more 'appropriate' methodology to set bonus rates provided that methodology is 'consistently applied and properly reflects its representations to with-profits policyholders'.

The definition of unsmoothed asset share is contained in COB 6.12.24. The methods to be applied are specified in PRU 7.41.19 to 123[2] but include amounts added as the result of a distribution from an inherited estate. COB 6.12.24(2) (c) makes clear that 'where the terms of the policy so provide' the effect of a participation in insurance business should be reflected. Losses which result from a failure to comply with COB 6.12 cannot, however, be deducted unless they

1   COB 6.12.23.
2   INS PRU 1.3.119 to 1.3.123.

cannot realistically be met from the estate or shareholder funds[1]. The reference to the terms of the policy so providing is probably a get out in most cases as historically very few (if any) policies will have detailed the particular pockets of insurance business in which groups of policies may have participated. In most cases this will therefore reduce the target value if strictly applied by the insurer.

A life office may calculate its unsmoothed asset share on an actual policy or on a specimen policy basis but it must specify in its PPFM which basis is applied to particular groups of policyholders[2].

COB 6.12.17 imposes requirements in relation to maturity values. Except where it is contractually obliged to provide a higher amount, a life office must set a target range, either for all its with-profits policyholders or for each group of with-profit policyholders. The target range is required to be expressed as a percentage of unsmoothed asset shares and must include 100% of unsmoothed asset share. This is interesting because 100% is merely required to be included somewhere within the range[3]. Once the life office has established its target range it must specify it in the PPFM, manage the fund with the aim of meeting the target range, and should have 'good reason' to believe that 90% of its maturity amounts are within the target range. In addition, as a long-term aim, the with-profits business should be managed to make aggregate maturity payments on its with-profits policies of 100% unsmoothed asset share.

This 'aggregate' target is designed to encourage life offices to treat generations of policyholders in the same way. However, the FSA accepts that this may not always be possible[4]. The target value is intended to be followed unless the life office has good reason to believe that it cannot, having taken into account any shareholder support arrangements and the benefit of provisions under any insurance business transfer scheme.

The *Equitable Life* decision looms large in many of the new provisions in COB 6.12. Further rules apply to the calculation of unsmoothed asset share relating to the life office's ability to deduct the cost of guarantees and similar policy benefits. In high-level terms, life offices are required to have a plan (having regard of course to legal considerations) specifying the basis on which charges can be applied. This should be consistent with and disclosed in a life office's PPFM[5]. Any deduction must be proportionate to and consistent with the costs that it is intended to offset and disclosed in key features and projections. The charges should also not change unless justified by a review carried out by changes in the business or economic environment or changes in the nature of the life office's liabilities as a result of policyholders exercising options in their policies.

6.21   COB 6.12.30–40 introduces fundamental obligations in relation to surrender values. Firstly, although a life office may use its own methods to calculate

1   COB 6.12.24(d).
2   COB 6.12.27.
3   COB 6.12.17.
4   COB 6.12.21.
5   COB 6.12.30.

surrender values, in aggregate they must be not less than the target maturity values less an amount 'necessary, in the opinion of the life office's governing body, to protect the interests of the life office's remaining with-profits policyholders'. COB 6.12.42G provides that this may include the life office's unrecovered costs (eg commission payments), amounts to reflect the true value of the underlying assets, the life office's costs in administering the surrender, and a fair contribution towards benefits under continuing policies which would otherwise result in higher costs falling on the continuing with-profits policies. This last point seems very broad and it remains to be seen how this will be dealt with in practice.

Similar provisions apply in relation to unitised with-profits contracts except they are limited to reductions in the value of the underlying assets or to allow for liquidity risk. Life offices may therefore now only apply MVRs where the market value of the underlying assets or liquidity problems will affect the life office's ability to realise the assets (eg when a high volume of surrenders is anticipated). The MVR must also be limited to the amount necessary to reflect these risks[1]. One of the criticisms post the *Equitable Life* judgment was based on the perception that the MVRs applied were penal. This provision, by limiting reductions to the amount 'necessary' to reflect the risk to the fund, should protect policyholders from such actions in the future.

C   Distributions

6.22   A life office must not make a distribution from a with-profits fund unless the whole of the cost of that distribution can be met without eliminating the regulatory surplus in that fund[2]. Realistic life offices (ie large with-profits life offices)[3] also need to ensure that there is a surplus on a realistic basis[4]. As the realistic basis of calculating liabilities includes discretionary and other non-contractual benefits, this should be higher than regulatory surplus and therefore potentially reduce the amount available for distribution. The life office must also ensure that the amount distributed to policyholders is not less than the required percentage of the total amount distributed. The required percentage is not less than 90% unless the company's constitution or a court order specifies otherwise. A life office that has an established practice specified in its PPFM to pay a different amount may also continue to do so. It is not clear how these rules fit with the rules in Rule 3.4 of IPRU (INS) but they are certainly much easier to follow.

---

1   COB 6.12.45.
2   COB 6.12.48.
3   With-profits liabilities of £500m or more.
4   COB 6.12.49.

D   Excess surplus

6.23   In order to prevent life offices building up future inherited estates they are now required to perform an annual assessment[1] to see if they have an excess surplus and, if so, normally to distribute it or carry out a reattribution. A life office will only not have to take one of these actions if it is consistent with Principle 6 and in the interest of customers to retain the surplus. This is clearly a matter of judgment in individual cases but it would be helpful to have some guidance from the FSA on when retaining a surplus, which is by definition excess to requirements, would not conflict with the customer's interests.

E   Restricting a life office's ability to make changes

6.24   A life office should only change its investment strategy when it is necessary or appropriate to take account of material changes in its, or the wider economic environment, changes in policyholder take up of an option, or the level of capital support available. Although this appears restrictive, changes in the company's or the wider economic environment are a broad basis on which to justify a change of strategy. In cases where support (eg from the estate, a scheme of shareholders) is made available to the fund and is properly subordinated to the fair treatment of policyholders, the strategy should be to manage the funds as if that support did not have to be repaid[2].

F   Restrictions in relation to new business

6.25   The life office's governing body also needs to be satisfied that its plans for new business are not likely to have a material adverse effect on its existing with-profits policyholders. COB 6.12.74 sets out circumstances in which it might be appropriate to establish a new bonus series to mitigate this risk. This can be useful where the life office wishes to impose additional charges on new business or where accepting the new business may necessitate a change in investment mix. If a new bonus series cannot contain the risk then it may be necessary to establish a new fund.

G   Procedure for material transactions

6.26   A life office must not enter into a material transaction (or a series of transactions which together are material) relating to a with-profits fund unless in the reasonable opinion of the life office's governing body it is unlikely to have a material adverse effect on the interests of the fund's existing policyholders[3].

---

1   COB 6.12.57.
2   COB 6.12.81.
3   COB 6.12.89.

Material transactions include a significant bulk outwards reinsurance, *any inwards* reinsurance, a financial engineering transaction and a significant restructuring of the fund. The governing body has to commission a report from the life office's actuary or appropriate professional advisers and should base its judgment on whether a knowledgeable policyholder would regard it as materially affecting his interests.

H Loans and guarantees to connected third parties

6.27 A life office can only make a loan to a connected person or give a guarantee in respect of them in specified circumstances. These are that the arrangement is on commercial terms and that it is believed to be beneficial to policyholders and will not expose them to undue credit or group risk.

Where a life office plans to purchase another business either directly or through a *connected person* it can only do so if it is fair to the with-profits policyholders. This should involve consideration of whether the actuary would regard it as fair[1].

I Charges

6.28 A life office should not charge a cost to a with-profits fund unless in the reasonable opinion of the life office's senior management the life office has incurred or will incur the cost in the operation of the fund[2]. Similarly, costs of compensation or redress or to cover a skilled person's report (because of an apparent failing of the life office) should not be borne by the fund (unless a mutual).

SECTION 4   COB 6.13 – PROCESS FOR REATTRIBUTION OF INHERITED ESTATES

A Background

6.29 The new rules relating to inherited estates seek to do two things: first[3] to prevent future *new* inherited estates being built up; and second to introduce rules and specific guidance relating to the process for reattribution of existing excesses in with-profits funds. To avoid the creation of new inherited estates life offices are now required to undertake an annual assessment of 'excess surplus'. Any such excess surplus not realistically required by the fund should normally be distributed or reattributed. The FSA accepts that life offices need some estate to run

---

1   See also other considerations in COB 6.12.86.
2   COB 6.12.61.
3   COB 6.12.57.

a with-profits fund but it is clearly concerned to see that policyholders get a fair share of profits generated by their money.

COB 6.13 specifies a new process for reattribution[1] of estates. A life office that is seeking to make a reattribution (an arrangement whereby policyholders give up rights in relation to the estate in return for a current or future benefit) must now appoint a policyholder advocate to act on behalf of its relevant with-profits policyholders. If the reattribution is not a Part VII scheme[2], the life office must also appoint an actuary as a reattribution expert. Provisions relating to the involvement of the FSA and rules relating to the costs of the reattribution are also set out in this section.

The division of assets in a reattribution needs in practice to be agreed with both the FSA and policyholders (although a 75% majority of policyholder voting may be sufficient on a scheme of arrangement[3]). The FSA appears to base its view very much on the advice of the appropriate expert (the independent, or if there is no Part VII scheme, in the future the reattribution expert). The life office must tell policyholders when negotiations with the policyholders advocate are complete, explain the outcome and, if appropriate, the life office's proposals. It must provide details of the effect of the proposals (including benefits calculated at an individual level) and send the report from the policyholder advocate explaining why he consider the proposals to be in their interests. A summary of the expert's report should also be included with details of how the report can be obtained. The policyholders must then be given the chance to either accept or reject the proposals, or if it is a scheme of arrangement to vote on them.

Inherited estates are often referred to as 'orphan assets' because they are surpluses that have been carried in the fund for some time and cannot really be said to belong to the fund's current policyholders. There are two diametrically opposed views as to who owns such assets. Proprietary life offices take the view that any surplus that they carry in with-profits funds from one generation to another belongs to the shareholders of the company. In that many traditional life offices were formed in the 17th Century, trying to work out how the surplus arose in the first place can be difficult. In some instances a surplus can be seen to have arisen as a result of particular actions (eg investment decisions). Shareholders would argue that they bore the risk of such decisions, particularly where the business contained guarantees, and that therefore they are entitled to any surplus that has been amassed over time. The view of consumer protection organisations is that any excess in the fund that is not realistically required to cover the existing or proposed business should be distributed in the usual way through the 90/10 or other appropriate gateway.

The new rules and guidance do not resolve the central issue of how the excess is shared. This will depend on the circumstances in each case and this is where the policyholder advocate comes in. The policyholder advocate will look at the expert's and the with-profits actuary's reports and will stand in the shoes of the policyholders to negotiate with the life office.

---

1   Unless a waiver is granted.
2   See Chapter 3.
3   Companies Act 1985, s 425.

B   The policyholder advocate

6.30   The FSA rules[1] require a life office to appoint a policyholder advocate where it is 'seeking' to make a reattribution. The policyholder advocate must be nominated or approved by the FSA before he or she is appointed[2]. The FSA is likely to nominate someone itself when it considers that the reattribution, or any part of it, is likely to be complex or controversial. Although the policyholder advocate is intended to have access to the professional advisers 'he regards as necessary to enable him to perform his functions', he should have the skills and knowledge necessary to act. This needs to be assessed in the context of the particular reattribution, so the life office will need to provide details about the proposed arrangement to the FSA to support the nomination. The FSA may in individual cases suggest consultation with groups of policyholders or the use of recruitment consultants to ensure the impartiality of the person proposed.

The role of the policyholder advocate will vary but will include negotiation with the life office on behalf of the with-profits policyholders on the deal on offer. This should include commenting on the methodology used to allocate benefits amongst the policyholder or groups of them, the criteria for eligibility, and the views expressed by the expert and the with-profits actuary[3]. The policyholder advocate is also expected to advise policyholders whether and if so, why, the life office's proposals are in their interests and if not, why not. At the end of negotiation if the proposal involves a Part VII scheme or an individual agreement, the policyholder will have the chance to accept or reject the proposals. Where a minority initially elect to reject the proposals another offer should be made at a later date. In the case of a scheme of arrangement, which can be accepted by majority decision[4], the policyholder will have the right to vote on the proposals[5].

The policyholder advocate's terms of appointment must define the relationship and how it can be terminated. It must stress the independent nature of the role[6]. The terms should also include the arrangements under which the policyholder advocate is to communicate with policyholders. This appears restrictive but should not in practice constrain the policyholder advocate as the terms should also require him to take such steps as 'he considers necessary to communicate with and receive views from' policyholders. Only when he is satisfied that he has had adequate time to communicate with policyholders should he be expected to start (and presumably continue) negotiating with the life office. The policyholder advocate must also have free and confidential access to the FSA.

The question of who bears the costs incurred is one for negotiation unless the reattribution does not go ahead, in which case the life office would normally be expected to pick up the costs. Otherwise, it is intended that the costs will split in a fair manner with shareholders paying a 'reasonable proportion'. The terms may

1   COB 6.13.8.
2   COB 6.13.9.
3   COB 6.13.14 and 6.13.44 in relation to the requirement to report.
4   75% by value voting.
5   COB 6.13.43.
6   COB 6.13.18.

include an indemnity from the life office in respect of 'certain claims' provided the indemnity does not extend to acts of bad faith.

Once a policyholder advocate's has been appointment is agreed in principle he should be given time to organise advisers and gather the appropriate information about the life office and the proposals being made. After that has happened, the life office must make an announcement marking the formal start of the negotiations. The FSA's guidance states that it would not normally expect the period from the announcement to the conclusion of a deal to be less than three months. In practice, depending on the complexity of the proposed arrangement, it could well be much longer than that.

C   Reattribution expert

6.31   The policyholder advocate will be a feature of all reattributions. Where the reattribution takes the form of a Part VII scheme (see Chapter 3), and many will, there will be an independent actuarial expert involved in the process. Where there is no Part VII scheme, and policyholders are asked to agree to another arrangement or scheme[1], a reattribution expert must be appointed[2]. The appointment must be approved by the FSA and the expert's terms of appointment must allow him to communicate freely, and at his discretion, in confidence with the FSA[3]. The role is very similar to that of the Part VII independent expert, as are the reporting requirements[4]. The report must be made available to the FSA, the policyholder advocate and the court (if relevant). An adequate summary of the report must be made available to all policyholders. One important difference between the reattribution expert/independent expert and the policyholder's advocate is that the latter's aim is to look at the proposals from the policyholder's perspective. The experts are required to be impartial in their assessment of the effect of the arrangements proposed. The expert's costs are to be borne by the life office.

SECTION 5   CLOSED LONG-TERM FUNDS

6.32   Exit strategies for life businesses are broadly similar to those available to non-life businesses. Arguably, the real difference comes in relation to investment contracts and in relation to with-profits contracts in particular. Closing life funds to all or most new business has become a popular way to deal with a contracting underlying market. It is one of a number of ways of capping a life office's liabilities and historically has often been the precursor to another exit strategy or the option taken when none of the other options are available. The other options most commonly used are:

1   Eg under the Companies Act 1985, s 425.
2   COB 6.13.22.
3   COB 6.13.25.
4   See COB 6.13.29 and 6.13.30 which incorporates requirements from SUP.

- Disposal – this is often the preferred route as it is the cleanest.

- Portfolio transfers – many transfers have been used to prevent insurance business withering on the vine (ie being left in a closed fund) but a transfer can also be used in order to ring fence liabilities.

- Reassurance – by effectively passing some or all liability on to a reinsurer a life office can achieve a level of certainty and release from its obligations in relation to long-term funds. It still, however, retains the underlying liability and needs to manage its relationship with the reinsurer. Reassurance of with-profits liabilities can be difficult to achieve in practice.

A closed fund is generally a fund which is not actively being marketed. The FSA's definition is in COB 6.12.95. Probably the most important thing to understand about closed funds is that they are a significant part of the long-term insurance savings market and many of them are still growing significantly year on year. This is because of increments or top-ups to new business. The most likely source of these increases is pension schemes business. An ongoing scheme may have new members and the existing scheme members' contributions would normally increase as their salaries increase. The FSA definition therefore makes clear that a fund can be closed even if it is accepting 'increments' on existing business. It can also be closed when the life office has not actually decided to close it but is not actively marketing it[1]. The other important point to note is that generally such funds remain subject to the same FSA rules as funds which are not closed.

Closed funds can be with-profits, non-profit or unit linked. Historically, funds have closed to allow a life office to concentrate on other types of business and it is fair to say that some, not all, such companies have invested the fund in a very conservative way so as to reduce ongoing involvement by the life office. This can have a very negative impact, particularly on pensions contract customers who will remain in that fund for a long time.

In the last few years there has been a significant increase in the number of funds closing to new business. There have been a number of reasons for this ranging from market forces, government intervention in the market place (imposition of a 1% cap on charges for stakeholder pensions), regulatory changes and practical issues such as mergers.

The FSA was subjected to criticism from policyholders when in 2004 Royal Sun Alliance agreed to sell its life business to the then almost unheard of Resolution Life. Resolution has now merged with Britannic to become a major player in this field. In September 2004 the FSA issued an Insurance Sector Briefing on the regulation of closed with-profits funds. This was against the backdrop of its ongoing TCF proposals for with-profits. Many of the issues identified in the paper have now been addressed by relevant provisions of COB 6.12. The first requirement of COB 6.12 is for the life office to notify the FSA and its customers if it closes a fund[2]. This should be done within 28 days of ceasing to

---

1   COB 6.12.95.
2   COB 6.12.94.

effect new contracts. Life offices cannot avoid the obligation by not making a formal decision to close. Life offices are then required to submit a run-off plan within three months. This must specify how the life office intends to ensure a 'full and fair distribution' of the fund's inherited estate. As investment of the fund's assets and its distribution are the most important issues for a closed fund, life offices are required to communicate with customers in plain language and to include an individual projection of future benefits. They must also explain the effect of run-off on the life office's investment strategy for the fund.

On an ongoing basis COB 6.12.85 seeks to restrict the life office's ability to change its investment strategy. Life offices can only change their investment strategy where necessary or appropriate to take account of material changes in its economic circumstances or the wider economy or to reflect policyholder action or capital support issues. Whilst this gives the life office quite a lot of scope to make changes, the customer-friendly PPFM sent to customers with their next annual statement should enable customers to see how the fund is invested (eg the proportion of equities as opposed to fixed-interest securities). The other requirements of COB 6.12, and indeed COB 6.10 in relation to PPFMs, will still apply to the fund. It will therefore need to specify target maturity values and manage the fund with the aim of achieving target maturity and surrender values in 90 per cent of cases. Life offices should also annually assess whether there is an excess surplus and unless there is a good reason not to, they should distribute it or do a reattribution.

In its briefing paper the FSA makes clear that they have no objection to closed funds as such and that it does not follow that because a fund is closed it will not perform as well as a fund which is still accepting new business, but it is clear that such funds need active management and are subject to regulatory provisions (eg capital/risk management) in much the same way as ongoing funds.

SECTION 6   GOVERNANCE

A   Actuaries

6.33   As part of its review of with-profits business the FSA has introduced the new and separate role of the with-profits actuary for UK with-profits insurance companies. This means that rather than just having one appointed actuary as previously, life offices will be advised by at least one actuary in relation to all classes of its long-term business and potentially by another in respect of its with-profits business. Both the 'actuarial' function and the 'with-profits actuary functions' are controlled functions and the people performing them (who should be at least two separate people) will need to be approved persons. This means that their appointment needs to be approved in advance by the FSA. SUP 4.3.1 requires a life office to appoint an actuary to fill any such vacancies at the time the vacancy arises or as soon as reasonably practicable after that. The FSA indicates that as it needs time to approve the person, life offices should ensure that they plan and make arrangements appropriately. Life offices also need to notify the FSA without delay when they are aware that a vacancy has or will arise. If the life office fails to make an appointment within 28 days the FSA may do so.

COB 4.3.9 specifies the requirements in terms of qualification, skill and experience required of an actuary of the life office. This requires life offices to seek appropriate references. A life office must also take reasonable steps to ensure that an actuary appointed or to be appointed docs not perform the function of chairman or chief executive and if he is to be the with-profits actuary he cannot be a member of the life office's governing body. He must also not perform any other function on behalf of the life office which could give rise to a significant conflict of interest[1].

The role of the actuarial function is mainly to advise the board appropriately in relation to material risk faced by the business, the life office's own risk assessment, and the capital needed to support the business. The actuary will also be involved in issues relating to the annual return to the FSA. SUP 4.3.15 sets out a list of areas where the FSA thinks a life office should take actuarial advice (which could be provided by the person(s) performing the actuarial function). This list includes risk and capital management issues and issues such as variation of charges, discretionary surrender charges and adequacy of reinsurance protection.

The main role of the life office's with-profits actuary is to advise in relation to the life office's discretions affecting the relevant classes of business to which he has been appointed and, in relation to realistic basis companies, the calculation of the with-profits insurance capital component. He must also, at least once in each calendar year, report to the life office's governing body in respect of the exercise of discretion, including, where relevant, reporting on the life office's application of its PPFM. He must also report to the with-profits policyholders, via a report to be included with the annual report, on whether in his opinion the life office's exercise of discretion has taken their interests into account in a reasonable and proportionate manner[2]. He should also advise the life office in relation to the data and systems that he reasonably considers necessary to be kept and maintained to provide him with the information he needs. The with-profits actuary should be kept informed by the life office of relevant information and changes (eg to business plans, etc). He should also have appropriate resources and access to the board.

B   With-profits committees

6.34   COB 6.11 provides guidance on governance arrangements relevant to the way with-profits life offices comply with SYSC. It also requires an annual report to with-profits policyholders to confirm compliance with its PPFM for each financial year.

The report should specify the reasons for the life office's belief that it has complied with its PPFM. It should detail the exercise of any discretion and address any competing or conflicting rights. This report must be annexed to the annual report of the with-profits actuary required by Sup 4.3.16 A R(4). In preparing its report the life office should take advice from the with-profits actuary. The life

1   SIP 4.3.12A.
2   SUP 4.3.16 A R (4).

office should make the report available to with-profits policyholders within six months of the end of the relevant financial year. In its annual statement to policyholders the life office should notify policyholders of how copies of the report can be obtained. In any event, the life office must deposit the report with the FSA when it makes its annual return[1]. Life offices are advised to use some 'independent judgment' to assess compliance of its PPFM and the management of conflicting interests. This independent judgment may take a number of forms including a review by a with-profits committee, an independent assessment, or, for small life offices, a review by the non-executive directors. Any adverse comment resulting should, if required, be included in the annual report[2].

Life offices are not required to have with-profits committees but one way to establish a level of independent assessment is to have an appropriate sub-committee of the board. This is more likely to be expected in the case of large companies.

1   IPRU (INS) 9.6(6).
2   COB 6.11.8.

CHAPTER 7

Prudential regulation

SUMMARY

SECTION I   INTRODUCTION TO PRU

7.1   The majority of the prudential regulation the FSA inherited was contained in the Insurance Companies Act 1982 and various insurance companies
regulations. Some of this regulation derived directly from EU legislation (eg the
First, Second and Third Life Directives now contained in the Consolidated Life
Directive[1]). This regulation principally dealt with defining contracts of insurance, specifying a minimum solvency margin and restrictions on the type of
business carried on by insurers. It also sought to reinforce the life/non-life divide
in terms of the way insurers operate. The FSA introduced its own slightly modified version of these rules in IPRU (INS)[2]. This applied until 31 December 2004
when the FSA introduced the Integrated Prudential Handbook ('PRU').

PRU provides a whole new basis for assessing an insurer's capital requirements (including an obligation to produce its own risk-based assessment) and the
assets (including derivatives) that it holds to cover its liabilities and its capital
requirements. In addition, much of PRU is taken up with guidance on risk
management and in particular the content of risk management policies. PRU also

1   2002/83/EC.
2   Note parts of IPRU (INS) are still in force.

specifies capital and other requirements for intermediaries and provides regulation of insurance groups and financial conglomerates (large groups with banking or investment business combined with insurance business).

Although the FSA intended PRU to be an integrated handbook applicable to banking, investment and insurance businesses authorised by the FSA[1], as originally implemented, the full regime only applied to insurers. The FSA has now moved away from the concept of a single integrated handbook As part of its implementation of the Capital Requirements Directive ('CRD') for banking and investment firms, provisions of PRU which are applicable to such firms and to insurers will be included in GEN PRU. The parts of PRU applicable to insurers only will become INS PRU. For consistency the risk management provisions of PRU (other than in relation to liquidity) moved to SYSC on 31 December 2006. Where possible the new references to GEN PRU, INS PRU and SYSC are shown in brackets next to the PRU reference in this chapter.

Finally, it is notable that whilst PRU has largely replaced IPRU (INS), IPRU (INS) still exists and it contains some rules which interact with the rules in PRU. These are described in the relevant parts of this chapter.

A   Overview

7.2   Although the FSA was unable in PRU to regulate the prudential risks of banks, investment firms and insurers, PRU was still a significant step towards harmonisation. Much of the framework on which the regulation of insurers is now undertaken is based on broadly similar requirements to those applicable to banks and investment firms. These requirements themselves stem from the Basel Framework (applicable to international banks) on which the CRD is also based. The framework can be explained as follows:

Basel 'Three Pillars'

Pillar 1: Provides minimum capital requirements;

Pillar 2: Provides for supervisory review which can lead to a requirement for capital above the minimum capital requirement; and

Pillar 3: Provides for market discipline through greater public disclosure of a firm's capital position.

The FSA has adopted this framework and introduced the concept of risk-based capital for insurers. The Pillar 1 requirements are based on the need to satisfy existing requirements (eg EU legislation). Under Pillar 2, the insurer discusses with the FSA its own 'risk'-based assessment of capital; if the FSA is unhappy with this it can provide individual capital guidance to the insurer. Additional transparency and reporting requirements have been introduced as part of the Pillar 3 process, particularly for with-profits business.

In producing PRU the FSA has not sought to anticipate the full effect of the proposed Solvency II Directive for insurers (currently expected to be in force by

---

1   Each section of PRU specifies who it applies to but generally small friendly societies are excluded.

2010). At the time of writing, the extent to which the Solvency II Directive will follow the FSA's risk-based approach is uncertain but it seems unlikely that the FSA will move away from the approach set out in PRU except to the extent that it is inconsistent with Solvency II requirements.

For life insurers with significant with-profits exposures, a completely new basis for specifying the minimum capital required has been introduced, known as the 'twin peaks' requirement. It is designed to improve transparency in with-profits funds by requiring large with-profits companies to calculate their assets and liabilities on a 'realistic' basis as well as on the standard 'regulatory' basis. The realistic value of liabilities takes into account the value of discretionary benefits (in keeping with customers' reasonable expectations and treating customers fairly) and options in policies. The regulatory calculation is based on the firm's mathematical reserves (contractual and guaranteed amounts); this should in many cases result in the realistic basis of calculating liabilities being higher than the regulatory basis. The life company is obliged to hold assets in the with-profits fund itself and capital based on whichever is the higher of the realistic and regulatory calculation of liabilities, which is why the FSA coined the phrase twin peaks.

SECTION 2   RISK MANAGEMENT AND LEGAL RISK ISSUES

7.3   The main requirement of PRU 1.2 (GEN PRU 1.2) (and indeed of PRU overall) is that a firm must at all times maintain overall adequate financial resources, including capital and liquidity resources which are adequate both as to amount and quality, to ensure there is no significant risk that its liabilities cannot be met as they fall due.

PRU 1.2 (GEN PRU 1.2) sets out rules requiring a firm to identify and assess the risks of it being unable to meet its liabilities as they fall due, how it intends to deal with those risks and the amount and nature of financial resources the firm will hold to cover the risk. The firm's assessment of risk should be proportionate to the nature, scale and complexity of its activities.

The processes and systems used by a firm to assess the adequacy of its financial resources must enable it to identify and assess how to deal with the major sources of risk to its ability to meet its liabilities as they fall due. These will include, but are not limited to, the following prudential risk:

- *Credit risk*: risk of loss resulting from another party failing to perform its financial obligations or failing to perform them in a timely manner.

- *Market risk*: risk of loss arising from fluctuations in the values of, or income from, assets, interest rates or exchange rates.

- *Liquidity risk*: risk of loss resulting from the inability to convert assets into cash in a timely manner.

- *Operational risk*: risk of loss resulting from inadequate or failed internal processes, people and systems or from external events.

275

- *Insurance risk*: risk of loss resulting from inherent uncertainties regarding the occurrence, amount and timing of insurance liabilities.

Firms may also be exposed to group risk (see Section 7). From 31 December 2006 there are additional prudential risk categories for concentration risk, residual risk, securitisation risk, business risk, interest rate risk and pension obligation risk.

7.4   In its focus on risk management and the effect on capital, PRU has effectively created a real cost for poor risk management. This is probably most novel in concept when applied to operational risks; (for example, poor systems or inadequate staff can now have a capital implication for a firm). Also, whilst firms can generally mitigate risk by holding appropriate loss-absorbing capital this will not always be possible and the firm may need instead to rectify the underlying issue.

For each major source of risk identified by it the firm must carry out appropriate stress tests and scenario analyses. Stress tests look at how the insurer's position is affected by an adverse occurrence or set of circumstances, such as falling equity values, systems problems or legal uncertainty. Scenario tests look at the effect of multiple occurrences at the same time (eg falling equity values, rising interest rates and a catastrophic external event). The idea is for the insurer to build in appropriate contingency funds for the happening of events which the insurer regards as reasonably foreseeable[1] even if unlikely. In PRU 2.3 the FSA gives guidance in relation to the application of these tests to the prudential risks as follows:

- *Credit risk*: firms should consider the effect of non-payment of reinsurance or other debtors such as intermediaries or policyholders (see also PRU 3/INSPRU 2.1).

- *Market risk*: firms should allow for reduced market values of investments, variations in interest rates, a lower level of investment income than planned and the possibility of counterparty default (see also PRU 4/INSPRU 3.1 and SYSC 16).

- *Liquidity risk*: firms should consider their cash-flow position and ability to withstand sharp, unexpected outflows of funds, via claims or an unexpected drop in premium (see also PRU 5/INSPRU 4.1).

- *Operational risk*: factors to consider should include reputational risk, including damage to brand, marketing and distribution risks and the impact of legal risk (see PRU 6/INSPRU 5.1).

- *Insurance risk*: firms should consider the potential for catastrophic loss, the cost of reinstatement premiums and reinsurance exhaustion. Other factors will differ depending on the business actually written (see also PRU 7/SYSC 17).

---

1   PRU 1.2 (GEN PRU 1.2).

7.5   Firms are required by PRU 4.2 (INSPRU 3.1) to calculate a risk capital requirement ('RCR')[1]. This is an additional amount of capital held to cover specified market-related risks (such as falls in the value of equities and property). This calculation was formerly part of the mathematical reserves (the 'resilience reserves'). When carrying out its risk-based capital assessment, a firm should consider the extent to which the market risk scenarios set out in PRU 4.2 (INSPRU 3.1) are appropriate to the nature of its asset portfolio. A firm may conclude that it needs to apply further stress tests to other forms of assets. The RCR should therefore be a *starting point* for the firm in assessing its own risk-based capital requirement and this is consistent with it forming part of the minimum capital requirements specified by PRU 2 (GEN PRU 2).

As part of its Pillar 2 activities the FSA will review a firm's capital against the minimum capital requirements and the firm's own risk-based assessment. The FSA will also look at the extent to which senior managers have been involved in the risk assessment process. FSA guidance[2] indicates that it will consider the results of other (ie economic capital or sophisticated modelling) techniques provided that the major risks are identified and that the model calculates the effect on a firm's financial position where they crystallise (or are assumed with a particular probability to crystallise). This could in theory (perhaps if there is significant diversification) lead to a lower capital requirement than would otherwise apply.

As a result of its review the FSA may give Individual Capital Guidance. Ultimately, if agreement is not reached between the firm and the FSA, the FSA may vary a firm's Part IV permission to require it to hold capital complying with the Individual Capital Guidance.

A   Systems and controls

7.6   The risk assessment required in PRU 1.2 (GEN PRU 1.2) is only one-half of the equation. Firms are also required to design and maintain systems and controls to ensure that senior management can make business planning and risk management decisions based on accurate information about risks and financial resources. These systems and controls (eg including risk policies) have been a very visible result of the introduction of PRU.

PRU 1.4 (SYSC 14) is made up predominantly of guidance, much of which reinforces other Handbook provisions – mainly SYSC and the FSA Principles. The main 'requirement' flowing from PRU 1.4 (SYSC 14) is to maintain, document and communicate appropriately a business plan including individual risk management policies in relation to the prudential risks set out above (see **7.3**). These policies need to set out the firm's appetite and tolerance for the risk in question. Later sections of PRU go on to give specific detailed guidance as to the content of each such risk management policy and to recommend other courses of action. Certain actions underpin each of the individual risk policies. In the FSA's view these are: use of risk management committees; management information

---

1   Under INSPRU this will apply only to the regulatory calculation.
2   PRU 1.2 (INSPRU 7.1.93).

adequate to enable proper oversight of the business and which is provided on a timely basis[1]; creation of separate risk assessment and internal audit functions; and appropriate segregation of duties for individuals. In addition, adequate internal controls must be in place to ensure the firm's business plan and risk management systems operate as expected to mitigate risks which can reasonably be foreseen. Firms are specifically directed, when considering the adequacy of their internal controls, to look at how they manage delegated (including outsourced) activities and are reminded of the guidance in SYSC 3A.9 on outsourcing.

The impact of this formalisation of risk management in insurance companies has been enormous. The FSA's guidance about what should be in each risk policy is detailed. In some areas the guidance covers issues that might also be dealt with by specific rules or which are designed to fit in with other FSA initiatives (eg treating customers fairly). For example, the insurance risk policy is expected to cover the firm's approach to pricing long-term insurance contracts including the determination of the appropriate level of any reviewable premiums (an issue which is topical at the time of writing)[2].

The insurance risk policy and the operational risk policy are those most likely to cut across legal issues[3]. The insurance risk policy requires firms to understand and manage legal risk in its policy documentation and its claims management process. Management of reinsurance exposure is also a key part of this. Non-insurance related legal risk (such as risk inherent in the systems and personnel of the firm) is normally dealt with as part of operational risk.

B   Legal issues in PRU

I   Legal risk and the legal risk policy

7.7   Legal risk can be a significant part of insurance risk (for example, contractual issues with policies) and operational risk (arising from the way the company operates). Similarly, changes in the business and legal environment can affect the nature of the underlying risks a firm is seeking to manage. As a transitional measure prior to the introduction of PRU the FSA specified[4] what it considered legal risk to be and how it expected firms to manage it. This was as follows:

'Definition of Legal Risk:

the risk that the law is proved to operate in a way adverse to the interests or objectives of the insurer where the insurer: did not consider its effect; believed its effect to be different; or operated with uncertainty as to its effect'.

---

1 In order to be useful, management information needs to be timely. The FSA guidance implicitly accepts that a balance will sometimes need to be struck in sacrificing an appropriate degree of accuracy for timeliness. Whilst in practice getting the balance right might be tricky, the information must enable a decision to be taken in time to control or mitigate the risk.

2 Rules on setting premiums at sustainable rates are included in PRU 7.2.41 (INS PRU 1.1.42).

3 See also PS140 and the transitional arrangements for PRU.

4 CP150/PS140 and subsequently the relevant Handbook Instrument (the interim Prudential Sourcebook Insurers (Systems and Controls) Instrument 2002).

Similarly, the FSA specified systems and controls that insurers should put in place to deal with legal risk. These were as follows:

C1 Insurers should have processes for identifying which legal risks the business is exposed to, including:

risks in existing products, including those where the interpretation of contracts could be challenged; the risk that a change in legislation may be overlooked or inadequately responded to; uncertainties surrounding existing or forthcoming court rulings; and risks in enforcing contracts with third parties, particularly reinsurance contracts.

C2 Insurers should also have processes for controlling (where possible) the risks that have been identified.

C3 There should be processes for reporting identified legal risks to the risk assessment function, risk committee, senior management and the 'governing body'.

C4 There should be processes for raising appropriate provisions against legal risk.

C5 Regular reviews of legal risk within the business units, including risk relating to new products, investment activities and reinsurance, should be undertaken.

7.8   With the introduction of PRU part of this wording found its way into the requirements for the insurance risk policy, and part of it pervades a number of the other risks. As legal risk in products result from general changes in the law, PRU provides that the identification of insurance risk should normally include:

- processes for identifying business environment changes (for example, landmark legal rulings) and for collecting internal and external data to test and modify business plans;
- processes at the point of sale for identifying potential claims for misselling;
- processes after the point of sale for identifying potential and emerging claims for the purposes of claims management and claims provisioning.

This could include:

(a)   identifying possible judicial rulings;

(b)   keeping up to date with developments in market practice; and

(c)   collecting information on industry-wide initiatives and settlements.

Firms will therefore need to be able to show how they monitor existing and future changes in the law and market practice and the process for dealing with them. This would normally be included in the firm's legal risk policy.

In relation to operational risk, PRU also provides that a firm should consider the risk resulting from the business environment and changes in that environment, including legal risks. Legal requirements can impact a firm's entire operation and a firm's assessment therefore needs to be wide-ranging. In risk management terms legal risk is often regarded as a sub-set of operational risk and many firms will evidence their management of legal risk through their legal risk policy.

Management of legal risk can also involve establishment of a legal risk committee or sub-committee of the risk committee. The legal risk policy may specify referral arrangements to such a committee or specify how the committee interacts with other risk committees. It is difficult to anticipate in advance the legal risk a firm may face. Legal risk policies sometimes seek to deal with this by specifying engagement arrangements (eg, to help the relevant business areas to establish the types of issue which require legal advice or input). As every risk cannot be catered for in advance, it is also advisable to raise awareness of legal risk within the organisation and include the issue of raising awareness in the legal risk policy. As with other risk policies, the legal risk policy should provide for audit of the policy and for it to be reviewed periodically.

2   Other legal issues in PRU

7.9   The provisions of PRU which either explicitly or implicitly require legal input include the following:

- the need to review policy and other contractual wording and to have appropriate controls for new product development;

- the need for legal input into reinsurance arrangements and appropriate assessment of risk transfer;

- the need to document agency/delegation of underwriting authority and outsourcing arrangements to comply with FSA rules;

- the need to monitor and act on developments in the law (including judicial rulings and prospective UK and EU legislation);

- managing litigation and claims and ensuring remedial action is taken when appropriate in light of past experience;

- ensuring documents securing collateral or guarantees or mitigating credit risk are valid and enforceable on an ongoing basis;

- ensuring documentation or arrangements relied upon to provide liquidity (including, for example, securitisations) is adequate and fit for the purpose;

- ensuring appropriate categorisation of assets into the relevant regulatory tiers;

- appropriate categorisation of admissible asset categories and interpretation of counterparty limits (including, in particular, the rules relating to 'approved derivative contracts');

- internal contagion risk issues (for example, restricting the activities of insurers and requiring separation of life fund assets); and

- applicability of the Group and Financial Conglomerate requirements.

Each of these categories is dealt with in more detail below except 'categorisation of assets' and 'tiers of capital' which are in Sections 5 and 4, internal contagion risk which is in Section 6 and Group and Financial Conglomerate requirements which are in Section 7.

3   Review of policy documentation

7.10   A firm's insurance risk policy should outline its objectives in carrying out insurance business, its appetite for insurance risk and its policies for identifying, measuring, monitoring and controlling insurance risk (namely, losses on insurance obligations). Provisions in PRU 7.1.30 (SYSC 17.1.30) require firms to pay close attention to the wording of their policy documentation and to consider: whether they have adequate in-house legal resources; the need for periodic independent legal review of policy documentation; the use of standardised documentation and referral procedures for variation of terms; reviewing the documentation used by other insurance companies ('peer review'); revising documentation for new policies in the light of past experience; and the operation of law in the jurisdiction of the policyholder.

These requirements are similar to the transitional arrangements referred to above and it is worth noting both the ongoing nature of the peer review and the desirability of periodic external assessment.

In addition, PRU 7.1.9 (SYSC 17.1.9) requires a firm as part of its insurance risk policy to consider its approach to the exercise of any discretion available in its long-term insurance contracts (eg, on charges or the level of benefits payable) bearing in mind applicable legal and regulatory constraints, the inclusion of options in its new long-term insurance contracts and the possible exercise by policyholders of options on existing contracts. These issues should also form part of any review or process for reviewing policy documentation.

4   Documenting reinsurance

7.11   If firms wish to take appropriate credit for reinsurance they need to ensure that reinsurance arrangements pass risk as they should, and do not distort the apparent financial condition of the insurer. In PRU the FSA emphasises the need for legal assistance in putting reinsurance in place. A firm's insurance risk policy should also therefore include:

- the firm's approach to the use of reinsurance or the use of some other means of risk transfer; and

- how the firm intends to asses the effectiveness of its risk transfer arrangements and manage the residual or transferred risks (for example, how it intends to handle disputes over contract wordings, potential payout delays and counterparty performance risks).

In addition, PRU 7.1.34 (SYSC 17.1.34) provides that before entering into or significantly changing a reinsurance agreement, or any other form of insurance risk transfer agreement, a firm should 'ensure there are adequate legal checking procedures in respect of the draft agreement' and understand the nature and limits of the agreement. Particular attention should be given to the wording of contracts to ensure that all of the required risks are covered, that the level of available cover is appropriate, and that all the terms, conditions and warranties are unambiguous and understood.

5   Delegation to third parties

7.12   There is a risk in any form of delegation or outsourcing that the delegate may either not perform as expected or may commit the firm to potential liabilities that it would not itself have been prepared to accept. In addition to the requirements of PRU (in relation to operational risk and insurance risk), firms must consider the provisions of Chapter 3 of SYSC relating to operational systems and controls and the FSA's guidance on outsourcing (SYSC 3A.9).

In general terms, the effect of the provisions of PRU and SYSC is that such delegations should be documented in such a way as to make clear the extent of the delegation and the respective responsibilities of the parties (including details of any underwriting limits for employees).

6   Managing litigation and claims

7.13   The actual management of claims falls within insurance risk and an insurer should have processes to monitor both the volume and type of claim (including fraudulent claims) and potential sources of group claim. In relation to assessment of the validity of claims, the FSA recommends 'procedures' to determine when experts such as lawyers should be used.

A firm will also, as part of its operational risk, be exposed to potential litigation from a number of sources and receive complaints from customers about actions of the firm or its staff. The FSA is keen for lessons learnt from previous disputes, claims or complaints to be reflected in future operations and documentation. It will look for a process to communicate such lessons learnt to all the appropriate areas of the business.

7   Appropriate documentation

7.14   There is much guidance in PRU reminding firms of the need for arrangements to be properly documented. There are also specific requirements to obtain either independent legal advice or the advice of a UK Queen's Counsel (or non-UK equivalent). See, in particular, the requirements of PRU 2.2 (GENPRU 2.2) in relation to innovative tier 1 capital and upper tier 2 capital. In other cases, as part of the scrutiny of the firm's governing body or auditors, legal advice may be sought to establish compliance with the rules.

C Adequate records

7.15 A firm is required[1] to take reasonable care to make and retain records to ensure that adequate information is available regarding its financial situation and business activities. A firm must make, regularly update and retain accounting and other records for at least three years. These must be sufficient to enable the firm to demonstrate its financial position and exposure to risk and that the firm is financially sound with appropriate systems and controls. The firm must also be able to demonstrate to the FSA that it is complying with PRU which is reinforced by a sign off by the governing body as part of the year-end process. The records must be kept in the UK unless they relate to business carried on outside the UK in which case they can be kept in that country, but an adequate summary of the records must periodically be sent to the UK.

SECTION 3 CAPITAL REQUIREMENTS

7.16 PRU specifies a minimum level of capital which a firm must hold in addition to the assets it is required to hold to cover its potential liabilities to policyholders. The absolute minimum level of capital is that required to comply with EU requirements ('the minimum capital requirement'). The FSA has taken the opportunity in PRU to change the minimum capital requirements for large with-profits life insurers (the 'enhanced capital requirement'). Further capital may also need to be held as a result of the firm's own risk-based assessment of its capital requirements.

The minimum capital requirement[2] applies to all insurers including pure reinsurers unless the insurer is within stated exceptions[3]. A separate calculation is required for composite insurers in respect of their long-term and general business. A composite firm may use excess assets held in respect of its general business to cover its long-term business capital requirements but may not use long-term assets to cover its general business capital requirements.

The requirement to hold a specified minimum level of capital is expressed as the capital resource requirement (the 'CRR')[4]. The amount of the CRR varies depending on the type of business carried on. For firms other than large with-profits insurers, the CRR is the minimum capital requirement. For large with-profit insurers, which for this purpose means firms having with-profits liabilities of £500m or more, the CRR is the enhanced capital requirement. Such firms are known as *realistic*-based or *twin peaks* life firms. Firms with lower with-profits liabilities may opt in to the requirement to maintain an enhanced capital requirement[5].

The CRR for each type of firm are set out in PRU 2.1.14 to 2.1.35 but are broadly summarised as follows:

1 By SYSC 3.2.30.
2 In PRU 2.1 (GENPRU 2.1).
3 In PRU 2.1.1 (GENPRU 2.1.1).
4 In PRU 2.1 (GENPRU 2.1).
5 PRU 2.1.17 (GENPRU 2.1.20).

capital resource requirement (CRR)	(for non-twin peaks firms) Equals MCR
	(for twin peaks firms) Higher of MCR and ECR
minimum capital requirement (MCR)	Higher of:
	• base requirement; and
	• sum of LTICR and RCR[1]. The LTICR is made up of:
	• insurance death risk capital component[2]; and
	• insurance health risk capital component[3]; and
	• insurance expense risk component[4]; and
	• insurance market risk capital component[5]
enhanced capital requirement (ECR)[6]	Sum of:
	LTICR[7]
	with-profit insurance capital component[8] (WPICC)

The 'base requirement' is the EU requirement and is set out in PRU 2.1.26 (GENPRU 2.1.30). For a large with-profits proprietary company it is 3m euros. In GENPRU that figure becomes 3.2m euros.

7.17   The RCR forms part of the calculation of the minimum capital required. The purpose of the RCR is to ensure that capital is set aside to mitigate the potential effect of market risk on the insurance company's asset and liability position. It works by applying a specified level of market movement (eg in relation to equities, fixed interest securities and real properties) to the insurer's assets and liabilities. Where the result is that the insurance company's assets would be less than its liabilities it is required to cover that amount by holding it as a capital reserve. The basis for calculating the RCR is specified in PRU 4.2.9 (INSPRU 3.1.10) with the factors set out in PRU 4.2.16 to 4.2.26 (INSPRU 3.1.16 to 3.1.26). A slightly different basis is assumed for significant interests outside the United Kingdom. It also includes provision to deal with temporary situations by including some averaging in the factors used (eg over 90 days).

1   PRU 4.2.9 to PRU 4.2.26/INSPRU 3.1.10.
2   PRU 7.2.81/INSPRU 1.1.81.
3   PRU 7.2.85/INSPRU 1.1.85.
4   PRU 7.2.88/INSPRU 1.1.88
5   PRU 7.2.89/INSPRU 1.1.89.
6   PRU also required (4.2.9) the addition of the RCR but this was removed from 31 December 2006.
7   INSPRU 1.1.80.
8   PRU 7/INSPRU 1.3.

A realistic basis life company will, as part of its realistic calculation, also have to calculate a risk capital margin ('RCM'). This can be confusing as the RCM covers market risk in a similar way to the resilience capital requirement. However, the RCM also covers credit risk and persistency risk.

The with-profit insurance capital component ('WPICC') is calculated as the amount by which the regulatory surplus exceeds the realistic surplus. This can be confusing as it is expressed in relation to 'surplus' rather than liabilities. Generally the realistic surplus should be less than the regulatory surplus because the realistic liabilities plus the RCM should be higher than the regulatory liabilities, plus the fund's share of the LTICR and resilience capital requirement ('RCR'). The flowchart in PRU 7 Annex 1G (INSPRU Annex 1G) sets out the calculation more clearly.

SECTION 4   TIERS OF CAPITAL

7.18   As part of the harmonisation of capital requirements the FSA adopted a new approach to determining the assets an insurer can hold to cover its capital resource requirement. Assets which may be held as capital are now divided into categories or 'tiers' which reflect differences in the extent to which the asset meets the characteristics of permanency and loss absorbency. The best form of capital (core tier 1), which includes permanent share capital, can be used without limit. Other assets which are either not perpetual or which contain cumulative obligations fall into other tiers.

There are two tiers of capital applicable to insurers, tier 1 and tier 2. Tier 1 capital is divided into three types (core, perpetual non-cumulative preference shares and innovative tier 1). Tier 2 capital is divided into two types (upper and lower tier 2 capital). Other forms of capital may be used with the FSA's consent in the form of a waiver.

The characteristics for tier 1 and tier 2 capital are set out in PRU 2.2.5 and 2.2.7 (GENPRU 2.2.93 to 197) respectively. The following table is a guide to the basic types of capital and their limits.

Tier of capital	Examples	Limit
Tier 1		
Core tier 1	Permanent share capital (ordinary shares, paid-up contribution by a member to a mutual, part of a mutual's initial fund) Reserves Share premium account Verified interim net profits	Unlimited
Perpetual non-cumulative preference shares	Perpetual non-cumulative preference shares	50% of MCR
Innovative tier 1	Capital instruments Innovative tier 1 instruments	15% of total tier

Tier of capital	Examples	Limit
Tier 2		
Upper tier 2	Perpetual cumulative preference shares Perpetual subordinated debt Perpetual subordinated securities	50% of total capital resources
Lower tier 2	Fixed term preference shares Fixed term subordinated debt Fixed term subordinated securities	50% of total capital resources
Other capital – **waiver required**	Unpaid share capital	25% of total capital resources
	Unpaid initial funds and calls for resources supplementary contributions Implicit terms	50% of total

PRU 2.2.15 to 2.2.26 (GENPRU 2.2.24 to 41) set out additional restrictions as follows:

(1) at least 50% of a firm's MCR must be made up of core tier 1 capital and perpetual non-cumulative preference shares (less deductions from tier 1 capital);

(2) life companies are required to meet the higher of 1/3 of the LTICR and the base requirement (see PRU 2.2.26 (GENPRU 2.2.34 and 2.2.41)) with core tier 1 capital and upper and lower tier 2 capital (less deductions from tier 1 capital); and

(3) a firm's tier 2 capital resources must not exceed its tier 1 capital resources.

A Innovative tier one capital

7.19   The concept of 'innovative tier 1' capital is new to insurers. It is intended to cover instruments which are likely (for example, because of their terms) to be redeemed and therefore not provide the desired permanency required for core tier 1 capital. For this reason innovative tier 1 capital is limited to 15% of the total tier 1 capital and it is therefore important to recognise instruments which are likely to be redeemed. One indication that an instrument is innovative is when the instrument includes what the FSA refer to as a step up (such as where although the instrument is marketed as a perpetual instrument it allows the issuer to increase the coupon). The table below reproduces the FSA's guidance in CP190 comparing typical characteristics of a tier 1 innovative instrument with an ordinary share (which is core tier 1 capital).

Characteristic	Ordinary share	Innovative instrument
Accounting treatment	Equity	Liability
Coupon payments	At the sole discretion of directors	May be deferred with any deferred coupons payable only in shares
Maturity	Cannot be redeemed	No specific redemption date but terms may include an issuer call which may coincide with an increase in the coupon
Subordination	Junior to all other claims	Normally ranks pari passu with preference shares
Ability to extinguish losses	Fully absorbs losses	Loss absorbency could be achieved by means of conversion into shares at predetermined trigger event

B   Other capital

7.20   Other forms of capital require a waiver from the FSA. Historically many life companies have included implicit items (eg reflecting the value of future profits). Despite the fact that the Consolidated Life Directive currently allows implicit items to be included, within limits, PRU 2.2.14 (GENPRU 2.2.17) does not permit implicit terms. PRU 2 Annex 2R states that the FSA may be prepared to grant a waiver to allow implicit terms to be included. However, this will be limited to 25% of the lesser of the LTICR and the total capital resources by 2007 and will be phased out by 2009.

A firm's total capital resources are broadly calculated as the tier 1 and 2 capital[1] less specified deductions which include inadmissible assets and assets in excess of counterparty or asset limits set out in PRU 3.

SECTION 5   VALUATION AND ADMISSIBLE ASSETS

7.21   One of the FSA's stated aims in the consultation process for PRU was to simplify the asset valuation rules for insurers and to create a more explicit link to relevant credit or market risk. Formerly the IPRU (INS) rules set out in detail how to value particular assets. The PRU rules mainly defer to accounting rules/practices and standards or market prices and apply unless otherwise stated in PRU (see PRU 7.3). This means that accounting treatment will determine the value a company can place on its assets. Shares in and debts due from related undertakings are treated differently.

---

1   Plus specified positive adjustments.

A Admissible assets

7.22   Once an asset has been valued appropriately it may also need to satisfy a requirement to be admissible. PRU 2.2.14 (GENPRU 2.2.17 and GENPRU 2 Annex 1R) requires a deduction from a firm's capital in respect of inadmissible assets. PRU 7.2.20 (INSPRU 1.1.27) requires a firm to ensure that its technical provisions are covered by admissible assets. Technical provisions are a firm's on-balance sheet provisions for liabilities under its insurance contracts. For life business, technical provisions will be the mathematical reserves which are actuarial estimates of a firm's liabilities in respect of future benefits due to policyholders.

Life companies carrying on with-profits business must cover the technical provisions in each of their with-profits funds with admissible assets. A realistic basis life firm must also ensure that the realistic value of assets in each of its with-profits funds is at least equal to the realistic value of liabilities in that fund (PRU 7.2.27 and 7.2.28 (INSPRU 1.1.28 and 1.1.29)).

To be admissible the asset must appear on the list of admissible assets which is set out in PRU 2 Annex 1R (GENPRU 2 Annex 7R) and reproduced below:

(1)   Investments that are, or amounts owed arising from the disposal of:

   (a)   *debt securities*, bonds and other money and capital market instruments;

   (b)   loans;

   (c)   *shares* and other variable yield participations;

   (d)   *units* in *UCITS schemes, non-UCITS retail schemes, recognised schemes* and any other *collective investment scheme* that invests only in *admissible assets* (including any *derivatives* or *quasi-derivatives* held by the scheme). (This changed from 31 December 2006 to permit other schemes where the insurer's investment is sufficiently small to be consistent with a prudent overall investment strategy)[1];

   (e)   land, buildings and immovable property rights;

   (f)   an *approved derivative* or *quasi-derivative* transaction that satisfies the conditions in PRU 4.3.5R or an approved stock lending transaction that satisfies the conditions in PRU 4.3.36R[2].

(2)   Debts and claims

   (a)   debt owed by *reinsurers*, including *reinsurers'* shares of technical provisions[3];

   (b)   deposits with and debt owned by ceding *undertakings*;

---

1   Having regard to the investment policy of the scheme and the information available to the insurer to enable it to monitor the investment risk being taken by the scheme (Annex 7, 1(d)(iv)).
2   INSPRU 3.2.
3   But from 31 December 2006 excluding amounts recoverable from an ISPV unless an FSA waiver is obtained.

(c)   debts owed by *policyholders* and *intermediaries* arising out of direct and *reinsurance* operations (except where overdue for more than three months and other than *commission* prepaid to agents or intermediaries);

(d)   for *general insurance business* only, claims arising out of salvage and subrogation;

(e)   for *long-term insurance business* only, advances secured on, and not exceeding the *surrender value* of, *long-term insurance contracts* issued by the insurer;

(f)   tax recoveries;

(g)   claims against *compensation* funds.

(3)   Other assets

(a)   tangible fixed assets, other than land and buildings;

(b)   cash at *bank* and in hand, *deposits* with *credit institutions* and any other bodies authorised to receive deposits;

(c)   for *general insurance business* only, *deferred acquisition costs*;

(d)   accrued interest and rent, other accrued income and prepayments;

(e)   for *long-term insurance business* only, reversionary interests.

Certain 'admissible' assets are not defined (eg bonds, capital market instruments and variable yield participations) leaving scope for interpretation. In relation to variable yield participations, it is understood that the FSA has stated that this could cover interests in limited partnerships. In practice, as the list of assets is fairly generic (eg shares), admissibility may not be too problematic except perhaps in relation to derivative contracts and collective investment schemes. It should be noted in relation to each of the categories that even if the asset satisfies the requirements of any other category of admissible asset it must be treated as a derivative or collective investment scheme (eg shares in a collective investment scheme entity must not be treated as shares).

PRU 7.2.30 (INSPRU 1.1.30) requires a UK firm to hold its admissible assets in any EEA State or (where admissible assets cover technical provisions in a currency other than pounds sterling) in any EEA State or the country of that currency.

The matching of assets and liabilities rules are found in PRU 7.2.34 (INSPRU 1.1.34).

B   Counterparty and concentration risk

7.23   The IPRU (INS) rules on admissibility also contained counterparty and asset limits. These limits now apply separately[1]. They apply in addition to the

1   PRU 3.2.33 (INSPRU 2.1.22).

general requirement[1] on a firm to restrict its exposure to counterparties and assets to prudent levels and to ensure that those exposures are adequately diversified. A deduction to a firm's capital is required in respect of assets in excess of the market risk and counterparty limits.

Counterparty exposure is the amount a firm would lose from its capital resources (calculated in accordance with PRU) if the counterparty were to fail to meet its obligations or if assets were to become worthless. In making this determination a firm must take into account exposures held by a subsidiary undertaking and synthetic exposures arising from derivatives or quasi-derivatives. A firm may take credit for collateral provided it is in the form of admissible assets and does not exceed the counterparty and asset limits set out in PRU 3.2 (INSPRU 2.1.22). Exposures which do not decrease the amount of a firm's capital are not taken into account, so, for example, holdings in relation to which the firm has not attributed any value will not form part of the counterparty exposure.

The limits are expressed in relation to types of counterparty (or similar counterparties within their group) and are calculated as a percentage of the firm's business amount. This is broadly its gross technical provisions plus other liabilities plus total capital (see PRU 3.2.22(4)/INSPRU 2.1.22(4)). Technical provisions in this case do not include those in respect of pure unit-linked liabilities.

The limits set out in PRU 3.2.22 (INSPRU 2.1.22) can be very broadly summarised as:

Counterparty	
Approved credit institutions	10% (plus 10% for short-term deposits so 20% in total)
Approved counterparty	5% (increased to 10% in certain cases*)
Corporate body	5%
Regulated institution	5% non-hybrid debt securities and 2.5% for unsecured debt
Individual(s) or partnership	1% (or 0.25% for unsecured debt)
There are also **asset limits** as follows:	
UCITS	Unlimited
Approved securities	Unlimited
Listed securities	5%
Unlisted investments (including securities)	1% (plus 10% all counterparties limit)[2]
Unsecured loans (other than with an approved counterparty)	5%
Cash in hand	3%
One piece of land	10%

*This additional exposure is only available where such exposures (ie to approved counterparties that are more than 5%) amount in total to less than 40%.

1 PRU 3.2 (SYSC 1.5.1).
2 Under INSPRU there is a 1% limit for individual collective investment schemes unless they are non UCITS UK authorised schemes in which case there is a 5% limit.

7.24   Where a counterparty could fall into more than one category the highest limit normally applies.

Approved counterparty means an approved credit institution or a firm authorised to write derivatives off market.

Approved credit institution means an EEA authorised/permitted banking institution.

Approved securities means a security issued guaranteed by Zone A country or
  a loan/deposit with an Approved Financial Institution or specified financial
  entities.

Corporate bodies means an entity which is not an individual or unincorporated
  association or closely related group of individuals or an approved counterparty. It covers regulated institutions except in relation to the assets for which
  there are specific rules for regulated institutions.

Hybrid securities means a debt security (other than an approved security) where
  the creditor cannot demand capital and interest to be fully repaid within 75
  years.

Listed/unlisted means dealt in/not dealt in on a regulated market.

Regulated institution means an EEA insurer, bank or firm authorised to write
  derivatives off market.

Limits do not apply to:

(1)   premium debt and loans covered by security in a long-term policy;

(2)   rights of salvage or subrogation;

(3)   deferred acquisition costs (as defined in the insurance accounts rules);

(4)   assets held to cover pure unit linked liabilities (eg without guarantees, etc);

(5)   debts from or guaranteed by a Zone A country; or

(6)   holdings in a UCITS.

The meaning of closely related[1] is broadly determined by control and the existence of a parent and subsidiary undertaking or consolidation relationship and
any similar relationship between a natural or legal person and an undertaking. It
is a very wide provision and will catch most of the scenarios which a firm could
envisage. In relation to specified collective investment schemes the connection is
with the issuer (eg either the authorised corporate director of an ICVC (ie UK
authorised open-ended investment company), or the ICVC itself, or the manager
of a unit trust). INSPRU will provide that parties are so interconnected if failure
of the issuer would be likely to affect the value of the units, in which case those
units should be aggregated with exposures to the manager.

Although the counterparty limits do not apply to exposures to reinsurers, firms
are required to notify the FSA as soon as they first become aware that a reinsurance exposure is reasonably likely to exceed 100% of their capital resources
(excluding capital resources held to cover property-linked liabilities) and to

1   PRU 3.2.39 and 3.2.40 (INSPRU 2.1.39 and 2.1.40).

demonstrate that they can either explain the arrangements or have a plan to manage them appropriately. In each financial year a firm should restrict its gross earned premiums paid to a reinsurer (or group of related reinsurers) to the highest of 20% of its gross earned premiums for that financial year or £4 million[1].

C   Derivatives and stock lending in insurance funds

7.25   To be an admissible asset, derivatives and quasi-derivatives (assets having the effect of a derivative contract) must be approved derivatives and stock lent by a firm must be under an approved stock lending transaction.

PRU 4.3 (INSPRU 3.2) sets out the applicable rules and guidance. The former extensive example-based guidance and 'Dear CEO' letters have been replaced by high-level guidance in PRU 4.3 (INSPRU 3.2). In the authors' view they are still worth looking at as some of the terminology is still the same and the examples help the reader to understand how the rules are applied in practice.

PRU 4.3 (INSPRU 3.2) provides that a derivative or quasi-derivative is approved if:

(1)   it is held for the purpose of efficient portfolio management ('EPM') or reduction of investment risk ('RIR');

(2)   it is covered; and

(3)   it is effected or issued on or under the rules of a regulated market or off market with an approved counterparty and (except for a forward transaction) on approved terms and is capable of valuation.

Although these requirements are very similar to the requirements in IPRU (INS) they impose new or restricted requirements on insurers, notably in the terms in which EPM is defined (see below).

D   EPM/RIR

7.26   Efficient portfolio management is defined in relation to:

(1)   generation of additional capital or income by taking advantage of *pricing imperfections* in assets which are equivalent to admissible assets or receiving a premium for selling a covered call option based on an admissible asset (even if in doing so the firm gives up the chance of greater capital or income);

(2)   *reducing tax or investment costs* in relation to admissible assets; or

(3)   acquiring or disposing of rights in relation to admissible assets or their equivalent *more efficiently or more effectively*.

---

1   Evidential provision in PRU 3.2.28 (INSPRU 2.1.28). Compliance with this provision may be relied upon in relation to the obligation of prudence and diversification.

The first limb of this definition is likely to give rise to most issues in practice. In particular it is not clear what assets are 'equivalent' to admissible assets (ie whether they should actually exist or can merely reproduce the same economic effect). It is also not clear to what extent the additional risk inherent in the pricing imperfection is acceptable.

Investment risk is defined for this purpose in PRU 4.3.12 (INSPRU 3.2.12) as the risk that the asset may not be equal to liabilities, be of appropriate safety, yield, marketability or in the appropriate currency. Additionally, where assets are held to cover unit-linked liabilities, it is the risk that they may not be appropriate cover for those liabilities.

Reduction of investment risk broadly replicates the previous requirement that it must reduce an aspect of investment risk without significantly increasing another aspect of that risk (ie any such increase in risk is small and reasonable or the risk is remote). The guidance specifically still contemplates that some adverse consequences (eg loss of premium) may arise through the use of derivatives.

E   Cover

7.27   The FSA requires cover for three reasons: to protect against loss; to protect against the risk of a firm not being able to deliver 'appropriate' (ie the right type of) assets; and to prevent excessive gearing in the investment portfolio. The requirement for cover arises in relation to a firm's obligation to transfer assets or pay a monetary amount under a contract (other than a contract of insurance) for the purchase, sale or exchange of assets or under a derivative or quasi-derivative. Cover must be in a form of assets, a liability, provision or an offsetting transaction. If a firm covers a liability with assets they must be admissible assets and it must reasonably believe that those assets will be sufficient to pay the amount of the obligation when it falls due. An obligation can be covered by a liability where the amount of that obligation would be offset by a decrease in the amount of liability. Similarly, a provision recognised by PRU 1.3 (GENPRU 1.3) at least equal to the value of the asset can be used as cover. The guidance makes clear that a derivative may be split to the extent it is uncovered and the uncovered portion treated as not being an approved derivative.

Cover from one transaction cannot be used for cover in respect of another and an offsetting transaction must provide the firm with the relevant assets *before* the obligation it is offsetting falls due. The guidance includes examples of the cover requirement and specifically states that borrowings may not be used to gear an investment portfolio (PRU 4.3.30 and 4.3.31 (INSPRU 3.2.30 and 3.2.31)). The FSA now specifically requires firms to cover options by holding the exercise price even though they may never actually exercise the option.

F   Over the counter transactions

7.28   The full PRU rules on OTC derivatives have never been brought into force. INSPRU provides that a derivative is on approved terms only if the firm reasonably believes that it could, in all reasonably foreseeable circumstances and under normal market conditions, readily enter into a further transaction with the counterparty or a third party to close out at the value attributed to the derivative by the firm (taking into account any valuation adjustments or reserves established by the firm)[1]. The FSA makes clear that the firm needs to be able to satisfy itself that the contract could be realised at the appropriate value. INSPRU also provides that a contract is only 'capable of valuation' if the firm reasonably believes it will be able to value it with reasonable accuracy on a reliable basis throughout the life of the transaction[2].

G   Stock lending

7.29   PRU also provides rules in relation to the basis on which an insurer can lend stock but still treat[3] the stock as its asset. There are no specific rules relating to the borrowing of stock by an insurer.

A *stock lending transaction* will be approved and therefore the assets lent will continue to constitute admissible assets if:

(1)   the assets lent are admissible assets;

(2)   the counterparty is an authorised person or an approved counterparty (eg a bank or firm authorised to write OTC derivatives or as specified in INSPRU 3.2.36 (including certain US authorised broker/dealers)); and

(3)   adequate and sufficient immediate collateral is obtained to secure the obligation of the counterparty.

The rules specify the type of collateral which can be used for these purposes. Assets must be adequate in quality, be admissible assets and be transferred to the firm or its agent at or before the time of the transaction in question (by end of the business day on which the loan is made). Collateral also continues to be adequate only if its value is at all times equal to the value of securities transferred to the firm.

SECTION 6   INTERNAL CONTAGION RISK

7.30   The provisions of PRU 7.6 (INSPRU 1.5) are concerned with what the FSA describes as 'internal contagion risk' and apply to insurers other than small friendly societies[4]. They are intended to protect a firm against different types of activity or business carried on within the firm.

1   INSPRU 3.2.34.
2   INSPRU 3.2.35.
3   PRU 4.3.36/INSPRU 3.2.36.
4   £5m premium income but parts of PRU 7.6 are disapplied in 7.6.2 (INSPRU 1.5 and 1.5.2 respectively).

A   The section 16 restriction

7.31   The first life directive required member states to restrict an insurer's ability to carry on non-insurance related activities. This control was for many years to be found in section 16 of the Insurance Companies Act 1982 ('ICA 1982'). This required insurance companies to limit their activities to insurance business and activities in connection with it. When IPRU (INS) was implemented, the FSA (in rule 1.3) rewrote the restriction to reflect more closely the provisions of the directives that had introduced the requirement in the first place. There were two perceived areas of concern. First, the 'in connection with' wording in section 16 was too vague and regarded as a 'gloss' on the derivatives' requirements. Second, that the restrictions only applied to activity being carried on by way of business. The substance of rule 1.3 is now set out in PRU 7.6.13 (INSPRU 1.5.13) which states that a firm 'must not carry on any commercial business other than insurance business and activities directly arising from that business'. FSA guidance indicates that activities directly arising from insurance business could include investing the firm's assets and employing staff.

Any non-insurance business which is permitted within this restriction (ie which 'directly arises' from the insurance business) should be limited, controlled and managed so that it does not lead to any significant risk that the firm might be unable to meet its liabilities as they fall due, and in quantifying this risk, a firm should consider how likely it is that financial risk from this type of business could diverge from expectations.

B   Separation of life funds and use of their assets

7.32   The FSA will not grant a firm a permission which incorporates both general and long-term insurance business[1]. Also, firms authorised to effect or carry out life and annuity business are permitted to carry out accident and sickness general insurance contracts on an ancillary or supplementary basis.

PRU[2] requires firms carrying on long-term insurance business to identify those assets which relate to their long-term insurance business, and to only apply such assets for the purpose of the long-term business. A firm must also not agree to, or allow, any mortgage or charge on its long-term insurance assets other than in respect of a long-term insurance liability.

Long-term insurance business includes payment of long-term insurance claims, expenses and liabilities, and also loans (provided that the loan was incurred for the purpose of the long-term insurance business). Long-term insurance assets include premiums, income and capital receipts and receivables in respect of long-term insurance business, and any other assets available to meet its long-term insurance liabilities (including assets to which these assets have been converted).

Separate accounting records must be maintained in respect of each long-term insurance fund. The question sometimes arises as to whether a firm has just one

---

1   PRU 7.6.17 (INSPRU 1.5.17). This does not prevent historic composites from continuing to carry on both types of insurance business, but the various systems and controls set out in PRU are designed to ensure that policyholders are adequately protected from the resulting risks.
2   PRU 7.6.30 and 7.6.31 (INSPRU 1.5.30 and 1.5.31).

long-term fund or a number of funds[1]. PRU provides that all long-term insurance assets constitute a firm's long-term insurance fund, unless a firm can identify particular life assets in connection with different parts of its life business, in which case the assets identified in relation to each such part constitute separate long-term insurance funds of the firm.

Further, the maintenance of separate funds may be necessary to ensure policy-holders are treated fairly where any surplus is shared between policyholders and shareholders in different ways for different blocks of business[2]. The most obvious example is where a proprietary life office writes some with-profits busi-ness. IPRU (INS) rule 3.5 also requires an insurer to avoid unfairness between its long-term funds or between a long-term fund and other assets of the insurer.

Firms may merge separate funds for different types of business[3] provided the merger will not result in policyholders being treated unfairly.

C Established surplus

7.33 Assets may not be transferred out of a long-term insurance fund unless the assets represent an established surplus, established no more than three months previously[4]. The established surplus can only be determined by actuarial investigation. Even where the investigation is still less than three months old a firm cannot make the transfer unless there are sufficient funds at the time of transfer to enable it to be made without breach of the requirements to cover its liabilities in PRU 7.2.20 and 7.2.21 (INSPRU 1.1.27 and 1.1.28).

These provisions are reinforced by regulations made under section 378 of the Financial Services and Markets Act ('FSMA'). The regulations provide that when an insurer is being wound up, the assets maintained in a long-term fund are to be available only to meet the liabilities of that fund unless on winding up there are surplus assets in the fund. It is therefore important for third parties dealing with UK long-term insurers to be clear whether the insurer is contracting on behalf of a long-term insurance fund and, if so, which one. This is particularly the case where they enter into a netting arrangement or where a charge over assets is proposed.

Firms are permitted to transfer non-life assets (eg assets referable to the general business) into the long-term insurance fund. However, once transferred, such assets may not be transferred out of the long-term insurance fund save where they represent an 'established surplus'.

D Appropriate assets, adequate premiums and fairness

7.34 PRU 7.2.34 (INSPRU 1.1.34) provides that save in relation to assets held to cover property-linked or index-linked liabilities, the assets held by firms to cover technical provisions must:

1 In practice this often seems to be determined based on historic and/or accounting practice.
2 PRU 7.6.27 (INSPRU 1.5.25).
3 PRU 7.6.26/INSPRU 1.5.26.
4 PRU 7.6.27 (INSPRU 1.5.27).

(1) have characteristics of safety, yield and marketability appropriate to the type of business carried on by the firm;

(2) be diversified and adequately spread;

(3) be of sufficient amount, and of appropriate currency and term, to ensure the cash inflows from those assets will meet expected cash outflows from the firm's insurance liabilities as they become due.

PRU 7.2.41 (INSPRU 1.1.41) provides that a firm must not enter into a long-term insurance contract unless it is satisfied on reasonable actuarial assumptions that the premiums are sufficient to enable it to establish adequate technical provisions covered by admissible assets and to maintain adequate overall financial resources. Guidance makes clear that adequacy may be assessed on a firm's total portfolio of business. It may therefore loss lead on individual products (ie firms relying on a single market home state authorisation or rights under the Treaty of Rome).

Note that if the FSA imposes a financial penalty on a life office, the firm is not permitted to pay such penalty from a long-term insurance fund. This rule does not apply to mutuals but is one of the few which does apply to EEA and Treaty Firms.

IPRU (INS) rule 3.2(b) continues to restrict a long-term insurer's ability to pay dividends where its long-term insurance assets are less than its long-term insurance liabilities (ie technical provisions and current liabilities).

E Unit-linked contracts

7.35 Much of the detail of PRU does not apply to unit-linked funds, particularly admissibility and counterparty limits in relation to property-linked and index-linked benefits. Certain provisions of PRU do, however, apply to property-linked funds.

PRU 7.6.35 (INSPRU 1.5.35) applies identification and maintenance provisions to property-linked funds and states that it should not apply those assets (as long as they are needed to cover property-linked benefits) for any other purpose. There is no equivalent provision on insolvency and typically unit-linked funds do not form separate long-term funds because the link to the underlying assets is notional. This means that on insolvency unit-linked assets are potentially available to satisfy other liabilities of the same long-term fund.

PRU 7.6.36 (INSPRU 1.5.36) provides for management of property-linked funds to cover, as closely as possible, its property-linked liabilities with the property to which those liabilities are linked taking into account both contractual and regulatory duties (eg treating customers fairly). PRU 4.2.57 (INSPRU 3.1.57) also requires a firm to cover its property-linked liabilities with assets which as closely as possible match those liabilities and/or a property-linked insurance contract.

Similarly, a firm must cover its indexed-linked liabilities with assets of appropriate marketability and security which correspond as closely as possible to the assets which form the index[1]. Alternatively, an insurer should hold a portfolio of

1 (PRU 4.2.58) INSPRU 3.1.58.

assets whose value or yield is reasonably expected to correspond closely with index-linked liabilities and indexed-linked to the insurance contract or an indexed-linked approved derivative or quasi-derivative contract. Unlike the situation with currency matching, a firm is not permitted to hold different assets and to cover the mis-matching by holding an excess of assets. Firms are also directed in particular to consider credit risk in accordance with PRU 3.2 (INSPRU 2.1).

F Reinsurance

7.36   There are specific requirements in relation to reinsurance (and other forms of risk transfer). The PRU obligations impose a general obligation to notify the FSA of changes to existing reinsurance arrangements or any new arrangements. The FSA is introducing further rules and guidance specific to financial engineering.

Additional provisions relating to reinsurance now apply to with-profits funds. These are set out in COB 6.12. COB 6.12.89R provides that a with-profits fund should not enter into a material transaction unless the firm's governing body reasonably believes it is unlikely to have a material adverse effect on the interests of the fund's with-profits policyholders. Material transactions include significant bulk outwards reinsurance, *any* inwards with-profits reinsurance and any financial engineering that would materially change the emergence of surplus on existing business.

Prior to entering into or significantly changing a reinsurance agreement, or any other form of insurance risk transfer agreement, a firm should conduct appropriate due diligence on the reinsurer, the contractual terms offered and the effect on the insurer's own regulatory position.

In managing its reinsurance agreements, a firm should have in place appropriate systems that allow it to maintain its desired level of cover including conducting regular stress and scenario testing.

SECTION 7   INSURANCE GROUPS AND FINANCIAL CONGLOMERATES

A   Group risk

I   Introduction

7.37   PRU 8[1] deals with group risk management and capital requirements including the new requirements of the Financial Groups Directive applicable to financial conglomerates (groups with significant interests in both the banking/investment sector and the insurance sector). These provisions mean that FSA regulated insurers now potentially face three levels of supervision:

---

1   See SYSC 12, GENPRU 3.1 and 3.2 and INSPRU 6.1.

(a)   prudential supervision on a stand-alone basis (which will be an 'adjusted' calculation where the insurer has significant interests in other insurers);

(b)   consolidated or supplementary supervision on a sectoral basis (ie banking, investment and insurance sectors);

(c)   supervision on a mixed-group-wide basis if they are a member of a financial conglomerate.

The rationale for the prudential supervision of corporate groups in the banking, investment and insurance sectors is the risk that weaknesses (such as inadequate capital or poor systems and controls) at group level could threaten the position of individual regulated firms within the group.

2   Group risk systems and controls

7.38   PRU 8.1 (SYSC 12) sets out prudential requirements applicable to all groups (including FSA-regulated EEA financial conglomerates)[1] requiring group-wide systems and controls to manage risks. All authorised firms (that are in the insurance, banking or investment sectors) within groups must have 'adequate, sound and appropriate risk management processes and internal control mechanisms for the purpose of assessing and managing their *own exposure to group risk*, including sound administrative and accounting procedures'[2]. Group risk also includes risk arising from non-regulated entities which are part of a group.

A similar requirement[3] applies *at group level*. The group level requirement is of more limited application. It applies in respect of financial conglomerates and groups only if regulated by the FSA. It also excludes the conglomerate's or its group's interest in any firms in which it (they) holds only a 'participation' (broadly a 20% holding but see below).

As with other areas of risk management, the FSA guidance states that what will constitute 'adequate, sound and appropriate' controls should be judged in light of the nature, scale and complexity of the group's business. Also, whilst appropriate systems and controls may be organised on a 'group-wide basis', with functions delegated to specific group members, each firm within the group retains individual responsibility for complying with its own obligations. A firm may rely upon its parent's systems and controls (where the parent is also subject to the group level requirement) provided it has made an appropriate assessment of such systems and controls.

An FSA-regulated EEA financial conglomerate's internal control mechanisms must include sound reporting and accounting procedures for the purpose of identifying, measuring, monitoring and controlling intra-group transactions and risk concentrations.

---

1   Broadly, where the ultimate EU parent company is established in the UK.
2   PRU 8.1.9(1) (INSPRU 12.1.8(1).
3   PRU 8.1.9(2) SYSC 12.1.8(2).

B Insurance groups

7.39 The Insurance Groups Directive ('IGD') (as amended) provides supplementary supervision for EU insurance groups (the sectoral supervision referred to above). The IGD requires that group level capital adequacy calculations must be reported to the group's supervisor (normally the supervisor of the ultimate EEA parent) and it also imposes additional reporting and system and control requirements. Companies regulated in the UK may therefore find that group supervision is conducted from another member state. The main aim is to prevent double counting of capital within an insurance group. The IGD used to only apply to group interests in insurance companies but has now been extended by the Financial Groups Directive ('FGD') to include other financial 'regulated' entities. It works by requiring a parent undertaking which has a significant interest in an insurance company to value its interest on a 'look-through' basis (ie it must look through to the capital of the insurance company and deduct the book value of the group's interest as shareholder). To allow limits on capital to be applied consistently at group level, group capital is aggregated and then the total deduction for total book values for each type of capital (tier 1, tier 2, etc) is made, producing a net total group figure for each type of capital.

The IGD does not require groups to actually hold capital calculated on a group basis. The FSA has announced that with effect from 31 December 2006, to provide consistency between the different types of group it regulates, the ultimate parent company in the insurance group (which may be an insurance holding company or an insurer) will be required to actually hold the required amount of group capital.

C Application of PRU 8.3/INSPRU 6.1

7.40 PRU 8.3 (INSPRU 6.1) applies to insurers that are either 'participating insurance undertakings' (ie holding a significant interest (20%) in other insurance undertakings) or are themselves members of an 'insurance group'. A firm may also be a participating insurer in relation to firms connected by an article 12 consolidation relationship (eg if they are managed on a unified basis or the administration, management or supervisory bodies of the undertaking consist of the same people). A firm is part of an insurance group if there is either sufficient cross shareholder control to amount to at least a participation (eg 20%) or control through the exercise of voting rights, rights to appoint directors or to exert a document influence. A group will normally constitute a company, its holding company and subsidiaries of the holding company but in each case extended to include companies in which another company in the group has a participation.

The group calculation, although based on these companies, is only conducted in relation to the ultimate EEA insurance parent. As that parent may be unauthorised (for example, an insurance holding company), the FSA has made all insurers in the group subject to the requirement to ensure the group is adequately capitalised. Such insurers are required[1], on a regular basis, to calculate the group capital resources ('GCR') (in accordance with the formula set out at PRU 8.3.36)

---

1 PRU 8.3.8 (INSPRU 6.1.8).

and group capital resources requirement ('GCRR') (in accordance with the formula set out at PRU 8.3.33). These calculations must be made in relation to the following entities known as the 'relevant calculating entities':

(a) the insurer itself, if it qualifies as a 'participating insurance undertaking' (ie if it holds at least a participation in another insurer);

(b) the 'ultimate insurance parent undertaking' (ie the ultimate parent of the insurance group which is either an insurer with at least a participation in another insurer or qualifies as an insurance holding company (ie its main business is to acquire and hold participations in subsidiaries which are either exclusively or mainly insurance undertakings, and at least one of which is EEA based); and

(c) the 'ultimate EEA insurance parent undertaking' (if different).

D Calculation of group capital adequacy

7.41   Calculation of GCR and GCRR involve looking at the individual capital resource requirements of each 'regulated related undertaking' in the group of a Relevant Calculating Entity. This includes firms in the investment, banking and asset management sectors as well as insurance undertakings, and the holding companies of the same (excluding holding companies of asset management companies).

Under article 3(3) of the IGD[1], an undertaking within an insurance group may be excluded from supplementary supervision (and therefore the requirement that its capital adequacy forms part of the GCR and GCRR) if it is not based in the EEA and there are legal impediments to the transfer of the necessary information, *or*, if in the opinion of the regulator responsible for supplementary supervision, its inclusion would be inappropriate/misleading or of negligible interest. For a UK group to take advantage of this (eg in relation to intermediate insurance holding companies) it is necessary to get a waiver from the FSA.

Normally, the GCRR of a relevant calculating entity is calculated as the *sum of the individual capital resources requirements of itself and each of its regulated related undertakings*.

The GCR is calculated as the proportional share (being the proportion of the total number of shares in the regulated related undertaking held by the relevant calculating entity or where an article 12(1) consolidation relationship exists, such proportion as the FSA decides in accordance with the FGD) of the sum of the tier 1 and tier 2 capital resources of the individual members of the group who qualify as regulated related undertakings, less the book value of investments in such group undertakings by all other group members.

Capital which a firm is itself required to hold cannot be assumed to be transferable intra-group. Capital which is not transferable for other reasons (for example surplus capital in the long-term fund) is also excluded from group capital calculations.

---

1   PRU 8.3.18 (INSPRU 6.1.18).

The group capital calculation involves deductions for inadmissible assets[1] and investments in 'ancillary services undertakings' (ie undertakings whose principal activity consists of owning/managing property, managing data-processing services, or any similar activity which is ancillary to the principal activity of insurance, banking or investment firms).

1   Limits on group capital

7.42   These limits are complicated not least because they are expressed by means of formulae but there are some areas of common ground with the individual company limits in PRU 2 (GENPRU 2), for example:

(1)   innovative tier 1 is limited to 15% of total tier 1;

(2)   core tier 1 must be at least 50% of total group tier 1;

(3)   total group tier 2 must be no more than total group tier 1; and

(4)   total group lower tier 2 must be no more than 25% of total group tier 1.

2   Adjusted solo calculation

7.43   A participating insurer will also have an adjusted solo calculation. This is because when doing its own capital calculations it must value interests in other insurers amounting to a participation on a look through basis. It must also make deductions in respect of assets in excess of market risk and counterparty limits as applied by PRU 8.3.70 to 8.3.78 (INSPRU 6.1.70 to 6.1.78) and ineligible surplus capital (eg capital which is not transferable – PRU 8.3.65 (INSPRU 6.1.65)).

E   Financial conglomerates (or cross-sector groups)

7.44   The FGD came into effect for financial years beginning on or after 1 January 2005. The Directive introduced rules to regulate financial conglomerates (groups with significant interests in both the insurance and banking/investment sector). The FGD was in the UK in PRU 8.4[2]. The rules provide for calculation and holding of adequate capital and a single EU supervisor at the financial conglomerate level. Financial conglomerates are also subject to risk concentration and intra-group transaction requirements (the mixed group-wide basis of supervision referred to above).

F   What is a financial conglomerate?

7.45   A group will be a financial conglomerate if:

1   PRU 8.3.59 (INSPRU 6.1.59).
2   Other than the amendments to the IGD which are incorporated in PRU 8.3 (INSPRU 6.1).

(1) at least 40% of its business is financial; and

(2) at least 10% or 6 billion euros of its financial business is in each of the insurance and the combined banking/investment sectors.

Whether a firm is a financial conglomerate is determined by applying the decision tree in PRU 8 Annex 4R[1] (GENPRU 8 Annex 4R) as follows:

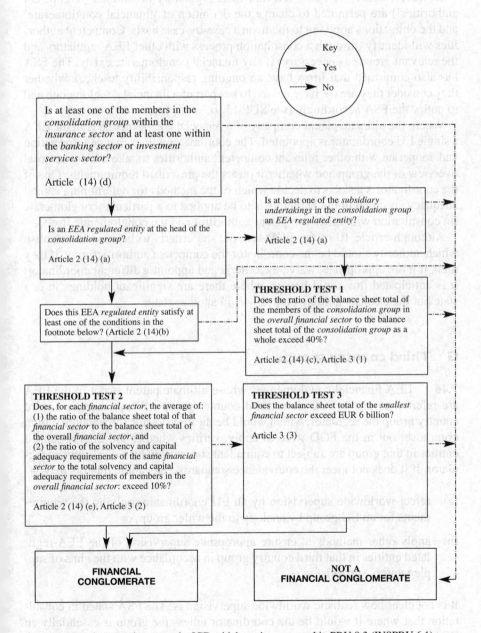

1 Other than the amendments to the IGD which are incorporated in PRU 8.3 (INSPRU 6.1).

Once identified as a financial conglomerate, the threshold limits to be included in the decision tree are reduced if/when the financial conglomerate would cease to qualify as a financial conglomerate based on the original figures and for three years following that date. This is to avoid sudden changes in status and the uncertainty that would bring. The reduction means that only 30% of its business needs to be in the overall financial sector and only 5 billion euros is required to be in each of the insurance and banking/investment sector.

However, under the FGD, relevant EEA regulatory authorities ('competent authorities') are permitted to change the definition of 'financial conglomerate' and the obligations applying to them, on a case-by-case basis. Competent authorities will identify (through a consultation process with other EEA regulators and the relevant groups as necessary) if any financial conglomerate exists. The FSA has also confirmed that firms have an ongoing responsibility to check whether they consider they are (or have ceased to be) part of a financial conglomerate and to notify the FSA accordingly (see SUP 15.9).

Where the ultimate parent company of a financial conglomerate is in the EEA a single EU coordinator is appointed. The coordinator will exchange information and cooperate with other relevant competent authorities to take a cross-sectoral overview of the group and whether it meets the prescribed requirements. One of the coordinator's tasks is to decide which of the methods for determining capital adequacy specified in the Directive is to be applied to a particular conglomerate (in consultation with other competent authorities and the conglomerate itself).

Although article 10 of the FGD sets out the criteria to be used to establish which authority should be the coordinator the competent authorities may, if they think it more appropriate, waive the criteria and appoint a different coordinator. It is anticipated this could happen where there are significant holdings in one state but the ultimate holding company is in another state.

G   Third country groups

7.46   EEA financial conglomerates whose ultimate parent is not in the EEA are referred to in the FGD as a 'third country group'. Where there is a third country group the regulator, which would be the coordinator if the identification criteria set out in the FGD were to apply, verifies whether the EEA regulated entities in that group are subject to equivalent supervision by a third country regulator. If it does not meet the equivalence standards, relevant regulators may:

(a)   effect worldwide supervision by an EU coordinator applying the requirements for an EU group by analogy to the wider group; or

(b)   apply other methods to ensure appropriate supervision of the EEA-regulated entities in that third country group in accordance with the aims of supplementary supervision.

It is not clear how realistic worldwide supervision is. The FSA stated in consultation that where it would be the coordinator unless the group is essentially an EEA group (eg only a holding company outside of the EEA) it is unlikely to seek to use worldwide supervision. UK authorised firms within a third country financial conglomerate may, as part of its Part IV Permission, be required to comply with PRU 8.5.8. This would require them to comply with additional systems and controls and capital adequacy requirements and perhaps to have to provide ring-fencing of capital held at the EEA level.

H   The financial conglomerates' capital requirements

7.47   A regulated firm that is a member of a financial conglomerate must at all times maintain capital resources of such an amount and type that results in the capital resources of the financial conglomerate taken as a whole being adequate.

Under the FGD there are four potential methods for calculating capital adequacy (both the capital requirements and the amount of capital):

Method 1	using accounting consolidation
Method 2	using a deduction and aggregation approach
Method 3	using book values and the deduction of capital requirements
Method 4	a combination of methods 1, 2 and 3, or any two of them

The relevant coordinator decides which method is to be applied. Where the FSA is coordinator, it has effectively chosen method 4. This should require the least amount of change as broadly each sector uses the method applied to it on a sectoral basis. For insurance companies within the group PRU 8.3 (INSPRU 6.1) applies whereas for other sectors their existing methods are used.

The rules work in a circular manner by requiring firms to hold capital to ensure that the conglomerate has the resources required under Part 4 of PRU 8 Annex 1R (GENPRU 8 Annex 1R), which in turn refers to the sectoral rules in para 4.2 of the Annex. Where the FSA is either not the coordinator or there are no capital ties within a group, the rules provide for more bespoke arrangements. These can be agreed with other supervisors and imposed as a requirement on a firm's Part IV Permission. The requirement will specify the appropriate method to be used or any share of deficit to be included.

I   Risk concentration and intra-group transactions

7.48   A firm must ensure that it complies with the sectoral rules regarding risk concentration (large exposure) and intra-group transactions of the most important financial sector in the conglomerate, in respect to that financial sector as a whole (including the mixed financial holding company). The effect of this is summarised in the table set out in PRU 8.4.36 (GENPRU 3.1.36).

For the insurance sector, there are no risk concentration requirements. The intra-group transaction requirements are specified in rule 9.39 of IPRU (INS). These require notification on specified forms of details of transactions that have taken place during the financial year in question. The idea is to give sufficient information on the financial impact of material connected party transactions (eg transactions with a connected party the value of which exceeds 5% of the insurer's liabilities from long-term business (other than unit-linked and net of reinsurance) or insurer's general insurance liabilities (net of reinsurance)).

CHAPTER 8

Life reassurance

SUMMARY

Section 1   What is reassurance?   **8.1**

Section 2   Analysis of reassurance contracts   **8.8**

Section 3   Reinsurance Directive   **8.15**

Section 4   Prudential standards relating to insurers: reassurance   **8.19**

SECTION 1   WHAT IS REASSURANCE?

8.1   Reassurance occurs when an insurer ('the primary insurer') passes some or all of the risk it has accepted from an insured person to another person ('the reassurer'). The term 'reassurance' is used in this chapter although from a life perspective both 'reassurance' and 'reinsurance' are used. For non-life assurance the reference would invariably be to 'reinsurance'. Other terms used to refer to the primary insurer are 'original insurer', 'direct insurer' and 'cedant'.

A precise legal definition of reinsurance has proved to be elusive. Indeed, much of the case law in this area has shied away from seeking to provide a definitive explanation (see, for example, Potter LJ in *Skandia International Corp v NRG Victory Reinsurance Ltd* [1998] Lloyd's Rep IR 439, 457). Generally, there must be a contract between an insurer and a reinsurer under which the insurer lays off some or all of its risk to the reinsurer for the payment of a premium in circumstances where the reinsurer has no contractual relationship directly with the ultimate insured. In *Forsikringaktieselskapet Vesta v JNE Butcher* [1989] 1 AC 852, 908 Lord Lowry stated that 'reinsurance is prima facie a contract of indemnity . . . under which the reinsurer indemnifies the original insurer against the whole or against a specified amount or proportion . . . of the risk which the latter has himself insured'.

The importance and purpose of reassurance lies in the ability of primary insurers to spread risk and so contribute to the function of the insurance market in distributing risk in a sustainable and economically efficient way. Reassurance can be continued beyond the first level so that a contract which reinsures a reinsured risk is known as a 'retrocession', the reassurer being termed the 'retrocessionaire' and the reassured as the 'retrocedant'. Multiple levels of reassurance can cause confusion and, more importantly, serious practical complications. Occasionally, the same insurer appears at different levels of the reassurance with the result that an insurer is effectively reassuring itself.

Essentially, the reassurance contract is another species of a contract of insurance although it does present its own special features.

A   Nature of reassurance contracts

8.2   The reassurance contract is solely between the reassured and the reassurer. The primary insured (normally) has no contract with the reassurer. Looking at insurable interest for reassurance contracts it is important to note that the risk which is insured under the reassurance contract is not the same as that which is covered by the primary insurance. The reassurance is against the risk that the liability under the primary contract will arise. Therefore, a reinsurer providing cover for pet risks does not need to be authorised as a pet insurer, because he is not providing pet insurance.

The primary insured normally has no contract with the reassurer. Therefore, the primary insured has no immediate concern whether the contract of reassurance is properly formed as his rights are purely against the primary insurer (although he may have a wider concern that the primary insurer is unable to meet his claim without the benefit of reassurance). Likewise, the reassurance contract is of no help to the primary insured if the primary insurer is insolvent or the primary insurance contract is defective as the reassurance contract cannot be called upon by the primary insured. One way to seek to deal with the potential problems this could cause is to insert 'cut-through' clauses under which the reassurer makes payment direct to the primary insured. These clauses are not dealt with any further here although it should be noted that they have encountered difficulty in many respects, for example, in terms of privity of contract, the Insolvency Act 1986 and whether this requires the reassurer to obtain the relevant regulatory status as a primary insurer.

B   Types of reassurance

8.3   The fundamental distinction in reassurance is between, on the one hand, compulsory or obligatory or treaty reassurance and, on the other, optional or facultative reassurance.

In the latter case the primary insurer approaches the reassurer to seek cover for a particular risk or category of risks. The contract is then negotiated in broadly the same way as a primary insurance contract. In the former case the agreement made between primary insurer and reassurer is that the reassurer will accept, subject to agreed limits and conditions, all the risks written by the primary insurer. Reassurance is therefore automatic on both sides. As soon as the primary risk is undertaken, it is automatically added to the risks reassured without the need for any further action from either party. The advantages of this type of reassurance is that it provides certainty, relative ease and cheapness of administration. The possible disadvantage for the reassurer is that he must accept the primary insurer's judgement of what risks should be accepted. Although, in many cases the treaty will provide for the primary insurer to follow the reassurer's underwriting criteria which are often set out in a dedicated handbook.

A 'halfway house' is a type of reassurance rather confusingly referred to as 'facultative/obligatory reassurance' (or colloquially as 'fac/ob' reassurance). In this case the primary insurer can choose which risks he will reassure, but the reassurer is obliged to accept those risks which the primary insurer passes onto him. From the reassurer's perspective this may be less satisfactory as the primary insurer can pick and choose which risks he wants to retain and those he does not, potentially passing on poor quality business to the reassurer. The practical value in this type of reassurance is that it enables the insurer to redistribute the risks which are particularly large compared to the general level of the business it transacts but which commercially they do not wish to decline completely.

C   Treaty reassurance – further issues

8.4   Reassurance treaties may be further distinguished into two main types, 'quota share' and 'surplus'. Under quota share a proportion of the risks written by the primary insurer are automatically ceded to the reassurer. This is quite a simple concept in that the reassurer reinsures a stated percentage of a given book of business. Possibly, different portions of the risk will be reassured in different places, and the primary insurer will generally retain at least some part of the risk himself.

For 'surplus' reassurance the insurer retains the risk completely up to a certain amount with the reassurer accepting the surplus of risk over and above that retention. The retention will be expressed either in relation to individual risks or in relation to the total of risks of a certain class.

With both quota share and surplus reassurance a proportion of the risk is 'ceded' and for this reason this type of reassurance is referred to as 'proportional'. Other types of reassurance are referred to as 'non-proportional', the most common examples of which are 'excess of loss' and 'stop loss'. The former provides cover against losses incurred on particular primary policies over and above a specified amount. This amount is usually fairly high. Excess of loss cover is usually arranged in a series of layers. The premium for the higher layers will be less than for the lower layers (reflecting the lower risk that the higher layers will be reached). It is a feature of this type of reassurance that it covers claims arising from a single event or occurrence. Issues tend to arise on what constitutes a 'single event'[1]. See **8.12**.

Stop loss insurance covers total losses on particular types or classes of policy during the period of insurance.

D   'Follow the settlements' clause

8.5   A common provision in reassurance contracts is a 'follow the settlements' clause. In broad terms this means that the reassurer is liable if the ceding

---

1   *Mann v Lexington Insurance Co* [2000] 2 All ER (Comm) 163.

company makes payment out and the main question it tends to raise is whether the insurer is able to hold the reassurer liable for settlements which may not be in accordance with strict legal liability. It has been held (*Insurance Co of Africa v Scor (UK) Reinsurance Co Ltd* [1985] 1 Lloyd's Rep 312, CA) that the effect of such a clause is that the reassurer must follow and honour any settlement entered in to by the ceding company unless the reinsurers can show lack of good faith or collusion or failure on the part of the ceding company to take all and proper businesslike steps to have the amount of the loss fairly and carefully ascertained. This would appear to impose quite a heavy burden on the reassurer and the 'follow the settlements' clause in modern reassurance contracts generally imposes certain responsibilities on the primary insurer designed to protect the reassurer. For example, certain claims data should be produced. Also, where the claims approval limit is exceeded reference may need to be made to the reassurer for approval. These are generally known as 'claims control and co-operation' clauses.

E   Foreign judgments

8.6   It is fairly common ground that in order to recover under a reassurance policy the insurers have to establish that they are liable under the primary insurance policy. The court ought to treat a foreign judgment as binding in respect of a reassured's liability under the original insurance contract, provided: (1) the foreign court was of competent jurisdiction; (2) the judgment had not been given in breach of any exclusive jurisdiction clause; (3) the reinsured had taken all proper defences; and (4) the judgment was not manifestly perverse[1].

F   Fronting

8.7   Having reinsurance available enables smaller insurers to accept risks which are beyond their capacity and possibly also their expertise by 'fronting' the insurance whilst reinsuring all, or the major part of, the risk to a reinsurer who specialises in that type of business (although 100% fronting can raise its own questions regarding whether, or the extent to which, the primary insurer is actually assuming any risk). Fronting is also used, perhaps more controversially, where the reinsurer is not permitted to conduct direct insurance business in a particular jurisdiction and therefore has to find a local reinsurer to notionally insure the risk. The result can be a reversal of the traditional course of business, with reinsurers agreeing to reinsure the entirety of a risk with a proposer and then having to find an insurance company willing to act as the fronting insurer[2]. From a regulatory perspective one of the issues raised is that the reinsurer will not be regulated in the UK although it will effectively be insuring individuals in the UK

---

1   *Commercial Union Assurance Co plc v NRG Victory Reinsurance Ltd; Skandia International Insurance Corpn v NRG Victory Reinsurance Ltd* [1998] 2 All ER 434, CA.
2   *Commonwealth Insurance Co of Vancouver v Groupe Sprinks SA* [1983] 1 Lloyd's Rep 67.

but without necessarily the same prudential protections which apply to FSA regulated insurers.

SECTION 2   ANALYSIS OF REASSURANCE CONTRACTS

A   Recent developments

8.8   Reassurance contracts have tended to lag behind the standards of most modern commercial agreements although it is probably true to say that they have made recent progress in making up lost ground. The authors have noted reassurance agreements from the early 1980s where provisions have specifically been structured on the basis of a 'gentleman's agreement'!

Not all disputes in connection with life reassurance are now resolved informally and amicably. Market attitudes have changed so that 'gentleman's agreements' are no longer considered satisfactory. In addition there has been an increase in the level of business ceded and in the sophistication of reassurance arrangements. The FSA have also started to take more of an interest in reassurance issues (see **8.19**). Crucially, Europe has woken up to the issue and has recently adopted a Reinsurance Directive (see **8.15**).

B   Major pitfalls in connection with reassurance contracts

8.9   Contracts are sometimes not fully documented and agreed before the parties enter into legally binding relationships. On occasions this is unavoidable due to commercial pressures and in the early days of a reassurance Treaty which is only reassuring new business for the primary insurer this may not be too much of an issue as the policies being reassured may be few in the early days and generally take some time to reach the cedant's books as a result of the sales and underwriting processes. However, it is not an ideal state of affairs and should not be allowed to continue for any longer than can be helped.

It has often been the case that reassurance contracts have had no legal vetting either by any in-house legal department or by external firms of solicitors. This state of affairs is changing not least because of FSA requirements in this area (see **8.19**). Other issues have been the use of one Treaty for all classes of business and a lack of consistency in wordings as a result of taking different wordings from a variety of sources.

C   Overview of the structure of reassurance treaties

8.10   The following is a possible structure. It is not intended to be definitive or exhaustive or to suggest that other structures are not equally valid. It is, however, a structure which has been broadly adopted by certain leading reassurers and reassurance brokers.

Schedule. This will set out the specific basic details of the contract. This will include some or all of the following: the parties; type of treaty (eg 'quota share'); treaty commencement date; date of coming into effect; termination date; primary policies covered; basis upon which premiums are charged; risks covered; any supplementary risks covered; geographical scope and currency; retentions; treaty limit; maximum benefit limit; 'Jumbo Risk' limit; claims approval limit; claims expense limit; benefit reinsured; benefit calculation date; reinsurance premium rates; brokerage (commission); accounts, information and data requirements; notice requirements. The Schedule may also include the signing provisions.

Special Conditions. These will tend to amend or add to the 'General Terms and Conditions' so is likely to be the category which will vary most from Treaty to Treaty. Possible areas it may cover include: review option (both reassurer and primary insurer having option to review or request a review); identification of reinsurance intermediary; detailed provisions relating to Jumbo Risks; distribution partners of the primary insurer (essentially a quality control method for the reassurer); alterations; underwriting and claims terms (set out in detail in the Appendix but referred to here to provide that adherence is a condition precedent to liability); terms of any co-reinsurance.

General Terms and Conditions ('GTCs'). In crude terms this is similar to the 'policy booklet' which a policyholder would receive in that it contains all of the standard terms and conditions which, as mentioned above, may be derogated from by the Special Conditions, etc.

Clauses it may well contain are as follows: Basic agreement – structure of Treaty, entire agreement clause, privity; definitions; regulatory warranty (ie that the parties are free and able to enter into this agreement); data protection and money laundering – consents, confirmations as to systems, indemnities (expanded on in Appendices); basis of agreement – accuracy of data and full disclosure at Treaty commencement date – ceding company confirmations; ongoing accuracy of information and data and full disclosure – ceding company confirmations, ability of reassurer to issue 'revision notice'; effect of breaching conditions precedent.

The GTCs are also like to include: underwriting and claims processes (generally it is a term of the contract that the ceding insurer must use the reassurer's underwriting/claims manual); retention – general provisions regarding assessment and variations; reassurance cession – the core term of Treaty, plus provisions for where Treaty limit breached and potential for offering such amounts on a facultative basis; reassurance premiums – details referred to in Schedule, provisions for where ages stated incorrectly, loadings, debts, liens, etc; accounts, information and data requirements – details set out in Schedule; provisions relating to alterations, cancellations, lapses and reinstatements; claims – exceeding claims approval limit, claims expenses, when claims must be referred to reassurer; change of underwriting or claims personnel at ceding office; limits – ability of reassurer to reduce underwriting and claims approval limits; aggregation and 'single event' provisions (see **8.12**); information, inspection and audit.

Wider and more general provisions may be included such as: notification of major business changes, eg changes in business practices; outsourcing – changes to current arrangements; set-off; interest; effect of transfers of business – eg under Part VII of Financial Services and Markets Act 2000; how amendments are made; provisions for termination for new business; termination provisions –

eg on insolvency; recapture terms; confidentiality; notice provisions; waiver; invalidity and severability; governing law; no joint venture or partnership; assignment – general prohibition unless agreement; force majeure.

Appendices. These may include some or all of the following: copies of the insurer's policies which are the subject of the reassurance; underwriting limits; specific provisions regarding reassurance premium rates; administration data; claims data; list of distribution partners; principal underwriting and claims personnel; claims approval limits and process; underwriting terms – granting of underwriting authorities, quality control, non-medical and financial limits, effect of non-disclosure, ratings (maximum/minimum extra mortality), length of validity of proposal forms, when to request health declarations, reinstatement of lapsed cases, length of validity of medical evidence, use of third party administrators; claims terms – granting of claims authorities, quality control, claims procedures and philosophy, minimum evidence requirements, investigation of non-disclosure, use of third party administrators; data protection agreement and principles – data sharing between the ceding company and the reassurer; expert determination – to resolve disagreement on certain terms; arbitration – (see further at **8.13**).

D   Aggregation

8.11   An aggregation clause enables two or more separate losses to be treated as a single loss for certain purposes where they are linked in some way. For example, the reinsurer may not be liable (or his loss will be limited) where the loss is over a certain monetary amount and arises from a 'single event'. Clearly, there will be occasions where what constitutes a single event will be unclear yet could have considerable implications for the reinsurer's liability. For example, a natural disaster may give rise to a large number of individual losses which cumulatively give rise to a very large total liability. Under an aggregation clause any excess or limit might fall to be applied on the aggregate of the claims, not to each individual claim. Aggregation is not necessarily always to the advantage of the reinsurer. For example, the individual value of a claim may fall below the 'deductible' so a reinsurer would only be liable if such claims could be aggregated.

The choice of language by which the parties describe the unifying factor in an aggregation clause is clearly of great importance. The more general the description of the unifying factor the wider the scope of the aggregation clause. Examples of unifying factors commonly used are an 'event' or 'occurrence', 'originating cause' and 'one source or original cause'. The first of these (and potentially the narrowest) is examined in more detail below.

E   Single event/occurrence

8.12   An 'event' is something which happens at a particular time, at a particular place and in a particular way[1]. Therefore, a state of affairs or an omission

1   *AXA Reinsurance (UK) plc v Field* [1996] 1 WLR 1026, 1035G, Lord Mustill.

cannot constitute an event. The 'unities' test was developed by Mr Kerr QC sitting as an arbitrator in Dawson's Field Arbitration Award in 1972. This arose out of the hijacking of four aircraft in 1970 by the Popular Front for Liberation of Palestine. Three of the aircraft were destroyed at Dawson's Field and the question was whether this arose out of 'one event'. As the hijacking occurred at different locations and by different perpetrators they could not be regarded as one event. However, their destruction on the ground in close proximity, more or less simultaneously, within a few minutes and as the result of a single decision was, he decided, one event. In the absence of unity in time or place, unity of intent or central orchestration is probably not sufficient.

F   Arbitration

8.13   Arbitration is the most common method of dispute resolution set out in reassurance contracts. From the parties' perspective it has the advantage of privacy and confidentiality and the ability to have the dispute resolved by arbitrators with expert knowledge of reassurance and a binding decision at the end of proceedings. Reassurance is a highly specialised field with its own complexities, customs and practices. However, it should be borne in mind that arbitration can be as costly and time consuming as court proceedings.

After internal dispute resolution procedures are exhausted the agreement will usually provide for the instigation of formal arbitration proceedings. Arbitration is likely to follow an agreed set of rules, for example the ARIAS Arbitration Rules ('ARIAS' stands for 'AIDA Reinsurance and Insurance Society of the UK', 'AIDA' standing for 'Assocation Internationale de Droite D'assurance'). An arbitrator is likely to be selected from both sides with a third arbitrator selected by the two party appointees. Arbitrators are likely to be required to be persons with life/reassurance experience of at least 10 years and to be lawyers or other professional advisers serving the industry. If the two arbitrators fail to appoint the third arbitrator then ARIAS themselves would do so. The place of arbitration will be stipulated and there is likely to be a time limit by which the decision of the arbitration must be issued together with any award. The usual agreement is to share the costs of arbitration except for legal costs which are usually the responsibility of the side incurring them. Importantly, the arbitration clause would normally survive any termination of the reassurance agreement.

G   Incorporation by reference

8.14   In **8.10** ('Appendices') it was indicated that the original policy may be incorporated by reference into the reassurance contract. The presumption in proportional reassurance is that the scope of cover is 'back-to-back' with the original policy. However, it is not likely to apply to ancillary or procedural provisions such as arbitration or choice of law clauses.

The purpose of the incorporation is not always totally clear and specific clauses should be included to clarify whether and in what way the underlying provisions are incorporated.

SECTION 3   REINSURANCE DIRECTIVE

A   Introduction

8.15   The EU Reinsurance Directive (RID) came into force on 10 December 2005[1] and the FSA have two years to make the required changes to the handbook in order to implement the Directive. Prior to this there have been no EU Directives directly applicable to reinsurance business. The aims of the directive mainly relate to bringing the prudential regulation of pure reinsurers in Europe into line with the standards applying to direct insurers with a view to giving them increased credibility in the world market. The RID is an interim measure that is intended to be in force until 'Solvency II' is developed. The long-term aim is to merge the regimes for both direct insurers and pure reinsurers when the Solvency II project is implemented in about 2011.

The RID applies to all firms exclusively conducting reinsurance business, including captive reinsurance undertakings. The existing EU Life and non-life insurance Directives are amended so that where direct insurance firms accept a significant amount of reinsurance business the RID reinsurance solvency requirements can be used.

The RID is largely based on the EU's non-life insurance Directives. In the UK most of the EU's insurance requirements are applied to reinsurance business, so the effect is limited for most UK firms. The main implementation issues will arise where the RID departs from the existing directives. The position will be less straightforward for certain other EU countries (for example, Belgium) which have not generally regulated reinsurers in the same way as primary insurers.

B   FSA's 'initial implementation considerations'

8.16   The FSA published this document on 11 November 2005. This identified three main areas where the RID diverges from the current UK regime for reinsurers:

(1)   Asset admissibility for reinsurance business will be based on 'prudent person' principles as opposed to the more prescriptive rules contained in the directives relating to direct insurance business and which currently apply in the UK to both insurers and reinsurers. In due course these principles may be extended to mixed insurers and direct insurers.

(2)   Application of the solvency provisions based on the non-life insurance rules to life reinsurance business.

(3)   A requirement to supervise insurance and reinsurance special purpose vehicles (ISPVs) and allow amounts outstanding or recoverable from them to be counted as regulatory capital or as reinsurance. Generally, ISPVs are set up and established in offshore jurisdictions which are lightly regulated and taxed. The RID recognizes that EEA member states need to be able to

---

1   Directive 2005/68/EC on Reinsurance.

compete on more even terms. Member states may therefore authorise ISPVs on a less onerous basis than applies to mainstream insurance and reinsurance companies. Solvency requirements will merely require that their liabilities are covered by their assets. Authorisation processes will be cheaper and quicker and reporting requirements less extensive than those for insurers and reinsurers.

However, a waiver will be required to enable credit taken by an insurer or reinsurer for amounts recoverable or outstanding from an ISPV (Financial Services and Markets Act 2000, s 148). Such waivers will be subject to rigorous vetting procedures by reference to, for example, the 'risk transfer principle' and the impact of the ISPV transaction on the ceding firm's individual capital assessment.

The 'risk transfer principle' has its origin in the FSA's attempts since 2002 to find a formula for ensuring that transactions such as securitisations (see ISPVs above), contingent loans and financial reinsurance only count for capital adequacy purposes to the extent that there is a real transfer of risk. The result is the inclusion of a set of principles in the FSA Handbook (see 1.1.19A R to 1.1.19F G of the Insurance Prudential Sourcebook – INSPRU) by which the firm or the FSA will determine whether and to what extent credit may be taken for the transaction. Indeed, this principle may be widened to all reinsurance transactions.

C Restriction of business to reinsurance

8.17   Ever since the first generation of EU directives relating to direct insurance there has been a requirement in broad terms that insurers should not carry on any commercial business other than insurance and other activities directly arising from that business (although the precise provisions have varied over time). Section 16 of the Insurance Companies Act 1982 contained the first version of this rule in the UK, which was then subsequently contained in the Interim Prudential Sourcebook for Insurers (IPRU(INS)). The provision has now moved to INSPRU 1.5.13R. It has often been difficult to determine precisely what is covered by this restriction. The corresponding provision for reinsurers in the reinsurance directive is in slightly different terms. It allows pure reinsurers to carry out reinsurance and related operations such as the provision of statistical or actuarial advice, risk analysis or research other related financial sector activities. Currently, this 'relaxation' will only apply to pure reinsurers but the position of mixed insurers and pure direct insurers may need to be considered in the context of Solvency II.

D Steps to implementation

8.18   The FSA issued a Consultation Paper in June 2006 (*06/12 Implementing the Reinsurance Directive*). This was slightly ahead of the schedule indicated in the FSA Business Plan for 2006/07 and the consultation period was only two months, the plan being to put in place the final rules for December 2006. This was designed to enable firms to benefit from proposed rule changes as at 31 December 2006 for year end reporting purposes.

However, this consultation paper did not include the provisions required to enable reinsurers authorised in one member state to passport into the UK which is one of the main aims of the Directive. This requires HM Treasury to make changes to the FSMA 2000. Amendments to the FSMA 2000 and regulations under it will also be required to implement the RID conditions for insurance business transfer. This is subject to separate consultation by HM Treasury.

SECTION 4   PRUDENTIAL STANDARDS RELATING TO INSURERS: REASSURANCE

8.19   The Prudential standards set out previously in the Integrated Prudential Sourcebook ('PRU') and now in the general Prudential Sourcebook ('GENPRU') and more specifically the Insurance Prudential Sourcebook ('INSPRU') and Senior Management Arrangements, Systems and Controls ('SYSC') (part of the FSA Handbook) set out the non-customer facing requirements for insurers etc in running their businesses. So, for example, it includes provisions relating to adequacy of financial resources, valuation of assets, risk management and associated systems and controls. SYSC 17 sets out the rules and guidance relating to 'Insurance Risk' and, for the purposes of this chapter, this contains several references to reinsurance.

SYSC 14.1.19R(2) requires a firm to document its policy for insurance risk, including its risk appetite and how it identifies, measures, monitors and controls that risk and SYSC 14.1.27R requires adequate internal controls to be established in order to maintain effective risk management systems. Part of that 'insurance risk policy' is 'the firm's approach to the use of reinsurance or the use of some other means of risk transfer' (SYSC 17.1.9G(12)). In terms of monitoring risk, SYSC 17.1.22G indicates that a firm should have appropriate procedures in place to allow managers to monitor the application and the effect of its reinsurance programme.

SYSC 17.1.34G gives specific guidance on 'reinsurance and other forms of risk transfer'. Therefore, prior to entering into or significantly changing a reinsurance agreement, or any other form of insurance risk transfer agreement, a firm should analyse how the proposed agreement will affect its exposure to insurance risk, its underwriting strategy and its ability to meet its regulatory obligations. It should also ensure there are adequate legal checking procedures in respect of the draft agreement. This seems to echo concerns that contractual documentation for reassurance contracts has often historically been found to be deficient. The insurer should also carry out appropriate due diligence of the reinsurer's financial stability (solvency) and expertise. A firm should also understand the nature and limits of the agreement (particular attention should be given to the wording of contracts to ensure that all the required risks are covered, that the level of available cover is appropriate, and that all the terms, conditions and warranties are unambiguous and understood). This should involve obtaining appropriate legal expertise as necessary.

When managing reinsurance agreements, or other insurance risk transfer agreements, a firm should have appropriate systems in place to enable it to maintain required cover levels. This could involve systems for: (1) monitoring the scope of risks covered by these agreements and the level of available cover; (2) keeping underwriting staff up to date regarding any changes in the scope or level of cover; (3) properly coordinating all reinsurance/risk transfer activities so that the aggregate required level and scope of cover is maintained; (4) ensuring the firm does not become overly reliant on any one reinsurer or other risk transfer provider; and (5) conducting regular stress testing and scenario analyses to assess the resilience of its reinsurance and risk transfer programmes to catastrophic events that may give rise to large and/or numerous claims (SYSC 17.1.35G).

When claiming under a reinsurance contract (known as 'reinsurance recoveries'), or some other risk transfer contract, a firm should ensure that it can identify and recover any money due in good time. It should also make adequate financial provision for the risk that it is unable to recover any money expected to be due, as a result of either a dispute with or a default by the reinsurer/risk transfer provider. Additional guidance on credit risk in reinsurance/risk transfer contracts is provided in INSPRU 2.1 (credit risk in insurance) (SYSC 17.1.36G).

Financial reassurance

8.20   The traditional purpose of reassurance has been to protect the life office against the adverse mortality and morbidity experience. However, reassurance is often employed with alternative or additional purposes in mind. Whilst the risk element must always remain, the primary purpose of financial reassurance is either tax planning or financing.

If a company is expanding rapidly it may find that it does not have enough capital available to finance its rate of growth. In such cases the reassurer is able to provide financing of the costs of acquiring new business (often known as 'new business strain'). Probably of more concern to most life offices is the explicit solvency margin requirement which has been in place since 1981 as a result of the implementation of EC Directives on life assurance regulation. In broad terms, as a life office grows it must show an increasing amount of free assets in its balance sheet. These are identifiable assets over and above the normal reserves required to meet insurance liabilities. Reassurance can be used to help a company optimise the statutory solvency margin which it needs to hold.

CHAPTER 9

Claims and title to life policies

The slightly archaic term 'title' in this respect means the right to the policy or evidence of such a right.

SUMMARY

SECTION I   DISCHARGE OF CONTRACT

A   General principles

9.1   When a contractual obligation is released and the contract (such as a life policy) brought to an end it is said to be 'discharged'. Discharge of a contract usually takes place in one of the following ways:

(1)   agreement;

(2)   novation;

(3)   breach; or

(4)   performance.

319

The obligations under a life assurance contract may be terminated in any one of such ways.

1 Agreement

9.2   As the parties form their contract by agreement, so it can also be ended by agreement. An agreement by the parties to an existing contract to extinguish the rights and obligations that have been created is itself a binding contract provided that it is either made by deed or supported by consideration.

In the case of a life policy, the policyholder and the life office may agree that on surrender of the policy for a cash payment the policy will cease. The consideration for the policyholder is the surrender value and for the life office it is the release from having to provide any further benefits under the policy. In many life policies there will be specific terms relating to the surrender of the policy and the calculation of any surrender value (assuming the policy has accumulated a surrender value).

The policyholder and the life office may similarly agree to vary the terms of a life policy. They may, for example, alter a whole life assurance so that premiums are reduced with a corresponding reduction in the sum assured. Evidence of such a variation may be provided by what is known as an 'endorsement' which may be attached to the original policy document. Alternatively, it may possibly just be evidenced by written correspondence between the life office and the policyholder.

2 Novation

9.3   Where the original obligations of one party are released by the other in consideration of obligations being undertaken by a third person the effect of this is a new contract and the original contract is said to have been discharged by novation[1].

The transfer of obligations under a life assurance contract from one insurance company to another will now generally be effected under the provisions of Part VII of the Financial Services and Markets Act 2000 (replacing section 49 and Schedule 2C of the Insurance Companies Act 1982), without the consent of the policyholder necessarily being obtained.

3 Breach

9.4   A breach of contract by one party, no matter what form the breach takes, always entitles the other to commence an action for damages. However, only nominal damages will be awarded where no loss has been suffered as a result of the breach and, in practice, it would not be worth pursuing an action.

The common law rule is that the right of a party to treat a contract as discharged by a breach arises where the party in default has repudiated the contract

1   *Re European Assurance Society* (1876) 3Ch D 391.

before performance is due or before it has been fully performed. He is deemed to have repudiated the contract where he has totally or partially failed to perform his obligations under the contract. However, if the said failure is only partial then it will be a repudiation of the contract only if the party in default has committed what is known as a fundamental breach, ie if, having regard to the contract as a whole, the promise that has been broken is of major importance. As stated by Chitty: 'Any breach of contract gives rise to a cause of action; not every breach gives a discharge from liability'. (See cases such *as Suisse Atlantique Societe v NVR Kolen Centrale*[1], *Hong Kong Fir Shipping Co Ltd v Kawasaki Kisen Kaisha Ltd*[2] and *Thompson v Corroon*[3]).

A written contract would usually contain within its own terms the circumstances in which it may be brought to an end as a result of breach; and that is ordinarily so for life policies. For example, the payment of the premium is always made a condition precedent. Payment of the premium is not ordinarily enforceable by the life office, and failure to pay it within the conditions defined by the policy or agreed by the parties is likely to result in the lapse of the policy or the reduction of the benefits covered on a basis defined in the policy. This latter consequence is known as the policy being made 'paid up'.

The contract may similarly be discharged if the life assured breaks one of the conditions of the assurance, eg if he engages in some hazardous pursuit, participation in which is a ground on which the policy is expressed to become void.

4 Performance

9.5   A contract is discharged by performance, ie by carrying out the obligations under the contract. Where the contract is to pay money, performance may be by payment or by tender. When a cheque is given in payment of the debt it is usually accepted merely as a conditional payment. The taking of the cheque suspends the right of action on the contract but does not extinguish the contract until the cheque is paid. If the cheque is not met, the right to payment in the original contract revives. The payee may refuse to accept the cheque and insist on cash; payment must then be made in legal tender, although the precise terms of the contract, where relevant, need to be considered to ascertain the precise position.

Tender other than legal tender does not discharge the debt but is a good defence to an action claiming the amount already paid. Legal tender is a tender of money which is in legal currency.

The policy terms relating to payment of claims are the first place to look. There is likely to be a requirement to execute the life office's standard claim form, which is likely to incorporate a formal discharge to the life office and possibly also an indemnity against third party claims. It is usual to provide that the claim under a life policy shall be paid at the principal office of the assurance company. The position where there is no such provision is not entirely free from doubt and it may be a question of what can be implied from the circumstances.

1   [1966] 2 All ER 61.
2   [1962] 2 QB 26; [1962] 1 All ER 474.
3   (1993) 42 WIR 157.

It is not thought that the debtor office must go to disproportionate lengths to seek out its creditor and pay him on the basis that the policyholder (or his successors in title) is in possession of all relevant facts (or should be).

As a result of the Second Life Directive[1] the law of the contract may be the law of the country in which the policyholder is habitually resident where there is no express or effective choice of law, in which case the question of mode of performance/discharge would be governed by the law of that country which could cause difficult practical problems. The policy should ideally also specify the currency in which payment is to be made.

B   Payment and discharge of life policies

9.6   The majority of life policies are expressed to be payable to the policyholder on survival of the life assured to the end of the term (where appropriate) or to his executors or administrators on proof of his death, subject in all cases to proof of title, and of age where that is required. 'Policyholder' would include 'successors in title' such as assignees or trustees of a trust which the policy was subject to. 'Policyholder' and 'life assured' are often (but not necessarily) the same person. Clearly, where the policy has been assigned, placed in trust, etc the chances of them being the same person are even more remote. By making payment to the person entitled (and that person acknowledges that fact), the life office is discharged or released from its obligation to make payment under the policy. If the life office pays to the wrong person it will not have discharged its liability under the contract. The term 'discharge' is often used loosely to refer to what is in fact a receipt which is merely evidence of payment of money. However, a formal receipt may be combined in one document with a discharge of all claims under the policy.

The policy terms are likely to contain provisions on how notice of a claim is to be given to the life office. Usually this must be given in writing[2]. The notice is likely to have to be given to the life office at a specified address and possibly within a certain time of the event giving rise to the claim. If not specified, such notice must be given within a 'reasonable time'[3]. Generally, with life assurance the time a claim is made is not normally as important as under, for example, general insurance or indemnity-based insurance and so a specific time limit is not common. However, it is possible to envisage situations where making a claim within a certain time period could be important, for example non-disclosure of a known medical condition where the passing of time may mean that vital evidence is no longer available. On receipt of notice, the life office will normally require the completion of a standard claim form or discharge form. This will take the form of an acknowledgement by the claimant that he will have no further

---

1 Council Directive 90/619, art 4; now see consolidating directive 'Directive Concerning Life Assurance' 2002/83/EC.
2 *Brook v Trafalgar Insurance Co Ltd* (1946) 79 LlL Rep 365 (CA).
3 *Hick v Raymond & Reid* [1893] AC 22. See also *Shinedean Limited v Alldown Demolition (London) Limited and AXA Insurance UK plc* [2006] All ER (D) 206 (Jun) for a consideration of time limits for claims in an indemnity insurance context.

claims against the life office in respect of that benefit. It may go further and contain an indemnity in favour of the life office regarding any subsequent claims by third parties. Clearly, the life office will not be protected where it can be shown that it was aware that it was not paying to the correct person.

The position of partial surrenders or withdrawals must also be considered as the remainder of the policy will remain in force. Some types of contracts expressly provide for the policyholder to take partial surrenders or withdrawals (usually investment bonds). There are likely to be terms relating to the level of withdrawals and the residual value of the policy and other matters so it is important to have regard to the precise contractual terms. It is also important to consider the taxation consequences of partial withdrawals.

9.7   A life office may only safely pay policy moneys to the person or persons entitled to them at the date when they become due. The life office should always obtain its discharge by paying the person entitled to sue at law for the policy moneys, or some person properly authorised by him to receive them. If the office accepts anything less than the discharge of the person entitled to sue at law, then it stands the risk of having to pay out twice on the policy. The person entitled to sue will either be the original policyholder himself (ie the person with whom the contract was made by the life office, known also as the 'grantee'), or his personal representatives; but may be his trustee in bankruptcy, or the trustees under a Married Women's Property Act policy[1], or the trustees of a trust declared in respect of the life policy, or a legal assignee of whose assignment the office has received notice, or a mortgagee. An appropriate payee may also be an attorney under a power of attorney or a receiver under a Court of Protection Order. The life office should not pay an equitable assignee without the agreement of the person entitled at law to sue. Where the office has notice of an equitable interest (other than a beneficiary's interest under a trust, will or on intestacy and other than the equity of redemption under a mortgage) the person entitled to such interest should be required to join in with the legal owner before the life office makes payment.

If the policy is expressed to be payable to a third party (ie some person other than the policyholder), such a person will normally have no right to sue and the policyholder (or his successors in title) alone can enforce the contract[2]. This is likely to be the case even after the Contracts (Rights of Third Parties) Act 1999, as the provisions of the Act are likely to have been expressly excluded. If the provision for payment to the third party is an essential term of the contract, the company can carry out the contract by paying him, and the carrying out of the contract will discharge it by performance[3]. Although such a payment may be a good discharge to the life office, the person to whom the payment is made may have to account to the personal representatives of the policyholder. Also, they will not normally be able to sue on the policy unless it is executed by deed or the Contracts (Rights of Third Parties) Act 1999 has not been excluded and the

---

1   Made under the provisions of the Married Women's Property Act 1882, s 11.
2   See *Re Engelbach's Estate, Tibbetts v Engelbach* [1924] 2 Ch 348.
3   *O'Reilly v Prudential Assurance Co Ltd* [1934] Ch 519.

contract gives benefits to the third party or expressly provides that he may enforce it. If the payee is named merely as an agent of the policyholder, his mandate may be withdrawn, and is normally withdrawn automatically by the policyholder's death. Therefore, if the policy is payable to a third party and payment to him is not expressed to be an essential part of the contract, the office should only pay to, or on the express authority of, the policyholder or those deriving title through him.

9.8 Formal discharges or authorities for payment by individuals are normally given under hand, ie signed by the said individuals and they need not be in the form of a deed.

Section 43 of the Companies Act 2006 provides that a company may contract by writing either under its common seal, or by any person acting under its express or implied authority. This section also provides that the same formalities required by law in the case of a contract made by an individual also apply unless a contrary intention appears, to a contract made by or on behalf of a company.

Therefore, where a company wishes to deal with a life office, for example if it wishes to insure an employee's life, the proposal form can simply be signed by an authorised signatory. The life office can always rely on section 40 of the Companies Act 2006, whereby a third party acting in good faith with a director or a person authorised to act on behalf of the company will bind the company even if the action in question is ultra vires (beyond the powers of) the company.

Since 1989[1], if a company wishes to execute a deed, it need not affix its common seal. Indeed, it need not even have such a seal. A deed signed by two authorised signatories (directors or the company secretary) or by one director in the presence of a witness and expressed to be executed by the company will have the same effect as if it had been executed under seal.

Where there is any doubt about the persons authorised to sign discharges on behalf of a company or corporation, the life office may either obtain a discharge under the company's seal, duly attested, or require evidence that the person signing is authorised to do so.

The Limited Liability Partnerships Act 2000 provided for the creation of limited liability partnerships (LLPs). The Limited Liability Partnerships Regulations 2001[2] regulate LLPs by applying to them, with modifications, the appropriate provisions of companies legislation.

9.9 Regarding payment of claims by cheque, the Cheques Act 1992 provides that a cheque crossed and marked with the words 'account payee' or 'a/c payee', either with or without the word 'only', will not be transferable.

In many cases the sum assured will be a fixed amount and so there is no question regarding the amount to be paid out. However, in other cases, for example with investment bonds, a calculation of benefits is required. With investment bonds, the death benefit is usually expressed as, for example, 101% of the value

---

1 Companies Act 1985, s 36A, as inserted by the Companies Act 1989, s 130(2). Now see s 44 of the Companies Act 2006.
2 SI 2001/1090.

of the units allocated to the contract, with the relevant value being taken as at the first valuation after notification of the death, but in all cases the precise terms of the policy would need to be examined.

It is unusual for the policy to provide for payment to be made at any particular time. Payment of benefits should normally be made within a reasonable time of the claim. If there is a need to investigate matters concerning the death and title to the policy this would obviously tend to extend the time between claim and payment.

When payment is made, any outstanding premiums will normally be deducted from the proceeds payable. Interest is payable on the policy proceeds either as the result of any relevant policy term or, if there is not one, a life office which is a member of the Association of British Insurers would ordinarily pay interest in accordance with the 'Long-Term Insurance: Statement of Normal Practice'. Essentially, the insurer will pay interest on claims delayed more than two months from the happening of the insured event (or for unit-linked policies from the cessation of the unit linking if later) unless the amount of such interest would be trivial. Interest is calculated at a relevant market rate from the end of the two-month period until the date of actual payment. For example, where there is a delay between death and the personal representatives obtaining a grant of probate, interest will be payable on the proceeds less any overdue premiums. A statement of account will be sent to the claimant explaining how the amount paid has been calculated.

Payment of a claim, whether by one sum or by instalments, may be made by cheque through the post although it is becoming increasingly common for the policy moneys to be paid directly into the claimant's bank account.

1   Treating Customers Fairly ('TCF')

9.10   More detail on TCF is contained in Chapter 5 and the reader is referred to that chapter for more background detail. The spectrum of TCF is wide ranging as it increasingly permeates the financial services industry as a result of the FSA making it clear that it will be a central part of their move towards a more principle-based regulatory regime. Clearly, in dealing with customers at the claims stage the organisation's approach to TCF will be brought sharply into focus. At the time of writing, claims handling has actually been specifically commented on by the FSA in the context of general insurance rather than life assurance and investment business but some of their comments would seem to be equally applicable to life assurance claims. Therefore, some of the points to look out for are:

(1)   Does the firm manage claims handling fairly so that genuine claims are paid properly while firms are taking reasonable steps to address claimant fraud?

(2)   Do firms rely on small print to avoid paying out even though it is unconnected with the event that gave rise to the claim?

(3)   Do firms provide adequate information to customers when they make a claim to manage their expectations, for example, timescales for processing the claim?

The FSA have also set out their findings in 'Cluster reports' relating to complaints management and handling.

In July 2006 the FSA issued a further paper entitled 'Treating Customers Fairly – towards fair outcomes for consumers'. The desired 'Outcome 6' is that 'consumers do not face unreasonable post-sale barriers imposed by firms to change product, switch provider, submit a claim or make a complaint'. The FSA explain that post-sale barriers to fair treatment can be cultural, contractual or competitive. The consumer should be able to change products or switch providers without incurring excessive penalty. The reference to 'penalty' is probably not used in a strictly legal sense as penalty clauses in contracts are not generally upheld anyway. Firms should also not make it unnecessarily difficult for consumers to make claims or to complain when something goes wrong.

2   Payment by mistake

9.11   Where the life office pays money under a mistake, prior to the case of *Kleinwort Benson Ltd v Lincoln City Council*[1] it was not possible to recover the amount paid if the mistake was one of law. In this case, with regard to the long-standing rule concerning mistake of law, it was held (Lords Browne-Wilkinson and Lloyd dissenting) that this should no longer be maintained as part of English law.

With regard to mistake of fact it has been clear for some considerable time, however, that where the mistake is one of fact material to the mistake[2], it may be able to recover the money in an action for money had and received. The mistake need not be mutual, nor need there be any fraud or misrepresentation by the payee. By way of example, in *Admiralty Comrs v National Provincial and Union Bank of England Ltd*[3] recovery was made of money paid into the current account of a deceased customer of the bank in the belief that he was alive. A person who accepts and keeps money to which he knows he is not entitled because of a mistake by the payer may furthermore be guilty of theft.

> ### *R v Gilks*[4]
>
> G kept £106 of £117 paid to him by a bookmaker which he knew he was not entitled to because of a mistake on the bookmaker's part. He admitted he knew of the mistake, but said it was 'hard lines' on the bookmaker and 'there is nothing dishonest about keeping the money'. Held, by the Court of Appeal that he was properly convicted of theft under section 1(1) of the Theft Act 1968, since he was guilty of theft at the moment he accepted the money. But the refusal to restore the money was not theft as he was under no obligation to restore a sum which arose out of a betting transaction.

1   TLR 30/10/98; ILR 4/11/98; (1998) 4 All ER 513; (1998) 3 WLR 1095; (1998) Lloyd's Bank Rep 387; (1999) LGR 1. (See also *Deutsche Morgan Grenfell Group plc v Inland Revenue Commissioners* [2006] All ER (D) 298 (Oct).)
2   *Bize v Dickinson* (1786) 1 Term Rep 285, ie which if true would have rendered the party under the mistake liable to pay the money in question or which is otherwise fundamental to the transaction.
3   (1922) 127 LT 452.
4   [1972] 3 All ER 280.

9.12   Where an office pays moneys under a mistake of fact, not realising the true position, it will still be entitled to recover even if it had been careless in its investigation of the facts. The general rule is that carelessness is irrelevant. Having the means to obtain the knowledge is not regarded as synonymous with knowledge for these purposes.

Kelly v Solari[1]

The plaintiff was the director of a life assurance company. The defendant's husband had been insured, but had not paid the last premium. The insurance therefore had lapsed, and the lapse had been noted by the company. The defendant claimed the policy moneys, on her husband's death, and the plaintiff, forgetting the lapse, paid them to her. Held, that the moneys could be recovered by the plaintiff.

In *Kelly*, Parke B laid down the principle that money can be recovered if paid:

'upon the supposition that a specific fact is true, which could entitle the payee to the money, but which fact is untrue, and the money would not have been paid if it had been known to the payer that the fact was untrue . . .'

This principle was cited with approval in the case of:

Barclays Bank Ltd v WJ Simms Son & Cook (Southern) Ltd[2]

A housing association, a customer of the plaintiff bank, drew a cheque in favour of a builder to cover an interim payment under a building contract. When the builder went into receivership the association immediately stopped the cheque. The defendant receiver, however, in good faith, had it specially cleared and, owing to an oversight by the plaintiff, paid. The bank sued the liquidator for money paid by mistake, relying on *Kelly v Solari*. They said that they had paid the cheque in the mistaken belief that it had not been stopped. It was held that they could recover.

9.13   However, it may be inequitable to require that the money be repaid, where there has been some representation by the life office which has misled the person to whom the money was mistakenly paid and caused that person to alter his or her position. This is the rule known as 'estoppel'. However, the fact that such a person cannot be put into the same position he was in before the money was paid will not necessarily prevent the money being recovered. If it can be shown that the payee would not have spent the money if he had not been influenced by the payer's mistake, the payer will not be able to recover.

Avon County Council v Howlett[3]

The defendant was injured in the course of employment with the plaintiffs and as a result was absent from work for nearly two years. The plaintiffs discovered that during that period they had overpaid the defendant to the extent of £1,007. They

1   (1841) 9 M & W 54.
2   [1980] QB 677.
3   [1983] 1 All ER 1073.

327

brought an action against the defendant claiming repayment of that sum on the ground that it had been paid by mistake. It was held that the plaintiffs were estopped from asserting their right to repayment. This was due to the fact that the plaintiffs made representations to the defendant which led him to believe that he was entitled to treat the overpaid moneys as his own. The misrepresentations were not caused by incorrect information given to them by the defendant and the overpayments were not brought about by the defendant's own fault. The defendant changed his position in reliance on the representations, by losing the claim for £86.11 social security benefit and expending the sum of £460.50 which he would not have incurred if he had not been paid the moneys in dispute. Therefore, the plaintiffs should be estopped from recovering the overpaid moneys at least to the extent of £546.61. However, Slade LJ held that estoppel was incapable of operating pro tanto, ie in respect of part only of the overpaid moneys, on the basis that it was contrary to principle and authority. He did add, however, that there may be exceptional circumstances where estoppel could operate to prevent the payer from recovering part but not all the overpaid moneys. However, such circumstances did not exist in the particular circumstances of the case.

9.14   The cases of *Kelly v Solari* and *Avon County Council* were considered in *Scottish Equitable plc v Gordon Derby*[1].

Scottish Equitable plc v Gordon Derby

Scottish Equitable (SE) claimed restitution of £162,000 paid to GD under a mistake of fact as to the amount of the final retirement benefits to which he was properly entitled. In calculating and paying out these benefits, SE failed to take into account certain benefits that GD had taken early. The total overpayment was £172,451. This was applied by GD in reducing his mortgage, on ordinary living expenses and the balance in a new pension fund with Norwich Union (NU). GD relied upon change of position and/or estoppel, contending also that carelessness was a bar to the recovery of money paid under a mistake. In the circumstances NU were prepared to unwind the policy and return him to the position he would have been in if SE's mistake had not been made. At first instance, Harrison J held that mere carelessness did not preclude the recovery of money paid under a mistake of fact, and GD could not rely on either change of position (there was no causal link) or estoppel by way of defence to SE's claim for the balance of the overpayment. The Court of Appeal held that the judge correctly applied the test set out in *Kelly v Solari*. The defence of change of position was not available to GD as the changes made by GD to his lifestyle were modest and not irreversible. The Court of Appeal also agreed with the judge that the defence of estoppel was precluded by the decision in *Avon County Council v Howlett* mainly because it is incapable of operating 'pro tanto'. It can only ever be a complete defence which would have been inequitable in this case.

C   Statute of Limitation

9.15   Section 5 of the Limitation Act 1980 provides that all actions founded on a simple contract must be commenced within six years from the date when the

1   [2001] 3 All ER 818.

cause of action arises. Therefore, any action to recover the sum assured under a life policy which has not been issued under seal must be brought within six years of the happening of the event upon which the benefits under the policy are expressed to be payable. Normally, the sum assured under a life policy is payable only after proof, satisfactory to the life office, of the death of the life assured and title to the policy (or simply title to the policy on maturity of an endowment assurance or surrender of an investment bond) has been provided. As the proof required by the life office relating to death and title are wholly within the power of the claimant the operation of the Limitation Act 1980 is not suspended in the meantime. However, where an action is based on fraud or mistake the period of limitation only begins to run when the fraud, concealment or mistake is discovered, or could with reasonable diligence have been discovered[1].

The relevant period during which an action must be brought is 12 years in the case of policies issued under seal[2].

D   Payment into court

9.16   If, in the opinion of the board of directors of a life office, no sufficient discharge can be obtained in any other way, the life office may pay the policy moneys into court under the Life Assurance Companies (Payment into Court) Act 1896[3]. The procedure for doing this is set out in Part 37 of the Civil Procedure Rules 1998 (Practice Direction – Miscellaneous Provisions about Payment into Court, paras 7 & 8). An office wishing to make payment into court must file an affidavit or witness statement made by its secretary or other authorised officer[4]. The receipt or certificate of the proper officer of the court is a sufficient discharge to the life office for the moneys paid into court. Payment may not be made into court under the Act if any other action is pending in England in relation to the policy unless the court gives leave to do so. The office is required to give immediate notice of a payment into court to every person appearing from the affidavit to be entitled to the moneys or to have an interest in them. The life office cannot deduct from the policy moneys any costs of or incidental to the payment into court and must bear the costs of payment in.

By proceeding under the 1896 Act the life office obtains an absolute discharge against all claims present and future and not only, as in the case of interpleader proceedings, in respect of an existing conflict between rival claimants. Payment into court therefore offers a remedy when the office faces the problem that the person legally entitled or the person who has given notice of his equitable claim cannot be ascertained or traced or where, perhaps, the title is unclear or unsatisfactory. For example, the identity of an assignee is not clear from a deed of assignment. Where the office claims a charge or other interest in the policy moneys it should deduct the amount it claims, paying only the balance into court.

1   Limitation Act, 1980, s 32.
2   Limitation Act 1980, s 8.
3   As amended by the Administration of Justice Act 1965, s 17 and the Courts Act 1971, s 56.
4   Para 7.1 (See Appendix 7).

Payment in of the whole amount may be taken as an admission by the office that it has no claim on the moneys in court.

The life office must bear the costs of payment in, unless it has agreed with the claimants that they will bear the costs. The office will not normally have to bear the costs of a subsequent application for payment out unless the original payment into court was not reasonable. However, the life office will avoid the cost of deciding the issue of entitlement as between competing claimants. Although possible, it should rarely be necessary to pay into court solely on the ground of the loss of policy documents (a statutory declaration as to the circumstances of the loss and/or an indemnity is likely to be more appropriate), unless conflicting claims to the policy are being made and cannot be reconciled.

9.17   Where the life office could be sued in different countries (eg England and Scotland) payment into court in one action is not an absolute bar to proceedings in the other country. However, generally, if payment into court is made in the country in which the claim is payable, the court in the other country would not allow proceedings to continue until there had been an adjudication on the claim against the moneys paid in.

The Life Assurance Companies (Payment into Court) Act 1896 applies to Northern Ireland but does not apply to Scotland. The office faced there with competing claims on the policy may be able to raise an action of multiplepoinding in the Court of Session. This process is similar to interpleader proceedings in England. It is only available when the policy money has become payable and the office admits liability to pay to the person or persons entitled. The only interest of the life office must be that of obtaining a discharge and there must be conflicting claims to the proceeds (the 'fund in medio'). The procedure of multiplepoinding is not available where the inability to obtain a discharge arises from the inability to find a claimant or from some doubt as to the validity of the title produced by a sole claimant.

SECTION 2   PROOF

A   Proof of death

9.18   Policy proceeds arising on death are usually made payable when proof satisfactory to the life office has been submitted of the death of the life assured and of the title of the claimant. Death must be proved by such evidence as the life office requires but its demands for proof must not be unreasonable – which will be a question of fact in the circumstances of the particular case[1]. It should be borne in mind that the life office is often being asked to pay out considerable sums of money hence it not being unreasonable to require a commensurate level of proof.

1   *Braunstein v Accidental Death Insurance Company* (1861) 1 B&S 782.

Death must be proved by:

(1)   direct evidence, ie by the oath of some person present at the death (eg a doctor);

(2)   death certificate, ie by production of a certified copy entry in the Register of Deaths or in some other public record which is admissible in evidence; or

(3)   evidence of prolonged absence or other facts from which the fact of death may be properly inferred.

In practice proof is usually provided in accordance with (2) above.

Generally, where a death claim arises under a life policy, an official certificate of death (ie a certified copy of the entry of death in an official register) should be produced to the life office. A certified copy of an entry, made in the General Register Office and bearing the seal of that office is, under section 34(6) of the Births and Deaths Registration Act 1953, sufficient evidence of death without any other proof of entry. In Scotland the relevant provisions are contained in the Registration of Births, Deaths and Marriages (Scotland) Act 1965. In Northern Ireland the provisions of the Births and Deaths Registration Act 1967 (Northern Ireland) are essentially similar to those in England.

9.19   In practice an official copy death certificate issued by a local Registrar is normally accepted. Because of the ease with which it is possible to produce falsified reproductions of death certificates by photographic or similar means, copy death certificates should not be accepted. Furthermore, from January 2001 the position with regard to copy certificates (whether for death, marriage or birth) changed in that the Crown now assert copyright over such documents so that only originals can be used unless a licence is obtained. Where the age of the life assured has not been admitted and the age in the death certificate does not correspond with the life office's records, proof of age should be called for. This may be established by:

(1)   direct evidence as to the date of birth;

(2)   birth certificate, ie by production of a certified copy entry in the Registry of Births, or in some other public record of the birth which is admissible in evidence; or

(3)   baptismal certificate (albeit that this is only evidence of the date and fact of baptism).

For certain policies, such as investment bonds with very little additional life cover, the age of the life assured is not important in terms of, for example, setting premium levels and so verifying age is likewise not so important.

In the case of jurisdictions outside of the United Kingdom, evidence may be provided by a certified entry in a foreign public register, the use of which is provided for by the Evidence (Foreign, Dominion and Colonial Documents) Act 1933 and the Oaths and Evidence (Overseas Authorities and Countries) Act 1963.

9.20 Where the life assured has disappeared and there is no direct evidence as to whether he is alive or dead then his death may be proved by either:

(1) circumstantial evidence, ie proof of facts from which a jury might reasonably infer the fact of death; or

(2) a presumption of common law arising from the life assured's disappearance and absence for seven years.

Where the life assured is also the policyholder, in order to obtain a Grant of Representation, it will be necessary for someone to apply to the district judge or registrar for leave to swear the death.

Leave to swear the death does not find as a matter of fact that the individual has died but is required in order to obtain a grant of representation where there is no direct evidence of death. The application to the High Court for leave to swear the death in these circumstances must be made only after the best possible enquiries and searches have been made amongst those who would be likely to hear of or from him if he were alive[1]. The application must be accompanied by an affidavit which should include particulars of all policies on his life. Notice should be given to the life office. No order will be made until the insurance companies in question have been notified of the application. If the life office opposes the application and is successful it will get its costs, but the life office may find it difficult to argue against the declaration if it does not take part in the proceedings. In a court action it may well be sufficient if the party who alleges death simply calls the missing person's nearest relatives in this country to give evidence that he was living here and disappeared more than seven years ago and that they have not heard from him or of him since he disappeared. The party alleging death must, however, show that reasonable enquiry has been made abroad if it was known that the missing person went or intended to go to a foreign country.

Where enquiries are made in respect of a missing person, rumours and reports may be heard from people who think they have seen him and these should generally be investigated. If, however, such rumours and reports are in fact without foundation, the fact that they have been received within the seven years does not prevent the presumption of death arising. Sometimes, a person disappears in circumstances which suggest that even if he were alive it would be unlikely that his relatives or friends would hear of or from him. There may be good reason why he would wish to disappear from the circles in which he moved previously. In such circumstances the presumption of death does not arise from the mere fact of seven years' absence without being heard of. The court will want further evidence[2].

9.21 Although death may be presumed after seven years' absence, there is no presumption of law as to the exact time of death within the seven-year period[3]. So if there is a need to establish death at or before any particular time during the

1 *Prudential Assurance Co v Edmonds* (1877) 2 App Cas 487.
2 *Watson v England* (1844) 14 Sim 28.
3 *Re Phené's Trusts* [1870] 5 Ch App 139 and *Chard v Chard* [1956] P 259, [1955] 3 All ER 721.

seven years (eg where a temporary assurance expired during that period) this must be proved as a fact by suitable evidence, eg by evidence of ill-health when he was last heard of. The position where the individual is in a 'persistent vegetative state' and would die but for a life support system can raise emotive issues (legal or otherwise) where such a state persists beyond the termination date of a temporary insurance.

As mentioned in (1) above, if the life assured has disappeared, it is not always necessary to wait for seven years before his death can be proved. The circumstances surrounding his disappearance (eg if he was a passenger on a ship that went missing) may be such that a court may reasonably find as a matter of fact that the life assured is dead, and so an application for leave to swear the death may be made within the seven years[1]. For example, in *National Trust v Sterling*[2] a person was lost at sea who had been on the SS Titanic. In this case it was enough for an affidavit to be produced that the insured had been lost on board at the time of sinking and had not been seen among the survivors.

No action can be brought against the life office where the life assured has disappeared until the personal representatives have completed their title by obtaining probate or letters of administration. The personal representatives are unable to do this until they have obtained leave to swear the death.

9.22   In cases of common disaster where it is likely that more than one application for leave to swear the death will emerge the Principal Registry will keep a record of all evidence accepted when the first application is granted for the guidance of subsequent applications, so that in such a case, enquiry should first be made to the Principal Registry. If passenger lists and evidence of death have been supplied to the Principal Registry by, for example, the shipping company or airline concerned then a circular may be issued listing the names of those who have died and no further evidence of death will be necessary and there will be no need for leave to swear the death. However, for disasters such as the World Trade Centre in New York destruction on 11 September 2001 and the tsunami in South East Asia on 26 December 2004, leave to swear the death in each case (in the absence of a death certificate) would be required in view of the difficulties in ascertaining the victims with complete accuracy.

If the courts of a foreign country where the presumed deceased was domiciled have made orders presuming his death and vesting his estate in the persons entitled, his death may (depending on the circumstances) be presumed without further evidence, but if there is only an order by the foreign court presuming the death but not vesting the estate, further evidence will certainly be required to show that the presumed deceased is in fact dead[3].

A life office will not necessarily be bound by an order for presumption of death made for some purpose other than that of obtaining a grant of representation, or even by an order of the Family Division giving leave to swear the death. It is still open to the office to defend proceedings against it either on the ground

---

1   *Re Norris's Goods* (1858) 1 Sw & Tr 6.
2   [1916] QR 51.
3   *Re Schulhof, Re Wolf* [1948] p 66, [1947] 2 All ER 841; *Re Dowds' Goods* [1948] P 256.

that there is no evidence of death or that there is no evidence of death before the date when the policy expired. But once the will has been proved or an administrator appointed, the office will then become liable to an action to enforce payment and may have to pay the costs of all subsequent proceedings. The advice to the life office may be to pay the claim and if it emerges that the life assured is still alive it can seek to reclaim the money paid out on the basis of a mistake of fact.

In Scotland the Presumption of Death (Scotland) Act 1977, which repealed the Presumption of Life Limitation (Scotland) Act 1891, now governs the position for presuming the death of a person who is thought to have died or has not been heard of for seven years in Scotland. The earlier statute did not apply to claims under life policies and the claimant had to prove the death as best he could. Under the 1977 Act, where a person, domiciled in Scotland (or resident there for a year prior to the action), is missing and is thought to have died or has not been known to be alive for a period of at least seven years then any person having an interest may raise an 'action of declarator' of the death of the missing person.

9.23   If two persons die in circumstances where it is uncertain which of them died first, the deaths are, for all purposes affecting the title to property, presumed to have occurred in order of seniority, and so the younger is deemed by section 184 of the Law of Property Act 1925 to have survived the elder. Therefore, if the elder has by will left his property to the younger, the bequest will not lapse. Conversely, a bequest in a will from younger to elder will lapse. These provisions are subject to the Law Reform (Succession) Act 1995[1], under which the intestate's spouse must survive the intestate by 28 days in order to be entitled. This statutory presumption in section 184 can be excluded by an express contrary provision in a will. This was the case in *Re Guggenheim*[2] where the deceased had made a declaration to the effect that in the event of he and his wife dying simultaneously, or in circumstances where there was no evidence as to who died first, his wife should be deemed to have predeceased him.

The statutory presumption does not apply for the purpose of incidence of inheritance tax. In this case the persons are treated as having died at the same instant and their property as having devolved accordingly[3].

9.24   The seniority rule applies even though the circumstances suggest that the victims probably died at the same time.

Hickman v Peacey[4]

> Four persons were killed when a bomb exploded in a small air raid shelter. There was no evidence to show whether any of them had survived the others. Held, that in the absence of such evidence it was uncertain which of them survived the other or others within the meaning of section 184 and the section applied. The fact that it appeared they had died simultaneously did not make the section inapplicable.

1   s 1(1), (3).
2   (1941) Times, 20 June.
3   Inheritance Tax Act 1984, s 4(2).
4   [1945] AC 304.

Section 31 of the Succession (Scotland) Act 1964 provides that where two persons have died in circumstances indicating that they died simultaneously, or rendering it uncertain which survived the other (known in Scotland as 'common calamity'), then for all purposes affecting the title to property or claims to legal rights or the prior rights of a surviving spouse[1], (a) where the persons are husband and wife it shall be presumed that neither survived the other, and (b) in any other case it shall be presumed that the younger survived the elder, unless the elder has left a testamentary disposition containing a provision in favour of the younger if he survives the elder and failing the younger in favour of a third person, and the younger person has died intestate, in which case it shall be presumed for the purposes of that provision that the elder survived the younger. In *Lamb v Lord Advocate etc*[2] it was held that no presumption arises for consideration if there is proof that one person survived the other and such proof is on a balance of probabilities.

B   Proof of survival

9.25   Where, as with a life annuity, payment by a life office depends on survival, evidence of continued existence is usually given by a certificate of a responsible independent person, or the annuitant himself.

Frequently, however, life annuity payments are made directly to the bank account of the annuitant. Evidence of survival can then be waived, on the understanding that the bank will inform the life office when it receives notice of the death of the customer. This obviously relies on the bank informing the life office appropriately and the bank would ordinarily exclude or seek to refuse liability for failure to do so. Although not ideal, it may be the most practical way to proceed given the administrative inconvenience to the life office in verifying the annuitant's continued existence.

This practice involves certain risks (eg that both husband and wife might be entitled to draw on the same account), but in practice the risk may be thought worth taking in the circumstances. Also, the life office should be able to recover amounts paid out in the mistaken belief that the annuitant is still alive[3].

C   Proof of title

9.26   A life office may need to examine the title to a policy in many different circumstances, but most cases will fall under one of the following heads:

(1)   Claim on death.

(2)   Claim on maturity (ie survival of term of endowment assurance).

---

1   See **9.60–9.62**.
2   1976 SLT 151.
3   See Section 1B, 'Payment by mistake', **9.11–9.14**.

(3)   Surrender.

(4)   Part surrender or surrender of bonus.

(5)   Conversion, eg to paid-up policy.

(6)   Exercise of option.

(7)   Loan.

1   Where no notice has been received

9.27   Where the claimant is the person who effected the policy, and the life office has received no notice (formal or informal, legal or equitable) of assignment, insolvency or incapacity, the claimant should in general be required to produce the policy, and to sign a suitable form of request, discharge or authority for payment.

2   Where notice has been received

9.28   Where the life office has received notice of any assignment or charge, it can call for production of the original deeds or documents relating to the title to the policy and examine them before it pays the proceeds to the claimant(s) or permits any other dealings with the policy. It would not normally be concerned with documents which evidence dealings with beneficial or equitable interests protected by trustees, or with second or subsequent mortgages, but the proper course is to call for all documents of which notice has been received. Until it has examined them the office cannot be certain that they affect only the beneficial interests. In addition, the life office is not able to ignore equitable interests where, for example, it has actual or constructive knowledge that actions in connection with a policy will prejudice such an interest.

D   Loss of policy documents

9.29   Life offices frequently have to decide what course of action to take where a claim is made (or other dealings are proposed) where the policy is stated to be lost or destroyed. In some cases, where the amount of money involved is modest the life office may take a pragmatic approach and simply make payment on request especially if payment is to be made to the account from which premiums were paid (although care needs to be exercised for joint accounts, trust policies, etc). Assuming the life office is not prepared to do this the following sets out the general position.

There are no statutory provisions as to the loss of life policies. The inability of the claimant to produce it or to account for it may amount to constructive notice to the life office of an equitable assignee.

The loss of a life policy is not in itself normally a sufficient ground for payment into court under the Life Assurance Companies (Payment into Court)

Act 1896, although the particular facts may sometimes justify this course[1]. The life office can require proof of the loss and of the searches that have been made in order to rebut constructive notice of any other interest. The claimant may be asked to make a statutory declaration (under the Statutory Declarations Act 1835) before a commissioner of oaths as to the facts surrounding the loss. This should include a statement that there have been no dealings with the policy, if appropriate, or if not, the statement should give particulars of all such dealings. If the loss is reported after the death of the policyholder, his executors are unlikely to be aware of the circumstances of the loss and can usually do little more than assert that they cannot find the policy.

All potential searches for the lost policy should be made and it is sometimes possible for the life office from its records to indicate suitable directions for enquiries. For example, it can give the names of any firm of solicitors who have served a notice of assignment.

If all searches and enquiries fail, payment under a statutory declaration and/or an indemnity by the claimant will in many cases be appropriate. Executors and trustees may hesitate to give an indemnity, and in such cases the indemnity of one or more of the principal beneficiaries may be thought sufficient. Even more problematical is the situation where the claimants allege that it is the life office (or an adviser) which has lost the policy document or that the document has never been received.

9.30   Life offices tend to have standard forms for the purpose of statutory declarations and indemnities and they would normally require a full history of the policy, details of any dealings and the circumstances surrounding the disappearance and details of the searches for the policy.

It is unlikely that a life office can insist on an indemnity[2]. If the matter went to court it is likely that the life office would be ordered to pay out, and the court order would be sufficient indemnity, but in view of the costs involved this must be viewed as an extreme measure for a life office to take in order to obtain a discharge.

If the policy was assigned as security for the repayment of a loan, there should be a reassignment on the loan being repaid in which case production of the reassignment will be sufficient evidence for the life office to be able to pay to the policyholder in the absence of any other indication that the policy has been assigned or otherwise dealt with. Failing this, a letter of disclaimer by the mortgagee or his personal representatives should be required.

1   *Harrison v Alliance Assurance Co* [1903] 1 KB 184.
2   *Crockett v Ford* (1855) 25 LJ Ch 552.

SECTION 3 SUICIDE AND UNLAWFUL ACTS

A Suicide

9.31 In order to avoid claims under policies effected with a view to suicide, some offices exclude death by suicide occurring within a specified period (usually 12 or 13 months). A few exclude suicide whilst sane at any time.

Suicide was (until 3 August 1961) a crime if committed voluntarily by a person of sound mind. It is contrary to public policy that a man should derive an advantage from his own criminal act and it followed that, until the law was altered, no benefit could have been taken by the personal representatives of a person who committed the crime of suicide.

The Suicide Act 1961 abolished the rule that suicide was a crime. The position now is that the policy moneys will often become payable on the life assured's death by suicide. However, payment may still be excluded expressly or impliedly by the terms of the contract or under general insurance law principles as described below.

If there is no express reference to suicide in the policy then two results follow:

(1) It appears from the remarks of Lord Atkin and Lord Macmillan in *Beresford v Royal Insurance Co Ltd*[1] that the life assured's personal representatives cannot recover if he commits suicide whilst of sound mind. This was on the ordinary principle of insurance law that a man cannot by his own deliberate act cause the event upon which the insurance money is payable. This is not the result of any rule of public policy but of a rule of construction of the contract, by which it is presumed that the insurers have not agreed to pay on that happening. In *Beresford*, Lord Atkin believed the life office could have resisted payment on the basis of public policy. Since the decriminalisation of suicide the public policy factor would no longer be relevant. Beresford's case would therefore now be decided differently as, in that case, the clause relating to suicide only prohibited payment on suicide during the first year of the policy[2]. So, if public policy was not a factor, the strict terms of the policy only excused payment in the first year. The general principle regarding payment not being made as the insured had brought about the event insured against was negated by the specific policy terms.

(2) This principle does not apply to suicide whilst insane and in that event the personal representatives can recover the sum assured[3].

Therefore, if the policy expressly deals with suicide (as in *Beresford*) one must look to the words of the policy to ascertain whether the sum assured is payable in that event. It may provide that suicide, sane or insane, is not covered at any time, or more commonly that it is not covered if it takes place within a limited period. If the life assured commits suicide after that period has expired, the life office

---

1 [1938] AC 586.
2 *Gray v Barr* [1971] 2 QB 554 CA at 582A, per Salmon LJ.
3 *Horn v Anglo-Australian and Universal Family Life Assurance Co* (1861) 30 LJ Ch 511.

may well, on the construction of the policy, be liable even if he was then of sound mind because the express protection is limited to that period and the implication is therefore that the life office has accepted the risk after that time[1]. The Court will, of course, normally give effect to a term wholly excluding suicide even if the life assured is insane at the time[2].

9.32   Where the life assured commits suicide and the sum assured is not payable either because of an exception in the policy or on general principles, the premium is not returnable, because there has not been a total failure of consideration. The life office has been on risk throughout to pay the sum assured on death from other causes.

The claimant is not normally required to disprove suicide[3]. Unless there is evidence suggesting otherwise (the death certificate may or may not indicate that suicide was the cause), there is a presumption that death was accidental. In seeking to resist a claim the burden of proof is on the insurer to prove suicide on the balance of probabilities.

Exclusion from payment on suicide potentially affects the value of a policy. This is of particular concern to an assignee or mortgagee. It is usual, therefore, to provide that in the event of suicide, whilst sane or insane, within the specified period (if any) the policy shall be valid to the extent of any interest acquired by a third party for consideration in money or money's worth. Such a clause has been upheld on the basis that it was not tending towards encouraging suicide and meant that the life policy was a safe security in the hands of the assignee. (See *Moore v Woolsey*[4] and *White v British Empire Mutual Life Assurance Co*[5].) The life office itself will not usually be considered a third party although the precise wording of the clause must be considered. *White v British Empire Mutual Life Assurance Co* was distinguished in:

Royal London Mutual Insurance Society v Barrett[6]

D borrowed from the life office on the security of a policy and leasehold property. The policy contained a suicide clause, but with the usual saving for 'the pecuniary interest of third parties bona fide acquired for valuable consideration'. D committed suicide. Held, that the life office was not a third party; that the policy was void; and that the life office could recover its debt against the leasehold property.

It would appear that a trustee in bankruptcy of the life assured would not be viewed as someone who had acquired an interest for value. Such interest arises solely through operation of law[7].

1   *Beresford v Royal Insurance Co Ltd* [1938] AC 586 at 596, per Lord Atkin.
2   *Ellinger v Mutual Life of New York* [1905] KB 31.
3   *Boyd v Refuge Assurance Co Ltd* 1890 17 R 955.
4   (1854) 4 E & B 243.
5   (1868) LR 7 Eq 394.
6   [1928] Ch 411.
7   *Jackson and others v Forster* (1859 and 1860) I El & El 463 and 470.

B Unlawful killing

9.33 A person who has insured the life of another cannot benefit under the life policy if he murders the person whose life he has insured[1]. Nor can he benefit in any other manner (ie other than as the assured under the policy). This is an application of the principle of 'ex turpi causa non oritur actio' (a right of action will not arise from a base cause) which was reaffirmed in the following case in the context of the Social Security Act 1975.

> *R v Chief National Insurance Comr, ex p Connor*[2]
>
> The applicant had stabbed her husband with a knife and was convicted of manslaughter. The court, affirming the Chief National Insurance Commissioner, held that it was contrary to public policy to admit her claim to a widow's allowance under the Social Security Act 1975.

This rule (known as the 'forfeiture rule') does not, however, apply where the murderer is insane[3]. The public policy which prevents a sane murderer recovering was held by the Industrial Assurance Commissioner to have no application when the verdict was 'guilty but insane' as that was not, properly speaking, a conviction[4].

The rule generally applies to manslaughter but its effect has been softened by case law and by statute. In *Gray v Barr*[5] the rule which appeared to emerge was that if the person responsible for the death was guilty of deliberate, intentional and unlawful violence, or threats of violence then the rule of public policy applied. However, if the case in question fell outside of this ambit then the public policy provisions will not apply. But the precise extent of *Gray v Barr* is not entirely clear. An application of this principle can be seen in *Re H (deceased)*[6] where it was found that the plaintiff could benefit under his wife's will where he had killed his wife but was found guilty of manslaughter on the ground of diminished responsibility.

Where the forfeiture rule applies it also bars all persons claiming through or under him such as his children. This has been criticised by the Law Commission in Consultation Paper 172, 'The Forfeiture Rule and the Law of Succession', published on 16 September 2003. This resulted in a Law Commission report 'The Forfeiture Rule and the Law of Succession' (Law Com No 295) who concluded that 'under our proposed reforms, the property will devolve in exactly the same way as if the killer had predeceased the victim'.

9.34 Statutory relief from the severity of the forfeiture rule was introduced in the Forfeiture Act 1982. In appropriate circumstances, this Act relieves persons

---

1 *Prince of Wales Assurance v Palmer* (1858) 25 Beav 605; *Davitt v Titcumb* [1989] 3 All ER 417.
2 [1981] QB 758.
3 *Re Batten's Will Trusts* (1961) 105 Sol Jo 529.
4 *Chaplin v Royal London Mutual* [1958] IAC Rep 2.
5 [1971] 2 QB 554.
6 [1990] 1 FLR 441.

guilty of unlawful killing from forfeiture of various rights such as inheritance, pensions and social security benefits. The Act does not apply to murder or suicide but could still apply to someone who assisted the deceased to commit suicide or to someone guilty of manslaughter. The Act gives the court a wide discretion to modify the effect and application of the forfeiture rule, but the court must take into account:

(1)   the conduct of the offender;

(2)   conduct of the deceased; and

(3)   other material circumstances.

In the light of these the justice of the case must require the effect of the rule to be modified (section 2(2)). Proceedings under the Act must be commenced within three months of the conviction.

In *S (deceased)*[1], the plaintiff and his wife effected a joint lives first death endowment policy. He subsequently killed her but although charged with murder was ultimately convicted of manslaughter on the grounds of diminished responsibility. In the application under the Forfeiture Act the plaintiff sought an order that the policy proceeds should be paid into a trust for the sole benefit of the son. In agreeing to the application the following factors were emphasised:

(1)   the plaintiff's responsibility was substantially impaired;

(2)   the order was for the benefit of the son, not the plaintiff;

(3)   no one else was interested in the policy proceeds.

The case of *Dunbar v Plant*[2] involved a suicide pact in which only one of the participants died. The Court of Appeal held that the survivor was guilty of aiding and abetting the suicide and the forfeiture rule applied. In applying the test set out in section 2(2) of the Forfeiture Act 1982 the court decided that, whilst there would be exceptions, the normal approach would be to grant full relief against forfeiture in the case of suicide pacts.

In *Dalton v Latham*[3] the claimant was convicted of the manslaughter of the deceased and his sentence was six years' imprisonment. He applied to modify the forfeiture rule to enable him to benefit under the will on the basis that he had cared for the deceased. His application was refused as the court decided he had taken advantage of the deceased and the conviction for manslaughter rather than murder merely reduced his responsibility for the crime.

1   [1996] 1 WLR 235.
2   [1997] 3 WLR 1261.
3   [2003] EWHC 796 (Ch), (2003) 147 Sol Jo LB 537.

C Repudiation of claims

9.35 Where the life office may repudiate a claim on the grounds that the policyholder caused the loss by his own wrongdoing, then his personal representatives and all who claim a share of his estate as a beneficiary under his will or on intestacy, as a creditor, as a trustee in bankruptcy, or as an assignee[1], are equally barred from claiming[2]. This extends also to the trustees of a trust declared by the policyholder of a policy effected on his life[3]. However, the position is different where the rights in question are 'alternative or independent'. So, for example, enforcement of the policy by a mortgagee of the policy would be possible. In *Davitt v Titcumb*[4] the right of a building society as mortgagee was in issue. A joint life policy was assigned to the building society and it was held that where one of the lives assured murdered the other the building society could still recover. However, the defendant was not to benefit, even indirectly.

To repudiate a claim on the basis of suicide or other wrongdoing, the life office must prove that the death was indeed caused by suicide or such other wrongdoing as appropriate[5].

SECTION 4 DEVOLUTION AND GRANTS

A Devolution of property on death

9.36 The broad rule is that on death *immoveable property* (ie all interests in land or 'real property') will pass to the person or persons who become entitled under the law of the country where the property lies (the 'lex situs'). Where property is abroad, consideration should be given to drawing up a separate will dealing solely with this property with the help of a local lawyer.

Conversely, for *moveable property* (ie 'personal property' (including life policies)) the general rule is that property will pass to the person or persons who become entitled under the law of the country in which the deceased died domiciled (the 'lex domicilii').

The question whether or not property is moveable or immoveable is decided by the lex situs[6].

Where the deceased dies domiciled in England, his real property in England and his personal property wherever situated therefore vest in the first instance in his personal representatives:

(1) where he has made a will and has appointed executors who accept office, this will be the executor or executors; and

---

1 *Amicable Society v Bolland* (1830) 4 Bligh (NS) 194; (1831) 2 Dow & Cl 1 (HL).
2 *Cleaver v Mutual Reserve Fund Life Association* [1892] 1 QB 147; referred to in *Davitt v Titcumb* above.
3 See *Cleaver v Mutual Reserve Fund Life Association* [1892] 1 QB 147.
4 [1989] 3 All ER 417.
5 *Walsh v Legal and General Assurance Society Ltd* (1935, unreported).
6 *Drummond v Drummond* (1799) 6 Bro Parl Cas 601.

(2)   where he has died intestate, or where he has made a will but has not appointed executors or has appointed executors who do not accept office, this will be the administrator or administrators.

An interest in a life policy which the deceased held jointly with another person as joint tenant who survives him will pass not to the personal representatives of the deceased but by survivorship to the other person. It will pass to the survivor who will hold it either as absolute beneficial owner or as trustee for himself and the deceased's personal representatives. This will depend on whether the legal joint tenants beneficially owned the interest in question as joint tenants or tenants in common.

The above analysis regarding joint tenancies of life policies now needs to be considered in the light of the decision in *Murphy v Murphy*[1] which surprised the authors and is not universally accepted. In particular, the judge at first instance and one of the judges in the Court of Appeal (Chadwick LJ) did not agree with the majority decision of the Court of Appeal. The position which appears to emerge form this case is that the death benefit under a jointly held temporary assurance policy constituted two separate interests rather than a joint tenancy capable of severance (which would have meant that half of the joint interest was potentially available for redistribution under the Inheritance (Provisions for Family and Dependants) Act 1975). It does seem clear that the decision was not intended to apply to non-temporary policies especially as the policy in question also contained an additional terminal illness benefit which was specifically stated not to be subject to separate interests.

I   Executors and administrators

9.37   An executor derives his title from the will and may act as such before obtaining probate (although a life office would naturally be reluctant to deal with an executor until probate had been obtained as they have no proof of his ability to act), whereas an administrator derives his title entirely from the grant of representation and has no power to do anything as administrator before letters of administration are granted to him[2]. The title of the administrator relates back to the date of death of the deceased (the doctrine of 'relation back'). However, this will only be the case if this would be beneficial to the estate from an objective point of view. Accordingly, relation back will not be allowed for the purpose of validating acts which were done before the grant with the subjective aim of benefiting the estate but which have not in fact benefited the estate at all[3].

No one is obliged to be an executor, but if a person shows an intention to act as executor, he must prove the will and act until the court releases him. A purported renunciation, before a grant of probate has been obtained, in order to purchase part of the estate is void if the executor has already acted as executor (ie joined in some act of administration of the estate). In the case of *Holder v*

1   [2004] 1 FCR 1.
2   *Wankford v Wankford* (1704) 1 Salk 299, 309.
3   *Mills v Anderson* [1984] 2 All ER 538.

Holder[1] the plaintiff sought to have the sale to the defendant of certain farms rescinded on the ground that the defendant had acted as executor. Before probate was granted, the defendant had with the other executors opened an executors' bank account, paid money into it, signed cheques for sums totalling £600 drawn on and paid out of the account, endorsed insurance policies and instructed solicitors to act for the estate. He had then decided not to accept the executorship because he wanted to purchase two farms which were part of the estate to be administered. It was held that though technically the defendant had joined in acts of administration which meant that his renunciation of executorship was invalid, the sale should not be rescinded in view of the special circumstances of the case which included the fact that the defendant had not interfered in the administration of the estate and that the beneficiaries knew that the defendant was a potential purchaser and did not look to him to protect their interests.

Where a will appoints a minor to be an executor, the appointment does not operate to vest in the minor the estate of the testator, or to constitute him a personal representative for any purpose, unless and until probate is granted to him in accordance with the probate rules[2] after he attains the age of 18.

If an executor has been appointed merely for a limited period, his powers will cease upon the expiration of such period.

2 Wills

9.38   Some fundamental provisions affecting English wills are as follows:

(1)   The testator (ie the person making the will) must be of full age and mental capacity.

(2)   It must appear that the testator intended by his signature to give effect to the will (the old requirement for the testator to sign at the end of the will is no longer applicable) or by some other person in his presence and at his direction. The signature must be made or acknowledged by the testator in the presence of two or more witnesses, present at the same time, each of whom must sign or acknowledge their signature in the presence of the testator, but not necessarily in the presence of each other.

(3)   Any additional testamentary document, known as a codicil, must be similarly signed and witnessed.

A will may be revoked:

(a)   by another will or codicil or a document signed and witnessed in the same way as a will, with the intention to revoke;

(b)   by destruction with the intention to revoke[3]; or

(c)   by marriage.

1   [1968] 1 All ER 665, CA.
2   Supreme Court Act 1981, s 118.
3   *Re Adams* [1990] 2 All ER 97 (obliteration of signature with ball point pen).

However, a will expressed to be made in contemplation of a particular marriage is not revoked by the occurrence of that contemplated marriage[1]. In the case of *Re Coleman, Coleman v Coleman*[2], a will made in September 1970 gave gifts and devised the testator's freehold house 'unto my fiancée' and disposed of the residue for the benefit of others. In November 1970 the testator married his fiancée and died in November 1972. It was held that the construction of the document as required by section 177 of the Law of Property Act 1925 failed to show that the whole of the will was made in contemplation of marriage (although certain clauses had been) and accordingly the will was revoked on the testator's marriage by virtue of section 18 of the Wills Act 1837. However, doubts were expressed about this decision, perhaps most notably by the Law Reform Committee[3]. Following the Administration of Justice Act 1982[4], the position now is that where it appears from a will that at the time it was made the testator was expecting to be married to a particular person and that he intended that a specific disposition in the will should not be revoked by that marriage, that disposition takes effect despite the marriage. Furthermore, any other disposition takes effect also, unless it appears from the will that he intended it to be revoked by the marriage. Effectively, this extends the concept to individual dispositions and not necessarily the will as a whole so the result in *Coleman* would be different if decided today.

Section 18A of the Wills Act 1837 (inserted by the Administration of Justice Act 1982, section 18(2)) dealt with the effect of divorce on wills. It provided that any appointment of the former spouse as executor be deleted and that any gift to that spouse be treated as having lapsed. The unfortunate effect of providing that the gift 'lapsed' was evident in the case of *Re Sinclair*[5] with the ultimate result being that Mr Sinclair's brother benefitted at the expense of the Imperial Cancer Research Fund whereas if the wife was treated as having predeceased the gift over to the charity would have survived. Subsequently, the Law Commission presented a report in September 1983[6] which was eventually enacted as sections 3 and 4 of the Law Reform (Succession) Act 1995. Essentially, this provides for the former spouse to be treated, in most cases, as having predeceased the testator. In particular, the substituted section 18A(1)(b) negatives the effect of *Sinclair*.

A soldier, sailor or airman (such terms being given a wide meaning) on active service or a mariner or seaman at sea may, whether or not of full age, make a valid will; and such a will need not be witnessed with the formalities required in the case of a civilian. It may even be made by word of mouth[7].

---

1 Law of Property Act 1925, s 177 (repealed and replaced by the Administration of Justice Act 1982, s 18 which has the same effect for wills made after January 1983).
2 [1976] Ch 1.
3 22nd Report, pp 14–16.
4 Section 18(1).
5 [1985] Ch 446.
6 Family Law: The Effect of Divorce on Wills (Law Com No 217).
7 Wills Act 1837, s 11.

3 Property vested in trustees

9.39   Property vested in trustees is held by them in joint tenancy and on the death of one of them vests in the survivor or survivors but, of course, still subject to the trusts. If there is a sole trustee or a sole surviving trustee, then on his death the trust property vests in his personal representatives despite any provision in the trustee's will or in the instrument creating the trust[1]. These personal representatives may either carry on the trust[2] or appoint new trustees in their place[3]; but, if there is a person nominated by the trust instrument to appoint new trustees, then he has priority in making an appointment ahead of the personal representatives.

Where there has been a change of trusteeship by, for example, appointment or retirement then the trustees would normally be required to produce evidence of this by production of the relevant deeds, etc.

B English grants of representation

9.40   A grant of representation will be issued by the Principal Registry of the Family Division, or by a District Probate Registry or a sub-registry, to evidence the title of the personal representatives to administer the estate of a deceased person where that person is domiciled in England and Wales at the time of his death.

Such grants are essentially of two kinds (although either may be limited in some way):

(1)   probate;

(2)   administration.

If the claimant does not wish to employ a solicitor, he can apply personally for a grant at any registry or sub-registry. If he decides not to use a solicitor, he will have to produce a death certificate or such other evidence of the death of the deceased as the registrar may approve[4], and supply all information necessary to enable the papers leading to the grant to be prepared in the registry[5].

Every application must be supported by an oath made by the applicant (and such other person as the registrar may require) which must state that the document of which probate is to be granted is the true and original last will of the deceased and must prove the marking of the will (ie the signatures of the applicant and the person before whom the oath is sworn)[6], the name and last address of the deceased and the date of death.

---

1   Administration of Estates Act 1925, s 1(2) and (3).
2   Trustee Act 1925, s 18(2).
3   Section 36.
4   Non-Contentious Probate Rules 1987, SI 1987/2024, r 5(5).
5   Rule 5(6).
6   Rule 10(1).

In addition the personal representatives must deliver to the Inland Revenue Commissioners an account specifying to the best of their knowledge and belief all appropriate property for inheritance tax purposes and the value of the said property[1]. A grant of representation will not be made until such an account has been produced and any inheritance tax payable has been paid. There are exceptions from having to provide a return for 'excepted' estates which, in this context, essentially means estates below the inheritance tax threshold (or 'nil-rate band').

1   Probate

9.41   The executors derive their title from the will and not from probate, and acts done by them before probate are binding on the estate. However, although they can begin an action as executors before probate they cannot proceed beyond the stage at which it becomes necessary to prove their title until probate is granted.

Probate is prima facie evidence that the will is valid, that it is the last will and also that any inheritance tax payable has been paid.

Where more than one executor is appointed, probate is sometimes granted to one or more of them, power being reserved to the others to come forward later and obtain a grant. Until that occurrence persons may safely deal with the executor(s) to whom probate has been granted. Such a later grant is called a double probate.

The probate comprises two parts:

(1)   the grant of probate; and

(2)   a copy of the will.

Any executor may decline to act if he so wishes. In such a case he is said to renounce probate.

2   Letters of administration

9.42   If the deceased has: (i) appointed executors who have predeceased him or who are unable or unwilling to act; (ii) has appointed no executors; or (iii) has died without leaving a will, letters of administration may be granted. There is a recognised order of priority in which persons may apply for a grant in such cases[2]. The person entitled to the grant has no title to act before the grant is made (except for matters of humanity and necessity) but when the grant has been made his title relates back to the death.

The following are examples of types of letters of administration:

(a)   *Administration with the will annexed ('cum testamento annexo').* Where there is a will but no available and willing executor. The court cannot

---

1   Inheritance Tax Act 1984, s 216.
2   Non-Contentious Probate Rules 1987, r 22 and Administration of Estates Act 1925, s 46.

appoint an executor and so it must grant letters of administration with the will annexed.

(b) *Administration pending suit (pendente lite).* Where legal proceedings are pending as to the validity of a will or obtaining or revoking any grant of representation. Often the grant is made to someone who is considered to be indifferent to the contesting parties.

(c) *Administration during mental incapacity.* Where the executor is incapable of managing his affairs by reason of mental incapacity the district judge or registrar may grant a limited administration to specified persons.

(d) *Administration de bonis non administratis.* Where a sole or last surviving executor has died intestate, or without executors (so that the 'chain of representation' is broken) or where a sole or last surviving administrator has died; in both cases before the estate is fully administered. The courts grant administration to a new representative for the purpose of completing the administration.

(e) *Administration for the use and benefit of a minor ('administration durante minore aetate').* This is a grant, limited as to time, which is made when (1) the person, or all the persons, entitled to administration is, or are, under age; or (2) the person appointed sole executor is a minor.

(f) *Administration ad colligenda bona.* Where there is delay in obtaining a grant with the result that the preservation of the estate is put at risk, an application may be made to the probate registrar for an order for a grant of letters of administration ad colligenda bona.

3 Cessate grant

9.43   A cessate grant is granted when a testator has directed that on the happening of a certain event, some other person is to be substituted for the original executor and that particular event occurs. Hence, this other person becomes entitled to a cessate grant. This second grant will also be granted on the death of a person who has taken a grant for the use and benefit of a person under disability (eg a mentally disordered person or a minor) or on removal of the said disability. It is a re-grant of all the remaining estate.

4 Probate in solemn form

9.44   Probate may be granted in common form or solemn form. Proof of a will in solemn form follows a court action, and is granted in cases where the validity of the will is open to question, or where there is a likelihood that it may be opposed.

5 Receipt by one personal representative

9.45   One of several personal representatives can give a life office a good discharge, but it is usual to ask for the signatures of all the executors who have proved the will, or all the administrators, as appropriate. Moreover, if the administration of the estate is complete and the executors have become trustees under a trust in the will, the receipt of all the trustees would generally be required[1].

6   Executor de son tort

9.46   Any 'intermeddling' with the deceased's assets by a person who is not an executor or administrator makes him accountable and he could potentially be sued by the rightful executors, administrators, beneficiaries or creditors. He is called an executor de son tort ('de son tort' means 'of his own wrong').

7   Payment without a grant

9.47   A life office is sometimes asked to pay without a grant but unless it has special power to do so, either in the policy or through its constitution, such a request should generally be treated with great caution, as it might later be found:

(1)   that even if an unproved will is produced to the office, it is invalid, or even a forgery, or is not the last will;

(2)   that the deceased left a will though the claimant is not aware of it;

(3)   that the claimant has not paid the debts and funeral expenses, in which a case a creditor can obtain a grant and compel payment;

(4)   that the life office (or others who 'intermeddle' with the estate assets) is liable for inheritance tax as though it was an executor[2].

An exception may sometimes be made for pragmatic purposes where the value of the policy and the estate are small and where there is little or no risk of insolvency, or of liability to tax or of dispute between rival claimants. The decision for the life office may be easier where there is a will and/or the deceased left a widow(er). Sometimes life offices adhere voluntarily to certain statutory provisions[3] which permit other types of assets such as national savings up to a limit of currently £5,000 to be paid without a grant of representation. Where the policyholder dies intestate and does not leave a widow(er), the life office might have particular difficulty in determining who is entitled to the money, for example, as yet unknown children from other relationships would be entitled to share in the estate. A grant of representation may be advisable in this case.

---

1   *Luke v South Kensington Hotel Ltd* (1879) 11 Ch D 121, 125; Trustee Act, 1925, s 14.
2   Inheritance Tax Act 1984, s 199(4) and s 200(4).
3   Administration of Estates (Small Payments) Act 1965 and Administration of Estates (Small Payments) (Increase of Limit) Order 1984, SI 1984/539.

8   Deaths of executors

9.48   Where one of two or more executors dies, whether before or after obtaining probate, the survivor(s) can act or continue to act, and so can the last survivor of them. The executors of the last survivor represent the original testator (on the basis that the last survivor proved the will) and so on, in what is known as the 'chain of representation'.

The effect of section 7 of the Administration of Estates Act 1925 is as follows:

(1)   An executor of a sole or last surviving executor of a testator is the executor of that testator.

The provision does not apply to an executor who does not prove the will of his testator. Also, in the case of an executor who on his death has not proved the will, the rights of that executor cease and the representation to the testator and the administration of his estate devolve in the same way as if the executor had never been appointed as such[1].

(2)   So long as the chain of representation is unbroken, the last executor in the chain is the executor of every preceding testator.

(3)   The chain of representation is broken by:

(a)   an intestacy;

(b)   the failure of a testator to appoint an executor; or

(c)   the failure to obtain probate of a will;

but is not broken by a temporary grant of administration if probate is subsequently granted[2].

(4)   Every person in the chain of representation to a testator effectively stands in the shoes of the original executor[3].

In any case where the chain of representation is broken before the administration is complete, it will be necessary to obtain letters of administration *de bonis non administratis* in order to complete the title.

C   Scottish grants

I   Scotland

9.49   There are two types of grant, the *confirmation nominate* and the *confirmation dative*. The confirmation nominate is granted where there is a will. Where

---

1   Administration of Estates Act 1925, s 5(i).
2   Administration of Estates Act 1925, s 7(3).
3   Administration of Estates Act 1925, s 7(4)(a) and (b).

there is no executor nominate appointed by the will, the Executors (Scotland) Act 1900 provides that the following persons will be deemed to be the executors nominate: the testamentary trustees failing whom, those legatees to whom the whole or the residue of the estate has been bequeathed. The confirmation dative is granted where there is no will. The court will appoint an executor dative in accordance with a recognised order of priority.

A Scottish grant gives power to collect only the property specified in a schedule (the inventory) attached to the grant; and if the executors subsequently discover additional assets, they have to obtain a further grant known as an *eik*. Where one of two or more executors dies, the survivor or survivors can act, but not the executors of the last survivor. There is no chain of representation as there is in England.

2   Resealing

9.50   The Administration of Estates Act 1971 abolished the necessity for a grant made in Scotland or Northern Ireland to be resealed in England before English assets could be collected. The Act provides that where a person dies domiciled in Scotland or Northern Ireland, the local grant of representation (provided it notes his Scottish or Northern Irish domicile) is treated as a valid grant in England, without any need for resealing. There are reciprocal provisions validating English grants in the other parts of the UK.

D   Grants made outside the United Kingdom

I   Section 19 of the Revenue Act 1889

9.51   Where a person dies domiciled abroad, the persons entitled must, as a general rule, obtain an English grant before they can collect his English assets; but there is an exception in the case of life policies, under section 19 of the Revenue Act 1889, which amends section 11 of the Revenue Act 1884, as follows:

> 'Provided that where a policy of life assurance has been effected with any insurance company by a person who shall die domiciled elsewhere than in the United Kingdom, the production of a grant of representation from a court in the United Kingdom shall not be necessary to establish the right to receive the money payable in respect of such policy.'

The UK does not include the Isle of Man or the Channel Islands.

Where section 19 applies, payment can be made on evidence of domicile and production of the appropriate documents identifying the person entitled to collect the policy moneys under the law of the country of domicile. If required by the life office, the claim should be supported by evidence of the validity of the grant and, where necessary, by evidence of the law of the country of domicile.

Haas v Atlas Assurance Co Ltd[1]

> H was the testamentary executor by Swiss law of a man who had effected policies on his life with an English life office and died domiciled in Switzerland. H claimed payment without an English grant. Held, that he was entitled to recover.

Section 19 of the Revenue Act 1889 concerns the requirements to establish title to the proceeds of a policy rather than liability for duty or tax on policies. Therefore, where the policy is a UK asset of the foreign domiciled policyholder, the life office should satisfy itself that any inheritance tax liability in respect of the policy has been discharged before payment of the proceeds otherwise the office may become accountable for the tax. Therefore, in practice the life office may well still seek the production of a grant of representation.

Section 200(1)(c) of the Inheritance Tax Act 1984 makes any person in whom the relevant property is vested at any time after the death liable for any inheritance tax payable, and this is so whether or not that person is beneficially entitled to the property. For this purpose, the meaning of the word 'property' is extended by section 200(4) of the 1984 Act to include any property directly or indirectly representing the original property. It may be argued that the 'property' of a life policy is the right to sue the office in respect of its obligation to pay a sum of money and that this 'property' is never vested in the life office. The life office may also be liable for inheritance tax if it has received notice that the policy in question is subject to a statutory charge for tax under section 237 of the 1984 Act.

9.52   There is another basis on which a life office may be liable for inheritance tax where it has made a payment without the production of an English grant of representation or under the provisions of section 19 of the Revenue Act 1889[2]. The life office may be held to have intermeddled with the policy proceeds so as to become liable as though it was an executor. The policy proceeds are then deemed to have vested in the life office[3] so that it becomes liable for the inheritance tax payable.

To assist in understanding the meaning of intermeddling, the case below is of assistance:

IRC v Stype Investments (Jersey) Ltd[4]

> In February 1979, Sir Charles Clore made a Jersey settlement of the shares in Stype Investments (Jersey) Ltd. In May 1979 he conveyed to that company an estate in Hertfordshire on terms that it should be held by the company as bare nominee for him. Shortly afterwards, he directed the company to sell the estate and completion was fixed for September 1979. Sir Charles died in July 1979. The sale proceeds were subsequently received by the company and transferred to its account in Jersey. The Revenue sought to serve process on the company in Jersey, alleging that it had 'intermeddled' with Sir Charles' property so as to

1   [1913] 2 KB 209.
2   See *New York Breweries Co Ltd v A-G* [1899] AC 62.
3   Inheritance Tax Act 1984, ss 199(4)(a), 200(4).
4   [1982] Ch 456.

become liable for capital transfer tax (the forerunner of inheritance tax) under section 25 of the Finance Act 1975[1]. It was held by the Court of Appeal that the conduct of the company in relation to receipt of the proceeds of sale of the estate constituted an intermeddling with the estate and so the company was an executor de son tort and therefore within section 25.

2 Domicile

9.53   A person's domicile must not be confused with his residence or nationality (although a person may be domiciled and resident in, and a national of, the same country). Domicile is a matter of fact. A person's domicile is the country where he either has (or is deemed by law to have) his permanent home, although he may be resident in some other country for other purposes.

Formerly, a woman acquired the domicile of her husband on marriage, and it changed with his throughout the marriage. Section 1 of the Domicile and Matrimonial Proceedings Act 1973 provides that the domicile of married women shall, after 1 January 1974, be ascertained by the same factors as for other individuals with an independent domicile. But a woman married before 1974 retains her husband's domicile until she acquires another.

A woman married before the 1973 Act and acquiring her husband's English domicile by dependence, has to retain it as her domicile of choice while she continues to live with him, even though she intends ultimately to return to her domicile of origin. Although the purpose of the 1973 Act was the abolition of the wife's dependent domicile, a woman married before 1974 wishing to revive her domicile of origin has not only to have an intention to cease living permanently in England but has also to take up residence permanently in another country, leaving her husband if necessary.

IRC v The Duchess of Portland[2]

The Duchess of Portland had a domicile of origin in Quebec and was a Canadian citizen. In 1948 she married the Duke (then Lord William Cavendish Bentinck) and so acquired a domicile of dependency in England. They lived in London but the Duchess always intended to return to Quebec should her husband predecease her or agree to go with her. She owned and kept for their use a house in Quebec and spent about 10 weeks there every year. It was held that the Duchess, who had a Quebec domicile of origin, did not acquire a domicile of choice in Quebec following the passing of the Act as she had not taken up permanent residence in Quebec. Her physical presence in Quebec for limited periods each year for the purposes of maintaining her links with Quebec was not enough to make her an inhabitant of it.

A person's domicile of origin is that of his father, except that a posthumous or illegitimate child takes that of his mother. His domicile may change to that of his mother if his parents are separated and he lives with her; and unless he goes back

---

1   Now replaced by the Inheritance Tax Act 1984, s 200(4).
2   [1982] Ch 314.

to live with his father, her domicile will in effect then become the child's domicile[1]. After age 16, a person may acquire an independent domicile of choice, but his domicile of origin will be restored if the domicile of choice is abandoned. The domicile of origin is never therefore entirely lost[2]. To acquire a domicile of choice it is necessary to reside in the country of choice, but residence alone is not sufficient, however long continued – there must also be the intention to remain permanently. To establish a domicile of choice it is necessary to show a clear unequivocal intention to remain in the country of choice permanently. There must be convincing evidence before a court will hold that a new domicile has been acquired[3].

For inheritance tax purposes a person will be deemed to be domiciled in the UK at the time of the transfer/death if:

(1) he was domiciled in the UK within the three years immediately preceding the transfer/death; or

(2) he was resident in the UK in not less than 17 of the 20 years previous to the date of transfer/death[4].

3   Resealing of grants made abroad

9.54   Under the Colonial Probates Act 1892, extended by the Colonial Probates (Protected States and Mandated Territories) Act 1927, and various Orders in Council, grants may be resealed in England if made by courts in certain countries which have generally been at some time British possessions, protected and trust territories.

When a grant of representation is obtained in a country to which the Act applies, and is then subsequently resealed in England, it will have the same effect as if it had been granted in England. The person who obtained the grant will have the same powers and duties as any person to whom a grant of representation was granted in England.

Section 109(1) and (2) of the Supreme Court Act 1981, as amended by the Inheritance Tax Act 1984, provides that an applicant for the resealing of a grant issued outside the UK is required to deliver an Inland Revenue Account and pay any inheritance tax.

SECTION 5   DISTRIBUTION

9.55   The executor or administrator must first ascertain the assets and liabilities of the deceased. On his application for probate or letters of administration he

1   Domicile and Matrimonial Proceedings Act 1973, s 4(1).
2   *IRC v Bullock* [1976] 1 WLR 1178, CA.
3   *Buswell v IRC* [1974] 1 WLR 1631, CA; *Re Clore (No 2), Official Solicitor v Clore* [1984] STC 609; *Plummer v IRC* [1988] 1 All ER 97, [1988] 1 WLR 292.
4   Inheritance Tax Act 1984, s 267.

must first pay inheritance tax on the net value of the deceased's estate after deduction of the liabilities payable out of it, and must swear that he will administer the estate according to law and render a true account whenever required by law to do so.

When the executor or administrator has obtained probate or letters of administration, he can collect, or establish his title to, the assets and pay the funeral expenses (where appropriate), debts, and any further inheritance tax. (The personal representatives may discover during the course of the administration that the deceased owns other assets which were not initially taken into account when calculating the inheritance tax payable.) The executor or administrator must then deal with the remainder of the property in accordance with the will or the law of intestate succession as appropriate. The rules relating to intestate succession also apply to any property which is not disposed of by the testator's will. This would be a 'partial intestacy'.

A   Distribution in England and Wales

I   Deaths on or after I December 1993

9.56   Where, on or after 1 December 1993, a person dies intestate, the law governing the succession to his property is to be found in Schedule 1 to the Intestates' Estates Act 1952 which conveniently sets out the appropriate sections of the Administration of Estates Act 1925 (as amended) but has itself been amended by section 1 of the Family Provision Act 1966 and by orders made under that Act, namely the Family Provision (Intestate Succession) Order 1993[1] and Intestate Succession (Interest and Capitalisation) Order 1977[2] (as amended)[3]. The position is summarised in the table below. These rules only apply where the deceased dies domiciled in England. For the Scottish law of intestate succession reference should be made to the Succession (Scotland) Act 1964 (as amended) summarised later in this section, and for Northern Irish law, to the Administration of Estates Act (Northern Ireland) 1955 and orders made under that Act, such as the Administration of Estates (Rights of Surviving Spouse) Order (Northern Ireland) 1993[4] and The Succession (Northern Ireland) Order 1996[5].

While a decree of judicial separation is in force, the separated spouses are not entitled to any rights of intestate succession in each other's estates – by section 18(2) of the Matrimonial Causes Act 1973 the property will devolve as if the other party to the marriage had then been dead.

If the intestate and the husband or wife of the intestate die in circumstances where it is uncertain which of them survived the other then if the deaths

1   SI 1993/2906.
2   SI 1977/1491.
3   Intestate Succession (Interest and Capitalisation) Order 1977 (Amendment) Order 1983, SI 1983/1374.
4   SR (NI) 1987/426.
5   1996/3163 (NI 26).

occurred on or before December 31, 1995, the provisions of section 184 of the Law of Property Act 1925 (under which the younger is deemed to have survived the older) do not apply and so the younger does not take on the intestate's death. Where the intestate dies on or after 1 January 1996, then in order to take any beneficial interest on his intestacy, his spouse must survive by 28 days (see section 1(1) of the Law Reform (Succession) Act 1995, which inserts a new subsection (2A) into section 47 of the Administration of Estates Act 1925).

9.57   England

Where the intestate leaves	Interest or share of estate taken

(1) a husband or wife, but
    (a) no issue (ie children, grandchildren and other lineal descendants), and
    (b) no parent or brother or sister of the whole blood, or issue of a brother or sister of the whole blood
	The surviving husband or wife takes the whole estate absolutely

(2) a husband or wife and issue (whether or not persons mentioned in (1)(b) above also survive)	The surviving husband or wife takes:
	 (i) the personal chattels (ie personal property)
	 (ii) the remainder up to £125,000 free of inheritance tax and costs with interest at 6% up to payment or appropriation and the residue (if any) is held:
	   (a) one half upon trust for the surviving husband or wife for life and thereafter on statutory trusts (see below) for the issue
	   (b) the other half on statutory trusts for the issue

(3) a husband or wife and one or more of the following, ie parent, brother or sister of the whole blood or issue of brother or sister of the whole blood but no issue	The surviving husband or wife takes: (i) the personal chattels (ii) the remainder up to £200,000 free of costs and inheritance tax with interest at 6% up to payment or appropriation (iii) one half of the residue (if any). The other half is taken by the parents and if more than one in equal shares or if no parent survives then it is held on statutory trusts for brothers and sisters of the whole blood or their issue (that is, nephews and nieces).
(4) issue but no husband or wife	The whole estate is held on statutory trusts for the issue

Where the intestate leaves no husband or wife and no issue, the distribution is as follows. (If any member of one class survive, those in a subsequent class cannot benefit):

Relatives surviving at death of intestate	Interest or share of estate taken
Both parents	The whole in equal shares
One parent	The whole
Brothers and sisters of the whole blood (or their issue)	The whole on the statutory trusts
Brothers and sisters of the half blood (or their issue (where deceased and beneficiary had one common parent))	The whole on the statutory trusts
Grandparents	The whole and if more than one then equally (not on statutory trusts)
Uncles and aunts of the whole blood (or their issue)	The whole on the statutory trusts
Uncles and aunts of the half blood (or their issue)	The whole on the statutory trusts
and if no relative takes an absolute interest	The Crown, Duchy of Lancaster, or Duke of Cornwall takes the whole as bona vacantia

9.58   Where a surviving husband or wife takes a life interest in part of the intestate's estate and elects to do so (within 12 months of the grant of representation unless the court extends this period), he or she is entitled to have it purchased or redeemed by the personal representatives for a capital sum. The capital sum is calculated by reference to various factors including actuarial tables incorporating a multiplier factor. These tables differ for surviving husbands and wives owing to the different life expectancies of men and women. The multiplier varies within each table according to the age of the surviving spouse and the prevailing rate of interest on medium term government stock. The capital sum is the product of the part of the residuary estate in respect of which the election has been exercised and the multiplier shown in the appropriate table[1].

In addition, where the estate includes an interest in a dwelling house in which the surviving husband or wife was resident at the death, he or she may require (again within 12 months of the grant of representation unless the court extends this period) the personal representatives to appropriate that interest in or towards satisfaction of any absolute interest taken by the survivor, including the redemption value of a life interest. The personal representatives may raise the sums of £125,000 or £200,000 or the capital value of a life interest by borrowing on the security of any part of the estate. Where there is a partial intestacy, the sum of £125,000 or £200,000 to be taken by the surviving spouse is reduced by the value at the death of any beneficial interests (other than personal chattels specifically bequeathed) acquired under the will of the deceased.

An adopted child is now treated as the child of the adopter (and not the child of any other person) for purposes of distribution on the death of an intestate after

---

1   Intestate Succession (Interest and Capitalisation) Order 1977, SI 1977/1491 and the amending SI 1983/1374.

357

the date of the adoption order. Under the Family Law Reform Act 1987, illegitimate children have the same right to share in their relatives' estates as if they were legitimate. However, where an illegitimate child dies intestate, it will be presumed that he was not survived by his natural father, or any person related to him only through his natural father, unless the contrary is shown[1].

2   The statutory trusts

9.59   The statutory trusts are briefly as follows:

(a)   *For issue.* In equal shares for the children who attain the age of 18 or marry. If any of those children predecease their parent(s), the children of that deceased child will take the deceased child's share per stirpes (ie they take in equal shares the share to which the deceased child would have been entitled).

(b)   *For persons other than issue.* In equal shares for members of the class who attain the age of 18 or marry. If any of these members predecease the deceased, the children of the deceased member will take the deceased member's share per stirpes.

B   Scotland – legal and other prior rights – intestate succession

I   Legal and prior rights

9.60   In Scotland the surviving spouse and issue of the deceased have legal claims against that person's estate, which take precedence over other claims on intestacy and which, with certain qualifications, cannot be defeated by testamentary disposition. These claims are known as 'legal rights'. They are not strictly rights of succession, but are more in the nature of debts, arising and being fixed at the moment of death, vesting then and requiring to be satisfied out of the net moveable estate before any other part of the estate can be distributed.

The common law entitlement to 'legal rights' was modified to some extent by the Succession (Scotland) Act 1964 and by subsequent legislation. Where a person has died after 10 September 1964, either totally or partially intestate, the 'legal rights' rank after statutory 'prior rights' as extended by that Act. But prior rights do not have the characteristic of legal rights in that legal rights prevail against a contrary testamentary disposition[2]. A beneficiary must elect whether or not to claim his or her legal rights and cannot claim both legal rights and entitlement under the will.

The rules of intestate succession operate only on the residual part of the deceased's estate which is not required to satisfy prior rights and legal rights. The legal rights are as follows:

1   Family Law Reform Act 1987, s 18(2).
2   Succession (Scotland) Act 1964, s 36(1).

(1)   *Jus relictae*: the right of a widow to one-third of her husband's moveable estate (essentially anything other than land) if he leaves any issue entitled to legitim (see below for definition); or to one-half if he leaves no such issue, or if all claims to legitim were discharged in his lifetime. The fund subject to the widow's claim consists of the free moveables net of debts, expenses and any deduction for prior rights.

(2)   *Jus relicti*: the equivalent right of a widower in his deceased wife's estate.

(3)   *Legitim*: the right of children (including illegitimate and adopted children and the surviving issue of deceased children who would have had a claim had they survived) to one-third of the net moveable estate if there is a surviving spouse claiming legal rights; or to one-half if there is no surviving spouse or if his or her claim has been discharged.

Where all the persons entitled to claim legitim are in the same degree of relationship to the deceased (eg if they are all children of the deceased), the division is on a per capita basis (ie they all receive an equal share). Where the persons claiming legitim are in differing degrees (eg if some are children and some are issue of a deceased child) then the division is per stirpes at the level of the nearest degree of relationship to the deceased in which there are surviving members (so a grandchild would be entitled to the share his parent would have received and if two or more grandchildren of the same parent then they would be entitled to an equal share of what their parent's share would have been).

9.61   In calculating the shares of legitim, any advances of moveable property made by the deceased during his lifetime to claimants on the fund must be *collated*. This is similar to the old hotchpot rule under English law. The amount of such advances must be added back to the legitim fund which is then divided with the amount of the advances being deducted from the share falling to the person to whom they were made.

Legal rights of spouses may be discharged in their lifetime by marriage contract. However, nothing in such a contract executed after the commencement of the Succession (Scotland) Act 1964 may exclude rights to legitim unless the child or issue entitled, being sui juris, consents. A spouse or child may also renounce legal rights.

Formerly, any bequest or other testamentary provision for a surviving spouse or child was additional to any legal rights, unless declared to be given in satisfaction of legal rights and so accepted. But testamentary dispositions executed after the commencement of the Succession (Scotland) Act 1964 which do not contain such a declaration are to have effect as if they contained one, in the absence of express provision to the contrary[1].

---

1   Succession (Scotland) Act 1964, s 13.

2 Statutory prior rights

9.62   As from 1 June 2005 the statutory prior rights of an intestate's surviving spouse are as follows[1]:

(1)   If the intestate's estate includes an interest as owner or tenant in a dwelling house in which the surviving spouse was ordinarily resident at the intestate's death:

(a)   where the value of the interest does not exceed £300,000 to the interest itself or in certain circumstances to its value instead; or

(b)   in any other circumstances, to the sum of £300,000.

(2)   If the intestate's estate includes the 'furniture and plenishings' of a dwelling house to which paragraph (1) above applies the surviving spouse is entitled to the whole of them if the value does not exceed £24,000, or in any other case to such part not exceeding £24,000 as the surviving spouse may choose.

(3)   The surviving spouse is entitled to a sum of money – £42,000 if the intestate is survived by issue and £75,000 if not; in either case with interest at a specified rate from the date of death to the date of payment. But if the surviving spouse, in the case of a partial intestacy, is entitled to a legacy (other than of property to which (1) or (2) above applies) then he or she is entitled only to the excess of the £42,000 or £75,000 over the legacy. This monetary provision is to be borne rateably by heritage and movable estate.

9.63   Under the 1964 Act[2], a deceased intestate's estate, net of prior rights and legal rights, devolves as follows. If there is any person in one group then no-one in a subsequent group may benefit:

(1)   children (includes adopted children and the issue of predeceasing children);

(2)   a parent or parents and brothers and sisters; half to the parents, half to the brothers and sisters;

(3)   brothers and sisters (or their issue) (brothers and sisters of the whole blood exclude those of the half blood);

(4)   a parent or both parents;

(5)   the surviving spouse;

(6)   uncles or aunts, irrespective of whether they are on the paternal or maternal side;

(7)   grandparent or grandparents;

(8)   brothers and sisters of any of the grandparents; or

---

1   Prior Rights of Surviving Spouse (Scotland) Order 2005, SSI 2005/252.
2   Section 2.

(9)   ancestors of the intestate, generation by generation successively, without distinction between paternal and maternal lines, the brothers and sisters of any ancestors having right before ancestors of the next more remote generation;

(10)   The Crown.

References above to brothers and sisters include those of the half blood only if none of the whole blood are entitled. If any person (other than a parent or spouse of the intestate), who would have been entitled had he survived, predeceases the intestate leaving issue who survive the intestate, then those issue take the whole or part to which the deceased person would have been entitled. If any person, who would have been entitled had he survived, predeceases the intestate leaving no issue who survive the intestate, then any other person who is also entitled takes his share and if there are more than one then the intestate's share will be divided equally between them if they are all related in the same degree to the intestate (for example, brothers and sisters) and per stirpes (for example, children of a deceased child taking in equal shares the share that the child would have taken had he survived) in other cases.

C   Northern Ireland – distribution on intestacy

9.64   The law governing intestate succession is to be found in the Administration of Estates Act (Northern Ireland) 1955 and in orders made under that Act, namely the Administration of Estates (Rights of Surviving Spouse) Order (Northern Ireland) 1993[1], the Intestate Succession (Interest) Order (Northern Ireland) 1985[2] and the Succession (Northern Ireland) Order 1996[3].

The following table sets out the position in Northern Ireland:

Northern Ireland

Where the intestate leaves	Interest or share of estate taken

(1)   a husband or wife, but
  (a)   no issue, and
  (b) no parent or brother or sister or issue of a brother or sister	

The surviving husband or wife takes the residuary estate absolutely	
(2) a husband or wife and issue (whether or not parents, brothers or sisters survive)	The surviving husband or wife takes: (a) the personal chattels (b) the remainder up to £125,000 free of costs, with interest at the specified rate up to payment.

1   SR (NI) 1993/426.
2   SR (NI) 1985/8.
3   1996/3163 (NI 26).

	The residue is distributed as follows:
	(i) Where only one child of the intestate survives, as to one half to the surviving husband or wife and as to the other half amongst the issue equally per stirpes.
	(ii) Where more than one child survives, as to one third to the surviving husband or wife, and as to the residue amongst the issue equally per stirpes.
	If a child of the intestate predeceased him leaving issue who survive him, the surviving spouse takes the same share as if the child had survived.
(3) a husband or wife and one or more of the following, namely parent, brother or sister or issue of brother or sister but no issue	The surviving husband or wife takes:
	(a) the personal chattels
	(b) the remainder up to £200,000 free of costs with interest at the specified rate up to payment
	(c) one half of the residue.
	The other half of the residue is taken by the parents and if more than one in equal shares, or if no parent survives, by brothers and sisters or their issue equally per stirpes.
(4) issue but no husband or wife	The whole estate is distributed amongst the issue equally per stirpes

Where the intestate leaves no husband or wife and no issue, the distribution is:

Relatives surviving at death of intestate	Interest or share of residue taken
Both parents	The whole in equal shares
One parent	The whole
Brothers or sisters or issue of deceased brothers or sisters	The whole estate in equal shares per stirpes

If the intestate leaves no husband or wife, issue, parent, brother, sister or issue of a deceased brother or sister, his estate is distributed to more remote relatives (the surviving issue of deceased uncles and aunts taking their parents' share per stirpes). If no person takes under the foregoing provisions, the estate passes to the Crown as bona vacantia.

Unlike the position in England, brothers and sisters and other relatives of the half blood are treated in the same way as and inherit equally with relatives of the whole blood in the same degree.

The references to 'spouse' in the above intestacy provisions now includes references to registered civil partners under the Civil Partnership Act 2004.

SECTION 6   RELEVANT STATUTORY PROVISIONS

A   **Children**

1   *Illegitimacy*

9.65   The Family Law Reform Act 1987 provides, subject to any contrary intention, certain rules of construction. No reference needs to be made to the terms 'legitimate' and 'illegitimate' as the term 'children' will encompass both legitimate and illegitimate children. Sections 1, 18 and 19 specifically provide that illegitimacy will not be taken into consideration when determining an illegitimate person's rights of succession on intestacy or under a will or inter vivos disposition. It is, however, open to a testator or donor to specifically exclude illegitimate children if he so wishes. The term 'illegitimate' and its derivations are no longer used in statutory references. Section 21 of the Family Law (Scotland) Act 2006 abolished the status of illegitimacy in Scotland.

2   *Adoption*

9.66   Prior to the Children Act 1975 an adopted child did not benefit as the child of his adoptive parents unless the disposition occurred after the adoption[1]. A will is regarded as made on the date of the testator's death, but that did not benefit children adopted after the testator's death. For example, a man may have made a will in 1964 leaving his estate to his wife during her lifetime and on her death to such of his grandchildren as are then living. If he died in 1968 a child *adopted* by his son in 1969 would not have qualified as a grandchild, whereas a child born to his son in 1969 would have done so. The same problem applied to inter vivos gifts for, unless the definition of 'child' was expressly extended, it did not include persons adopted after the date of the gift.

The Children Act 1975 changed this. The provisions relating to adoption were re-enacted in the Adoption Act 1976, and the Children Act 1975 was then repealed by virtue of Schedule 4 to the Children Act 1989. The Children Act 1989 made certain amendments to the Adoption Act 1976.

The Children Act 1975 (now repealed but the relevant provisions survive) provided that the adopted child qualified as a child of his adoptive parents' marriage[2]. This principle applies, subject to any contrary intention, to:

(1)   the construction of wills of testators dying on or after 1 January 1976;

(2)   intestacies occurring on or after that date; and

(3)   settlements, etc made on or after that date.

An adopted child was therefore brought more fully into the adoptive family so far as property rights are concerned. But, as a corollary, he lost any succession rights as a member of his natural family.

---

1   Adoption Act 1958, ss 16, 17.
2   Now Adoption Act 1976, s 39(1)(a)

Where a child is adopted whose natural parent has effected an insurance policy with a friendly society or an industrial assurance company for the payment on the child's death of money for funeral expenses, the rights and liabilities under the policy are transferred to the adoptive parents who will be treated as the person who took out the policy[1].

If a disposition depends on the date of birth of a child then, by section 42(2) of the Adoption Act 1976, it is to be construed as if: (1) the adopted child had been born on the date of the adoption; and (2) two or more children adopted on the same date had been born on that date in the order of their actual birth. This rule regulates, for example, the relative seniority of children where there is a provision in a will or trust 'to the eldest son of A' and A adopts a child or children.

Where it is necessary to determine for the purposes of a disposition of property effected by a trust, etc whether a woman can have a child, it is presumed (rather curiously) that, following execution of the trust, once a woman has attained the age of 55 she will not adopt a child. If she does, the child will not be treated as her child for the purposes of the instrument[2].

3   Trustees and personal representatives

9.67   Both the Adoption Act 1976 and the Legitimacy Act 1976 contain useful provisions to protect trustees and personal representatives. According to this legislation, a trustee or personal representative is not under a duty to enquire, before distributing any property, whether any adoption has been effected or revoked[3], or whether any person is illegitimate[4] if that fact could affect entitlement to the property.

However, trustees and personal representatives have to enquire whether an illegitimate person exists with an interest in the property before they distribute it. Section 20 of the Family Law Reform Act 1987 provides that trustees and personal representatives do not have the special protection provided by section 17 of the Family Law Reform Act 1969. Being similar in terms to section 7 of the Legitimacy Act 1976, section 17 of the 1969 Act enabled trustees and personal representatives to distribute property without having ascertained whether any person, who claims through such person, is or may be entitled to an interest in the property.

However, section 20 did not remove the protection given to trustees and personal representatives in section 27 of the Trustee Act 1925 which provides that as long as they advertise for claims to the property, they will be exempt from liability to all claimants except those of whom they had notice. Another means by which personal representatives can safely make a distribution is by obtaining a 'Benjamin Order' which gives personal representatives leave to distribute assets on the basis set out in the order[5]. A Benjamin Order does not require advertising or searches to have been made.

1   Adoption Act, 1976, s 49.
2   Adoption Act, 1976, s 42(5).
3   Adoption Act, 1976, s 45.
4   Legitimacy Act 1976, s 7(1).
5   *Re Benjamin* [1902] 1 Ch 723.

B   Family provision

9.68   The Inheritance (Provision for Family and Dependants) Act 1975 implemented the recommendation of the Law Commission in their second report on family property[1]. It replaced all existing legislation on family provision and gave the courts, on application to it, wider powers to order financial provision out of the estate of the deceased for his family and dependants if the court is of the opinion that under the will (or intestacy), the deceased failed to make reasonable financial provision for them.

The persons who may apply to the court are set out in section 1(1) of the 1975 Act, and are as follows:

(1)   the wife or husband of the deceased;

(2)   a former wife or former husband who has not remarried;

(3)   a child of the deceased;

(4)   any person (not a child of the deceased) who was treated by the deceased as a child of the family;

(5)   any other person who immediately before the death was being maintained wholly or partly by the deceased;

(6)   a cohabitee of the deceased for at least two years immediately before the death of the deceased (provided the deceased died after 1 January 1996). This last provision was added by section 2 of the Law Reform (Succession) Act 1995.

References to wife, husband and former wife or husband now include references to same-sex civil partners and former civil partners following the coming into force of the Civil Partnership Act 2004.

The 1975 Act lists the types of order in section 2(1) which the court may make when it decides that reasonable financial provision has not been made for the applicant and in particular specifies methods by which periodical payments may be provided out of the estate, which is explained in section 2(2). The Act also sets out the matters which the court must have regard to when deciding whether reasonable financial provision has been made for an applicant.

The property which is available for financial provision is extended by the 1975 Act to include in the estate any property or money comprised in a nomination or donatio mortis causa and, if the court so decides, the deceased's severable share of property jointly owned with others. In *Powell v Osborne*[2] the court ordered that half the proceeds of a life policy that the deceased held as a joint tenant should be paid to his wife. The deceased had left his wife to live with another woman with whom he had purchased a property on mortgage supported by the policy on their joint lives. The case effectively turned on the value of the policy

---

1   Family Provision on Death (Law Com no 61) (1971).
2   [1993] 1 FLR 797, CA.

immediately before the husband's death[1]. The policy had no surrender value immediately before death. However, it was held that as the value of the policy depended on death, its value was for these purposes the same immediately before death as on death.

9.69   The courts also have the power to review certain transactions effected by the deceased within six years before his death other than for full valuable consideration, which were made with the intention of defeating claims for family provision. The courts may require that the property comprised in those transactions be made available for financial provision[2]. This therefore makes inter vivos gifts or part-gifts vulnerable in the hands of any person for the prescribed length of time.

By section 146 of the Inheritance Tax Act 1984, any inheritance tax paid on property, which is required to be made available for family provision, may be reclaimed from Her Majesty's Revenue and Customs. Effectively, the property is added back into the deceased's estate, the order by the court is treated as a disposition by the deceased on his death, and a new calculation of the inheritance tax, if any, is made. For example, the court order may provide for property to be redistributed to the deceased's spouse in which case the new calculation will provide that no inheritance tax will be payable with respect to the redistributed property due to the spouse exemption.

'Maintenance' for which an applicant might receive financial provision under section 1 of the Inheritance (Provision for Family and Dependants) Act 1975 cannot include provision for liability for inheritance tax[3].

Failure by the deceased to discharge his responsibilities to the applicant, during his minority, did not in itself entitle the applicant to receive financial provision from the deceased's estate under the Act[4].

An application to the court cannot normally be made, without the permission of the court, after the end of six months from the date on which representation to the estate is first taken out. Personal representatives are protected from liability for distributing any part of the deceased's estate after this six-month period notwithstanding the fact that the court might make further orders or vary an existing order.

The 1975 Act does not apply in Scotland where provision for dependants is secured by the legal rights and statutory prior rights mentioned in the previous section[5]. It was, however, extended to Northern Ireland by the Inheritance (Provision for Family and Dependants) (Northern Ireland) Order 1979[6].

1   Inheritance (Provision for Family and Dependants) Act 1975, s 9.
2   Inheritance (Provision for Family and Dependants) Act 1975, s 10.
3   *Re Dennis, Dennis v Lloyd's Bank Ltd* [1981] 2 All ER 140.
4   *Harlow v National Westminster Bank plc* (1994) 138 Sol Jo LB 31, CA.
5   See **9.60–9.62**.
6   SI 1979/924.

C Income support and other state benefits

9.70   Section 134(1) of the Social Security Contributions and Benefits Act 1992 and associated regulations provide that a person is not entitled to income support if his capital exceeds £16,000[1]. Also, a claimant is treated as possessing income and capital of which he has deprived himself for the purpose of securing entitlement to income support or increasing the amount of that benefit[2]. This question tends to arise in relation to the holding of single premium or other life assurance policies where the policyholder requires nursing home care and fees are payable. The upper capital threshold is actually £21,000 where the reference is to eligibility to local authority assistance with care home fees.

The surrender value of a policy is treated as capital, however, the Income Support (General) Regulations 1987[3] provide that the surrender value can be disregarded in assessing the claimant's eligibility for income support[4]. Interesting questions arise when a claimant invests (deliberately or not) in a single premium life policy which would appear to have the effect of reducing his capital. It is not obviously a disposal of capital as the claimant would still retain ownership of the asset (ie the policy). In a case before the Social Security and Child Support Commissioners[5] the claimant had invested £10,000 into a single premium investment bond. The Commissioner decided that the surrender value was to be disregarded. However, he also decided that where a significant amount was invested then this operated as a 'deprivation' and an adjudication officer should always consider whether the investment was made for the purpose of securing income support.

SECTION 7   ASSENT AND APPROPRIATION

A   Assent

9.71   Where a policy on the life of the testator is, by his will, made the subject of a specific legacy, the policy (or the sum assured if the testator was the sole or last surviving life assured) will pass in the first instance to his executors. If, however, the policy is on the life of another person or the policy money is payable by instalments it will have a continuing existence and where the executors do not need it for purposes of administration they may vest it in the legatee.

An assent is some action which activates the gift of the property to the beneficiary concerned (even if further formalities are required to transfer the subject matter to the person entitled) and show that the executors do not require the property for administration. The beneficiary derives his title from the will; the assent

---

1   Income Support (General) Regulations 1987, SI 1987/1967 and the Social Security (Miscellaneous Amendments) (No 2) Regulations 2005, SI 2005/2465.
2   Income Support (General) Regulations 1987, SI 1987/1967, regs 42, 51, 51A; For care home fees see the National Assistance (Assessment of Resources) Regulations 1992, reg 25.
3   Income Support (General) Regulations 1987, SI 1987/1967.
4   Income Support (General) Regulations 1987, SI 1987/1967, Sch 10, para 15.
5   R(IS) 7/98.

merely makes the gift operative. Once the personal representatives have effectively assented they hold the property on trust to carry out the further requirements. Some form of documentation is often needed in order to vest the legal title to the property in the beneficiary. An assent, by itself, is often of little practical use except in relation to tangible moveable property such as jewellery, furnishings, etc. For a life policy an assignment would be required.

Assents to the vesting of personal estate such as a life policy need not be in writing or in any particular form. This is different to the vesting of a legal estate in land which is required to be in writing. Stamp duty is no longer payable on a written assent relating to non-land transactions (except for some documents relating to stocks, shares and marketable securities)[1].

B Appropriation

9.72   An appropriation of a policy may be made under section 41 of the Administration of Estates Act 1925 or under an express power in the will in or towards satisfaction of a legacy or of any other interest or share in the deceased's property.

SECTION 8   MISCELLANEOUS MATTERS

A   Surrender by personal representatives

9.73   Under section 33 of the Administration of Estates Act 1925 (as amended by the Trusts of Land and Appointment of Trustees Act 1996), the personal representatives (administrators) of an intestate hold the personal estate upon trust with the power to sell. Where the deceased leaves a will, the section has effect subject to any provisions contained in the will. It seems, accordingly, that if an application to surrender a life policy is made by personal representatives, the application can be accepted subject to production of the grant of representation.

B   Legacy of policy subject to a loan

9.74   A specific legacy of property subject to a charge passes on death subject to the charge. If, for example, a testator makes a specific bequest of a policy on which there is a policy loan, the legatee will, unless a contrary intention appears from the will, take the policy subject to the loan. He cannot require the executor to pay off the loan out of other property of the testator[2].

---

1 Finance Act 2003, s 125.
2 Administration of Estates Act 1925, s 35. See *Ross v Perrin-Hughes* [2004] EWHC 2559 (Ch), [2004] All ER (D) 159 (Nov), where a 'contrary intention' was found. This case examined the construction of a gift in a will of a property subject to a mortgage together with surrounding evidence. In this case it was held that the lease should be taken free of the mortgage.

C Donatio mortis causa

9.75   When a document which represents, or is evidence of, a chose in action (such as a life policy) is delivered by a person in contemplation of death on condition that it shall be the property of the donee only in the event of the death of the donor in the circumstances threatening him, there is a donatio mortis causa of the chose in action. The court will uphold this against the personal representatives. It is a question of fact whether the delivery of a document was made as a gift inter vivos or mortis causa, and to establish the latter there must be evidence that the donor made the gift in contemplation of death.

A life policy can be the subject of a donatio mortis causa[1]. If it is delivered by a person in contemplation of death in circumstances which indicate an intention to give, the court will presume that it was given to be retained only in the event of death and to be returned if the donor should recover. An essential part of the validity of a donatio mortis causa is that the donor should part with dominion over the policy so as to prevent it being dealt with by him in the interval between the gift and his death or recovery. It is also possible to pass certain other property by donatio mortis causa, such as chattels, but with other property (for example, land) the position is not clear.

D Mentally disordered persons

9.76   The affairs of mentally disordered persons in England are administered by the Court of Protection in accordance with the Mental Health Act 1983 and various Court of Protection Rules[2]. The Court of Protection may make orders affecting a patient's property and may appoint a receiver who must act in accordance with the court's directions. The patient cannot deal with his own property whilst the appointment is in force. Before making a payment to the receiver, the life office must be satisfied that the court has made an order authorising the receiver to give a discharge. There is a summary procedure for use where the patient's assets do not exceed a certain amount or where the patient's estate is straightforward under which an officer of the Court of Protection may be enabled to give a discharge. If the patient recovers and becomes capable of dealing with his own affairs, the receiver is discharged by a further order of the Court of Protection; the receiver's powers cease automatically on the patient's death.

It should be noted that a mentally disordered person cannot grant a valid power of attorney, and any ordinary power he may have given before his incapacity arose will cease to be effective. However, if he gave an enduring power of attorney before his incapacity, and provided the said power is registered, it will not cease to be effective[3].

The Court of Protection has power to make a settlement of the patient's

1 *Amis v Witt* (1863) 33 Beav 619.
2 SI 2001/824; SI 2001/825.
3 Enduring Powers of Attorney Act 1985, s 1.

property[1]. It may, if it considers the patient is incapable of making a valid will, direct or otherwise authorise the execution of a will or codicil for an adult patient whose affairs it manages. This is known as a 'statutory will'. A patient may make a valid will for himself in a lucid interval even if the appointment of a receiver is in force but the person propounding the validity of the will would have to show that it was made during such an interval[2].

9.77   Where a policyholder domiciled abroad becomes mentally disordered, the person able to deal with his affairs is the officer appointed by the proper court of the country of domicile. Therefore, a foreign curator or administrator of a mentally disordered person domiciled and resident abroad may sue for that person's personal estate in England.

Didisheim v London and Westminster Bank[3]

G was entitled to securities deposited with the bank. She was domiciled and resident in Belgium. She became mentally disordered and D was appointed by the Belgian court as her curator. Held, that D could give the bank a good discharge and that on general principles of private international law the English court was bound to recognise the order of the Belgian court.

Pelegrin v Coutts and Co[4]

A domiciled Frenchman resident in Paris deposited securities with Coutts and Co. He became of unsound mind and an administrator was appointed by the Civil Tribunal of the Seine with express power to receive the securities. Coutts and Co refused to act without an order of the English court. Held, that in refusing to act on the order of the French court, Coutts and Co had shown undue and unreasonable excess of caution and must bear their own costs.

At the time of writing the Mental Capacity Act 2005 had received Royal Assent (7 April 2005) but had not yet been brought into force. The Act will come into force in April 2007 and has received a lot of media attention for its 'living wills' provisions but it will also affect Enduring Powers of Attorney which will be replaced by 'Lasting Powers of Attorney' ('LPAs'). These will be wider than EPAs in that they can cover personal and healthcare issues as well as financial matters. Therefore, an attorney could be in conflict with the donor's doctors with regards to 'life sustaining treatment'.

9.78   Unlike EPAs, LPAs will only take effect upon registration with the public guardian. Therefore, donors who wish their attorneys to act on their behalf, even though they retain capacity, will either have to register the LPA or

---

1   Mental Health Act 1983, s 96(1)(d) and (e). (Repealed by the Mental Capacity Act 2005, ss 66(1)(a), (2), 67(2), Sch 7 although not yet brought into force.) See, in particular, section 18 of the Mental Capacity Act 2005 for broadly equivalent provisions.
2   *Cartwright v Cartwright* (1793) 1 Phill 90. (See *Banks v Goodfellow* (1870) LR 5 QB 549 for the test of testamentary capacity.)
3   [1900] 2 Ch 15.
4   [1915] 1 Ch 696.

complete a separate ordinary power of attorney. This seems a backward step in that some donors currently find it helpful to rely on their unregistered EPAs. For example, a donor may be in hospital or nursing home, unable for practical reasons (as opposed to mental incapacity) to attend to their affairs or simply disinclined to get involved with certain issues. EPAs can be used to ease the burden in these circumstances. However, EPAs can be open to abuse and the new system requiring registration of LPAs has the advantage of requiring a greater degree of supervision by the Public Guardianship Office. Another new safeguard is that a 'prescribed person' must certify that the donor understands the effect of the LPA and that no undue pressure has been placed upon him to sign it. This would appear to be quite an onerous obligation upon the doctor or other prescribed person.

Where someone loses mental capacity without having an EPA in place the present position is that a receiver may be appointed to manage the patient's property. The parallel role under the new act is that of the 'deputy'. The Court of Protection will have power to make decisions on behalf of the incapacitated patient and power to appoint a deputy to make decisions. The same potentially emotive issues relating to 'personal welfare' arise in this context as they do with LPAs, although the code of practice states that such powers should only be delegated to deputies in extreme circumstances.

CHAPTER 10

Assignments

SUMMARY

SECTION I   ASSIGNMENTS GENERALLY

10.1   An assignment of a life policy is a document or action which is effective to transfer the ownership of a policy from one person or persons to another or others. Assignments may be made for a variety of reasons, including:

- sale or exchange;

- gift or voluntary transfer;

- trust or settlement, transferring the policy to trustees;

- transfer to beneficiaries in pursuance of the trusts;

- mortgage; transfer of mortgage; or reassignment on repayment;

- assignment to a trustee for the benefit of creditors; or

- assignments by operation of law (eg on insolvency).

Before the Policies of Assurance Act 1867 (see Appendix 2), assignments of life policies were not recognised at law. The power to discharge the life office on payment or to sue on it in default was vested in the original policyholder. He had made the contract and could give a good discharge even if he had later made an assignment. But the courts of equity recognised assignments and would assist an assignee by permitting him to join the assignor as plaintiff or, if he refused, as defendant in an action brought by the assignee. Policies of assurance were accordingly said to be assignable in equity, with the effect that the assignee could acquire the *beneficial* interest but not the *right to sue without joining the assignor*. Additionally, all choses in action (not limited to life policies[1]) became assignable at law in 1873, by virtue of section 25(6) of the Judicature Act 1873 (re-enacted as section 136 of the Law of Property Act 1925).

To constitute a legal assignment under the Policies of Assurance Act 1867 or the Law of Property Act 1925, certain conditions laid down by those statutes need to be complied with. Where such conditions are not satisfied, it is still possible that there will be an equitable assignment.

Although a life office may get a legal discharge from an assignee following a legal assignment under the 1925 Act, the assignee will still be subject to any equities which have priority. However, an assignment under the 1867 Act is, unlike the 1925 Act, subject to that person also being the person entitled in equity to the proceeds of the policy.

As a general rule where there are competing claims, either equitable or legal, the person entitled will be the first assignee, without knowledge (constructive or actual) of prior equitable interests, to serve notice on the life office[2]. The main benefit of a legal assignment is therefore the procedural and practical advantages of not having to join the assignor into the proceedings or involve him in any dealings with the life office.

SECTION 2 LEGAL ASSIGNMENTS

A The Policies of Assurance Act 1867

10.2 The Policies of Assurance Act 1867 (set out at Appendix 2) provides that an assignee can sue in his own name if:

(1) as a result of assignment or other derivative title he becomes entitled to a policy of life assurance and possesses at the time the action is brought the right in equity to receive[3] and the right to give a valid discharge to the assurance company for the policy moneys (ie it is a pre-condition that he be beneficially entitled to them at the time of the claim, the purpose being to ensure that the assignee under this Act does not obtain a better title than he would have done as an equitable assignee before the Act);

---

1 *Re Moore* (1878) 8 Ch D 519.
2 See **10.36**.
3 *Scottish Amicable Life Assurance Society v Fuller* (1867) IR 2 Eq 53.

(2)   he has obtained an assignment, either by endorsement on the policy or by separate instrument, in the words or to the effect as set out in the Schedule to the Act[1]; and

(3)   written notice of the assignment has been given to the assurance company.

Notice must be given to the life office's principal place of business, or if more than one, at any one of them in England, Scotland or Ireland. Life offices must state in every policy their principal place of business at which notices of assignment may be given.

Under the 1867 Act, a policy of life assurance is defined as 'any instrument by which the payment of moneys, by or out of the funds of an assurance company, on the happening of any contingency depending on the duration of human life, is assured or secured'.

Assignments under the 1867 Act must be in, or to the effect of, the prescribed wording but it is not necessary to follow that wording precisely. It is not necessary for the assignment to be by deed (although it usually is). They need not be for consideration and the assignee cannot get priority over a prior assignee who has given notice to the life office. This can cause difficulties for the life office in making payment out as the life office cannot get a legal discharge if there is a prior equitable assignee. For this reason assignment under the Law of Property Act 1925 may be preferable since, although such assignments are 'subject to equities. . .', this is not a precondition of it being a legal assignment[2].

In addition, the person giving notice may require the assurance company to deliver a written acknowledgement of receipt of notice (on payment of a fee not exceeding 25p)[3].

See Chapter 12 for taxation effects of assignments for consideration.

B   The Law of Property Act 1925

10.3   Section 136 of the Law of Property Act 1925, re-enacting section 25(6) of the Judicature Act 1873, provides a method for assigning the legal title to 'debts and things in action'. A policy of life assurance (or, more correctly, the right to receive payment under a policy) is a chose or 'thing' in action. The provisions of section 136 are as follows:

'(1) Any absolute assignment by writing under the hand of the assignor (not purporting to be by way of charge only) of any debt or other legal thing in action of which express notice in writing has been given to the debtor, trustee or other person from whom the assignor would have been entitled to claim such debt or thing in action, is effectual in law (subject to equities having priority over the right of the assignee) to pass and transfer from the date of such notice:

(a)   the legal right to such debt or thing in action;

---

1   See Section 4A, **10.7**.
2   See, Priority, **10.38**.
3   Section 6.

(b)   all legal and other remedies for the same; and

(c)   the power to give a good discharge for the same without the concurrence of the assignor.

Provided that, if the debtor, trustee or other person liable in respect of such debt or thing in action has notice:

(a)   that the assignment is disputed by the assignor or any person claiming under him; or

(b)   of any other opposing or conflicting claims to such debt or thing in action;

he may, if he thinks fit, either call upon the persons making claim thereto to interplead concerning the same, or pay the debt or other thing in action into court under the provisions of the Trustee Act 1925.'

Effect of the section compared to the Policies of Assurance Act 1867. Under both Acts the assignee takes subject to any existing equities. But unlike the 1867 Act, the operation of section 136 is not dependent on the assignee having the right in equity, at the time an action is brought, to receive the policy money. All that is necessary is an absolute assignment and express notice in writing. Once an absolute written assignment under the Law of Property Act 1925 has been obtained by an assignee and he has given notice then, provided he is the first assignee so to do, he obtains the right to sue at law (even if there is a prior equitable assignment). The life office can obtain a legal discharge from the legal assignee in these circumstances even if it has notice of the previous equitable assignment. This is not the case with an assignment under the 1867 Act.

Is it possible to have a legal assignment of a life policy under both Acts at the same time? The answer is thought to be yes but the matter is not entirely free from doubt. The problem stems from the fact that the Law of Property Act 1925 provides that section 136 'does not affect the provisions of the Policies of Assurance Act 1867'[1]. It is at least arguable, therefore, that section 136 was only intended to cover choses in action other than life policies. Although in practice the substance of an assignee's interest in the policy will rarely depend on whether or not the assignment is under the 1867 Act or the 1925 Act, it does mean that the life office may not get a good legal discharge without joining the assignor under the 1867 Act. An alternative view is that section 136(2) is making it clear that the 1867 Act continues in force providing another remedy for the assignee and that it was not impliedly repealed by the 1925 Act. From the life office's point of view, the safest course in such circumstances is not to pay out on the policy unless the assignee can make out a good title under the Policies of Assurance Act 1867 (ie he must have the right in equity to receive the policy moneys). If the assignment is (unusually) expressly subject only to section 136 of the Law of Property Act 1925 then this would not be necessary.

In practice assignments documents do not tend to distinguish whether they are being made under the 1867 Act or under the 1925 Act.

---

1   Section 136(2).

SECTION 3   EQUITABLE ASSIGNMENTS

A   General

10.4   The 1867 and 1925 Acts did not affect the validity of equitable assignments and 'whether or not what has been done in any particular transaction amounts to an equitable assignment is a matter of inference from the facts and documents concerned'[1]. So an oral assignment would be possible but may have evidential problems[2]. An assignment or agreement to assign is binding as between the parties without notice to the life office but notice to the life office can be crucial for priority purposes[3]. A direction by the policyholder to the life office to pay the policy moneys to a third party is (without more) merely a revocable mandate, at any rate until the policyholder's intention to give that third party the benefit of the policy has been conveyed to him[4]. The mere delivery (or deposit) of a policy for valuable consideration is an equitable assignment, even without a memorandum of deposit or notice to the life office[5]. An example of this is the deposit of the policy with a bank or building society as security.

There is also authority for mere delivery (without consideration) being sufficient but the position is not entirely clear[6]. The precise circumstances surrounding the delivery would therefore be important[7]. Mere physical possession of the policy document would not in itself give the holder any rights as the bank (or other holder) may be holding it for a variety of reasons other than as security.

Unlike a legal assignment it is possible to assign part of a life policy by an equitable assignment.

The essential requirement is that the intention of the assignor to assign the rights in question should be clear. If the assignment is in writing, no particular form of words is necessary[8].

Where there has not been a legal assignment but the assignee has given *consideration*, equity will (subject to the rules on priority)[9] assist him to perfect his title against third parties, even though he may not have obtained a formal assignment.

If, however, a *voluntary* assignee seeks the support of equity, he will succeed only where:

(1)   the assignment is complete as between assignor and assignee, ie everything necessary has been done by the assignor to make a present transfer and render the assignment binding (even if there remains something to be done by the assignee (for example, give notice))[10]; or

1   Per Cohen LJ in *IRC v EMI Ltd* [1949] 1 All ER 120, CA; affd sub nom *EMI v IRC Ltd* [1950] 2 All ER 261, HL.
2   *Brandt's Sons & Co v Dunlop Rubber Co Ltd* [1905] AC 454.
3   See **10.36**.
4   *Re Williams, Williams v Ball* [1917] 1 Ch 1.
5   *Maughan v Ridley* (1868) 8 LT 309.
6   *Cook v Black* (1842) 1 Hare 390 cf *Howes v Prudential Assurance Co* (1883) 49 LT 133.
7   *Chapman v Chapman* (1851) 13 Beav 308.
8   *Brandt's Sons & Co v Dunlop Rubber Co Ltd* [1905] AC 454.
9   See further Section 6, **10.36**.
10   *Milroy v Lord* (1862) 4 De G F & J 264 at p 274, per Turner LJ.

(2)   the assignor has constituted himself as trustee for the assignee.

10.5   The assignee will not, however, succeed if there is only an agreement or intention to assign in the future as opposed to a present unconditional intention to transfer the policy, unless there is consideration for the promise to assign.

> *Re Williams, Williams v Ball*[1]
>
> The policyholder gave his housekeeper a policy with the following signed endorsement: 'I authorise X to draw this insurance in the event of my predeceasing her'. Held, that the assignment was inoperative as it contained no present words of gift and was without consideration and conditions; and it did not take effect as a testamentary disposition because it was not executed as such.

> *Re Westerton, Public Trustee v Gray*[2]
>
> A man handed to his landlady an envelope in which were enclosed a bank deposit receipt, a signed order directing the bank to pay to her, and a letter addressed to her stating that in view of her kindness he desired to make some return by giving her the amount on deposit. Held, that there was a valid and complete gift by way of assignment.

In relation to (1) above it is possible to construe everything necessary to transfer title to a life policy as requiring a valid legal assignment. A parallel may be drawn with cases dealing with the transfer of company shares and the distinction between tasks to be completed by the assignor and those which are outside his control (eg directors of the company actually registering the shares subject to the transfer, in the name of the transferee)[3]. Failure to serve notice (and therefore no valid legal assignment) does not prevent the assignment being a valid equitable assignment[4]. The principle has been developed further in *Pennington v Waine*[5] where it was held that for an equitable assignment of shares by way of gift, although delivery of the share transfer form was generally thought to be required it could be dispensed with in some circumstances. In this case there was a clear finding that the donor intended to make an immediate gift. The intended recipient had been informed of it and it would have been unconscionable for the donor to have recalled the gift once the recipient had signed the prescribed form of consent to act as a director. In the circumstances delivery of the share transfer form before the donor's death was unnecessary so far as perfection of the gift was concerned. In any event applying the principle that a benevolent construction should be placed upon words of gift in order to give effect to the donor's clear wishes, the words used by the company's auditor in a letter to the recipient should be construed as meaning that the donor (and the company's auditor through her) had become agents for the purpose of submitting the share transfer to the company.

In the absence of a better right in equity the debtor cannot refuse to pay an

1   [1917] 1 Ch 1.
2   [1919] 2 Ch 104.
3   See *Re Rose* [1952] Ch 499.
4   *Holt v Heatherfield Trust Ltd* [1942] 2 KB 1.
5   [2002] EWCA Civ 227.

assignee who is a volunteer merely on the grounds of lack of consideration[1]. If the debtor does pay to such an assignee, the assignor will be unable to sue the debtor as the assignment as between the assignor and assignee was complete.

Express notice of the equitable assignment should be given to the life office so that it is in no doubt as to the situation. Otherwise the life office is entitled to pay the assignor and thereby obtain a discharge[2]. Whether or not notice is given to the life office does not affect the position between the assignee and assignor[3]

The effect of an equitable assignment is that the assignee acquires the beneficial interest in the insurance but not the right to sue. He will have to sue with the assignor as co-claimant with his consent or join him as a co-defendant if he does not consent.

B   Scotland

10.6   There was never a separate equity jurisdiction in Scotland, law and equity having always been administered together by the same courts. Although the Policies of Assurance Act 1867 (though not the Law of Property Act 1925) applies to Scotland, it was not required there to give recognition at law to assignments of life policies. The Transmission of Moveable Property (Scotland) Act 1862 already applied to assignments of policies issued by Scottish companies whether the policyholder was resident in Scotland or not. The provisions of the Policies of Assurance Act 1867 now apply to provide an alternative form of assignment.

SECTION 4   FORM OF ASSIGNMENT

A   Form of legal assignments

10.7   An assignment may be under hand (by just writing) or made by deed. The use of the word 'assign' is not necessary. Any words indicating assignment, for example, 'transfer', 'convey', or 'make over', will suffice. It is, however, for the reasons mentioned above, important to distinguish between a legal assignment and an equitable assignment and indeed, it will usually be the form of the assignment which determines its nature.

The requirement in the Policies of Assurance Act 1867 is that there be a written assignment either endorsed on the policy or by separate instrument in the words or to the effect set out in the Schedule to the Act[4]. Stamping is no longer required[5].

The prescribed wording is as follows:

1   *Walker v Bradford Old Bank* (1884) 12 QBD 511.
2   See **10.36**.
3   *Fortescue v Barnett* (1834) 3 My & K 36.
4   Policies of Assurance Act 1867, s 5.
5   Finance Act 2003, s 125.

'I, AB of, &c in consideration of, &c do hereby assign unto CD of, &c, his Executors, Administrators and Assigns, the [within] Policy of Assurance granted, &c [here describe the Policy]. In witness, &c.'

Despite the brevity of this form, the wording of an assignment of a policy is usually expanded and, for example, expressed to assign not just the policy but all sums assured by or to become payable under or by virtue of it and all benefits and advantages of the policy as well. Any benefit by way of bonus or otherwise will in any event pass under the assignment unless express terms are used to exclude it[1]. This would include policies effected in substitution for the assigned policy under an option in the original policy[2]. Also, where the policyholder assigned as a gift a policy on his life for a one-year term, and later extended the policy and died during the extended term, it is presumed that the extension was effected for the benefit of the assignee who was entitled to claim the whole of the policy moneys[3].

Although section 136 of the Law of Property Act 1925 does not provide a pre-scribed wording, it states that the assignment must be under the hand of the assignor and notice must be given to the life office. It need not be in the form of a deed (although in practice normally would be). It also states that it must be an absolute assignment of the chose in action and not merely an assignment by way of charge only. It is submitted that due to the nature of the right under the Policies of Assurance Act 1867 (ie the requirement of being beneficially entitled to receive the policy moneys), an absolute assignment is also implicitly required by that Act as well[4].

To constitute an absolute assignment, the instrument must express a clear and final intention to make an immediate and outright transfer of the whole policy[5]. An assignment subject to a condition for defeasance and revesting in the assignor upon the happening of a future event, and an assignment subject to a condition precedent, or an agreement to assign at a future date (even if supported by con-sideration)[6] do not therefore constitute valid legal assignments. An assignment expressed to be as security does not necessarily prevent the assignment being absolute. However, if it is combined with conditions as to defeasance, it will not be absolute. An assignment by way of charge would not be an absolute assign-ment as it does not transfer any property[7]. By way of contrast an assignment by way of mortgage may, however, be absolute if there is a provision, express or implied, for reassignment on repayment of all outstanding moneys[8]. The govern-ing principle is that the life office must not be placed in a position of uncertainty as to the person to whom it should pay the money[9]. Therefore, with a mortgage

1   *Gilly v Burley* (1856) 22 Beav 619.
2   *Nesbitt v Berridge* (1864) 10 Jur (NS) 53.
3   *Royal Exchange Assurance v Hope* [1928] Ch 179.
4   *Re Williams, Williams v Ball* [1917] 1 Ch 1 at p 4, per Astbury J.
5   *Williams v Atlantic Assurance Co Ltd* [1933] 1 KB 81.
6   *Spencer v Clarke* (1878) 9 Ch D 137.
7   *Tancred v Delagoa Bay Railway Co* (1889) 23 QBD 239.
8   See *Tancred v Delagoa Bay Railway Co* (1889) 23 QBD 239 and *Durham Bros v Robertson* [1898] 1 QB 765.
9   *Durham Bros v Robertson* [1898] 1 QB 765.

the proviso as to reassignment is important because it enables the life office to know where the title to the policy is, without knowing the state of the borrowings on which the policy is secured.

It is generally considered that part of a policy cannot be the subject of a valid *legal* assignment.

> *Re Steel Wing Co Ltd*[1]
>
> A creditor purported to assign part of a debt. Held, that the assignment would not pass the right to sue for that portion of the debt under the Judicature Act 1873, but that it would operate in equity.

An assignment of one segment or sub-policy under a contract issued as separate policies (sometimes known as a 'cluster' policy) would not be treated as an assignment of part of a policy, even where the policy is subject to certain conditions which apply across all the segments (for example, the investment funds in which the segments are invested). In such cases the assignee is free to encash the whole segment and there is no uncertainty from the life office's point of view as to the person entitled to payment.

I   Joint tenancy and tenancy in common

10.8   Generally, in law, personal property (as opposed to real property) may only be held subject to a 'joint tenancy'. In equity both a 'tenancy in common' and a joint tenancy may exist. On the death of one joint tenant the beneficial interest passes to the survivors or survivor of the joint tenants and on the death of the last survivor to his personal representatives. On the death of a tenant in common his share passes to his personal representatives and not to the surviving tenants. In certain cases equity will presume a tenancy in common of the beneficial interest, eg where property is purchased by two persons with money provided in unequal shares, mortgages made to two persons jointly[2] and where the property is acquired by business partners.

As indicated above, at law (but not in equity) a chose in action can only be owned jointly and not in common. In the case of *McKerrell, McKerrell v Gowans*[3] which related to an assignment of a policy held jointly by a husband and wife, it was said 'whatever else the assignment by the husband may have been it did not affect the right of the wife as survivor to sue at law on the policy'. Accordingly, there was no legal assignment under the Judicature Act 1873 (the predecessor of section 136 of the Law of Property Act 1925).

Similarly, it has been submitted[4] that section 136(1) of the Law of Property Act 1925 (which requires an absolute assignment of the whole chose in action) apparently does not permit one joint owner to effect a severance of the legal title by assigning his interest to the other joint tenant. To enable the life office to obtain a legal discharge, the assignment would have to be from both joint owners

1   [1921] 1 Ch 349.
2   *Morley v Bird* (1798) 3 Ves 629, 631 per Arden, MR.
3   *McKerrell, McKerrell v Gowans* [1912] 2 Ch 648 at 653.
4   See 35 *Halsbury's Laws* (4th edn Reissue) para 1245, n 5.

to the sole future owner. In practice, an assignment by one joint owner to the other of the former's interest in the policy should create a valid equitable assignment. Provided there are no existing or prior interests of which the assignee has knowledge, or which have been notified to the life office, then the assignee's interest is well established. However, in order to get around the inability of a person without the legal title to give a good discharge and in the absence of the legal owner, a life office may ask for an indemnity before it pays out to a person with only the equitable title to the policy.

2   Equity

10.9   No special form of words or writing is necessary to pass equitable rights to the proceeds of a policy so long as the intention of the parties that those rights should pass is clear.

B   Assignments by way of sale

I   Assignments on sale[1]

10.10   Where a policy is sold, the consideration is usually the payment of money. The vendor should be required to prove his title to the purchaser.

The purchaser should ask the life office what notices have been received and whether all premiums due have been paid. If he cannot obtain possession of all the earlier documents he should require an acknowledgement of his right to production, which may be incorporated in the assignment itself or in a separate form. The vendor may assign with full title guarantee, with limited title guarantee or with no title guarantee although often the assignment is silent in this respect[2]. The assignment, which in practice is usually made by deed, should contain a receipt for the purchase money. The purchaser should serve notice on the life office.

Ideally, the purchaser should make arrangements to be kept in touch with the life assured, so that if the life assured dies he can claim under the policy. In practice this may not be easy or practical.

The traded life policy market, in particular endowment policies, has grown enormously. Today, there are numerous companies who have established themselves as intermediaries for sellers and buyers and the sale of such policies is regulated under the Conduct of Business Sourcebook (COB 6.5.44R). Generally speaking, the prices obtained by the sale of life policies comfortably exceed the surrender values offered by the life office. There are also companies who conduct auctions of life policies.

---

1   This can be more advantageous than surrendering the policy particularly for with-profits endowments where a large amount of the return would normally be derived from terminal bonuses.
2   See Chapter 1 for implied covenants under the to Law of Property (Miscellaneous Provisions) Act 1994.

2   Sale of policy subject to mortgage

10.11   Where a vendor sells a policy subject to a mortgage all that the purchaser obtains is the equity of redemption and the price will be adjusted accordingly.

3   Void and voidable assignments

10.12   The assignment of a policy, or an agreement to assign, where without the knowledge of the contracting parties the life assured is already dead, is void ab initio.

> *Scott v Coulson*[1]
>
> C purchased from S a policy on the life of D, and it was assigned to him. It was subsequently discovered that at the date of the contract and unknown to both parties, D had already died. Held, the contract was void on the ground of mutual mistake and must be set aside.

A sale or gift of a life policy is voidable and may be set aside by the court on the ground of misrepresentation, even if innocent[2], duress, or undue influence, and this should be borne in mind, for example, if on examination of an assignment, the consideration recited appears to be grossly inadequate.

There are certain cases of fiduciary relationship where, unless the contrary be shown, the court will *presume* an undue influence. For example, the relationship between trustee and beneficiary; solicitor and client; doctor and patient; parent and child; guardian and ward; and also husband and wife. In the context of this type of relationship there is no need to produce evidence to show that actual undue influence was exerted. This is presumed unless the contrary is shown.

C   Assignments for nominal consideration

10.13   Sometimes the assignment may be expressed to be for nominal consideration even though it does not represent the true consideration. This may be the case where in fact no consideration passes hands but there is a concern that if the assignment is not in the form of a deed, and is expressed to be for nil consideration, it would not be binding on the parties. However, no consideration need be mentioned in the assignment, nor indeed is consideration necessary[3].

D   Assignments by way of gift

10.14   A gift of a policy should be described as such on the face of the instrument, so that no doubt can arise that the assignor intends to pass the beneficial

---

1   [1903] 2 Ch 249.
2   Misrepresentation Act 1967.
3   *Re Westerton, Public Trustee v Gray* [1919] 2 Ch 104.

interest. Unless the intention to make a gift is clear, there may be a presumption that the donee holds the policy on a resulting trust for the donor.

Where the donee is the wife or a near relative of the donor, the assignment is sometimes expressed to be in consideration of natural love and affection, although this practice largely seems to have died out. A gift or settlement made before and in consideration of marriage is made for value (ie it is not a 'gift')[1], as is one made after marriage if it is made in pursuance of a binding ante-nuptial agreement.

If the policy is subject to a mortgage the deed should, unless the contrary be intended, provide that, as between the assignor and the assignee, the assignee shall be liable for the repayment of the mortgage debt, ie so the gift in effect is only of the amount in excess of the mortgage debt. This is advisable in the light of the decision in the following case:

> *Re Best, Parker v Best*[2]
>
> B mortgaged a policy to the life office, entering into the usual covenant to repay the mortgage. He later assigned the policy as a gift to his wife, but the deed did not refer to the mortgage. The life office deducted the mortgage debt from the claim. Held, that the widow must be reimbursed by the executors of the husband.

An assignment of a policy made for an *illegal* consideration is not enforceable against the assignor. Also, where an assignment is made otherwise than for full consideration in the five years preceding the petition for an assignor's bankruptcy or commencement of winding up, it may be capable of being reversed by the trustee in bankruptcy or liquidator.

E Assignments made abroad

10.15 Where there is a foreign element to an assignment the question as to which country's law (the 'proper law') governs the assignment between assignor and assignee, or between two assignees with conflicting claims, will be determined by the Contracts (Applicable Law) Act 1990 which gives statutory force in the UK to certain international conventions on Conflicts of Laws. The position is, however, similar to the common law rules of private international law which it replaced.

A distinction has to be drawn between the law which governs the assignment and the law of the life policy itself. Where the question is the liability of the life office to be sued in the name of the assignee, or whether the latter can give a discharge to the life office, the rights of the assignee will be determined according to the proper law of the original contract. For a UK insurer, where the policyholder is habitually resident in a member state of the EU, this is determined in accordance with the Financial Services and Markets Act 2000 (Law Applicable to Contracts of Insurance) Regulations 2001, SI 2001/2635, implementing the relevant parts of the Second and Third Life Directives (now the Consolidated

---

1 *Moore v Woolsey* (1854) 4 E & B 243.
2 [1924] 1 Ch 42.

Life Directive)[1]. Subject to any choice of law the proper law would normally be the law of the country in which the policyholder has his habitual residence. The term 'habitual residence' is defined in the Glossary to the FSA Handbook as (where the policyholder is an individual) 'the address given by the policyholder as his residence if it reasonably appears to be a residential address and there is no evidence to the contrary'. In relation to non-EU policyholders the provisions of the Contracts (Applicable Law) Act 1990 would apply in the absence of a choice of law.

In relation to the law of the assignment, the 1990 Act essentially provides that the law applicable to the assignment is the law chosen by the parties. This choice may either be expressly specified in the assignment (which is not common) or implied by the circumstances of the case. It also provides that the parties may agree to change the law governing the assignment. Where no choice has been made, the law applicable to the assignment is the law of the country with which the assignment has the closest connection. There is a presumption that the assignment is most closely connected with the country where the assignor has his habitual residence.

Voluntary assignment is specifically provided for by Schedule 1 to the 1990 Act (Article 12 of the Rome Convention). The law governing the right to which the assignment relates shall determine its assignability, the relationship between the assignee and debtor (eg the life office) and any question whether the debtor's obligations have been discharged[2].

It is interesting to note that Article 1, paragraph 3 specifically excludes contracts of insurance from the application of Schedule 1 although contracts of reinsurance are specifically included by virtue of paragraph 4.

10.16   The following cases illustrate the operation of the application of the proper law of the assignment:

Lee v Abdy[3]

A policy with an English life office was effected by a man domiciled in the Cape of Good Hope and was subsequently assigned by him to his wife. Under the law of the Cape, a husband could not assign a policy to his wife. Held, that the assignment was a nullity.

Pender v Commercial Bank of Scotland Ltd[4]

A husband domiciled in Scotland effected with an English life office a policy on his life under the Married Women's Property Act 1882 for the benefit of his wife. The wife mortgaged her interest in it to a Scottish bank. Under English law she could validly do this but she could not do so under the law of Scotland. Held, that her capacity must be determined by the law of Scotland and that the mortgage was invalid.

1   Second Life Directive; Council Directive 90/619; Third Life Directive; Council Directive 92/96; Consolidating Life Directive of 5 November 2002 (No 2002/83/EC).
2   See *Raiffeisen Zentralbank osterreich AG v Five Star General Trading LLC and others* [2001] EWCA Civ 68, CA.
3   (1886) 17 QBD 309.
4   1940 SLT 306.

Scottish Provident Institution v Cohen & Co[1]

A Scottish life office issued a life policy in Scotland to a domiciled Scotsman. Afterwards, then being resident in England, he deposited the policy with a domiciled Englishman as security for an advance, notice being given to the office. The policyholder was made bankrupt in Scotland. The trustee raised the question as to whether the policy should not vest in him. It was held that, although under the law of Scotland the deposit would not have been a good assignment, in view of the fact that the transaction was completed in England the law of England would apply, and the deposit was good (as an equitable assignment) against the trustee acting for the general creditors in Scotland[2].

Conversely, an assignee whose assignment is valid by foreign law, but does not entitle him to give a discharge in England, may nevertheless have an equitable right which will be recognised by English law.

F   Miscellaneous

1   Examination of title

10.17   Before making any payment under a policy, or agreeing to any variation in the terms of a policy or where the policyholder seeks to exercise an option under the policy (or any other dealings with the policy are proposed), the life office must examine title to ascertain the person or persons entitled to give a discharge for the amount payable or undertake any other dealings with the policy. This may be the grantee(s) (the original contracting party or parties), or persons deriving title from the grantee(s) either by assignment or by operation of law (eg his personal representatives or trustee in bankruptcy).

In the absence of any notice affecting the policy or an interest in it, the person or persons who effected the policy can enforce it or deal with it with the consent of the life office where necessary.

2   Payment to nominee

10.18   It is possible that a good discharge can be given by persons other than the original contracting parties or persons deriving title under them. If it is an essential term of the policy that payment shall be made to a specified third party, then the life office is entitled to carry out the precise terms of the contract. It follows that a good discharge can be obtained by paying the third party although the right to sue may remain with the policyholder or his personal representatives. However, the payment to the third party cannot be intercepted by the policyholder[3]. The principle of 'privity of contract' was fundamentally affected by the

---

1   (1888) 16 R (Ct of Sess) 112.
2   It would appear that a mere deposit of the policy is not sufficient in England without a memorandum in writing to effect an assignment in England. See *United Bank of Kuwait plc v Sahib* (1994) Times, 7 July; [1997] Ch 107, [1996] 3 All ER 215, CA.
3   *Re Schebsman, ex p Official Receiver, Trustee v Cargo Superintendents (London) Ltd* [1944] Ch 83.

Contracts (Rights of Third Parties) Act 1999 so that the third party may now have an enforceable right of his own unless the effect of this Act is excluded.

In most cases the correct interpretation of the contract will be that payment is to be made to the named person. However, it is always safer to obtain an authority from the policyholder or his personal representatives for the payment to be made to the named person and an acknowledgement that such a payment will discharge the contract.

Where a policy contained a proviso that the receipt of the husband or wife or certain relatives of the policyholder was a good discharge, it was held that the proviso was an integral part of the contract and was not repugnant to the preceding obligation to pay to the executors or administrators of the policyholder. The payment by the life office to a relative without knowledge that a grant of representation had been taken out must be accepted in satisfaction of their obligation in view of the express provision in the policy that such payment was conclusive evidence that all demands against the life office had been fully satisfied. However, this did not mean that any person other than the executors could actually enforce the contract[1].

Life offices are sometimes placed in a difficult position when the policyholder purports to make a 'nomination' of a policy. As such, a nomination in connection with a life policy is not recognised under English law (although it is under certain continental and other systems of law). The nomination may amount to a declaration of trust under section 11 of the Married Women's Property Act 1882 or otherwise (see Chapter 9 for the interpretation of wordings which have been held to create a trust). Also, as mentioned above, it could be a contractual term in that A may have agreed with B to make payment to C (potentially for C's own benefit in view of the Contracts (Rights of Third Parties) Act 1999 where the Act has not been expressly excluded). The case of *Gold v Hill*[2] generated considerable interest in view of the references to 'nominations' in connection with a life policy. However, it was held that the 'nomination' had the effect of establishing a secret trust at the time of death rather than establishing that a nomination, as such, was an effective means of transferring the benefits of a life policy. In addition, it was also held that it was not a disposition of an equitable interest and so section 53 of the Law of Property Act 1925 did not need to be complied with.

The sum payable under certain Friendly Society policies may be transferred by nomination under section 66 of the Friendly Societies Act 1974 provided the sum in question does not exceed £5,000.

3 Enjoyment of benefit

10.19 The person or persons entitled to sue and to receive the policy moneys will not, of course, necessarily be entitled to enjoy them beneficially. The claim may, for example, be made by executors, whose duty it is to collect the policy moneys and to deal with it in accordance with the will of the testator, or by

---

1 *O'Reilly v Prudential Assurance Co Ltd* [1934] All ER Rep 672.
2 TLR 24/8/98: (1999) 1 FLR 54; [1998] Fam Law 664, 142 Sol Jo LB 226. Applied in *Beddar and others v Prestidge* [2001] All ER (D) 254.

trustees who will deal with it in accordance with the instrument constituting the trusts and general trust law.

4   Equitable interests

10.20   The right to sue and to receive the policy moneys is not affected by equitable interests under wills, trusts and mortgages which are protected by executors, trustees or mortgagees. Such interests concern the life office only if it has notice that the executors, trustees or mortgagees have exceeded or propose to exceed their powers or have committed or propose to commit a breach of trust. The life office may, however, be affected by having notice of equitable interests not otherwise protected and it cannot disregard them. Normally, in such circumstances the life office should seek a discharge from all interested (or potentially interested) parties.

5   Policy provision that policy cannot be assigned

10.21   It is possible for the policyholder and the life office to agree that the policy is to be non-assignable with the result that any purported assignment is not binding. However, it may still be possible for an equitable assignment or declaration of trust to be effected[1].

SECTION 5   NOTICE

A   Summary of reasons for service of notice

10.22   Service of notice is required for four main reasons:

(1)   In the case of a legal assignment to give the assignee the right to sue at law in his own name under the Policies of Assurance Act 1867, or under the Law of Property Act 1925.

(2)   To bind the life office and to prevent it from paying to the assignor.

(3)   To acquire, in the case of an assignee for value, priority over earlier equities of which notice has not been served on the life office and which are unknown to the assignee.

(4)   To preserve priority against interests subsequently acquired.

B   Notice to agents

10.23   If notice is given to an authorised agent it is as good as notice to the life office itself. However, policy documents often contain a condition that agents of

---

1   *Re Turcan* (1889) 40 Ch D.

the company are not permitted to accept notice of any assignment and that assignment can only be given at the company's head office. In including such a provision the life office predominantly has in mind the representatives (or 'tied agents') of the life office. As a result of such a provision the notice given to such an agent would not constitute a formal notice and priority (where relevant) would not be acquired as a result. However, if the agent actually communicates the notice to head office this could still constitute informal notice to the life office.

C Notice under the Policies of Assurance Act 1867

1 Effect of the Act

10.24 The Policies of Assurance Act 1867 enables an assignee to sue in his own name. The 1867 Act is concerned only with the determination of the person to whom the life office may pay. It does *not* affect the *priorities* of equitable interests in the policy money although it requires the assignee to have 'the right in equity to receive' the policy moneys.

The Act gives the assignee the right to sue in his own name, provided that:

(1) He has the right in equity to receive the policy money and to give an effectual discharge.

(2) He has a written assignment in the appropriate form.

(3) A written notice of the date and 'purport' of the assignment has been given to the life office[1].

2 Notice

10.25 The provisions of the 1867 Act with regard to notice are as follows:

(1) A written notice of the date and purport of the assignment must be given to the assurance company at its principal place of business, for the time being, or, if it has two or more principal places of business, then at one of those principal places.

(2) The assurance company must on every policy specify the place or principal places of business at which notices may be given.

(3) The assurance company must, upon payment of a fee not exceeding 25p, give in writing, under the hand of its manager, secretary, treasurer or other principal officer, an acknowledgment of the receipt of the notice.

The Act does not indicate whether more than one fee of 25p can be charged if the notice affects more than one policy or deed. In practice, life offices do not generally make any charges for acknowledgment of receipt of notice.

---

1 Policies of Assurance Act 1867, ss 1, 3 and 5.

The Policies of Assurance Act 1867 provides that a bona fide payment made by a life office before receipt of notice shall be as valid against the assignee giving notice as if the Act had not been passed. Therefore, notice and consequently legal title to the policy will only be complete on receipt by the life office of the notice.

D Notice under the Law of Property Act 1925

1 Debts and choses in action

10.26 Section 136[1] of the Law of Property Act 1925 provides that express notice in writing must be given, but there are no provisions on the subject of acknowledgement of notice. Without notice there can be no assignment under section 136 although it may still amount to an equitable assignment.

2 Content of notice

10.27 The production of the assignment instrument itself is service of notice, as the document is in writing (and for the purposes of the 1867 Act its date and purport are shown). In one case[2] the Court of Appeal held that a letter referring to an assignment of a debt but without giving any date and wrongly stating that notice had previously been given was, nevertheless, itself a sufficient notice of assignment. However, if a notice identifies a document by its date, and the date is wrong, the notice is bad. Denning LJ in *W F Harrison & Co v Burke*[3] (approving an earlier case of *Stanley v English Fibres Industries Ltd*[4]) declared that it was clear from section 136(1) of the Law of Property Act 1925 that notice in writing was 'an essential part of the transfer of title to the debt and, as such, the requirements of the Act must be strictly complied with, and notice itself . . . must be strictly accurate – accurate in particular in regard to the date which is given for the assignment'. It is possible that this may have amounted to an equitable assignment.

3 Provisions as to notice

10.28 Section 196 of the 1925 Act provides that:

(1) Any notice required to be served or given shall be in writing.

(2) That it shall be sufficient to leave the notice at the last known business address (of the insurance company) in the UK.

---

1   See Section 2B concerning legal assignments.
2   *Van Lynn Developments Ltd v Pelias Construction* [1969] 1 QB 607.
3   [1956] 1 WLR 419 at 421.
4   (1899) 68 LJQB 839.

(3)   That notice may be served by registered post and if the letter is not returned undelivered, it is deemed served when the letter would in the ordinary course be delivered. Under the provisions of the Recorded Delivery Service Act 1962 the notice may be sent by recorded delivery instead of by registered post.

There are no provisions as to the time within which notice must be given, but it must be given before an action to enforce the assigned rights[1]. Indeed, valid notice may even be given after the death of the life assured[2]. No mention is made in section 136 as to any requirement of communication to the assignee.

E   Constructive notice

10.29   Section 199 of the Law of Property Act 1925 provides that a purchaser shall not be prejudicially affected by notice of any instrument or matter or any fact or thing unless:

(1)   it is within his own knowledge, or would have come to his knowledge if such enquiries and inspections had been made as ought reasonably to have been made by him; or

(2)   in the same transaction with respect to which a question of notice to the purchaser arises, it has come to the knowledge of his counsel, as such, or of his solicitors or other agent, as such, or would have come to the knowledge of his solicitor or other agent, as such, if such enquiries and inspections had been made as ought reasonably to have been made by the solicitor or other agent[3].

'Purchaser' in the section means a person acquiring an interest in good faith for valuable consideration and includes a mortgagee; while valuable consideration includes marriage and formation of a civil partnership it does not include nominal consideration in money.

Section 199 of the 1925 Act is consistent with the established equitable rule of constructive notice, namely that a person who is aware of such facts as would have put a reasonable man on inquiry is deemed to be aware of facts which a reasonable inquiry would have revealed. Failure to produce the policy may fix the purchaser with implied or constructive notice of an earlier charge[4].

I   Production of policy

10.30   It may be argued that the life office should require production of the policy for every transaction with it, even though the transaction does not bring the policy to an end. Examples of such transactions are:

1   *Bateman v Hunt* [1904] 2 KB 530 at p 538.
2   *Walker v Bradford Old Bank* (1884) 12 QBD 511.
3   Conversely, notice by the assignee to a broker does not generally constitute valid notice. See *Amalgamated General Finance Co Ltd v C E Golding & Co Ltd* [1964] 2 Lloyd's Rep 163.
4   *Spencer v Clarke* (1878) 9 Ch D 137. See **10.38** for a summary of the facts of the case.

(1)   Partial surrenders and surrenders of bonuses.

(2)   Payments of sums assured by instalments (as in family income policies).

(3)   Payments of annuities.

(4)   Exercise of options or variations to policy.

In practice, however, where small or regular and frequent payments are to be made, the production of the policy on each occasion is waived in the interests of convenience. Usually this may be done without serious risk.

2   Production of deed

10.31   Where a deed which affects two policies with the same life office is produced in connection with a transaction under one of them, it is thought that this amounts to notice of the dealing with the other policy. However, it would presumably need to be clear on the face of the deed that it affected two such policies.

F   Withdrawal of notice

10.32   The Policies of Assurance Act 1867 does not contain any provisions about withdrawal or amendment of notice.
   A person who serves notice sometimes desires to amend it on the ground that it contains some error and may serve a second notice to that effect. He may, on the other hand, desire to withdraw his notice altogether because:

(1)   it was served in error;

(2)   the deed to which it relates is no longer operative (eg a mortgage that has been paid off);

(3)   the deed to which it relates has been superseded by a fresh deed;

(4)   no deed or document was in fact executed.

The rules for payment into court under the Life Assurance Companies (Payment into Court) Act 1896[1] (see Appendix 7) contain a reference to withdrawal of notice. It seems obvious that notice can be withdrawn only by the person who served it or by the person on whose behalf it was served. In any event, withdrawal of notice should be treated with great caution for the following reasons:

(1)   The deed in question may contain recitals or references to other interests of which notice has not been served.

(2)   The deed said to be superseded may contain an assignment of the policy which does not become a nullity merely because another deed (perhaps in the same form) is subsequently executed by the assignor.

1   CPR Pt 37 Practice Direction – Miscellaneous Provisions about Payment into Court (paras 7 and 8).

If notice is withdrawn, it is desirable, in practice, to examine the title immediately and to obtain lodgement of any cancelled or superseded documents.

G   Recording receipt of notices

10.33   The Policies of Assurance Act 1867 did not forbid equitable assignments or impair their efficiency, and a life office should still record an equitable interest of which it has received notice.

It is important, therefore, for a life office to record, as well as the dates of receipt of notice, the following:

(1)   The date and effect of every assignment of which it receives notice (statutory or otherwise).

(2)   The date and effect of any event whereby the title passes by operation of law (eg on appointment of a trustee in bankruptcy).

(3)   The date of death of any assignee, etc and the date and details of the grant of representation to his estate.

(4)   The date and particulars of any equitable interest (eg charge by memorandum of deposit) of which it receives notice.

The recording system is increasingly incorporated as part of the life office's computer systems. If individual notices are not retained, there should be some other record than the computer entry (eg microfilm records, hard copy notices of assignment or telephone attendance notes) which shows all notices, referring to each individual policy, in the order of date of receipt.

I   Information as to notices

10.34   The Policies of Assurance Act 1867 does not state whether the life office must give an enquirer information about notices received but the general practice is to do so and it would usually be in its best interests to do so. Generally, it is accepted that information should be given on receiving a written request from a known interested party. It will also normally be given where the enquirer is a solicitor, banker or accountant as the life office would normally accept the enquirer's statement that he is making the enquiry with the consent or on behalf of some person known by the life office to be interested in the policy.

In *Re Weniger's Policy*[1], it was assumed that the life office would on request give such information, for it was stated that if a first mortgagee makes a further advance on a fresh bargain he must, to preserve priority, enquire whether notice of another charge has been received. When giving information, the life office should disclaim responsibility for any error or omission in the information given.

---

1   [1910] 2 Ch 291.

SECTION 6   PRIORITY

10.35   This section deals with the effect of notice on priorities of equitable interests. As far as *priorities* are concerned, a legal assignee is in the same position as an equitable assignee. It is also worth noting the following statement regarding section 136 of the Law of Property Act 1925[1]:

> '[S]ection [136] enables the assignee to acquire a title that has all the procedural advantages of legal title but as far as priorities are concerned his position is no better than if the assignment had been effected prior to that Act. It follows that even if the assignment is effected for value without notice of a prior equity, priorities fall to be determined as if the assignment had been effected in equity, not in law.'

A   Effect of notice on priorities of equitable interests

1   The Policies of Assurance Act 1867

10.36   As indicated, this Act gives a simpler remedy against a life office by avoiding the need for the assignee to join the assignor of the policy in actions against the life office; and to make it easier for a life office to settle a claim.

Newman v Newman[2]

> A had an equitable interest in a policy and served notice on the life office but which was not in accordance with the 1867 Act. Later B, with notice of that interest, took an assignment and served notice which did comply with the Act. Held, that B did not take priority. The statute was not intended to affect the priorities of interested parties between themselves where the subsequent assignee had notice of the prior interest.

The Policies of Assurance Act 1867 was *not* intended, for example, to provide that a person who has advanced money on a second charge with notice of a first charge (and subject to it) should, by giving statutory notice to the life office, take priority over the first charge – nor does it have this effect. If, when taking an assignment, the assignee has notice of some existing equitable interest, he cannot take priority over that interest merely by giving notice to the life office, and that is so whether or not the life office has notice of the equitable interest. The 1867 Act does not affect the position as between the assignee and the person with the equitable interest. In these circumstances, if the assignee has actual or constructive notice of the existing equitable interest, the person with that interest is entitled to the policy proceeds. An example of constructive notice is the case of *Spencer v Clarke*[3] (see **10.38**). In simple terms, constructive notice is where the assignee fails to make a reasonable investigation with the consequence that he will be deemed to have notice of what would have been discovered had he made reasonable enquiries.

1   Per Phillips J in *E Pfeiffer Weinkellerei-Weineinkauf GmbH & Co v Arbuthnot Factors Ltd* [1988] 1 WLR 150.
2   (1885) 28 Ch D 674.
3   (1878) 9 Ch D 137.

The priority in point here is priority in the right to sue. The 1867 Act does not determine the priority of conflicting interests in the policy money. This follows the ordinary rules of priority of equitable encumbrances (see **10.38**).

2   The Law of Property Act 1925

10.37   'The statute does not forbid or destroy equitable assignments or impair their efficiency in the slightest degree'[1]. This point, although in some respects fairly well established ever since the Judicature Act 1873, has been doubted in some cases, for example, by Robert Goff J in *Ellerman Lines Ltd v Lancaster Maritime Co Ltd*[2]. There is dicta in that case that there is a distinction between the priority of legal and equitable assignments although the case did not turn on that point. The apparent discrepancy has, however, been addressed by Mummery J in the case of *Compaq Computer Ltd v Abercorn Group Ltd*[3], Mummery J preferring the view expressed in *E Pfeiffer Weinkellerei-Weinenkauf GmbH & Co v Arbuthnot Factors Ltd*[4]. He stated the following in relation to section 136:

> 'Section 136(1) provides that the assignment is subject to equities having priority over the right of the assignee. The effect of those words is to create, in the case of a statutory assignment of a chose in action, an exception to the general rule that equity will not prevail against a bona fide purchaser of a legal estate for value without notice of the prior equity.'

Thus it would appear that the priority of assignments, whether legal or equitable, is determined by the rules for equitable encumbrances.

B   Priorities of equitable encumbrances

10.38   The priorities of equitable encumbrances of choses in action such as life policies are, apart from the doctrine of notice, determined by the date of the encumbrances. Where, however, there is a life office, trustee or other person to whom notice can be given to restrain the holder of the fund from parting with it, priority is prima facie determined by the date of giving notice. This is known as the rule in *Dearle v Hall*[5]. It is worth noting the statement of Phillips J in *Pfeiffer*[6]:

> 'The rule in *Dearle v Hall* is an exception to the general principle that equitable interests take priority in the order in which they are created. The rule applies to dealings with equitable interests in any property and in particular to equitable assignments of legal choses in action. Under the rule priority depends upon the order in which notice of the interest created by the dealing is given to the person affected by it, ie in the case of assignments of a debt, the debtor.'

1   *William Brandt's Sons & Co v Dunlop Rubber Co* [1905] AC 454 at 462.
2   *The Lancaster* [1980] 2 Lloyd's Rep 497 at 503.
3   [1993] BCLC 602.
4   *E Pfeiffer Weinkellerei-Weineinkauf GmbH & Co v Arbuthnot Factors Ltd* [1988] 1 WLR 150.
5   (1828) 3 Russ 1.
6   *E Pfeiffer Weinkellerrei-Weineinkauf Gmbh & Co v Arbuthnot Factors Ltd* [1988] 1 WLR 150.

No encumbrancer can, however, by giving notice obtain priority over an encumbrance prior in point of time if he had actual or constructive notice of that earlier encumbrance at the time. He will have to show that he has given value and he must have acted in good faith, without notice, actual or constructive, of any earlier assignment. If a person lends money on the security of a life policy which is not delivered to him and is in the hands of an earlier mortgagee, he has constructive notice of the earlier mortgage.

Spencer v Clarke[1]

The holder of a policy deposited it with A, who retained it but gave no notice to the life office. Later B, in ignorance of the deposit with A, agreed to lend on the policy and when the borrower alleged he had left the policy at home by mistake, B completed his loan by means of a memorandum of charge under which the borrower undertook to execute a mortgage upon request. B served notice on the life office. Held, that B was put on enquiry by the conduct of the borrower and was fixed with constructive notice of A's security; and that the title of A, who held the policy, must prevail.

Re Lake, ex p Cavendish[2]

A solicitor misappropriated his client's money but later executed a mortgage of his life policies in favour of the client to secure part of the appropriated money. He did not inform the client or give notice to the life office. Later, he executed a second mortgage to another client without disclosing the first mortgage and the second client gave notice to the life office. Held, that the second mortgage had priority.

10.39 The case of *Re Weniger's Policy* may help to illustrate the above mentioned rules.

Re Weniger's Policy[3]

W charged a life policy as follows:

Date	Action
20 Dec 1897 13 Dec 1899	Memoranda of deposit with the life office for £250.
14 July 1905	Memorandum of charge to Kapp for £146, subject to the life office charge.
1 Sept 1905	Charge to Metropolitan Credit Co for £115.
27 Nov 1905	Charge to Telegraph Co for £600, out of which the life office was repaid. Telegraph Co accordingly then held the policy. It paid premiums of £115.
30 April 1906	Charge to Kapp for £73.
9 May 1906	Charge to Cohen.
25 May 1906	Charge to Ramsay.

1 (1878) 9 Ch D 137.
2 [1903] 1 KB 151. This case followed *Foster v Blackstone* (1833) 1 My & K 297, 2 LJ Ch 84.
3 [1910] 2 Ch 291.

No notice had at this stage been given by any encumbrancer.

Notices were then given in the following order:

(1)   Metropolitan Credit Co.

(2)   Ramsay.

(3)   Kapp (both charges).

(4)   Cohen.

(5)   Telegraph Co.

The life office is deemed to have notice of its own charge.

The court determined the priorities as follows and for the reasons shown:

(1)   Telegraph Co for £250 (ie transfer of the life office charge) and the premiums paid to preserve the security.

(2)   Metropolitan Credit Co, being first to give notice, but having constructive notice of the life office charge by reason of the fact that it had been deposited with the life office. They had no notice of Kapp's interest and therefore took priority over it.

(3)   Kapp, as to his original charge, which was subject to the life office charge. He had no constructive notice at that time affecting his position, for had he enquired for the policy he would have found it to be with the life office, as he would have expected his interest being subject to the life office charge. (Ramsay, although second to give notice, was postponed because if when making his advance he had enquired for the policy he would have found that Telegraph Co had it.) He would, however, have lost priority had they not all been fixed with constructive knowledge.

(4)   Telegraph Co for remainder of its charge (Kapp's second charge and Cohen are postponed for the same reason as Ramsay's ie constructive notice of potential prior interests).

(5)   Ramsay in order of notice as all had constructive notice of potential prior interests.

(6)   Kapp's second charge.

(7)   Cohen.

An important practical point to emerge from the above is that an assignee should therefore always insist on the production of the policy or a satisfactory explanation for its non-production. Otherwise he will be unable to gain priority over any prior equity of which he had no actual notice because he will be fixed with constructive notice of previous assignments.

I   Position of voluntary assignees and trustees in bankruptcy

10.40   While a person who takes an equitable interest bona fide and for valuable consideration can by service of notice obtain priority over an earlier equitable interest of which he had no notice, a voluntary assignee cannot obtain priority in that way[1]. However, giving notice still has the advantage for the voluntary assignee that this will prevent subsequent assignments for value gaining priority by giving notice.

The trustee in bankruptcy as statutory assignee takes the assets of the bankrupt subject to all equities affecting the property in the hands of the debtor, and as he is not an assignee for value he cannot, therefore, by giving notice obtain priority over an earlier equitable interest of which no notice has been given[2] (except that if any assignment is for less than full consideration it may be impeached in certain circumstances by the trustee in bankruptcy as a transaction at an undervalue or preference)[3].

He should nevertheless give notice of his appointment to the company to prevent subsequent assignees who took their assignment without notice of the bankruptcy from gaining priority over him by giving prior notice. From a purely practical point of view as well it prevents the life office from innocently paying out the policy moneys to the bankrupt with the resulting difficulties which could arise (see *Rooney v Cardona*[4]).

C   Summary

10.41   In summary, therefore:

(1)   The priority of equitable and legal assignments are determined primarily in accordance with the date on which notice is served on the life office.

(2)   However, the question of knowledge or constructive knowledge at the time of giving notice can affect priority.

(3)   Failure to produce the policy documents without a valid explanation will normally be constructive knowledge of prior interests except (eg in cases such as Kapp's in *Re Weniger's Policy*[5] above), where an interest is expressed to be subject to a prior assignment, in which case the second assignee would not expect the assignor to have the policy. If there were two such subsequent interests with notice of the earlier interest but not of each other then priority will be in order of service of notice (eg Metropolitan Credit in the example above).

(4)   The sub-assignee from an original assignee with a prior equity, even with knowledge of the subsequent assignments, will get priority to the extent of that original assignee's interest.

---

1   *Justice v Wynne* (1860) 12 Ir Ch R 289.
2   *Re Wallis, ex p Jenks* [1902] 1 KB 719 and *Re Russell's Policy Trusts* (1872) LR 15 Eq 26.
3   See Chapter 9.
4   [1999] 1 WLR 1388, [1999] 2 FLR 1148, [1999] Fam Law 542, [1999] All ER (D) 124.
5   [1910] 2 Ch 291.

SECTION 7   STAMP DUTY

10.42   From 1 May 1987, assignments of policies, where there was no consideration, have been exempt from stamp duty provided they contained the relevant certificate. As a result of section 125 of the Finance Act 2003, stamp duty was abolished on all instruments (except those relating to stock or marketable securities) so that the requirement for a stamp duty certificate has similarly disappeared.

SECTION 8   MORTGAGES

A   Nature of mortgage

1   General principles

10.43   Life assurance policies are sometimes used as security for loans either on their own or as collateral security in house purchase. This practice used to more common than it is now, essentially because lenders increasingly view their security in the property as sufficient in itself. Life offices may themselves grant loans on the security of policies issued by them.

A mortgage is a transfer of property (real or personal) from one person (*the mortgagor*) to another (*the mortgagee*), as security for a debt. It is defined by section 205(1)(xvi) of the Law of Property Act 1925 as including 'any charge or lien on any property for securing money or money's worth'.

Where an individual has borrowed money, to purchase his home, the lender may require the borrower to effect a policy (with the sum assured equal to the value of the outstanding loan) to ensure that on the death of the borrower, there is sufficient money to cover the outstanding loan. Such a policy may be an endowment policy which will also act as an investment vehicle so that the borrower may be able to repay the sum borrowed before his death. The lender may or may not require the borrower to mortgage the policy as security to the lender.

The lender is technically able to effect a policy on the life of the borrower to protect its position in the event of the borrower's untimely death. It can do this as it has an insurable interest in the life of the borrower to the extent that it would incur a pecuniary loss if the borrower died before repaying the debt. This is not a common occurrence.

More generally, an existing policyholder may wish to raise money and he may use a life assurance policy on his own life as security for a loan.

(a)   Background to mortgages

10.44   A mortgage (usually of land) used to take the form of a conveyance by the mortgagor to the mortgagee on condition that the mortgagee reconveyed it to the mortgagor if the loan was repaid on a date mentioned in the conveyance (usually fixed at six months from the date of the loan). Such a conveyance or transfer was strictly construed, so that if the mortgagor failed to repay the loan on the fixed date, there was no obligation on the mortgagee to reconvey the land. The mortgagee could (and often did) retain the land for his own benefit.

(b)   Equity of redemption

10.45   Eventually, equity intervened and gave relief to the mortgagor under the maxim 'once a mortgage always a mortgage'. As a result, where a mortgagor intended a conveyance to be by way of security, he can now compel the mortgagee to reconvey the property on repayment of the loan, not only on the day fixed for its repayment (customarily six months) but also any time thereafter. This right is called the equity of redemption. The equity of redemption essentially distinguishes a mortgage from an absolute assignment.

The mortgagor will always have this right, unless he defaults on his interest payments and the mortgagee sells the mortgaged property or obtains a court order of foreclosure which vests the property in the mortgagee free from the mortgage.

(c)   Clog on the equity of redemption

10.46   An agreement between the mortgagor and mortgagee which prejudicially affects or acts as a fetter on the equity of redemption (ie the mortgagor's right to redeem the mortgage) is known as a 'clog on the equity' and is unenforceable by the mortgagee.

(d)   Legal mortgages

10.47   A legal mortgage transfers the legal interest in the mortgaged property. For life policies it must be by written assignment and comply with the Policies of Assurance Act 1867 or section 136 of the Law of Property Act 1925. A mortgage deed which transfers the property, with a proviso for redemption and reconveyance, satisfies the requirements of this section.

(e)   Equitable mortgage

10.48   An equitable mortgage transfers the equitable but not the legal interest in the property. This can be by way of an oral agreement between the parties, where the intention to create a mortgage is clear, or by a deposit of the policy document with a memorandum of deposit, a method sometimes used by life offices to secure policy loans on policies issued by them. Where deposit of the policy occurs without any accompanying memorandum this may still constitute an equitable mortgage provided this is the intention of the parties[1]. Possession of the policy in itself is not enough to establish the existence of a mortgage as the policy may have been deposited for other reasons. However, on the face of it if the deposit is made as security for a debt it will be presumed (unless there is a contrary intention) that he intended to mortgage the policy[2].

1   *Shaw v Foster* (1872) LR5 HL 321, 340.
2   *Norris v Wilkinson* (1806) 12 Ves 192.

(f) Differences between legal and equitable mortgages

10.49 Where the mortgagor defaults, a mortgagee who has only an equitable mortgage cannot, without further action, exercise his power of sale under the Law of Property Act 1925[1] because he has not acquired the legal title. He will have to apply to the court for an order to enable him to sell.

With an equitable mortgage, the mortgagor has a right to the return (where relevant) of the title deeds on repayment of the loan. There need be no reassignment of the mortgaged property as, under an equitable mortgage, there has been no assignment of the legal interest. For legal mortgages, there will need to be a formal reassignment of the mortgaged property.

(g) Liens

10.50 Although there is no transfer of property liens provide a third party with an interest in the property in question. A precise definition is elusive although many definitions assume actual possession of the property. These would be 'legal' liens whereas the lien which arises in the context of a life policy will tend to be an equitable lien. A voluntary payment of premiums under a policy does not, as a general rule, give any lien or interest in the policy to the payer. The circumstances under which an equitable charge or lien can be asserted on a policy by reason of payment of a premium were discussed in *Re Leslie, Leslie v French*[2] where a husband voluntarily paid premiums on a policy on the life of his wife and it was held that he had no lien.

A lien may be acquired if a person pays a premium or premiums in the following circumstances (the first four of which were set out by Fry LJ in *Re Leslie, Leslie v French*):

(1) By contract with the beneficial owner of the policy.

(2) By reason of the right of trustees to an indemnity out of the trust property for money expended by them to preserve it. For example, where the trustee has paid premiums out of his own funds in order to maintain the policy. Where, however, the relationship of parent and child or husband and wife exists as between the trustee and beneficiary, the payment of premiums is presumed to be for the benefit of the beneficiary and so cannot be recovered (unless the presumption is rebutted). In addition, in many cases the proposer and the settlor will be the same person and he will also be a trustee so the normal right of indemnity would be negated by the presumption that, as settlor, he intended to benefit the beneficiaries (but see *Clack v Holland*[3]).

(3) By subrogation to the right of trustees where some person, at their request, advances money to preserve the trust property.

(4) By reason of the right of mortgagees to add to their security with money paid by them to preserve the mortgaged property. Therefore, where the

1 Law of Property Act 1925, s 101(1)(i).
2 (1883) 23 Ch D 552.
3 (1854) 19 Beav 262.

lender pays the premiums to prevent the policy from lapsing or being made paid up.

(5)　Where a married woman has paid premiums on a policy taken out at her husband's request in their joint names. (In a case where the trustee in bankruptcy had knowledge that the premiums were being paid by the wife the court ordered that the trustee repay her out of the policy moneys although this was not on the basis of the existence of an equitable lien (*Re Tyler*[1])).

(6)　Where the person paying the premiums did so under the mistaken belief that the policy benefits belonged to him, and the true owner allows this to be done[2].

(7)　Where an assignee has paid premiums although a prior interest in the policy had been created.

10.51　In *Foskett v McKeown*[3] the House of Lords disagreed with the Court of Appeal that the purchasers were entitled to a lien on the proceeds of a life policy to secure repayment of premiums paid with their money. Lord Millett (House of Lords) explained that an equitable lien is a '. . . proprietary interest by way of security. It is enforceable against the trust property and its traceable proceeds. The finding of the majority that the purchasers had no proprietary interest in the policy or its proceeds should have been fatal to their claim to a lien'. The Court of Appeal reasoning was that the purchasers were entitled (by subrogation to Mr Murphy's lien) to be repaid the premiums. They believed he was 'entitled to the Trustee's ordinary lien to indemnify him for expenditure laid out in the preservation of the trust property'. This was in accordance with cases (2) and (3) in *Re Leslie, Leslie v French*. This was rejected by Lord Millett as although he was a trustee of the policy he did not pay premiums in this capacity. He paid them as a settlor. In any event, Lord Millett went on to state that the main reason for rejecting the Court of Appeal's argument was that '. . . it makes the purchaser's rights depend on the circumstance that Mr Murphy happened to be one of the trustees of his children's settlement'. This reasoning depended on the chance that Mr Murphy happened to be a trustee of his children's settlement. Lord Millett concluded this part of his judgment by stating 'The purchaser's rights cannot turn on such chances as this'.

This raised the question how the purchaser's rights were to be protected. In summary, Mr Murphy effected a policy on his own life and declared a trust of it for his children. He paid the first two premiums out of his own funds but subsequent premiums were paid from funds held under express trust for purchasers of plots of land to be developed in Portugal. These funds had become mixed up with Mr Murphy's own funds via various bank accounts. Mr Murphy committed suicide and the sum assured of £1 million was paid out. The purchasers claimed at least a 40% share of the proceeds, a share proportionate to their contribution to the premium paid. The Court of Appeal held that the purchasers were only enti-

---

1　[1907] KB 865.
2　*Re Foster, Hudson v Foster (No 2)* [1938] 3 All ER 610.
3　(2000) WLR 1299; (2000) 3 All ER 97; ILR 3/7/2000.

tled to a lien equal to the premiums they had paid. The House of Lords reversed this. Where a trustee wrongfully used trust money to provide part of the cost of acquiring an asset, the beneficiary was able to claim a proportionate share of the asset. In every case, the value inherent in the trust property had become located within the value inherent in the new asset. A conclusion that the beneficiary could only assert a lien over the new asset would result in any appreciation in value going to the trustee. The process of tracing involved the purchasers tracing the premiums through mixed substitutions not into the insurance money directly but firstly into the policy. That policy represented the traceable proceeds of the premiums and so the purchasers were entitled to a proportionate share of the policy and this was the case whether it was immediately before or after death. The fact that the policy had increased in value was not relevant. Lord Millett described this case as '. . . a textbook example of tracing through mixed substitutions'.

2   Form of mortgage of life policies

(a)   Creation of a mortgage of a life policy

10.52   Mortgage deeds of life policies will contain all the usual provisions of a mortgage deed and also provisions which relate specifically to life policies.

(I)   USUAL PROVISIONS

10.53   The usual provisions include date; parties; details of the property mortgaged; amount borrowed; various covenants (eg to repay the loan on a fixed date, and to pay interest) and the required notice periods.

(II)   SPECIFIC PROVISIONS TO BE INCLUDED IN MORTGAGES OF LIFE POLICIES

10.54   These generally contain certain specific provisions:

(1)   A covenant by the mortgagor to pay the premiums as they fall due and any other moneys required to keep the policy in force and that he will restore the policy if it is made paid up or lapses.

(2)   A covenant by the mortgagor that the policy is valid (and that it will not become void) and that if it does become void he will effect a new policy for an equivalent amount and assign it to the mortgagee and will effect and assign a further policy in the same way if any such substituted policy becomes void.

(3)   A power to the mortgagee to pay any premium in arrears and add the amount to the principal (ie the outstanding loan).

(4)   A power in the case of default for the mortgagee to pay premiums and for any such payments to be a charge on the policy (although there will be a right to do this even without express provision)[1].

---

1   *Gill v Downing* (1874) LR 17 Eq 316.

(5)   A power to the mortgagee to exercise his power of sale by surrender to the life office[1].

(6)   A power to the mortgagee, if his power of sale has arisen, to convert the policy to a fully paid-up policy.

(b)   Types of policy used in connection with mortgages

(I)   LIFE OFFICE LOAN

10.55   Life offices may make loans to policyholders, on the security of their policies. A policyholder may wish to raise money for general purposes or he may wish to finance his premium payments. If a policyholder would otherwise have no option but to let his policy lapse it may be better for the life office to grant a loan within the policy's surrender value, rather than for the policyholder to completely surrender his policy. In this way, the life office will continue to receive the premiums and would also receive interest payments on the loan. The advantages for the policyholder are: he is able to maintain his life cover; for with-profits policies, he does not lose any terminal bonus on maturity of the policy (generally the right to a terminal bonus is forfeited on complete surrender of a policy before maturity); and, assuming the surrender value increases over time, the policy may be used as security for future loans[2].

Life offices will not normally loan more than 90% of the surrender value of a policy. They may limit themselves to a lower amount on unit-linked policies as opposed to with-profits policies, due to the volatility of the price of units.

(II)   POLICIES USED IN CONNECTION WITH MORTGAGES OF REAL PROPERTY

10.56   As mentioned at **10.43**, policies are sometimes used in connection with mortgages of real property (eg home purchase), as collateral security for the loan used to purchase the property. Where the lender requires a policy to be taken out, it may also require it to be mortgaged to it (either legally or equitably by the deposit of the policy document). The type of policy used will depend upon the type of mortgage which has been chosen:

(1)   *Repayment mortgage.* The capital element of the loan is repaid in regular instalments, together with the interest payable. A lender may require that a policy be taken out to ensure that if the borrower dies before the loan is repaid, the balance outstanding on the loan can be repaid with the policy proceeds. It is generally a wise precaution for the borrower to effect such a policy irrespective of the borrower's requirements. The sum assured under such a policy should, at the outset, equal the value of the outstanding loan. The policy may be a whole life, a level term or a decreasing term and may or may not be mortgaged to the lender.

---

1   See **10.66–10.67**.

2   However, a loan on a life policy may cause a chargeable event in certain circumstances giving rise to a liability to higher rate tax. See Chapter 12.

(2) *Endowment mortgage*. During the term of the mortgage, the borrower repays the lender only the interest accruing on the outstanding capital sum, whilst also paying premiums towards an endowment policy with the same term as the mortgage so that the proceeds from the endowment policy will be used to repay the principal on maturity (or on death before that).

(3) *Pension mortgage*. During the mortgage term, the borrower repays only the interest accruing on the outstanding capital sum. A lender may accept as 'security' an undertaking from the borrower that he will use any cash lump sum he is entitled to on retirement to repay the principal. However, this undertaking would not give the lender any right against the life office to the cash lump sum. The life office would pay this sum to the policyholder at retirement, if so requested.

(c) Assignments absolute in form

10.57 Where a policy is effected by the debtor on his own life and assigned to a creditor in order to give security to that creditor, the question may arise whether the creditor is entitled to the policy absolutely or only as mortgagee. The maxim 'once a mortgage always a mortgage' applies[1].

If he is entitled only as mortgagee he must account to the debtor for the balance of the policy moneys after satisfaction of his debt. The court will look at the substance of the transaction and not merely the form[2]. Parol evidence is admissible to show that an apparent absolute assignment is, in fact, a mortgage. As a general rule the policy belongs to whichever of the mortgagee or debtor is (as between themselves) liable to pay for it. If the debtor has agreed to pay the premiums, or that they should be debited to his account, he is entitled to an equity of redemption even though the policy is in the name of the creditor or has been assigned to him[3]. Therefore, the creditor is deemed to be a mortgagee and is only entitled to have the debt repaid. On repayment of the debt, the debtor is entitled to have the policy reassigned to him, or, if he is dead, his personal representatives are entitled to the balance of the policy moneys.

But if the creditor has effected and paid for the policy, the debtor has no right to any part of the policy money purely on the basis that he has repaid the debt.

3 Capacity

(a) Capacity to borrow

(I) MINORS

10.58 The general rule is that contracts to create a mortgage or charge, for the repayment of money lent or a charge over his equitable interest[4] are voidable at

---

1 *Salt v The Marquess of Northampton* [1892] AC 1.
2 *Re Watson* (1890) 25 QBD 27.
3 *Courtenay v Wright* (1869) Giff 337, 351.
4 Goods and services which are necessary to the minor such as food, drink, clothing, lodging, medicine and medical and legal services.

the minor's option until a reasonable time after reaching the age of majority, although they are binding on the lender. In practice, life offices would rarely lend to minors.

(II) COMPANIES

10.59   The capacity of a company or other corporation to borrow depends primarily on its constitution although any company engaged in commerce has for a long time had an implied power to borrow for the purposes of its business and this has been, in effect, extended even further by the Companies Act 2006 under which all companies have unlimited objects unless they choose to restrict them.

The mortgagee can, in any event, rely on section 40 of the Companies Act 2006 which means that if the life office has no notice of any restriction on the company's power to borrow and is acting 'in good faith', any loan agreement with the company will be binding.

Every limited company must keep a register of charges affecting the company's property.

(III) TRUSTEES

10.60   Where trustees hold a policy on trust, they can borrow on the security of the policy if there is express provision for that purpose in the trust instrument, or if they need money to pay premiums to preserve the policy, or under section 16 of the Trustee Act 1925 which gives the trustees statutory power to do so[1], or if all the beneficiaries, being legally capable and between them entitled to the whole beneficial interest, authorise them to do so.

(b)   Capacity to release security

10.61   Where a mortgagee considers that he holds ample security, he may be prepared to release a part of it. If, for example, he holds a life policy, he may allow the mortgagor to surrender the reversionary bonus for his own benefit.

B   Rights and remedies of the mortgagor

I   Rights of the mortgagor

10.62   The mortgagor retains an interest in the mortgaged property in the form of the equity of redemption.

Therefore, he can:

---

1   The trustees will have the power to mortgage a life policy under s 16 if they are authorised by the instrument, if any, creating the trust or by law to pay or apply capital money subject to the trust for any purpose or in any manner. However, this section does not apply to trustees of property held for charitable purposes, or to trustees of a settlement for the purposes of the Settled Land Act 1925, not being also the statutory owners.

(1)   give the mortgagee a further charge on the property;

(2)   mortgage the property (subject to the first mortgage and any further charges) to a second, third or subsequent mortgagee (subject to prior encumbrances).

If the mortgagor later wishes to give a first mortgage to a second mortgagee, he may be able to arrange with the first mortgagee that the second mortgagee shall have priority. In such a case the first mortgagee must either be a party to the second mortgage in order to postpone his interest or must execute a separate document to that effect.

If, for example, a policyholder has mortgaged his policy to X and later wishes to borrow on it from the life office, he will probably find the life office unwilling to lend unless X is prepared to postpone his mortgage and rank his security after that of the life office.

2   Remedies of the mortgagor

(a)   Legal mortgage

10.63   The mortgagor has the following remedies:

(1)   The right at law to have the property reassigned if, *on* the day fixed in the mortgage, he pays the principal, interest and costs.

(2)   The right in equity to have the property reassigned if, *after* the day fixed in the mortgage, he pays the principal, interest and costs. He must, however, normally give six months' notice of his intention to repay or pay interest in lieu of notice[1]. (In practice, modern mortgage deeds will usually provide for much shorter notice periods.)

(3)   The right on repayment to require the mortgagee to transfer the mortgage to a third party as the mortgagor may direct. Such a right is useful if the mortgagee calls in the loan and the mortgagor has to arrange another loan to repay it.

(4)   The right at his own expense to inspect and make copies of or extracts from the documents of title to the mortgaged property in the custody or power of the mortgagee. This right cannot be excluded by contract[2].

(b)   Equitable mortgage

10.64   The mortgagor of an equitable mortgage has the right to the return of the documents of title of the mortgaged property on payment of principal, interest and costs[3].

1   See *Smith v Smith* [1891] 3 Ch 550.
2   Law of Property Act 1925, s 96(1).
3   The mortgagor should give reasonable notice.

C   Remedies of the mortgagee

I   General

10.65   At any time after the date for repayment mentioned in the mortgage has passed, the mortgagee can give the mortgagor notice requiring him to repay the mortgage money. If within three months the mortgagor fails to repay, the mortgagee has various remedies which are summarised below):

(1)   The right to sue the mortgagor on his personal covenant to repay the loan. This right is very rarely exercised as at this stage, the mortgagor is unlikely to have sufficient funds to perform the covenant.

(2)   The right to sell the mortgaged property. The mortgage may contain an express power of sale but otherwise the mortgagee can rely on the statutory power.

(3)   The right to appoint a receiver. The receiver is deemed to be the agent of the mortgagor under the statutory power and collects the income from the property. He pays out of it the outgoings, interest, premiums and other disbursements. The appointment of a receiver may be a convenient remedy for a mortgagee on the security of real property or of a life interest, but is not used in connection with life policies.

(4)   The right to transfer the mortgage to another person.

(5)   The right to tack further advances on to the original mortgage to rank in priority to subsequent loans.

(6)   The right to marshall against another mortgagee's security to the extent that the security the two mortgagees have in common has been exhausted by the other mortgagee.

(7)   The right to apply to the court for an order of foreclosure. On an order of foreclosure absolute, the mortgaged property is vested in the mortgagee absolutely, free from the mortgage, and the right of the mortgagor to redeem is gone. This is a drastic measure and it is more usual for a sale to be ordered.

(8)   The right to consolidate two or more mortgages from the same mortgagor if that power is expressly reserved in the mortgage deed or one of them. On consolidation, the mortgagee can refuse repayment under any of the consolidated mortgages unless he is repaid under all. The power is of considerable value where one of the mortgages is well secured and another only partially secured.

If the mortgagor does not pay the premiums on a policy which he has mortgaged there is authority that the mortgagee has an implied power to pay the premiums and add the amount which it has paid out (with interest) to the security[1]. There may, of course, be an express power to this effect[2].

1   *Hodgson v Hodgson* (1837) 2 Keen 704.
2   *Browne v Price* (1858) 4 CB (NS) 598.

A mortgagee is also entitled to all reasonable costs charges and expenses incurred by him in relation to the mortgage, and in particular his legal costs

(a)   Relevance of the statutory power of sale for life policies

(I)   MORTGAGES MADE BY DEED

10.66   Where a policy is mortgaged by deed, its surrender to the life office, so far as the mortgagor is concerned is, in effect, equivalent to the exercise of the power of sale and can, it is generally considered, be made under the statutory power but technically the position is not clear as there is no specific reference to surrender as an alternative to sale.

In addition, the surrender of a policy may not be a permissible exercise of the statutory power of sale if the surrender value is not equal to the sort of price the mortgagor could reasonably expect to obtain on the market. This is particularly pertinent in the case of endowment policies. The market in 'second-hand' or 'traded' policies has grown considerably. It is quite likely, therefore, that the open market value of endowment policies which have been running for at least five years will be more than the surrender value. It is questionable, therefore, whether the mortgagee should exercise his power of sale by surrendering the policy or whether he should, instead, sell the policy on the open market. The mortgagor will clearly want the mortgagee to get the best price for the policy as he will benefit from any balance of the sale or surrender proceeds after the loan has been repaid. However, the mortgagee is under no duty to obtain the best possible price for the mortgagor although the mortgagor owes a duty in equity to take reasonable care to secure a proper price[1].

Where the policy is charged only to the extent of the debt, it would appear that a purchaser from the mortgagee would not get full legal title as the 'subject of the mortgage' for the purposes of section 104 would be the charge and not the policy. However, it is arguable that the mortgagee could surrender the policy under the power of sale and that the life office could get a discharge from the mortgagee on the basis of section 107 of the Law of Property Act 1925[2].

(II)   MORTGAGES NOT MADE BY DEED

10.67   In such cases the statutory power does not apply, even if the document contains an assignment of the policy. However, there may be an express power of sale in the mortgage instrument or even an implied power of sale.

A life office will not be concerned to see whether the power of sale is properly exercised where:

(1)   the mortgage is by deed and the deed gives power to the mortgagee to surrender and the office accepts a surrender from a mortgagee in exercise of the power; or

---

1   *Downsview Nominees Ltd v First City Corporation Ltd* [1993] AC 295, [1993] 3 All ER 626, PC.
2   See **10.74**.

(2)   the office acts on a title derived by a purchaser from a mortgagee exercising
the power.

The life office must not, however, accept a title from a purchaser where it is clear
that the power of sale has been improperly exercised[1].

If the mortgagor and the mortgagee join in surrendering the policy the office is
not, of course, concerned whether the power of sale has arisen or not.

(b)   Conditions affecting exercise of the mortgagee's rights

(I)   OVERRIDING INTERESTS IN THE MATRIMONIAL HOME

10.68   A mortgagee will not be able to exercise his power of sale if a third party
has a beneficial interest in the property and the mortgagee has made no enquiry
as to that third party's rights, if any[2].

The decision in *Williams & Glyn's Bank Ltd v Boland*[3] caused great concern
to conveyancers and lenders. The difficulty the case creates is that a mortgagee
or purchaser, despite having searched the Land Register, cannot be certain
whether or not a third party has an equitable right to occupation of the property
which binds the mortgagee or purchaser. And there is no procedure which can
provide a complete safeguard.

The perceived problems do not appear to be as great as initially feared (including by the Law Commission). Mortgagees now normally adhere to a code of
practice which ensures that the necessary enquiries are made. These enquiries
enable them to ascertain whether persons other than the mortgage applicant are
or will be occupying the property and if there are or will be other occupants,
whether any of them claim an overriding interest.

If an overriding interest is claimed, the mortgagee will have to ensure that the
persons with such an interest relinquish their rights before it advances the
moneys the mortgagor wishes to borrow. Although inquiry need not be made of
the children of the vendor as their occupation is only through their parents[4].
Subsequent cases such as *Bristol & West BS v Henning*[5] which concerned a
cohabitee may have limited the effect of the *Boland* case (albeit that *Boland* was
not cited in this case).

(c)   Undue influence

10.69

Barclays Bank plc v O'Brien[6]

The defendant O'Brien was a shareholder in a company which had a substantial
unsecured overdraft. He arranged with the company's bank an overdraft facility

1   *Selwyn v Garfit* (1888) 38 Ch D 273.
2   *Williams and Glyn's Bank Ltd v Boland* [1981] AC 487.
3   [1981] AC 487, [1980] 2 All ER 408, [1980] 3 WLR 138.
4   *Hypo-Mortgage Services Ltd v Robinson* [1997] 2 FLR 71.
5   [1985] 2 All ER 606.
6   [1993] 4 All ER 983.

for the company on the security of his guarantee of the company's indebtedness. O'Brien's liability was secured by a second charge over the matrimonial home he jointly owned with his wife. The wife signed the legal charge without reading it. The company's indebtedness increased beyond the agreed limit and the bank brought possession proceedings to enforce payment under the guarantee. In her defence, the wife contended that she had signed the charge under undue pressure from her husband who had also misrepresented to her the effect of the legal charge.

Held (HL), that because the bank knew that the transaction was not to Mrs O'Brien's advantage and because there is a substantial risk in transactions of this kind that there has been undue influence the bank should have been put on inquiry as to the circumstances in which Mrs O'Brien had agreed to act as surety. It should, therefore, have taken reasonable steps to ensure her agreement was properly obtained. The bank could have asked her to attend a private meeting to warn her of the amount of the potential liability under the charge and the risks involved and also advised her to take independent legal advice. Having failed to do this, it was fixed with constructive notice of the undue influence and wrongful misrepresentation made by the husband. On this basis, it was held that the legal charge should be set aside.

Subsequent cases have built upon the principles established in *Barclays Bank plc v O'Brien*. In *RBS v Ettridge (No 2)*[1], for example, the mortgagee would be put on enquiry if the relationship between the surety and the debtor is known to the mortgagee and raises a legal presumption of undue influence. In *Bank of Scotland v Bennett*[2] it was emphasised that the risk must be sufficiently real and substantial in order to conclude that the mortgagee ought reasonably to have made further enquiries to satisfy himself that the surety's consent was not obtained improperly. The mortgagee is not put on enquiry simply because the surety has no control or involvement in the business whose liabilities are secured or because the loan exceeds the value of the mortgaged property[3]. A mortgagee is not required to inquire as to the relationship between debtor and surety or as to the personal motives of the surety for wanting to help the debtor[4]. Where the transaction was so improvident that it is inexplicable on any other basis the mortgagee was put on inquiry[5].

To avoid constructive notice of the surety's rights the mortgagee should take reasonable steps to allay his suspicions. Therefore, for example, the mortgagee should insist that the surety attend a private meeting on their own with the mortgagee's representative at which she is told of the extent of her liability, alerted to the risk and advised to take independent legal advice.

(d)   Jointly mortgaged policies

10.70   Many couples, whether married or not, effect policies where the death benefit is payable on the failure of their joint existence, in order to cover the amount

---

1   [1998] 4 All ER 705. See also *First National Bank plc v Achampong* [2003] EWCA Civ 487, [2004] 1 FCR 18.
2   [1999] 1 FCR 641.
3   *Britannia Building Society v Pugh* [1997] 2 FLR 7, 29 HLR 423, CA.
4   *Banco Exterior Internacional SA v Thomas* [1997] 1 All ER 46.
5   *Credit Lyonnais Bank Nederland NV v Burch* [1997] 1 All ER 144.

borrowed under a mortgage. The policy may be assigned to the mortgagee (although increasingly lenders do not take a mortgage of the policy). Where the policy is mortgaged the normal intention is that the maturity value or the death benefits are used to repay the mortgage and the mortgage is thereby discharged. If the mortgage is satisfied out of other funds then on the first death the surviving assured will be entitled to the policy proceeds and not the estate of the deceased assured[1].

D Discharge of mortgage

I Repayment and reassignment

10.71 The mortgagor or any person entitled to any interest in the equity of redemption, may redeem the mortgage. As mentioned above the money secured is usually made payable on a fixed day, usually six months from the date of the mortgage. The mortgagor cannot redeem before then unless the mortgagee has taken steps to procure repayment by taking possession of the property or otherwise (for example, by surrendering a mortgaged policy[2]); but he has a legal right to redeem on the fixed day. Thereafter he has a right in equity to redeem on giving (customarily) six months' notice or on paying six months interest instead. Clearly, the specific terms of the mortgage deed must be consulted and currently the trend is towards shorter, or even non-existent, notice periods.

On repayment, the mortgagor must at his own expense take whatever steps are necessary to have restored his title to the property free from the mortgage. He may perhaps ask for a re-assignment of the policy by the mortgagee. A receipt is, however, usually sufficient to show that all money secured by the mortgage has been repaid and that the mortgagee has no further interest in the property.

Many life office standard mortgage deeds have pre-printed reassignments contained within or on the reverse of them. These simply require dating and signing by the mortgagee at the appropriate time.

(a) Statutory receipt

10.72 Section 115(1) of the Law of Property Act 1925 provides that, on repayment, a receipt endorsed on (or written at the foot of, or annexed to) the mortgage operates to discharge the mortgage and reconvey the mortgaged property to the person entitled to the equity of redemption. A form of the statutory receipt is given in Schedule 3 to the Law of Property Act 1925.

(b) Delivery of documents of title

10.73 On repayment, the mortgagee should return the policy document to the mortgagor. The mortgagee is not liable if he delivers the document to a person not having the best right to them unless he has notice of such a right[3].

---

1 *Smith v Clerical Medical and General Life Assurance Society* [1993] 1 FLR 47. See also *Ross v Perrin-Hughes* [2004] EWHC 2559 (Ch), [2004] All ER (D) 159 (Nov).
2 *Bovill v Endle* [1896] 1 Ch 648.
3 Law of Property Act 1925, s 96(2).

2 Claims under mortgaged policies

10.74 When a claim is made by a mortgagee, the life office may, subject to satisfactory proof of title, pay the policy proceeds to the mortgagee relying on section 107(1) of the Law of Property Act 1925:

> 'The receipt in writing of a mortgagee shall be a sufficient discharge for any money arising under the power of sale conferred by this Act, or for any money or securities comprised in his mortgage, or arising thereunder; and a person paying or transferring the same to the mortgagee shall not be concerned to inquire whether any money remains due under the mortgage.'

'Mortgage' is defined by section 205(1)(xvi) of the 1925 Act as including 'any charge or lien on any property for securing money or money's worth'.

In view of these sections, it is considered that a mortgagee can give a good discharge for the policy moneys payable on the life assured's death, or on his survival until the maturity of an endowment assurance, whether his mortgage is by deed or not, and whether or not it contains an assignment.

The life office is not concerned with the state of account between the mortgagor and the mortgagee or with equitable interests in a legal mortgage where it is dealing in good faith (see section 113 of the Law of Property Act 1925). However, it can, if desired, examine the accounts and pay to the mortgagee only the amount due to him, and the balance of the policy moneys to the person with the equity of redemption.

If a life office has notice that no money is owing under a mortgage, it cannot properly pay to the mortgagee without the concurrence of the mortgagor or persons deriving title under him. In such a case the mortgagee has no right in equity to receive the policy money.

In the same way, where a mortgagee makes a claim and the life office has notice of another mortgagee who has priority over the mortgagee making the claim, the life office should notify the mortgagee with priority and only pay out if the latter has given its consent.

(a) Simple receipt

10.75 Discharge of a mortgage is usually evidenced by a statutory receipt (which also has the advantage of operating as a reconveyance), but a simple receipt would suffice and the receipted mortgage might be returned to the mortgagor to evidence his title to the policy[1].

In practice, most life offices, when investigating title to a policy for the purpose of payment of a claim or on surrender, will accept a simple receipt as sufficient evidence of the discharge of a mortgage. A formal reassignment or a statutory receipt may be required, however, if the office is proposing to grant a loan on the security of the policy or to carry out any other transaction which does not involve the encashment of the policy.

---

1 *Edwards v Marshall-Lee* (1975) 119 Sol Jo 506.

(b)   Equitable interests

10.76   When investigating title to a mortgaged policy, the life office need not make enquiries about equitable interests of which it has actual or constructive notice.

Section 113 of the Law of Property Act 1925 provides:

> '(1)   A person dealing in good faith with a mortgagee, or with the mortgagor if the mortgage has been discharged, released or postponed as to the whole or any part of the mortgage property, shall not be concerned with any trust at any time affecting the mortgage money or the income thereof whether or not he has notice of the trust, and may assume unless the contrary is expressly stated in the instruments relating to the mortgage:
>
> (a)   that the mortgagees (if more than one) are or were entitled to the mortgage money on a joint account; and
>
> (b)   that the mortgagee has or had power to give valid receipts for the purchase money or mortgage money and the income thereof (including any arrears of interest) and to release or postpone the priority of the mortgage debt or any part thereof or to deal with the same or the mortgaged property or any part thereof;
>
> without investigating the equitable title to the mortgage debt or the appointment or discharge of trustees in reference thereto.'

The life office can get a good discharge from the trustees to whom the property was mortgaged who have not died unless it has been notified of the appointment of additional trustees or the discharge of existing trustees, in which case the life office will only get a good discharge from the current trustees.

Where property has been mortgaged to more than one person jointly or to secure a sum advanced from money belonging to them on a joint account, then, unless a contrary intention is expressed, a good discharge may be obtained from the survivor or survivors alone in the event of one or more having died (or from the personal representatives of the last survivor)[1].

In view of the wide meaning given to 'mortgage' in section 205(xvi) of the Law of Property Act 1925, section 113 enables an equitable mortgagee by deposit to give a valid receipt.

1   Law of Property Act 1925, s 111.

CHAPTER 11

Trusts and life assurance[1]

SUMMARY

SECTION I   INTRODUCTION

11.1   The common practice of declaring trusts of life assurance policies, and of including policies as part, or all, of the property in a trust means that those involved in life assurance should understand at least the nature and basic principles of the law relating to trusts. Trusts also play a large part in the mitigation of inheritance tax and in estate planning and so a knowledge of trusts is also of great benefit to advisers and their customers. Readers are recommended to consult more specialist texts for more detailed coverage[2].

A   The nature of trusts

I   *Definitions and uses*

11.2   There is no universally accepted definition of a trust. Perhaps one of the most satisfactory definitions is set out in *Underhill and Hayton*[3]:

---

1 See generally, Underhill and Hayton *Law of Trusts and Trustees* (17th edn, 2007).
2 See also Chapter 14.
3 Article 1, Underhill and Hayton *Law of Trusts and Trustees* (17th edn, 2007) p 2.

'an equitable obligation, binding a person (called the trustee) to deal with property (called trust property) owned by him as a separate fund, distinct from his own private property, for the benefit of persons (called beneficiaries or, in old cases, cestuis que trust), of whom he may himself be one, and any of whom may enforce the obligation'

Likewise, there is no universally accepted definition of the term 'settlement' which is often used as an alternative term for a trust but is generally wider. Parliament has from time to time defined the word for the purposes of particular tax statutes. For example, the Income Tax (Trading and Other Income) Act 2005 (ITTOIA 2005)[1] defines the word for the purposes of income tax, to include 'any disposition, trust, covenant, agreement, arrangement or transfer of assets'.

Trusts are created for many reasons and may take a variety of forms. Their origins lie in medieval times with the object of preserving landed estates intact for as long as possible. Trusts today are used for a variety of purposes, for example, to enable property to be held for persons (eg minors) unable to hold it themselves; to tie up property for the enjoyment of persons in succession; to protect family property from creditors and from particular members of the family with reckless or extravagant tastes; to enable provision to be made for dependants privately; to provide a framework for charitable giving, for causes or non-human beneficiaries; to enable investment to be made through unit trusts; to provide pensions for retired employees and their dependants; and for estate planning and to minimise the incidence of various taxes.

11.3   The practical uses of trusts in connection with life policies are explained more fully in Chapter 14 but it is useful to bear in mind that the main uses centre around:

(1)   speed of payment (no need to wait for a Grant of Representation provided there is a surviving trustee);

(2)   taxation mitigation (the reader is referred to Chapter 13 in particular for a commentary on the provisions in the Finance Act 2006, which drastically affect the inheritance tax treatment of trusts);

(3)   the ability to benefit a certain beneficiary outside of the will (which is ultimately publicly available); and

(4)   in some cases, protection against the effects of bankruptcy.

Modern trusts tend to be flexible rather than fixed or absolute and are usually designed so that the interests in the trust property may be altered in the light of changes in taxation legislation or practice or in family or personal circumstances.

Trusts are classified in a variety of ways. One classification of trusts is by the degree of instruction given to the trustees. If the trustee is given no active duties to perform in relation to the trust property, eg S assigns a life policy to T1 and T2 to hold on trust for B, the trust may be described as a *simple* trust (or an absolute,

---

1   Section 620(1).

fixed or bare trust). In such a trust, the beneficiaries are absolutely entitled as against the trustees. If, however, duties are declared, eg S transfers £10,000 to T on trust to pay the income to A, B and C at T's discretion, it may be classified as a *special* trust.

Trusts are further categorised by how they come into existence: express; resulting or implied; and constructive, but reference should be made to more specific works for a detailed explanation of this[1]. Trusts are further classified for the purposes of taxation and a more detailed examination of this can be found in Chapter 13.

A common question which arises in relation to trusts in general and very often with regard to life policy trusts is where a person is both a beneficiary and a trustee. It is sometimes thought that the two are incompatible. However, it is very often the case with a life policy trust and, in practice, it is rarely an issue. Presumably, the settlor is happy with this state of affairs in view of the fact that he will have selected both trustees and beneficiaries and provided that the trustee-beneficiary acts in accordance with the terms of the trust and the rules of common law, equity and statute there should not be a problem. However, to put the matter beyond doubt the settlor may wish to insert a provision in the trust instrument that the trustee is able to benefit himself personally.

B   Trusts distinguished from powers

11.4   A power is an authority vested in a person to deal with or dispose of property which is not his own. It may take effect at law, as with a power of attorney; or it may be equitable only, as in the case of a power of appointment, which enables the donee to declare in whom and in what manner property is to vest without giving him any right of ownership over the property.

The main distinction, however, is that a trust is mandatory, a mere power is discretionary; a trustee is bound to carry out the terms of a trust and if he does not, the court will do so for him, but the donee of a mere power cannot be compelled to exercise it, and if he does not, the property will pass to the persons entitled in default of its exercise.

The distinction between trusts and powers is not always entirely clear. What at first sight appears to be a mere power may in fact be a trust, and this will often happen where there is no 'gift over' in default of appointment. The question depends on what the intention of the donor was: if he intended that in any event the objects of the power should benefit, it is a power in the nature of a trust, a 'trust power'. Otherwise it will be a mere power. In *Burrough v Philcox*[2] a testator gave property to his two children for their lives, with power to the survivor of the children to dispose of the property by will amongst the testator's nephews and nieces or their children 'either all to one of them or to as many of them as my surviving child shall think proper'. It was held that a trust was created in favour of the testator's nephews and nieces, subject, however, to a power of selection by

---

1   See Underhill and Hayton *Law of Trust and Trustees* (17th edn, 2007).
2   (1840) 5 My & Cr 72. See also *Schmidt v Rosewood Trust Ltd* [2003] All ER (D) 442 (Mar).

the surviving child. As this power had not been exercised, the property had to be divided equally amongst the members of the class in accordance with the equitable maxim 'equality is equity'.

C Creation of trusts

I Requirements of a valid trust

11.5 A trust may be created by will, deed or some other form of written instrument. For a trust of personal property such as a life policy (also known as 'personalty'), writing is not essential and a trust may be created orally or even by conduct. It should be borne in mind that section 53 of the Law of Property Act 1925 requires a trust of an equitable interest in either real or personal property to be in writing.

11.6 For the creation of a trust the following conditions, known as 'the three certainties'[1], must be present:

(1) the words used must be construed as imperative. There must be an intention to create a trust and 'precatory' words are not sufficient;

(2) the subject matter of the trust must be certain; and

(3) the objects, ie the beneficiaries, must be certain.

Where a life assurance policy is effected with the intention that it should benefit someone other than the grantee (the person to whom the policy is 'granted' by the life office), a trust should be created by the use of language which clearly indicates such an intention, rather than language which infers a general intention to benefit a third party. Where a policy is effected and expressed to be for the benefit of a third party, then, except in the case of trusts created under the Married Women's Property Act 1882, the policy moneys will belong to the policyholder's estate, unless he has effectively constituted himself a trustee for that third party. Numerous cases have demonstrated this requirement, both in the context of trusts generally and in trusts specifically of life assurance policies[2]. Some examples are given below[3].

In *Re Foster, Hudson v Foster*[4], a father effected a deferred assurance on the life of his son, expressed *to be payable* to the representatives or assigns of the son at death on or after the age of 21. The father paid the premiums during his life and after his death the premiums were paid by or on behalf of the son until he died. It was held that (1) the father had not constituted himself a trustee for his

1   *Knight v Knight* [1840] 3 Beav 148.
2   See *Re Engelbach's Estate, Tibbetts v Engelbach* [1924] 2 Ch 348; *Re Foster, Hudson v Foster* [1938] 3 All ER 357; *Re Sinclair's Life Policy* [1938] 3 All ER 124; *Re Webb, Barclays Bank Ltd v Webb* [1941] 1 All ER 321 and *Re Foster's Policy, Menneer v Foster* [1966] 1 All ER 432.
3   See also *Swain v Law Society* [1982] 2 All ER 827.
4   [1938] 3 All ER 357.

son and that the policy moneys were payable to the personal representatives of the father; and (2) that, as all parties had acted under the mistaken belief that the policy belonged to the son, his personal representative was entitled to a lien on the policy for the premiums paid by the son or on his behalf.

In *Re Engelbach's Estate, Tibbetts v Engelbach*[1], a father effected an endowment policy to provide for the payment of the sum assured on 3 February 1923, if his daughter should be alive at that time. In the proposal form, opposite the words 'full name and description of the proposer', he had inserted the words 'Edward Coryton Engelbach for his daughter Mary Noel, aged one month'. The father died on 7 March 1916, and the daughter survived to the fixed date when the policy moneys were paid to her. She was, however, persuaded to pay them to a stakeholder pending a decision as to the legal rights of the parties. The question to be decided by the court was whether the policy created a legal estate in the daughter, or whether the policy moneys when paid belonged to the father's estate. It was held that as the daughter could not sue on the contract nor did her father constitute himself a trustee for his daughter, the policy moneys belonged to the father's estate and must be paid to his executors.

In *Re Sinclair's Life Policy*[2], S effected an endowment policy under which the benefit was expressed *to be payable* at the end of 17 years to his godson, H. S had handed the policy to H's father and told him to retain it so that he could collect the money. S died in 1924 and the policy matured in 1936 when the life office paid the money into court. Farwell J held that the evidence was insufficient to establish a trust in favour of H. There was no doubt that A's intention was to make provision for his godson, but he did not constitute himself a trustee of the moneys payable.

11.7   Where a policy is effected by an adult *as trustee* for a child, however, it would create a trust and give the child an enforceable right. Such a trust is usually created by express words and this is the safest course, but it seems that in some circumstances a trust may be implied, eg by provisions which indicate that after a certain period the beneficial interest will pass to the child and the adult will cease to have a beneficial interest.

In *Re Webb, Barclays Bank Ltd v Webb*[3] a father effected a deferred assurance 'on behalf and for the benefit of' his child. The policy money was expressed to be payable to the personal representatives or assigns of the child, provided that he survived to his 21st birthday. Under the policy the father could exercise various options, including to borrow or surrender, *on behalf of the child*, until the child attained 21, at which time, all the rights and powers of the father or his personal representatives were to cease and the child was to become entitled, subject to any assignment or charge, to the policy absolutely. It was held that the form of the policy *established a trust* in favour of the child, as there was a sufficient showing of intention to create a trust. Farwell J stated:

1   [1924] 2 Ch 348.
2   [1938] 3 All ER 124.
3   [1941] 1 All ER 321.

'The whole matter rests entirely upon the true construction of the policy in question. I think that one must take it that unless there is in the policy something which does establish reasonably clearly that the assured was in fact constituting, and intending to constitute, himself a trustee for the third party of the assurance moneys, the third party is not and the personal representatives of the assured are, entitled to the money payable.'

Further:

'It is for a person to make clear by the language used that he is constituting himself a trustee and the absence of any clear words to that effect makes it difficult to establish a trust.'

In *Vandepitte v Preferred Accident Insurance Co of New York*[1], Lord Wright stated:

'The intention to constitute the trust must be affirmatively proved.'

11.8   In *Re Foster's Policy, Menneer v Foster*[2] a father effected a deferred assurance 'for and on behalf of myself and the . . . child'. The policy was on similar lines to that in the *Webb* case, except that there was no specific provision that the father should cease at the end of the deferred period to have any beneficial interest in the policy. It was held that on the true construction of the policy, the father's interest ceased at the end of the deferred period and a trust was therefore *implied* for the child, for whose benefit the policy was expressed to have been effected. The fact that from the end of the term of deferment the right to surrender the policy, etc became vested in the child for her own benefit was inconsistent with the father retaining any beneficial interest thereafter.

In *Davis v Davis*[3] the court was required to construe the intentions of the deceased. On the evidence available it was held that the deceased's sister held a property as nominee for the deceased and that a life policy which had been assigned to her was not for her own benefit but for the purpose of discharging a mortgage over the property. It was established that a secret trust in favour of the deceased's step-daughters existed. This was on the basis of wholly oral statements.

The difficulties created by not clearly evidencing certainty of intention can be seen from the case of *Simpson v Simpson and another*[4] where the existence of a trust created orally was eventually decided in favour of those seeking to establish the existence of the trust but not without the great inconvenience and expense of court proceedings.

Where premiums are paid by a father in respect of a policy taken out by him on his child's life, the premiums may be rebuttably presumed to be made by way of advancement, in which case the child's estate will (subject to any rebuttal) be entitled to the policy moneys.

1   [1933] AC 70 at 79–80.
2   [1966] 1 All ER 432.
3   [2001] All ER (D) 352.
4   [2005] EWHC 2098 (Ch).

Where two parties have demonstrated a clear joint intention and have acted in pursuance of an agreement, equity will protect their beneficial rights under such an agreement. In *Smith v Clerical Medical and General Life Assurance Society*[1], D and E bought a house together with a 100% mortgage and effected an endowment policy, which was designed to pay off the full amount of the mortgage if either of them died within 25 years. When E died, D sold the house and paid off the mortgage from the sale proceeds. There was then a dispute as to whether the policy monies should be paid to E's personal representatives or to D. The Court of Appeal held that D was beneficially entitled to the money in pursuance of the joint intention of the deceased and D.

11.9 Certainty of the subject matter of the trust can cause difficulties (see, for example, *Boyce v Boyce*[2]) although it will almost invariably be clear that a particular policy is the subject matter of the trust, although difficult questions can arise when settlors attempt to declare trusts of only part of a policy or of certain sums payable under the policy or where only one of two joint policyholders attempts to declare a trust of the policy or part of the policy.

11.10 The test for certainty of objects will differ depending on the type of trust. For a fixed trust to be valid, it must be possible to ascertain each and every beneficiary: it must be possible for the trustee to compile a complete list of those entitled[3]. For other trusts (and for powers) the test is now whether it can be said with certainty that any given individual is or is not a member of the class[4].

Unless the trust gives the trustees a discretion or a power of appointment, the precise share which each beneficiary is to take must also be certain.

Another essential to the establishment of a trust is that of 'complete constitution'. When this has been achieved the beneficiary will be able to enforce the trust and this will be the case whether or not he is a 'volunteer' (ie whether or not he has given consideration). A leading case in this area is *Milroy v Lord*[5] where Turner LJ stated that this was achieved by the settlor having 'done everything which, according to the nature of the property comprised in the settlement, was necessary to be done in order to transfer the property and render the settlement binding upon him'. Essentially, there are two methods of achieving this. One is by the settlor declaring himself as a trustee. Clarity is required and so establishing certainty of intention is important. The other is by the effective transfer of the property to trustees. The transfer must be appropriate to the nature of the property being transferred so in the case of a life policy this would be by assignment in accordance with the Policies of Assurance Act 1867, or under section 136 of the Law of Property Act 1925. Some uncertainty has more recently crept into this area of the law with the case of *Pennington and another v Waine and others*[6]

1 [1992] 1 FCR 262, CA.
2 (1849) 16 Sim 476.
3 *IRC v Broadway Cottages Trust* [1955] Ch 20.
4 *McPhail v Doulton* [1970] 2 All ER 228 and *Re Baden's Deed Trust (No 2)* [1972] 2 All ER 1304.
5 (1862) 4 De GF & J 264 at pp 274–275.
6 [2002] 1 WLR 2075.

where the donor did not do all she was able to do to divest herself of the property (shares), but Arden LJ stated that the donor clearly intended to make an immediate gift and the stage had been reached where it would have been unconscionable to have recalled the gift. The possibility of this third method was considered in *T Choithram International SA v Pagarani*[1] and *Pennington v Crampton*[2]. Essentially, this relies on the fact that it would have been unconscionable (and hence contrary to equitable principles) for the donor to recall a gift after a certain length of time.

It is also usually possible for a corporate body to create a trust. A minor cannot create a trust although if he purports to do so then at his majority it will become binding unless he repudiates it within a reasonable time of attaining the age of 18[3]. Trusts may be created in the ways listed below.

2 Statutory trusts

11.11 Some trusts are expressly created or implied by the operation of statute. For example, a policy effected by a man or a woman on his or her own life and expressed to be for the benefit of his or her spouse and children or any of them will create a trust under section 11 of the Married Women's Property Act 1882.

A common form of statutory trust arises where two or more people co-own a legal estate[4]. The co-owners will hold the property on trust for themselves. Also, where an individual dies intestate, the Administration of Estates Act 1925 (as amended) provides that the estate shall be distributed in a specified manner, which may include the creation of a trust.

3 Express trusts

11.12 An express trust is one which has been intentionally and deliberately created. This expression covers all trusts created in this manner. For example, 'fixed trusts', 'power of appointment trusts', 'inheritance trusts', etc. The trust may also be referred to by its taxation status, for example, 'interest in possession', 'discretionary' or 'accumulation and maintenance'.

4 Implied trusts

11.13 An implied trust is not expressed in any form but is to be implied from the actions or relationship of the parties. Where, for example, partners purchase property and direct the vendor to convey it to one partner, he may hold it upon implied trust for all the partners.

A 'species' of implied trust is the 'resulting trust', which may arise on the failure of an express trust, either wholly or partially, in which event the beneficial

---

1 [2001] WTLR 277.
2 [2002] WTLR 387.
3 *Edwards v Carter* [1893] AC 360.
4 Law of Property Act 1925, s 36.

interest may 'result' back to the settlor or his estate. Where, accordingly, a man effected a policy for the benefit of his wife and she had murdered him, she was barred from receiving any benefit and there was a resulting trust to his estate and thus for the beneficiaries of his estate[1].

5   Constructive trusts

11.14   These are a species of implied trust imposed by equity, irrespective of the intention of the owner of the property, in order to satisfy the demands of justice and good conscience. The concept of constructive trusteeship can be elusive and can arise from different sets of circumstances. For example, if a third party knowingly receives trust property and also knows that it is transferred to him in breach of trust, equity will deem him to hold it upon a constructive trust for the beneficiaries[2]. Actual receipt of trust property is not essential for a third party to be deemed to be a constructive trustee. A person can still become a constructive trustee on the basis of 'intermedelling', ie if he knowingly enables a fraudulent purpose to be effected. The question of the requisite state of mind was considered in *Royal Brunei Airlines v Tan*[3]. Lord Nicholls referred to 'a person who dishonestly procures or assists in a breach of trust or fiduciary obligation'. This would seem to suggest that a finding of constructive trusteeship would be difficult to achieve, although Lord Nicholls went on to indicate that the meaning of dishonesty in this context is not the same as would apply in a criminal matter. He went on to say that '. . . for the most part dishonesty is to be equated with conscious impropriety'. So, for example, a life office who was aware that a trustee of a policy who had applied to surrender the policy intended to use the proceeds for his own benefit must refuse to pay to him otherwise it could be held to be a constructive trustee of those moneys.

The test relating to dishonesty was also explored more recently in *Barlow Clowes International Ltd (In liquidation) v Eurotrust International Ltd*[4] where, in broad terms, an objective approach to dishonesty was stated to be required.

The knowledge need not be actual, it may be constructive. Constructive knowledge for these purposes is very difficult to define. It obviously falls short of actual knowledge but must be sufficiently obvious so as to put the third party on notice that something is amiss. It may require that he should investigate further, as he is not entitled to 'shut his eyes' to the obvious.

Constructive trusteeship can arise in other scenarios. One of the oldest cases involved a fiduciary using his position to obtain an unauthorised profit (renewal of a lease held as trust property by a trustee in his own favour)[5].

In another case, where one of two joint tenants murdered the other, the Ontario High Court held that although the normal rule of survivorship applied and the

---

1   *Cleaver v Mutual Reserve Fund Life Assurance* [1892] 1 QB 147. See also *Davitt v Titcumb* [1989] 3 All ER 417.
2   See *BCCI (Overseas) Ltd v Akindele* [2000] 4 All ER 221.
3   [1995] 2 AC 378; [1995] 3 WLR 64.
4   [2006] 1 All ER 333.
5   *Keech v Sandford* (1726) Sel Cas Ch 61.

full interest accrued to the survivor, the court would impose a constructive trust so that he held the property as to an undivided one half interest for the benefit of the deceased joint tenant's next of kin[1].

In a more recent case, a Crown employee purchased property with the proceeds of bribes accepted during the course of his employment. It was held that the property was held on constructive trust for his employer[2].

Constructive trusts have also been found to exist where a common intention between the parties can be inferred. A constructive trust was not held to exist in the case of *Pratt v Medwin*[3]. O and M purchased a house as tenants in common with a mortgage. They were required to have a supporting insurance policy which, amongst other benefits, guaranteed to pay off the mortgage if O died. The payments came out of their partnership account but equivalent amounts were deducted from O's personal drawings account in the partnership. M, however, was unaware that the accountant was deducting these sums from O's personal drawings account and was under the impression that the purpose of the policy was to guarantee the mortgage debt and hence was intended to be shared beneficially. It was held in dismissing the appeal that a party was not bound by any inference which the other party drew to his attention unless that inference was one that could reasonably be drawn from his own words and conduct. The policy was separate from the property and was in the name of O and the payments were made by O. There was no evidence, apart from M's 'impression' that there was a common intention that the proceeds of the policy be shared. This can be contrasted with the case of *Oxley v Hiscock*[4] where a common intention was found and a constructive trust held to exist.

6   Creation of a trust of a life policy

11.15   There are a number of ways in which a life assurance policy can become the subject of a trust:

(1)   A policy may be effected for the benefit of the grantee's spouse and/or children and create a trust by reason of the Married Women's Property Act 1882.

(2)   The grantee may assign the policy to trustees to hold for the beneficiaries.

(3)   The grantee may declare an express trust of the policy. This may be on the basis of a 'trust request' (submitted with the proposal/application form to form part of the contract between the grantee and the life office) for use prior to the policy being effected, or a declaration of trust of the policy any time after the policy is effected.

---

1   *Schobelt v Barber* (1966) 60 DLR (2d) 519.
2   *A-G for Hong Kong v Reid* [1994] 1 All ER 1, PC. See *Rockbrook Ltd v (1) Khan (2) Miracles by Design Limited* [2006] EWHC 101 Ch for an example of the difficulties which can be encountered in seeking to establish a constructive trust.
3   [2003] EWCA Civ 906.
4   [2004] 3 All ER 703.

An interesting case on the subject of declaring trusts of life assurance policies and which concerns certainty of words is *Pappadakis v Pappadakis*[1]. A document provided by the life office, which was described as a 'Declaration of Trust', was used purportedly to create a trust of a policy in favour of the proposer's wife and children. This was subsequent to an initial trust document (about which there was no dispute) under which the proposer himself was a potential beneficiary along with family members.

Following the birth of his son the proposer effected three further documents. The first appointed an additional trustee. Under the second the trustees irrevocably appointed the policy benefits to the proposer and assigned the policy to the proposer free of trust. The third document (which was the document under consideration by the court) provided that the Declaration was made by the person whose name appeared in a blank space and was expressed to take effect as an assignment of the policy by the settlor to named persons who were described as trustees, to be held by them as trustees for the persons whose names appeared in the space provided for the names of the beneficiaries. The space for the trustees was left blank. This form was signed by the proposer alone.

Before he died the proposer and his wife executed a deed of gift which recited that there were doubts about the validity of the Declaration of Trust and that it was believed that the proposer was absolutely entitled (at both law and in equity) to the policy, by which the proposer assigned the policy to his wife absolutely. It was held that the Declaration of Trust was invalid and the widow was entitled to the whole proceeds of the policy. Although headed a Declaration of Trust it was in fact worded and structured as an assignment of the policy to trustees. It could not be effective because the trustees (the assignees) were not named and it was not possible to assign something to nobody. As the assignment was voluntary and gratuitous, but failed to take effect as such, it could not be saved by equity holding it to be a declaration of trust. The proposer had not intended it to be a declaration of trust and as a matter of construction it was clearly not a declaration of trust. It was not possible to overrule this by an inference to be drawn from the absence of certain manuscript words which should have been added to the document. Nor could the document be rectified as there was no clear and convincing evidence as to what it was intended that the Declaration should have said.

In view of the confusion and issues which arose, *Pappadakis* might be viewed as supporting the view that those seeking to declare trusts of life assurance policies should not rely on trust documentation supplied by life offices, which is necessarily of a standard and non-specific nature and should instead seek to obtain a bespoke trust document from his own legal advisers. However, it should be borne in mind that the vast majority of life policies which are effected subject to such trusts fully achieve the objectives of the settlor at little or no cost. Perhaps the best course of action is for the settlor to take the life office's specimen trust (where available) to his own legal advisers, preferably those with knowledge and experience in this area. Hopefully, this will involve less expense than a trust instrument which has been drafted specifically for that case. Indeed, this is the approach suggested by most life offices which provide specimen documentation.

---

1   TLR 19/1/2000.

Realistically, for policies with relatively low sums assured the cost of independent legal advice to the proposer will often be prohibitively expensive.

A further example of the confusion surrounding specimen life office trust documentation arose in the case of *Strover v Strover*[1] where partnership protection trusts were entered into with what appeared to be the understanding on the part of the deceased that if he left the firm the beneficial interest would revert to him. Hart J stated that the partners had not '. . . collectively or individually . . . directed their minds to what was to happen in the event of a retirement'. The actual wording of the trust provided for the benefits to continue to be payable to the surviving partners. The court ultimately decided that there was a 'proprietary estoppel' so that the deceased's estate was the ultimate beneficiary.

7   Scotland

11.16   There are important differences between English and Scots law as to what is required to create a valid trust. Also, the trust terminology differs. To create a valid trust, 'delivery', or some other overt act signifying irrevocability, is necessary if the trust is not to be revocable by the *truster* (settlor). Delivery is the requirement that the subject matter of the trust must be delivered to the trustees, or to some person on their behalf, with the intention of transferring the rights in such subject matter so that they are held against the *truster* for *behoof* (on behalf of) the beneficiaries. (Delivery need not be physical delivery and, in fact, only in rare cases would there be actual physical delivery.) If there is no delivery there must be one of the permitted equivalents, such as intimation[2] or possibly registration of the trust deed in the Books of Council and Session.

If a Scottish trust is not properly constituted because the requirements as to delivery or its equivalent have not been fulfilled, there is likely to be a resulting trust for the truster. In *Allan's Trustees v IRC*[3] it was held by the House of Lords that a person could create a valid trust by declaring himself a trustee of the policy and giving intimation to one of several beneficiaries. Intimation of the deceased life assured's intentions prior to the policy coming into force does not constitute delivery; and a parent is not an appropriate person to whom intimation, on behalf of an adult beneficiary, may be given[4].

In the case of policies under the Married Women's Policies of Assurance (Scotland) Act 1880, the provisions of the Act create an irrevocable trust, without any need for delivery or intimation of the policy, since the Act provides that the policy vests immediately on its being effected in the life assured and his legal representatives in trust for the beneficiaries expressed, or in any trustee nominated in the policy or appointed by separate writing duly intimated to the life office.

---

1   [2005] EWHC 860 (Ch).
2   Intimation is accepted as being the equivalent of delivery: *Clark's Trustees v Inland Revenue* 1972 SLT 189.
3   1971 SLT 62.
4   *Kerr's Trustees v Inland Revenue* [1974] SLC 193.

The Married Women's Policies of Assurance (Scotland) Act 1880 can there-fore create a trust where one would not otherwise exist. In the case of *Re A Policy No 6402 of the Scottish Equitable*[1] a policy was effected by A on his own life 'for behoof of' his wife's sister. It was held that such words did not create a trust. There was a resulting trust in favour of A. Had the words been in favour of his wife then a trust under the Act would have arisen.

D   Variation of trusts made in contemplation of or during marriage[2]

11.17   On granting a decree of divorce, nullity of marriage or judicial separa-tion, the court may, under the 'property adjustment orders' powers contained in the Matrimonial Causes Act 1973, make an order varying, for the benefit of the parties to the marriage and/or the children of the family, any ante-nuptial or post-nuptial settlement made on the parties to the marriage, or an order extinguishing or reducing the interest of either of the parties to the marriage under any such set-tlement. In this context, 'settlement' is given a wide interpretation. Divorce in itself will not destroy the interest of a named spouse, but the interest may be varied as a result of any order the court makes. The Civil Partnership Act 2004[3] introduces the same provisions for same sex couples relating to, for example, property adjustment as apply under the Matrimonial Causes Act 1973.

In *Gulbenkian v Gulbenkian*[4], a husband effected two endowment assurances on his life; one payable to him at maturity if he was living, or if he died during the term, to his wife; and the other payable to him at maturity if he was living, or if he died during the term, to his wife if she was living, and if she was not, to the personal representatives of the husband. The husband divorced the wife and asked for an order varying the trusts. It was held that the name of the wife should be struck out.

SECTION 2   TRUST PROVISIONS

A   The trust property

11.18   All types of property, real or personal (eg a chose in action such as a life policy), legal or equitable, in possession, remainder or reversion and whether vested or contingent may be the subject matter of a trust.

The following paragraphs consider some of the common provisions, trusts and powers which will be encountered in trust documentation.

---

1   [1902] 1 Ch 282.
2   See also *Bown v Bown and Weston* [1948] 2 All ER 778; *Gunner v Gunner and Stirling* [1948] 2 All ER 771; *Lort-Williams v Lort-Williams* [1951] 2 All ER 241, CA.
3   Section 72 and Schedules 5, 6 and 7.
4   [1927] P 237.

B   Life interests

11.19   A person who has a life interest (a 'life tenant') has an interest in the property of the trust only during his lifetime. If the trust property is land, he would only be entitled to the use and enjoyment of it, or the rents and income from it and if the trust property is personalty, he would only be entitled to the income from the trust property. Life tenants (who have no other interest in the trust property) cannot therefore (unless there is a specific power to advance or appoint capital to the life tenant or it is possible to vary the trust) receive any capital from the trust, nor can a capital investment be made on their behalf. A life tenant will have an 'interest in possession' in the property to which his income entitlement refers[1]. It is not common to solely create a life interest in a trust of a life policy as it is a non-income producing asset. However, a life interest is often created in conjunction with some sort of capital interest.

C   Protected life interest

11.20   The life interest may be framed in such a way that it will come to an end if the life tenant attempts to dispose of it, or becomes bankrupt. Although a life interest can be given to a person *until* bankruptcy, an individual cannot settle his own property on *himself* with an interest determinable on bankruptcy, for to do so would be an attempt to defeat his creditors[2].

D   Protective trusts

11.21   A protective trust combines a determinable interest with a discretionary trust. Under a protective trust, the interest of the beneficiary is determinable upon bankruptcy or attempted alienation, upon which a discretionary trust arises in favour of himself and other beneficiaries (usually family members). The original beneficiary may then receive such income as is necessary for his maintenance with the surplus directed to any spouse and/or issue. These trusts may be created by using express terms, but such settlements became so popular that section 33 of the Trustee Act 1925 enables creation of such a trust by merely directing that property is to be held 'on protective trusts'.

E   Powers of appointment

11.22   Settlors often prefer to retain flexibility over future interests under the trust and so confer upon the trustees (one of which will usually be the settlor), or themselves, a power of appointment. This is a power to declare at some future date the persons in whom the future benefits of the trust are to vest, the extent of

---

1   Inheritance Tax Act 1984, s 49: see further Chapter 13.
2   See the cases collected in *Mackintosh v Pogose* [1895] 1 Ch 505.

their interests, and the time at which they are to vest. Such appointments may be authorised to be made by deed, will, or simply in writing, and may be revocable or irrevocable. The appointor, if he appoints at all, can do so only in favour of one or more persons of the specified class or classes set out in the original trust instrument, which may include the settlor (where the trust is not designed to mitigate inheritance tax)[1]. It must be distinguished from a *general* power of appointment which may be exercised in favour of any person the appointor may choose.

Where the power of appointment is being exercised, the appointors must take care to specify whether they are appointing revocably or irrevocably. Otherwise, it would appear that the appointment will be irrevocable and cannot therefore be further altered[2].

The recent case of *Sieff and others v Fox and others*[3] analyses the rules relating to what trustees should take into account (and what they should not take into account) when exercising their powers. In this case the trustees exercised a power of appointment without regard to the correct capital gains tax consequences. It was held that if they had the correct information they would not have exercised the appointment in question and, as a result, it was held that the appointment should be set aside.

The flexible power of appointment trust is commonly used in relation to trusts of life policies. This is discussed further in Chapter 14.

F Fraud on the power

11.23 Normally, an appointor is under no duty to exercise the power of appointment, but if he chooses to exercise it, he must do so honestly[4]. It must be exercised for the purposes intended by the trust and not for corrupt or extraneous reasons, for otherwise the exercise of the power will in equity be regarded as a fraud on the power and be void[5]. The word *fraud* in this connection does not imply or require any intention of fraud in the criminal legal sense. The appointment may be void, not only where the appointer is seeking a benefit for himself but also in some cases where he is arranging a disposition of the trust fund for some purpose foreign to the power or as a result of a bargain with the appointee to benefit persons who are not objects of the power[6].

---

1 See, generally, *In Re Baden's Deed Trusts (No 2)* [1972] 2 All ER 1304; *In Re Manisty's Settlement Manisty v Manisty* [1973] 2 All ER 1203 and *In Re Hay's Settlement Trusts* [1981] 3 All ER 786. Refer also to *Turner v Turner* [1983] 2 All ER 745 in which it was held that where trustees exercised a power of appointment but without exercising their discretion – simply acting at the behest of the settlor – they would be in breach of their duty and the purported appointments would be set aside.
2 *Worrall v Jacob* (1817) 3 Mer 256.
3 [2005] 3 All ER 693. *See also Re Hastings-Bass [1975] Ch 25.*
4 *Cloutte v Storey* [1911] 1 Ch 18.
5 *Re Brook's Settlements, Brook v Brook* [1968] 3 All ER 416.
6 *Vatcher v Paull* [1915] AC 372. See *Re the X Trust* 5 ITELR 119 (Judgment date 13 June 2002 – Jersey) for an example of a case where a non-beneficiary benefited but where the exercise of the power was nevertheless upheld.

It is not, however, in itself a fraud on the power to *release* the power so that it cannot be exercised, even though the person who releases the power does so in order to obtain some benefit for himself under the trusts in default of appointment or otherwise[1].

G Hotchpot clause

11.24 A hotchpot clause is intended to ensure that the shares of all the children who are beneficiaries in the trust fund shall be equal. The clause provides that if a power to advance or appoint part of the fund is exercised in favour of one child, the amount advanced or appointed is to be taken into account when the shares of the children in the remaining part of the fund fall to be determined, unless the person exercising the power has a power to direct otherwise.

Suppose, for example, there are two children, John and Mary, that there is a fund of £4,000, and the trust provides for them to benefit in equal shares and that an appointment of £1,000 is made to John. If there were no hotchpot clause and no further appointment, distribution of the unappointed part of the fund would be in equal shares to John and Mary (namely, £1,500 each), the result being that John would have £2,500 altogether and Mary only £1,500. If, however, there is a hotchpot clause, John must bring into account the £1,000 appointed to him, so that finally, the children would take in equal shares. The precise wording of the clause must be closely analysed.

H Care of children

I Maintenance, education and benefit

11.25 It is clearly desirable in a trust providing for minor children that the trustees should have power to apply the income of the trust fund for their maintenance and education. Trusts normally contain express powers for this, but if they do not (unless excluded expressly or by implication), the statutory power will apply.

The statutory power of maintenance is to be found in section 31 of the Trustee Act 1925.

(1) Before the beneficiary attains the age of 18 the trustees *may*, subject to contrary direction in the trust instrument, express or implied, pay to his parent or guardian, or otherwise apply, the whole or part of the income of the trust property for his maintenance, benefit or education.

(2) This power is discretionary, but is exercisable irrespective of any other fund available for the same purpose, or the existence of some person bound by law to provide for such maintenance or education[2]. In considering whether

---

1 See *Re Radcliffe, Radcliffe v Bewes* [1892] 1 Ch 227.
2 Section 31(1)(ii).

to exercise this power, the trustees should, however, have regard to the beneficiary's age, requirements, the general circumstances of the case, and of what other income, if any, is applicable for the same purposes.

(3)   The amount of the income which is not so applied for maintenance or education *must* be accumulated at compound interest. The trustees may, during the beneficiary's minority, apply the accumulations or any part thereof as if they were income of the current year[1].

(4)   On attaining the age of 18, if the beneficiary does not have a vested interest, then the trustees *must* pay the whole of the income and any accumulations of income to the beneficiary until he either attains a vested interest or dies, or until failure of his interest[2]. This would also give the beneficiary in question an interest in possession for inheritance tax purposes in the relevant share of the trust fund. This is explained further in Chapter 13. Although it is more common for an interest in possession to be expressly provided under the terms of the trust rather than to rely on section 31.

2   Application of section 31 of the Trustee Act 1925

11.26   The section only applies if the trust property carries the intermediate income and if there is no express contrary indication in the trust instrument, ie a direction to accumulate. (Essentially, for these purposes 'carrying the intermediate income' means that the income or interest produced by the trust property is to be applied for the benefit of the relevant beneficiary).

Where section 31 is applicable, the trustees must apply their discretion, rather than simply paying out the income automatically to the parent or guardian of the beneficiary[3]. The circumstances of the beneficiary should be reviewed regularly. In particular, there should be a review a few months prior to the minor beneficiary attaining the age of 18, since on attaining 18, the statutory power to so apply income expires.

Since the power is discretionary, the court will not interfere with the trustees' discretion, so long as they exercised it bona fide[4].

Sums of income paid by trustees in the exercise of this discretionary power form part of the income of the beneficiary for tax purposes. An exception to this rule is to be found in section 29 of the Income Tax (Trading and Other Income) Act 2005 where, if any income (or accumulated income) in excess of £100 is distributed to a minor and unmarried child of the settlor, during the settlor's lifetime, it will be taxed as the income of the settlor in the tax year in which the income is distributed.

The court has an inherent jurisdiction to allow a minor's trust property to be used for his maintenance. Usually the court will only apply income for this purpose, but it can also use capital from the trust. The court also has a statutory

1   Section 31(2).
2   Section 31(1)(ii). The beneficiary's right to income creates an interest in possession: *Swales v IRC* [1984] 3 All ER 16 at 24. See Chapter 13.
3   *Wilson v Turner* (1883) 22 Ch D 521.
4   *Re Senior, Senior v Wood* [1936] 3 All ER 196.

power to sell or otherwise deal with a minor's property to provide funds for his maintenance[1].

3 Advancement

11.27 Older trusts often contained an express power for the trustees to raise and apply capital for the 'advancement' of any of the remaindermen (the persons entitled to the capital of the trust after the expiry of a life interest). In every post-1925 trust of, in effect, personal property, the statutory power of advancement applies by virtue of section 32 of the Trustee Act 1925, unless excluded by express words or necessary implication.

Modern trusts usually rely on the statutory power, making minor alterations, often with power to advance the whole instead of one half of the beneficiary's presumptive or vested share or interest.

An 'advancement' is strictly a payment out of capital, historically intended for the purpose of advancing a child in life, by for instance, enabling him to study for some profession or occupation, or to set him up in business. In view of the quite restricted meaning of 'advancement' it became more common in trusts to add the words 'or benefit' and indeed this is the approach of section 32. More modern uses therefore include paying school fees, paying tax on behalf of the beneficiary, or in any other way using the capital to 'benefit' the beneficiary. A payment under section 32 is an advance distribution to the beneficiary of part of his expectant share. The power applies even if there is a possibility that the beneficiary's interest may be defeated but does not apply to a beneficiary who does not have an interest in capital, eg the life tenant.

In *Re Pauling's Settlement Trusts, Younghusband v Coutts & Co*[2], the Court of Appeal held that a power of advancement can be exercised only if there is some good reason for it – and the good reason must be beneficial to the person to be advanced. The power cannot be exercised capriciously or with some other benefit in view.

The other limitations of the statutory power of advancement are:

(1) the capital advanced must not exceed half the beneficiary's vested or presumptive share (unless expressly altered);

(2) when the beneficiary's interest vests, any advances must be brought into account in calculating his share ('hotchpot'); and

(3) the advance must not prejudice the prior life, or other, interest of any person (eg a life tenant) unless he is sui juris and gives his consent.

In *CD v O*[3] the court varied a trust of two life policies by extending the statutory power of advancement to the whole of a beneficiary's share in a fund.

---

1 Section 53.
2 [1963] 3 All ER 1.
3 [2004] EWHC 1036 (Ch).

I Other clauses

11.28   A trust may also contain some or all of the following clauses. Following the coming into force of the Trustee Act 2000, certain provisions (for example, regarding extending investment powers) are now automatically incorporated into trusts unless specifically excluded. Nevertheless, it is still common to see express provisions dealing with such matters:

(1)   Trustees' indemnity clause. There have been several cases addressing the effectiveness of such clauses. *Armitage v Nurse*[1] and *Bogg v Raper*[2] indicated that such clauses were, surprisingly to many observers, firmly established in terms of their effectiveness unless the trustee had been 'dishonest'. Although in cases of doubt such clauses would be construed against a trustee seeking to rely on such a clause. See for example, *Wight v Olswang*[3]. However, this view was modified in *Walker v Stones*[4] where it was held that, at least in the case of a solicitor-trustee, it was necessary to take into account the fact that where the trustee's 'honest belief', though actually held, is so unreasonable that no reasonable solicitor-trustee could have thought that an action was for the benefit of the beneficiaries. Further, in *Twinsectra v Yardley and others*[5] a combined test was introduced. Here it was held that a solicitor would be liable as an accessory to a breach of trust if he acts dishonestly. This required that (a) his conduct was dishonest by the standards of ordinary and reasonable people, and (b) he himself realised by their standards this conduct was dishonest.

In December 2002 the Law Commission consulted on trustee exemption clauses. Their favoured proposal seemed to be that trust corporations and other 'professional' trustees[6] should not be able to exclude liability arising from 'negligence'. The final report was published on 19 July 2006. The report recommends that the trust industry adopt a non-statutory rule of practice which should be enforced (so far as this is possible) by the regulatory and professional bodies who govern and influence trustees and the drafters of trusts. The Law Society and the Institute of Chartered Accountants in England and Wales have both already moved towards introducing regulation for their members. The Society of Trust and Estate Practitioners ('STEP') has launched a version of the rule that will bind its members in England and Wales.

The recommended rule of practice governs the disclosure and explanation of clauses in trust instruments which have the effect of limiting or excluding liability for negligence. The rule requires paid trustees to take reasonable steps to ensure that settlors understand the meaning and effect of such

---

1   [1998] Ch 241, [1997] 2 All ER 7095, CA.
2   (1998) Times, 22 April, CA.
3   (1998) Times, 17 September.
4   [2001] 2 WLR 623.
5   [2002] 2 AC 164.
6   Trustee Act 2000, s 28.

clauses before including them in trust instruments. The Report recommends that the drafters of trusts should also be subject to the rule.

(2) Charging clause. Without such a clause trustees were historically not able to charge more than their out of pocket expenses. Under the Trustee Act 2000, trust corporations and professional trustees are entitled to reasonable remuneration for their services to the trust, provided, in the case of professional trustees, that he is not a sole trustee and that each other trustee has agreed in writing to the remuneration[1]. This is the case even if the services are capable of being provided by a lay trustee. Clearly, an express charging clause could provide even greater flexibility.

(3) A clause specifying who has the power of appointing additional trustees.

(4) An investment clause. Until the Trustee Act 2000 such a clause was very important as the statutory investment provisions were comparatively limited (see below).

(5) A specific power to effect insurance or life assurance policies. Again, the Trustee Act 2000 means that a specific clause to this effect is no longer necessary in trusts, although in practice one is often included.

J Society of Trust and Estate Practitioners ('STEP') Standard Provisions

11.29 A trust document can be extremely lengthy – there are many more administrative provisions which may be used in addition to those mentioned above. It is now possible and arguably preferable to avoid all this by incorporating a standard set of administrative provisions.

STEP have produced a standard form which may be incorporated by the words 'the standard provisions of the Society of Trusts and Estate Practitioners (1st edition) shall apply'. The standard form shortens the length of a document and reduces the risk of accidental omissions. However, many settlors and trustees prefer to have all the relevant provisions set out in full in the trust document and independent legal advice should be taken on this.

SECTION 3   THE DUTIES AND POWERS OF TRUSTEES

11.30 The duties of a trustee are onerous, and must be strictly complied with if the trustee is not to commit a breach of trust and potentially be personally liable for any resulting loss to the trust. Both statute and case law impose many duties and powers which may be expressly amended by the terms of the trust.

The common law rule was that unless the trust instrument expressly indicated to the contrary, the trustee was not entitled to be paid for carrying out the trustee-

---

1   Sections 28 and 29.

ship[1]. However, the Trustee Act 2000 provides that trust corporations or professional trustees can receive remuneration from the trust for their services[2]. It is a basic principle that a trustee is entitled to recover his out of pocket expenses and this is embodied in statute[3].

A   Standard of care

11.31   The common law duty of care has largely been codified by the Trustee Act 2000, although the precise extent to which this codification extends is not totally clear and is examined further below. The position at common law (which is not necessarily replaced) is that an unpaid and non-professional trustee must perform his duties and exercise his discretionary powers in accordance with certain standards of care. In discharging his *duties* the equitable duty on the trustee is take the same care as an ordinary prudent man of business would use in the management of his own private affairs[4]. When performing his *duties of investment*, however, the trustee has a slightly higher duty of care, that of a prudent man of business investing for persons for whom he felt morally obliged to provide[5].

If trustees are professional trustees, eg a solicitor or bank, and are paid for performing their duties, an even higher standard is expected, that of the degree of care and skill which could reasonably be expected of persons with the same professional attributes as the trustees. A professional trustee is liable for loss through neglect to exercise the special care and skill it professes to have.

Bartlett v Barclays Bank Trust Co[6]

A settlement created in 1920 for the benefit of the settlor's wife and issue consisted of 99.8% of the debenture stock and shares in a private company. The bank was the trustee of the settlement. By 1960, following the death of the settlor and his wife, no beneficiary or member of the family was on the company's board, which comprised two surveyors, an accountant and a solicitor. No director regarded himself as the bank's representative. The bank did not attend the board's monthly meetings, and without the bank's knowledge the board embarked on two very hazardous property deals, one at Guildford and one at Old Bailey. The Guildford project succeeded, and the proceeds were used to invest in the Old Bailey project. It failed and the company suffered a large loss. As the board did not provide regular information to the bank and the bank was content to receive only that information it gleaned at annual general meetings, the bank was unaware of the hazardous nature of the property deals. The beneficiaries took proceedings against the bank for breach of trust. It was held that a prudent businessman would not have been content only with information from annual general

1   *Robinson v Pett* (1734) 3 P Wms 249.
2   Section 29.
3   Trustee Act 1925, s 30(2).
4   *Speight v Gaunt* (1883) 9 App Cas 1. See also *Bartlett v Barclays Bank Trust Co Ltd* [1980] 1 All ER 139.
5   *Learoyd v Whiteley* (1887) 12 App Cas 727.
6   [1980] 1 All ER 139.

meetings in the conduct of his own affairs. Moreover, the bank, as a professional corporate trustee owed a higher duty of care, and was liable for loss caused by failure to exercise the special care and skill which it professed to have. The bank was therefore held to be in breach of trust and was liable for the loss that had arisen. However, other cases have displayed a more lenient attitude towards professional trustees.

Nestle v National Westminster Bank plc[1]

This case has been heavily criticised. The bank was sole trustee of a trust fund which achieved very little real growth over the investment period. The bank had not understood the clause in the trust instrument relating to the scope of its investment powers and had not taken steps at any time to obtain legal advice on the matter. The Court of Appeal held that the bank had failed in its duty to review the investments regularly and should have taken legal advice about the scope of its powers under the will which created the trust. Although it had failed in its duties, the bank was not liable to the plaintiff who failed to prove loss as a result of the bank's breaches of duty, ie there was no breach of trust which was proved to have caused a loss.

11.32   The statutory duty of care as set out in section 1 of the Trustee Act 2000, applies in the circumstances specified in Schedule 1. These are quite limited and include the exercise of investment powers, powers in relation to land, powers to compound liabilities, power to insure trust property and powers in relation to reversionary interests, valuations and audit. It also applies when trustees enter into arrangements for the appointment of agents, custodians or nominees and when reviewing their activities. It would appear from the way in which it is drafted that the duty only applies to acts and not to omissions, so in respect of omissions the action will only be possible for a breach of the common law duty of care (which does not seem to be wholly replaced by the new statutory provisions). Another feature of section 1 of the Trustee Act 2000 (set out in subsection (1)) is that whilst the common law duty looks at objective standards of care, the statutory duty takes account of subjective factors[2] so differences could arise depending on whether a beneficiary's complaint relates to an act or omission.

The statutory duty of care does not apply to the extent that the trust instrument itself excludes its application[3].

Whenever the duty does apply the trustee must exercise such care and skill as is reasonable in the circumstances, having regard in particular to any special knowledge or experience that he has or holds himself out as having, and if he acts in the course of a business or profession he must have regard to any special knowledge or experience that it is reasonable to expect of a person acting in that kind of business or profession[4].

1   [1994] 1 All ER 118, CA.
2   Section 1(1)(a).
3   Schedule 1, para 7.
4   Section 1(1).

B   Summary of main duties of the trustee

1   On acceptance of the trust

11.33   Assuming a person named as trustee accepts trusteeship then on accepting the trust, the trustee should immediately:

(1)   make himself familiar with the terms of the trust, the contents of any document handed to him as trustee (including the trust instrument) and any relevant deeds or title papers and, generally make himself aware of the assets of the trust;

(2)   (if this has not already happened) arrange for all of the trust property to be transferred into the joint names of himself and his co-trustees[1];

(3)   investigate any circumstances indicating a possible prior breach of trust and, if necessary, seek to recover the trust fund if such a breach has occurred (for if he does not do this, he may be personally jointly liable);

(4)   consider the investments.

2   Possession and control of trust property

11.34   The trustees (whether original or appointed subsequently) must immediately, on their appointment, obtain possession and control of the trust property by the appropriate legal method in relation to the particular property of the trust. For example, if the trust property is cash, the trustees should jointly open a bank account and pay in the cash; if it is land, they should obtain (where necessary) a conveyance; if it is stocks and shares, they should obtain the appropriate certificates or registration in the names of the trustee (CREST is an electronic system which records share transactions and provides details of who owns shares without the need for a share certificate) and deposit bearer bonds with a bank where it will be held in their joint names; if it is life assurance policies, they should obtain the policy and (where necessary) an assignment of it. They should serve notice on the life office and enquire from the life office about notice of any earlier assignments.

The trustees should retain control of the trust property separately from any of their own property. Where the money is paid into a personal bank account (whether intentional or not), the trustee will be deemed to have spent his own money before that of the trust[2].

(a)   Vesting declarations

11.35   Section 40 of the Trustee Act 1925 removes the need for a formal conveyance or other appropriate means of transferring the property of the trust from

---

1   See 'Vesting declarations' at **11.35**.
2   *Re Hallett's Estate* [1880] 13 Ch D 696.

the old trustees to the new, or to the remaining trustees upon a retirement of other trustees. The section provides that, with some exceptions, and subject to any express provision to the contrary, if the appointment or retirement is by deed, it operates as if it contained a vesting declaration. It does not apply where the property is held by personal representatives, rather than trustees[1].

One of the exceptions set out in section 40(4) is that the automatic vesting declaration cannot extend to 'property which is only transferable . . . in a manner directed by or under Act of Parliament'. One view is that as life policies are assignable *at law* only as directed by the Policies of Assurance Act 1867, or section 136 of the Law of Property Act 1925, they are excluded from the automatic vesting provisions of section 40. However, a life policy is not *only* transferable in this way so it is thought that the exception would not apply to life policies.

3 Duty not to profit from the trust

11.36 'Equity prohibits a trustee from making any profit by his management, directly or indirectly'[2]. A trustee who acquires a benefit in his position as a trustee must surrender that benefit to the beneficiaries. This rule does not apply where the person who created the trust and appointed the trustee also grants the conflicting interest to that trustee[3].

4 Duty against a conflict of interest or self-dealing

11.37 A trustee must not put himself in the position where his duty to the trust and his own personal interest may conflict. This, in the view of the authors (unless the trust instrument expressly provides to the contrary), should require that independent intermediaries, representatives and appointed representatives refuse trusteeship of life policy trusts if investments are to be made upon their recommendations. They would, from the outset, be in a position of conflict and, in particular, ought properly to return any commission earned as a result of any trust investments made on their recommendation. (This must be contrasted with the position where the trust instrument allows fees for professional charges, although the precise terms should be considered.)

A trustee cannot generally purchase trust property for himself, even if he pays a fair price for it[4].

5 Duty to maintain an even hand between the classes of beneficiaries

11.38 The trustees must administer the trust honestly and impartially for the benefit of all the beneficiaries. Where the trust has life tenants (entitled to

---

1 *Re Cockburn's Will Trusts* [1957] Ch 438, [1957] 2 All ER 522.
2 *Regal Hastings Ltd v Gulliver* [1942] 1 All ER 378.
3 *Sargeant v National Westminster Bank plc* (1990) 61 P & CR 518, CA.
4 *Tito v Waddell (No 2)* [1977] 3 All ER 129.

income) and remaindermen (entitled to capital), the trustee must keep an even balance between the respective interests, and in particular, ensure that their investment strategy does not favour one at the expense of the other. Where the life tenant and the remaindermen are the same then issues in this respect are less likely to arise. The position is of particular relevance to life assurance policies as they are not income producing assets so there may be concerns about balancing the interests of beneficiaries under such trusts[1].

6   Duty to account

11.39   Trustees must keep accounts[2] and produce them when requested by the beneficiaries. They must also give the beneficiaries all reasonable information as to the running of the trust and must allow inspection of any title deeds or other documents relating to the trust, if so requested.

7   Duty to act unanimously

11.40   Unless the trust instrument provides for a majority decision, the trustees must act unanimously; their decisions and actions must be undertaken by all the trustees, as one body.

8   Duty to act personally and not delegate

11.41   Each trustee must act in his personal capacity except to the extent that delegation is authorised, either by law or specifically by the trust instrument (or by the beneficiaries where they are all mentally capable and over the age of 18). This is perhaps particularly relevant in relation to investing trust funds. The trustees may wish to delegate this function to an investment manager. There may be a specific power in the trust instrument, or the trustees can rely on the statutory powers to delegate set out in the Trustee Act 2000. The Trustee Act 2000 contains specific provisions regarding the appointment of asset managers by trustees (see further **11.43**).

Regarding appointment of an agent for other purposes, section 3(3) of the Enduring Powers of Attorney Act 1985 allowed a trustee to delegate his functions by using an enduring power of attorney. This was criticised on the basis that it did not involve as many of the safeguards for beneficiaries as a power of attorney under section 25 of the Trustee Act 1925. For example, under section 25, delegation is not permitted to a sole co-trustee and notice of the power of attorney must be given to the co-trustees. Under section 3(3), however, an appointment could be made to a sole co-trustee and notice was not required to be given to any party. Also, a section 3(3) delegation was indefinite. Further, a power of attorney under section 25 will be extinguished upon the mental incapacity of the

---

1   *Re Fisher, Harris v Fisher* [1943] Ch 377.
2   *Springett v Dashwood* (1860) 2 Giff 521.

donor, whereas under section 3(3), the grant of the power can survive[1]. These unintended effects in the law were the subject of a Law Commission report, 'The Law of Trusts, Delegation by Individual Trustees'[2]. It examined the circumstances and manner in which an individual trustee should be authorised to delegate and made recommendations for change, contained in a draft Bill. Further reference should be made to the Law Commission report, available from HMSO. The report made reference to collective delegation (particularly in relation to the investment of trust funds) by stating that this 'important topic needs to be considered'.

11.42   The Trustee Delegation Act 1999 implemented, with minor modifications, the changes recommended by the Law Commission in their report. It should be noted, however, that sections 1 and 2 only apply in respect of attorneys of trustees with beneficial interests in land. Section 4 of the Trustee Delegation Act 1999 repealed section 3(3) of the Enduring Powers of Attorney Act 1985 subject to various transitional provisions. The repeal implemented the policy that trustees should only be able to delegate their trustee functions by statute subject to the safeguards under section 25 of the Trustee Act 1925. This repeal ended the existence of the inconsistent but overlapping regimes for delegation by individual trustees and applies to all enduring powers of attorney (EPAs) created after the 1999 Act came into force[3].

A new section 25 of the Trustee Act 1925 was introduced by section 5 of the 1999 Act. The previous section 25 prohibited delegation to a sole co-trustee (unless a trust corporation). Both the existing and previous sections require that notice of appointment be given to specified persons and provided that the trustee remained liable for the acts and omissions of the attorney. The powers conferred under both existing and previous sections can be excluded or restricted by the trust document. Section 5(1) of the 1999 Act sets out the new section 25. The power of attorney can define the period for which it is to be effective (subject to a 12-month maximum) but if nothing is stated then the default period is 12 months.

The new section 25(3) no longer prohibits a sole co-trustee being the donor of a section 25 power but is subject to the practical difficulties which would arise as a result of the application of the 'two-trustee' rules.

A new prescribed form of power of attorney which may be used by a *single* trustee wishing to delegate all of his or her trustee functions in relation to a single trust to a single attorney is provided by section 25(6). Section 6 repealed section 2(8) of the Enduring Powers of Attorney Act 1985 so that an EPA can now be used to delegate trustee functions under section 25 of the Trustee Act 1925 (and so is, of course, subject to the protections of the new section 25).

Section 7 specifies the various 'two-trustee' rules (generally that moneys accruing to a trust should always be dealt with by two trustees) and that these cannot be satisfied by one person acting in two capacities.

---

1   For a discussion on powers of attorney generally, see Thurston *A Practitioners' Guide to Powers of Attorney* (5th edn, 2003).
2   Law Com No 220, January 1994.
3   Section 4(1).

Section 36 of the Trustee Act 1925 relating to the appointment of new or additional trustees is amended to give the attorney under an EPA a new but limited power of appointment of new trustees in certain circumstances. These are necessary to prevent the strengthened 'two-trustee' rules from frustrating the new power for an attorney under an enduring power to exercise the trustee functions of the donor.

11.43   The trustees' powers to *collectively* delegate under the 2000 Act are wide ranging. Trustees may now delegate any of the defined 'delegable functions'. With regard to non-charitable trusts these are any function other than (a) any function relating to whether or in what way trust assets should be distributed; (b) any power to decide whether fees or payments should be paid from capital or income; (c) power to appoint trustees; (d) any power to delegate or to appoint a nominee or custodian. For trustees of charitable trusts the definition is much narrower.

Almost anyone may be appointed as an agent except a beneficiary[1]. Where 'asset management functions' are delegated to an agent additional requirements are imposed. The appointment must be made in an agreement made or evidenced in writing. Furthermore, trustees must prepare a policy statement providing guidance to their agent as to how the delegated investment powers should be used. This must be done with a view to ensuring the powers are exercised 'in the best interests of the trust'. In addition, any agreement with an investment manager must have a confirmation that the investment manager will secure compliance with the Policy Statement and the trustees must assess whether the Policy Statement is being complied with. The trustees must also review the Policy Statement from time to time.

Regarding the terms upon which the delegation is made the agent is bound by the same restrictions as the trustee. The trustee can specify the terms of the delegation including reasonable remuneration for services provided and reimbursement for expenses properly incurred. Certain terms can only be agreed so far as 'reasonably necessary'. These are sub-delegation, limitation of liability of the agent and acting despite conflicts of interest[2].

9   Duty to invest

11.44   The trustees must seek to safeguard the value of the trust property by investing it in accordance with the terms of the trust instrument or (if the trust is silent on this point) in accordance with the Trustee Act 2000. Until the implementation of this Act on 1 February 2001 the relevant statutory provision was the Trustee Investments Act 1961. Unless the trust instrument contained wide investment powers, the trustees did not have power to invest in a life assurance policy under the 1961 Act. The provisions of the 2000 Act relating to investment are far-reaching and the 1961 Act has been repealed. There is a 'general power of investment' which enables them to make any investment they could make if

---

1   Section 12(3).
2   Section 14(1) to (3).

they were absolutely entitled to the trust assets except land other than loans secured on land[1]. It is sometimes mistakenly stated that this empowers the trustees to invest in anything they like. However, this is not quite the case as this is subject to the 'standard investment criteria', the need to obtain and consider 'proper advice', and the imposition of the statutory duty of care on trustees exercising those duties. The standard investment criteria are virtually identical to those in the 1961 Act. Trustees must have regard to the suitability of the investments and the need for diversification[2]. Trustees must further review the trust instrument from time to time to consider any possible variations[3]. In considering suitability the trustees must firstly look at the type of investment to see if it is a good investment for the trust and then look at the specific investment of that type, taking into account such things as performance. Trustees must also obtain and consider proper advice[4] when reviewing the investments of the trust[5]. However, a trustee need not obtain such advice if he reasonably believes that in all the circumstances it is unnecessary or inappropriate to do so[6].

The general power of investment is in addition to powers otherwise conferred on trustees[7], but is also subject to any restriction or exclusion imposed by the trust instrument, or by any enactment or any subordinate legislation[8].

10 Nominees and custodians

11.45 The 2000 Act also introduced new provisions regarding nominees and custodians. Previously, there was no existing general power to use custodians and nominees so, for example, it was technically impossible to use CREST (an electronic settlement system for shares – see **11.34**), etc without an express power (although many trustees were prepared to accept the risk where the status of the nominee or custodian was such as to give them reasonable comfort). Sections 16–20 now contain express powers in this respect. Writing is required and the statutory duty of care applies to the trustees in making such an appointment. Sections 16 and 17 (power to appoint custodians or nominees) do not apply where there is a 'custodian trustee'. There are restrictions on who can be a nominee or custodian. Only those who carry on such a business or a body corporate controlled by trustees can be nominees or custodians. As with a standard delegation certain aspects can only be agreed if reasonably necessary (sub-delegation, limitation of liability and conflicts of interest)[9].

With both a standard delegation and an appointment of nominees and custodians (and in most cases whether or not the appointment is under the 2000 Act)

1 Section 3(1).
2 Section 4.
3 Section 4(2).
4 Section 5(1).
5 Section 5(2).
6 Section 5(3).
7 Section 6(1)(a).
8 Section 6(1)(b).
9 Section 20.

there is a duty to review such arrangements[1]. Intervention must be considered if necessary and where relevant the 'policy statement' must be kept under review[2].

There is no general liability for acts of agents, etc appointed under the 2000 Act provided the duty of care is complied with[3]. Third parties have no need to check compliance with the terms of the 2000 Act[4].

(A)   Reform of trust powers

11.46   The Trustee Act 2000 came into force on 1 February 2001. It implemented, with some amendments, the recommendations of the Law Commission and the Scottish Law Commission Reports entitled *Trustees' Powers and Duties (1999) Law Com No 260, Scot Law Com No 172*.

(B)   Trustees duty while investing

11.47   Trustees must seek to obtain the best rate of return available irrespective of their own, or the beneficiaries', political, social or moral views[5].

I I   *Duty to consider powers*

11.48   Whilst under a discretion as to whether or not to actually exercise their powers and under no duty to actually exercise them, the trustees are under a duty to actively consider whether or not to use them[6].

C   Breach of trust

11.49   Failing to comply with any of their duties will constitute a breach of trust, for which the trustees will be personally, jointly and severally liable. A breach of trust, whatever its nature, will be taken very seriously by the courts. A defence may be available in the form of section 61 of the Trustee Act 1925, which provides that the court may relieve, in whole or in part, the trustees' potential liability if he has acted honestly and reasonably and ought fairly, in all the circumstances, to be excused.

I   *Indemnity*

11.50   An indemnity may be available under section 62 of the Trustee Act 1925 if the breach of trust is at the instigation, request, or with the consent in writing

1   Section 22.
2   Section 22(2).
3   Section 23(1).
4   Section 24.
5   See *Cowan v Scargill* [1985] Ch 270 and *Harries Church Comrs for England* [1993] 2 All ER 300.
6   *Re Hay's Settlement Trust* [1981] 3 All ER 786.

of a beneficiary. In this case, the court may impound all or any part of the particular beneficiary's interest in the trust property by way of indemnity to the trustee. This provision, however, will not be allowed to benefit a trustee who is also a beneficiary.

2 Participation, consent, release or acquiescence by the beneficiaries

11.51 If they are sui juris (having full legal capacity), such consensus will prevent the beneficiaries in bringing a claim against the trustees[1].

D Powers

11.52 Various powers are conferred upon trustees by statute and the trust instrument may (and often will) extend or alter these. Apart from the powers of maintenance and advancement already considered, the Trustee Act 1925 gives, for example, powers of sale; power to give receipts; power to insure; power to partition property; powers of compromise, etc. The Trustee Delegation Act 1999 and the Trustee Act 2000 have also expanded the trustee's statutory powers.

The full range of powers may be detailed in the trust instrument or the settler may simply rely on the general law although this would be unusual in an express trust. As mentioned earlier, a set of standard powers may be incorporated by using STEP's short form.

E Position of the beneficiaries

11.53 The beneficiaries cannot, generally, control the trustees while the trust remains in being. The trustees are guided by the trust instrument, the rules of equity and statutory provisions, and in the exercise of their functions they are entitled to use their own judgment and are not ordinarily obliged to consult the wishes of the beneficiaries[2].

The beneficiaries do have a right to compel proper administration of the trust either by insisting on an audit of the accounts by a solicitor or accountant acceptable to the trustees[3], or by making an application to the court for the determination of a specific question[4] or for the general administration of the trust[5].

If the beneficiaries are sui juris and together entitled to the whole beneficial interest they can put an end to the trust and direct the trustees to hand over the trust property[6].

1 *Fletcher v Collis* [1905] 2 Ch 24.
2 *Re Brockbank, Ward v Bates* [1948] 1 All ER 287.
3 Public Trustee Act 1906, s 13.
4 CPR Part 64, para 1.
5 CPR Part 64, rule 2(1).
6 *Saunders v Vautier* (1841) 4 Beav 115.

SECTION 4   DEALINGS WITH LIFE POLICIES IN TRUST

A   Introduction

11.54   The first duty of trustees is to preserve the trust property for the benefit of the beneficiaries. Dealings with the trust property by the trustees should only be effected:

(1)   under a direction or authority in the trust itself, which may be express or implied;

(2)   by direction of the beneficiaries, being sui juris and between them entitled to the whole beneficial interest;

(3)   under the authority of statute; or

(4)   by order of the court.

I   Authorisation in the trust instrument

11.55   In many cases it will be clear from the trust instrument that the trustees can authorise or enter into the proposed transaction. Where a trust of a life policy has been created using one of the life office's standard trust forms, the life office should still check the terms of that trust, as the settlor may have altered the standard terms to suit his particular circumstances.

If the trust instrument specifically authorises the trustees to carry out the transaction, the life office may safely accept the trustees' discharge or request, subject however to any notice of the purpose of the transaction being inconsistent with the purposes of the trust.

B   Trustees' powers to deal with life policies

I   Power to sell or mortgage

11.56   In modern times trustees will almost always be given express power to sell or mortgage by the trust instrument and, in any event, this may be possible under statute for property 'in possession'[1].

2   Power to surrender

11.57   A modern trust instrument will usually give the trustees a power (either specific or general) to sell or surrender the policy and hold the proceeds as part of the trust property or to exercise any options under the policy (although sometimes the power to exercise options, make investment switches, etc is reserved by

---

1   Eg Trustee Act 1925, s 16.

the settlor to himself). From *Re Steen Trusts, Steen v Peebles*[1] it would seem that a trustee may, without a specific power, surrender a life policy in exchange for a fully paid up policy of less value in cases where the party liable to pay the premiums cannot possibly do so.

Where a trustee has a power of sale, but not expressly a power to surrender, it is thought that the power of sale is sufficient to authorise the trustees to surrender the policy as a surrender is in substance a sale of the policy to the life office but the matter is not entirely free from doubt.

3 Power to raise money by sale, mortgage, etc

11.58   Section 16 of the Trustee Act 1925 provides:

> 'Where trustees are authorised by the instrument, if any, creating the trust or by law to pay or apply capital money subject to the trust for any purpose or in any manner, they shall have and shall be deemed always to have had power to raise the money required by sale, conversion, calling in or mortgage of all or any part of the property for the time being in possession.'

This section applies notwithstanding anything contrary contained in the trust instrument (but does not apply to certain types of trust such as charitable trusts).

A policy is, however, unlikely to be treated as 'property in possession' within the meaning of section 16 of the Trustee Act 1925: 'All personal things are either in possession or in action. The law knows no *tertium quid* between the two'. (A 'tertium quid' essentially being a third possibility[2].) A policy is a chose in action, ie a thing of which the owner does not have the possession, but only a right to recover it by a suit or action at law. Cash in a person's pocket is an example of a thing in possession.

'Property' is defined by section 68 of the Trustee Act 1925 as including real and personal property, any thing in action, and any other right or interest, whether in possession or not. 'Possession' is defined as including receipt of rents or profits, or the right to receive the same, if any. A life policy does not produce an income[3], although it is clear that there can be an interest in possession in a policy even though it produces no income[4].

In view of the lack of authority, it is perhaps undesirable to rely on section 16 as conferring a power to sell, surrender or mortgage a policy.

4 Power of sale implied in order to invest

11.59   Section 3 of the Trustee Act 2000 enables any kind of investment to be made by a trustee as if he were absolutely entitled. It is probably reasonable to conclude that he would have an implied power to sell the current trust assets in order to make an investment.

---

1   (1890) 25 LR Ir 544.
2   *Colonial Bank v Whinney* (1885) 30 Ch D 261, per Fry LJ.
3   *Re Fisher, Harris v Fisher* [1943] 2 All ER 615.
4   See Chapter 14.

5   Powers to raise tax

11.60   Under section 212 of the Inheritance Tax Act 1984, where a trustee is liable for inheritance tax, he has the power to sell or mortgage or create a terminable charge on the property to which the inheritance tax is attributable in order to raise the amount of the tax or any interest and expenses properly incurred by him in respect of the tax. Section 212(3) further enables any money held on the trusts of a settlement to be expended in paying the inheritance tax attributable to the value of any property comprised in the settlement and held on the same trusts.

6   Protection to purchasers and mortgagees dealing with trustees

11.61   Section 17 of the Trustee Act 1925 provides that a purchaser or mortgagee paying or advancing money on a sale or mortgage purporting to be made under a trust or power vested in trustees shall not be concerned to see that the money is necessary, or that no more than is necessary is raised, or otherwise as to its application.

7   Power to borrow

11.62   The trust instrument will often confer on the trustees a specific power to borrow to pay the premiums in respect of a life policy. Such a power is in any case implied if the trustees have no funds to keep up a policy which is in danger of lapse[1]. If a trustee pays a premium with his own funds, he will have a lien on the policy for the amount of the premium[2]. A voluntary payment by a third party is not, however, sufficient to give a lien[3].

8   Liens on premiums

11.63   In *Re Smith's Estate, Bilham v Smith*[4], B effected an endowment assurance on his life under the Married Women's Property Act 1882 for the absolute benefit of his wife (W). W died, but B maintained the policy until maturity. He died shortly after maturity and his second wife, as his executrix, claimed a lien on the policy money for premiums paid by B after W's death. It was held that the claim of the executrix on behalf of B's estate was enforceable. It was for money expended by B as a trustee to preserve the property of a beneficiary[5].

It is thought that no lien would be acquired if B had continued paying premiums after the death of W with the intention of benefiting the persons entitled

---

1   *Clack v Holland* (1854) 19 Beav 262, 24 LJ Ch 13.
2   *Re Smith's Estate, Bilham v Smith* [1937] 3 All ER 472.
3   See *Re Leslie, Leslie v French* (1883) 23 Ch D 552 and *Re Jones' Settlement, Stunt v Jones* [1915] 1 Ch 373.
4   [1937] 3 All ER 472.
5   See also *Re Roberts* [1946] Ch 1.

through her. If, therefore, a husband (or other person in such circumstances) does not wish to acquire a lien, he should take steps to see that there is evidence available as to his intention. Some life offices incorporate in their forms of proposal and request for trust policies, a declaration by the proposer that no premiums he may pay shall give rise to a lien, it being his intention in paying them to make a gift to the persons beneficially entitled to the policy.

9 Power to raise a loan on the security of a policy

11.64 Assuming there is the right (or facility) to raise a loan on the security of the policy from the life office in the policy terms this is sometimes restricted to the 'absolute owners' of policies. This would presumably not include trustees, even if the trust instrument provides that they shall have the investment power of an absolute owner on the basis that they hold the legal, but not the beneficial, interest. The trust instrument may, however, specifically authorise the trustees to raise money in this fashion. The trust instrument and the policy terms should therefore be examined closely.

10 Power to exercise options

11.65 Where the policy contains options they become part of the trust property and the trustees must exercise them for the benefit of the beneficiaries under the trust, and not so as to defeat their interests. The rights conferred by the options are part of the assets of the trust, unless specifically excluded (sometimes the settler reserves the right in the trust to exercise these). In *Re Fleetwood's Policy*[1] the settlor exercised an option to surrender the policy for cash and it was held that the trusts continued to attach to the resulting surrender value, which consequently had to remain in court until it was clear who was entitled to it.

In *Re Policy of Equitable Life Assurance Society of the United States and Mitchell*[2] a policy had been effected in favour of a named wife, if living, at the life assured's death, or if she was not living then for his children, and if none survived him, for his executors, administrators or assigns. The named wife and one child died. The husband remarried and assigned all his property to a trustee for his creditors. The trustee proposed to exercise the option of taking the cash value of the policy for the benefit of the creditors. The court decided that the options could be exercised by the assured only as trustee for the beneficiaries under the policy, and that the proper course was to issue a paid-up policy for the benefit of the children who survived the life assured, but if none survived, then for his estate.

11 Power of trustees to exercise contractual rights

11.66 If, under the policy, the assured has a right to surrender, convert to a paid-up assurance, raise a loan or exercise an option, it seems that his right to do any of those things will pass to the trustees of a trust to which the policy has been

1 [1926] Ch 48.
2 (1911) 27 TLR 213.

assigned. It seems, therefore, that, unless they are expressly prohibited, the trustees are entitled to exercise any such right in the policy in whatever manner they think is most beneficial to the beneficiaries, unless the exercise of the option would be inconsistent with the purposes of the trust. It is also possible for the settlor to specifically retain for himself in the trust the right to exercise certain options. Most trusts would give the trustees specific power or powers to deal generally with the policy or other trust assets and so in practice the point in unlikely to arise. If they have the necessary powers it is for the trustees to decide how they shall exercise their powers and the life office is not concerned with their reasons unless it has notice that a breach of trust is intended, or that the proposed transaction is inconsistent with the trust purposes, in which case it should be concerned as a potential constructive trustee.

An alternative (but not widely held) view, however, is that trustees can only exercise a contractual right under a policy if they are authorised to do so by their trust instrument.

12   Power to compound liabilities

11.67   Under section 15 of the Trustee Act 1925, a personal representative, two or more trustees acting together or (where authorised by the trust instrument or by statute) a sole trustee, are given a wide discretion to settle claims (and ancillary matters) which may be made by third parties against the trust or vice versa. Section 15 of the Act is not concerned with disputes arising within the trust.

Without such a wide power the trustees might be obliged to litigate every possible claim in order not to be in breach of trust. Section 15 only protects trustees who have acted or at least exercised an active discretion and will not relieve them where they have ignored the claim[1]. The trustees may apply to the court for directions or to sanction a compromise where the court will consider the most desirable compromise as is fair between all the beneficiaries[2].

There is considerable disagreement as to whether section 15 allows the trustees, in exercise of their wide powers of compromise, to surrender a policy. In the absence of authority, it seems unsafe to rely on this section alone. In *Wrightson v IRC*[3], it seems to have been accepted that because there was no power in the settlement to surrender the policies, the trustees could not do so; it was not suggested in argument that there might be power under section 15 of the Trustee Act 1925, or any other statutory provision.

13   Maintaining the policy

11.68   The trust instrument may include any of the following provisions:

(1)   A covenant by the settlor to pay the premiums; if the policy should become voidable, to restore it; and, if it should lapse, to effect a further policy for

1   *Re Greenwood* (1911) 105 LT 509.
2   *Re Earl of Stafford, Royal Bank of Scotland v Byng* [1979] 1 All ER 513, CA.
3   *Wrightson v IRC* [1957] 2 All ER 745.

the amount which would have been payable at death under the lapsed policy. This is a rare provision in modern trusts in view of the fact that the settlor is imposing an onerous obligation upon himself.

(2)   A power to the trustees to pay the premiums out of the income or capital of the trust fund if the settlor fails to pay them.

(3)   A proviso that the trustees shall not be responsible for seeing that the policy is kept up and that it shall not be a breach of trust for them to allow it to become void.

Trustees are not bound to pay the premiums under a settled policy where they have no funds available to enable them to do so but, if they have funds provided for the purpose, they have power to use them to pay premiums if the policy would otherwise lapse. If they pay them out of their own funds they will be entitled to be indemnified out of the trust property for the amount they have paid out[1]. If the assured does not pay the premiums and the trustees cannot do so, they must take whatever course is likely to be in the best interest of the beneficiaries. It might be in their interest that the policy should be converted into a paid-up assurance, in which case, the life office would be safe in accepting their application to do so. It must, however, be remembered that if the policy could be maintained without forfeiture, this might prove more advantageous to the beneficiaries than conversion to a paid-up assurance. This would almost certainly be the case if the life assured were to die whilst the policy was in force.

14   Dealings with the policy at the direction of beneficiaries

11.69   Even if not authorised by the trust instrument, or by statute, surrenders and other dealings with policies are possible provided that the persons entitled to the beneficial interest are all ascertained, and are of full age and capacity, and all of them concur in the transaction[2].

In *Re Smith, Public Trustee v Aspinall*[3], the trustees held property upon trust at their discretion to pay or apply income or capital for the maintenance or support of a wife, with trusts over for the children. All the beneficiaries were ascertained and of full capacity. It was held that the trustees must give effect to a mortgage of the trust assets executed by the beneficiaries, who were able if they so desired to require the trustees to hand over the trust fund to them.

15   Powers of the court

11.70   Under section 57 of the Trustee Act 1925, where a sale, mortgage, surrender or other disposition of the policy, or other transaction, is, in the opinion of

---

1   *Re Smith's Estate, Bilham v Smith* [1937] 3 All ER 472 (but see *Clack v Holland* (1854) 19 Beav 262, 273, 277).
2   *Saunders v Vautier* (1841) 4 Beav 115.
3   [1928] Ch 915.

the court, expedient but the trustees have no power to effect it, the court may by order confer upon the trustees the necessary power for the purpose.

16 Settlor's powers of revocation

11.71   It is a common misconception that the trust is in some way 'owned' by the settlor and so he can therefore do what he wants with it. However, once the settlor has effectively constituted a valid trust of the policy he has given up control of the policy and it is then owned by the trustees to deal with in accordance with the terms of the trust. It is open to the settlor to reserve the right to withdraw the policy from the trust by including appropriate provisions in the trust and the extent of these provisions is subject to the construction of the trust document. This is subject to the trust not being held to be a 'sham'[1]. The settler is also usually a trustee and so may exercise a degree of control in that capacity.

17 The extent of the trust property

11.72   It is also a question of construction as to the extent of the trust property. In most cases there is little doubt that the whole of the policy and anything deriving from it or accruing to it is the subject of the trust. However, in some cases there has been some doubt as to whether bonus payments are subject to the trust or are retained by the settlor[2].

18 Summary

11.73   Policies held by trustees may be surrendered or otherwise dealt with by the trustees alone if power to do so is conferred on them by the trust instrument or by statute. Probably, a right to surrender set out in the policy can be exercised by trustees, even in the absence of specific power in the trust instrument provided that its exercise is not inconsistent with the trust purposes. In the cases of policies specifically settled, however, it seems likely that in most cases it will be inconsistent with the purposes of the trust for the trustees to surrender the policy in the absence of an express power to this effect. Any transaction may, however, be carried out if the beneficiaries are all ascertained and sui juris and they all join with the trustees in effecting it; or the transaction may be carried out if authorised by the court under section 57 of the Trustee Act 1925.

C Dealings with the beneficial interest in trust policies

1 Assignments

11.74   A beneficiary may deal with his interest in the policy in the same way and under the same conditions as he could deal with any interest under a trust.

---

1   See, for example, *Rahman v Chase Bank (CI) Trust Co Ltd* [1991] JLR 103.
2   *Gilly v Burley* (1856) 22 Beav 619; *Roberts v Edwards* (1863) 9 Jur (NS) 1219.

The assignee or mortgagee of such an interest should serve notice on the trustees of the policy.

D   Claims by trustees: examination of title[1]

11.75   When a claim under a life policy is made by trustees at death or maturity, the trust document and all deeds of appointment or retirement of trustees must be produced. If they are in order, the life office may safely pay the policy moneys to the trustees, unless it has knowledge of an intended breach of trust. If the life office has such knowledge, it should not pay out, as it may subsequently find itself liable as a constructive trustee for any loss suffered by to the beneficiaries.

Where any appointment of new trustees has been made by the survivors or survivor of two or more persons in whom the power to appoint new trustees was vested, evidence of death of the deceased appointor or appointors should be produced.

If a trustee dies, his office passes to the remaining trustees. When the last remaining trustee, or a sole trustee dies, the trust property will devolve upon his personal representatives[2]. The person on whom the deceased trustee's estate devolves cannot be compelled to act in the trusts which have devolved upon him[3], nor can he insist upon doing so against the wishes of a donee of a power of appointing new trustees in place of the deceased trustee(s)[4].

If the claim is made by the personal representatives of a last surviving trustee, evidence of the deaths of trustees should be produced, together with the grant of representation to the estate of the last survivor.

Where the trustees apply to surrender a policy, to convert it to a paid-up assurance, to borrow on its security or to exercise any option, the life office must satisfy itself: (1) as to the title of the trustees; (2) that they have the power to carry out the desired transactions; and (3) that the office has no notice that the power is being exercised for a purpose not permitted by the trust instrument.

I   Notice of breach of trust

11.76   If the life office is satisfied that the trustees have power to effect a proposed transaction, it is entitled, in the absence of notice to the contrary, to assume this is consistent with the general purposes of the trust. But where it is apparent from the trust instrument itself that the trustees' actions are inconsistent with the trust purposes, or where the office is aware that a breach of trust is intended, it should not agree to the trustees' request. If the life office agreed, it could be liable as a constructive trustee if it had actual or constructive knowledge of the breach.

---

1   For a general discussion on this subject see Chapter 9.
2   Trustee Act 1925, s 18(2).
3   *Re Benett* [1906] 1 Ch 216; see also *Re Ridley* [1904] 2 Ch 774 and the cases cited therein.
4   *Re Routledge's Trusts* [1909] 1 Ch 280.

In most cases, however, it is probable that there would be some trust purpose that could be served by the particular transaction. So long as there is some such purpose which could be served, the life office is under no obligation to enquire what that particular purpose is, and still less to satisfy itself that the proposed course of action is the best one in the circumstances. In some cases, the life office may require the beneficiaries to join in the transaction; or if it identified a particular issue, for example, there were minor or unascertained beneficiaries, the attention of the trustees may be drawn to their obligations. However, in seeking to protect its own position and in looking to provide a service to its customers the life office cannot of course act as a legal adviser to the trustees and must confine itself to remarking upon its own position although this may assist the trustees in understanding their own position. If the life office knows the purpose for which the money or the transaction is required, it must satisfy itself that it is within the trust purposes. A life office paying money to the trustees with knowledge that it will be applied in breach of trust will not get a good discharge.

In practice the life office is likely to wish to seek to avoid any questions being raised regarding its conduct. So where it has notice of dispute it should proceed with caution, perhaps delaying payment until all parties have reached agreement.

2 Method of payment

11.77 Normally, payment should be made to *all* the trustees (or on the instructions of all the trustees). Although a sole trustee would appear to have a statutory power to give a complete discharge to the life office conferred by section 14 of the Trustee Act 1925 provided land is not included. It provides that the receipt in writing of *a* trustee for any money, securities or other personal property or effects payable, transferable or deliverable to him under any trust or power shall be a sufficient discharge to the person paying, transferring, or delivering the same and shall effectually exonerate him for any loss or misapplication thereof. Section 14 applies, notwithstanding anything to the contrary in the instrument (if any) creating the trust[1].

Where there is more than one trustee, it is not entirely certain whether it is sufficient for one trustee to give a receipt, or whether all trustees must join in the receipt. The section clearly refers to *a* trustee. However, this does conflict with the fundamental principle that trustees must act unanimously. Further, certain texts[2] also state that only a receipt by *all* the trustees will give a good discharge to a purchaser. The texts which support this view cite cases in support[3] which were decided prior to the passing of the Trustee Act 1925. The safest course to take where there is more than one trustee is for the life office to insist on the receipt of all of them, unless the trust instrument allows a majority of trustees to give a good receipt and discharge or possibly even one of their number.

---

1 Section 14(3).
2 See *MacGillivray and Parkington on Insurance Law* (10th edn, 2003) paras 24–203.
3 *Lee v Sankey* (1872) LR 15 Eq 204, *Re Flower and Metropolitan Board of Works* (1884) 27 Ch D 592.

Instead of acting personally, the trustees may, by a power conferred upon them by statute[1] employ and pay an agent to exercise any or all of their 'delegable functions'. This does not include, for example, deciding whether or in what way any assets of the trust should be distributed.

A life office must accordingly pay, for example, a banker or solicitor who, by producing the policy and the receipt, gives evidence of his appointment as agent to receive the money.

A personal representative is a trustee within the meaning of the Trustee Act 2000[2]. It is clear that, on express direction in writing from the trustees, the life office can pay a solicitor, banker, stockbroker or similar professional person. It should not ordinarily, however, pay to:

(1) just one of the trustees, who is not a solicitor, banker or stockbroker or similar professional person;

(2) a bank, if the account to be credited is not the account of the trustees or of their appropriate professional agent; or

(3) a beneficiary;

unless, perhaps, the life office is satisfied that the payment is being made in the due course of the performance of the trusts, or the terms of the policy[3] and that there have been no dealings with the beneficial interest of which the trustees or the life office have notice and which is inconsistent with such payment. It is, of course, possible that the life office will take a pragmatic view regarding payment where the sum of money at stake is not large and there is nothing which otherwise arouses suspicion.

Where the trustees receive money as a result of any transaction, eg on surrender, they must pay or apply it in accordance with the provisions of the trust instrument or their statutory powers (eg of maintenance or advancement), or invest it as part of the trust fund, unless the beneficiaries being sui juris and between them entitled to the whole beneficial interest, direct otherwise.

E Trust policies and cancellation

11.78 The requirements for an insurer to issue a cancellation notice are explained in Chapter 5. There is nothing in statute or the regulations or rules (in particular COBS 6.7) which explain the consequences of a cancellation by the proposer of a policy which has been written under trust from the outset. The following is therefore only one possible view. The right to cancel would appear to be vested in the proposer as the cancellation rights vest in the 'retail customer' under the COB Rules. It is difficult to see how the trustees could be viewed as the 'retail customer' in this context. The trust is properly and completely constituted

---

1 Trustee Act 2000, s 11.
2 Section 35.
3 See *O'Reilly v Prudential Assurance Co Ltd* [1934] All ER Rep 672.

prior to the expiration of the cancellation period (as the trust property is in existence). The proposer's right to cancel does not affect the validity of the trust (albeit that the trust could subsequently have no trust property if cancellation rights were exercised and so would cease as a result).

Assuming that the proposer is under no contractual liability to maintain the policy (which might arise in the case, for example, of cross partnership or shareholder policies) there will be no breach of duty if the proposer serves a notice of cancellation in respect of a trust policy. The beneficiary of the trust takes the beneficial interest in the trust property subject to all the restrictions and provisions attaching to it, including the power vested in the proposer to cancel the policy during the cancellation period.

Where the insurer returns sums to the proposer from cancellation of a trust policy, the question arises as to the capacity in which the proposer holds the returned sums. Much here depends upon a proper construction of the trust instrument. No general statement can be given in view of the variety of trust wordings in use. One view is that the returned sums would not normally constitute trust property because the settlor has sought to declare a trust of a life policy at the outset, so where that policy is cancelled the intention of the settlor is not fulfilled with the result that the trust fails. However, it can also be argued that a policy was in existence and the proceeds are therefore trust assets. The life office discharges its legal duties on returning the premiums and any other appropriate sums to the 'retail customer'[1], who will be the proposer.

It is thought that the right of cancellation expires on the proposer's death as there is no one who would be a 'retail customer'. It is also thought that the power to cancel vested in the proposer is personal to him and is not capable of assignment.

SECTION 5   THE APPOINTMENT, RETIREMENT AND REMOVAL OF TRUSTEES

A   Who can be a trustee?

11.79   In general, any individual, limited company or other body able to hold property may be appointed a trustee. Apart from persons under 18 there is no statutory prohibition upon the appointment of any person as a trustee. However, there are some persons who, whilst they have the legal capacity, are so undesirable as trustees that the court may, upon application by a beneficiary or co-trustee, remove them if they are appointed, eg:

(1)   if there is financial irresponsibility leading to bankruptcy[2];

(2)   if there is conviction of crimes involving dishonesty[3];

---

1   COB 6.7.52R.
2   *Re Barker's Trusts* (1875) 1 Ch D 43.
3   *Coombes v Brookes* (1871) LR 12 Eq 61.

(3) where appointment as trustee would conflict with an individual's interest as a beneficiary (but this does not mean that a trustee cannot be a beneficiary)[1].

It is common for banks, insurers, solicitors, accountants and other financial services organisations to establish 'in house' trust companies for either their own internal purposes or for commercial reasons.

B Number of trustees

1 Maximum

11.80 For trusts of property such as life policies (there are different provisions for land, etc), there is no legal restriction upon the number which may be appointed and also hold legal title to the particular property (except as provided by section 36(6) of the Trustee Act 1925 relating to the appointment of additional trustees).

2 Minimum

11.81 One trustee is sufficient except where it is necessary to give a good receipt for the purchase money of land in England or Wales. At least two trustees must remain after the retirement of a trustee under section 39 of the Trustee Act 1925 or after the discharge of a trustee under section 37(1)(c) (except where only one trustee was originally appointed).

C Appointment of first and new trustees

1 First (or additional) trustees

11.82 When an inter vivos (ie during lifetime) trust is created, the settlor will usually appoint the first trustees himself so that there are trustees in addition to the settlor at the outset. The original trust deed is therefore likely to include a clause appointing the trustee(s) who may be the settlor himself and/or other persons. The settlor will almost certainly also, in the trust instrument, give someone the power to appoint further trustees or he may reserve the power himself. But if he makes any future appointment under that power he will do so because he is the person named or specified in the trust instrument as having that power, and not simply because he is the settlor.

2 Effective vesting of policy in first trustees of life policy trusts

11.83 It is common practice to appoint additional trustees from the outset, in the same document used to declare the trust perhaps with a direction to issue the

---

1   *Re Parsons, Barnsdale and Smallman v Parsons* [1940] 4 All ER 65.

policy to the trustees (usually the settlor and the additional trustees). In the case of new policies the question arises whether or not such an appointment will result in a legally effective vesting of title to the policy in the trustees.

Where an existing policy is assigned to a pre-existing trust, there will invariably be existing trustees, in whom the policy can vest so long as it is properly assigned. Where a new policy is effected in accordance with the Married Women's Property Act 1882, the statutory provisions provide for the effective vesting of property in the trustees. Where an existing life policy is to be subject to a declaration of trust, the settlor may assign the policy to the trustees (one of which may be the settlor himself) by specific wording to this effect. Often, even without any conveyance or assignment, the declaration of trust and appointment of trustees will be by way of deed and thus the title to the policy will automatically vest in the trustees by reason of section 40 of the Trustee Act 1925.

Where, however, the trust is created by using what has been termed a 'trust request', whereby the proposer requests the life office to effect and issue the policy to him and the additional trustees, on trust, there is a school of thought that there will not be an effective vesting of title of the policy in the additional trustees as, at the time of the appointment, the policy is 'future property', which is not, in law, capable of being assigned. This might, it is argued, require a subsequent, formal assignment of the policy (once it is in existence) to the trustees in order for the life office to recognise their status as trustees. The question would seem to concern the precise legal position of the trustees in relation to the life office and the beneficiaries. Even if legal title to the policy may not be technically vested in the trustees this does not affect the fact that they have been validly appointed as trustees by the settlor. The terms of the policy would require payment to be made to the trustees so the life office is doing no more than complying with its contractual duties in making payment to them[1]. Once payment has been made to the trustees they would be required to account to the beneficiaries (in the same way as they would be if the policy had been properly vested in them) at the very least on the basis that they were trustees de son tort.

11.84   The effect of the Contracts (Rights of Third Parties) Act 1999 could also be of relevance here in that where a contract expressly provides that a third party is able to enforce a term of the contract or the term in question purports to confer a benefit on him then such third party may enforce such a term. However, it is open to the parties to exclude the effects of the Act.

Another possible route which could be used to deal with the possible non-vesting of the trust property in the additional trustees is for the settlor (who is clearly a trustee) to appoint the additional trustees as his agents under the trust. Whilst the policy is not vested in such additional trustees in their capacity as such they would nevertheless be in a position to deal with the trust property in their capacity as agents of the settlor.

In practice, the authors are not aware of the technical issues surrounding vesting of life policies in additional trustees ever having been a contentious issue and the question currently appears to be a purely academic one.

---

1   *Re Schebsman decd* [1944] 1 Ch 83.

3 Appointment of new trustees

11.85 A will or trust instrument will usually name the persons entitled to appoint new trustees. If the document is silent on this point, the statutory provisions apply. Section 36(1)(b) of the Trustee Act 1925 provides that 'the surviving or continuing trustees or trustee for the time being, or the personal representatives of the last surviving or continuing trustee' may, in writing, appoint new trustees although only in place of an outgoing trustee.

A common approach in trusts of life policies is to expressly give the power of appointing additional trustees to the settlor during his lifetime and to the trustees for the time being thereafter.

Unless there is a contrary provision in the trust instrument, the section 36 power provides that a *replacement* trustee may be appointed where the trustee:

(1) is dead;

(2) remains outside the UK for a continuous period exceeding 12 months (this ground is often expressly excluded);

(3) wants to retire;

(4) refuses to act or disclaims before accepting office;

(5) is unfit to act;

(6) is incapable of acting (this includes physical and mental illness, old age and in the case of a corporation, dissolution);

(7) is an infant; or

(8) is removed under a power in the trust instrument.

A common issue facing life offices when being asked to make payment under a life policy under trust is that not all of the trustees are available to give a discharge to the life office. This may be for a variety of reasons, for example, they are refusing to act or they simply cannot be found. The latter presents a particular difficulty if there is no express power of removal as this does not fit neatly into any of the above categories. It may be that the sum of money at stake is relatively small or the beneficiaries are clearly established in which case the life office may take a pragmatic view in making payment out at the direction of the available trustees. However, a 'missing' trustee may also raise the suspicions of the life office (for example he may not actually be untraceable but simply disagrees with the other trustees). In appropriate circumstances the only solution may be to seek the directions of the court.

4 Method of appointment under section 36

11.86 An appointment under section 36 of the Trustee Act 1925 is merely required to be in writing, although it is common practice to appoint by deed which also has the benefit of the automatic vesting provisions contained in section 40 of the Trustee Act 1925.

5   Appointment by the court

11.87   Where it is inexpedient, difficult or impracticable to appoint a new trustee, the court has wide power to appoint new trustees 'either in substitution for or in addition to any existing trustee or trustees, or although there is no existing trustee'[1]. An order can be made on the application of a trustee or a beneficiary[2].

6   Delegation of trustee functions[3]

11.88   A trustee who, for example, goes abroad for a limited period, or is about to undergo a serious operation, will not necessarily desire to retire from the trusts. Under section 25 of the Trustee Act 1925, as amended by section 9 of the Powers of Attorney Act 1971, and as substituted by section 5(1) of the Trustee Delegation Act 1999, he may appoint an attorney to act for him in his absence. The power need not state the reason why it is given (and the reasons are not confined to those mentioned, or limited in any way); but the notice mentioned below must do so. The period of delegation must not exceed 12 months[4]. The power of attorney may define a shorter period but, if nothing is stated, the default period is 12 months from the date of execution of the power by the donor. The following points should also be noted (and see also **11.41–11.43**):

(1)   The previous rule that a trustee cannot appoint as attorney his only other co-trustee unless that co-trustee is a trust corporation was removed essentially because the original prohibition was ineffective. Protections were better secured by other means[5].

(2)   The appointor is liable for the acts and defaults of the attorney as if they were his own[6].

(3)   Before, or within seven days after, giving the power the donor must give written notice of it to each of the other trustees and to the persons having power to appoint new trustees. The notice must specify the date on which the power came into operation, its duration, the name of the donee, the reason it is given and what trusts and powers are delegated, where they are not all delegated. Failure to comply with these requirements will not (in favour of a person dealing with the attorney) invalidate any act the attorney may do or instrument he may execute.

(4)   The section applies to, amongst others, a personal representative in the same way as it does to a trustee[7].

1   Trustee Act 1925, s 41.
2   Trustee Act 1925, s 58.
3   See **11.41**.
4   Section 25(2).
5   Section 7.
6   Section 25(7).
7   Section 25(10).

(5)   The 1999 Act introduced a prescribed form which can be used by a single trustee wishing to delegate his trustee functions under a trust to a single attorney. This is similar to the prescribed form in section 10 of the Power of Attorney Act 1971, which cannot be used by trustees but which is widely used generally[1].

D   Ending trusteeship

1   Disclaimer

11.89   An individual is not bound to accept the onerous duties of a trustee. If he desires, a 'trustee' may disclaim before he does any act indicating acceptance of his office.

2   Retirement

11.90   A trustee may retire by deed, provided that:

(1)   either a trust corporation or two trustees will remain after his retirement; and

(2)   his co-trustees and the person, if any, entitled to appoint new trustees, consent by deed[2].

The deed of retirement will normally contain a declaration by the retiring and continuing trustees vesting the property in the continuing trustees and, except in certain cases, one will be implied unless there is a contrary intention in the trust instrument[3].

3   Replacement

11.91   A trustee may retire under section 36(1) of the Trustee Act 1925 on being replaced by someone else.

4   Removal

11.92   A trustee may be removed from his office in four situations. The first is under an express power contained in the trust instrument; the second is under the powers of section 36 of the Trustee Act 1925; the third is by the court appointing a new trustee in his place under section 41 of the Trustee Act 1925; and the fourth is under the court's inherent jurisdiction (eg if there is a permanent condition of hostility with his co-trustees and the beneficiaries)[4].

---

1   Section 25(5) and (6).
2   Trustee Act 1925, s 39(1).
3   Trustee Act 1925, s 40(2), (3).
4   *Letterstedt v Broers* (1884) 9 App Cas 371 at 386.

5   Death of trustee

11.93   The trustees hold property as joint tenants so that by the jus accrescendi (the 'right of survivorship'), on the death of one trustee, the property passes automatically to the surviving trustees. If a sole or last surviving trustee should die the office of trusteeship, by operation of law, passes to his personal representatives[1]. They can, if they wish, act as trustees, until the person entitled to appoint new trustees makes an appointment. This provision does not impose any obligation upon the personal representative to act and 'such a personal representative of a deceased trustee has an absolute right to decline to accept the position and duties of trustee if he chooses to do so'[2]. If they do not wish to act and the trust instrument is silent as to who may appoint additional trustees, they may make an appointment themselves.

SECTION 6   PERPETUITIES AND ACCUMULATIONS

A   Perpetuities

11.94   It is against public policy that property should be settled on trusts which may last for an indefinite period. The rule against perpetuities prevents the settlor 'ruling from the grave'. Due to the Perpetuities and Accumulations Act 1964 (the 1964 Act), there are two 'systems' in operation: the common law system applying to those trusts effected prior to the commencement of the 1964 Act and the system applying to trusts created thereafter.

I   The common law rule

11.95   The rule lays down that unless it is certain, at the date of the settlement, or in the case of a will, at the date of death of the testator, that the interest under a settlement *will* vest within the perpetuity period, the trust is void. The common law perpetuity period is a maximum of 21 years after the death of an expressly or impliedly relevant 'life in being' at the creation of the trust (with a further period for gestation).

2   The 'wait and see' rule

11.96   The 1964 Act is not retrospective and only applies to instruments coming into operation after 15 July 1964. Where an interest would have been void under common law, one now 'waits and sees' what actually happens. The interest is valid until it becomes absolutely clear that the interest cannot vest within the perpetuity period. The 1964 Act sets out a list of statutory lives in being[3].

1   Trustee Act 1925, s 18.
2   *Re Bennett* [1906] 1 Ch 216 at 225, CA, per Vaughan Williams LJ.
3   Section 3(5).

3 The 80-year period

11.97 The 1964 Act allows a settlor or testator, if he wishes, to provide for a perpetuity period of any fixed period not exceeding 80 years. The modern practice is to use the 80-year period.

The property need not vest *in possession* during the period so long as every benefit under the settlement will vest *in interest*. It must be possible during the period for the beneficiaries to act together to put an end to the trusts. While, therefore, every valid life interest under the settlement must *commence* during the period, it need not *end* during the period.

The 1964 Act provides that so far as the rule is concerned, there is a presumption that a female can have a child only between the ages of 12 and 55 and that a male under the age of 14 years cannot father a child.

The rule against perpetuities does not apply to certain charitable trusts[1] nor to certain pension schemes.

4 Pension schemes

11.98 Despite concerns that the exemptions of certain pension schemes from the rule against perpetuities were going to be removed they continue to be governed by section 69 of the Social Security Act 1973 (as amended)[2]. This exempts pension schemes which fulfil the conditions specified in that section and in the Regulations made from time to time. The basic condition is that the scheme is registered[3].

The Perpetuities and Accumulations Act 1964 did not validate trusts which were already void under previous law; and schemes which cease to qualify become subject to the perpetuity rules after two years (or such longer period as the Secretary of State may consider reasonable)[4].

B Accumulations

11.99 A further consequence of the general principle that property and wealth should be free to circulate has been the statutory control of accumulations of income from property in trust.

Section 164 of the Law of Property Act 1925 and section 13 of the Perpetuities and Accumulations Act 1964 provide that income may not be accumulated for longer than one of six, alternative, periods. The periods are:

---

1 *Christ's Hospital v Grainger* (1849) 1 Mac & G 460.
2 Prior to this Act, the only statutory provisions exempting certain pensions from the perpetuity rules were contained in the Superannuation and Other Trusts Funds (Validation) Act 1927.
3 Personal and Occupational Pensions Schemes (Perpetuities) Regulations 1990, SI 1990/1143; Taxation of Pension Schemes (Consequential Amendments of Occupational and Personal Pension Schemes Legislation) Order 2006, SI 2006/744.
4 Personal and Occupational Pension Schemes (Perpetuities) Regulations 1990, SI 1990/1143.

(1)   the life of the settlor (this period is taken for trusts set up during lifetime where no other period is specified);

(2)   21 years from the death of the testator or settlor (this period is taken for trusts set up by will where no other period is specified);

(3)   the duration of the minority or minorities of any persons living or 'en ventre sa mere' (conceived but not yet born) at the death of the testator or settlor (this period begins from the death of the settlor or testator);

(4)   the duration of the minority or minorities of any persons entitled (or would be entitled if of full age) to the income directed to be accumulated (this period is not restricted to the minority of persons in existence when the trust came into force);

(5)   the period of 21 years from the date of making the disposition; and

(6)   the duration of the minority or minorities of any persons in being at that date.

The last two periods were added by the 1964 Act and are only for trusts coming into operation after 15 July 1964.

Where income is directed to be accumulated for one of the authorised periods and, at the end of that period, the income has to be accumulated under the general law or some other statutory provision[1], the further period of accumulation is declared valid by section 165 of the Law of Property Act 1925.

If there is a direction in the trust instrument to accumulate for a period longer than one of the above then (1) if the period is also longer than the perpetuity period then the direction to accumulate is totally void[2], and (2) if the period is not longer than the perpetuity period then only the excess over the nearest of the six authorised periods is invalid. The income released as a result of (1) or (2) passes to the person who would have been entitled had no accumulation been directed[3].

The rules against accumulations do not apply where the settlor is a corporation provided the company is not acting merely as a nominee for an individual, as a company is not a 'person' for the purposes of section 164(1) of the Law of Property Act 1925[4].

C   Reform

11.100   In November 1993, the Law Commission published a consultation paper[5] to examine the policy behind the rules on perpetuities and accumulations and to see if in modern conditions they can be justified, and if so how the rules

1   Eg Trustee Act 1925, s 31.
2   Law of Property Act 1925, s 164(1).
3   Law of Property Act 1925, s 164(1).
4   *In Re Dodwell & Co Ltd's Trust* [1978] 3 All ER 738.
5   *The Law of Trusts, The Rules against Perpetuities and Excessive Accumulations* (Law Com no 133).

can be simplified and brought up to date. In 1998 they issued a report based on this consultation paper[1] the proposals in which were generally viewed as desirable but there is currently no sign of any reforming legislation.

SECTION 7   STAMP DUTY

A   Provisions from 1 December 2003

11.101   Stamp duty was first imposed by the Stamp Act 1694. There have been various consolidating and amending acts, for example the Stamp Act 1891 and the Stamp Duties Management Act 1891 which were in turn amended by various Finance Acts. Section 125 of the Finance Act 2003 introduced a major reform of stamp duty. With regard to transactions in land, stamp duty was replaced by stamp duty land tax. In other respects stamp duty was abolished in respect of all documents and in respect of transfer of most assets, the exceptions being shares and securities and certain partnership assets.

B   Stamp duty on life assurance policies

11.102   The liability to pay stamp duty on policies of life insurance or assurance was abolished for instruments with effect from 31 December 1989[2].

C   Stamp duty on assignments of life assurance policies

11.103   The assignment of a policy used to attract 'ad valorem' duty under the head 'conveyance or transfer' on a sale but this could be avoided by certification that the instrument fell within the Category L exemption where there was no consideration for the assignment[3]. There is, of course no need to include such a certificate now but it is still common at the time of writing to see the certificate on such documents.

D   Stamp duty on trusts of life assurance policies

11.104   From September 1999, the categories of exempt instruments under the 1987 Regulations was extended to include declarations of trust of life policies as

---

1   Law Com, Report No 251, 1998 (and further Consultation Paper in September 2002 on the 'Rule Against Excessive Accumulations'). See also The Rule Against Perpetuities and the Law Commission's Flawed Philosophy (TP Gallanis, The Cambridge Law Journal, Volume 59, Issue 02, Jun 2000, pp 284–293 for the arguments in favour of abolition rather than reform.
2   Finance Act 1989, s 173.
3   Stamp Duty (Exempt Instruments) Regulations 1987, SI 1987/516.

defined[1]. These added a new Category N provision. Both the 1987 Regulations and the 1999 Regulations were made under the Finance Act 1985[2].

Trusts of life policies which sought to avoid stamp duty therefore contained an exemption certificate worded along the following lines: 'It is hereby certified that this instrument falls within Category N in the Schedule to the Stamp Duty (Exempt Instruments) Regulations 1987'. Again, although unnecessary today in view of the Finance Act 2003, it is still common to see trust documents with this certificate.

1   Stamp Duty (Exempt Instruments) (Amendment) Regulations 1999, SI 1999/2539.
2   Section 87(2).

CHAPTER 12

Insolvency and MWPA trusts

SUMMARY

Section 1   Life policies and bankruptcy and insolvency   **12.1**

Section 2   Bankruptcy   **12.6**

Section 3   Other individual arrangements   **12.25**

Section 4   Corporate arrangements   **12.29**

Section 5   Protective trusts   **12.37**

Section 6   Married Women's Property Act 1882 (MWPA)   **12.39**

SECTION I   LIFE POLICIES AND BANKRUPTCY AND INSOLVENCY

12.1   Bankruptcy of an individual or insolvency of a company are relevant to both ownership and any dealings in a life policy. A life office needs to understand the various types of arrangement that can affect ownership or prevent dealings in relation to a policy. The later sections of this chapter give a brief overview of the types of insolvency and other proceedings, arrangements and personnel with whom a life office may have to deal. For a fuller understanding of a particular process readers are referred to specialist works on insolvency.

In practice life offices have more issues with individual bankruptcy than the insolvency of companies. In part this is because of the 'statutory assignment' of an individual's policy into the name of the trustee in bankruptcy. This necessitates a reassignment of the policy by the trustee when the bankrupt is discharged. Other issues tend to arise in relation to policies that the bankrupt either forgot about or asked someone else to pay premiums on, particularly where the policy had no surrender value and would otherwise have been worthless to the trustee.

There is also a preliminary issue around the effect of the statutory assignment to the trustee in bankruptcy. The traditionally accepted view is that an assignment may not be completed without notice to the life office. This is because even if a policy is transferred beneficially by an assignment, notice is still required to perfect that assignment (under both the policies of the Assurance Act 1867 and

467

section 36 of the Law of Property Act 1925). Section 311 of the Insolvency Act 1986 provides that notice should be served where it is required to protect the priority of the trustee. In practice trustees in bankruptcy do normally serve notice. However, the case of *Rooney v Cardona*[1] seems to indicate that such notice is not required.

The essential facts of this case were that the life office involved paid the policy moneys to Mr Cardona at a time when he was an undischarged bankrupt. Mr and Mrs Cardona had effected a policy in 1992 with themselves as grantees and lives assured. The policy was not subject to any express declaration of trust and did not contain any reference to it being for the benefit of anyone else or to it being subject to the Married Women's Property Act 1882 (MWPA). In 1995 Mr Cardona was adjudicated bankrupt and notice of this bankruptcy was published in the London Gazette. The decision of the Court of Appeal assumes that as the policy was beneficially owned by the trustee and there were no conflicting priorities (ie ie no third parties had registered an interest) no notice was required to protect the trustee's position as against the life office.

This case is interesting in that the life office was partly at fault because it relied upon an indemnity for the lost policy without doing a bankruptcy search. It is not clear whether the case would have been decided differently if the policy had been produced to the life office.

A   Trustees refusal to pay premiums

12.2   Where a trustee in bankruptcy refused to pay premiums on the bankrupt's policies and disclaimed all interest in them, and the bankrupt died, his legal personal representatives were held entitled to the policy moneys as against the trustee[2]. Where, however, during the bankruptcy, a policy lapsed through non-payment of premiums and the life office voluntarily endorsed it as a paid-up policy for a reduced amount, it was held that the trustee in bankruptcy was entitled to the benefit of the policy so endorsed[3].

B   Undisclosed policy

12.3   Difficulties sometimes arise, either because the bankrupt considers the policy valueless and does not disclose it in his statement of affairs, or because the trustee does not take any action. The bankrupt or anyone that he may get to pay premiums for him may be unaware that the policy remains the property of the trustee and they may pay subsequent premiums so that an asset of considerable value is built up for the benefit of the creditors. Two cases illustrate the point:

1   [1991] WLR 1388.
2   *Re Learmouth* (1866) 14 WR 628.
3   *Re Shrager* (1913) 108 LT 346.

Tapster v Ward[1]

T effected a policy and his affairs were liquidated when only one premium had been paid and the policy had no surrender value. The policy was not disclosed to the trustee but was kept up by T until his death. Held, the trustee in bankruptcy was entitled and was under no obligation to repay any part of the premiums to the bankrupt's personal representative.

Similar difficulties arise where a policy is effected by an undischarged bankrupt who does not realise that it may be vested in the trustee or appreciate the consequence.

Re Phillips[2]

An undischarged bankrupt effected a policy. He was later discharged, but again became bankrupt. The policy was disclosed in the second bankruptcy, but not in the first. Held, that the trustee in the first bankruptcy was entitled.

Re Stokes, ex p Mellish[3]

S effected a policy while his affairs were in liquidation by arrangement under the Debtors Act 1869. Unknown to the trustee he paid the premiums out of his salary and continued to do so after his discharge. Held, that the trustee was entitled to the policy. The principle of *Re Tyler* (see **12.4**) did not apply as the trustee was ignorant of the existence of the policy.

The position is now largely covered by section 307 of the Insolvency Act, which allows the trustee in bankruptcy, on service of notice, to augment the bankrupt's estate to include property acquired after the commencement of the bankruptcy (subject to prior interests of third parties acquired without notice of the bankruptcy in good faith, and for value). This is supplemented by a duty on the bankrupt[4] to give the trustee notice of the relevant facts within 21 days of becoming aware of them and not to dispose of the property within 42 days commencing on the date of the notice unless the trustee consents in writing[5]. Where the bankrupt does dispose of the property there are provisions enabling the trustee to serve notice on the recipient of the property to vest it in the trustee[6]. In practice, life offices are likely to require the trustee's written consent before they issue a new policy to an undischarged bankrupt.

C Knowledge of the trustee

12.4   The trustee in bankruptcy is neither bound to pay the premiums nor disclaim the policy: but if the policy is disclosed and the trustee knows that

1 (1909) 101 LT 503.
2 [1914] 2 KB 689.
3 [1919] 2 KB 256.
4 Section 333(2).
5 Rule 6.200(2).
6 Section 307(3) and r 6.201.

premiums are being paid by a third party, he may have to allow a lien for the premiums, even though such payment of premiums would not in other cases afford any claim for a lien.

> *Re Tyler, ex p Official Receiver*[1]
>
> A husband had effected a policy and, being in difficulty, requested his wife to pay the premium and the interest on a loan on it. She continued to do so after the adjudication in bankruptcy of the husband. The trustee claimed the policy free from any lien by the wife. He was aware that payments were being made by her. Held, that the lien must be allowed. The trustee as an officer of the court must be even more straightforward and honest than an ordinary person in the affairs of everyday life.

D Reassignment

12.5   Also, it is emphasised that discharge of the bankrupt does not operate to re-vest in the bankrupt any life policy owned by him at the time of the bankruptcy or acquired by him before discharge, even though it may have little or no surrender value. If he wishes to maintain such a policy, he should ask the trustee in bankruptcy either to disclaim the policy or to agree to assign it to him after his discharge.

SECTION 2   BANKRUPTCY

12.6   When people think of insolvency in relation to individuals, most people think automatically of bankruptcy, however, over the years other methods have evolved (which have significantly increased in number of cases in recent years) of dealing with situations where a person is in financial difficulty and, therefore, technically insolvent. The aim of many of these procedures is to avoid bankruptcy. This section will look principally at the law relating to bankruptcy and reference to the act or to sections are references to the Insolvency Act 1986 and to the Insolvency Rules 1986[2]. Section 3 will look at individual voluntary arrangements, and briefly at summary administration, county court administration orders, and deeds of arrangement under the Deeds of Arrangement Act 1914.

A Obtaining a bankruptcy order

12.7   The aim of the law of bankruptcy is to take the property of a debtor and distribute it among his creditors, and then, subject to certain safeguards and with certain exceptions and after the expiry of a certain time period, to grant the debtor himself a discharge so that he can start afresh. The bankruptcy

---

1   [1907] 1KB 865.
2   SI 1986/1925, as amended by SI 1987/1919, SI 1991/495 and SI 1993/602.

proceedings will therefore (with certain exceptions) divest the bankrupt of all property he owned at the time of the bankruptcy and (on service of notice), property acquired subsequently but before discharge. At the same time, it will, on the whole, release him from his obligations at the time of bankruptcy. A bankruptcy action is commenced by a petition to the court for a bankruptcy order. It is a prerequisite that there be a debtor and that he be personally amenable to the jurisdiction of the courts in England and Wales[1]. The essential determinant of the place of presentation of the petition is the debtor's place of residence or where he has carried on business during the six months before the presentation of the petition. The petition may be brought by creditor(s), the debtor himself, the supervisor of (or a person bound by) a voluntary arrangement[2]. Except in cases where the debtor petitions for his own bankruptcy on the grounds that he is unable to pay his debts, the debt in question must be for £750 or more, it must be a liquidated sum payable immediately or at some certain future time and it must be unsecured. In order to be successful in obtaining a bankruptcy order, it is necessary to show that the debtor is unable, or it appears that there is no reasonable prospect of him being able, to pay the debt and that this is not affected by any application to set aside a statutory demand.

The grounds on which inability to pay are to be shown, are exclusively those in section 268:

(1)   that the debtor has not complied with a creditor's statutory demand; or

(2)   there is an unsatisfied execution in favour of the creditor on a judgment debt against the debtor.

Similarly, no reasonable prospect of being able to pay can also be established where the debt is not immediately payable by non-compliance with a statutory demand, provided certain conditions are fulfilled[3]. A statutory demand is not a document issued by the court. However, it must be in the prescribed form[4] and served upon the debtor or his solicitor, although there are provisions for advertising it in a newspaper in the case of a judgement debt where the debtor has absconded or is keeping out of the way with a view to avoiding service. After three weeks and on production of an affidavit proving service of the demand, the petitioner will be entitled to the bankruptcy order (assuming the debtor has not succeeded in having the statutory demand set aside). Similarly, in relation to an unsatisfied execution or other process, it needs to be shown that this has been returned unsatisfied in whole, or in part.

If there is a serious possibility that the property will be significantly diminished during that period it is possible for a bankruptcy petition to be presented before the end of the three-week period, this being known as an expedited petition[5].

---

1   Section 265 and see *Zvonko Stojevic* (1) *Komercni Bank SA* (2) *Yvonne Venvil (the Trustee in Bankruptcy of Zvonko Stojevic* (3) the Official Receiver (2006).
2   See under voluntary arrangement, **12.25**.
3   Section 268(2).
4   See Insolvency Rules 1986, r 6.1.
5   Section 270.

1 Secured debts

12.8   Section 285[1] provides that a secured creditor is free to enforce his security in the event of the debtor's bankruptcy, but he may equally petition for bankruptcy if he is either willing to give up his security, which would normally only happen if the value of the security was small, or if his petition is expressed to not be made in respect of the secured part of the debt and it contains a statement of the estimated value of the security at the date of the petition. The scheme of things is that the debts are then effectively treated as two separate debts, one secured, and one unsecured as to the balance.

2 Set-off

12.9   Section 323 provides that amounts owed by a creditor may be set off against amounts owed by the bankrupt at the commencement of the bankruptcy (namely the date the order is made) if they arise out of mutual credits, mutual debts or other mutual dealings. This right is wider than the general right of set-off but is subject to a number of limitations, for example:

(1)   The parties must owe each other money in the same right[2], not in any representative or fiduciary situation.

(2)   The right will not apply where the creditor had notice that a bankruptcy petition was pending at the time the debt became due.

(3)   The mutual dealings must be such as would lead to a money claim and not to any other remedy.

(4)   It had been thought that mutual credits may not be set off where the creditor's right is contingent and that contingency has not yet occurred, however, Hoffman LJ held[3] that the requirement for dealings to be mutual is 'unreasonable' and that all that is required for mutuality is that the obligations the subject of set-off are incurred by the same parties in the same right or capacity.

It is also worth noting that where there is sufficient mutuality (eg where the debts arise out of the same contract) it is impossible by contract to exclude the statutory right of set-off. Further, in relation to debtor companies, there is a similar provision in the Insolvency Rules[4].

---

1   Subsections 4 and 5.
2   See *National Westminster Bank Ltd v Halesowen Presswork and Assemblies Ltd* [1972] AC 785 at 821.
3   *Re a Debtor (no 340 of 1992)* [1996] 2 All ER 211 and *Skarzyvnski v Chalford Property Co Ltd* [2001] BRIR 673.
4   Rule 4.90 and rule 2.85.

3 Interim receiver and the Official Receiver

12.10 An application may also be made in extreme cases for the Official Receiver to be appointed as an interim receiver to prevent dissipation of the potential bankrupt's property[1]. Normally, the Official Receiver will become receiver and manager of the bankrupt's property from the date the bankruptcy order is made. In either event, if the bankruptcy order is made, either the Official Receiver will be appointed as trustee in bankruptcy or an insolvency practitioner will be appointed for the purpose. An insolvency practitioner is essentially someone who holds a valid authorisation, either by membership of a recognised professional body, or by virtue of a licence granted directly by the DTI. Accompanying the petition, the potential bankrupt is required to prepare a statement of affairs (verified by affidavit) and submit it to the Official Receiver. The Official Receiver may require further disclosure[2] and may decide to apply for the holding of a public examination of the bankrupt at a duly convened sitting of the court. The Official Receiver's other main responsibility is to decide whether the assets are sufficient to justify the summoning of a meeting of creditors to appoint a trustee in bankruptcy.

4 Bankruptcy order and provable debts

12.11 The order made by the court is required to state the date of presentation of the petition and the date of the making of the order. The Official Receiver will cause the order to be published in the London Gazette and a newspaper. The order takes effect on the beginning of the day on which it is granted and, although the property of the bankrupt remains in his name until the trustee is appointed, he has no ability to deal with it. That power is with the Official Receiver. It is worth noting that, by virtue of section 284, any disposition of property by the bankrupt between the dates of the presentation of the petition and the making of the order is void, except to the extent that it either has the consent of, or is subsequently ratified by, the court. However, subsection 4 provides that where a person has received any property or payment from the bankrupt before the commencement of the bankruptcy (ie the making of the order) and has done so in good faith, for value without notice that the petition has been presented, or where another person obtains an interest in such a property from someone who satisfies those criteria, then those dispositions will not be void.

The effect of the bankruptcy order is that, subject to limited exceptions, the bankrupt may not be sued in respect of debts which are provable in the bankruptcy, namely debts or liabilities to which he is subject at the time of the bankruptcy order[3].

---

1   Section 286(2).
2   Insolvency Rules 1986, r 6.66(1).
3   Section 285.

B Appointment of trustee

12.12 The Official Receiver must decide as soon as possible, within 12 weeks from the date of the bankruptcy order, whether or not to appoint a trustee in bankruptcy. However, where a summary administration order for small bankruptcies is issued under section 275 the Official Receiver automatically acts as the trustee in bankruptcy in most cases. Otherwise the trustee in bankruptcy would be appointed at the first creditors' meeting, or the Official Receiver could refer the matter of appointing the trustee in bankruptcy to the Secretary of State, who would then appoint a trustee. If no reference is made by the Official Receiver, then the Official Receiver will become the trustee in bankruptcy from the date on which he notifies the court of his decision not to refer the matter to the Secretary of State. The appointment of a trustee in bankruptcy will take effect only if the person accepts the appointment in accordance with the Insolvency Rules. On appointment of the trustee in bankruptcy, the bankrupt's property ('his estate'), including any life policies, vests in the trustee in bankruptcy without conveyance, assignment or transfer[1]. However, this is subject to the rule that the trustee in bankruptcy takes subject to the equities. He is not considered to be an assignee for value and cannot therefore gain priority over existing equities by giving notice. This is often explained as the trustee merely stepping into the shoes of the bankrupt.

> *Re Wallis, ex p Jenks*[2]
>
> A husband deposited a policy with his wife to secure advances made by her to him. He was adjudged bankrupt. The trustee gave notice to the life office and claimed the policy free from any charge on the ground that he first gave notice. Held, that the trustee takes subject to equities and cannot obtain priority by notice.

Section 311(4) provides that notice of assignment need not be given 'except in so far as it is necessary' in a case where the deemed assignment is from the bankrupt himself, for protecting the priority of the trustee. It is submitted that because of the Policies of Assurance Act 1867 registration of any assignment is necessary to protect the assignee from a purchaser for value without notice of the bankruptcy. It is not clear how this fits with the case of *Rooney v Cardona* where the Court of Appeal held that as against the life office itself notice was not required. If that case were followed to its logical conclusion it could mean that section 311(4) would be redundant as priority could never be obtained over the trustees' interests. This could cause a major problem in markets like the second-hand endowment market which relies upon the life office's register of interest. Also, it is worth noting that *Rooney v Cardona* did not deal with this issue in these terms and there is dicta in the judgment re-enforcing the effect of section 311(4) and emphasising that notice in the London Gazette is not constructive notice to the world of the bankruptcy. It may be that the only person who is at risk in not

1 Section 306(1) and (2).
2 [1902] 1KB 719.

receiving notice is the life office which does not have a competing claim. Much will also depend on the circumstances as it may be possible (eg where the trustee leaves the policy with the bankrupt) or the life office completes reasonable searches to rely upon some of the other authorities in this area. Also, in practice, if trustees need to register their interests as against third parties[1] notice is likely to continue to be served.

C Property subject to a bankruptcy order

12.13 The bankrupt's estate is defined for these purposes primarily in section 283 as all property belonging to the bankrupt at the commencement of a bankruptcy and all property which, by virtue of provisions in that part of the Insolvency Act, is to be comprised or treated as falling into the estate[2]. Property is given a very wide definition in section 436, including all present and future property and specifically including things in action (such as life contracts).

Section 307 provides the framework and power for the trustee to vest 'after-acquired property' into the estate by service of notice on the bankrupt. This power does not, however, apply where such property is disposed of to a person for value, or if a banker enters into a transaction, in both cases in good faith without knowledge of the bankruptcy[3]. However, there is authority for the proposition[4] that money received and paid away by the bankrupt, even to a person with notice, may be treated as valid against the trustee if the trustee has not intervened. In relation to income, the bankrupt is allowed to retain the amount of income deemed necessary to maintain him and his family in reasonable circumstances and subject to that the trustee may apply for an income payments order under section 310. It is also worth noting the effect of protective and MWPA trusts (see Section 6).

D Power to avoid prior transactions

12.14 Additionally, there are powers in the Insolvency Act for the trustee to apply to the court effectively to retrieve property or restore a previous situation, in relation to the estate of the bankrupt. There are three grounds on which this can be done:

(1) where there is a transaction at an undervalue (ie for less than full consideration) in the five years before presentation of the petition;

(2) where there is a preference (ie one creditor is put in a better position than another);

---

1 *Re Russell's Policy* (1872) LR 15 Eq 26 and s 311.
2 See **12.18** for excluded property.
3 This maintains and clarifies the position formerly contained in the Bankruptcy Act 1914, s 47.
4 *Re Vanlohe* (1871) 7 Ch App 1985.

(3)   where there is a transaction effectively delaying or defrauding creditors at any time.

1   A transaction at an undervalue

12.15   A transaction at an undervalue is defined[1] as either a gift or a transaction in consideration of marriage, or a transaction, the consideration for which in money's worth is significantly less than the value in money or money's worth of what is provided. However, in order to be impeached the transaction must have been entered into at a relevant time, which is defined in section 341. The basic rule is that any transaction at an undervalue within *two years* of the presentation of the petition can be attacked. Transactions which occurred *between two and five years* before presentation of the petition can only be set aside if, at the time of the transaction, the bankrupt was already, or became, insolvent in consequence of it. Insolvent for this purpose means unable to pay debts as they fall due, or the value of a person's assets are less than the amount of his liabilities, taking into account contingent and prospective liabilities. In respect of a transaction which is not to an associate[2] of the bankrupt, the burden of proof to show that the person was or became insolvent is on the trustee. However, if the other party to the transaction was an associate then the burden of proof is reversed and is, therefore, placed on the associate. Thus, if a bankrupt gratuitously or for much less than full consideration assigns or declares a trust of property (eg a life policy in favour of his wife and children) then, unless it is an MWPA trust[3], it will be a transaction at an undervalue for these purposes. It may, therefore, be attacked by the trustee in bankruptcy if it took place less than five years before presentation of the petition, unless the beneficiaries can show that the settlor was not and did not became insolvent because of the gift.

The court may make such order as it thinks fit for restoring the position to what it would have been if the bankrupt had not entered into the transaction. Additionally, the court has wide general powers to order restitution and trace the proceeds of transactions. Although protection is afforded[4] to third parties acquiring an interest in property or a benefit from a transaction in good faith for value without knowledge of the relevant circumstances, that would render the transaction voidable.

2   Preferences

12.16   Preferences are essentially advantages being given to one creditor over another. To be capable of being attacked by the trustee in bankruptcy a preference has to take place at the 'relevant time' and the court has power to put the parties back into the position they would have been if the preference had not

---

1   Section 339.
2   See **12.16**.
3   See Section 6, **12.39** et seq.
4   Section 342(2).

taken place. The term 'preference' is defined[1] in relation to a person who is a creditor, a surety or a guarantor of debts or liabilities of the bankrupt, as the bankrupt suffering something to be done which has the effect of putting that person in a better position, in the event of the debtor's bankruptcy, than he would have otherwise been in. There is also a requirement that the bankrupt 'desired' to produce this effect, although this need not be his dominant motive in acting in any particular way. This can be a difficult concept to ascertain. Guidance was set out by Millett J in *Re MC Bacon*[2]. The court is required to presume that the motive is satisfied where a preference is given to an associate of the debtor (otherwise than by reason of his being an employee), although this presumption is rebuttable. The relevant time is two years in the case of a preference to an associate, or six months in any other case. However, it is worth noting that unlike the situation with transactions at an undervalue, it is necessary for the trustee in every case of preference to establish that the bankrupt was insolvent[3] at the time the preference was given.

The term 'associate' is defined very widely in the Insolvency Act[4] and covers most forms of blood or marital relationship, including a former spouse or a reputed spouse. It also extends to business associates and partners, and employment relationships. A company can also be an associate of an individual if it is controlled by that individual or if that individual and his associates together control the company, either by securing that the company acts in accordance with their instructions or by exercising control of more than one-third of the voting rights of the company. Trustees and beneficiaries can also be associates if the bankrupt or his associates are beneficiaries, or if the settlor is a potential beneficiary.

3   Transactions defrauding or delaying creditors

12.17   Sections 423 to 425 contain what is loosely called 'transactions defrauding or delaying creditors', although there is no actual condition of fraud. These sections, unlike those relating to transactions at an undervalue generally and preferences, do not relate merely to insolvency. They apply at any time where it can be shown that a transaction at an undervalue was entered into for the purpose either of putting assets beyond the reach of a person who is making or may at some time make a claim against a person, or otherwise prejudicing the interest of such a person in relation to the claim which he is making, or may make. Because of the presumptions available in respect of transactions at an undervalue, particularly where associates are involved, it is likely that these provisions will only be used in an insolvency situation when the transaction took place more than five years before the bankruptcy. It is worth remembering that transaction is defined as including a gift, agreement or arrangement. The motive of defeating or

---

1   Section 340(3).
2   [1990] BCLC 324.
3   See **12.15** in relation to transactions at an undervalue.
4   Section 435.

delaying claims of creditors is essential and has to be proved in each case. While there is not an insolvency situation the claim can be brought by the person who would be defeated or delayed, but it is provided that in the appropriate cases only the person acting in the insolvency or the supervisor in a voluntary arrangement have the right to bring such a claim. Similarly, there are wide powers to order restitution and protection for innocent third parties for value without notice of the circumstances giving rise to the impeachability of the original transaction.

E Excluded property

12.18 Having seen the definition of property and the ability to draw further property into the bankrupt's estate, it should also be noted that there are various exceptions to the assets which would be included in the bankrupt's estate. First, there are two categories of exempt assets provided by section 283(2), as follows:

'(a)   such tools, books, vehicles and other items of equipment as are necessary to the bankrupt for use personally by him in his employment, business or vocation; and

(b)   such clothing, bedding, furniture, household equipment and provisions as are necessary for satisfying the basic domestic needs of the bankrupt and his family.'

Neither of these would extend to life policies.

Second, section 283(3)(a) provides that property held on trust for any other person will not form part of a bankrupt's estate. The trust need not be a formal trust and it is thought this would therefore extend to the assignor of an equitable assignment holding on behalf of the equitable assignee. In relation to powers of appointment[1], the property subject to the power will not be included where it is not for the time being included in the bankrupt's estate and where either it is exercisable at a time after the bankrupt's discharge or the bankrupt is not a potential beneficiary, provided, of course, in both cases that the bankrupt is not the settlor and that the trust, assignment or other transaction is not capable of being avoided under the powers discussed in Section D above.

Further, it is specifically provided[2] that the ambit of a bankrupt's estate is subject to the provisions of any enactment not contained in the Insolvency Act 1986 under which any property is to be excluded from a bankrupt's estate. It is worth noting section 159(5) of the Pension Schemes Act 1993 which excludes protected rights under a personal pension scheme from being passed from the bankrupt's estate to a trustee in bankruptcy. Section 95 of the Pensions Act 1995 provides that in respect of bankruptcies taking place on or after 29 May 2000 all pension rights are excluded (ie including those held under occupational schemes).

1   See s 283(4).
2   Section 283(6).

F   Forfeiture

12.19   It is also possible for property to fall out of the bankrupt's estate by virtue of a forfeiture clause[1] in a settlement to which the property belongs. In order to be valid, such a clause must be expressed to operate upon the *presentation* of a bankruptcy petition, the settlement should contain a gift over of the interest to be forfeited[2] and the settlor cannot be the bankrupt[3]. Where the settlement comprises property from other sources, such a clause in favour of the partial settlor may be effective to the extent of that other property not provided by the bankrupt. However, it should be possible for trustees of a settlement containing a power of appointment to appoint away from the settlor prior to commencement of the bankruptcy, namely between the date of the petition and the order. This effectively takes such property out of the settlor's estate[4], as it would not be a disposition by the bankrupt in that period. On the other hand, amounts receivable by the bankrupt from a discretionary trust may be treated like income, with the trustee in bankruptcy being entitled to the balance over the amount required for the deemed needs of the bankrupt and his family. Forfeiture wordings are still included in occupational pension schemes and personal pension schemes to cater for pre-29 May 2000 bankruptcies. Since they contain a gift over and since the settlor is not (usually) a settlor of the scheme, they generally work. However, in respect of pensions which are already in payment at the time of bankruptcy, pension payments may be treated as income for the purposes of income payments orders under section 310, even though the pension could not itself vest in the trustee in bankruptcy because of a forfeiture or non-assignment clause in the pension scheme[5].

G   Discharge of the bankrupt

12.20   When the bankrupt is discharged from bankruptcy, the effect is to release him from all of the debts which were provable in the bankruptcy, such that creditors no longer have the right to claim for any outstanding amounts. A bankrupt will be automatically discharged after one year unless an order is made by the court, on the application of the Official Receiver, to suspend discharge due to the bankrupt's failure to fulfil his obligation under the Insolvency Act[6] or the Official Receiver has agreed an earlier discharge if appropriate (section 279(2)). By virtue of section 281, discharge of the bankrupt will not extend to secured debts and will have no effect on the remaining functions, duties and powers of the trustee in bankruptcy.

As distinct from a discharge, the bankrupt may also apply for the bankruptcy order to be annulled on the grounds either of facts existing at the time of the

---

1   See also Section 5, **12.38**.
2   *Brandon v Robinson* (1811) 18 Ves 429; 34 ER 379.
3   *Re Johnson* [1904] 1KB 134.
4   *Re Balfour's Settlement* [1938] Ch 928.
5   *Re Garrett* [1930] 2 Ch 137.
6   Section 279.

order, such that the order should not have been made, or if all of his debts have been paid or secured[1] or the bankrupt has agreed an individual voluntary arrangement with his creditors (section 261).

H Death of an insolvent person

12.21 The Administration of Insolvent Estates of Deceased Persons Order[2] provides a slightly modified but analogous system to deal with situations where a person dies insolvent, both where proceedings in bankruptcy have and where they have not already been commenced. Where proceedings have not been commenced, creditors may petition for an order for the administration of the deceased person's estate according to the laws of bankruptcy. Equally, the personal representative may petition for this purpose. Where proceedings in administration have already begun, it is necessary to apply to have them transferred. The court may transfer them to the bankruptcy court, although this power is discretionary. Where the modified provisions apply the powers to make adjustments to prior transactions, namely, at an undervalue, or preferences and the ability to disclaim onerous property, all still apply.

I Insolvent partners or partnerships

12.22 Section 420 made provision for the position of insolvent partnerships to be dealt with by statutory instrument[3]. As a result of the original order made in 1986, the position with regard to partnerships was that there were effectively three ways of dealing with an insolvency situation:

(1) individual members of the partnership could be the subject of proceedings in bankruptcy without the partnership being involved;

(2) the partnership could be wound up under the provisions in the Act dealing with unregistered companies[4]; or

(3) there could be a winding up of the partnership together with the bankruptcy of two or more of its members. The same insolvency practitioner would act in both matters.

The original order was revoked and replaced by the Insolvent Partnerships Order 1994[5] with effect from 1 December 1994. The subsequent order maintains the basic premise of the original order but makes separate provision, depending on who has presented the petition for winding up. Notably, the new order provides

1 Section 282(1) and Insolvency Rules 1986, r 6.206.
2 SI 1986/1999.
3 See the Insolvent Partnerships Order 1994, SI 1994/2421; Insolvent Partnerships (Amendment) Order 1996, SI 1996/1308.
4 See the Insolvency Act 1986, Pt V.
5 SI 1994/2421, subject to transitional provisions in art 19.

for the availability of voluntary arrangements and administration orders (suitably modified) for insolvent partnerships[1]. Other changes to the provisions of the 1986 order include a change to (3) above, so that on a creditor's petition, at least one partner (not two) now needs to be made insolvent, together with the partnership. On an individual partner petitioning for their own bankruptcy the court may issue a certificate of summary administration of the estate of any of the partners (if the requisite conditions are satisfied)[2]. Specified provisions of the Company Directors Disqualification Act 1986 will apply in certain circumstances to an insolvent partnership[3].

It is also possible that one partner may be bankrupt but that the partnership itself is solvent. In that case the individual could be made bankrupt without the partnership being involved although it is possible, depending on the partnership deed, that such a bankruptcy would cause a dissolution of the partnership.

J   Undischarged bankrupts and subsequent debts

12.23   Debts arising after the commencement of an individual's bankruptcy which are not in respect of obligations incurred before the bankruptcy commenced are not provable in the bankruptcy. This means that unless the bankrupt subsequently enters into a voluntary arrangement, it will be necessary to seek a second bankruptcy order to try to protect the interests of those creditors. There is unfortunately no means of consolidating successive bankruptcies. The rules relating to second bankruptcies whilst still undischarged from the effects of a previous bankruptcy are set out in sections 334 and 335 of the Insolvency Act.

K   Searches in bankruptcy

12.24   Information as to bankruptcy proceedings can be obtained through agents who keep records made from the London Gazette and other sources. The information given at any time may, however, be incomplete, for sometimes advertisement of a receiving order may be stayed pending appeal and it is possible that proceedings against the particular individual may have taken place under a name other than that by which he is known to the person making the enquiry or search.

SECTION 3   OTHER INDIVIDUAL ARRANGEMENTS

A   Voluntary arrangements

12.25   Sections 252 to 263 inclusive in Part VIII of the Insolvency Act govern the making of voluntary arrangements by individuals. Essentially, a voluntary

1   SI 1994/2421, arts 4–6.
2   Schedule 7, para 6.
3   See arts 16 and 18 and the Insolvent Partnerships (Amendment) Order 2001.

arrangement either enables a person who is insolvent to avoid bankruptcy, or enables a bankrupt to bring the bankruptcy to an end in a shorter period of time, by making arrangements which are acceptable to the required majority of his creditors. The arrangement operates such that once the requisite majority is obtained, then all creditors who were entitled to receive notice of the creditors' meeting, even those who did not agree to the arrangement, are bound by it and are normally bound to accept a lesser amount than that to which they were originally entitled.

Given the ability to lessen the amount that creditors receive, certain safeguards have been built into the arrangement, namely the debtor's statement of affairs and proposal must undergo preliminary scrutiny by a qualified insolvency practitioner (called the 'nominee') who must report to the court stating whether, in his opinion, the proposal should be carried forward and submitted to a meeting of the debtor's creditors for possible approval. Then, only if the court is satisfied, will the meeting of creditors be convened. The meeting will be chaired by the nominee or his delegate and a majority of three-quarters in value of the creditors present in person or by proxy and voting on the resolution must be obtained. If the consent is obtained then the nominee (thereafter called the 'supervisor') supervises the arrangement. Both the nominee and anybody bound by the arrangement have the right under section 276 to petition for bankruptcy if a debtor fails in his obligation under the arrangement or they can show that the information in his statement of affairs, as presented to the meeting, was false or misleading[1].

I Interim order

12.26 In order to allow a debtor the ability to make the necessary arrangements, an interim order is made under section 252 (save where a 'fast-track' IVA is proposed in the case of an undischarged bankrupt). This provision prevents any petition being presented or proceeded with, and no other proceedings, execution or other legal process may be commenced or continued without leave of the court during the period of the order. Once the voluntary arrangement has been approved, the interim order ceases to have effect and any pending petitions for bankruptcy are normally automatically discharged, although there is a 28-day challenge period for such an arrangement. As has already been stated, a voluntary arrangement may be used to bring a bankruptcy to an end and the court then has power, at its discretion, to annul the bankruptcy under section 261, on which happening (subject to the arrangements and supervision of the supervisor) the property reverts to the individual under the voluntary arrangement subject to any terms the court may direct or may vest in such other person as the court may appoint.

---

1 *Cadbury Schweppes plc v Alimudin Amiraly Somji* (2001) WLR 615.

B County court administration order

12.27 Under Part VI of the County Courts Act 1984, if a debtor is unable to pay a judgment debt and his whole indebtedness is less than the 'County Court Limit' he may apply to the county court for a county court administration order. The order will make provision for the payment of debts by instalment or otherwise. While such an order is in force no creditor included in the list of creditors may petition or join in a bankruptcy petition unless certain criteria are satisfied.

C Deeds of arrangement and other procedures

12.28 Deeds of arrangement made under the Deeds of Arrangement Act 1914 are little used today. They operate by a debtor giving up his property to a trustee in return for a release from his creditors' claims. The deed has to be registered with the DTI within seven days of execution otherwise it is void. A disadvantage of these deeds of arrangement is that, unlike the procedure under the Insolvency Act 1986, they cannot be used to bind dissenting creditors. There is no equivalent of an interim order to prevent such creditors petitioning for bankruptcy. Non-statutory contractual composition agreements with creditors similar to a deed of arrangement and other informal procedures dealing with debtor's debts in a certain manner may involve inherent risks for creditors and are subject to the same problem as deeds of arrangement. However, they are commonly employed in practice.

SECTION 4   CORPORATE ARRANGEMENTS

12.29 This section deals briefly with the variety of methods of dealing with the insolvency of a company, the relevant personnel in each case and their powers. Briefly, these are an administrator, an administrative receiver, a liquidator, provisional liquidator or a supervisor of a voluntary arrangement, all of whom must be qualified insolvency practitioners.

A Administrative receiver

12.30 A receiver is normally appointed by a debenture holder and the court is not usually involved. The Insolvency Act 1986 gave statutory effect to much of the existing common law relating to receivership and introduced the concept of an administrative receiver. An administrative receiver is a receiver who has been appointed in respect of the whole or substantially the whole of a company's property, and who holds a charge which when created was a floating charge over part (or all) of the company's property. This basically excludes receivers appointed under a charge of a specific asset (ie a fixed charge) only. Whereas the powers of a receiver are set out in the instrument or court order appointing the receiver, the powers of an administrative receiver are deemed to include the powers set out in Schedule 1 of the Insolvency Act 1986, unless they are otherwise inconsistent with the instrument under which he was appointed. Moreover, section 42(3) of that Act provides that a person dealing with an administrative receiver in good faith and for value is not concerned to enquire whether he is acting within his powers. A receiver is deemed to be the agent of the company until the company goes into liquidation.

B Administration

12.31   Administration is a procedure introduced by the Insolvency Act 1986 to provide the benefits of receivership (see **12.33**) where no floating charge exists. A company is put into administration and an administrator (who tends to be an insolvency accountant) is appointed. Before the Enterprise Act 2002 came into force on 15 September 2003, the powers of an administrator were set out in Part II of the Insolvency Act 1986. These powers have now been replaced by those inserted by the Enterprise Act 2002 at Schedule B1 of the Insolvency Act 1986. The administrator's powers are wide and allow him to effectively manage the business of the company.

Since the Enterprise Act 2002, the administrator's objectives are three-fold. Primarily the objective is to rescue the company as a going concern. If this is unachievable, the administrator must try to achieve a better result for the company's creditors than would have been possible if the company had been wound up. Finally, if it is not reasonably practicable to achieve the first two objectives, the administrator has a third objective which is to realise the property of the company so that a distribution may be made to one or more secured or preferential creditors. The administrator is obliged to perform these functions in the interests of all the company's creditors and to do so as quickly and efficiently as possible. The administrator acts as the company's agent and cannot be held liable on the contracts made as agent of the company.

Prior to the Enterprise Act 2002, administration could only be effected by the granting of a court order. However, it is now possible for the shareholders of the company, its directors or holders of qualifying floating charges to appoint an administrator out of court too. This route is seen as being cheaper and more flexible for companies in financial difficulties. Before the 'out of court' route was established, a floating charge holder was able to block the making of an administration order as floating charge holders had to be given notice of any petition to seek an administration order. One of the main advantages of the current administration procedure is the protection it receives from a statutory moratorium, which prevents creditors from taking action against the company's assets (including the enforcement of security), therefore allowing the administrator to carry on the running of the business of the company. An exception to the moratorium exists for financial collateral arrangements in the Financial Collateral Arrangements (No 2) Regulations 2003. It should also be noted though, that for floating charges created before 15 September 2003 the right to veto an administration order and put in place an administrative receiver still exists.

The effect of a company going into administration is that on the making of an administration order, any petition for winding up of the company is dismissed. If a qualifying floating charge holder appoints an administrator, any petition for winding up is suspended. Further, subject to the exceptions made in financial collateral arrangements, on the making of any administration order, any winding-up petition is dismissed and any administrative receiver must vacate office[1]. The administrator also has the ability to require receivers of any of the company's property to vacate office.

Similar to liquidators[2], an administrator has powers to set aside transactions at an undervalue, transactions defrauding creditors and preferences. However, unlike liquidators, administrators do not have powers to disclaim onerous contracts nor to seek an order of the court against directors for a contribution to the company's assets for wrongful or fraudulent trading.

C Arrangements with creditors

12.32 There are two types of statutory arrangement available to a company. First, like an individual, a company may enter into a voluntary arrangement under section 1 of the Insolvency Act, and secondly, the company may enter into a scheme of arrangement under section 425 of the Companies Act 1985. Although both mechanisms may be used where a company is in financial difficulty and wishes to come to an arrangement with creditors, they are rarely used in such circumstances because they provide no protection against persons seeking to wind up the company, nor do they allow the company to continue trading without the threat of the directors being subsequently made personally liable for any losses occurring during that period[3]. In this way they are similar to the deed of arrangement for individuals.

A section 425 scheme is often used for company reorganisations where the company is solvent. This scheme takes effect only after it has been approved by meetings of the relevant classes of creditors and members, by the requisite majority, by the company and by the court. Once approved the scheme will bind all the members and creditors of the relevant classes. A voluntary arrangement, on the other hand, allows a company to enter into a binding composition with its creditors, and was mainly intended to be used following an administration order (which would itself include the 'moratorium' on actions) or during a liquidation (either by its administrator or liquidator as appropriate – the directors cannot propose a composition or scheme if the company is in liquidation or under administration). It is very similar to an individual voluntary arrangement in that an insolvency practitioner supervises the arrangement and every creditor with notice of the meeting is bound by the voluntary arrangement once the requisite majority has been obtained. However, as has been previously noted, unlike an individual arrangement there is no protection against creditors before the proposal is approved unless there is an administration order in place.

1 Section 11(1).
2 See further Section 4D, **12.33**.
3 ie for wrongful or fraudulent trading: ss 213 and 214.

D Liquidation

12.33   Liquidation is a means by which a company's affairs are wound up, leading to the dissolution of the company as a legal entity. There are effectively three types of liquidation, one compulsory and two voluntary: a members' voluntary liquidation and a creditors' voluntary liquidation and a compulsory liquidation. A members' voluntary liquidation is slightly at odds with the rest of this chapter, in that it is of such a liquidation that the directors declare that the company is solvent. A creditors' voluntary liquidation takes place where such a declaration has not been made. It should be noted that a winding-up petition may be presented and an order for compulsory liquidation made in respect of a company which is already in voluntary liquidation.

A voluntary liquidation commences at the time when the resolution to wind up the company is passed[1]. Whereas a compulsory liquidation commences on the date of presentation of the winding-up petition, unless a resolution for voluntary liquidation has previously been passed, in which case it commences at the time of the passing of that resolution[2].

The situation is similar to that found in bankruptcy cases in that, after the commencement of a winding up, any disposition of the company's property and any transfer of shares or alteration in the status of the company's members is void, unless the court orders otherwise[3].

1   Provisional liquidator

12.34   At any time after the petition for a compulsory liquidation is presented to the court and before the court makes an order, an application may be made to appoint a provisional liquidator to maintain the status quo. The order appointing a provisional liquidator will specify the functions he is to carry out and may limit his powers. The appointment will terminate when the court so orders and will normally terminate if the petition for winding up is dismissed or granted.

2   Powers of directors and liquidators

12.35   In a voluntary winding up where no liquidator has been appointed or nominated, a provision exists[4] similar in effect to section 284 relating to individual bankruptcy (which prevents individuals from dissipating assets prior to the bankruptcy order). This prevents the directors from exercising powers other than those necessary to preserve the assets of the company, or in a creditors' winding up, relating to their statement of affairs or the convening of the creditors' meeting. In a compulsory liquidation, on the making of the court order the Official Receiver becomes the liquidator until another person is appointed,

---

1   Section 86.
2   Section 129.
3   Section 127.
4   Section 114.

unless the company was, prior to the winding-up order, subject to an administration order or a voluntary arrangement, in which case the court may appoint the administrator or supervisor[1].

In both voluntary and compulsory winding up, the powers of the directors cease on appointment of a liquidator. In the case of voluntary arrangements, this cessation is provided by the Act but in the case of compulsory liquidation it is established by the case of *Re Farrows Bank*[2]. The company cannot deny the apparent authority of its directors until, in the case of voluntary liquidation, the suspension of their power is notified in the London Gazette or, in the case of a compulsory liquidation, the making of the winding-up order is notified[3].

The powers of the liquidator are set out in sections 165 to 167 and in Schedule 4. The powers are divided into those that require a sanction and those that do not. Generally, the liquidator acts as the company's agent and will not be personally liable on contracts made expressly as liquidator on behalf of the company.

3   Avoiding prior transactions

12.36   A liquidator may apply to the court to restore the company's position in relation to transactions at an undervalue[4] and preferences[5]. The relevant time for this purpose in relation to both a transaction at an undervalue and a preference given to a connected person (other than a mere employee) is two years before the date of commencement of the winding up[6], unless the recipient can show that the company was not insolvent[7] or becomes unable to pay its debts in consequence of the transaction or preference. In the case of any other preference, the time period is six months before the date of the winding-up order[8]. In either case it is a relevant time during the period between the presentation of the petition for and the making of an administration order. In relation to preferences it is also necessary to show that the company was influenced in deciding to give the preference by a desire to put that person in a better position in the event of the company's insolvent liquidation[9]. However, this will be presumed if the preference is given to a person connected with the company (otherwise than by reason only of his being an employee). A 'connected person' for these purposes is defined in sections 249 and 435 as a director, shadow director or an associate of either of them or the company.

Additionally, floating charges may be invalid if created in the period of 12 months (or two years in the case of a connected person) before the date of the presentation of the petition or commencement of the winding up, except to the

1   Section 140(1) and (2).
2   [1921] 2 Ch 164.
3   Companies Act 1985, s 42.
4   Section 238; *Knights (Liquidator of Taylor Sinclair (Capital) Ltd) v Seymour Pierce Ellis Ltd* LTL 27 July 2001.
5   Section 239.
6   Or in relation to an administration order the date of presentation of the petition.
7   See s 123.
8   Or in relation to an administration order the date of presentation of the petition.
9   Section 239.

extent of the value of any new consideration given at the time of execution of the charge.

A liquidator, like a trustee in bankruptcy, will realise assets, pay debts (there are provisions relating to expenses and preferential debts similar to those for bankruptcy) and distribute any surplus to shareholders. Once the company's affairs are fully wound up, the liquidator in a voluntary liquidation will prepare an account of the winding up and lay it before a shareholders' meeting, which is advertised in the London Gazette, at least one month prior to it taking place. Any remaining property of the company on dissolution will be treated as bona vacantia. In the case of a compulsory liquidation a final meeting of creditors is called. Following such meetings the Registrar of Companies is informed and the company is normally dissolved three months later.

SECTION 5   PROTECTIVE TRUSTS

12.37   As has already been seen above[1] it is not possible for a person to create a trust which contains a forfeiture clause relating to their own interest under the trust. It is equally not possible to declare a trust with a condition subsequent that the trust will terminate if the beneficiary in question is made bankrupt. However, it is possible to include a forfeiture clause in a trust which operates in cases of an alienation by, or bankruptcy of, the beneficiary or which can operate on an alienation prior to bankruptcy of the settlor. For example, in *Re Detmold*[2] the settlor created a trust which contained a life interest for himself subject to a gift over to his wife and children in the event of alienation of his interest either voluntarily or involuntarily by process of law. The condition as to alienation was breached and the settlor subsequently became bankrupt. It was held that the forfeiture having taken place prior to the bankruptcy, it was valid to defeat the interest of the trustee in bankruptcy. The distinction here is that the trust created a determinable interest for a person until he attempted to alienate rather than attempting to alienate property which has already been given absolutely.

One means of creating such a trust is to use what are called protective trusts. Such trusts can be useful to provide an income for life for a spendthrift or financially naive beneficiary and his dependants. A protective trust is essentially a trust of income to a beneficiary for his lifetime provided that if he alienates the interest or is made bankrupt, his life interest will cease and be replaced by a discretionary trust for the benefit of himself and/or his family[3]. Before the Trustee Act 1925, it was necessary to include a clause to this effect in the settlement[4]. However, section 33 of that Act provides a 'shorthand arrangement' so that a reference to protective trusts will bring the protective trust set out in that section into play. This effectively provides that where any income, including an annuity or other periodical income payment, is directed to be held on protective trusts for

---

1   See forfeiture clauses Section 2F, **12.19**.
2   [1889] 40 Ch D 585.
3   In this respect it is similar to the clauses found in occupational pension schemes.
4   *Re Walker* [1939] Ch 974.

the benefit of any person (called 'the principal beneficiary') for the period of his life or for any lessor period, then during that period ('the trust period') the income shall without prejudice to any prior interest be held on the following trusts:

(1)   upon trust for the principal beneficiary during the trust period or until he does or attempts to do any *act or thing* or until any event happens (other than an advance under any statutory or express power) whereby if the income was payable during the trust period to the *principal beneficiary* absolutely during that period, he *would be deprived of the right to receive the same or any part thereof in any of which cases the said trust of the income* shall fail or determine;

(2)   if the *trust fails or determines* during the trust period then for the rest of that period the income is to be held upon trust to be applied as *the trustees in their* absolute *discretion* (without being liable to account for the exercise of such discretion) think fit, for the maintenance or support or otherwise *for the benefit* of all or any of the following persons:

(a)   the principal beneficiary and his or her wife or husband if any and his or her children or more remote issue if any; or

(b)   where there is no wife or husband or issue in existence the principal beneficiary and the persons who would, if he were dead, be entitled to the trust property or the income.

In addition to the statutory trust, it is still possible to have an express protective trust. It should also be noted that the express wording of the section excludes advances made under any statutory express powers.

It is also provided that nothing in that section operates to validate any trust which, if contained in the trust instrument, would be liable to be set aside. This has the effect of preserving the pre-existing law so if the settlor himself is to take the income until the happening of the event then if that event is bankruptcy the income will go to his creditors.

A   Conditions causing forfeiture

12.38   The condition that will cause forfeiture under section 33 is any act or event whereby the principal beneficiary would be deprived of the right to receive the income during the trust period. This is very wide and has not surprisingly been held to extend to bankruptcy or assignment by the principal beneficiary.

One problematic area with forfeiture under protective trusts is the effect of court orders on divorce. There is authority in *General Accident Fire and Life Assurance Corpn Ltd v IRC*[1] that an order of the divorce court to pay a sum of money to the principal beneficiary's wife during her life did not bring about a

---

1   [1963] 1 WLR 1207.

forfeiture of her husband's protective interest. This was not an event contemplated by section 33(1). In *Re Richardson's Will Trust*[1], however, an unsatisfied court order that the principal beneficiary charge his interest to create an annual payment for his wife created an equitable charge, which therefore caused a forfeiture. Similarly, in *Edmonds v Edmonds*[2] an attachment of earnings order to secure a former wife's maintenance was held to cause a forfeiture of a pension held on protective trust.

Conversely, acts which have been held not to cause a forfeiture include appointment of an attorney to receive income[3] or appointment of a receiver where the principal beneficiary was a person of unsound mind[4]. Also, an order of the court under section 57 of the Trustee Act 1925 giving power to trustees to raise capital moneys for the benefit of a life tenant has been held not to cause a forfeiture since all settlements are subject to this overriding section[5].

Although provisions to create a protective trust can be included in a settlement from the outset, it has been held that, in a trust containing a power of appointment, the donee of the power is unlikely to be able to make an appointment on a protective trust basis because of the discretionary nature of the trust following forfeiture of the principal beneficiary's interest. This would, in effect, be a delegation of that person's power which would not be possible unless the settlement itself made provision for it[6].

One point to note about protective trusts is that the case law[7] is not clear regarding payment by the trustees (once the forfeiture has occurred) of the income to the principal beneficiary even though this accords with the express wording of the section. The reasoning appears to be that the principal beneficiary would be bound to hand over to the creditor/assignee whose interest caused the forfeiture any part of the income paid to him and that the trustees having notice of such interest are equally bound not to pay the income to him. The cases, however, rather strangely establish that the trustees may expend such income for the principal beneficiary's benefit[8].

SECTION 6   MARRIED WOMEN'S PROPERTY ACT 1882 (MWPA)

A   Protection against creditors

12.39   A transaction at an undervalue[9] to an associate, which includes wife and children, can be overturned for up to five years if a petition in bankruptcy is presented within the period, unless it can be shown by the wife and/or children (as

---

1   [1958] Ch 504, [1958] 1 All ER 538.
2   [1965] 1 All ER 379n.
3   *Re Tancred's Settlement* [1903] 1 Ch 715.
4   *Re Oppenheimer's Will Trust* [1950] Ch 633.
5   *Re Mair* [1935] Ch 562.
6   *Re Boulton's Settlement Trust* [1928] Ch 703.
7   See eg Stirling LJ in *Re Fitzgerald* [1904] 1 Ch 573 at 593.
8   *Re Bullock* (1891) 64 LT 736.
9   See Section 2D, **12.14**.

appropriate) that the donor was not and did not thereby become insolvent. In view of the fact that 'insolvent' for this purpose means unable to pay debts as they fall due it can be quite difficult to establish. Section 11 of the Married Women's Property Act 1882 (MWPA) provides protection in such circumstances in relation to life policies. It provides (in part) in respect of an MWPA trust that:

> ' . . . the moneys payable under any such a policy shall not, so long as any object of the trust remains unperformed, form part of the estate of the insured or be subject to his or her debts: Provided, that if it shall be proved that the policy was effected and the premiums paid with intent to defraud the creditors of the insured, they shall be entitled to receive, out of the moneys payable under the policy, a sum equal to the premiums so paid.'

It would appear from cases decided under the Bankruptcy Act 1914[1] and section 172 of the Law of Property Act 1925 (now repealed), that the wording in section 11 will be effective to prevent the trustee in bankruptcy seeking to avoid such trusts as prior transactions.

There appears to be some uncertainty as to the extent of a creditor's right to recover premiums where it can be shown that there was an intention to avoid creditors. The wording in section 11 of the MWPA is that the creditors are entitled 'to receive out of the *moneys payable under the policy*, a sum equal to the premiums so paid'. There is some authority on the point. First, in *Holt v Everall*[2] it was held that the surrender value of an earlier policy used to pay premiums on a second policy could be recovered by the creditors. In relation to when the amount can be recovered (ie on bankruptcy or death), there is a Scottish case[3], which indicates that under similar wording in the Scottish Act of 1880, the creditors claim their interest when the 'policy comes to be realised'. In that particular case, it was when the policy came to pay out on death. However, in relation to policies with a surrender value or unit-linked policies, there appears to be no authority on the question of whether the creditors would be entitled to the moneys earlier than on death.

B   Conditions and benefits of an MWPA trust

12.40   The relevant part of section 11[4], which defines what an MWPA trust is, provides as follows:

> 'A policy of assurance effected by any man on his own life, and expressed to be for the benefit of his wife, or of his children, or of his wife and children, or any of them, or by any woman on her own life, and expressed to be for the benefit of her husband, or of her children, or of her husband and children, or any of them, shall create a trust in favour of the objects therein named . . . The insured may by the

---

1   *Re Harrison and Ingram, ex p Whinney* [1900] 2 QB 710.
2   [1876] 2 Ch D 266.
3   *Stewart v Hodge* 1901 SLT 436.
4   As amended by the Law Reform (Married Women and Tortfeasors) Act 1935 and the Statute Law (Repeals) Act 1969.

policy or by any memorandum under his or her hand, appoint a trustee or trustees of the moneys payable under the policy, and from time to time appoint a new trustee or new trustees thereof, and may make provision for the appointment of a new trustee or new trustees thereof, and for the investment of the moneys payable under any such policy. In default of any such appointment of a trustee, such policy, immediately on its being effected, shall vest in the insured and his or her legal personal representatives, in trust for the purposes aforesaid. [.....] [repealed by Statute Law (Repeals) Act 1969 Schedule Part III] The receipt of a trustee or trustees duly appointed, or, in default of any such appointment, or in default of notice to the insurance office, the receipt of the legal personal representative of the insured shall be a discharge to the office for the sum secured by the policy, or for the value thereof, in whole or in part.'[1]

From this it can be seen that in addition to the protection afforded to creditors, the effect of section 11 of the MWPA 1882, is to enable:

(1)   the creation of a trust of life policies without the formalities otherwise required[2];

(2)   the appointment of trustees and vesting of the policy in those trustees from the outset[3].

C   Trustees of MWPA policies

I   Method of appointment

12.41   The assured may by the policy or by a memorandum under his hand appoint a trustee or trustees, and may from time to time appoint new trustees and he may vest the power to appoint new trustees in himself or some other person or persons. If he makes no appointment, or until he makes an appointment, he will himself be the trustee and if he dies his executors or administrators will be the trustees.

The assured does not under modern practice execute the policy himself, but he may be said to have made the appointment by the policy if he accepts a policy naming trustees. An appointment by memorandum under hand may be incorporated in the proposal (which may itself be incorporated in the policy by reference), or may be a separate document. It is customary to record such an appointment in the policy if made at the time the policy is effected. If the policy is for the benefit of the wife, the husband may think it suitable to appoint her as trustee jointly with himself. He can then retain some control of the policy during his life and at his death the wife can as surviving trustee collect the

---

1   The section replaced the Married Women's Property Act 1870, s 10, the terms of which were somewhat similar, though there are important differences; namely, under the 1870 Act, the trust was created only where a policy was effected by a *married man*.

2   As mere use of the words 'on behalf' of would not be sufficient to satisfy the certainty of words requirement.

3   See Chapter 11 on the issues relating to this.

policy money without any formality other than proof of his death and production of the policy.

Section 11 refers to the appointment of a new trustee and there is some doubt as to whether this includes an additional, as opposed to replacement, trustee. In practice there will rarely be an issue as there will either be express provision to this effect in the trust or section 36(6) of the Trustee Act 1925, will apply.

D   Requirements for an MWPA trust

12.42   In order that a policy may create a trust under the section, it must fulfil the following requirements:

(1)   *It must be a policy effected by a man on his own life or by a woman on her own life.* The Act mentions any man or any woman. A bachelor or spinster, widower or widow may effect a policy under the Act. It does not therefore include a life of another contract.

In *Re Oakes' Settlement*[1] it was held that a policy is effected by the person who signs the proposal form and the fact that some other person is generous enough to pay the first or subsequent premiums is not relevant. This decision was, however, made for the purpose of interpreting a provision regarding estate duty (the forerunner of inheritance tax) on policies which has since been repealed and should not therefore be taken as necessarily having general application.

The decision in *Griffiths v Fleming*[2] is sometimes cited as authority for the proposition that a husband and wife can effect a joint lives policy under the MWPA for the benefit of, say, a child. But the judges, although they were prepared to treat the policy as effected in trust under the MWPA, preferred not to do so and in any case expressly based their opinions on the fact that there were two proposals and two contracts and that the life office had issued the wrong policy. Vaughan Williams LJ said that the joint policy was not within the MWPA. It is therefore submitted that, if any view at all can be formed regarding joint lives policies as a result of this case, it is that such policies are not within the provisions of the Act.

Griffiths v Fleming[3]

Husband and wife each signed a proposal form for a policy on his or her own life, and each paid a proportion of the first premium corresponding to their representative ages. The company issued a policy for a joint lives assurance payable, on the death of the first of them to die, to the survivor. The wife committed suicide. The insurance company refused to pay on the ground that the husband had no insurable interest in her life. The plaintiff pleaded that he had such an interest and alternatively that each of the lives had effected an insurance in favour of the other. It was held by the Court of Appeal that a wife has an insurable interest in

1   [1951] Ch 156.
2   [1909] 1 KB 805, CA.
3   [1909] 1 KB 805.

her husband's life without need of proof. Two of the judges said that separate proposals to insure the respective lives were accepted by the insurance company and
there was nothing to show any intention to have one joint life policy. The
company could not set up a form of policy which was not in accordance with the
proposals so as to defeat their liability. The policy should therefore be read as two
assurances, and the court preferred to treat them as two assurances effected by
one spouse on the life of the other, rather than as two assurances each effected by
one spouse on their own life for the benefit of the other. Therefore, each policy
fell within the terms of section 11 of the MWPA.

In *Rooney v Cardona*[1] the Court of Appeal took the view that an ordinary joint
life endowment contract on the lives of a married couple was not within section
11 despite the conclusions reached at first instance. In this case the parties had
not referred to section 11 and the policy was not expressed to be for the benefit
of the lives assured. Also, unlike *Griffiths v Fleming*, there were not separate proposal forms.

12.43

(2) *The policy must be a policy of assurance on life.* The MWPA does not
contain a definition of 'policy of assurance' but a policy is nevertheless on
life because it covers death only from a particular cause (such as a personal
accident policy) or provides benefits payable on other events than death.

> *Re Gladitz, Guaranty Executor and Trustee Co Ltd v Gladitz*[2]
>
> G effected a Lloyd's policy covering payments to be made in the event of death
> by accident and of disablement. The policy contained the following memoran-
> dum: 'It is understood and agreed that all claims under this policy shall be
> payable to Winifred Gladitz, wife of the assured, if she is living at the happening
> of the event upon which the claim becomes payable'. Held, (1) that a policy
> which, besides including provision for payment upon the happening of a man's
> death by a particular cause, also provides for payment upon other events is nev-
> ertheless a policy of assurance effected by a man on his own life within the
> MWPA, even though that Act is not mentioned in the policy, and (2) that the
> memorandum printed at the foot of the policy sufficiently expressed it to be for
> the benefit of the wife.

The MWPA accordingly extends to whole life, temporary and endowment assurances, family income and most other life assurance policies including whole of
life policies with dread disease or critical illness cover.

(3) *The policy must be expressed to be for the benefit of husband, wife and/or
children only.* It is not necessary to mention the MWPA in the policy but it
is preferable to do so in order that, in any case of conflict of law owing to
differences in domicile of the proposer, the beneficiaries and place of establishment of the life office, there shall be no doubt that the policy is intended
to create a trust under the MWPA and is not subject to the law of some other

1   [1999] 1 WLR 1388.
2   [1937] Ch 588.

country. It is not necessary to use words expressly declaring a trust, nor indeed does it seem that there need be a positive intention to effect the policy under the Act, so long as it is expressed in such a way as to bring it within the MWPA. However, a policy not 'effected' in trust for any object within the MWPA cannot later be the subject of a declaration of trust under the MWPA (although it can be subject to a trust outside of the Act).

E   Beneficiaries under MWPA trusts and the nature of their interests

1   Objects of the trusts

12.44   Reference must in every case be made to the policy to ascertain the objects of the trust, and the nature and extent of the interests which the beneficiaries are to take[1].

2   Class of beneficiaries

12.45   The class of beneficiaries comprises wife or husband, and children, including illegitimate[2], and adopted children. It does not, however, extend to stepchildren or grandchildren whether legitimate or not.

If a policy is expressed to be for the benefit of any person other than the wife or child of the life assured, it may not be protected by section 11 of the Married Women's Property Act 1882 except possibly to the extent that it benefits the wife or children[3]. The life assured may, however, have constituted an effective trust outside the MWPA for the other beneficiaries, though the mere statement in the policy that it is effected for the benefit of those persons would not be sufficient in itself to create such a trust. Where there is no effective trust for those other beneficiaries there will be, to that extent at least, a resulting trust for the life assured.

Re *Parker's Policies*[4] has been cited as authority for the proposition that a policy expressed to be for the benefit of any person other than the wife or child of the life assured is not protected by section 11 even to the extent of the interests of wife or child named as beneficiaries. Certainly, no such decision was made in that case and on analysis it does not appear that the judge's obiter remarks can afford any support for it; it is submitted that the opinion expressed in *Re Clay's Policy* is more likely to be followed. However, the question is clearly not free from doubt and the proposer would be well advised to be specific about both the Act and the beneficiaries where it is desired that such a policy is to be subject to the MWPA.

---

1   *Cousins v Sun Life Assurance Society* [1933] Ch 126.
2   With effect from 1 January 1970, Family Law Reform Act 1969, s 19.
3   *Re Clay's Policy of Assurance; Clay v Earnshaw* [1937] 2 All ER 548.
4   [1906] 1 Ch 526.

3 Named and unnamed beneficiaries

12.46 Where a policy is effected for the benefit of a named wife or child the identity of the beneficiary is clear, but in a case where there is a reference to relationship only, it is necessary to construe the policy in order to ascertain who the beneficiaries are to be. Where, for example, a policy is effected by a man, and expressed to be for the benefit of his wife (without naming her), the policy will have to be construed to determine whether the beneficiary is the wife living at the date of the inception of the policy or whether a second or subsequent wife living at the life assured's death is to take. In *Re Browne's Policy, Browne v Browne*[1] the proposer's first wife died and he remarried. It was held that his second wife took an interest on his death where the policy was expressed to be 'for the benefit of his wife and children'.

4 Named wife

12.47 A policy expressed to be for the benefit of or to be payable to a named wife, husband or child without further words will give the beneficiary an immediate vested interest in the whole policy. The following expressions all have the same construction:

(1) For the benefit of Lilian, wife of the life assured.

(2) For the benefit of Lilian, wife of the life assured, absolutely.

(3) For the benefit of Lilian, wife of the life assured, her executors, administrators or assignees.

The last of these expressions is not perhaps a very happy choice of words since it is clearly not the intention of the husband to personally *benefit* his wife's executors or administrators. Prior to the following case there were some cases which expressed a contrary opinion.

> *Cousins v Sun Life Assurance Society*[2]
>
> A husband effected a policy on his life under the MWPA, for the benefit of his wife, Lilian. She died in his lifetime and he applied to surrender the policy. Held, that the wife took an immediate vested interest from the commencement of the policy, which passed, on her death in the husband's lifetime, to her personal representatives as part of her estate.

5 Limited interests

12.48 The interest of the beneficiary need not be the whole extent of the policy money but may be *limited* in various ways by the use of appropriate words.

---

1 [1903] 1 Ch 188.
2 [1933] Ch 126.

Re Fleetwood's Policy[1]

A husband effected a policy whereby the life office agreed to pay to his wife if she should be living at his death but otherwise to his executors. The policy reserved to the husband various options, one of which he exercised. This was the option to receive cash with its share of accrued profits and to discontinue the policy. Held, that he had exercised the option as trustee, and that the trusts attached to the resulting benefit. Moreover, the policy was expressed to be for the benefit of the wife in a certain event only, but the fact that her interest was of a limited or contingent character did not prevent the policy from being a policy within the MWPA. Unless the husband and wife came to an agreement the fund must be accumulated in court until it could be ascertained, by the death of either party, who was entitled to it.

Re Ioakimidis' Policy Trusts, Ioakimidis v Hartcup[2]

A husband effected an endowment assurance expressed to be for the benefit of his wife only in the event of his death before 28 May 1938, leaving her surviving him. The assured died in 1924 and his creditors claimed the policy money. Held that the policy was within the MWPA and created, in the event which happened, a valid trust for the wife.

The interest of a named wife under an endowment assurance may accordingly be:

(1)   for her absolutely;

(2)   for her if she is living on survival of the husband to the end of the term or on his previous death;

(3)   for her only if the husband dies before maturity leaving her surviving.

If the proposer wishes, he may give the wife or other beneficiary a life interest only or, it is submitted, reserve a power of appointment among his wife and children.

6   Interests of children

12.49   The interests of children may be made contingent on attaining majority or surviving the assured, or may be limited in such other manner as the proposer may think fit.

Before drafting any policy which is to be for the benefit of children, it is important to determine:

(1)   whether the children are to be named, so that any further children born will be excluded;

(2)   whether, if not named, the class of children is to be limited to the children of the existing marriage or to any children of the life assured. After 1969 a

1   [1926] Ch 48.
2   [1925] Ch 403.

provision for children without further description will include any illegitimate children of the life assured; and

(3)   whether any child's interest is to continue for the benefit of his or her estate:

(a)   if he or she predeceases the assured, or dies before the event upon which the sum assured becomes payable; or

(b)   if he or she dies before attaining majority or marrying.

7   Maintenance, education, and advancement of children

12.50   The trustees will have the statutory powers to use income for maintenance, education or benefit, and capital for advancement or benefit. If further powers are required, eg to use the whole of the capital for education (the statutory power only allows one half), they must be specifically given in the trust provisions.

8   Policy effected by an unmarried person

12.51   A policy under the MWPA can be effected by an *unmarried* man or woman for the benefit of his or her legitimate or illegitimate child or children; or for any person the life assured may marry. If the proposer is already engaged to be married, it may be suitable to express the interest of his fiancée as contingent on her marriage to the proposer and to be effected in consideration of marriage.

9   Divorce

12.52   Divorce will not *of itself* destroy the interest of a named wife; but she may lose it on divorce if the husband applies to the court for an order to vary the settlement made by the policy.

On granting a decree of divorce, nullity or judicial separation the court may make an order varying, for the benefit of the parties to the marriage and of the children of the family, or either or any of them, any ante-nuptial or post-nuptial settlement made on the parties to the marriage[1]. The court also has power to make an order extinguishing or reducing the interest of either of the parties to the marriage under any such settlement[2]. 'Settlement' is given a wide interpretation and would include trusts of life assurance policies.

The following are cases under previous enactments which gave the court powers similar to, but not as wide as, those under the Matrimonial Causes Act 1973.

1   Matrimonial Causes Act 1973, s 24.
2   Matrimonial Causes Act 1973, s 24(1)(d).

Gulbenkian v Gulbenkian[1]

A husband effected two endowment assurances on his life as follows:

(1)   A policy payable to him at maturity if then living, or, on his death during the term, to his wife.

(2)   A policy payable to him at maturity if then living, or, on his death during the term, to his wife if living, and otherwise to his personal representatives.

The husband divorced his wife and asked for an order varying the trusts. Held, that the name of the wife should be struck out.

Gunner v Gunner and Stirling[2]

A husband effected under the MWPA a whole life policy for the benefit of a named wife absolutely. He divorced her and applied to the court to vary the policy as a settlement. Held, that the settlement of the policy could be varied.

Lort-Williams v Lort-Williams[3]

A husband took out a policy on his life under the MWPA 'for the benefit of the widow or children or any of them of the assured in such shares and proportions and interests and generally in such manner as the assured shall by will or deed revocable or irrevocable appoint or may have so appointed'. The wife divorced him and applied to the court to vary the terms of the policy, the husband having in the meantime married again. The Court of Appeal held that the policy could be varied notwithstanding that the wife's interest was contingent on her surviving the husband and uncertain, and even though the use of the word 'widow' contemplated that a second wife might benefit.

F   Notes on MWPA policies construed by the court

12.53

Wording	Construction
Policies issued under section 10 of the Married Women's Property Act 1870 (very similar predecessor to 1882 Act).	
For the benefit of his wife, Susan, and of the children of their marriage[4].	(1) The children who take are those living when the fund comes into existence. (2) The wife and surviving children take as joint tenants. If a life interest for the wife had been intended, the policy could have used the words 'for the benefit of my wife for life with remainder to our children'.

1   [1927] P 237.
2   [1949] P 77.
3   [1951] P 395.
4   *Re Seyton, Seyton v Satterthwaite* (1887) 34 Ch D 511.

Wording	Construction
For the benefit of his wife and children[1].	The wife and children take as joint tenants.
For the benefit of his wife or if she be dead between his children in equal proportions[2].	The widow (who was a second wife and not the wife living at the date of the policy) was not entitled. The children of both marriages take in equal shares. The words 'if she be dead' pointed to the wife living at the date of the policy.
For the benefit of his widow or widow and children or some or one of them in such shares and proportions and interest and generally in such manner as the assured shall by any will or codicil or by deed revocable or otherwise appoint[3]. Note – the assured by deed appointed to his second wife if she should survive him.	The second wife survived the assured. The appointment was good and the second wife takes absolutely.
For the benefit of his wife[4].	The wife living at the date of the policy died in the lifetime of the husband. She was not named in the policy. The words 'for the benefit of his wife' mean in these circumstances 'for the benefit of her who by surviving the assured shall become his widow'.
Policies issued under section 11 of the Married Women's Property Act 1882.	
For the benefit of L the wife of the assured.	The specifically named wife takes an immediate absolute vested interest in the policy, which passes on her death in the husband's lifetime to her personal representatives[5].
For the benefit of his wife and children[6].	The wife living at the date of the policy died. The assured was survived by a second wife and children of both marriages. The second wife and all the children take as joint tenants. Note – had the policy been effected after 1969 any illegitimate children would have been entitled to share equally with the second wife and lawful children.

1   *Re Davies' Policy Trusts* [1892] 1 Ch 90.
2   *Re Griffiths' Policy* [1903] 1 Ch 739.
3   *Re Parker's Policies* [1906] 1 Ch 526.
4   *Re Collier* [1930] 2 Ch 37.
5   *Cousins v Sun Life Assurance Society* [1933] Ch 126.
6   *Re Browne's Policy, Browne v Browne* [1903] 1 Ch 188.

G   Scotland

I   The MWPA (Scotland) Act

12.54   The corresponding Scottish Act is the Married Women's Policies of Assurance (Scotland) Act 1880, which extended to Scotland facilities already available in England under the English Act of 1870. It was amended in 1980 by the Married Women's Policies of Assurance (Scotland) (Amendment) Act 1980 to extend to men and women whether married or not.

Section 2 of the MWPA (Scotland) Act, as amended, makes provisions which in general are similar to those in the English MWPA with regard to trustees, protection against creditors, and receipts for sums secured by the policy or for the value thereof, in whole or in part. The provision entitling the creditors to claim a return of premiums applies if the life assured is made bankrupt within *two years* of the date of the policy, as well as if it is proved that the policy was effected and premiums paid with intent to defraud creditors.

A man or woman can therefore now effect a policy in trust under the MWPA (Scotland) Act and any one or more members of the classes known as 'spouse and children' can be beneficiaries. 'Children' includes children which the person effecting the policy has, or may have in the future, including illegitimate children and adopted children. It does not, however, extend to children of a spouse and another person unless the person effecting the policy has adopted them.

The MWPA (Scotland) Act, as amended, further provides that where a policy vests in trust by virtue of section 2 of the 1880 Act then:

(1)   that trust constitutes a trust within the meaning of the Trusts (Scotland) Act 1921; and

(2)   any person in whom such a policy vests is a trustee within the meaning of that Act. The sometimes onerous requirement for delivery is not essential for MWPA (Scotland) Act trusts.

Moreover, a policy is not prevented from vesting in a trustee merely because it contains a provision that a trustee may in his professional capacity charge a reasonable remuneration for his services. The powers of trustees are clarified by the 1980 amendment act. Trustees under such trusts will therefore have all the powers of trustees within the meaning of the Trusts (Scotland) Act 1921. One particularly interesting provision introduced by the 1980 amendment act was that a beneficiary under such a trust may now assign or renounce his interest[1]. This is the case whether or not the policy was dated before or after 29 October 1980.

This Act extends to Scotland only and although the effect of this is not clear it seems wise to use the 1880 Act only for policies payable in Scotland effected by people resident and domiciled in Scotland.

---

1   Section 3(1) and (3).

CHAPTER 13

Income tax and capital gains tax

SUMMARY

SECTION I   INTRODUCTION

13.1   The effect of the Finance Act 1984 was to remove income tax relief for premiums payable in respect of life policies effected after 13 March 1984. In addition, any policy effected prior to 14 March 1984 loses relief if it is varied after 13 March 1984 so as to increase the benefits or extend the term of the policy.

This introduction gives a brief outline of the subject to be dealt with in more detail in later sections.

A person who paid the premium on a life policy on his or her own life, or the life of his or her spouse, could, subject to certain conditions, have obtained a reduction in income tax liability. This relief applied only to basic rate, not to tax at the higher rate.

For premiums under a policy effected after 19 March 1968 to have been eligible for income tax relief, the policy, besides satisfying the other rules prescribed in the Income and Corporation Taxes Act 1970 (ICTA 1970), had to satisfy (or be exempt from) a number of qualifying conditions: ie it must have been a 'qualifying policy' within the meaning of Schedule 1 to that Act. These conditions, which were intended primarily to prevent tax avoidance, were first introduced by

503

the Finance Act 1968 but were later consolidated in ICTA 1970. However, because it was believed that the rules under the 1968 Act were deficient in some respects, further qualifying conditions were imposed by Schedule 2 to the Finance Act 1975 with effect from 1 April 1976. The 1975 Act also provided for the taking over by the Inland Revenue (HMRC) from the life offices of the function of testing and certifying policies as 'qualifying' under the statutory requirements.

The status of a policy as 'qualifying' continues to be important subsequent to the Finance Act 1984. If a policy is non-qualifying, a potential liability to higher rate tax will arise under sections 461–546 of the Income Tax (Trading and Other Income) Act 2005 (ITTOIA 2005) – (formerly sections 539–554 of the Income and Corporation Taxes Act 1988 (ICTA 1988)) – on the profit (or gain) derived from the contract. Even if the contract is a qualifying policy, such a tax charge may arise in the event, for example, of termination of premium payments within ten years of commencement or within three-quarters of the term, if less.

SECTION 2   TAX RELIEF ON LIFE PREMIUMS – POSITION PRIOR TO THE FINANCE ACT 1984

13.2   In view of the fact that this is now mainly only of historical interest it is dealt with only briefly in this edition. For a fuller treatment the reader is referred to the tenth edition of this book.

A   Premiums ranking for relief – conditions applicable to all policies[1]

13.3

(1)   The premium must have been one payable on a policy effected with an insurance company legally established in the UK or any branch in the UK of an insurance company lawfully carrying on life assurance business in the UK, or on a policy effected with a registered friendly society, or on a policy issued by underwriting members of Lloyd's or any other approved association of underwriters.

HMRC previously interpreted the old section 19(2)(i) of ICTA 1970 as meaning that relief was not due unless the management of a policy issued overseas had been transferred to the UK branch. They ultimately concluded, however, that the legislation did not impose such a condition and so if the premium on such a policy is paid to the UK branch and the conditions for relief were otherwise satisfied, relief would have been due[2].

1   See now ICTA 1988, s 266.
2   Inland Revenue Press Release, 4 February 1981.

(2)   The policy must have been a policy of insurance made by a man on his own life or on that of his wife; or a woman on her own life or the life of her husband.

A premium on a joint life policy would not normally have ranked for relief, unless the lives were husband and wife.

> *Wilson v Simpson*[1]
>
> Two directors, W and M, effected a policy on their joint lives and paid the premium in equal shares. One director claimed relief on his half-share of the premium. Held, that as the assurance had been made jointly with another person, it was not a contract made by him only, nor was the assurance made on his life, but on their joint lives. The payments he had made were his contribution towards the joint payment. Relief, was, therefore, not available.

(3)   The policy must have secured a capital sum on death.

> *Gould v Curtis*[2]
>
> G effected a double endowment assurance, the benefit being £100 if death should occur during a term of years or £200 on survival to the end of the term. Held, that the whole of the premium was available for relief and not only that part charged to provide the capital sum on death.

B   The extent of relief

13.4   After 5 April 1979 a fixed percentage of each premium is deducted from the life assurance premium on payment and retained by the taxpayer. The premium limit from 6 April 1990 is the larger of one-sixth of total income (after charges) and £1,500 for each spouse. Different rules applied prior to 6 April 1990. There is no actual limit on the deduction from premiums as life offices never know if the one-sixth limit is being exceeded. Tax relief may therefore be deducted irrespective of the size of the premium and so it is up to HMRC to ensure that the limit is not exceeded. In the event that the limits are exceeded, HMRC are able to recover the excess tax relief by issuing an assessment to the policyholder. It can also issue a 'Paragraph 4' notice. This is a notice to the policyholder and the life office specifying that premiums must henceforth be paid gross[3].

If such a notice is received from HMRC, the life office must make arrangements to collect premiums without deduction of tax relief from the date specified in the notice.

From 6 April 1989 the rate of relief is 12.5%.

---

1   [1926] 2 KB 500.
2   [1913] 3 KB 84.
3   ICTA 1988, Sch 14, para 4.

C Conditions and limits of relief

13.5

(1) The policy, if effected after 19 March 1968, must be either a qualifying or exempt policy within the provisions laid down in what is now Schedule 15 to ICTA 1988 (see Section 3). A policy effected on or before that date is treated as one made after that date if varied after that date so as to increase the benefits secured, or to extend the term of the assurance.

(2) The total maximum relief in any year is relief in respect of one-sixth of the 'total income' of the taxpayer. 'Total income' for this purpose is the aggregate of the income from all sources reduced by all charges and other deductions but before deducting personal allowances[1]. The capital element of a purchased life annuity is not included in total income for this purpose.

(3) The premium must have been *paid* by the claimant. The relief is not lost if the assured raises the money by borrowing from his bank or elsewhere on another or even the same policy. A premium is not, however, regarded as *paid* if it is charged against the benefits under the express terms of the policy. Thus, where the premiums are only partly paid in cash and the balance is advanced by way of loan by the life office, then relief is only available on the part of the premium paid in cash.

> *Hunter v R*[2]
>
> A policy provided for a sum assured of £1,500 payable on death and the premium was £66 per annum. Of this, £33 was paid in cash and the remaining £33 plus interest thereon was to be deducted from the proceeds. The taxpayer contended that the £33 was paid by an advance from the life office. Held, that relief was available only on the £33 actually *paid* by the taxpayer. Payments can be made net of relief via a third party, such as a broker or employer, but must come ultimately from the assured or his spouse.

There is no requirement that premiums should be paid out of income; relief can be obtained even if they are paid out of capital.

(4) The relief for any year of assessment should be based on the premiums paid in that year. The renewal date is not material. If accordingly the premiums fall into arrears and several premiums are subsequently paid in one year, all the payments rank for that year. Where an advance of the premium is made by the life office and is subsequently paid off, the payment will be treated as a payment of premium on which relief can be claimed but relief will be allowed only if such an advance of premium is actually repaid. Cancellation of the debt by way of set-off is not sufficient.

---

1   ICTA 1988, s 835.
2   [1904] AC 161.

R v Income Tax Special Commrs, ex p Horner[1]

H effected an endowment assurance and on maturity the portions of premium advanced by the life office were deducted from the policy money. Held, that no relief could be made in respect of amounts so deducted.

Watkins (Inspector of Taxes) v Hugh-Jones[2]

H-J effected a policy entitled to share in profits in the form of reduction of premium. He claimed that he had paid the full premium and received a set-off of the reduction. Held, that the reduced premium only was available for relief.

(5)   The policy must not have been varied after 13 March 1984 so as to increase the benefits or extend its term[3].

The following are not regarded as increasing the benefits or extending the term:

(a)   reduction of term of endowment assurance if premiums remain unchanged but sum assured is reduced;

(b)   change in premium frequency (eg annual to monthly);

(c)   conversion from without to with-profits if premiums are not increased but sum assured is reduced;

(d)   removal of a debt premium loading or exclusion imposed because of an exceptional risk of death, even if premiums consequently increase;

(e)   commutation of future premiums (although this is still a 'significant variation' for qualification purposes, and hence may disqualify the policy anyway).

(f)   the reinstatement on original terms of a pre-14 March policy which has lapsed or become paid up through non-payment of premiums, provided it occurs within 13 months of the due date of the first unpaid premium and all arrears, including interest, are paid;

(g)   switching funds under a unit-linked policy;

(h)   variation in sum assured under a unit-linked policy where no increase in premium;

(i)   automatic increases in premiums at set intervals in accordance with the original terms of the policy;

(j)   increases in premiums, sums assured or extension of premium paying period as a result of a 'review clause' in a unit-linked policy in line with the performance of the underlying investments or mortality experience;

1   [1932] 17 TC 362.
2   [1928] 14 TC 94.
3   ICTA 1988, Sch 14, para 8(4).

(k) variation in premiums within defined limits specified in the policy;

(l) changes to premiums or sum assured, or extension of term, to correct bona fide misstatement of age.

The following (although not intended to be exhaustive) are, however, regarded as removing eligibility:

(a) alteration from one class of assurance to another;

(b) conversion from an endowment assurance to a low cost endowment assurance and vice versa;

(c) reduction of term of endowment type assurance, if premiums are simultaneously increased;

(d) conversion from without-profits to with-profits (or to unit-linked) for same sum assured;

(e) addition of disability or accidental death benefits or the addition of any new option;

(f) extension of term of an endowment policy whether or not for an increased premium;

(g) extension of premium paying term of whole life assurance where premiums were payable for a limited period;

(h) the rewriting of a pre-14 March policy from 'non-Married Women's Property Act 1882 (MWPA 1882)'[1] to 'MWPA 1882'.

If an alteration does remove eligibility, it is the whole premium which is disallowed, not just that part attributable to the increased benefits or extended term.

D Title

13.6 The relief is normally independent of any question of title. If a father effected a policy and, having assigned it to his daughter, continued to pay the premiums, he may claim relief notwithstanding that he has no longer any title to the policy. If he effected the policy subject to the MWPA 1882, or under any form of trust, relief may similarly be claimed.

SECTION 3 TAX RELIEF BY DEDUCTION FROM PREMIUMS

13.7 The Finance Act 1976 contained provisions for the introduction of the system ('premium relief by deduction') of allowing tax relief on life assurance premiums by deduction at source (commencing with the year of assessment 1979–80).

1 Married Women's Property Act 1882, s 11.

The central feature of the system is that relief for eligible premiums is normally allowed without the intervention of a tax office. Any person who pays an eligible premium is entitled to deduct and retain an appropriate sum for relief (12.5% since 6 April 1989) from the amount of the premium, and the life office receives, under a system of bulk repayments, reimbursements from HMRC for the 'deficiencies' in its premium receipts. Tax offices are involved only when, in particular cases, it becomes necessary to make an adjustment at the end of the year of assessment because circumstances have led to over or under allowance of relief under the deduction system. Prior to 6 April 1989 the relief was 15% of premiums and had been more.

The legislation which implemented the system was contained in Schedule 4 to the Finance Act 1976 and is now contained in section 266(5) of ICTA 1988. The legislation comprised basic provisions establishing the system and a number of supporting provisions making changes in the rules and conditions for premium relief. There was also a series of regulations and HMRC practice notes for the guidance of life offices and individual policyholders.

Under this system relief is not dependent on a claim being made and, somewhat strangely, is available although the policyholder has no income against which to set relief. Thus, individuals with income below the tax threshold receive relief under the system which previously was not available to them. The policyholder is authorised to deduct the tax relief from his premiums and the life office is obliged to accept the reduced amount in full satisfaction of the policyholder's liability.

A   Limits

13.8   The overall limit on relief as previously set out under section 19 of ICTA 1970 was amended for this system so as to allow tax relief on life premiums up to a maximum of £1,500 or one-sixth of the policyholder's total income whichever is higher.

The Finance Act 1976 provided that the aggregate amount of the premiums on which relief is available *by deduction* would be restricted to £1,500 in any one year (being any period of 12 months beginning with an anniversary of the effecting of the policy). This was achieved by reducing the amount of each premium eligible for relief by the proportion that £1,500 bears to the aggregate of premiums for that year. However, as the operation of this *deduction* limit would have proved an administrative burden, amending legislation was introduced in the Finance Act 1978 to remove the restriction. This meant that offices can accept premiums net of income tax relief whatever the amount of premium, provided they are within the *overall* limit mentioned above.

Where the correct relief has not been given under the deduction system, an adjustment is made. This may occur, for example, where a person is paying premiums under more than one policy and there is an over-allowance of relief. In cases of over-allowance the Inspector of Taxes has power to make any necessary assessments to recover the difference. HMRC is empowered also, in cases where it appears that the relief to which a person is entitled has been or might be exceeded, to issue a notice to both policyholder and life office requiring future premiums to be paid gross.

B Husband and wife

13.9 Under the system of premium relief by deduction, once premiums are established as eligible for relief they will broadly continue to be eligible throughout subsequent changes in marital status. The legislation ensures, therefore, that, in the case of policies on the life of a spouse, relief is preserved on divorce provided that the marriage was subsisting on 6 April 1979, when the new rules came into force.

Relief is also available for policies effected prior to 14 March 1984 if marriage (or a registered civil partnership) takes place after that date.

C Residence

13.10 The policyholder must be resident in the UK to be able to pay premiums net of tax relief[1]. Residence has been explained by HMRC in the following terms[2]:

> 'An individual can be regarded as resident in the United Kingdom if his "home" in the ordinary sense is here, who if he goes abroad on business or pleasure goes for short periods only. For taxation purposes the United Kingdom comprises England, Scotland, Wales and Northern Ireland only, and does not include the Channel Islands or the Isle of Man.'

This definition is provided as a simple test which will apply to the vast majority of cases. Residence for this purpose is not necessarily the same as for other taxation purposes.

Residence under the Income and Corporation Taxes Act 1988 is normally determined for the whole of an income tax year. A person who is in the UK for part only of a tax year will be treated as resident or not, as the case may be for the whole of the year.

Members of the armed forces and their spouses are counted as UK residents. Other persons resident abroad but taxed as UK residents, such as diplomatic staff are, however, not eligible to pay premiums net of relief. Policyholders resident abroad may be able to claim tax relief direct from HMRC under section 278 of ICTA 1988. This includes British subjects, Crown Servants and Isle of Man or Channel Islands residents.

D Industrial assurance

13.11 Generally speaking, the system of relief by deduction applies to industrial assurance policies and policies issued by friendly societies. Under previous rules the premiums on certain categories of industrial assurance policies were not eligible for relief. Paragraph 11 of Schedule 4 to ICTA 1970 (now Schedule 14

---

1 ICTA 1988, s 266(5).
2 Notes on Statements Prescribed under the Income Tax (Life Assurance Premium Relief) Regulations 1978, SI 1978/1159, reg 2.

to ICTA 1988), provided that virtually all such policies issued before the passing of the Act would be eligible for relief under the new system. Two categories of policy, viz 'statutory' policies (effected by a child on the life of a parent or grandparent), or 'juvenile' policies (effected by a parent or grandparent on the life of a child) became eligible for relief, subject to certain restrictions.

E   Temporary assurances

13.12   The Finance Act 1976 excluded from the category of qualifying policies temporary life policies where the term is less than one year. Thus no relief was available in respect of premiums paid under short-term policies such as holiday or travel insurance.

SECTION 4   QUALIFYING POLICIES

A   Policies effected after 19 March 1968

13.13   For premiums under a policy effected (or in some cases varied – see below) after 19 March 1968, but before 13 March 1984, to be eligible for income tax relief and for any gains arising under such a policy to avoid any possible liability to the higher rate of income tax, the policy must be a 'qualifying policy' as defined in Schedule 15 to ICTA 1988, or be exempt from the provisions of that Act. For the premiums to be eligible for income tax relief, it must also of course satisfy the rules set out in Section 2[1] of this chapter and the amount of relief may be limited as mentioned in that section. Qualifying status is also one of the factors relevant to a possible charge to the higher rate of income tax on the profit (or gain) under the policy (see Section 6). But the two aspects (ie premium relief and qualification) must not be confused. Thus a life of another policy may be a qualifying policy for this purpose, and be free from the charges to tax on policy gains, although it will not normally have been eligible for life assurance premium relief.

These provisions do not apply at all to life policies issued in connection with schemes approved under Chapter I of Part XIV of ICTA 1988, and its forerunner, the Finance Act 1970 (ie 'new code' schemes). So far as life assurance premium relief from income tax is concerned, exemption is irrelevant for policies effected under pension schemes which are 'exempt approved', as employees' contributions will be treated as a deduction from earned income. HMRC has indicated that policies effected under schemes approved by it will be treated as exempt, irrespective of how much of the cost is borne by the employer[2]. 'Salary sacrifice' arrangements (ie where an employee agrees to forgo part of his salary on inclusion in a scheme) are treated as paid for by the employer.

1   See **13.2–13.6**.
2   Inland Revenue Press Release, 6 March 1980.

Schedule 15 to ICTA 1988 does not apply to a policy effected on or before 19 March 1968 unless it has been 'varied after that date so as to increase the benefits secured or to extend the term of the insurance', in which case it will be treated in the same way as a policy effected after 19 March 1968. The expression 'increase the benefits secured' is not defined. The allocation of a reversionary bonus to a policy would not be within the meaning of the term; but the conversion of a without-profits policy to a with-profits or a conversion from whole life to endowment assurance for the same sum assured would be regarded as increasing the benefits secured by the policy; so would the introduction of disability benefits not previously included.

I Conditions for eligibility as a qualifying policy

13.14 The conditions for eligibility as a qualifying policy vary according to the class of assurance. They are set out in Part I of Schedule 15 to ICTA 1988 and are summarised below together with a note of any special HMRC treatment or concession, where relevant.

(a) Whole life assurances

13.15

(1) The policy must secure a capital sum or series of capital sums payable only on death (or on death or earlier disability), and must not secure any other benefits. It is not regarded as securing other benefits by reason only that it:

(a) participates in profits;

(b) has a guaranteed surrender value;

(c) contains an annuity option;

(d) provides for waiver of premiums during disability, or secures disability benefits of a capital nature;

(e) provides for effecting further policies without evidence of insurability.

HMRC has issued guidance in respect of variations of qualifying policies. Certain policies which may be converted or restructured in certain ways will no longer be certified as qualifying policies[1].

(2) The premiums must be payable at annual or shorter intervals, over a period of at least ten years or until the earlier death (or disability) of the life assured.

(3) The total premiums payable in any period of 12 months must not exceed twice the total premiums payable in any other such period (medical and occupational loadings being disregarded).

1 Inland Revenue Press Release, 22 January 1988.

(4)   The total premiums payable in any period of 12 months must not exceed one-eighth of the total premiums payable over the premium paying term (or where premiums are payable throughout life, over the first ten years). Again, medical and occupational loadings are disregarded.

The following further points should be noted:

(1)   The words in paragraph 1(1) of Schedule 15 to ICTA 1988 'if a policy secures a capital sum which is payable only on death' do not mean that the capital sum must be of the same amount whenever death occurs. It may vary not only according to the date of death but also according to the manner of death (eg natural causes or accident).

(2)   No objection will be raised in cases such as whole life limited premium payment policies where, for example, the first premium is a half-yearly premium with annual premiums thereafter and there is a final half-yearly premium. This would not be treated as an infringement of the 'two times' or 'one-eighth' rules, and the policy will be regarded as qualifying.

(b)   Temporary assurances – term exceeding ten years

13.16

(1)   The policy must secure a capital sum or series of capital sums payable only on death (or on death or earlier disability), and must not secure any other benefits. It is not regarded as securing other benefits by reason only that it:

   (a)   participates in profits;

   (b)   has a guaranteed surrender value;

   (c)   contains an annuity option;

   (d)   provides for waiver of premiums during disability, or secures disability benefits of a capital nature;

   (e)   provides for effecting further policies without evidence of insurability.

   HMRC has issued guidance in respect of variations of qualifying policies. Certain policies which may be converted or restructured in certain ways will no longer be certified as qualifying policies[1].

(2)   The premiums must be payable at annual or shorter intervals, over at least ten years, or for at least three-quarters of the term, whichever is the shorter period. Therefore, the ten-year term will apply for terms over 13 years and four months.

---

1   Inland Revenue Press Release, 22 January 1988.

(3) The total premiums payable in any period of 12 months must not exceed twice the total premiums payable in any other such period (medical and occupational loadings being disregarded).

(4) The total premiums payable in any period of 12 months must not exceed one eighth of the total premiums payable over the whole term (medical and occupational loadings being disregarded).

(c) Temporary assurances – term ten years or less

13.17

(1) The policy must secure a capital sum or series of capital sums payable only on death (or on death or earlier disability), and must not secure any other benefits. It is not regarded as securing other benefits by reason only that it:

    (a) participates in profits;

    (b) has a guaranteed surrender value;

    (c) contains an annuity option;

    (d) provides for waiver of premiums during disability, or secures disability benefits of a capital nature;

    (e) provides for effecting further policies without evidence of insurability.

HMRC has issued guidance in respect of variations of qualifying policies. Certain policies which may be converted or restructured in certain ways will no longer be certified as qualifying policies[1].

(2) The policy must provide that any payment made by reason of surrender shall not exceed the premiums paid.

(d) Endowment assurances

13.18

(1) The policy must secure a capital sum payable either on survival to end of term or on earlier death (or disability). This includes a sum payable on death only if it occurs after the attainment of an age not exceeding 16, in which case the benefit on earlier death must not exceed the total premiums paid before the death. In applying this rule any loading for premiums payable more frequently than annually is ignored. Unlike whole life and temporary assurances, other benefits may be included, except benefits of a capital nature payable before death, disability or survival (except by surrender or cashing bonuses).

(2) The term of assurance must be at least ten years and premiums must be payable at annual or shorter intervals over at least ten years.

---

1 Inland Revenue Press Release, 22 January 1988.

(3)   The total premiums payable in any period of 12 months must not exceed twice the total premiums payable in any other such period (medical and occupational loadings being disregarded).

(4)   The total premiums payable in any period of 12 months must not exceed one-eighth of the total premiums payable over the whole term. Medical and occupational loadings are disregarded.

In the case of policies where the sum assured is payable by instalments, the capital sum is taken as the total of the instalments and not the cash sum for which they could be commuted when the sum assured becomes payable.

Again, the words 'a policy which secures a capital sum payable either on survival for a specified term or an earlier death' do not mean that the capital sum must be of the same amount whenever death occurs or that the capital sum on maturity must be the same amount as the capital sum on death. The capital sum payable on maturity can in fact be different from that payable on death and the capital sum on death may also vary according to the date and manner of death.

(e)   Other types of policy

13.19

(1)   *Mortgage protection policies.* Policies effected solely to cover a mortgage of the taxpayer's residence or his own business premises are exempt from the provisions relating to qualifying policies provided the sum assured is substantially the same as the amount outstanding under the mortgage. The principal amount secured must be repayable by instalments payable annually or at shorter intervals. The policy should thus be purely a decreasing term assurance to which no permanent benefit is attached[1].

(2)   *Family income policies.* The same conditions apply to family income policies as to temporary assurances. If a whole life or endowment assurance policy includes income benefits the policy will be a qualifying policy either:

   (i)   if both the basic assurance and the income benefits would have qualified separately; or

   (ii)   if the policy fulfils the conditions for a whole life or endowment assurance as the case may be.

(3)   *Pure endowments.* Pure endowments (ie policies securing a capital sum payable only on survival for a fixed period, with or without a provision for return of premiums on death) if issued after 19 March 1968 are non-qualifying policies.

(4)   *Contingent assurances.* Contingent assurances (ie policies payable on the death of the life assured, provided another person (the 'counter-life') is still

---

1   ICTA 1988, Sch 15, para 9.

alive) are treated in the same way as if payment on the death of the life assured did not depend on the continued existence of the counter life.

(5)   *Industrial life policies.* Industrial life policies are specially dealt with in paragraph 7 of Schedule 15 to ICTA 1988.

(6)   *Policies with increasing premiums.* If there is provision for an increase of the premium to more than twice its original amount, the policy will be non-qualifying.

(7)   *Last survivor policies.* Premiums ceasing on first death. Where a last survivor policy is written with the premium paying period ceasing on the first death, HMRC takes the view that this will not be a qualifying policy as it will not comply with paragraph 1(2)(a) of Schedule 15 to ICTA 1988, in as much as the premium paying period may not be for ten years. If premiums are expressed to be payable until the first death but subject to a minimum premium paying period of ten years the policy will qualify.

(8)   *Children's assurances.* Policies on the lives of young children often have life cover deferred to, for example, age 16. In order to qualify, the policy must provide that if life cover is deferred until 16 or some lower age, any payment made on death during the deferred period must not exceed the total premiums paid.

2   Dating back

13.20   For the purpose of the conditions for qualification, in particular the 'one-eighth' rule, policies may be dated back for a period of up to three months without causing an otherwise qualifying policy to become non-qualifying. This is because in such circumstances the assurance will be regarded as having been made on the effective date of assurance, ie the date to which the policy is back-dated. But if the assurance is dated back more than three months it will be regarded as having been made on the actual date of assurance and this may mean that an otherwise qualifying policy is non-qualifying.

3   Variations and substitutions

13.21   The rules relating to variations in the terms of policies and substitutions are to be found in paragraphs 17 to 20 of Schedule 15 of ICTA 1988 and are summarised below.

(a)   Assurances effected after 19 March 1968

13.22   In applying the following rules 'old policy' means the policy as it stood immediately prior to the alteration, and 'new policy' includes the converted policy viewed as if it were a new policy commencing at the date of the conversion, ie ignoring previous premiums and benefits.

   If the old policy did not qualify the revised policy does not qualify. An exception to this is where the person making the insurance was an infant when the old policy was effected and the policy secured a capital sum payable not later than one month after his 25th birthday or on the anniversary of the policy immediately following that birthday. If the old policy was a qualifying one and the new policy is also a qualifying one then the policy as converted will normally also qualify. The only exception to this rule is where the old policy has been in force less than ten years at the time of variation, in which case the revised policy will qualify only if the highest revised premium payable in any period of 12 months during the remainder of the ten years is not less than one half of the highest total paid over any period of 12 months under the old policy (or any related policy).

It follows that conversions from whole life to endowment assurance or from a longer to shorter term endowment assurance will usually result in the revised policy continuing to qualify provided the new unexpired term after conversion is ten years or more.

Variations which do not affect the terms of the existing policy in any significant respect are disregarded. These include changes in the intervals at which premiums are payable within one year and most changes due to misstatement of age.

It is not possible to define precisely what variations would be regarded as significant. Prima facie, however, variations in the following would all be significant and would require a policy issued after 19 March 1968 to be retested:

(1)   sum assured;

(2)   type of benefit which alters the premium or benefit paid (historically HMRC stated that a change from without-profits to with-profits or vice versa would be significant but changes between without-profits, with-profits, unit-linked and unitised with-profits are only significant if the premium and/or benefit also change. This change is effective from 5 November 2005);

(3)   policy term;

(4)   premium paying term;

(5)   change in premium payment, including payment in commutation of future premiums. A mere change in frequency of premium payments is not a significant variation.

13.23   In section 540(1)(b)(i) of ICTA 1988, reference is made to surrender, assignments or conversion into a paid-up policy 'before the expiry of ten years from the making of the insurance or, if sooner, of three-quarters of the term for which the policy is to run' ('the chargeable event period'). In the case of varied policies which are subsequently surrendered or made paid-up, if the premiums did not increase as a result of the variation then the chargeable event period runs from the date of the original policy. If the premiums payable were increased as a result of the variation then the chargeable event period runs from the date of the variation. HMRC has confirmed that in deciding whether or not the premiums payable have been increased the rate of premium payable before and after the variation should be compared. For this purpose it ignores any increase due solely to a change in the frequency of payment.

Where the existing policy was qualifying, and was effected more than ten years before the conversion, but the revised policy would on the face of it be non-qualifying (eg, an endowment assurance maturity within the next ten years or an infringement of the spread of premium rules ie 'twice the premium' and 'one-eighth' rules) then the revised policy will nevertheless be a qualifying policy if:

(1) the premiums payable in any period of 12 months under the revised policy are not greater than the smallest total paid over any period of 12 months before the conversion; or

(2) the old policy was issued outside the UK and the conversion is in the following special circumstances as set out in paragraph 17(3) of Schedule 15 to the 1988 Act.

(b) Offshore policies effected before 17 November 1983

13.24 The new policy satisfies the normal rules relating to substitutions referred to above (the offshore policy will also need certification by HMRC) and:

(1) the policyholder became resident in the UK in the 12 months before the issue of the new policy;

(2) the issuing company certifies that the new policy is in substitution for the offshore policy and that it has arrangements with the offshore company to issue such substituted policies; and

(3) the new policy confers benefits which are substantially equivalent to those under the old policy.

(c) Offshore policies effected after 17 November 1983

13.25 The offshore policy must have been capable of being certified as a qualifying policy under the pre-18 November 1983 rules, and the new policy must satisfy the normal substitution rules, and the conditions laid down in (1), (2) and (3) above.

An offshore policy effected on or before 17 November 1983 will be deemed to have been effected after the said date if it is varied after that date (whether by exercise of an option or otherwise) so as to increase the benefits secured or to extend its term.

When a policy is varied more than once, on each occasion the 'old policy' dates from the last preceding variation.

(d) Assurances effected before 20 March 1968

13.26 Such policies will remain exempt from the provisions of Schedule 15 unless the alteration increases the benefit secured or extends the term of the assurance, in which cases the same rules apply as where the existing assurance was effected after 19 March 1968, the existing policy being treated as a qualifying policy if it would have been a qualifying one had it been effected after 19 March 1968.

(e)   Variation of term assurance policies

13.27   If under a term assurance of ten years or less, the original sum assured is reduced to less than half or the term is extended to cover an additional period (but the total term is still more than ten years), any resulting reduction in premium to less than half is not treated as disqualifying the policy under paragraph 17(2)(b) of Schedule 15 to ICTA 1988.

4   Certification of qualifying policies

13.28   Under paragraph 22 of Schedule 15, the life office must issue a Qualifying Life Assurance Policy Certificate when requested by the policy-holder. The certificate must show the name of the life assured, the policy number, the sum assured, the amount and due dates of the premiums. For policies issued on or after 1 April 1976 it must also show the HMRC certification reference. This will state that in the life office's opinion the policy does qualify.

B   Policies effected on or after 1 April 1976: additional requirements

13.29   The practical operation of the 1968 qualifying rules had given rise to some difficulties. Moreover, the rules had proved inadequate in some circumstances to prevent what was regarded as an abuse of the tax relief. In particular, it was believed that the life assurance element of some contracts was too low and that a minimum requirement ought to apply.

Accordingly, further qualifying conditions were introduced by the Finance Act 1975 to supplement those already in operation from 1968. In consequence, for life policies taken out on or after 1 April 1976, life assurance relief was given in respect of premiums, and any gains arising under a policy avoided any possible liability to the higher rate of income tax, only if the policy was a qualifying policy within the provisions of what was Part I of Schedule 1 to ICTA 1970, as amended by Part II of Schedule 2 to the Finance Act 1975[1]. All such provisions are now contained in Schedule 15 to ICTA 1988.

The changes introduced by the Finance Act 1975 applied to 'insurances made' on or after 1 April 1976. Thus, for example, a whole life assurance or a term assurance policy which does not comply with the 75% rule (see below), but which was effected before that date, continues to qualify. However, such a policy which is 'significantly' varied on or after 1 April 1976 has to comply with the 75% rule in respect of premiums payable from the date of variation.

---

1   Note that not all of the changes introduced by the Finance Act 1975, Sch 2 were consolidated into ICTA 1970, Sch 1 and so the Finance Act 1975 should be referred to separately.

1 Whole life and temporary assurances

13.30 The qualification rules relating to whole life and term assurances were therefore amended by the imposition of a condition *additional* to the 1968 provisions.

To be a qualifying policy, a whole life or temporary assurance must assure a capital sum on death of not less than 75% of the premiums which would be payable under the policy if death were to occur at age 75. If a capital sum is payable under a joint life policy (ie on the first death), the period taken is to the seventy-fifth birthday of the older of them. In the case of a last survivor policy it is the age of the younger of the lives assured which is relevant. In the case of a policy which does not secure the payment of a capital sum if death occurs before age 16 or lower, the policy must not provide for any payment which exceeds the total premiums previously paid on the policy.

A temporary assurance policy which makes no provision for any payment on total or partial surrender, and where the term of the policy does not run beyond age 75 of the life assured, is excluded from the application of the 75% rule.

If the capital sum on death may be payable as a single sum, or a series of sums, the 75% calculation is to be made applying the smallest total sum payable. This rule prevents avoidance of the qualification rules by giving an option to take a series of payments where in reality this option is unlikely to be taken up.

Any addition to a premium made where the payment is otherwise than annually is to be disregarded.

2 Endowment assurances

13.31 The qualification rules relating to endowment assurances were added to by Part II of Schedule 2 to the Finance Act 1975.

To be a qualifying policy, an endowment assurance must secure a capital sum in the event of death of at least 75% of the premiums payable during its prospective term. But as this rule might operate harshly in the case of policies on older lives (where the premiums are likely to be high in relation to the capital sum assured), the 75% standard is reduced by 2% for each year by which the age of the life assured exceeds 55 years.

3 Options

13.32 Paragraph 3 of Schedule 2 to the Finance Act 1975 introduced changes in the rules for determining whether a policy which includes one or more options is a qualifying policy.

It was previously the practice, when a policy was tested for qualification at its inception, to test it initially without regard to options and to retest it if and when an option was exercised. This basis of testing continues in respect of policies issued before 1 April 1976 and, if an option is exercised, any change in the terms is treated as a variation to which the substitution and variation rules of paragraph 17 of Schedule 15 to ICTA 1988 apply.

For policies issued on or after 1 April 1976 the policy is tested taking into account at the outset the existence of the options, but with no retesting on the subsequent exercising of any option. This is achieved by testing at the outset all the hypothetical policies which would result from exercising all or any of the options to see whether all of them would be qualifying policies. Only if this is so is the policy a qualifying policy.

In practice, rather than spell out only the options which can be allowed, the policy can contain a clause limiting the options available, which require to be tested as 'significant' variations, to those which would allow the policy to remain a qualifying one when tested under the variation rules. HMRC have indicated that the following would be acceptable as a modification to options to convert, to meet the qualifying rules:

> 'The right of conversion under this option is limited to making such changes in the terms of the policy (and/or substituting a new policy) as would be compatible with the requirements of paragraph 19(3) of Schedule 15 to ICTA 1988 for this to be a qualifying policy.'

When the option is actually exercised in a particular case, the test has to be carried out but the alteration does not constitute a variation (the option having been provided in the policy from the outset) and no new ten-year period, which could affect a subsequent variation, has started.

4   Maturity or surrender value as first premium

13.33   Under the 1968 rules a new policy sometimes failed to qualify solely because the initial premium was inflated by the inclusion in it of the maturity or surrender value of an old policy – thereby infringing the provisions requiring an even spread of premiums. For policies issued on or after 1 April 1976 in appropriate circumstances this value is left out of account of the first premium for the purpose of testing the new policy for qualification. The maturity or surrender value of the previous policy must have been retained by the life office in the following circumstances:

(1)   where the previous policy was a qualifying policy and has been in force for at least ten years and the person or persons effecting the new policy are the same as under the previous policy and are acting in the same capacity (ignoring any change in trustees) although the life assured may be changed; or

(2)   whether or not the previous policy was qualifying it was issued when the person effecting the new policy was an infant and the capital sum secured under the previous policy was payable not later than one month after the child's 25th birthday or on the policy anniversary following that age.

5   Certification of qualifying policies

13.34   With effect from 1 April 1976, the certification of qualifying policies was taken over from the life offices by HMRC[1]. Thus, a policy issued or varied on or after that day must, if it is to be a qualifying policy, be so certified by HMRC, or must conform to a standard form which is certified by it.

In 2005 HMRC introduced new legislation to assist life companies who restructured as part of an insurance business transfer scheme[2]. While re-certification of the company name was still required, any variation, which alters the basis on which the benefits secured by the policy are to be determined, did not require to be tested as a significant variation. This part of the legislation was retrospective.

In addition, the legislation also adopted the same rule for all variations of that nature as from 7 October 2005. This is particularly useful for policies which allow switches between unit-linked funds and unitised with-profit funds without affecting the premium or sum assured. If such a policy is nearing maturity customers will no longer need to defer the maturity date so there would still be ten years to maturity. Whether it is wise to switch into a unitised with-profit fund close to maturity is another matter.

Strictly this legislation also means that a change from non-profit to with-profit or to unit-linked (and vice versa) no longer needs to be tested as a variation for qualification. However, such variations usually occur simultaneously with variations to the premium and sum assured which still have to be tested as significant variations.

6   Industrial life policies

13.35   In general terms, paragraph 7 of Schedule 15 to ICTA 1988 provides that certain types of industrial assurance policies which would not qualify under the normal rules are none the less qualifying policies, provided that the total capital sums involved on all such policies held by one policyholder do not exceed stipulated monetary limits.

7   Reinstatement

13.36   HMRC have agreed that non-forfeiture provisions of a qualifying policy may allow premiums to remain outstanding for a period of up to 13 months from the date of the first unpaid premium during which application may be made by the policyholder to reinstate the policy. Reinstatement of a policy within 13 months will not, therefore, affect its status and this applies regardless of whether in the meantime the policy has lapsed, been paid up or converted into a term assurance.

1   ICTA 1988, Sch 15, para 21.
2   Schemes falling within section 105 of FSMA 2000, sanctioned by a court under Part 1 of Schedule 2C to the Insurance Companies Act 1982 or by a court under section 49 of that Act with regard to certification.

A provision in the policy allowing reinstatement (or simply deferment of premiums) during a longer period than 13 months disqualifies the policy ab initio. Similarly, if regardless of policy conditions, the policy is allowed to be reinstated outside the 13-month period it would be deemed to be varied.

For policies effected before 20 March 1968 the 13-month period referred to is extended to five years provided neither the benefits nor the term of the policy are increased.

8   Combination of policies

13.37   Section 30 of the Finance Act 1980 was introduced in order to put an end to the exploitation of life assurance premium relief by the issue of certain contracts, known generally as 'short-term bonds'. In the typical case these consisted of a combination of policies under which one policy attracted a very high rate of return which depended on the availability of premium relief on another policy. Section 30 denied the premium relief, that made possible the high return on these bonds, by disqualifying any policy forming part of such an arrangement which would otherwise be a qualifying policy. The section provides that a policy will not be treated as qualifying if it is connected with another policy, the terms of which provide benefits which are greater than would reasonably be expected if any policy connected with it were disregarded. The section operates therefore if two or more policies are connected and one or more of them is uncommercial. A policy is regarded as connected with another policy if they are at any time simultaneously in force and either of them is issued with reference to the other or with a view to the issue of the other policy on particular terms. These provisions now appear in paragraph 14 of Schedule 15 to ICTA 1988[1].

The following features where they occur in relation to a policy are not in themselves regarded as bringing the policy concerned within the scope of the section:

(1)   the policy fee is reduced or a higher unit allocation allowed where a policyholder is taking out more than one insurance, providing the reduction or increase (as the case may be) reflects only the saving in the life office expenses;

(2)   an insurance is split into a cluster of separate policies (known as 'segmentation') each of which is a qualifying policy and provides identical benefits for an identical premium;

(3)   owing to the existence of other policies:

(a)   a policy is issued on terms not taking into account an exceptional risk of death; or

(b)   less than normal underwriting information is sought;

(4)   a policy is issued simultaneously with a temporary purchased life annuity which is intended to fund the premiums payable under the policy (a 'back-to-back arrangement');

1   The Finance Act 1984 introduced adjustments to cover 'capital and income bonds'.

(5) a policy is issued in exercise of an option contained in a convertible term assurance where the latter policy remains wholly or partly in force.

9 Restructuring of qualifying policies issued on or after 25 February 1988

13.38 As a result of taking legal advice, HMRC issued a Press Release on 22 January 1988. This announced a change in their interpretation of the qualifying provisions. Certain policy alterations, whether by exercise of an option or by agreement, are viewed as sufficiently fundamental as to create a new contract, even though they do not give rise to the issue of new policies. Consequently, the new contract may not satisfy the qualifying rules.

Changes which give rise to new contracts are, for example, conversions changing the event upon which benefits under policies become payable, for example, whole life to endowment policy. One common example was the 'pep-percorn option' under which a qualifying endowment policy is converted at maturity to a whole life policy. All or part of the policy proceeds are reinvested and premiums of, eg £1 a year, are paid. Such changes almost invariably result in the rescission of the existing contract thus giving rise to a new non-qualifying policy and so any gains may give rise to a tax charge.

However, the following changes are not affected by the new interpretation:

(1) those resulting from policy reviews under unit-linked whole life assurance policies;

(2) variations of sums assured/premiums within the qualifying rules.

In 2005, HMRC introduced new legislation to assist life companies who restructured as part of:

(3) changes between with-profits and without-profits and unit-linked switches (these changes are to be treated as 'insignificant' with effect from 7 October 2005);

(4) cessation of premiums (within qualifying rules);

(5) extension of term;

(6) change of life or lives assured;

(7) reduction of term of endowment assurance; and

(8) conversion to paid up, commutation, part surrender or partial conversion to paid up, provided there is no simultaneous change in the nature of the event on which the benefits are payable[1].

---

1 Under IPTM8210 and IPTM8215 HMRC (currently in draft form 24/04/2006) state that a conversion to paid up is not even a 'variation' if it arises as part of the policy's 'non-forfeiture' provisions. Similarly, a policy containing an option to convert to paid up is not even a 'variation' provided the conversion to paid up takes place after ten years after the completion date of the policy or when it was last significantly varied.

10 Free gifts

13.39 Insurance companies frequently offer incentives in connection with policies of life insurance, contracts for life annuities and capital redemption policies. These are often described as 'free gifts' and may take a variety of forms, such as small consumer goods, store vouchers, or discounts offered by hotels or travel agents.

So long as the aggregate cost to the insurer of all 'gifts' provided in connection with an insurance does not exceed £30, no account will be taken of the gifts in assessing whether policies are qualifying life insurance policies nor in computing any gain under the chargeable event legislation[1].

SECTION 5 'CLAW-BACK' OF TAX RELIEF

13.40 HMRC became concerned at the number of qualifying policies which were effected with the deliberate intention of being surrendered in the first ten years. The surrender value paid out would result in a profit, the essential source of which was the tax relief rather than investment by the life office.

The Finance Act 1975 therefore introduced provisions, effective from their introduction in the Budget of 26 March 1974, designed to recover part or all of the tax relief allowed on premiums for qualifying policies, on the happening of certain events.

A Surrender, etc within first four years

13.41 The relevant rules were originally set out in section 7 of the Finance Act 1975 and apply to qualifying policies effected after 26 March 1974. They are now set out in section 268 of ICTA 1988. However, these provisions are now of no practical importance in view of the fact that more than four years have passed since the withdrawal of life assurance premium relief on 13 March 1984.

B Surrender, etc after four years

13.42 There are further rules in section 269 of ICTA 1988 which provide for tax relief to be recovered if certain events occur in the fifth or any later year from the inception of the policy. These rules which apply to qualifying policies effected after 26 March 1974 were introduced to counter an avoidance device whereby tax relief was obtained for premiums paid out of periodic partial surrenders or cashing of bonus. Their effect is to ensure that tax relief on an established policy is only granted to the extent that the current year's premium, in effect, remains invested.

1 Inland Revenue Extra Statutory Concession B42.

Thus, where, during the fifth or any later year from inception of a policy, there is:

(1) a total or partial surrender;

(2) bonus encashment; or

(3) a policy loan at a non-commercial interest rate, except for a loan to a full-time employee of the issuing company for house purchase or improvement[1], *and any of these events has happened before* in connection with the policy, then the life office by whom the policy was issued is required to deduct from the proceeds becoming available an appropriate amount by way of recovery of tax relief which must be paid over to HMRC. It will be noted that the claw-back under section 269 of ICTA 1988 does not apply in the case of the first surrender, etc (even total surrender) since the start of a policy. Nor does the recovery apply to conversion of a policy into a paid-up or partly paid-up policy.

The recovery under these rules is at a rate equal to the rate allowed on premiums for the year of assessment in which the event giving rise to the recovery occurs. This rate is applied to the lower of:

(1) the total premiums *payable* during the year; or

(2) the sums *payable* on surrender or otherwise falling due.

If, during the course of a year, more than one surrender, etc takes place, the sums payable on each occasion are aggregated for the purpose of calculating the amount of claw-back. The deduction from proceeds, made by the life office, is to take account of the amounts of claw-back already retained during the same year. The total amount recovered is not to exceed one half of the basic rate of tax on the premiums for the year on the policy concerned.

The calculation is modified if the policy concerned is one which, by reason of an increase in annual premiums by more than 25% of their former amount, is deemed to have given rise to a new and separate policy to the extent of any additional rights attributable to the increase. In such cases a new four-year period is deemed to commence.

C Collection procedure

13.43 Any office which deducts and retains from proceeds arising on surrender, etc any amount by way of recovery under section 269 of ICTA 1988, must make a return to HMRC of all such sums falling due during each return period. The return is made annually.

A life office which has accounted for any such recoveries must within 30 days thereof provide the policyholder with a statement specifying the amount recov-

---

1 See ICTA 1988, s 271.

ered and indicating how it has been calculated[1]. Although claw-back is potentially payable under qualifying policies the policyholder may not have received the tax relief on the premiums because, for example, the policy was written on a life of another basis or he was non-resident. The life office must still deduct claw-back but if the policyholder has not had any, or full, tax relief on the premiums, he can reclaim the excess claw-back from HMRC using his claw-back certificate.

SECTION 6   TAXATION OF GAINS ON POLICIES

13.44   A gain realised on a life policy, life annuity contract or capital redemption policy effected after 19 March 1968, which does not satisfy certain conditions, is subject to income tax at the higher rate. The statutory provisions are to be found in Chapter 9 of Part 4 of ITTOIA 2005 (formerly sections 539–554 of ICTA 1988). It should be borne in mind that capital gains tax is not relevant in this context[2]. This can be quite confusing. The correct terminology in this context is 'gains chargeable to income tax'.

The charge to higher rate tax on gains arising on the realisation of policies extends to:

(1)   all life policies effected after 19 March 1968 which are non-qualifying, including of course single premium bonds;

(2)   qualifying life policies in certain circumstances;

(3)   all capital redemption policies and annuity contracts effected after 19 March 1968 in most circumstances – although from 9 February 2005 separate rules for capital redemption bonds effected by UK companies were introduced.

A policy will be classed as a qualifying or non-qualifying policy as the case may be and the question of whether a charge to tax arises on the realisation of the policy will be dealt with accordingly. Exempt policies do not come within the charge. Policies effected before 20 March 1968 are not subject to the charge unless varied on or after that date so as to increase the benefits or extend the term and therefore the policy has been 'retested'.

A   Chargeable events and computation of gains under policies in years falling wholly after 13 March 1975

I   Life policies

13.45   The gain arises and tax becomes chargeable only upon the occurrence of a 'chargeable event' defined, in relation to a life policy, in section 484 of

---

1   ICTA 1988, s 272.
2   See **13.71** and **13.72**.

ITTOIA 2005 and subject to the exclusions in relation to qualifying policies set out in section 485 of ITTOIA 2005.

In the case of single premium bonds and other non-qualifying policies, this means:

(1)   death giving rise to benefits under the policy;

(2)   maturity;

(3)   total surrender;

(4)   assignment for money or money's worth;

(5)   part surrender (including bonus encashment) or part assignment where the amount payable by way of surrender or an assignment exceeds the total of the 5% annual allowable credits.

In the case of qualifying life policies it means:

(1)   death;

(2)   maturity;

(but in either event, only if the policy is made paid up within ten years of inception or, if sooner, three-quarters of the term of the policy)

(3)   surrender of the policy;

(4)   assignment for money or money's worth;

(5)   part surrender or part assignment (see (5) above);

(but for each of the latter three events, only if it occurs within the above mentioned period or the policy has been converted into a paid-up policy within that date).

These time limits run from any variation to a policy by which the premiums are increased. The maturity of a policy is not a chargeable event if a new policy is issued under an option conferred by the maturing policy and the whole maturity value is transferred to the new policy.

No event is a chargeable event once the rights under the policy have been assigned for money or money's worth, unless the contract has been reassigned so that at the time of the event the contract is held by the original beneficial owner. This is a change which was introduced by the Finance Act 1975, with effect from 10 December 1974, designed to prevent the avoidance of the tax charge by the device of assigning the policy to a second person who then reassigns it to the original beneficial owner.

13.46   A further change was introduced by section 18 of the Finance Act 1983 to counter the tax avoidance device known, generally, as 'second-hand bonds'. These contracts were single-premium life policies which were sold by the original purchaser (often a broker or other agent) to the person who was intended to hold the policy ultimately. As a result of this transaction, the policy was taken out of the income tax charge to gains on non-qualifying life policies and became an asset subject to the then lower rate of capital gains tax. Section 18 provided that after 26 June 1982 (when the Chancellor's announcement was made) an income tax charge is imposed on gains arising from non-qualifying policies and annuities which are assigned for money or money's worth and not held by the original beneficial owner.

No account is taken of assignments of policies on mortgages or discharges thereof, and assignments between spouses or registered civil partners living together are similarly ignored.

The amount to be treated as a gain on a policy depends on the nature of the chargeable event giving rise to it. The amounts are as follows:

(1)   On death, the excess of the surrender value immediately before death, plus the amount of any relevant capital payments *over* the sum of the total premiums paid under the policy, plus the total gains on previous chargeable events.

(2)   On maturity or full surrender, the excess of the amount payable, plus the amount of any relevant capital payments *over* the sum of the total premiums paid, plus the total of gains on previous chargeable events (where there is a right to receive periodical payments the amount taken as payable is the capital value of those payments).

(3)   On assignment, the excess of the consideration, plus the amount of any relevant capital payments or previous assignments *over* the sum of the total premiums paid, plus the total of gains on previous chargeable events (where a policy is assigned as a gift, surrenders or assignments taken up to the time of the assignment are charged on the assignor and not on the person beneficially interested in the policy at the end of the relevant year).

(4)   On part surrender (including bonus encashments) or part assignments, the amount payable by way of surrender or assignment over the 5% allowable credits (see **13.50** under 'partial surrenders').

'Relevant capital payments' means any sums or other benefits of a capital nature paid or conferred under the policy before the chargeable event, eg previous part surrenders. Surrender of bonus is treated as though it were a surrender of rights conferred by the policy.

2   Life annuity contracts

13.47   A chargeable event in relation to a life annuity contract is defined in section 484 of ITTOIA 2005 and means:

(1)   total surrender (the taking of a cash option instead of the annuity payments is treated as a surrender and from 10 December 1974 so too is the payment of a capital sum on death);

(2)   assignment for money or money's worth;

(3)   certain part surrenders or part assignments (see (5) at **13.45** in relation to non-qualifying life policies).

The amount to be treated as a gain depends on the nature of the chargeable event giving rise to it. The amounts are as follows:

(1)   on surrender, the excess of the amount payable plus the amount of any relevant capital payments over the sum previously paid under the contract by way of premium or as a lump sum (reduced by the capital element of any annuity instalments which have been paid), plus the total gains on previous chargeable events;

(2)   on assignment, the excess of the consideration plus the amount of any relevant capital payments or of any previously assigned share *over* the sum previously paid by way of premium or as a lump sum (reduced by the capital element of any annuity instalments which have been paid), plus the total of gains on previous chargeable events (where a contract is assigned as a gift, surrenders or assignments taken up to the time of the assignment are charged on the assignor and not on the person beneficially interested in the policy at the end of the relevant year).

(3)   (See (4) at **13.45**, in relation to life policies.)

The definition of the term 'relevant capital payments' is broadly similar to that applying in respect of life policies. Surrender of a bonus or other sum is, again, treated as a surrender of rights conferred by the contract.

3   Capital redemption (or sinking fund) policies

13.48   A chargeable event in relation to a capital redemption policy is defined in section 484 of ITTOIA 2005, subject to the exclusions contained in section 486 of ITTOIA 2005, and means:

(1)   maturity (except where the sums payable on maturity are annual payments already subject to tax under Schedule D);

(2)   total surrender;

(3)   assignment for money or money's worth; or

(4)   certain part surrenders or part assignments (see (5) at **13.45** in relation to non-qualifying life policies).

The computation of the taxable gain under capital redemption policies is broadly similar to that under life policies.

4   Policy loans

13.49   As it would otherwise be possible to avoid the charges to tax on gains by withdrawing funds from policies and annuity contracts in the form of loans rather than by surrender, the Finance Act 1975 provided that such loans are treated as equivalent to surrender for this purpose. This only applies where the loan is made by, or by arrangement with, the company issuing the policy. These provisions do not apply in respect of a qualifying policy if either interest is payable at a commercial rate or money is lent to a full-time employee of the company issuing the policy for the purpose of purchase or improvement of his only or main residence.

5   Partial surrenders

13.50   Many modern policies allow partial surrenders at frequent intervals and so, in order to reduce the work involved in what could be a complex calculation both for life offices and HMRC, the previous system for charging higher-rate tax on partial surrenders was replaced by a new system[1] involving fewer and simpler calculations and freedom from the tax charge so long as the amount withdrawn by partial surrenders does not exceed certain limits. Thus, for policy years falling wholly after 13 March 1975, a chargeable event occurs only if the value of surrenders and assignments not brought into account on previous chargeable events exceeds the allowable credits (the annual twentieths referred to below) of all premiums paid.

The main elements of the system can be summarised as follows:

(1)   Action is related to policy years (ie years running from the start of the policy or its anniversary) instead of to individual partial surrenders.

(2)   Each year there is an allowance of:

(a)   one-twentieth of any premium paid during the year, and

(b)   one-twentieth of any premium on which an allowance has been due in previous years, up to a maximum of 20 twentieths.

In other words, the policyholder is able to withdraw 5% per annum of a single premium for a maximum of 20 years or, in the case of an annual premium policy, 5% per annum of the premiums paid in that year. Allowances, so far as not used in any one year, will be carried forward cumulatively.

(3)   At the end of each policy year the cumulative figure of partial surrenders is compared with that of the aggregate of the allowable credits (the annual 5% allowances). If the former exceeds the latter a chargeable event arises and the amount of the excess will be the chargeable sum. Where this happens the allowances up to that point will be deemed to be used up and the process of accumulation of allowances and annual comparison with surrenders taken will start afresh.

(4)   These rules are applied in relation to policy years and a period from an end of a policy year to final termination of the policy is treated as a policy year. If the period to final termination begins and ends in the same year of assessment, both the final period and the year preceding it are together treated as one year.

---

1   ITTOIA 2005, s 507.

(5) On final termination of the policy there will be a charge on the total profit on the policy (final proceeds plus any previous partial surrenders less total premiums paid and any chargeable gains arising on previous chargeable events). Withdrawals under the 5% limit are thus technically tax-deferred rather than fully tax free.

6   Assignments of jointly owned policies

13.51   The assignment of the whole of a policy for no consideration does not constitute a chargeable event. The life insurance industry has, for many years, held the view that where a policy is owned jointly by one or more persons and one of those persons assigns their share in the policy to the other or others, that action constituted an assignment of the whole policy and thus no tax would be payable. However, during the course of 1996/97 it emerged that HMRC did not share this view and considered such a transaction to be a part-assignment which could give rise to a chargeable event under the 'reckonable excess' rules even if no consideration is involved. Furthermore, they considered that the person who should suffer the tax charge should be the assignor although the legislation appeared to indicate that any tax charge should be assessed on the assignee.

Following long correspondence between HMRC and the Association of British Insurers (ABI) on this subject, section 83 and Schedule 28 of the Finance Act 2001 clarify the position in these circumstances. This legislation took effect for ownership changes occurring in policy years on or after 6 April 2001. The changes are broadly as follows:

(1) All ownership changes where joint owners transfer ownership of the policy to one of the previous joint owners will be deemed to be part-assignments for tax purposes. This will also apply where an individual who was previously the sole owner of a policy assigns ownership to himself and another person or persons.

(2) Although these part-assignments will continue to give rise to chargeable events in accordance with the 'reckonable excess' rules, an exception will be made for transactions by way of gift. Thus the treatment of part-assignments will be aligned with that of assignments of the whole policy.

(3) It will be the person assigning their share in the policy who will be liable to any tax charge arising on the transaction, not the assignee.

B   Assessment to tax

I   Method of charging tax (sections 465–467 of ITTOIA 2005 – formerly section 547 of ICTA 1988)

13.52   The gain computed in accordance with the principles set out above will form part of an individual's income if, immediately before the chargeable event, the rights under the policy or contract were held:

(1) by the individual as beneficial owner;

(2) as security for a debt owed by the individual; or

(3) on trusts created by the individual, including trusts under the Married Women's Property Act 1882, or the corresponding Scottish or Northern Irish Acts (although he can recover the tax from the trustees: section 551 of ICTA 1988).

If the policy is vested in personal representatives, the gain is deemed for this purpose to be part of the deceased's aggregate income.

The gain will be chargeable only to higher-rate tax in the tax year in which the chargeable event took place and at the rate applying in that tax year, assuming the policy is effected with a UK-based life company. If the person chargeable is not liable to such tax for that year, after the gain calculated as above has been added to his income, no assessment will arise.

13.53 The effect of the application of the old section 547 gave rise to what became known by tax planners as the 'dead settlor' provisions. If the chargeable event could be postponed until a tax year beyond that in which the settlor under a trust died (eg by a joint lives (last survivor) policy on the lives of two spouses effected by, typically, the older of the couple or where a single premium bond or similar policy was effected by trustees under a trust where the settlor had already died) then there would be no one on whom HMRC could assess the gain and thus on any subsequent chargeable event (eg death or surrender) no tax liability should arise.

As a result of advantage being taken of this very generous tax treatment, the legislation was changed in the Finance Act 1998. The previous rules relating to the tax treatment of policies effected subject to trust will only continue to apply where the policy was already in force before 17 March 1998, provided that the policy had not been varied on or after that date so as to increase the benefits payable or extend the term and that the person who had created the trust had died before that date.

If any of these criteria cannot be met, the new rules[1] state that if, immediately before the happening of a chargeable event, the policy was held on trust and the person who created the trust was either non-UK resident or had died in a tax year prior to the occurrence of the chargeable event, or the policy was held as security for a debt owed by the trustees, the amount of the gain shall be deemed to form part of the income of the trustees for the year of assessment in which the chargeable event occurred and shall be charged at the rate applicable to trusts for that year. The rate for 2006/07 is 40% but credit is available for savings rate tax deemed to be paid within the fund (assuming again that the policy is effected with a UK life company) and thus the actual rate of tax will be 20%.

If it is not possible to assess the trustees to tax as would be the case if they were offshore, HMRC can take advantage of section 740 of ICTA 1988 to assess the gain to tax on any UK resident beneficiaries who derive benefit from the policy proceeds.

1 ITTOIA 2005, s 467.

2 'Top-slicing'

13.54   The relevant provisions are now set out in section 535 of ITTOIA 2005 (formerly section 550 of ICTA 1988). The rate of tax to be charged on the gain following a chargeable event is assessed on the 'top-slicing' basis as follows:

(1)   The gain is divided by the number of complete relevant years between the effecting (or variation) of the policy and the chargeable event. This sum is the 'top-sliced' gain.

(2)   The top-sliced gain is added to the total income for tax purposes in the appropriate year and tax is calculated on the total thus arrived at.

(3)   The total tax liability without the top-sliced gain is then calculated, and deducted from (2).

(4)   From this difference is deducted tax at the savings rate (20% for 2006/07) on the top-sliced gain included in (2).

(5)   The result is multiplied by the number of complete years in (1) to determine the tax liability on the whole gain.

When adding in the top-sliced gain, it is important that the computation is made in the correct order. Earned income is taxed first, then rental income, then savings income, then dividend income, then the gain.

For gains arising in policy years falling wholly after 13 March 1975 the period of 'spread' (referred to in (1) above) for calculating the 'top-slicing' relief is:

(1)   on the first chargeable event – back to the start of the policy;

(2)   on any later chargeable event other than final termination – back to the previous chargeable event;

(3)   on final termination – the number of whole years from the start of the policy.

It is stressed that top-slicing relief can only be used to obtain relief from the higher rate of income tax. It cannot be used to mitigate starting or basic rate tax, nor can it be used to ascertain the availability of the age-related allowances. It should also be noted that, for offshore policies, on the occurrence of a chargeable event, the top-slice divisor is always calculated back to the start of the policy even if there had been previous chargeable events subsequently.

3 Basic rate charge

13.55   The general rule is that gains are charged only to the higher rate of tax, but an exception arises in the case of chargeable gains on deferred annuities when a cash option is taken in lieu of an annuity. This contract was an essential element of guaranteed income bonds which relied, in part, for their attraction on the cash return under the deferred annuity. Because it was believed that income bonds exploited the rules relating to the taxation of annuities and of a life office's annuity business, measures were introduced by paragraph 17 of Schedule 2 to the Finance Act 1975 (amending ICTA 1970) and now contained in section 547(5A) and (6) of ICTA 1988 which provided that any gain arising when a cash sum was taken under any deferred annuity, effected after 26 March 1974, was subject to basic rate as well as higher rate tax. The computation of 'top-slicing' relief for the higher rate charge remains unaffected.

Most 'income bonds' offered since March 1974 rely on a combination of an immediate annuity and endowment assurance and are not affected by the above provision.

4   Certificates of chargeable events

13.56   By virtue of section 552 of ICTA 1988, a UK life office was required in cases where a chargeable event occurs to give a certificate to its Inspector of Taxes. The certificate, in addition to specifying the name and address of the policyholder and the nature and date of the event, had to set out the surrender value or the sum payable by reason of the event, the amount or value of any relevant capital payments, the premiums (or other consideration) paid and the number of full years for the top-slicing procedure. The certificate had to be given within three months of the event or its written notification to the life office.

A certificate did not have to be issued automatically if no gain has arisen by virtue of the event or if the amount paid out (except on a part surrender, bonus encashment or surrender) does not exceed £500. However, an Inspector of Taxes can still request a certificate in these cases. If so requested it must be delivered within 30 days of receipt of the notice.

On the introduction of self-assessment for income tax purposes from the tax year 1996/97, HMRC felt that section 552 should be amended to fit better with the needs of policyholders in having to self-assess chargeable gains under life policies. New legislation was therefore included in the Finance Act 2001 which applies to chargeable events occurring on or after 6 April 2002.

Insurers now have a statutory duty to report all chargeable event gains of which they are aware to policyholders. The existing de minimis limit of £500 mentioned above no longer applies although there is a threshold figure (half the higher rate tax threshold) below which it is not necessary to send copies of the notification of potential chargeable event certificate gain to HMRC.

In place of the information formerly required, the new notification of potential chargeable event certificate gains will need only to state information needed to complete tax returns, namely:

(1)   the amount of the gain;

(2)   the date of the event giving rise to the gain;

(3)   the number of years for top-slicing relief purposes;

(4)   whether credit for savings rate tax is available in respect of the gain.

Insurers will, of course, be able to provide additional information if they wish to do so.

13.57   As far as offshore life offices are concerned, section 552A of ICTA 1988 provides for the appointment of UK-based fiscal representatives by offshore insurers to provide details of chargeable gains made by UK resident policyhold- ers to HMRC. However, regulations which supplement section 552A came into force from 6 April 1999 and exempt offshore insurers from the requirement to appoint fiscal representatives in certain circumstances such as where the insurer is resident in a state in the European Economic Area in which it is a criminal offence to disclose information to HMRC (Luxembourg and Switzerland for example), where the amount of premiums from relevant insurances is nil or negligible, or where the insurer enters into an agreement to supply information relating to chargeable events to HMRC. Insurers must agree to issue chargeable event cer- tificates to UK-based policyholders in the following circumstances:

(1)   For policies written prior to 6 April 2000, when the amount paid out is greater than twice the higher rate income tax threshold in the tax year when the chargeable event occurs, ie from 6 April 2006, £33,300 × 2 = £66,600.

(2)   For policies written on or after 6 April 2000, details of the amounts of all chargeable gains. Copies of the chargeable event information must be sent to HMRC where the gain is greater than half the higher rate income tax threshold in the year the gain is made, ie from 6 April 2006, 50% of £33,300 = £16,650.

5   Non-resident policies and offshore capital redemption policies

13.58   Section 528 of ITTOIA 2005 (formerly section 553 of ICTA 1988) has the effect of modifying the rules for computation of tax on gains in respect of off- shore policies effected after 17 November 1983 which are not substituted by a qualifying policy effected by a UK life office and offshore capital redemption policies effected after 22 February 1984. On the happening of a chargeable event under such policies, any gain arising thereunder will be subject to a starting rate, a savings rate and a higher rate tax. 'Top-slicing' relief will, however, be allow- able in determining the higher rate tax liability and for a part surrender or part assignment the number of complete relevant years can be computed from the start of the policy rather then back to the previous chargeable event. Where the policyholder was resident in the UK for only part of the period since the policy was effected chargeable gains will be reduced to:

$$\frac{\text{Total gains under the policy} \times \text{Period of residence in the UK}}{\text{Total period the policy has been in force}}$$

For the purposes of top-slicing relief, the reduced gains as computed above will be spread over a period equal to the complete number of years the policy has been in force less the complete number of years during which the policyholder was not resident in the UK.

There is an anti-avoidance provision which prevents a deduction being claimed for a period of non-residence in respect of policies issued after 19 March 1985 held by non-resident trustees. This provision also applies to policies issued before 19 March 1985 where the trustees subsequently become non-resident.

6   Personal Portfolio Bonds (PPBs)

13.59   Where an offshore bond is of a highly personalised nature, HMRC, in the past, attempted to assess all the investment income of the bond on the policyholder, using section 739 of ICTA 1988. However, this approach was deemed incorrect by the House of Lords in the case of *IRC v Willoughby*[1].

As a result of this, in March 1999, new regulations were laid before Parliament under section 553C of ICTA 1988 concerning the tax treatment of PPBs. A PPB is defined as a policy which allows the policyholder to choose the investments that determine the benefits under the policy. Personalised investments include stocks and shares quoted on recognised stock exchanges including the Alternative Investment Market, shares in family companies and also more unusual assets such as fine wines, vintage cars, etc. There is still, however, a wide range of permissible investments including unit trusts and other collective investment funds.

For PPBs, a taxable gain will arise each year from 6 April 2000. This gain is calculated as 15% of the sum of the total amount of premiums paid under the bond and the aggregate total of similarly calculated 15% amounts for earlier years since the bond was first taken out. Tax is charged at the individual's marginal rate on the gains each year. The legislation concerning personal portfolio bonds is now contained in sections 515–526 of ITTOIA 2005.

PPBs taken out prior to 17 March 1998 can continue to hold stocks, shares, warrants and options listed on a recognised stock exchange or the AIM. However, pre-17 March PPBs must not be enhanced in any way.

C   Companies effecting life policies

13.60   Major changes to the taxation of gains under life assurance policies effected by companies were contained in section 90 and Schedule 9 of the Finance Act 1989. Previously, gains arising under life policies were generally assessed to tax only if the company was a close company and the policy was a non-qualifying policy. Qualifying policies were normally not subject to these rules unless such a policy was surrendered or made paid-up within the first ten years or three-quarters of its term if sooner. Gains were computed as laid down in section 6, ie by reference to the surrender value of the policy immediately before death, where appropriate, and in general were apportioned to shareholders who were potentially liable to higher rate tax thereon.

1   [1997] STC 995.

Following the Finance Act 1989, the method of computation of gains remains the same as before, but:

(1)   the legislation covers all companies, whether close or not;

(2)   qualifying as well as non-qualifying policies are chargeable to tax on their gains;

(3)   instead of apportionment of the gains to shareholders, these are now treated as income gains of the company (ie chargeable to corporation tax). Withdrawals within the 5% entitlements can still be taken tax free at the time of withdrawal for up to 20 years by companies but any withdrawal in excess of 5% is potentially liable to corporation tax. However, top-slicing relief is not available on a policy effected by a company. Furthermore, companies do not receive the benefit of a credit for any tax paid within the fund – ie the entire gain will be taxable.

The new legislation applies to policies issued after 13 March 1989. Policies issued on or before this date would not be affected unless they are varied after that date so as to increase the benefits secured or extend the term of the assurance (any exercise of rights conferred by the policy would be treated as a variation for this purpose). Where a policy was effected prior to 14 March 1989 and is not varied thereafter, it would appear that any gains can be taken tax free as the new legislation makes no provision for the taxation of such policies.

I   Companies effecting capital redemption policies

13.61   Prior to 9 February 2005, capital redemption bonds (CRB) owned by UK resident companies were exempted from the 'loan relationship rules' by virtue of legislation in paragraph 1A(1)(b) of Schedule 9 to the Finance Act 1996. Instead, a chargeable event arising from a CRB owned by a UK resident company was subject to corporation tax under Chapter II of Part XIII of the Income and Corporation Taxes Act 1988 (ICTA 1988).

As a consequence of disclosures made to HMRC under Part 7 of the Finance Act 2004 that CRBs were being used in alleged artificial tax avoidance schemes, legislation was introduced removing the exemption referred to above. As a result, a CRB owned by a UK resident company will generally now be taxed under the loan relationship rules rather than the chargeable event legislation.

The new legislation was effective from 9 February 2005 and as no transitional relief was available, all existing and new CRBs owned by UK resident companies are affected.

Policies of life assurance owned by UK resident companies were and remain outside the scope of the loan relationship rules by virtue of the exemption in paragraph 1A(1)(a) of Schedule 9 to the Finance Act 1996.

2   The impact of the loan relationship rules

13.62   In effect, the loan relationship rules deal with the tax treatment of interest bearing assets held by companies. The important thing to note is that the tax treatment arising from the loan relationship rules should follow the accounting treatment adopted by the company, provided that the accounting treatment follows 'generally accepted accounting practices'. The following points may be useful:

(1)   If the capital redemption bond is being held as a quasi bank account then it should be shown on the company's balance sheet as a current asset. The effect of this is that the asset should be held at current cost. This means that any change in the value of the asset will be reflected in the company's profit and loss account. Consequently, tax deferral will not be possible.

(2)   If the capital redemption bond is being held as a long-term investment for the company then it should be held on the company's balance sheet as a fixed asset. In these circumstances the company might be able to choose between showing the asset at either historic cost or current cost. If a current cost basis is adopted then the position described in the previous paragraph applies. Alternatively, if an historic cost basis is chosen then it is possible that tax deferral might be possible.

However, a number of points need to be considered:

(i)   If the company already owns other investments then the accounting policy that it has adopted for them will also apply to the capital redemption bond.

(ii)   In choosing the accounting basis, the company must comply with the principles such that the accounting policy results in a true and fair picture of the company and that the accounting treatment is prudent. There is no single correct approach. Indeed, two companies in similar situations might adopt a different policy. On balance, where the investment is essentially in cash, there is probably a stronger case for using current cost rather than historic cost.

(iii) Regardless of the accounting policy adopted by the company, HMRC has the power to disregard the accounts produced by the company if it considers that they do not follow 'generally accepted accounting practices' and substitute accounts that, in its opinion, do. Consequently, the company might adopt a historical cost basis, but HMRC could substitute a current cost basis if it thinks that this is a more appropriate treatment.

(iv)   It is likely that the company will, at some future point in time, want access to the capital redemption bond in order to use the proceeds in the business. The effect of this is that once the company starts to access the capital redemption bond, HMRC could reclassify it as being a current asset. This means that it would have to be valued at current cost.

3   Existing policies

13.63   The new legislation deals with companies that have already invested into a capital redemption bond. In these circumstances the company will be deemed to have fully assigned the capital redemption bond on 9 February 2005 and reacquired it on the following day so bringing the policy into the loan relationship rules.

If this assignment creates a chargeable gain there is no immediate liability to corporation tax. This gain is brought into charge when the capital redemption bond is finally surrendered. Where there is a loss, there are no provisions to provide relief.

D Group life assurance policies: application of section 541(1)(a) and (5)(a)

13.64 An anomaly arises from HMRC's interpretation of the chargeable event legislation with regard to group life assurance policies which are not exempt under the provisions of Chapter I of Part XIV of ICTA 1988. Where one policy is effected on the lives of more than one person so that more than one death benefit can be paid under the policy, in the event of second or subsequent deaths, previous death benefits will be treated as 'relevant capital payments' when calculating chargeable gains.

This can lead to very harsh results. For example, where an employer has effected a group life policy on the lives of, say, 50 employees, on each death (other than the first), chargeable gains would be computed by taking into account all the previous payments of death benefits.

This can be compared with the position of the employer effecting separate policies for each employee. No gains as described in the previous paragraph would have arisen as there would be no relevant capital payments.

In view of the lack of tax avoidance motive in most such group policy cases, HMRC approach represents a rigid adherence to the words of the statute. The result, however, is surely unintended.

A possible solution was proposed in a Revenue Press Release of 3 July 1992. Paragraph 3 states that:

> 'this potential difficulty is avoided by utilising a separate policy of life insurance for each insured life or the type of master/subordinate group policy where each subordinate policy is separate and covers one life only.'

The Association of British Insurers' release on 8 July 1992 on this subject (following discussions with the Inland Revenue) reveals that such master/subordinate policies will usually be regarded as 'interconnected policies' for chargeable event purposes and thus the problem will not have been solved. Indications of interconnected policies are where:

(1) there is cross subsidy between lives assured;

(2) each employee must effect a policy;

(3) the insurance benefits are not independent of benefits under other contracts;

(4) terms or options under the contract cannot be exercised independently of the terms of any other contract; or

(5)   the life assured or his dependants are not entitled to receive the benefits and the life assured does not pay premiums or is not chargeable to income tax on the premiums paid by the employer.

An example of (1) above would be free cover limits which apply to proposers within the group that would not apply to an independent proposer.

This effectively rules out a number of the benefits of a group policy where, for example, an employer can bargain for better life assurance terms for his employees as a group of individuals.

Whilst it may be difficult for arrangements to be structured in the future to escape the application of these rules, their application seems particularly harsh in the case of some already established schemes (post-18 March 1991) – not just employer/employee schemes but also group credit card, hire purchase and group personal loan cover.

It is to be hoped that a practical solution can be found to the problems created by the application and interpretation of this legislation.

HMRC are currently drafting an 'Insurance Policyholder Taxation Manual (April 2006). In Chapter 7, Part 1, HMRC are preparing an improved definition which should exclude more policies from being defined as group life policies.

SECTION 7   ANNUITIES AND INCOME TAX

A   Deduction of tax from annuities

13.65   Income tax is deductible from annual payments and annuities[1]. The deduction is made by the person or company that makes the payment, and the payee is bound to allow the deduction[2]. The person making the payment must, however, notify the payee that the deduction is being made[3].

Where an annuity payment is made by a life office under an annuity contract, the life office must, therefore, (except where a special arrangement has been made) deduct income tax at the basic rate from the payment, and account to HMRC for the amount deducted. In the case of a payment made under a purchased life annuity (see later), the life office must deduct income tax at the rate applicable to savings income (20% for 2006/07) from the taxable portion of the annuity.

B   Annuities payable without deduction

13.66   As a matter of convenience for annuitants of modest means and to reduce the number and amount of claims for repayment of income tax, HMRC

---

1   ICTA 1988, ss 18 and 19.
2   ICTA 1988, s 348.
3   ICTA 1988, s 352.

has made special arrangements under which life offices may, in certain circumstances, pay life annuities without deduction of income tax.

I Residents in the United Kingdom

13.67 The limits within which the arrangement operates vary from time to time and are amended where rates of tax and personal and other allowances are varied by Finance Acts, but by way of illustration the following shows the limits of income for the year 2006/07.

Age of annuitant	For payment without deduction of income tax
	Single
Under age 65	£5,035
Age 65–74	£7,280
Age 75 and over	£7,420

These limits may be higher in the case of married couples or registered civil partners where one or other of the couple was aged 65 or over as at 6 April 2000.

The annuitant has to make, on the appropriate official form, a declaration that his income falls below the appropriate limit, and changes in his circumstances must be notified to HMRC. He must, if required, renew his declaration.

If the annuity is one which is regarded, for income tax purposes, as containing a capital element, the capital element is excluded in assessing the annuitant's total income.

13.68 The arrangements do *not* extend to any proportionate payment to the date of death.

> *Bryan v Cassin*[1]
>
> S was entitled to an annuity payable quarterly. On his death his executor claimed repayment of income tax deducted from the proportionate payment to the date of death. If the payment had been made during the lifetime of S, he would, because his income was small, have been entitled to repayment of the amount of tax deducted. Held, that the proportionate payment formed no part of the income of the deceased, and that the executors were not entitled to any repayment of the tax deducted.

In practice, however, where during life an annuity is being paid without deduction of income tax, the same arrangement can concessionally be applied to the proportionate payment.

In applying the arrangements, the life office should be satisfied that the title to the *beneficial* interest is vested in the annuitant in the following cases:

1   [1942] 2 All ER 262.

(1)   where an annuity is purchased by executors or trustees;

(2)   where a joint life annuity is purchased by two or more persons jointly;

and in the latter case the life office may have to sever each instalment of annuity into appropriate parts if, during the joint life, it is enjoyed in shares to each of which a different tax treatment is to be applied.

The arrangements do not affect the income tax liability of the life office, for, in the computation of its liability or claim for repayment, the treatment of annuities paid under the arrangements is taken into account.

2   Residents abroad

13.69   Similar arrangements can sometimes be made in the case of certain persons resident abroad.

Part XVIII of ICTA 1988 provides for relief from double taxation in the case of residents in territories outside the UK which make conventions with the UK.

Conventions have been made with many countries under which annuities purchased in the UK or in respect of pensions arising in the UK are, where taxable abroad, exempt from UK income tax; and such annuities and pensions can be paid without deduction of income tax under the procedure laid down by the Double Taxation Relief (Taxes on Income) (General) Regulations 1970[1].

C   Annuities containing a capital element

1   Purchased life annuities

13.70   Prior to 1956, all purchased life annuities were treated, for taxation purposes, as consisting wholly of income but the Finance Act of that year provided that such annuities, with certain exceptions, should be regarded as containing a 'capital element' not subject to tax. The balance of the annuity payment is taxable as investment income. The relevant provisions are now contained in sections 656–658 of ICTA 1988. They apply, subject to the exceptions mentioned, whether or not the life on which the annuity depends is that of the purchaser and whether or not it is for his own benefit.

The capital element is a fixed amount of the purchase price, and is determined on the basis of rules laid down in ICTA 1988 and in regulations made in pursuance of the 1988 Act. The effect of the rules is that if the annuitant survives for precisely the period of his expectation of life according to the prescribed mortality table, he will have received in the form of tax-free payments exactly the amount paid by way of premiums.

The capital element is a function of mortality and the younger the age the lower the capital element of any given type of annuity. In the case of a temporary annuity the effect of mortality is smaller and the capital element represents a

---

1   SI 1970/488.

greater percentage of the annuity than in the case of a whole life annuity commencing at the same age.

The practice is for the office granting the annuity to provide the annuitant with the official claim form which the annuitant completes and returns to the office, which forwards it to its own Inspector of Taxes. In due course the annuitant and the office are officially advised by HMRC whether or not the annuity qualifies as one which contains a capital element and, if it does, what the amount of capital element is.

SECTION 8   CAPITAL GAINS TAX AND LIFE POLICIES

A   Life policies and deferred annuity contracts

13.71   Section 210 of the Taxation of Chargeable Gains Act 1992 (re-enacting section 143 of the Capital Gains Tax Act 1979) provides that no chargeable gain accrues on the disposal of rights under a policy of assurance or contract of deferred annuity, except where the person making the disposal is not the original beneficial owner and acquired the rights for consideration in money or money's worth. Where a gain does arise, the payment of the sum assured under a life policy (including the transfer of investments or assets to the policyholder where applicable)[1], or the first instalment of a deferred annuity or the surrender of either contract will be a chargeable disposal of rights under the contract.

It follows, therefore, that where the beneficial ownership of a life policy or a deferred annuity contract remains vested in the same person throughout its duration, there will be no charge to capital gains tax on its becoming payable or being surrendered. Where beneficial ownership changes, no liability will arise at any time provided the new beneficial owner acquires his interest as a result of a gift inter vivos, a bequest, or under the law of intestate succession. Only if he acquires his interest for consideration in money or money's worth does a liability arise when the policy is subsequently disposed of; there will be no liability on the original beneficial owner when he sells the policy.

Where there is a chargeable gain on the disposal of a contract for a deferred annuity, the amount of the consideration for the disposal will be the market value at the time of the right to the first and further instalments of the annuity.

Where the gain on a non-qualifying policy which has been assigned for money or money's worth is charged also to income tax under ITTOIA 2005 then the income tax charge takes precedence and by section 37 of the Taxation of Chargeable Gains Act 1992 a double liability is avoided.

B   Calculation of tax

13.72   It will be seen that it will not often be necessary to calculate the chargeable gain on an assurance policy, but where this is necessary the computation

---

1   Taxation of Chargeable Gains Act 1992, s 210(3)(b).

must be made according to the provisions of Schedule 2 to the Taxation of Chargeable Gains Act 1992.

The chargeable gain is computed by deducting from the proceeds of 'disposal' (which term includes payment of the policy moneys) the total cost of acquisition. This includes all premiums paid by the person making the disposal, and, in the case of a purchased policy, the purchase price. Indexation relief and taper relief will be available in the normal way to reduce the gain. Finally, a deduction may be claimed for incidental costs of acquisition and disposal, eg legal fees.

Premiums which have been allowed as a deduction in computing profits for income tax or corporation tax purposes must be excluded from the computation of gain.

C   Business assurance

13.73   The application of section 210 can have particularly pernicious effects in relation to policies effected for business assurance purposes (partnership and private company protection). Further details are set out in Chapter 17.

D   Annuities and pensions

13.74   A chargeable gain does not accrue to any person on the disposal of a right to or to any part of:

(1)   any allowance, annuity or capital sum payable out of any superannuation fund or under any superannuation scheme established solely or mainly for persons employed in a profession, trade, undertaking or employment and their dependants;

(2)   an immediate annuity granted by a life office, whether or not including instalments of capital; or

(3)   annual payments under a covenant not secured on any property[1].

---

1   Taxation of Chargeable Gains Act 1992, s 237.

CHAPTER 14

Inheritance tax

SUMMARY

SECTION I   INTRODUCTION

14.1   From 1894 transfers of capital on death were subject to estate duty. The Finance Act 1975 replaced estate duty with capital transfer tax (CTT) from 26 March 1974. This taxed not only transfers of capital on death but also lifetime gifts and was codified by the Capital Transfer Tax Act 1984. The Finance Act 1986 replaced CTT with inheritance tax (IHT) which applies to all transfers made on or after 18 March 1986 and renamed the codifying act the Inheritance Tax Act 1984 (IHTA 1984).

A   Nature of IHT

14.2   The general principle is that transfers of capital out of an individual's estate are liable to IHT. The essential features of IHT are that:

547

(1)   it applies (subject to certain exceptions) to transfers by way of gift during lifetime, as well as to the value of an individual's estate on death;

(2)   it is generally charged on the donor, not the donee, ie, the tax is applied by measuring the loss suffered by the transferor, not the benefit received by the transferee;

(3)   it is cumulative, ie, it is chargeable on the cumulative total of chargeable transfers made by an individual during a seven-year period (on transfers in excess of the 'nil rate band', a threshold of £285,000 from 6 April 2006), and any transfers made more than seven years before the transfer in question will not be taken into account; and

(4)   it is levied separately from any other tax, so that it is possible for a transfer to be liable to both IHT and capital gains tax (CGT), without any allowance in one for the other.

IHT is not restricted to cases where an individual actually makes a gift during lifetime or the value of his estate on death. It also applies to cases which are treated as if a transfer had occurred, eg in connection with settled property and the failure to exercise a right. IHT applies to individuals. However, special rules exist to charge individuals in respect of dispositions made by close companies and to bring trustees within the scope of the tax.

The tax applies to the whole of the United Kingdom (UK), including Northern Ireland.

B   Relationship to life assurance

14.3   Life assurance itself is linked with IHT because it plays a large part in mitigating and providing for the tax. Life assurance practitioners should, therefore, be aware of at least the basic principles of IHT for this reason and also to be able to appreciate fully the IHT consequences of movements of certain assets within the client's estate. This chapter sketches the general scheme of the tax[1] and looks more closely at the relevant IHT provisions relating to life assurance contracts. Chapter 15 will then examine the effect of IHT on various types of life policy trust wordings and consider the role and use of life assurance in estate planning.

SECTION 2   LIFETIME TRANSFERS

A   The charge

14.4   IHT is charged on the *value transferred* by a *chargeable transfer*[2] which, in the case of a lifetime gift, means any *transfer of value* made by an

1   For a detailed treatment of IHT see one of the major works on the subject, eg Foster *Inheritance Tax*.
2   IHTA 1984, s 1.

individual which is not exempt[1] and which is in excess of the nil rate band (£285,000 for transfers made on or after 6 April 2006). For IHT purposes, certain lifetime transfers are potentially exempt transfers (PETs)[2] which are assumed to be exempt at the time of transfer and do not enter the cumulative total until death[3]. A *transfer of value* is a *disposition* made by a person (the transferor) as a result of which the value of his *estate* immediately after the disposition is less than it would be but for the disposition and the amount by which it is less is the 'value transferred' by the transfer[4].

IHT is levied, therefore, by reference to the *reduction* in the transferor's estate, as a result of making the gift, not by reference to the increase in the transferee's estate. This means that if tax on the gift is paid by the transferor, the reduction in his estate includes the amount of the tax, as this forms part of his loss. To calculate the total tax payable in these circumstances it is necessary to 'gross up' the value transferred at the appropriate rate[5].

On a transfer for partial consideration, only the balance, ie the element of gift, is chargeable. Similarly, if the transferee assumes responsibility for a liability of the transferor (eg where he pays CGT arising on the gift) the value of the transfer is reduced accordingly.

B   Transfers which are not transfers of value

14.5   There is no transfer of value, and thus no IHT, if the transfer was not intended to confer any gratuitous benefit on any person and either the transaction was at arm's length between unconnected persons, or was such as might be expected to be made in a transaction at arm's length between unconnected persons[6]. 'Connected persons' means, essentially, a spouse, registered civil partner, or relative (including uncle, aunt, nephew and niece)[7].

If the transfer was of a sale of shares or debentures in an unquoted company it is also necessary to show that the price was freely negotiated at the time of the sale or that the price was that which would have been expected had it been freely negotiated at the time[8]. (This is to avoid the possibility of avoiding IHT by imposing a fetter on the disposition of shares in the company's articles of association.)

Certain other 'transfers' are also deemed not to be transfers of value, including dispositions for the maintenance of one's family[9] and transfers of property by a close company to trustees to hold on trust for the benefit of employees (excluding any shareholder with 5% or more of the shares[10]).

---

1 Section 2(1).
2 Section 3A.
3 See Section 4C, **14.32**.
4 IHTA 1984, s 3(1).
5 See Section 5A, **14.41**.
6 IHTA 1984, s 10(1).
7 IHTA 1984, s 270 and Taxation of Chargeable Gains Act 1992, s 286.
8 IHTA 1984, s 10(2).
9 Section 11.
10 Section 13. (See also ss 12, 14, 15, 16.)

C   Disposition

14.6   This term is not defined and carries its ordinary wide meaning which includes, inter alia, the payment of money, the conveyance, transfer or assignment of property (by sale or gift), and the creation of a settlement[1], ie any transaction by which a person disposes of an interest in an asset or creates a new interest in another person in an asset. Where an individual deliberately omits to exercise a right, which as a result reduces his estate and increases another's, the omission is treated as a disposition[2]. This could, for example, cover the failure to collect a debt or to vote in respect of shares in a company. In relation to settled property a surrender of a life interest has been held to be a disposition[3].

D   Associated operations

14.7   A disposition includes one made by 'associated operation', which is where a transfer of value is made by any two or more operations of any kind by the same or different persons and whether simultaneous or not affecting the same property, or where one operation affects a further operation[4]. Note that 'operation' includes an omission.

The 'same property' means property which represents directly or indirectly the property or income (including accumulations) arising from it. Similarly, operations which in any way provide for, or facilitate, the performance of other operations will be associated with them.

Where the associated operations provision applies, the composite transfer (ie the value of the overall loss to the estate) will be treated as being made at the time of the last of the operations.

This provision is designed to counter avoidance measures whereby an individual's estate is reduced through a series of transactions or where property is transferred in stages, the aggregate value of the constituent transfers being less than the value of the property as a whole; or where a gift is made of property worth little at the time but which subsequently increases in value by reason of some other act of the donor. This matter will be raised again in connection with 'back-to-back' arrangements and certain other arrangements referred to in Chapter 15.

HMRC does not view the sharing of one spouse's or registered civil partner's estate with another, where that other makes gifts out of the money received as an associated operation, unless it is a blatant case of a gift conditional upon using it to make gifts to others[5].

1   *Ward v IRC* [1956] 1 All ER 571 (an estate duty case).
2   IHTA 1984, s 3(3).
3   *IRC v Buchanan* [1958] Ch 289 at 296 (an income tax case). See also *Grey v IRC* [1959] 3 All ER 603.
4   IHTA 1984, s 268(1), see *IRC v Macpherson* [1988] STC 362, HL.
5   See HC Official Report, SC A, 13 February 1975, Col 1596.

E Estate

14.8   IHT only arises if a disposition reduces the value of the transferor's estate[1]. Broadly, an individual's estate comprises the aggregate of all property to which he is beneficially entitled (not including excluded property)[2], less his liabilities. In addition to tangible property, equitable rights, debts and other choses in action, an individual is treated as beneficially entitled to all property, other than settled property, over which he has (or would if he were sui juris) a general power to appoint or dispose as he thinks fit or on which he can charge money. An individual beneficially entitled to an interest in possession in settled property (such as a life interest) was treated as entitled to the property in which the interest subsists[3]. However, this position was altered by the Finance Act 2006. This will only remain the case for settlements created before 22 March 2006 provided the existing beneficiaries at that date have not been changed, unless that change occurred before 6 April 2008 in which case the new beneficiaries will be treated as having been the beneficiaries in existence at 22 March 2006. For new settlements created on or after 22 March 2006, the former treatment will continue to apply only if the settlement is made for the benefit of disabled persons as defined in section 84 of the IHTA 1984. If this is not the case, such settlements will be treated for IHT purposes as trusts without an interest in possession and will be taxed accordingly.

SECTION 3   TRANSFERS ON DEATH

A   The charge

14.9   On the death of an individual, IHT is chargeable as if immediately before his death, the deceased had made a transfer of value equal to the value of his estate at that date[4]. In valuing the estate, any changes brought about by the death (eg the cessation of a life annuity, or the proceeds payable on a claim under a single life policy owned solely by the deceased) are to be taken into account[5]. This provision does not apply, however, to the termination on the death of any interest or the passing of any interest by survivorship[6] (eg the interest under a jointly owned, joint lives, last survivor contract) which would, therefore, be valued at the full open market value at death[7]. No grossing up is required in determining the value transferred, since the tax is payable from the estate by the personal representatives.

Any PETs within seven years prior to death become chargeable at the value of the property at the time of the PET, subject to any claim for a fall in the value of the property from the date of the gift to the date of the transferor's death or earlier

1 IHTA 1984, s 5.
2 Section 6, see Section 4A, **14.22**.
3 Section 49(1).
4 Section 4(1).
5 Section 171.
6 Section 171(2).
7 Sections 160 and 167(2)(a).

sale by the transferee[1] and taper relief. If there are any available annual exemptions, they may be applied retrospectively. If a PET does become chargeable by virtue of the donor dying within seven years, it will be necessary to look back over the seven years before the PET to see whether any chargeable lifetime transfers have been made. If this is the case, account needs to be taken of such transfers in determining the amount of tax, if any, due on the failed PET.

If an individual dies within seven years of making a chargeable transfer, the IHT death rates will retrospectively apply with credit for any lifetime tax already paid and taper relief as appropriate[2]. The donee is liable for the extra IHT and so no grossing up is required.

B   Estate

14.10   The meaning of estate is similar to that for lifetime transfers, and is the aggregate of property to which, immediately before his death, the deceased was beneficially entitled, other than excluded property. Certain property is left out of account, however, for the purpose of the IHT charge on death. Thus, where the deceased had an interest in possession in property settled before 22 March 2006, and on his death (1) the property reverts to the settlor during the settlor's lifetime, or (2) the settlor's spouse or registered civil partner becomes beneficially entitled to the property, then its value is excluded from the deceased's estate – unless the settlor or the settlor's spouse or registered civil partner acquired the reversionary interest for money or money's worth[3]. (Spouse includes widow or widower in cases where the settlor died less than two years before the deceased.) Also left out of account are interests in certain superannuation schemes and certain overseas pensions. The value transferred is the value representing the sum which the estate might reasonably be expected to raise if sold in the open market (less liabilities)[4].

C   Gifts with reservation of benefit

14.11   The Finance Act 1986[5] introduced the concept of 'gifts with reservation of benefit' (a similar concept existed under the estate duty regime). Where property is disposed of by way of gift (on or after 18 March 1986) but either:

(1)   possession and enjoyment of the property is not bona fide assumed by the donee at least seven years before the donor's death; or

(2)   at any time within seven years of the donor's death ,the property is not enjoyed to the entire exclusion, or virtually[6] to the entire exclusion, of the donor and of any benefit to him by contract or otherwise,

1   Section 131.
2   See **14.40**.
3   Section 53.
4   Sections 5(3) and 160. For a discussion on 'excluded property', see Section 4A, **14.22**.
5   Finance Act 1986, s 102, Sch 20.
6   For the Inland Revenue's interpretation on gifts with reservation of benefit and their interpretation of the de minimis rule see FRPI/80 and Tax Bulletin Issue 9 (November 1993).

the property is deemed to be 'property subject to a reservation', ie property to which the donor was beneficially entitled immediately before his death, and it will be added to and form part of his taxable estate for IHT purposes. Furthermore, no CGT uplift will be available on the donor's death.

If the reservation ceases before the donor's death, he will be treated as having made a PET at that time. If the cessation was more than seven years before the death, the PET will have fallen out of account, but if not, IHT will be assessed on normal principles[1]. Note that the value of the PET cannot be reduced by any of the available annual exemptions.

The rules relating to gifts with reservation involving land were tightened with effect from 9 March 1999 in response to the House of Lords ruling in *Ingram and another v IRC*[2]. Section 102A of the Finance Act 1986, as inserted by the Finance Act 1999, extends the existing provisions to prevent the avoidance of IHT on death by way of a lifetime gift where the donor or his spouse enjoy a significant right or interest or is a party to a significant arrangement in respect of land. Where this happens, the interest disposed of will be treated as a gift with reservation. A right, interest or arrangement is significant if it entitles or enables the donor or his spouse to occupy all or part of the land (or enjoy some other right) otherwise than for full consideration in money or money's worth. The right, etc is not significant if it:

(1)   cannot prevent another person or persons enjoying the land virtually or entirely to the exclusion of the donor;

(2)   does not enable the donor to occupy the land immediately after the disposal but would have done so were it not for the disposal; or

(3)   was granted or acquired more than seven years before the gift.

Similar provisions also apply to gifts of undivided shares in land under section 102B.

14.12   The gift with reservation of benefit rules do not apply to any disposals which are exempt within any of the provisions of the IHTA 1984 (see below), except for the £3,000 per annum and normal expenditure exemptions[3].

Thus any property enjoyed by or benefiting the donor's spouse did not automatically fall within these provisions but this situation came to an end with effect from 19 June 2003[4]. Prior to that date, the opportunity existed for a settlor to create a trust for the benefit of his or her spouse. The settlor could be a potential beneficiary under the trust without infringing the gift with reservation rules. Some months after the creation of the settlement, the trustees made an appointment away from the settlor's spouse in favour of the children or grandchildren. This course of action constituted a PET by the spouse but a situation had been created whereby a trust had been set up for the benefit of the settlor's children or grandchildren, but under which both the settlor and his spouse were potential

1   See Section 5, **14.40**.
2   [1999] STC 37.
3   Finance Act 1986, s 102(5).
4   Sections 102(5A) and 102(5B).

beneficiaries and the gift with reservation rules had not been breached. From 19 June 2003 onwards, however, this is only the case whilst the settlor's spouse actually has the interest in possession. Once this is appointed away, if the original settlor is still a potential beneficiary, the gift with reservation rules would apply.

Where the disposal by way of gift was made in connection with an insurance policy (issued before 18 March 1986), the gift with reservation provisions will not apply unless the policy is varied on or after that date so as to increase the benefits secured or extend the term of insurance. Any change made in the policy terms in pursuance of an option or other power conferred is deemed to be a variation, apart from the exercise of an indexation option with respect to benefits or premiums before 1 August 1986 if the option or power could only be exercised before that date[1].

The following are examples of changes which will be regarded as increasing the benefits or extending the term[2]:

(1) altering from one class of assurance to another;

(2) converting from an endowment assurance to a low cost endowment assurance or vice versa;

(3) reducing the term of an endowment assurance if premiums are being simultaneously increased;

(4) converting from a without- to a with-profits policy for the same sum assured;

(5) adding premium waiver benefit or double accident benefit or the addition of an option not previously included in the policy.

D Pre-owned assets tax

14.13 In recent years, HMRC have sought to litigate in situations where they feel that the gift with reservation rules have been infringed. Where they have lost cases (*Ingram and another v IRC*[3] and *IRC v Greenstock*[4]) they have amended the legislation to render planning of that nature ineffective. However, HMRC were becoming increasingly frustrated that tax advisers were finding ever more complex ways to circumvent the gift with reservation legislation.

It was therefore decided to introduce a completely new tax, pre-owned assets tax which, from 6 April 2005, has the effect of imposing an income tax charge

---

1 Sections 102(6) and 102(7).
2 See Life Insurance Council Circular 139/86 in a letter dated 21 November 1986 from the Life Insurance Council of the Association of British Insurers to LIC members following clarification from the Inland Revenue confirming that in deciding whether a policy is varied as mentioned in the Finance Act 1986, s 102(6), account would generally be taken of the Inland Revenue's interpretation of the corresponding wording used in the provisions relating to life assurance premium relief (see Chapter 13).
3 [1999] STC 37.
4 [2003] STC 825.

each year on the benefit people enjoy when they have arranged free continuing use of major capital assets that they once enjoyed.

The legislation concerning the tax is contained in Schedule 15 of the Finance Act 2004. Three classes of assets are covered by the new rules: land, chattels and intangible property which includes policies of life assurance.

Each class of assets has its own rules, but for life assurance policies, a pre-owned assets income tax charge can arise where any income arising under a settlement would be treated by virtue of sections 624 and 625 of the Income Tax (Trading and Other Income) Act 2005 (income arising under a settlement where the settlor retains an interest) as income of the settlor.

The life assurance policy would be valued at the time that it first falls within the charge and thereafter HMRC has stated in correspondence with the ABI that it should be sufficient for policies to be revalued every five years. This would hold good for regular premium policies too assuming the chargeable person remains in normal health throughout the five-year period. Once valuation has taken place, a rate of interest equal to the official rate of interest (5% at the time of writing) would be applied. There is a de minimis limit of £5,000 on the value of the benefit assessable so if the amount calculated as above was below this figure, no tax would be payable. Note that where the same settler has made a number of gifts all of which are potentially liable to pre-owned assets tax, the taxable benefits of each gift must be added up to see whether the overall £5,000 limit has been breached. If the benefit is in excess of £5,000, pre-owned assets tax will be payable on the whole benefit at the settlor's marginal rate of tax.

It should be noted that it is not possible to make a gift with reservation and also to pay pre-owned assets tax on the same gift. It must be either one or the other. The combination of the two taxes does, however, mean that it is now very difficult to make a gift, retain a benefit under it and avoid being liable for one of the taxes.

E Variation of dispositions taking effect on death

14.14 When an individual has been left property by will, under the intestacy rules, or under the right of survivorship, any transfer of that property would, prima facie, be a transfer of value, and potentially liable to IHT. Provisions exist[1] to mitigate this where the original donee is simply redirecting (or disclaiming) the deceased's dispositions. In certain circumstances, such a variation (or disclaimer) will not be treated as a transfer of value and will be treated as if the deceased had effected the variation (or the disclaimed benefit had never been conferred).

A variation occurs when the individual who benefits or would benefit under the deceased's will (or intestacy or otherwise) redirects property to another party of his choosing; a disclaimer occurs when the property is merely refused by the individual and the property falls into residue. The provisions apply equally to variations and disclaimers (referred to hereafter as variations), but do not apply to settled property in which the deceased had an interest in possession[2] or to

1 IHTA 1984, ss 17(a), 142.
2 See ss 142(5), 49(1).

property which is deemed to be included by virtue of the gift with reservation of benefit provisions[1].

To be within these provisions, the following conditions must be satisfied:

(1)   The variation must be made within two years after the death of the testator or intestate.

(2)   The variation must be made by an instrument in writing made by the individual(s) who benefit or would benefit under the dispositions. Any such individual must be aged 18 or over and must be of sound mind. A deed is usually used[2], although any instrument in writing will be effective. In *Crowden v Aldridge*[3], a unanimous direction by residuary legatees by memoranda (even though it was executed in contemplation of executing a formal deed which never in fact was executed) was held to be an effective variation of the estate.

(3)   An election in writing must be submitted to HMRC that the provisions should apply. This election can be contained within the deed itself. The election must be made by the individual(s) who effected the instrument (and also by the personal representatives, if the variation causes more IHT to be payable) within six months of the date of the instrument (or such longer period as the board may allow).

(4)   The variation must not be made for a consideration in money or money's worth unless the consideration is itself a qualifying variation or disclaimer relating to another of the deceased's dispositions.

A deed of variation may be rectified[4] and there may be more than one deed of variation in respect of the same estate, but each deed can only vary property that has not already been varied.

A deed of variation can be used to set up what would otherwise be a gift with reservation. For example, if a grandfather leaves property on trust to his son in his will, the son could redirect that property onto trust for himself and his own children as the beneficiaries. For IHT purposes, this variation will be treated as being made by the testator, not by the son and thus would not be a gift with reservation of benefit.

F   Redirection of severable share of joint property

14.15   Under the provisions set out in Section E, it is possible to sever the beneficial interest in a joint tenancy with, for IHT purposes at least, retrospective effect. It would normally be used where property is owned jointly by husband and wife or by two registered civil partners and one party dies without making

1   See s 142(5), (6), Finance Act 1986, s 102, Sch 19, para 24.
2   See *Law Society Gazette* 18 December 1991.
3   [1993] 3 All ER 603.
4   *Russell v IRC* [1988] STC 195, *Matthews v Martin* [1991] STI 418, *Schneider v Mills* [1993] 3 All ER 377.

use of the nil rate band, and with insufficient assets in the free estate for the surviving spouse or registered civil partner to redirect other property. It would then be appropriate to sever the beneficial joint tenancy to pass the deceased's share of the property to other beneficiaries to use up the nil rate band, whilst utilising the remaining free assets for the benefit of the surviving spouse or registered civil partner.

G   Inheritance (Provision for Family and Dependants) Act 1975

14.16   A court may order financial provision for family and/or dependants of a deceased person out of his net estate. Property so redirected is treated for IHT purposes as having devolved on death subject to the provisions of the court's order[1].

H   Surviving spouse election

14.17   Where a surviving spouse or registered civil partner elects under section 47A of the Administration of Estates Act 1925 to take the capital value of his or her life interest in the residuary estate in lieu of the income for life, the election is not a transfer of value. The surviving spouse or registered civil partner is treated as having been entitled not to the life interest, but to a sum equal to the capital value of the interest[2].

I   Commorientes[3]

14.18   When two individuals die in such circumstances that it is impossible to know which died first, the general law, and the law of succession to property, presumes that the older was the first to die[4]. For transfers on death, this rule is excluded, and it is presumed instead that the deaths occurred at the same instant[5], thus avoiding a double charge.

Example

If mother and daughter die in a road traffic accident, the general law would treat any property bequeathed by the mother to the daughter as passing to the daughter's estate and then to the beneficiaries under the daughter's will (or intestacy). However, because of section 4(2), IHT is charged only on the transfer to the daughter's estate and not again on the transfer to the daughter's ultimate beneficiaries.

1   IHTA 1984, s 146(1).
2   Sections 17(c) and 145.
3   See Chapter 4.
4   Law of Property Act 1925, s 184.
5   IHTA 1984, s 4(2).

J Survivorship clauses

14.19 Where under the terms of a will, or otherwise, property is held for a person if he survives another for a specified period of not more than six months, the dispositions at the end of the specified period (or that person's earlier death) are treated as having had effect from the beginning of that period[1].

K Quick succession relief

14.20 Relief is available from the IHT charge on death where the value of the deceased's estate has been increased by a chargeable transfer to him within the preceding five years.

For property not comprised in a settlement, the tax charged on the death is reduced by a percentage of part of the tax paid on the earlier chargeable transfer[2]. The percentage varies according to the period between the transfer and the death as follows:

Not more than 1 year	100%
1 to 2 years	80%
2 to 3 years	60%
3 to 4 years	40%
4 to 5 years	20%

SECTION 4   EXEMPTIONS AND RELIEFS

14.21 It was stated earlier that IHT is charged on the *value transferred* by a *chargeable transfer* which, in the case of a lifetime gift, means any *transfer of value* made by an individual which is not exempt. The IHTA 1984 provides for fully exempt transfers[3]. The Finance Act 1986 introduced PETs[4]. Further, there will be no IHT if the property transferred is excluded property.

A Excluded property

14.22 In measuring the loss to an individual's estate following a transfer (or the value of the estate upon death), no account is to be taken of 'excluded property'. The main categories of excluded property are:

(1)   property situated abroad belonging to an individual not domiciled or treated as not domiciled in the UK[5], and

1   Section 92.
2   Section 141.
3   IHTA 1984, Part II, Ch I.
4   Section 3A.
5   Sections 6(1), 48(3).

(2)   reversionary interests, eg interests following life interests (other than those acquired for money or money's worth), or those, for settlements made after 15 April 1976, where either the settlor or his spouse are beneficially entitled[1].

B   Exempt transfers

14.23   An exempt transfer is the most efficient transfer for IHT purposes as, following the transfer, the property is immediately treated as being out of the estate of the transferor. The exemptions are not mutually exclusive and a transfer may fall within one or more of the exemptions and be freed from IHT partly by one exemption and partly by another. If a transfer is exempt, no IHT is ever payable. Some exemptions apply to a transfer whether made during lifetime or on death. Others apply either only to lifetime transfers or only to transfers on death. The following is not an exhaustive list, but does contain the principal exemptions for most practical purposes.

I   Spouse exemption

14.24   Transfers between spouses or registered civil partners from 5 December 2005 (whether living together or not) during lifetime and on death are exempt[2]. The exemption does not apply where the transfer:

(1)   depends on a condition which is not satisfied within 12 months after the transfer; or

(2)   'takes effect' on the termination after the transfer of any interest or period[3].

The exemption is not excluded merely because the gift is dependent on the recipient surviving the other spouse for a specified period. It is therefore quite common for a will to be drawn so that the surviving spouse or registered civil partner is not to benefit unless surviving for, say, 28 days (but the period must not be any longer than six months) and the exemption will apply[4].

If, immediately before the transfer, the transferor is domiciled in the UK, but the spouse or registered civil partner is not, the exemption is limited to a cumulative total of transfers of £55,000[5] (which is in addition to the nil rate band). After 17 March 1986 gifts in excess of £55,000 may qualify as PETs.

The separate taxation of spouses or registered civil partners is important for a number of reasons. They are each entitled to the benefit of the reliefs and exemptions and in calculating the rate of tax on a chargeable transfer by one spouse, gifts made by the other are not taken into account. These principles

1   Section 48(2).
2   Section 18(1).
3   IHTA 1984, s 18(3).
4   See 'Survivorship clauses', **14.19**.
5   Section 18(2).

obviously have great significance for estate planning as will be considered in Chapter 15. The relationship between them is not overlooked entirely, however, and for certain valuation purposes[1], spouses or registered civil partners are treated as one.

For the purposes of the remainder of this chapter, apart from the next paragraph, references to spouse also apply to registered civil partner.

2 Surviving spouse exemption

14.25 Where an individual's spouse died before 13 November 1974, leaving an interest in possession in property to the surviving spouse, estate duty would have been payable on that first death. To avoid a double charge to tax, there is no charge to IHT on either the subsequent death of the surviving spouse, or on the lifetime termination of that interest, provided that there would have been no charge on death[2].

3 Annual exemption of £3,000

14.26 Transfers of value made by a transferor (including the termination of an interest in possession in settled property created before 21 March 2006 – assuming that no further capital had been added to the settlement since then)[3] during lifetime in any one tax year[4] are exempt up to £3,000 in total[5]. For this purpose, transfers are not required to be grossed up. If the exemption is not utilised, or not fully utilised in any one tax year, it may be carried forward to the following year and used to relieve transfers in that year only. If the exemption is unused by year three, it cannot be carried forward into that year.

Subject to two exceptions, the £3,000 annual exemption is available in addition to the other exemptions and reliefs, ie it applies to the residue of value remaining after applying any other reliefs or exemptions. It is not cumulative with the 'small gifts' exemption (see below), nor is it applicable to PETs arising as a consequence of a donor releasing his interest in property subject to a reservation[6].

4 Small gifts not exceeding £250

14.27 Transfers of value made by a transferor during lifetime in any one tax year by outright gifts to any one person are exempt up to £250 (without grossing up) per transferee[7].

Gifts to the trustees of a settlement are not 'outright' and so fall outside the exemption. This exemption is available only if the total of all gifts made by the

1 See s 161 (ie related property).
2 Schedule 6, para 2.
3 Section 57(2)(b).
4 6 April–5 April.
5 IHTA 1984, s 19(1).
6 Section 19(3A)(a).
7 Section 20.

transferor to the transferee in any tax year does not exceed £250. (It should be remembered that this actually refers not to the value received but the loss to the transferor's estate.) There is no carry forward facility for this exemption.

5   Normal expenditure out of income

14.28   A transfer of value is exempt if or to the extent that it fulfils, during life-time, the following conditions:

(1)   it was made as part of the transferor's normal expenditure;

(2)   it was made out of his income (taking one year with another); and

(3)   after allowing for all transfers of value forming part of his normal expenditure, the transferor was left with sufficient income to maintain his usual standard of living[1].

A gift is regarded as part of the transferor's 'normal' expenditure if its amount and type are consistent with his usual pattern of gifts. 'Normal' is regarded as broadly equivalent to regular or habitual[2]. The first gift in a series can qualify as 'normal' provided there is evidence that further gifts are intended, for example, a contract with a life office. This would cover the payment of the first premium under a regular premium life assurance policy written in trust. If there is no such evidence, but in fact further normal payments are made, the first premium may, retrospectively, qualify for this exemption.

'Income' for this purpose means net income and is determined with normal accountancy (rather than income tax) rules. The exemption is not lost merely because of fluctuations of income from one year to another; nor if the transferor makes a gift from income and, having met some exceptional expense, is obliged to resort temporarily to capital to meet ordinary living expenses.

The capital element of a purchased life annuity bought after 12 November 1974 is not regarded as part of the transferor's income for this purpose in relation to transfers of value made after 5 April 1975[3]. Furthermore, where an individual has effected a life policy as part of a 'back-to-back' arrangement[4], the premiums payable would not automatically qualify for the normal expenditure exemption. Similarly, withdrawals taken from single premium bonds would not qualify.

6   Gifts in consideration of marriage

14.29   Certain gifts in consideration of marriage are exempt up to various limits (without grossing up). The limits are as follows:

(1)   £5,000 if the transferor is a parent of a party to the marriage;

---

1   Section 21(1).
2   *Bennett and others v IRC* 1995 STC 54.
3   Section 21(3), (4).
4   See Section 7C, **14.71**.

(2) £2,500 if the transferor is a remoter ancestor of a party to the marriage;

(3) £2,500 if the transferor is a party to the marriage;

(4) £1,000 if the transferor is any other person[1].

The exemption applies to gifts made at the time of, or shortly before, the marriage. Strict proof is required when a gift made after the marriage is alleged to be in consideration of it.

7 Gifts for maintenance of family

14.30 A disposition is not a transfer of value if it is made by one party to a marriage in favour of the other party or of a child of either party and is for the maintenance of the other party or for the maintenance, education or training of the child in any period up to the year in which he attains the age of 18 or, if later, when he ceases to undergo full-time education or training[2]. 'Marriage' in relation to a disposition made on the occasion of the dissolution or annulment of a marriage, and in relation to a disposition varying a disposition so made, includes a former marriage[3]. A disposition in favour of a dependent relative is exempt if it constitutes reasonable provision for the relative's care and maintenance[4]. Note that 'child' includes illegitimate, legitimated and adopted children.

8 Miscellaneous

14.31 There are some other exemptions, including: gifts to charities[5], gifts to qualifying political parties[6], gifts to registered housing associations[7], gifts for national purposes[8] and gifts for the public benefit provided they were made before 17 March 1998[9]. Further, there is no charge to IHT where a member of the armed forces dies from a wound inflicted, accident occurring or disease contracted on active service[10]. Exemptions which have particular reference to life assurance are dealt with in Section 7A, **14.66**.

C Potentially exempt transfers

14.32 A PET is a transfer of value made by an individual (on or after 18 March 1986) which would otherwise be a chargeable transfer to:

1 IHTA 1984, s 22.
2 Section 11.
3 Section 11(6).
4 Section 11(3). See Inland Revenue Pamphlet IR 1 (1992) F12 for the considerations applying as to whether a disposition is exempt if made by a child in favour of his unmarried mother.
5 Section 23.
6 Section 24.
7 Section 24A.
8 Section 25.
9 Section 26, but subsequently repealed by Finance Act 1998, s 143(1).
10 Section 154.

(1)   another individual or property which becomes comprised in his estate or increases the value of his estate;

(2)   an absolute or bare trust (although it should be borne in mind that, at the time of writing, HMRC take the view that the creation of an absolute trust for the benefit of a minor beneficiary would constitute a chargeable lifetime transfer rather than a potentially exempt transfer);

(3)   an accumulation and maintenance trust provided the transfer was made before 22 March 2006[1];

(4)   a disabled person's trust[2];

(5)   an interest in possession trust on or after 17 March 1987 but before 22 March 2006.

A transfer out of an interest in possession trust is also a PET (since 17 March 1987) if the transferee is an individual, an interest in possession trust, an accumulation and maintenance trust, or a disabled person's trust provided that the trust was created before 22 March 2006 and that the beneficiaries with the interest in possession have not been varied since that date (or, if they have, such variation took place before 6 April 2008).

If the transferor survives for seven years after the date of the PET, it becomes fully exempt and is never taxed, but if the transferor dies within seven years, the PET becomes a chargeable transfer and there will be an IHT computation[3] based on the value of the property at the time of the gift, the transferor's seven-year cumulation at the time of the gift and the death rates in force at the time of death or the rates in force at the time of the gift if this results in a lower amount of tax being payable. (Note that unless and until a PET becomes chargeable, it is regarded as exempt for all purposes, so that it would not be aggregated with a later chargeable transfer (eg a transfer to a discretionary trust) for the purposes of establishing the appropriate rate of tax for the chargeable transfer.)

D   Reliefs

14.33   There are a number of reliefs available from the charge to IHT. This section deals with two main areas of relief, namely agricultural property relief and business property relief.

I   *Agricultural property relief*[4]

14.34   Agricultural property relief is available for transfers of the 'agricultural value' of agricultural property, during lifetime, on death and on transfers into and

---

1   Section 71.
2   Section 89.
3   In accordance with IHTA 1984, s 7. See Section 5.
4   Sections 115–124.

out of settlements. The relief also extends to certain transfers of shares in companies which own or occupy farms[1].

For the purposes of this relief, 'agricultural value' is the value the property would have if it were subject to a perpetual covenant not to use it otherwise than for agricultural purposes. 'Agricultural property' is agricultural land or pasture in the UK, the Channel Islands and the Isle of Man and includes woodland and any building used in connection with the intensive rearing of livestock or fish if the woodland or building is occupied with agricultural land or pasture and the occupation is ancillary to that of the agricultural land or pasture; and also includes such cottages, farm buildings and farmhouses, together with the land occupied with them, as are of a character appropriate to the property[2].

The relief operates before deduction of the annual exemption and other exempt transfers and before grossing up (if applicable) by reducing the value transferred (automatically, without claim) by the following percentages[3]:

(1) 100% if immediately before the transfer the transferor had the right to vacant possession of the property or the right to obtain it within 12 months;

(2) 100% subject to the old limits (£250,000 or 1,000 acres per transferor) where the transferor would have been entitled to 50% relief under the old rules and had been entitled to his interest since before 10 March 1981 and satisfies certain conditions;

(3) 100% if the property is let subject to an agricultural tenancy commencing after 31 August 1995;

(4) 50% in all other cases.

14.35 To qualify for relief, the transferor must, immediately before the transfer, either:

(1) have occupied the agricultural property for agricultural purposes for at least two years; or

(2) have owned the agricultural property for the last seven years and throughout the period the property must have been occupied for agricultural purposes (whether by him or another)[4].

For this purpose:

(1) If the transferor inherited the property on the death of another, his period of ownership is regarded as beginning on the date of that death. Where the transferor was a spouse, the spouse's period of occupation may be added[5].

1 Section 122.
2 Section 115.
3 Section 116.
4 Section 117.
5 Section 120.

(2)   Occupation by a company controlled by the transferor is treated as occupation by the transferor[1].

(3)   If at the time of the transfer, the transferor had occupied the property for agricultural purposes for less than two years but it replaced property he had previously occupied for agricultural purposes, the occupation condition is treated as satisfied if he had occupied one or other of the properties for a combined period of at least two out of the five years preceding the transfer[2].

(4)   In similar circumstances to (3) the ownership condition is treated as satisfied if the transferor had owned one or other property for a combined period of at least seven years out of the ten preceding the transfer and, throughout, they had been occupied for agricultural purposes[3].

14.36   Agricultural relief at the rate of 100% also apples where shares or securities in a company are transferred[4], if:

(1)   agricultural property forms part of the company's assets and part of the value of the shares and securities can be attributed to it;

(2)   the company was controlled by the transferor immediately before the transfer;

(3)   the agricultural property had been occupied for agricultural purposes by the company or the transferor for the two years immediately before the transfer or owned by the company and occupied for agricultural purposes for seven years immediately before the transfer; and

(4)   the shares or securities had been owned by the transferor for a corresponding period.

The relief in these circumstances extends to that part of the value of the shares or securities transferred which is attributable to the agricultural value of qualifying agricultural property.

Relief is not available if at the time of the transfer, the agricultural property or the shares or securities are under a binding contract for sale[5].

Where the transfer falls within seven years of the transferor's death, relief is given only if the property was owned by the transferee throughout the period from the date of the transfer to the date of death and throughout that period the property was agricultural property occupied either by the transferee or another for the purposes of agriculture[6].

---

1   Section 119.
2   Section 118.
3   Section 118.
4   Section 122.
5   Section 124.
6   Sections 124A and 124B.

2 Business property relief[1]

14.37   Relief is available for transfers of 'relevant business property' at a reduction (before any grossing up) of 100% or 50%, according to the category in which it falls. The relief is available for transfers during life, on death and also for transfers of settled business property.

Subject to certain conditions, relief is available on transfers of the following categories of 'relevant business property' at the rates shown:

(1)   100% relief for:

(a)   a sole proprietor's business or an interest in a partnership; or

(b)   a holding of unquoted shares or shares in a company quoted on the Alternative Investment Market (AIM).

(2)   50% relief for:

(c)   land, buildings, plant or machinery owned by a partner or controlling shareholder and used wholly or mainly in the business of the partnership or company immediately before the transfer, provided that the partnership interest or shareholding would itself, if it were transferred, qualify for business relief;

(d)   settled business property used by a life tenant in his own business; or

(e)   a holding of shares giving control of a public company either by itself or in conjunction with the related property rules.

The relief takes the form of a percentage reduction in any value transferred which is attributable to relevant business property, and any exemptions or other reliefs applying are given after the business relief has been given.

14.38   Relief is given only if:

(1)   the transferor owned the business property for the two years immediately before the transfer[2]; or

(2)   it replaced other relevant business property and one or other property had been held for a combined period of at least two years out of the five immediately prior to the transfer[3].

A holding of shares is treated as giving an individual control of a company if he has voting control on all questions affecting the company as a whole[4]. Shares which form 'related property'[5] (eg owned by the spouse) are taken into account for this purpose.

---

1   Sections 103–114. For specific reference to Lloyd's underwriting interests, see Section 7C, **14.72**.
2   Section 106.
3   Section 107.
4   Section 269.
5   Section 161.

Relief is not available where the business is engaged wholly or mainly in dealing in securities, stocks or shares, land or buildings or holding investments[1] – unless it is the holding company of a trading group. Relief is also denied if the business or shares are subject to a binding contract for sale[2].

In addition, the value attributable to an excepted asset within a business does not qualify for relief. The main excepted assets are property rented to third parties, investments (for example unit trusts, single premium bonds) and large cash balances which are in excess of future business requirements — see *Barclays Bank Trust Co Ltd v IRC*[3].

The relief also applies to PETs[4] in a way similar to that for agricultural property, covering situations where the transfer was within seven years of the transferor's death. The relief will only be available where the transferee has retained ownership of the original property from the date of the transfer to the date of death and the property must qualify as relevant business property at the latter date (apart from the minimum two-year ownership requirement).

3   Miscellaneous

14.39   In addition to the above reliefs, there are provisions which relieve, inter alia, woodlands[5] from a charge to IHT on death and also relieve voidable transfers[6] (eg those set aside as a result of an order under the Inheritance (Provision for Family and Dependants) Act 1975).

SECTION 5   RATES AND CALCULATION OF TAX

14.40   IHT is levied by reference to the transfers of value made in the previous seven years[7] (the principle of cumulation) as well as by reference to the value (in terms of loss to the transferor's estate) of the particular transfer. The rates at which IHT is charged are set out in Schedule 1 to IHTA 1984. There is currently a 'nil rate band' within which chargeable transfers do not attract tax. The value of the nil rate band for transfers made on or after 6 April 2006 is £285,000. Chargeable lifetime transfers in excess of the nil rate band are charged at the life-time rate which is half the death rate[8] (currently, therefore, 20%). However, where the transferor dies within seven years of that transfer, subject to the avail-ability of taper relief, additional tax may be payable. Transfers on death are charged at the death rate in force (currently 40%), although PETs which prove chargeable may be charged at the death rate in force at the date of the gift if this results in less tax. Many transfers of value during lifetime are not immediately

---

1   Section 105(3).
2   Section 113.
3   1998 (STC 125).
4   Sections 113A and 113B.
5   Sections 125–130.
6   Section 150.
7   From 27 July 1981 to 17 March 1986, a ten-year period applied.
8   IHTA 1984, s 7(2).

chargeable transfers, but PETs, upon which IHT will not be payable unless the transferor dies within seven years of effecting the transfer. If death so occurs, the PET becomes chargeable and tax is levied on a tapering scale[1] as shown below:

number of years before death	*% of applicable death rate*
less than 3	100%
more than 3 but less than 4	80%
more than 4 but less than 5	60%
more than 5 but less than 6	40%
more than 6 but less than 7	20%

When computing the tax, the value of each transfer is the amount of the original transfer (not the current value of the property representing it) and the taper relief applies to the figure of IHT due, not to the value of the property.

PETs made within three years of death are charged at the full death rate. Chargeable transfers made more than five years before death on which the lifetime rate was charged will not bear any further IHT, but transfers made more than three years but less than five years before death, will. The extra tax is effectively the difference between the relevant percentage of taper relief and the percentage of the property on which tax has already been paid (ie 50%). For example, after four years, but less than five, the extra tax would be 60%, less 50%, namely 10%.

A   Grossing up

14.41   As IHT is charged on the loss to the transferor's estate resulting from the chargeable transfer, if the transferor pays the IHT, this will increase the loss and must be taken into account by 'grossing up' the net transfer to find the sum that, after the deduction of the IHT, leaves the net value transferred. (Tax is paid on the grossed-up value, which must be added to the transferor's cumulative total.)

The IHTA 1984 does not provide a specific method of grossing up. One example is by using fractions. On a chargeable lifetime transfer (eg transfer to a discretionary trust) the tax due (on the current rates) is 20% of the total, therefore the value actually transferred is 80% of the total. The fraction to find the tax due is therefore: (value actually transferred x 20/80).

If the transferee pays the IHT there is no need to gross up. (Even when the transferee pays the IHT, the amount of tax is calculated by reference to the transferor's cumulative total.)

PETs are not grossed up because no tax is chargeable at the time of the PET and should the PET prove chargeable upon the transferor's death, the primary liability will fall upon the transferee.

---

1   Section 7(4).

B Liability[1]

14.42 The primary liability to pay IHT on a chargeable lifetime transfer always lies with the transferor, with secondary liabilities on any person whose estate is increased in value by the transfer, any person in whom the property becomes vested or who has an interest in possession in it and, where the property becomes settled, any person for whose benefit the property or income from it is applied[2].

As to transfers on death, (other than property comprised in a settlement), the deceased's personal representatives have the primary (personal) liability. If, as a result of death, a PET proves chargeable or additional tax is due on lifetime transfers, the liability rests with the transferee, although if this is not paid within 12 months, the liability rests with the deceased's personal representatives[3].

For the liability arising under settlements, the primary liability lies with the trustees[4], although it may be paid, by agreement, by the beneficiaries, and where tax is payable on the death of an individual with an interest in possession, there is a secondary liability on the deceased individual's personal representatives.

C Limitation of liability

14.43 The liability of the persons above is not without limit. A person acting in a representative capacity is only liable to the extent of the value of the assets which they hold or have control over[5].

SECTION 6 SETTLEMENTS

14.44 It was stated in Section 2A, **14.4** that IHT is charged on transfers of value made by individuals[6]. However, special provisions exist to bring into charge dispositions in respect of settled property[7]. For IHT purposes, settlements are divided into two types, and two entirely different methods of taxation exist, depending on whether or not there exists a person(s) beneficially entitled to an interest in possession in the settled property. The following is a broad outline of the position.

It should be noted that the IHT treatment of gifts into settlements changed fundamentally from 22 March 2006 when all gifts into settlements (unless for the benefit of disabled persons as defined in section 89 of IHTA 1984) became chargeable transfers.

---

1 Sections 199–210.
2 Section 199(1).
3 Section 200.
4 Section 201.
5 Section 204.
6 Section 2(1).
7 See Part III of the 1984 Act.

A Settlement

14.45 For the purposes of IHT, a settlement is defined as any disposition whereby property is:

(1) held in trust for persons in succession or for any person subject to a contingency;

(2) held by trustees on trust to accumulate income or under discretionary powers; or

(3) charged with the payment of any annuity or periodic payment otherwise than for full consideration[1].

It will not, therefore, include a bare trust although, at the time of writing, HMRC was of the opinion that the creation of a bare trust for a minor beneficiary would be a settlement.

B Settlements with an interest in possession

14.46 Although the IHTA 1984 contains specific rules in relation to interests in possession[2], it does not define it. HMRC's understanding of the term, however, is as follows:

> 'An interest in possession in settled property exists where the person having the interest has the immediate entitlement (subject to any prior claim by the trustees for expenses or other outgoings properly payable out of income) to any income produced by that property as the income arises – but that a discretion or power, in whatever form, which can be exercised after income arises so as to withhold it from that person negatives the existence of an interest in possession. For this purpose a power to accumulate income is regarded as a power to withhold it, unless any accumulations must be held solely for the person having the interest or his personal representatives.'[3]

The term was the subject of an important House of Lords case:

Pearson v IRC[4]

Three beneficiaries were absolutely entitled to a trust fund, subject to powers in the trustees of appointment and accumulation. The trustees exercised their powers of appointment by deed dated 20 March 1976 to appoint irrevocably to one of the beneficiaries a capital sum to be held on trust to pay the income to that beneficiary during her lifetime or the trust period, whichever was the shorter. HMRC sought to collect tax on what they considered to be the creation of an interest in possession. The question was therefore whether or not an interest in possession existed prior to the appointment (as if it did, there would be no charge to tax when the power of appointment was exercised). The Chancery Division

1 Section 43.
2 Sections 49–54.
3 Inland Revenue Press Release, 12 February 1976.
4 [1980] 2 All ER 479.

and the Court of Appeal found in favour of the trustees, holding that an interest in possession did so exist. The House of Lords, however, (by a bare majority) agreed with HMRC's approach. It was stated that the term 'interest in possession' must be given its ordinary meaning which implies that there must be a present right to present enjoyment. As the trustees had a discretionary power to accumulate, there was no such present right in this case, merely a right to later payment of such income as the trustees, either by deliberate decision or by inaction for more than a reasonable time, did not cause to be accumulated.

14.47 In short, it can be said that a beneficiary has an interest in possession if he has a present right to present enjoyment of the *net income* of the settled property without any requirement for any further decisions of the trustees.

The test is not whether the beneficiary is entitled to all the income, but whether he is entitled to the net income as it arises. To determine what constitutes *net income*, a distinction must be drawn (and was in *Pearson*) between two types of powers exercisable by the trustees: *dispositive* and *administrative*. Net income refers to the income arising after the payment of trust expenses (which are payable out of trust income in accordance with general trust law principles). These expenses will be met by the trustees exercising their administrative powers. Where, however, the trustees have a dispositive power, ie the power to appropriate the income in favour of any person other than the beneficiary in question, that beneficiary cannot have an interest in possession[1]. It should be noted that an overriding power of appointment does not prevent the existence of an interest in possession.

Where the property does not actually produce any income (eg a life assurance policy), it is still possible to have an interest in possession (life office specimen trust forms have generally contained a deeming provision to this effect). The relevant question is whether the beneficiary would be entitled to the income as it arose if the property were income-producing[2].

However, it is felt that the practice of life offices may change following the Finance Act 2006 which stated that, from 22 March 2006, all gifts into interest in possession trusts and accumulation and maintenance trusts would be taxed for IHT purposes, in the same way as gifts into a settlement without an interest in possession.

1 Scotland

14.48 The legislation provides[3] for Scotland that an interest in possession is a right under a settlement to enjoy property. Thus, the term has the same meaning as it has, albeit undefined, in England and Wales.

2 The charging provisions

14.49 There are three parties to consider: the settlor, the primary beneficiaries (the life tenant(s)) and the remaindermen.

---

1 See also *Miller v IRC* [1987] STC 108.
2 See *Westminster Bank Ltd v IRC* [1957] 2 All ER 745.
3 IHTA 1984, s 46.

(a) The settlor

14.50 A transfer into an interest in possession settlement made before 22 March 2006 was a PET, which will only become chargeable if the settlor dies within seven years of the transfer. A transfer into such a settlement from 22 March 2006 onwards will be a chargeable lifetime transfer.

(b) The primary beneficiaries

14.51 A fundamental rule for property settled before 22 March 2006 is that a beneficiary with an interest in possession is treated as beneficially entitled to the whole of the property in which the interest subsists[1]. Where there is more than one beneficiary with an interest in possession, beneficial entitlement of the property for IHT purposes is apportioned according to their shares of the income[2]. When that interest ceases, a transfer of value for IHT purposes takes place[3].

If the cessation occurs during lifetime (whether by selling, surrendering or assigning), and the primary beneficiaries are those either that were actually in place as at 22 March 2006 or if there was a variation of the primary beneficiaries subsequent to that date and such variation took place before 6 April 2008, the transfer may be a PET (if it satisfies the conditions of section 3A of IHTA 1984, see Section 4C, **14.32**), eg a transfer to another individual. If the beneficiary whose interest in possession remains as a potential beneficiary under the trust, HMRC's current view is that he would be treated as having made a gift with reservation of benefit in these circumstances. If the cessation occurs during lifetime and after 6 April 2008, and the primary beneficiaries have been varied since that date, the transfer will be a chargeable transfer, assuming the trust continues in force – see **14.55** – again subject to the comments above regarding gifts with reservation.

If there is a depreciation in the value of the trust property as a result of the trustees entering into certain transactions, the beneficiary's interest will be treated as having come to an end to the extent of the depreciation[4]. It may be possible, however, to claim the exemption of 'no intention to confer any gratuitous benefit'[5].

If the cessation occurs on the death of a beneficiary, the capital value of the trust fund representing his income entitlement will be treated as part of his estate. If the death of the primary beneficiary occurs on or after 6 April 2008 and the trust continues in force, the trust will become a 'relevant property' trust and the principal charge and exit charge as described at **14.57** and **14.58** will apply.

There is no charge to IHT on a cessation of an interest in possession in the following instances[6]:

(1) where the beneficiary becomes absolutely entitled to the property;

1 Section 49(1).
2 Section 50(1).
3 Section 52(1).
4 Section 52(3).
5 Section 10.
6 See s 53.

(2)   where the property reverts to the settlor or the settlor's spouse (or within two years of the settlor's death, the widow or widower), provided that the interest was not acquired for consideration in money or money's worth and the spouse or widow or widower is domiciled in the UK. This applies to trusts created before 22 March 2006 only;

(3)   if the transfer is a PET.

If the interest is disposed of for a consideration in money or money's worth, the amount of the consideration will reduce the value transferred.

(c)   The remaindermen

14.52   The interest of the remaindermen comes into effect only when a prior interest (that of the primary beneficiary, or life tenant) ends and is a reversionary interest and is thus excluded property[1].

3   Rate of tax and liability

14.53   The liability for any IHT falls on the trustees of the settlement[2] and the rate of tax will be determined by the beneficiary's cumulative total of chargeable transfers within the preceding seven years.

4   Quick succession relief

14.54   There is a relief for IHT where a second charge arises within five years of the first charge. The conditions for the relief are that the transferor must be entitled to an interest in possession, the first transfer was of the same property and the property became, or it was already, settled property on the first transfer[3]. The relief is calculated as a percentage reduction in tax payable on the first transfer and is allowed as a deduction against tax due on the second transfer.

C   Settlements with no interest in possession[4]

14.55   Prior to 22 March 2006, the settlements within this class were primarily discretionary trusts. However, with effect from that date, gifts into interest in possession trusts and accumulation and maintenance trusts are now treated in the same way for inheritance tax purposes and hereafter the term 'discretionary trusts' will be used to cover any trust which is not an absolute or bare trust. It will be useful to state some basic points and define some relevant terms in relation to the taxing of discretionary trusts for IHT purposes:

1   See ss 53(1) and 48(3).
2   Section 201.
3   See s 141.
4   See generally ss 58–85.

(1) Once property is the subject of a discretionary trust, only half the normal IHT rates are relevant.

(2) The IHT charges apply to *relevant property*, which is settled property in which there is no *qualifying interest in possession*[1].

(3) A q*ualifying interest in possession* is an interest to which an individual or a company is beneficially entitled[2]. (As stated earlier, there is no statutory definition of the term and so the principles established in *Pearson v IRC*[3] are equally relevant here – but the new rules applicable to trusts created on or after 22 March 2006 mean that for settlements created on or after that date, even where an interest in possession exists, this will still be a relevant property trust – that is subject to possible entry, ten yearly and exit charges.)

(4) The *ten-year anniversary* is the tenth anniversary of the date on which the settlement commenced and each subsequent tenth anniversary (although no ten-year anniversary could fall before 1 April 1983)[4].

(5) A *related settlement* is one made by the same settlor which commenced on the same day as the settlement in consideration (unless one or both of them are charitable)[5].

An IHT charge for a discretionary trust can arise in any of the following situations:

(1) on its creation, as a chargeable transfer;

(2) on every tenth anniversary (the 'principal charge', known formerly as the 'periodic charge');

(3) on distribution of capital by the trustees or on its termination ('exit charges').

I   Creation

14.56   A transfer into a discretionary trust is always a chargeable transfer. If the settlor has utilised his nil rate band, IHT will be due and may be paid by the settlor (after grossing up) or by the trustees. Thereafter, the tax treatment of the trust varies depending on whether the trust was created before 27 March 1974 (ie pre-CTT) or after 26 March 1974. The discussion below refers primarily to settlements created after 26 March 1974.

1   Section 58.
2   Section 59.
3   [1980] 2 All ER 479.
4   Section 61.
5   Section 62.

2 The principal charge

14.57 The principal charge is levied where, immediately before a *ten-year anniversary*, a settlement contains *relevant property*. The rate of IHT is three-tenths of the *effective rate* applied to the *relevant property* in the settlement at the date of the charge.

The *effective rate* is the average rate of tax that would be charged by applying half the IHT rates on a *notional transfer* made by an individual with a *hypothetical cumulative total of transfers*. The *notional transfer* is the sum of (a) relevant property in the settlement, (b) the value of any property in the settlement which has never been relevant property and (c) the value of any property in a related settlement. The *hypothetical cumulative total of transfers* is the sum of (a) the cumulative total of transfers, if any, made by the settlor in the seven years before the settlement commenced (ten years for transfers before 18 March 1986) and (b) the amount which was subject to the 'exit charge' (see below) in the previous ten years, ie the value of the property which has left the settlement in the preceding ten years and on which an exit charge was payable.

To calculate the *effective rate*, one must calculate the tax payable on a transfer of the notional transfer by a person with the hypothetical cumulative total as stated above. The *effective rate* is then the tax payable divided by the value of the notional transfer, expressed as a percentage.

Example

On 1 May 1996, S effects a whole life assurance policy subject to a discretionary trust with a sum assured of £250,000 and an annual premium of £3,000. There are no related settlements and S has made previous chargeable transfers of £275,000 during the preceding seven years.

The first ten-year anniversary is 1 May 2006. On that day, the amount of relevant property (ie the policy) in the settlement is £30,000 (ie the premiums paid).

The effective rate of tax would be calculated as follows:

(1) *Calculate the value of the notional transfer*

There is no non-relevant property, nor any related settlement, so the value of the notional transfer is equal to the value of the relevant property: £30,000.

(2) *Calculate the transferor's previous chargeable transfers plus any values which have been the subject of exit charges*

There are previous chargeable transfers of £275,000 and no amounts subject to exit charges.

(3) *Calculate the tax on such a notional transfer*

	Cumulative total	*Tax*
Previous transfers £275,000	275,000	Nil
Notional transfer £30,000	305,000	4,000
Total tax		4,000
Tax on the notional transfer		4,000

The effective rate is therefore $(4,000/30,000) \times 100 = 13.33\%$.

(4) *Calculate the actual rate*

Three-tenths of the effective rate is 4.0%.

(5) *Calculate the actual IHT payable on the ten-year anniversary*

4.0% of the relevant property (£30,000) is £1,200.

There are further provisions, and necessary calculations in situations where the *relevant property* was either not relevant property or not comprised in the settlement for the whole of the ten-year period[1]. Basically, the rate at which tax is charged is reduced by one-fortieth for every complete quarter in which it was not relevant property or not comprised in the settlement.

Further, if there were additions to the settled property after the commencement date, in calculating the hypothetical cumulative total, one can take the values of the chargeable transfers made by the settlor in the seven years prior to the commencement date of the settlement, or prior to the date of the addition, whichever is the higher[2].

It should be noted that on the current rates, the maximum possible rate is 6%.

3   The exit charge

14.58   A charge to IHT arises where property in a discretionary settlement ceases to be *relevant property*[3]. This may occur due to the settlement coming to an end, when the property is distributed to the beneficiaries, when an individual becomes beneficially entitled to an interest in possession in the settled property, when the property is held on an accumulation and maintenance trust or when the property becomes *excluded property*.

A charge to tax will also arise when the trustees make a disposition, ie do some act or deliberately fail to exercise a right that results in a reduction in the value of the settled property (although it may be possible to claim the exemption that the disposition was not intended to confer any gratuitous benefit)[4].

The rate of the exit charge is a fraction of the rate which was applied at the ten-year anniversary. The fraction is calculated as one-fortieth for each complete period of three months that has elapsed since the last ten-year anniversary[5]. The tax is charged on the amount by which the value of the relevant property in the settlement is diminished as a result of the event giving rise to the charge. Note that no tax is payable if the event in question occurs in the first quarter of a ten-year period.

1   Section 66(2).
2   Section 67.
3   Section 65(1).
4   Section 10.
5   See s 69.

Example

Using the figures from the previous example, the last ten-year anniversary IHT charge was £1,200 in respect of the £30,000 relevant property in the settlement. Five years (ie twenty-quarters) later, the life assured dies and the sum assured of £250,000 is paid out by the trustees. Assuming no changes in the general rates of tax since the last ten-yearly charge, the £250,000 will be taxed at the fraction of 20/40 of the rate of 4.0% (ie 2.0%) so that £5,000 will be payable.

Again, special rules apply if any property has been added to the settlement or any property in the settlement has become relevant property since the last ten-year anniversary.

(a) Rate before first ten-year anniversary[1]

14.59 Where an exit charge falls due before the first ten-year anniversary, the rate of tax is a fraction of the 'effective rate' calculated in much the same way as the *effective rate* for the ten-yearly charge. The value of all the property in the settlement at the time of creation is taken together with all the property in any related settlement. The hypothetical cumulative total of the settlor's chargeable transfers in the seven years (ten years for transfers before 10 March 1986) prior to the creation of the settlement is also brought into the calculation. The actual rate is three-tenths of the 'effective rate' so calculated. The fraction is again calculated as one-fortieth for each complete period of three months which has elapsed since the creation of the settlement. The actual rate is, therefore, the sum of the 'effective rate' × (3/10) × (number of complete quarters since the trust was set up/40).

(b) Pre-27 March 1974 settlements

14.60 The calculation of the rate of tax is modified if the settlement was created before 27 March 1974.

In calculating the ten-yearly charge, the settlor's cumulative total of chargeable transfers, the value of other non-relevant property and the value of property in related settlements are all disregarded.

In calculating the exit charge arising before the first ten-year anniversary, the rules were modified[2], in particular as to the calculation of the notional transfer. Further, the rate was simply three-tenths of the 'effective rate' (as modified), there was no account of the number of quarters elapsing between commencement and the time of the disposition.

(c) Exemptions

14.61 Although no qualifying interest in possession subsists in them, the property in the following types of trust is not to be treated as *relevant property*[3]:

1 Section 68.
2 Section 68.
3 Section 58.

(1)   charitable purpose trusts[1];

(2)   accumulation and maintenance trusts[2];

(3)   protective trusts[3];

(4)   employee and newspaper trusts[4];

(5)   maintenance funds for historic buildings, etc[5]; and

(6)   temporary charitable trusts[6].

D   Accumulation and maintenance trusts

14.62   The life assurance practitioner should be aware of these trusts, which are basically settlements with no interest in possession which were introduced on 15 April 1976. Prior to 22 March 2006, to come within the definition of an accumulation and maintenance trust and thereby avoid the principal charge or any exit charges, certain conditions had to be satisfied[7]:

(1)   There must be no interest in possession in the settled property and income not applied for the maintenance, benefit or education of the beneficiaries must be accumulated.

(2)   One or more beneficiaries had to become entitled to the settled property, or to an interest in possession in it, by the age of 25 at the latest. This was an absolute requirement and means that a beneficiary must not be able to be disentitled from acquiring the necessary interest under the terms of the settlement[8]. By concession[9], HMRC regarded the age requirement as being satisfied if it is clear that a beneficiary would in fact become entitled by the age of 25, even if it was not specified in the trust instrument.

(3)   Either not more than 25 years have elapsed since the commencement of the settlement, or, at such later time as the conditions in (1) and (2) have become satisfied, all the beneficiaries must be or were grandchildren of a common grandparent, or children, widows or widowers of such grandchildren who were themselves beneficiaries but died before they became entitled. If this criteria is satisfied, the trust could continue indefinitely (subject to the trust rules on perpetuity).

If the trust has been for the benefit of children who do not have a common grandparent, then it can only last for 25 years. After 25 years, it will revert to being a

1   Section 76.
2   Sections 71 and 58.
3   Section 73.
4   Section 72.
5   Section 77.
6   Section 70.
7   Section 71.
8   See *Lord Inglewood v IRC* [1983] STC 133.
9   Extra Statutory Concession F8(1992).

regular discretionary trust and would incur the usual ten-year anniversary and exit charges to inheritance tax. In addition, the trust fund would incur an inheritance tax charge of 21% of the value of the property in the trust fund on losing its accumulation and maintenance status.

If the trust is caught by this, the trustees will have to consider the implications of paying the charge, which will reduce the cash held in the trust and may result in having to sell investments with a possible CGT charge.

It may be possible to avoid the charge by appointing or advancing the capital of the fund onto fixed interest trusts, bare trusts or absolutely for the benefit of any beneficiaries or to re-settle the funds on new accumulation and maintenance trusts. It should be noted that if the settlor was non-UK domiciled when the property was settled on trust, the charge would only apply to the extent that the trust holds UK assets.

If the trust was created on 15 April 1976, the 25-year period will end on 15 April 2001 and thus, this is the earliest time when the 21% tax charge could apply.

I A&M trusts created on or after 22 March 2006

14.63 Following the Finance Act 2006, all transfers into A&M trusts on or after 22 March 2006 are treated as chargeable transfers and are thus taxed in the same way as discretionary trusts as described above, that is that there may be an immediate charge to IHT to the extent that the value transferred, after deducting any available exemptions and taking account of any existing chargeable transfers made by the same settlor within the previous seven years, exceeds the current nil rate band.

Ten yearly charges and exit charges may also be payable.

However, an exception to this general rule is a trust created in a will or on intestacy in favour of a minor child of a deceased parent which can vest the benefit absolutely in the child between the ages of 18 and 25 (a so called '18 to 25 trust'). If the benefit vests absolutely at age 18, then no charge to tax will arise at that time. If the trust continues after age 18, then at age 18 the trust will become subject to the 'relevant property' trust regime but there will be no entry charge.

This means that, if the child becomes absolutely entitled at the last possible time for 18 to 25 trusts – ie at the age of age 25 – then the discretionary trust regime will apply, but the trust will be treated as having started when the beneficiary attained age 18 for the purpose of determining the appropriate fraction of the effective rate to charge.

The maximum exit charge that can therefore arise when the beneficiary becomes absolutely entitled at age 25 is 4.2% which is 28 quarters into the first ten yearly charge period. If the beneficiary became absolutely entitled, say at age 21, then the maximum exit charge would be 1.8%, that is, three-tenths of 6%.

If the value of the gift to the trust on death plus the cumulative total of chargeable transfers made by the deceased in the seven years prior to death is less than the nil rate band applicable when the beneficiary becomes absolutely entitled, there will be no tax charge.

2   A&M trusts created prior to 22 March 2006

14.64   Transfers to A&M trusts before 22 March 2006 were classed as PETs and consequently fell outside the regime for 'relevant property' trusts.

The original proposals in the Finance Bill 2006 stated that if such a trust was not amended before 6 April 2008 to give the beneficiary an absolute right to the trust capital on attaining age 18, then it would automatically become a 'relevant property' trust from that date with the ten yearly charges starting on the first ten yearly anniversary of the creation of the trust after 6 April 2008 (albeit on a proportionate basis in view of the fact that the trust property had not been 'relevant property' for the whole of the ten-year period).

However, these proposals were amended by the Finance Act 2006 so that the tax treatment outlined above in connection with '18 to 25 trusts' is also generally available for pre-22 March 2006 A&M trusts irrespective of the identity of the settlor where the beneficiary is currently under 18, provided that the trust is amended to meet the '18 to 25 trust' rules as above.

SECTION 7   LIFE ASSURANCE

14.65   Although the IHTA 1984 contains certain provisions specifically relating to life assurance, one is left, generally, to apply the basic charging principles of IHT to situations involving life assurance contracts and policy trusts.

A   Lifetime transfers

I   Premiums

14.66   Premiums paid by the life assured on an own-life, own-benefit policy, or by the grantee on a life-of-another policy for the grantee's benefit, are not liable for IHT as there is no transfer of value.

Premiums paid on trust policies are transfers of value because they reduce the payer's estate. Where life assurance premium relief is available, the amount of the transfer is the net premium paid.

From 22 March 2006, gifts into new interest in possession trusts become chargeable lifetime transfers. However, in most cases, premiums will fall within one of the available exemptions, eg the £3,000 annual exemption[1] or the normal expenditure out of income exemption[2]. Any premiums in excess of the available exemptions will be chargeable lifetime transfers and will need to be taken into account in computing the settlor's IHT liability if he should die within seven years.

Prior to 22 March 2006, where the trust in question was an interest in possession trust, the first premium over and above any available annual exemptions

1   Section 19.
2   Section 21.

constituted a PET[1] since the value transferred was attributable to property (the policy) which by virtue of the transfer (the payment of the first premium) became comprised in the estate of another individual. Subsequent premiums were treated as PETs[2] only to the extent that the value of the estate of the beneficiary(ies) was increased, ie to the extent that the value of the policy is increased[3]. Premium payments in the early years of a policy may not have increased the value of the policy, eg where there is no surrender value and the payments are taken up by charges. It was advisable, therefore, to gift cash to trustees (the cash then becoming settled property, which was comprised in the estate of an individual). The trustees then used this cash to pay the premiums directly to the life office. In this instance, the transfers will prove chargeable only if the payer dies within seven years of effecting the transfer.

For regular premium policies written subject to interest in possession trusts which were in force on 22 March 2006, HMRC have confirmed that they view the payment of ongoing premiums as merely maintaining the policy in force rather than adding to the trust property and thus the existing IHT treatment will remain and the trust will not become a 'relevant property' trust. It should, however, be noted that if the practice of the settlor gifting cash to the trustees to enable them to pay any premiums over and above the exemptions is continued, this will have the effect of placing the trust within the new relevant property regime as each payment to the trust will be viewed as a new gift.

HMRC have also confirmed in guidance notes issued to the ABI that where there are increases in premiums due to ten-yearly plan reviews or the exercise of cost of living or indexation options or where the policy provides for premiums to automatically increase over the term of the policy then provided such increases occur as a result of options contained within the policy or of specific policy terms, the exercise of these options would not be sufficient to place the policy in the relevant property regime. This is also true of paying further single premiums under an existing pre-22 March 2006 single premium bond provided there is an option in the original policy to do this.

2   Transfer of existing policy into trust

14.67   Where an existing policy is put into trust, the transfer of value is measured by the special rules of valuation in relation to life assurance policies (see **14.70**).

3   Transfer of interest

14.68   If the individual beneficially entitled to an interest in a life policy (eg the life assured under an own-benefit policy or a beneficiary with an interest in possession in a trust policy) transfers his interest during his lifetime then, unless the transfer is for full consideration, there is a transfer of value for IHT purposes.

1   IHTA 1984, s 3A.
2   Section 3A(2)(b).
3   See letter dated 28 October 1987 from the Life Insurance Council (LIC) of the Association of British Insurers to LIC members following clarification from the Inland Revenue.

The transfer will be a PET if the usual conditions apply[1] (and subject to **14.60** if the trust was created prior to 22 March 2006). One of the available exemptions may apply to the transfer, eg the spouse exemption[2], however, the small gifts and normal expenditure out of income exemptions do not apply. The same principles apply to the transfer during lifetime of an interest in an annuity.

Where the trust was created on or after 22 March 2006, the trust will be treated for IHT purposes as one without an interest in possession and thus, the alteration of a beneficiary will have no IHT implications.

B   Transfers on death

14.69   On the death of the life assured under an own-benefit policy, or a policy written under a trust in which the settlor reserved a benefit (unless effected before 18 March 1986 and not subsequently varied so as to increase the reserved benefits or to extend its terms), the value of the policy (ie the proceeds payable on death) will form part of his estate for the charge to IHT on the transfer on death[3]. Note that where the settlor's spouse is a beneficiary, there is no reservation of benefit provided that there is no intention that benefits accruing to the spouse will be used or are in fact used for the benefit of the settlor.

The death of the grantee under a life-of-another policy and the death of a beneficiary with an interest in possession in a settled policy (provided that the settlement had been created prior to 22 March 2006) (or a beneficiary under a simple trust policy) will constitute transfers and form part of the deceased's estate for IHT purposes.

The death of the life assured, other than the settlor under a trust policy, will not be a chargeable transfer unless the beneficiaries have predeceased him and he has acquired an interest in possession through the will or intestacy of the last of them to die.

The spouse exemption may apply to any of the transfers on death mentioned above.

C   Special provisions

I   Valuations

14.70   If there is a transfer of value of the interest in a life policy or reversionary annuity *during lifetime* then special rules apply for determining the value transferred[4]. The value is taken to be not less than the total of the premiums or other consideration paid under the policy or contract less any sums previously paid to the policyholder by way of partial surrender. The market value (either the surrender value or the second-hand value) will apply if it is higher.

1   Section 3A.
2   Section 18.
3   Section 171.
4   Section 167.

The special valuation rule does not apply to term assurances of three years or less or where, if the term exceeds three years, premiums payable in any one year are not more than twice those in any other years. There is a relaxation of the rule for unit-linked assurances[1], in that any drop in the value of units allocated is allowed as a deduction from the total premiums. In both these cases the value taken is broadly the market value which, in the case of term assurances, will depend upon the state of health of the life assured and the remaining length of the term.

2   'Back-to-back' arrangements (annuity purchased in connection with a life policy)

14.71   These arrangements involve the purchase by A of an immediate purchased life annuity and a whole life policy on A's life written in trust for B. In this way, A reduces the value of his estate by purchasing the annuity (which ceases on his death and therefore does not fall back into his estate) and also creates a source of income for his life which enables him to pay premiums under the policy. The policy proceeds should normally be free of IHT as they are in trust for B and thus are not part of A's estate. Thus A's dutiable capital is replaced by non-dutiable assets in the form of a policy belonging beneficially to B.

However, great care should be taken to avoid the potential impact of section 263 of IHTA 1984 which concerns 'associated operations' as defined by section 268 of that Act. Where a life assurance policy is taken out on or after 27 March 1974 and, at the time the insurance is made, or at any earlier or later date, an annuity on the life of the insured person is purchased and the benefit of that policy is vested in another person, then unless it can be shown that the effecting of the contracts is not an associated operation, the purchaser of the annuity shall be treated as making a transfer of value at the time the policy became so vested, of the lesser of:

(1)   the purchase price of the annuity plus the premium under the policy; or

(2)   the value of the greatest benefit capable of being conferred by the policy at any time.

HMRC have stated that the purchase of an annuity and the effecting of a life assurance policy will not be treated as an associated operation if it can be shown that the policy was issued after full medical evidence of the assured's health had been obtained and that it would have been issued on the same terms had the annuity not been purchased – see HMRC Statement of Practice E4. With effect from 31 December 1987, HMRC have regarded a policy as being issued on full medical evidence if it can be shown that the life office has, as a minimum, obtained a private medical attendant's report and has used it as the basis of its normal underwriting procedures in the same way as it would have done had the annuity not also been purchased. HMRC can ask for the medical evidence to be produced in any case.

1   Section 167(4).

Perhaps the best way to establish that the two contracts do not constitute an associated operation is to use different life offices for each contract. This will also be beneficial in that the best rates can be obtained in both cases.

The normal expenditure from income exemption may not be available to exempt the premiums from tax because the capital element of the annuity would not be regarded as income for this purpose. If, however, the investor has enough other income which could have been utilised, this exemption may be available provided the investor does not have to resort to capital to maintain his standard of living.

3 Lloyd's underwriting interest[1]

14.72 A Lloyd's underwriter is entitled to business property relief at 100% on the value of his underwriting interest.

Business property relief is available on the value of the whole underwriting interest, which includes investments and cash held in the Lloyd's deposit (which underwriters are required to deposit up to a stated amount); underwriting reserves (the member's personal reserves and his special reserve); and profits on the open years' accounts at death.

If, however, the underwriting interest is thought to be excessive in comparison to the level of business written, the excess will not attract relief, as it cannot be categorised as 'relevant business property'.

Where an underwriter has funded his deposit or underwriting reserves by a letter of credit or guarantee from a bank or a life office, assets held by the bank or life office as security for those arrangements (eg a charge on a life policy) will also qualify for 100% relief up to the value of the guarantee or the letter of credit[2]. In this way, the proceeds of any life policy may qualify for business property relief.

Note. The impact of IHT on life assurance is greater than it has been possible to consider in this section, which has dealt only with the direct effect of the tax on life assurance contracts. Accordingly, Chapter 15 looks more closely at matters such as the role and use of life assurance in estate planning for IHT, the considerations which should be applied to an assured's existing policies, and the effect of IHT on various policy trust wordings.

SECTION 8 ANNUITIES

A Single life annuities

14.73 An annuity involves the payment of a capital sum to an insurance company in return for an (immediate or deferred) payment of income, commonly for the rest of the annuitant's life. A single life annuity (unless there is a

---

1 See Tolley's *Taxation of Lloyds Underwriters* (9th edn 2000). Note that this section does not refer to corporate membership of Lloyd's, which has been possible since 1 January 1994.
2 See *IRC v Mallender* [2001] STC 514.

guaranteed capital return element) will cease on death and thus there will be nothing in the estate on which to charge IHT.

Where the annuity provides a capital return upon death of the annuitant, if that capital benefit is paid to the deceased's personal representatives, it will form part of his estate for IHT purposes and be taxable accordingly. It is possible, however, to place the capital return element in trust, in which case the value of the gift will need to be determined for IHT purposes. The CTO drew attention to this point[1], and stated that the value of the gift for IHT purposes will generally be substantially more than the value of the death benefit the right to which has been gifted. This is because the value is determined in accordance with the loss to the transferor's estate principle, under which the value would be the difference between the purchase price of the annuity and the open market value of the right to receive the unprotected annuity payments during the annuitant's lifetime. The CTO have pointed out that the open market value is likely to be less than the amount for which the insurance company would have sold an unprotected annuity on the same individual's life. The main reason for this difference is due to the fact that a purchaser in the open market (unlike an insurance company) would need to buy life cover to protect his investment, the cost of which would vary in accordance with the usual underwriting considerations.

B Joint lives annuities

14.74 Most joint annuities are on the lives of husband and wife, either purchased by one of them or by both jointly. Because of the spouse exemption, no IHT charges will arise on the purchase of the annuity or on the death of one annuitant leaving the other surviving, and this will be so whether the contract is (1) a joint annuity payable to them jointly and thereafter to the survivor or (2) a single life annuity for one followed by a reversionary annuity for the other.

Where a proposer purchases an annuity in joint names, to be payable during the joint lifetime of himself and his wife and then during the life of the survivor and the policy provides for payments after the first death to be made to the survivor, it may be that the law will presume, in the absence of evidence to the contrary, that the husband intended to provide for the wife. But in view of the opinions expressed in *Pettitt v Pettitt*[2] to the effect that the former presumption of advancement in favour of a wife is now of little force, it is perhaps desirable on the comparatively rare occasions when the annuitants are not both contributing to the purchase price that the purchaser should make clear, at the time of making the proposal, that he intends his wife to take beneficially any annuity payable after his death.

Where the wife is the purchaser or in any case where the purchaser is not the husband or parent of the other life, there will not be any presumption that the purchaser intended the other to enjoy the annuity beneficially, and if that is indeed the intention the annuity policy should express a trust for that person.

1 See Life Assurance Council Circular 160/1994 in a letter dated 26 July 1994 from the Association of British Insurers to all LIC members and the Taxation (Life Policies) Panel.
2 [1970] AC 777.

SECTION 9   REGISTERED PENSION SCHEMES

14.75   This book covers the law of life assurance and not the law of pensions. However, it would not be complete without some mention of the subject, as the life assurance practitioner will invariably need to consider pension arrangements and the IHT implications for individuals whose assets are large enough to bring them within the IHT net. (Further details of pension arrangements are given in Chapter 16, Section 3.)

A   Structure of pension arrangements

14.76   Prior to 6 April 2006, the legislation governing tax-approved pension arrangements was contained in Part XIV of the Income and Corporation Taxes Act 1988. Because of the way the legislation had been developed and modified over many years (starting with the Finance Act 1970), a total of eight different tax regimes had emerged. Each regime had its own complex rules limiting the amount an individual could contribute to a pension scheme and the benefits a scheme could pay out. So, following a lengthy period of consultation and development, which started in 2002, the government has swept away all the existing pensions tax legislation and introduced a single set of rules. The new rules are contained in Part 4 of the Finance Act 2004, and came into effect from 6 April 2006.

Because the new pensions tax legislation lays down a single set of rules, it does not need to distinguish between the different types of pension arrange-ments. The legislation uses the general term 'registered pension scheme'. This means a pension scheme that has been registered with HMRC as being a scheme that meets all the requirements of Part 4 of the Finance Act 2004. But it must be borne in mind that simply because every pension arrangement is called a 'registered pension scheme' for the purposes of the tax legislation, there are still many different types of 'registered pension schemes', each with their own characteristics. It does not matter whether the arrangement is a multi-member scheme (such as an occupational pension scheme) or a single contract (such as a retirement annuity), each will be classified as a 'registered pension scheme'.

14.77   Pension arrangements that are categorised as 'registered pension schemes', and involve insurance contracts, can take various forms:

(1)   Retirement annuities

- This type of arrangement takes the form of a contract between the insurer and the individual – ie the policy is written in the name of the individual, and the individual has both beneficial and legal ownership. All the terms governing the operation of arrangement are laid down in the policy.

(2)   Provider-sponsored personal pension schemes (including stakeholder pension schemes)

- This type of arrangement normally takes the form of a contract between the insurer and the individual – ie the policy is written in the name of the individual, and the individual has both beneficial and legal ownership. Unlike retirement annuities, the contract is held within a 'scheme' structure. The terms governing the operation of the arrangement are contained in the scheme rules, as well as the policy. The scheme itself would have been established by the insurer executing a deed poll, which adopts the rules and appoints the scheme administrator (usually the insurer itself).

- It is possible for the insurer to establish the scheme under trust, but this creates a more complex structure and is a method rarely used for fully insured arrangements. Trust-based schemes will be encountered where the scheme is operated as a self-invested personal pension scheme, or where the scheme has been set up by an employer. In addition, the trust-based approach has been used for some stakeholder pension schemes set up by providers other than insurers.

(3)   Employer-sponsored occupational pension schemes

- This type of arrangement is established by the employer executing the trust instrument which adopts the rules and appoints the trustees. The terms governing the operation of the arrangement are set out in the scheme rules. The contract will be between the insurer and the trustees, and the policies will be written in the name of the trustees.

- Occupational pension schemes can take many forms:

  (i)   defined benefit schemes;

  (ii) group money purchase schemes (fully insured or self-administered);

  (iii) insured money purchase schemes tailored for individuals (executive pension plans);

  (iv) small self-administered schemes (SSASs).

(4)   Provider-sponsored free-standing additional voluntary contribution schemes

- This type of arrangement is established by the provider executing the trust instrument which adopts the rules and appoints the trustees. The terms governing the operation of the arrangement are set out in the scheme rules. The contract will be between the insurer and the trustees, and the policies will be written in the name of the trustees.

(5)   'Left scheme' policies – to secure benefits outside the terms of occupational pension schemes

- Such policies are effected by the scheme trustees in the name of the individual, for the purpose of providing deferred benefits for an individual who has left service (a 'section 32' buy-out policy), or where the scheme has wound-up (a 'trustees' buy-out policy), or for providing a pension in the form of an annuity (a 'compulsory purchase annuity' policy), or for providing a pension in the form of income withdrawals (an 'income withdrawal' policy).

- Similar 'left scheme' policies can also arise from policies originally effected in the name of the trustees being assigned to the individual on leaving service or on the scheme winding up. The benefits cease to be covered by the rules of the scheme, and all the terms governing the operation of the arrangement are laid down in the policy. The individual has both beneficial and legal ownership.

14.78 The benefits under 'registered pension schemes' can take various forms as set out below. It should be noted that the forms of benefits available under a particular 'registered pension scheme' will depend on what is allowed by the rules governing the scheme or the provisions of the insurance contract.

(1) On the member's death before drawing retirement benefits:

- a lump sum;

- a pension to a dependant – which can be provided in various ways:

  (i) on the 'secured pension' basis by the purchase of an annuity;

  (ii) where the dependant is under age 75, on the 'unsecured pension' basis; or

  (iii) where the dependant is aged 75 or over, on the 'alternative secured pension' basis.

(2) On the member drawing retirement benefits – which can be at any time from age 50 (55 from 6 April 2010), but must be before the 75th birthday:

- a lump sum (referred to in FA 2004 as a 'pension commencement lump sum');

- a pension – which can be provided in various ways:

  (i) on the 'secured pension' basis by the purchase of an annuity, which may include a guaranteed period of up to ten years and/or a reversionary annuity payable to a dependant;

  (ii) on the 'secured pension' basis by means of a 'scheme pension', which may include a guaranteed period of up to ten years and/or a reversionary pension payable to a dependant;

  (iii) whilst the member is under age 75, on the 'unsecured pension' basis; or

  (iv) when the member reaches age 75, on the 'alternative secured pension' basis – which may include a guaranteed period of up to ten years.

(3) On the member's death after drawing retirement benefits:

- where the member's pension was being paid on the 'secured pension' basis (ie by means of an annuity):

  (i)   continuation of pension payments for any remaining guaranteed period; and/or

  (ii) payment of a lump sum associated with the pension (under 'annuity protection'); and/or

  (iii) commencement of any associated pension to a dependant.

- where the member's pension was being paid on the 'unsecured pension' basis, the remaining fund would be disposed of by:

  (i)   payment of a lump sum (less 35% tax); or

  (ii) provision of a pension for a dependant on the 'secured pension' basis by the purchase of an annuity, or on the 'unsecured pension' basis where the dependant is under age 75, or on the 'alternative secured pension' basis where the dependant is aged 75 or over.

- where the member's pension was being paid on the 'alternative secured pension' basis, the remaining fund would be disposed of as follows:

  (i)   If there is a dependant, the fund must be used to provide a pension for that dependant. The pension could be on the 'secured pension' basis by the purchase of an annuity, or on the 'unsecured pension' basis where the dependant is under age 75, or on the 'alternative secured pension' basis where the dependant is aged 75 or over.

  (ii) If there is no surviving dependant, the fund can be paid as a lump sum to a charity, or transferred to another arrangement within the scheme for the benefit of another individual. (This would normally be in accordance with directions given by the member to the scheme administrator.)

  (iii) It is also possible to treat the member's 'alternative secured pension' as being guaranteed for ten years. Hence on death in that period, the pension payments would continue until the end of the guaranteed period. This could be used in conjunction with (i) or (ii).

(4)   On a dependant's death whilst in receipt of a pension:

- where the dependant's pension was being paid from an annuity, no further benefit would arise;

- where the dependant's pension was being paid on the 'unsecured pension' basis, the remaining fund would be disposed of by payment of a lump sum (less 35% tax);

- where the dependant's pension was being paid on the 'alternative secured pension' basis, the remaining fund would be disposed of as follows:

(i) if, exceptionally, there is another surviving dependant of the member, the fund must be used to provide a pension for that dependant. The pension could be on the 'secured pension' basis by the purchase of an annuity, or on the 'unsecured pension' basis where the dependant is under age 75, or on the 'alternative secured pension' basis where the dependant is aged 75 or over; or

(ii) if there is no other surviving dependant, the fund can be paid as a lump sum to a charity, or transferred to another arrangement within the scheme for the benefit of another individual. (This would normally be in accordance with directions given by the member, or the dependant, to the scheme administrator.)

B   Impact of the IHT legislation

14.79   It can be seen from the above that there are a wide range of structures for registered pension schemes, and a wide range of benefits that might be provided. In addition, the individual often has a good deal of flexibility in tailoring the form of the benefits for his or her personal circumstances, and deciding when to start drawing the benefits. This makes the interaction with the IHT legislation some-what complex. However, there are a number of exemptions and concessions which mean that, for most cases, the value of the benefit will not form part of the estate for assessing IHT. Particular issues for each type of registered pension scheme are considered later, but first a few general observations can be made.

1   Contributions paid by an individual

14.80   Any contribution made by an individual to his or her registered pension scheme will not be classified as a transfer of value (section 12 of IHTA 1984).

It should be borne in mind that it is possible for an individual to make contri-butions to another individual's pension arrangement (for example, a grandparent paying contributions into a stakeholder pension scheme for a grandchild). Looking at the situation from the perspective of the contributing individual's estate, HMRC has advised that, where such contributions do not fall within either the £3,000 annual exemption or normal expenditure out of income exemption, the contributions will constitute potentially exempt transfers.

2   Individual dies whilst in receipt of a pension on the 'secured pension' basis

14.81   Section 151 of IHTA 1984 applies to pensions being paid on the 'secured pension' basis (ie by means of an annuity or 'scheme pension'). It provides that an interest in a pension or annuity, that comes to an end on the death of a member, shall not be taken into account in determining the value of the estate for IHT purposes. This means that any capital value that could otherwise have been placed on the pension at the time of death will be left out of account.

Where there are remaining pension payments due under a guaranteed period (which can be up to ten years from the date the 'secured pension' commenced):

(1)   if the remaining payments are payable as of right to the legal personal representatives, a capital value will be ascribed to those payments and included in the value of the estate for IHT purposes;

(2)   if the remaining payments are payable at the discretion of the trustees or scheme administrator of the 'registered pension scheme', no IHT charge will arise.

3   Individual dies whilst in receipt of a pension on the 'unsecured pension' basis

14.82   Where the member dies and the remaining fund is paid as a lump sum (less 35% tax), the situation will be as described in Section 9B5.

Where the member dies and the remaining fund is used to provide pension benefits for a dependant, there will not normally be a value to include in the member's estate for IHT purposes although there is a possibility that the situation described in Section 9B6 could arise.

Where the remaining fund is used to provide pension benefits for a dependant, the following situations could arise:

(a)   The pension for the dependant could be provided on the 'secured pension' basis (by means of a scheme pension or lifetime annuity). On the dependant's death, the pension would simply come to an end and there would be no further value to consider. So, no IHT charge would arise in respect of the dependant's estate.

(b)   Where the dependant is under age 75, the pension could be provided on the 'unsecured pension' basis. On the dependant's death whilst still under age 75, the remaining fund will be paid as a lump sum (less 35% tax). The situation will be as described in Section 9B5.

(c)   Where the dependant's pension started on the 'unsecured' pension' basis, and was then changed to the 'alternatively secured pension' basis on the dependant attaining age 75, the remaining fund would be dealt with as follows on the dependant's subsequent death:

●   Where, exceptionally, there is another individual who qualifies as a dependant of the member, the fund must be used to provide a pension for that individual.

●   Where the fund is paid to a charity, or charities, there will be no IHT charge.

●   Where the fund is disposed of by means of an unauthorised payment (ie paid out of the scheme to a recipient other than a charity, or transferred to another arrangement within the scheme for the benefit of another individual), there will be a charge to IHT on the dependant's estate based on the value of the remaining fund (section 151C of

IHTA 1984). The IHT due will be paid by the scheme administrator from the fund. The balance will then be paid as an unauthorised payment subject to the relevant tax charges. (At the time of writing it is not yet clear how the IHT charge and the unauthorised payment tax charges will interact. Potentially there could be a total tax charge of 82% – ie 40% IHT charge followed by a tax charge of 70% on the unauthorised payment.)

The amount of IHT due will be notified to the scheme administrator by HMRC Inheritance Tax. It will be calculated based on the aggregate value of the dependant's personal estate and the remaining fund, and then apportioned between the two. So, the personal estate and the pension scheme will each benefit from a share of the nil-rate threshold.

(d)   Where the dependant is aged 75 or over when the member dies, such that the dependant's pension starts on the 'alternatively secured pension' basis, on the dependant's subsequent death the situation will be as described in (c).

4   Individual dies whilst in receipt of a pension on an 'alternatively secured pension' basis

14.83   Where there is no 'dependant' the following situations could arise:

(a)   Where the remaining fund is to be paid as a lump sum to a charity, or charities, there will be no charge to IHT in respect of the member's estate.

(b)   Where the fund is disposed of by means of an unauthorised payment (ie paid out of the scheme to a recipient other than a charity, or transferred to another arrangement within the scheme for the benefit of another individual), there will be a charge to IHT in respect of the member's estate based on the value of the remaining fund (section 151A of IHTA 1984). The IHT due will be paid by the scheme administrator from the fund. The balance will then be paid as an unauthorised payment subject to the relevant tax charges. (At the time of writing it is not yet clear how the IHT charge and the unauthorised payment tax charges will interact. Potentially there could be a total tax charge of 82% – ie 40% IHT charge followed by a tax charge of 70% on the unauthorised payment.)

The amount of IHT due will be notified to the scheme administrator by HMRC Inheritance Tax. It will be calculated based on the aggregate value of the member's personal estate and the remaining fund in the pension scheme, and then apportioned between the two. So, the personal estate and the pension scheme will each benefit from a share of the nil-rate threshold.

Where there is a 'dependant' the situation is quite complex. The pensions tax legislation in the Finance Act 2004 requires the remaining fund to be used to provide pension benefits for the 'dependant'. But the inheritance tax legislation in IHTA 1984 has different provisions depending on the relationship between the dependant and the member. Accordingly it is necessary to split the range of possible 'dependants' into two categories:

A   the member's wife, husband, civil partner, or any other individual financially dependent on the member (defined as a 'relevant dependant' in IHTA 1984).

B   any individual who would fit into the definition of 'dependant' but who is not a 'relevant dependant', for example, a child of the member under age 23 who is not financially dependent on the member.

Where the remaining fund is used to provide a pension for a dependant in category A, there is not an immediate IHT charge on the member's estate. However, the charge is only treated as deferred until the dependant's death, at which time a charge is levied against any fund remaining – the charge still being in relation to the member's estate (section 151B of IHTA 1984).

The following situations could arise on the death of the category A dependant:

(a)   Where the pension for the dependant is being provided on the 'secured pension' basis (by means of a 'scheme pension' or 'lifetime annuity'), the pension would simply come to an end and there would be no further value to consider. So, no IHT charge would arise.

(b)   Where the pension for the dependant is being provided on an 'unsecured pension' basis (dependant dies under age 75), there will be a charge to IHT based on the value of the remaining fund (section 151B of IHTA 1984). The IHT due will be paid by the scheme administrator from the fund in the pension scheme.

The amount of IHT due will be notified to the scheme administrator by HMRC Inheritance Tax. The tax is charged as if the remaining fund was the top slice of the member's estate. The rate of tax and the nil-rate threshold will be those applicable as at the date of the dependant's death.

The remaining fund after the IHT charge will then be paid as a lump sum, subject to a 35% tax charge as described in Section 9B5. So, potentially the fund could be hit with a 40% IHT charge and then a further 35% tax charge – making a total tax charge of 61%.

(c)   Where the pension for the dependant is being provided on the 'alternatively secured pension' basis (dependant dies aged 75 or over), the remaining fund will be dealt with as follows:

●   Where, exceptionally, there is another individual who qualifies as a dependant of the member, the fund must be used to provide a pension for that individual.

●   Where the fund is paid to a charity, or charities, there will be no IHT charge.

●   Where the fund is disposed of by means of an unauthorised payment (ie paid out of the scheme to a recipient other than a charity, or transferred to another arrangement within the scheme for the benefit of another individual), there will be a charge to IHT based on the value of the remaining fund (section 151B of IHTA 1984). The IHT due will be paid by the scheme administrator from the fund. The balance will then be paid as an unauthorised payment subject to the relevant tax charges. (At the time of writing it is not yet clear how the IHT charge and the unauthorised payment tax charges will interact. Potentially there could be a total tax charge of 82% – ie 40% IHT charge followed by a tax charge of 70% on the unauthorised payment.).

The amount of IHT due will be notified to the scheme administrator by HMRC Inheritance Tax. The IHT charge arises on the basis that it was a charge on the member's estate that was deferred on the member's death (as the fund was used for the benefit of a dependant in category A). The tax is charged as if the remaining fund was the top slice of the member's estate. The rate of tax and the nil-rate threshold will be those applicable as at the date of the dependant's death.

Where the remaining fund is used to provide a pension for a dependant in category B, there will be an immediate charge to IHT on the member's estate based on the value of the remaining fund (section 151A of IHTA 1984). The IHT due will be paid by the scheme administrator from the fund. The balance will then be used for the benefit of the dependant.

The amount of IHT due will be notified to the scheme administrator by HMRC Inheritance Tax. It will be calculated based on the aggregate value of the member's personal estate and the remaining fund, and then apportioned between the two. So, the personal estate and the pension scheme will each benefit from a share of the nil-rate threshold.

The following situations could arise on the death of the category B dependant:

(a)   Where the pension for the dependant is being provided on the 'secured pension' basis (by means of a 'scheme pension' or 'lifetime annuity'), the pension would simply come to an end and there would be no further value to consider. So, no IHT charge would arise in respect of the dependant's estate.

(b)   Where the pension for the dependant is being provided on the 'unsecured pension' basis (dependant dies under age 75), the remaining fund will be paid as a lump sum (less 35% tax). The situation will be as described in Section 9B5.

(c)   Where the pension for the dependant is being provided on the 'alternatively secured pension' basis (dependant dies aged 75 or over), the remaining fund will be dealt with as follows:

   •   Where, exceptionally, there is another individual who qualifies as a dependant of the member, the fund must be used to provide a pension for that individual.

   •   Where the fund is paid to a charity, or charities, there will be no IHT charge.

- Where the fund is disposed of by means of an unauthorised payment (ie paid out of the scheme to a recipient other than a charity, or transferred to another arrangement within the scheme for the benefit of another individual), there will be a charge to IHT based on the value of the remaining fund (section 151C of IHTA 1984). The IHT due will be paid by the scheme administrator from the fund. The balance will then be paid as an unauthorised payment subject to the relevant tax charges. (At the time of writing it is not yet clear how the IHT charge and the unauthorised payment tax charges will interact. Potentially there could be a total tax charge of 82% – ie 40% IHT charge followed by a tax charge of 70% on the unauthorised payment.).

The amount of IHT due will be notified to the scheme administrator by HMRC Inheritance Tax. It will be calculated based on the aggregate value of the dependant's personal estate and the remaining fund, and then apportioned between the two. So, the personal estate and the pension scheme will each benefit from a share of the nil-rate threshold.

5   Lump sums payable on the death of an individual

14.84   Any lump sum payable as of right to the legal personal representatives on the individual's death will clearly form part of the estate for IHT purposes. This situation would normally be encountered where the individual has legal ownership of the policy and all the terms governing the pension arrangement are contained in the policy. Retirement annuity policies and 'left scheme' policies would come within that category.

A retirement annuity policy, or 'left scheme' policy, can be made subject to a discretionary trust (whether at the outset or by a later declaration of trust and assignment). The whole of the policy must be made subject to the trust, but the terms of the trust will specify that the retirement benefits will be retained for the benefit of the individual. The trustees will only have power to dispose of the moneys that become available on the individual's death. The normal IHT exit charge will not arise so long as distribution takes place within two years of the date of death. If the moneys remain in the environment of a discretionary trust for more than two years, the normal rules for periodic and exit charges will apply. Making the policy subject to a discretionary trust would constitute prima facie a transfer of value for IHT purposes – but the value of the death benefit transferred is regarded as nominal provided the individual was not in serious ill-health when the transfer was made. HMRC would only investigate further if the individual died within two years of the date of setting up the trust (see Section 9B6).

Occupational pension schemes normally contain provisions such that the lump sum is distributed at the discretion of the scheme trustees to beneficiaries selected from a specified range, such distribution to take place within two years of the date of death. In these circumstances, the value of the benefit will not normally be included in the estate for IHT purposes. The legal personal representatives can be included in the range of potential beneficiaries, and if the trustees decide to make payment to the legal personal representatives through the exercise of the discretionary powers, then the benefit will not normally form part of the estate for IHT purposes.

Personal pension schemes and stakeholder pension schemes established by deed poll fall between the retirement annuity policy and occupational pension scheme structures. The individual has legal ownership of the policy, but the provisions for the payment of benefits are contained in the scheme rules. For a lump sum death benefit, the scheme rules will usually provide that the lump sum would be paid to a discretionary trust set up for the policy by the individual (which is possible because the individual is the legal owner), or, if there is no trust, the lump sum would be paid by the scheme administrator through the discretionary provisions.

14.85   The whole of the policy must be made subject to the trust, but the terms of the trust will specify that the retirement benefits will be retained for the benefit of the individual. The trustees will only have power to dispose of the moneys that become available on the individual's death. The normal IHT exit charge will not arise so long as distribution takes place within two years of the date of death. If the moneys remain in the environment of a discretionary trust for more than two years, the normal rules for periodic and exit charges will apply. Making the policy subject to a discretionary trust would constitute prima facie a transfer of value for IHT purposes – but the value of the death benefit transferred is regarded as nominal provided the individual was not in serious ill-health when the transfer was made. HMRC would only investigate further if the individual died within two years of the date of setting up the trust (see Section 9B5).

Where there is no trust, the lump sum will be distributed at the discretion of the scheme administrator to beneficiaries selected from a specified range, such distribution to take place within two years of the date of death. In these circumstances, the value of the benefit will not normally be included in the estate for IHT purposes. The legal personal representatives can be included in the range of potential beneficiaries, and if the trustees decide to make payment to the legal personal representatives through the exercise of the discretionary powers, then the benefit will not normally form part of the estate for IHT purposes.

Where the individual dies before drawing the benefits, but after the date that the benefits could have been drawn, there is a possibility that the situation described in Section 9B6 could arise. So, despite the fact no IHT charge would arise through the process of paying the lump sum (for example, where it is paid through the discretionary provisions in the scheme rules), there could be an IHT charge arising from another direction.

6   Failure to exercise an option in connection with pension rights under a registered pension scheme (sections 3(3) and 12(2A)–2(D) of IHTA 1984 – omission to exercise a right)

14.86   An IHT charge might be considered under section 3(3) of IHTA 1984 where decisions have been made by the individual prima facie with the aim of benefiting others on death, rather than to make provision for the individual's own retirement. Sections 12(2A)–2(D) provide that, in certain circumstances, the failure to exercise an option in connection with the pension rights, which was available before death, can give rise to a lifetime charge to IHT under section 3(3). The circumstances where a claim might arise are where there is evidence to indicate that the individual had become aware he or she was in ill-health and was likely to die within two years, and at or after that time took some action which affected the value that could otherwise have formed part of the estate.

HMRC has stated that, in practice, they expect to see very few cases where a claim would even be considered. HMRC would not pursue a claim where the death benefit was paid to the individual's dependant (ie spouse, civil partner or any other individual financially dependent on the individual) or to a charity. In addition, a claim would not be made where the individual survived for two years or more after making the relevant decision.

Examples of the scenarios where a claim might arise are as follows:

(a) An individual sets up a trust for the lump sum death benefit that would be payable under a policy of which the individual is the legal owner – ie a retirement annuity policy, a personal pension policy, or a 'left scheme' policy.

(b) An individual reaches the age at which retirement benefits become due under the terms of the pension arrangement (eg the vesting date under a retirement annuity or personal pension scheme). He decides to defer drawing the benefits because he is in ill-health and wishes the fund to be available as a lump sum death benefit for the benefit of his family.

Where the death benefit would automatically go to the estate anyway (eg under a retirement annuity where there is no trust), the act of deferring the benefit would not have any significance in itself. But if the individual set up a trust for the policy after the vesting date, or paid extra contributions to a policy already under trust, HMRC might raise a claim.

Where the death benefit would not automatically go to the estate (eg under a personal pension scheme where the benefit would be payable through the discretionary provisions), the act of deferring the benefit would be sufficient in itself for HMRC to consider raising a claim. But no claim would be made if the lump sum was paid to a dependant or to a charity.

(c) An individual is in ill-health and decides to take pension on the 'unsecured pension' basis rather than purchasing an annuity – the reason being that there will be a fund available on his death for the benefit of his family.

(d) An individual becomes ill whilst taking pension on the 'unsecured pension' basis and decides to reduce the amount of income being taken so that the fund on death is higher than it otherwise would have been.

In the case of (a), the value to be added to the estate would be the amount of the lump sum paid to the trust.

In the case of (b), (c) and (d), the value to be added to the estate would be the capital value of the ten years worth of payments that would have been paid from an annuity with a ten-year guaranteed period which could have been purchased with the relevant fund.

C Retirement annuities

1 Death of member before the vesting date – lump sum

14.87 The lump sum can derive from:

(1) the retirement fund;

(2) any separately insured lump sum death benefit.

The insurer will deal with payment of the lump sum as follows:

(a) where the policy is subject to an individual discretionary trust, payment will be made to the trustees of that trust;

(b) where (a) does not apply, payment will be made to the legal personal representatives.

Where the lump sum is payable as of right to the legal personal representatives, as in (b), then it will clearly form part of the estate for IHT purposes.

Where payment is made to an individual discretionary trust, no IHT liability will normally arise if the money is distributed within two years of the date of the individual's death. If distribution does not take place within two years, the normal rules for discretionary trusts will apply from that time, and periodic and exit charges will arise. Many policy trusts become fixed trusts in favour of the default beneficiary(ies) if distribution does not take place within the two-year period. In these circumstances, the relevant value would form part of the beneficiary's estate.

Where the individual sets up the policy trust whilst in ill-health, and dies within two years, HMRC might raise a section 3(3) claim as explained in Section 9B6.

Prior to 6 April 2006 it was possible to formally assign a separately insured lump sum to a lender in connection with a mortgage (although that practice had become largely defunct in the latter years). The legislation from 6 April 2006 prohibits all assignments of benefits, apart from assignment to a trust for the purpose of holding lump sum death benefits. Where an assignment to a lender was made before 6 April 2006, it appears that payment to the assignee can be made without infringing the new legislation, and no IHT charge will arise.

2 Death of member after deferring drawing the benefits beyond the vesting date – lump sum

14.88 Registered pension schemes are free to lay down their own conditions on when a member can draw benefits within the range from the 50th birthday (55th birthday from 6 April 2010) up to the day before the 75th birthday. The retirement annuity policy will have a specific vesting date that falls within the age range 60 to 75, with an option to draw the benefits before or after that date within the approved range. If the benefits are not drawn at the vesting date because the individual was in ill-health and death occurs within two years, HMRC might raise a section 3(3) claim as explained in Section 9B6.

3   Death of member in annuity guaranteed period

14.89   The annuity can be set up with a guaranteed period of up to ten years. On death in the guaranteed period, the remaining guaranteed payments will be payable as of right to the legal personal representatives. A capital value will be determined for the remaining payments which will be added to the value of the estate for IHT purposes as described in Section 9B2.

HMRC has expressed the opinion that it is not possible to create a trust for such an annuity.

4   'Unsecured pension' and 'alternatively secured pension'

14.90   Retirement annuity policies were all established before the 'unsecured pension' and 'alternatively secured pension' options became available. In theory, an insurer could add the options, but most likely it would be necessary to transfer the fund, before vesting, to the insurer's personal pension scheme to gain access to the options. If, exceptionally, an insurer does add the options then the same principles would apply as described for personal pension schemes in Section 9D4–D6.

D   Personal pension schemes (including stakeholder pension schemes)

1   Death of member before vesting date – lump sum

14.91   The lump sum can derive from:

(1)   the Non-Protected Rights Fund; and

(2)   any separately insured lump sum death benefit.

The rules for most schemes will provide for the scheme administrator to deal with payment of the lump sum as follows:

(a)   in accordance with any specific provision regarding payment of such sums under the contract;

(b)   if (a) is not applicable, and the contract is subject to an individual trust (under which no beneficial interest in a benefit can be paid to the member, the member's estate or the member's legal personal representatives), payment will be made to the trustees of the trust; or

(c)   if (a) and (b) are not applicable, payment will be made at the discretion of the scheme administrator to beneficiaries determined from a specified range of potential beneficiaries.

Scenario (a) is now rare. It is likely that the specific provision under the contract will mean that the lump sum is payable as of right to the legal personal representatives. In those circumstances, the lump sum will clearly form part of the estate for IHT purposes.

In scenario (b), where payment is made to an individual discretionary trust, no IHT liability will normally arise if the trust distributes the money within two years of the date of the member's death. If distribution does not take place within two years, the normal rules for discretionary trusts will apply from that time, and periodic and exit charges will arise.

Many policy trusts become fixed trusts in favour of the default beneficiary(ies) if distribution does not take place within the two-year period. In those circumstances, the relevant value would form part of the beneficiary's estate.

Where the member sets up the policy trust whilst in ill-health, and dies within two years, HMRC might raise a section 3(3) claim as described in Section 9B6.

In scenario (c), the lump sum will be distributed at the discretion of the scheme administrator to beneficiaries selected from a specified range, such distribution to take place within two years of the date of death. In those circumstances, the value of the benefit will not normally be included in the estate for IHT purposes. The member can give the scheme administrator an 'expression of wish' form, indicating who he would like the scheme administrator to consider paying the lump sum to. But this form will not be binding on the scheme administrator (otherwise the IHT exemption would not apply). The legal personal representatives can be included in the range of potential beneficiaries, and if the trustees decide to make payment to the legal personal representatives through the exercise of the discretionary powers, then the benefit will not normally form part of the estate for IHT purposes.

14.92   There is a possibility that the situation described in Section 9B6 could arise. For example, a member who is over the age of 50 (and would therefore be eligible to draw the benefits) might become ill, but does not draw the benefits. If that member then dies within two years, an IHT charge could arise in respect of any lump sum paid from the scheme – unless the lump sum is paid to a dependant or to a charity (section 12(2D) of IHTA 1984).

If there is a Protected Rights Fund under the scheme, and the member leaves a widow(er) or civil partner, then the Protected Rights Fund must be used to provide a pension for that individual. However, if there is no widow(er) or civil partner, the Protected Rights Fund will be paid as a lump sum in accordance with the following rules:

(a)   in accordance with any direction given by the member in writing; or

(b)   if (a) is not applicable, to the member's estate.

If no directions have been left for the payment of the Protected Rights Fund as a lump sum, it will be payable as of right to the legal personal representatives, and will clearly form part of the estate for IHT purposes.

Where the member has left a binding direction in writing in respect of the Protected Rights Fund, such a direction will form a transfer of value.

Prior to 6 April 2006 it was possible to formally assign a separately insured lump sum to a lender in connection with a mortgage (although that practice had become largely defunct in the latter years). The legislation from 6 April 2006 prohibits all assignments of benefits, apart from assignment to a trust for the purpose of holding lump sum death benefits. Where an assignment to a lender was made before 6 April 2006, it appears that payment to the assignee can be made without infringing the new legislation, and no IHT charge will arise.

2   Death of member after deferring drawing the benefits beyond the vesting date – lump sum

14.93   Registered pension schemes are free to lay down their own conditions on when a member can draw benefits within the range from the 50th birthday (55th birthday from 6 April 2010) up to the day before the 75th birthday. The personal pension policy will have a specific vesting date that falls within the age range 50 to 75, with an option to draw the benefits before or after that date within the approved range. If the benefits are not drawn at the vesting date because the individual was in ill-health and death occurs within two years, HMRC might raise a section 3(3) claim as explained in Section 9B6.

3   Death of member in annuity guaranteed period

14.94   The annuity can be set up with a guaranteed period of up to ten years. On death in the guaranteed period, the remaining guaranteed payments may, or may not, be payable as of right to the legal personal representatives. That depends on the provisions in the scheme rules.

The rules of most personal pension schemes will provide for the scheme administrator to decide who should receive the payments. Hence the payments will not be due as of right to the legal personal representatives and no IHT liability should arise.

Where, exceptionally, the rules of the particular personal pension scheme provide for the remaining guaranteed payments to be payable as of right to the legal personal representatives, a capital value will be determined for the remaining payments which will be added to the value of the estate for IHT purposes as explained in Section 9B3.

HMRC has expressed the opinion that it is not possible to create a trust for such an annuity.

4   Death of member whilst taking income on the 'unsecured pension' basis

14.95   The member can make various arrangements for the disposal of the remaining fund on his or her death.

The member can leave written instructions that the remaining fund is to be used for the benefit of a named dependant (ie the widow(er), civil partner or other individual who is financially dependent on the member). In those circumstances, the fund would not form part of the member's estate for IHT purposes.

The dependant would normally have the following options:

(a)   take the fund as a lump sum (less the 35% tax charge);

(b)   use the fund to provide income on the 'unsecured pension' basis if under the age of 75, or on the 'alternatively secured pension' basis if aged 75 or over; or

(c)   use the fund to purchase an annuity.

Where the member does not specify that the remaining fund is to be used for the benefit of a dependant, or the dependant has predeceased the member, the fund (less the 35% tax charge) will be paid as a lump sum as described in Section 9D1.

It is possible that a section 3(3) claim could arise as explained in Section 9B6.

If, exceptionally, HMRC decides to pursue a section 3(3) claim, the value is determined from the loss to the estate at the instant before death. At that point the individual had the right to use the whole remaining fund for the purchase of an annuity. The section 3(3) claim is therefore determined as follows:

(a)   The 'unsecured pension' provider will determine the annuity that could have been purchased, using its current annuity rates, on the basis of single life only, guaranteed ten years, non-escalating, payable monthly in advance. (If the provider does not write annuity business, HMRC will determine the annuity.)

(b)   HMRC will then determine a value for the ten years' guaranteed payments that would have been made.

It should be noted that the value is determined as the 'loss to the estate'. The rules for most Personal Pension Schemes will provide for the scheme administrator to decide who should receive the payments. Hence the payments will not be due as of right to the legal personal representatives, and hence there is no 'loss to the estate'. So, a section 3(3) claim will only have a value where the rules of the personal pension scheme provide for the remaining payments under an annuity guaranteed period to go to the legal personal representatives as of right. However, HMRC has indicated that a claim could also arise under section 3(1) on the basis that the member could have exercised his statutory right to transfer his benefits to another personal pension scheme, and hence would have had the opportunity to choose a scheme under which it would be possible to redirect the benefits to the estate. It is not clear whether this argument is ever likely to be pursued.

5   Death of member whilst taking income on the 'alternatively secured pension' basis

14.96   The methods of dealing with the remaining fund, and the IHT charges that could arise (see Section 9B4), are as follows:

(a)   If there is a dependant, the fund must be used to provide a pension for that dependant. The pension could be on the 'secured pension' basis by the purchase of an annuity, or on the 'unsecured pension' basis where the dependant is under the age of 75, or on the 'alternatively secured pension' basis where the dependant is aged 75 or over.

There would be no IHT charge at this stage for a category A dependant (see **14.83**).

There would be an immediate IHT charge for a category B dependant (see Section 9B4). The charge will be paid by the scheme administrator from the fund held in the scheme, and only the balance will be used for the benefit of the dependant.

(b)   If there is no surviving dependant, the fund can be paid as a lump sum to a charity, or charities. There would be no IHT charge.

This would normally be in accordance with directions given by the member to the scheme administrator in writing. If the member has not left any such directions, the scheme administrator can choose the charity.

(c)   If there is no surviving dependant, the fund can be disposed of by means of an unauthorised payment (ie paid out of the scheme to a recipient other than a charity, or transferred to another arrangement within the scheme for the benefit of another individual). There will be a charge to IHT based on the value of the remaining fund. The charge will be paid by the scheme administrator from the fund. The balance will then be paid as an unauthorised payment subject to the relevant tax charges. (At the time of writing it is not yet clear how the IHT charge and the unauthorised payment tax charges will interact. Potentially there could be a total tax charge of 82% – ie 40% IHT charge followed by a tax charge of 70% on the unauthorised payment.)

6   Death of dependant whilst in receipt of a pension

14.97   The various scenarios, and the IHT charges that could arise, are as follows:

(a)   Where the dependant's pension was being paid from an annuity, no further benefit would arise. Hence there would be no IHT charge.

(b)   Where the dependant's pension was being paid on the 'unsecured pension' basis, having been derived from the member's 'unsecured pension' fund, the remaining fund would be paid as a lump sum (less the 35% tax charge), as described in Section 9D1.

(c)   Where the dependant's pension was being paid on the 'alternative secured pension' basis, having been derived from the member's 'unsecured pension fund', an IHT charge could arise as described in Section 9B4.

(d)   Where the dependant's pension was being paid on the 'unsecured pension' basis, having been derived from the member's 'alternative secured pension fund', an IHT charge could arise as described in Section 9B4.

(e)   Where the dependant's pension was being paid on the 'alternatively secured pension' basis, having been derived from the member's 'alternatively secured pension fund', an IHT charge could arise as described in Section 9B4.

E Occupational pension schemes

1 Death of member before the normal retirement – lump sum

14.98 Under a defined benefits scheme, the benefits payable would be specified in the rules of the scheme. The benefit would typically be:

(1) a lump sum based on a defined multiple of salary (up to 4 times), the liability for which would usually be insured under a group life assurance contract;

(2) a return of the individual's own contributions, with or without interest;

(3) a pension payable to a dependant.

Under a money purchase scheme, the benefits are not specifically defined. What will normally happen is that moneys will become available to the trustees which will derive from:

(1) the retirement fund;

(2) any separately insured lump sum death benefit.

The rules of the scheme will normally give the trustees power to pay the lump sum to beneficiaries determined from a specified range of potential beneficiaries, such distribution to take place within two years of the date of the individual's death. In these circumstances, no IHT liability will arise. The individual can give the trustees an 'expression of wish' form indicating who he would like the trustees to consider paying the lump sum to. This form will not be binding on the trustees (otherwise the IHT exemption would not apply). The legal personal representatives can be one of the potential beneficiaries considered by the trustees, and an exercise of discretion in favour of the legal personal representatives will not give rise to an IHT liability.

2 Death of member after deferring drawing the benefits beyond the normal retirement – lump sum

14.99 Registered pension schemes are free to lay down their own conditions on when a member can draw benefits within the range from the 50th birthday (55th birthday from 6 April 2010) up to the day before the 75th birthday. But it is likely that most occupational pension schemes will remain fairly inflexible about the time at which a member can draw benefits.

So, the extent to which an individual can influence the time at which benefits are drawn is much more restricted where the benefits arise under an occupational pension scheme, than it is where the benefits are under a personal pension scheme. Usually when an individual reaches the normal retirement age specified in the rules of the scheme, the benefits will come into payment automatically (unless the individual continues in the employment, in which case the benefits will be deferred until the individual actually leaves).

So, the likelihood of a section 3(3) claim arising is remote. However, there may be odd circumstances where it could arise. For example, if an individual deferred drawing the benefits on reaching the normal retirement age because he was in ill-health, it is possible that a section 3(3) claim might arise as described in Section 9B6.

3   Death of member in pension guaranteed period

14.100   The pension can be set up with a guaranteed period of up to ten years. On death in the guaranteed period, the remaining guaranteed payments may, or may not, be payable as of right to the legal personal representatives. That depends on the provisions in the scheme rules.

The rules of most occupational pension schemes will provide for the trustees to decide who should receive the payments. Hence the payments will not be due as of right to the legal personal representatives and no IHT liability should arise.

Where, exceptionally, the rules of the particular occupational pension scheme provide for the remaining guaranteed payments to be payable as of right to the legal personal representatives, a capital value will be determined for the remaining payments which will be added to the value of the estate for IHT purposes as described in Section 9B3.

4   Death of member whilst taking income on the 'unsecured pension' basis

14.101   An option to take income on the 'unsecured pension' basis can only be provided under money purchase schemes. It is likely to be encountered mainly under executive pension plans and SSASs.

The issues to be aware of will be the same as those described for personal pension schemes in Section 9D4.

5   Death of member whilst taking income on the 'alternatively secured pension' basis

14.102   An option to take income on the 'alternatively secured pension' basis can only be provided under money purchase schemes. It is likely to be encountered mainly under executive pension plans and small self-administered schemes.

The issues to be aware of will be the same as those described for personal pension schemes in Section 9D5.

6   Death of dependant whilst in receipt of a pension

14.103   The various scenarios, and the IHT charges that could arise, will be the same as those described for personal pension schemes in Section 9D6.

F Free-standing additional voluntary contribution schemes

14.104 The provisions outlined in Section 9E for occupational pension schemes apply equally to free-standing AVC schemes.

G 'Left scheme' policies

1 Death of member before the vesting date – lump sum

14.105 The lump sum can derive from:

(1)   the retirement fund;

(2)   any separately insured lump sum death benefit.

The insurer will deal with payment of the lump sum as follows:

(a)   where the policy is subject to an individual discretionary trust, payment will be made to the trustees of that trust;

(b)   where (a) does not apply, payment will be made to the legal personal representatives.

Where the lump sum is payable as of right to the legal personal representatives, as in (b), then it will clearly form part of the estate for IHT purposes.

Where payment is made to an individual discretionary trust, no IHT liability will normally arise if the money is distributed within two years of the date of the individual's death. If distribution does not take place within two years, the normal rules for discretionary trusts will apply from that time, and periodic and exit charges will arise. Many policy trusts become fixed trusts in favour of the default beneficiary(ies) if distribution does not take place within the two-year period. In these circumstances, the relevant value would form part of the beneficiary's estate.

Where the individual sets up the policy trust whilst in ill-health, and dies within two years, HMRC might raise a section 3(3) claim as explained in Section 9B5.

2 Death of member after deferring drawing the benefits beyond the vesting date – lump sum

14.106 Registered pension schemes are free to lay down their own conditions on when a member can draw benefits within the range from the 50th birthday (55th birthday from 6 April 2010) up to the day before the 75th birthday. The 'left scheme' policy will have a specific vesting date that falls within the age range 60 to 75, with an option to draw the benefits before or after that date within the approved range. If the benefits are not drawn at the vesting date because the individual was in ill-health and death occurs within two years, HMRC might raise a section 3(3) claim as described in Section 9B6.

3   Death of member in annuity guaranteed period

14.107   The annuity can be set up with a guaranteed period of up to ten years. On death in the guaranteed period, the remaining guaranteed payments will be payable as of right to the legal personal representatives. A capital value will be determined for the remaining payments which will be added to the value of the estate for IHT purposes as described in Section 9B2.

HMRC has expressed the opinion that it is not possible to create a trust for such an annuity.

4   'Unsecured pension' and 'alternative secured pension'

14.108   The extent to which these income options will be available under a 'left scheme' policy will depend on whether the particular insurer is prepared to allow them. It may be necessary to transfer the fund, before vesting, to the insurer's personal pension scheme to gain access to the options. (Care is needed when considering a transfer as there may be protected tax-free lump sum rights.)

If, exceptionally, an insurer does add the options then the same principles would apply as for personal pension schemes as described in Section 9D4–D6.

SECTION 10   EMPLOYER-FINANCED RETIREMENT BENEFIT SCHEMES

14.109   'Employer-financed retirement benefit schemes' (EFRB schemes) is the term used for schemes which are not registered with HMRC and therefore do not obtain the various tax reliefs available to registered pension schemes.

Many of these schemes were set up before 6 April 2006 as 'unapproved schemes'. They became important since the introduction of the 'earnings cap' in 1989 and had their own tax treatment which was broadly set out in the Inland Revenue Guide entitled 'The Tax Treatment of Top-up Pension Schemes'. The benefits can be funded in advance by the employer (in which case the scheme will usually be established under a trust), or the benefits can be unfunded (in which case the arrangement will usually be contractual between the employer and the individual). The terms 'funded unapproved retirement benefit schemes' (FURBS) and 'unfunded retirement benefit schemes' (UURBS) became established.

From 6 April 2006 there will be no tax-advantages to EFRB schemes. HMRC will treat them in the same way as any other arrangement operated by an employer to provide benefits for employees.

Despite the fact that lump sum death benefits may be payable through discretionary provisions in scheme rules, there will be no IHT exemption.

However, the pre-6 April 2006 IHT treatment will continue to apply to the portion of the fund accrued up to 6 April 2006, as described below:

(1)   Where the documentation governing the arrangement provides for the lump sum to be paid at the discretion of the trustees (in the case of a scheme set

up under trust), or the employer (in the case of a contractual arrangement), an IHT liability will not normally arise, so long as the range of potential beneficiaries does not include the legal personal representatives. (If the legal personal representatives are included, there may be an IHT 'gifts with reservation' charge.)

(2) It has been confirmed by HMRC that if an individual reaches the age of 75 and decides not to take his benefits at that time, the benefits can remain subject to the trust and can be paid free of IHT on his subsequent death. However, having taken that decision at the age of 75, it will never subsequently be possible for the individual to buy an annuity at some stage in the future should his circumstances change.

SECTION 11 MISCELLANEOUS

A 'Buy and sell' agreement

14.110 It is sometimes the practice for partners or shareholder directors of companies to enter into an agreement (known as a 'buy and sell' agreement) whereby, in the event of the death before retirement of one of them, the deceased's personal representatives are obliged to sell and the survivors are obliged to purchase the deceased's business interest or shares, with funds for the purchase frequently being provided by means of appropriate life assurance policies.

This arrangement, and its variants, are considered in more detail in Chapter 17. However, it is appropriate to state in this chapter that, in HMRC's view, such an agreement, requiring as it does a sale and purchase and not merely conferring an option to sell or buy, is a binding contract for sale within section 113 of IHTA 1984[1]. As a result, IHT business property relief will not be available on the business interest or shares.

B Valuation

14.111 There are a number of special rules applying to certain kinds of property, eg life policies, debts, options[2], but the general principle of valuation for IHT is that the value at any time of any property is taken to be the open market value[3], with no reduction on the grounds that the whole property is hypothetically to be placed on the market at one time.

In determining the open-market price of unquoted shares or securities[4] it is assumed that a prudent prospective purchaser has all the information he might reasonably require if he were proposing to purchase them from a willing vendor by private treaty and at arm's length.

1 See Section 4D2, **14.37–14.38**.
2 See generally IHTA 1984, ss 160–170.
3 Section 160.
4 Section 168.

In valuing property, no account is taken of the value of property owned by others unless it is 'related property'[1]. Property is related to the property comprised in a person's estate if either (1) it is comprised in the estate of his spouse; or (2) it is, or has been within the preceding five years, the property of a charity, charitable trust or one of the political national or public bodies to which exempt transfers may be made. Where a person transfers related property, he is regarded as transferring the value of his proportion of the total value of all the related property. Thus, for example, where husband and wife own 40% each of shares in a company and husband transfers all his shares to his son by gift, he is treated as having transferred property equal in value to one-half of an 80% holding and not a single 40% holding.

C   Domicile and residence

14.112   For persons domiciled in the UK, IHT applies to all of their property wherever it is situated; whilst for persons domiciled outside the UK, it applies to any property situated in the UK. Domicile has its usual meaning, ie the country of permanent home, birth, dependency or choice. However, a person who would not under the general law be regarded as domiciled in the UK may nevertheless, for IHT purposes, be deemed to be domiciled at the time of a transfer if:

(1)   he was domiciled in the UK on or after 10 December 1974 within the three years immediately preceding the transfer (ie three years' domicile outside the UK is needed to acquire a foreign domicile); or

(2)   he was resident in the UK on or after 10 December 1974, in not less than 17 of the 20 years of assessment ending with the year of assessment in which the transfer was made[2].

For the purposes of (2), 'resident' has the same meaning as for income tax purposes.

1   Policies under seal

14.113   The general rule is that a chose in action, such as a life policy, is situated in the country where it is properly recoverable or can be enforced[3]. Thus, if an individual who is not domiciled in the UK owns a policy issued by a life office in the UK, the policy moneys would, in the normal course of events, be regarded as situated in the UK and be liable to IHT. However, if the person beneficially entitled to the chose in action is domiciled outside the UK and the property is situated outside the UK, the property is 'excluded property' for the purposes of IHT[4], as stated above. The general rule stated above does not apply to specialty

---

1   Section 161.
2   Section 267.
3   See Dicey and Morris *The Conflict of Laws* (11th edn) vol 2, p 907.
4   IHTA 1984, s 6(1).

debts (which will include a life policy effected under seal), in that a debt due on a specialty is treated as situated in the country where the specialty itself is situated. It is possible therefore for a non-UK domiciliary to avoid IHT by ensuring that the policy is effected under seal.

D   Payment of tax[1]

14.114   Generally, IHT is due six months after the end of the month in which the chargeable transfer is made or, in the case of a transfer made after 5 April and before 1 October in any year otherwise than on death, at the end of April in the next year[2].

As previously stated, the primary liability to pay the tax lies on the transferor for lifetime gifts, the personal representatives of the deceased for transfers on death, the trustees where the transfer is of settled property and the donee when a PET or a chargeable transfer become liable for IHT or for additional IHT upon the death of the transferor. If tax is not paid by the due date it can be recovered from the donee or other persons who come into possession of the property trans-ferred[3]. A right of recovery of tax from a transferor's spouse is provided but the sum recoverable is limited to the market value of the transfer when it was made to the spouse[4].

There are provisions for the optional payment of IHT in ten annual instal-ments[5] on certain property passing on death, notably land of any description, shares or securities giving control (as defined) of a company and other shares or securities not quoted on a recognised stock exchange in respect of which certain conditions are satisfied. The provisions apply also to (1) lifetime transfers where the IHT is paid by the transferee; and (2) settled property, where the property is retained by the trustees. Interest is chargeable on the whole of the unpaid tax at each instalment date; the rate with effect from 6 May 2001 is 4%[6].

Instalments of IHT are to be free of interest, however, where the value trans-ferred represents land which qualifies for agricultural relief, a business or shares or securities in a company (including land and buildings if held as business assets).

Where any tax or interest is unpaid, an 'HMRC charge' may be imposed for the due amount on any property to which the tax is attributable by its transfer; and any property comprised in a settlement where the charge arises in connection with the settlement[7].

1   Sections 226–232.
2   Section 226.
3   Section 199.
4   Section 203.
5   Section 227.
6   See Inland Revenue Press Release, 24 April 2001.
7   IHTA 1984, s 237.

CHAPTER 15

Estate planning and life assurance

SUMMARY

Section 1   Planning for IHT with life assurance   **15.1**

Section 2   Declaring trusts of policies   **15.19**

Section 3   Life office specimen trust forms   **15.20**

Section 4   Policy trust wordings   **15.27**

Chapter 9 dealt with the general principles and fundamentals of settlements and trusts; Chapter 14 dealt with the general principles and structure of inheritance tax (IHT). This chapter considers IHT, IHT mitigation, the relationship between IHT and estate planning using life assurance, the appropriate policies, and the appropriate trusts to consider in each case. Reference is made to the rationale behind the common specimen trust forms of life offices and also to specific trust wordings which may be required.

Individuals (and their advisers) should consider estate planning in order to minimise the IHT liability on their estates[1] and to create certainty as to the holding and devolution of their personal assets upon death. Further, a grant of representation will not normally be issued (unless the estate is '*excepted*')[2] until the HMRC account giving full details of the deceased's estate is lodged and any IHT due has been paid[3]. This can often cause financial difficulties and may require, for example, a loan to be taken for this purpose. There is an agreement between HMRC and the British Bankers' and Building Societies' Association that participating institutions will accept instructions from personal representatives to transfer sums standing to the credit of the deceased direct to HMRC in payment of inheritance tax before the issue of the grant. This is of considerable practical help where the personal representatives do not have ready access to other funds outside the estate, such as life policy proceeds written in trust.

---

1 'Estate' is defined by IHTA 1984, s 5 as the aggregate of all property to which an individual is beneficially entitled (not including excluded property), less liabilities. See Chapter 14.

2 Capital Transfer Tax (Delivery of Accounts) Regulations 1981, SI 1981/880 (as amended). See Inland Revenue Press Release 14 February 2000.

3 Supreme Court Act 1981, s 109(1).

However, despite this, the use of life assurance policies effected to cover the IHT liability is still very important. It does not in itself ensure that the right sum of money is in the right hands at the right time, because (if the policy is subject to a trust) the policy proceeds will be paid to the trustees (for the benefit of the beneficiaries) whereas the IHT liability must be met by the deceased's personal representatives, out of the estate. Quite often, however, the policy proceeds will subsequently be paid by the trustees to the beneficiaries which will effectively replace the tax which has been paid out of the estate.

This chapter looks at some wider aspects of the role and use of life assurance in estate planning. It considers various methods of reducing an individual's estate for IHT purposes, of ensuring that capital growth is outside the estate and of allowing retention of, control over and access to some of the investments made. Central to many of these methods is the use of trusts and settlements and the final section considers the specimen trust forms provided by life offices, some of the more common trust wordings which may be appropriate, and their effect.

SECTION I   PLANNING FOR IHT WITH LIFE ASSURANCE

A   Importance of life assurance

15.1   Before considering particular plans, it is appropriate to summarise some of the reasons why life assurance policies are so important in estate planning:

(1)   A policy can provide funds on the death of the life assured to meet tax or other liabilities which may arise at that time.

(2)   The proceeds are payable in cash and if the policy is qualifying and written under trust, payment can be made free of income tax and capital gains tax to the recipient (note that the underlying funds may have been subject to corporation tax) and may be paid free of IHT. (There may be IHT to pay as a result of a potentially exempt transfer (PET) proving chargeable or on death within seven years of a chargeable lifetime transfer: see further Chapter 14.)

(3)   A life policy effected on a with-profits or unit-linked basis can provide capital appreciation which may not be taxed in the assured's hands (but note the possible taxation of the underlying funds).

(4)   A person wishing to divest himself of capital over a number of years may do so very effectively by paying premiums, for example, within the £3,000 annual exemption or the normal expenditure out of income exemption to effect a life policy under trust.

(5)   Trusts of life policies may be created quite simply at the outset of the assurance, and the trustees may prevent minor beneficiaries from having control of gifted funds until later in their lifetime.

(6)   Payment of the proceeds on the death of the life assured under a trust policy

can generally be made without waiting for grant of representation and may, in the case of Married Women's Property Act (MWPA) 1882 trusts, provide protection from creditors generally.

(7)   A life policy is a flexible investment which, generally, can be surrendered, sold, used as security for a loan, gifted, charged, made paid up or varied.

(8)   Finally, and most importantly of all, life assurance can provide protection for an estate owner's dependants in the event of his premature death.

B   Estate planning

15.2   There are several things which an individual may do, both during his lifetime and by making provisions in his will, to mitigate IHT. Since the introduction of capital transfer tax (CTT) (the predecessor to IHT), various schemes designed to reduce the value of an individual's estate or transfer assets without an IHT charge have been promulgated. Many of these schemes have been artificial, and others of such an esoteric nature that many an individual (hereafter referred to as an 'investor') has been reluctant to commit himself to the convoluted and often circular transactions necessary to achieve the desired aims.

It is important to bear in mind the result of a series of decisions by the courts, notably *W T Ramsay Ltd v IRC*[1] and *Furniss v Dawson*[2]. The essential principle emerging from these (and other) cases is that where there is a preordained series of transactions or a single composite transaction, which includes steps which have no commercial (business) purpose apart from the avoidance of a liability to tax, the steps inserted for no commercial purpose may be ignored. More will be mentioned of this principle later.

Life assurance can play a vital part in conserving estates by ensuring that funds are available to replace the capital that would otherwise have been lost as a result of paying the tax. Where no, or only restricted business property relief is available, life assurance may be the only means of helping small firms and private companies to stay in business. Similarly, where agricultural property relief is restricted or is not available at all, a life assurance policy could be the only way of making certain that funds are available to ensure that the agricultural assets pass intact to the desired beneficiaries (see **14.34–14.36**).

Before deciding on the appropriate type of policy or policies, sums assured and other arrangements to minimise the charge to IHT and meet the IHT liability, it is necessary to know the investor's intentions for disposing of his estate upon his death, of any substantial lifetime transfers he may wish to make and his current (and likely future) requirements for income and capital. It is also necessary to consider the beneficiaries whom the investor wishes to benefit at these

1   [1979] 3 All ER 213; affd [1981] 1 All ER 865, HL.
2   [1982] STC 267; affd [1984] STC 153, HL. See also *Craven v White* [1988] STC 476, HL and *Fitzwilliam v IRC* [1993] STC 502, HL, *IRC v McGuckian* [1998] STC 908, HL and *MacNiven v Westmoreland Investments Ltd* [2001] STC 237, HL.

times and to consider the most suitable assets, in terms of tax efficiency and personal preference, to use for estate planning purposes. A balance will usually have to be found between the competing interests of the desire to pass property as tax efficiently as possible to an investor's children (or other desired beneficiaries) and the need to provide income for the investor and his spouse or registered civil partner for the remainder of their lives. For the remainder of this chapter, spouse includes registered civil partner.

If one is solely considering the reduction of IHT, it may be advantageous to equalise the estates of husband and wife or registered civil partners during their lifetime so that each can pass up to the amount of the nil rate band of their estate on death by means of his or her will in favour of the children (or other potential beneficiaries), rather than leaving the whole estate on death to the surviving spouse, with the aggregated estates passing ultimately to the children, (or others), on the death of the surviving husband or wife or registered civil partner. Any tax on the second death is thereby reduced and could be provided for by means of a joint lives last survivor policy.

However, it may not be possible to do this in individual cases, if, for example, there are insufficient assets remaining for the surviving spouse to afford to maintain the required lifestyle.

In estate planning, whether estates should be shared and in what proportion will depend on the circumstances; in particular on the size of and the assets comprising the estates, the situation of the respective parties and their intentions. There is no simple answer and each case must be considered according to its own facts.

Discretionary will trust

15.3 If the position of the surviving spouse is a concern, an alternative use of the nil rate band is to leave by will the unused amount of any available nil rate band to a discretionary trust for the benefit of a wide class of beneficiaries which could include the spouse, children and grandchildren. As the surviving spouse would be a beneficiary he or she could therefore receive income or capital at the discretion of the trustees. (In practice, many testators leave a non-binding expression of wishes to the trustees expressing their desire that the trust should provide primarily for the spouse as his or her needs require during his or her lifetime.) As the trust is discretionary, the value of the trust would not pass into the surviving spouse's estate. Income would only form part of the surviving spouse's total income to the extent that it was actually distributed and the distribution of capital within ten years would not give rise to an IHT charge[1]. If the survivor is likely to survive the tenth anniversary of the discretionary trust, consideration would have to be given as to whether it would be better to pay the principal charge[2] at

---

1   This is because the exit charges before the ten-year anniversary are calculated by reference to the initial value of the trust fund, together with any chargeable transfers made by the settlor in the preceding seven years. If that total does not exceed the nil rate band, no tax is payable. See Chapter 14, Section 6C.
2   See Chapter 14, Section 6C.

the ten-year anniversary or to break the trust before that time. The decision may well depend upon the likely value of the property within the trust at the time of the ten-yearly charge (as the rate of IHT charge will depend, in part, upon the value of the property). It should be noted, however, that, on current rates, the maximum charge is 6% of the value.

Example

A man has an estate of £500,000 and his wife has assets of her own totalling £400,000; neither of them have made any previous chargeable transfers. They have children but do not propose to make any substantial lifetime gifts to them.

(i) If the estates are passed to the survivor on the first death and then on to the children on the death of the surviving husband or wife, the position (assuming the current IHT rate on death of 40%) would be as follows:

	Husband		*Wife*
Estates	£500,000		£400,000
IHT on first death	NIL		NIL
Total in hands of surviving spouse		£900,000	
IHT on second death		£246,000	
Total net estate to children		£654,000	

The appropriate policy to provide for the IHT in this case would be a last survivor whole life assurance. The proceeds would be payable on the death of the second of them (ie when the joint estate finally passes to the children) and if the policy is written under trust for the benefit of the children (assuming the premium payments were exempt), the proceeds should be payable free of IHT.

(ii) If the wills are redrawn in such a way so that on the first death the available nil rate band is left subject to a discretionary trust with the balance of the estate passing to the surviving spouse, the position (assuming the husband dies first) would be as follows:

Husband's estate	£500,000
Less nil rate band to discretionary trust	£285,000
Balance to wife	£215,000
Wife's subsequent estate on death	£400,000
Plus inheritance from husband	£215,000
Total estate	£615,000
Less nil rate band	£285,000
Taxable estate	£330,000
IHT payable	£132,000
Amount passing to children	£483,000
Plus amount in discretionary trust	£285,000
Total available	£768,000

The amount passing to the children in this case is £96,800 more, due to the nil rate band being utilised in full.

15.4   Despite the tax saving possibilities (as illustrated above) from maximum utilisation of the nil rate band, it is not always possible to take advantage of this type of planning, particularly where the major asset of the joint estates is the family home and there are insufficient other assets to be able to use the nil rate band in full.

From 22 March 2006, all gifts into trusts created under a will are treated as gifts into a discretionary trust for inheritance tax purposes unless the trust falls within any of the following three criteria:

(1)   it was created for the benefit of a minor child who will become absolutely entitled to the trust property on attaining age 18;

(2)   it constitutes an Immediate Post Death Interest (IPDI) as set out in section 49A of the Inheritance Tax Act 1984. Briefly, to qualify as an IPDI, the settlement must have been created by the will of the deceased or under the intestacy rules, the life tenant must have become beneficially entitled to the interest in possession on the death of the testator or the intestate and the 'bereaved minor' rules as set out in section 71A of the Inheritance Tax Act 1984 do not apply, nor is the trust for the benefit of a disabled person. These latter two conditions have to apply for the whole of the period that the individual in question had the interest in possession; or

(3)   it was created for the benefit of a disabled person as described in section 89 of the Inheritance Tax Act 1984.

Thus, any settlement not falling within these three criteria will be liable to the principal and exit charges in the same way as a discretionary trust.

2   The family home

15.5   As mentioned above, a significant practical problem when considering IHT planning is often that the principal asset is the family home, which is owned jointly by husband and wife or by registered civil partners. Where husband and wife own the home as joint tenants, before any planning can be undertaken it will be necessary to sever the joint tenancy to create a tenancy in common. Once this has been achieved, each spouse may then leave their interest in the home to, for example, the children. This strategy may work perfectly well but it also could cause problems of a very practical nature. Assume a husband dies first and leaves his share of the home to his married son. In the event of the son subsequently getting divorced, the value of his interest in the home would be taken into account in the divorce settlement. He would also be entitled to move back into the home and, presumably, move in any new partner and/or children which might well not be to the liking of his mother. In the worst scenario it may even be possible for the son to subsequently force a sale of the home, leaving his mother looking for a new place to live.

There are, of course, other planning possibilities available involving the private residence but these should not be considered without taking specialist legal advice. The gifts with reservation of benefit legislation (see **14.11** and **14.12**) is a major problem in this area and this legislation was significantly tightened in the Finance Act 1999 following the decision in *Ingram v IRC*[1] and in the Finance Act 2004 following the decision in *IRC v Greenstock*[2].

In addition, since 6 April 2005, not only is there the gifts with reservation of benefit legislation to be aware of but there is also the pre-owned assets tax legislation to take into account – see **14.13**.

3   Business assets

15.6   The planning of estates will need different consideration when the estates comprise business assets such as shares in a private trading company, a professional or trading partnership or a farm (any of which may attract either business property relief or agricultural property relief – see **14.34–14.38**). In those circumstances, children, other relations and non-family members might well have contributed considerably to the wealth which has been accumulated and may feel quite strongly that part of that wealth should find its way into their hands – especially if the principal estate owner is the first of the parents to die. With such estates it might be wise for more assets to be passed to the children on the first death, or a planned programme of lifetime transfers considered, although the capital gains tax (CGT) implications of lifetime gifting should be borne in mind. Life assurance can assist in such planning by providing funds to enable the surviving spouse to have an adequate income. In any event, assets qualifying for 100% business or agricultural property relief should ideally not be left to exempt persons, such as the surviving spouse, as this course of action effectively wastes the relief. Such assets should be left to non-exempt persons such as children, grandchildren or perhaps to a discretionary trust under which the surviving spouse could be a potential beneficiary. Another provision to consider is to effect a registered pension plan (depending on the business situation) which could provide dependant's income benefits after death. The contributions are tax effective as tax relief should be available subject to HMRC's normal requirements (ie the 'wholly and exclusively' test[3] see Chapter 14, Section 3). If the death benefits payable from a registered pension arrangement are held subject to a discretionary trust, in general there will not be a charge to IHT in respect of the death benefits[4].

If the premiums paid towards the trust policies mentioned in the various situations above are not exempt, under the normal expenditure out of income exemption or the £3,000 annual exemption, the tax treatment of the premiums will be as set out at **14.66**.

C   Other uses of life assurance

I   Estate planning – lifetime transfers

15.7   In addition to providing funds to meet IHT liabilities when they arise, another role for life assurance in estate planning is to mitigate the IHT ultimately

---

1   [1999] STC 37.
2   [2003] STC 822.
3   ICTA 1988, s 74(1)(a).
4   IHTA 1984, ss 151, 210; SP10/86 (9 July 1986) set out in Appendix 10.

payable through a reduction of the individual's estate. This is achieved by creating a medium for the tax-effective transfer to others of funds which will achieve capital growth in the estate of the recipient, not that of the transferor. A common additional objective of the transferor is to retain control over, and have access to, the investment. A common misconception is that this type of planning will provide the transferor with an income in the true sense of the word – it will not. Life assurance policies are non-income producing investments. The marketing material of many policies, notably the single premium bond, states that they provide an 'income' for the policyholder. This is not actually income, but a return of capital, (hence, the term 'income' often being presented in inverted commas in the marketing material). Some of the range of available options are described below.

(a) Discounted gift plans

15.8 Discounted gift plans aim to provide an immediate reduction in the investor's estate for IHT purposes; a regular tax-efficient income for the investor and death benefits for nominated beneficiaries which are free of IHT.

(I) PETA PLANS

15.9 Before the introduction of inheritance tax these types of plans were well known. The investor purchased two plans: a pure endowment (ie without death benefit, the benefit only being payable on survival) under which a fixed 'income' (usually within the 5% tax-deferred entitlements so as not to attract a charge to higher rate tax)[1] was taken, and a term assurance which was written under a flexible power of appointment trust to ensure that the sum assured (which was equal to the bid value of the units under the pure endowment) was out of the investor's estate. For IHT purposes, the transfer of value, which would, under the legislation in force before 22 March 2006, have been a PET, would be the sum of the total investment into the plan less the value of the investor's retained interest under the pure endowment policy, at the time of effecting the arrangement. (This will be calculated on actuarial principles, depending on age, sex and health at the time the trust is declared.)

Following the tax avoidance line of cases referred to above and the Finance Act 1986, these plans were thought to have been rendered wholly ineffective for IHT purposes. The effect of the Finance Act 1986[2] is that such an arrangement (where the benefits accruing to the donee under a life assurance policy are measured by reference to benefits accruing to the donor under that or another policy) is thought to be treated as a gift with reservation of benefit.

However, similar plans are now once again available in the market. The companies which offer these plans have tried to avoid the effect of the Finance Act 1986 by having a *fixed* sum assured under the term assurance (which would be the value of the original investment of capital in the endowment policy) rather than one which varies with reference to the value of the endowment policy.

1 ITTOIA 2005, s 465 and Chapter 13.
2 Finance Act 1986, s 102 and Sch 20, para 7.

(II) CAPITAL REDEMPTION BOND 'CARVE OUT' SCHEMES

15.10 Capital redemption bonds may be used to avoid the gift with reservation of benefit provisions of paragraph 7 of Schedule 20 of the Finance Act 1986, which refer to a policy on the *life* of the donor or his spouse. A capital redemption bond is not written on a life, but is a contract of insurance for a fixed term, and should not therefore fall within the above provisions. Under the plan, the bond is written subject to a trust under which the right to regular withdrawals is retained by the investor absolutely, whilst all other rights and benefits are written subject to a flexible power of appointment trust, under which the investor is excluded as a beneficiary. As the bond is effected through an offshore company, the investment benefits from a tax-free growth of fund (apart from possible withholding taxes). As with the PETA plan concept, the discount is arrived at by calculating the present day actuarial value of the settlor's right to enjoy the stipulated level of regular withdrawals based on his age at the time the policy is effected and his state of health. This amount is outside the settlor's estate from commencement.

In recent years, variants of this plan have appeared on the market where the underlying asset is a life assurance policy. This is achieved by the carve out being over the trust rather than over the individual property.

(III) REVERTER TO SETTLOR PLANS

15.11 Under these plans, a series of endowment assurances are effected which are set to mature at yearly intervals. These policies cannot be surrendered. The policies are all written subject to trusts under which the right to the maturity proceeds of the policies is retained by the investor for his own benefit but should the investor die before the maturity date of a policy, the death benefits are held for the remaining beneficiaries. Each year, a policy will mature and the proceeds will be paid to the investor which he can use as 'income'. Again the discount is calculated by reference to the actuarial value of the policy proceeds which the investor is likely to receive back by way of maturing policies.

Traditionally, all the above plans have used interest in possession trusts to take advantage of the fact that the initial gift involved in creating the trust was a PET. However, with effect from 22 March 2006, all transfers into such trusts will be chargeable transfers and thus there may be inheritance tax to pay at the outset if the amount of the gift (together with any previous lifetime transfers made within the last seven years) is more than the nil rate band in force at the date of the gift. In any event, if the amount of the chargeable lifetime transfer is in excess of £10,000 or the settlor's cumulative total of chargeable transfers within the last ten years has exceeded £40,000, HMRC will need to be notified of the transfer by completion of Form IHT 100. In addition, the trust may also be liable to the principal charge on the ten-year anniversary, depending on the value of the trust property at that date, and the exit charge when capital leaves the settlement.

It may be that, from 22 March 2006, gifts into these arrangements will be restricted so that the amount of the initial transfer is within the nil rate band. Care will also be needed regarding the ten-yearly charges. It could be that the use of absolute or bare trusts in connection with these arrangements will become more widespread as transfers into trusts of this nature will continue to be PETs.

(b) Inheritance trusts

15.12 There are a wide variety of these arrangements which are known generically as 'inheritance trusts', and more commonly as 'gift and loan' schemes. The basic principle of these arrangements is that the investor establishes a settlement with a nominal sum, generally in favour of his children, and appoints additional trustees. The investor then lends a lump sum to the trustees of the settlement, expressed to be free of interest and repayable on demand (usually evidenced by a deed of loan agreement). The trustees invest the lump sum as a single premium in a unit-linked life assurance policy, typically a single premium bond, on the life of the investor (or the beneficiaries). By part surrender, the trustees withdraw from the single premium bond each year (for up to 20 years) a sum usually within the 5% pa tax deferred allowance[1] of the original investment to repay the loan. Any amount withdrawn in excess of the 5% allowance may result in a higher rate tax charge on the investor (as settlor of the trust) or possibly on the trustees if the withdrawal occurs in a tax year subsequent to the death of the settlor.

The investor thus receives an 'income' whilst the capital sum and any growth upon it (less the amount of the outstanding loan) is held as part of the trust fund for the beneficiaries outside the investor's estate and therefore free of IHT. On the death of the investor/settlor, the outstanding loan will be paid to the personal representatives and form part of the estate for IHT purposes. The initial gift is a transfer of value which will usually be covered by the £3,000 annual exemption. If it is not, it will be a PET if made before 22 March 2006, which will only prove chargeable if the investor dies within seven years of the declaration of trust[2].

There has been some concern about the efficacy of such arrangements due to section 102 of the Finance Act 1986 which provides that where an individual 'disposes of any property by way of gift' and either it is not bona fide assumed by the donee or not enjoyed to the entire exclusion or virtually to the entire exclusion of the donor, then it constitutes a gift with reservation of benefit and will be treated as property to which the donor was beneficially entitled immediately before his death.

It may be argued that such an arrangement does not constitute a 'gift' as it is not given freely (in as much as the loan is repayable), although HMRC has expressed the view[3] that an interest-free loan is not a transfer of value for IHT purposes, but may be a gift, the gifted element being the interest forgone. They have stated further that an interest-free loan in itself is not a gift with a reservation of benefit but it may be if, for example, (1) there is a statutory provision to this effect, or (2) there is some other arrangement between the lender and the borrower related to the interest-free loan which has the effect of making the loan into a gift with reservation of benefit. Such an arrangement might include the use

---

1 ITTOIA 2005, s 507 and Chapter 13.
2 See Chapter 14.
3 See letter dated 6 April 1987 from the Life Insurance Council (LIC) of the ABI to all members of the LIC following clarification from the Inland Revenue, LIC Circular no 60/87.

and enjoyment of other property or arrangements which were in some way *collateral* to the interest-free loan.

15.13   The IHT regime clearly contemplates the situation whereby a donor lends money to the trustees of a settlement. Schedule 20[1] to the Finance Act 1986, which supplements section 102, contains a provision relating to settled gifts[2]. It provides that where there is a gift into settlement, the property comprised in the settlement shall be treated as the property comprised in the gift and where property comprised in the settlement is directly or indirectly derived from a loan made by the donor to the trustees of the settlement, it shall be treated as property originally comprised in the gift.

The effect of this could be that everything in the settlement at the material date (the donor's death) is treated as derived from property originally comprised in the gift and could, therefore, bring the loan and the entire growth on any policy into the gift with reservation of benefit provisions.

However, having said that, such arrangements have been quite commonly entered into since the advent of IHT and, as far as the authors are aware, the Capital Taxes Office has yet to mount a successful challenge to them using the above legislation.

There are several variations of this arrangement in existence, all trying to avoid the difficulties stated above. Three of the common variants are: (a) gift and bare trust; (b) gift and flexible trust using two policies; (c) loan-only scheme using a flexible trust.

(a)   *Gift and bare trust.* This follows the basic arrangement described above. The rationale of having a bare (or absolute) trust is that it falls outside the definition of 'settlement' for IHT purposes[3] and so should not be caught by the anti-avoidance provisions, which refer to a gift into *settlement*. However, it may fall within the 'collateral arrangements' argument referred to above. This variant has not generally been popular in any event, as the trend has been to prefer power of appointment trusts, hence the second variant. However, for trusts created on or after 22 March 2006, this may change.

(b)   *Gift and flexible trust using two policies.* The 'gift into settlement' is nominal, being either a capital sum or a single premium bond for a small initial premium. The settlor then appoints additional trustees and makes a substantial loan to the trust. The trustees invest the loan in a single premium bond, usually on the lives of the beneficiaries. The companies offering this variant take the view that this is outside the effect of paragraph 5(4) of Schedule 20, as the 'gift into settlement' is the initial nominal sum (in which the investor can have no possible beneficial interest under the terms of the trust), with the loan being completely separate, therefore keeping the growth on the single premium bond purchased with the money loaned to the trust out of the gift with reservation of benefit provisions.

---

1   FA 1986.
2   Schedule 20, para 5(4).
3   IHTA 1984, s 43.

(c) *Loan-only scheme using a flexible trust.* The rationale behind this variant is that section 102 refers to a 'disposal of property by way of gift' and that if there is no gift, the gift with reservation of benefit provisions have nothing to bite on. The settlor merely makes a loan to the trustees who then use the loan monies in order to purchase a single premium bond from which they then take withdrawals to repay the loan.

All of these schemes have traditionally used power of appointment trusts and so the comments made at the end of **15.7** also apply. Generally however, for arrangements of this sort, as the initial gift tends to be very small (or non-existent in the case of the loan only schemes) the gift would normally be within the £3,000 annual exemption and thus there would be no chargeable lifetime transfer. The main issue would therefore appear to be the principal charge at the ten-yearly anniversary. This would be calculated by reference to the value of the trust property at that time less the outstanding loan. Again, for larger amounts, use of an absolute trust may become more popular to avoid this potential charge.

(c) Retained interest trust

15.14 The purpose of this arrangement is to take advantage of the investor being able to take the full 5% annual allowance as 'income', until his interest is exhausted, whilst being able to gift away a percentage of the capital sum. The investor effects a single premium bond and carves out two separate interests in trust under it: an interest for himself absolutely (the retained or the donor's part) and the donee's part which is held on flexible trusts for his chosen beneficiaries. The investor is excluded from the donee's part and so there is no gift with reservation in relation to that part.

The 5% tax deferred withdrawal provisions refer to the initial investment in the single premium bond, not to the proportional part of the policy which the investor retains under his part of the trust. Therefore, at any time, the investor can ask the trustees to pay part of his entitlement. To be tax efficient, they would normally do this from the 5% annual entitlement, and such trusts often contain a provision to this effect. All the withdrawals must be deducted from the donor's part, which may, therefore, if the donor's part grows at a lesser rate than the total withdrawal, erode. In this way, the donor's part may be progressively reduced, or even eventually extinguished, leaving an increasing proportion of the bond in the gifted part. Once the donor's part has been completely exhausted, there can be no further payments to the investor, by way of withdrawal or otherwise, as this would constitute a gift with reservation and therefore not be IHT effective.

Prior to 22 March 2006, assuming the trust was an interest in possession trust, the transfer would have been a PET and if the death of the donor occurred within seven years, the PET would prove chargeable and the usual provisions would apply (see Chapter 14, Section 3). The balance, if any, of the donor's part, would be paid to the investor's estate and would be aggregated with his estate for IHT purposes. From 22 March 2006 onwards, gifts into such trusts would be chargeable lifetime transfers unless the trust used was an absolute trust.

It can thus be seen that the true value of this type of arrangement lies with the ability to take withdrawals from the total original investment thus enabling a greater 'income' to be enjoyed. The IHT benefits are no different from the settlor simply effecting two bonds, one for his own benefit and the other in trust for the selected beneficiaries.

2   Life policies as trustee investments

15.15   Traditionally most trusts have invested in portfolios of quoted securities although this has perhaps always been a slightly questionable policy, particularly in the case of smaller trusts where a collective investment scheme or a single premium bond could offer all the advantages of diversification and professional fund management at a reasonable cost. However, since the passing of the Trustee Act 2000 which imposed on trustees the duty to ensure the suitability of any investments they make, the arguments in favour of this type of investment have increased. Furthermore, the above Act now gives wide investment powers to virtually all trustees and thus there should no longer be a question about whether or not trustees have the power to make investments in life assurance policies.

In considering insurance policies five factors need to be taken into account:

(1)   *Insurable interest.* The trustees will need to exhibit an insurable interest in the life of a beneficiary on whose life the policy is to be effected.

(2)   *Investment powers.* This should no longer be a problem as modern trusts will generally have sufficiently wide investment powers to invest in such policies and the Trustee Act 2000 now confers wide investment powers on all trustees unless their powers are specifically restricted by the terms of the trust.

(3)   *Power of advancement.* It is advisable (as most modern trusts do) to extend the statutory power of advancement under section 32 of the Trustee Act 1925 to apply to the whole of the trust fund (the statutory power only extends to one half of the trust fund). The trustees may then exercise this power either from time to time or on a more regular basis to make capital payments to a beneficiary.

(4)   *Other taxation consequences.* As a single premium bond is a non-qualifying policy a chargeable event could arise on its encashment or if withdrawals in excess of the 5% annual entitlements are taken. If this happens then any gains arising are assessable to tax in the manner described later in this section, and in more detail in Chapter 13.

(5)   *Life tenant.* If there is a life tenant such an investment may not be appropriate as no income would be produced and capital could not normally be advanced to him. Even if a power exists to advance capital to a life tenant, care should be exercised – see later in this section.

A single premium bond as a trustee investment has the advantage of much simplified administration from the trustees' viewpoint. As a life assurance policy, it is outside the scope of capital gains tax and thus there is no need for the trustees to concern themselves with the trustees' annual CGT exemption or with the complexities of taper relief. Furthermore, as a non-income producing asset, completion of the trust tax return is again simplified.

15.16   The ability for trustees to utilise the 5% tax deferred annual entitlement as a means of making tax-efficient payments to beneficiaries is also a big advantage, especially when one bears in mind the changes to the system of dividend tax credits from 6 April 1999 which affect discretionary and accumulation and maintenance trusts and may result in a serious reduction in net income for beneficiaries where the original source of that income is dividends.

The tax treatment of any such capital payments in the hands of beneficiaries should also be considered. In certain situations, capital payments out of a trust (eg 5% withdrawals from a single premium bond) may be treated by HMRC as adopting the nature of income for income tax purposes, in the hands of the recipient beneficiary, based on the decision in *Brodie's Trustees v IRC*[1]. In this case, the trustees of a will held property upon trust to pay the income to the testator's widow for life with a provision that if, in any year, the income did not amount to £4,000, the trustees were to use capital to ensure that no less than £4,000 was paid to the widow. On the occasions when this happened, HMRC contended that these capital payments were made to satisfy an income entitlement and should thus be taxed as income in the widow's hands. This view was subsequently supported by the Court. However, this should be contrasted with the later case of *Stevenson (Inspector of Taxes) v Wishart*[2].

This case concerned regular monthly capital payments made from a discretionary trust to the beneficiary who was in a private nursing home. In making them, the aim of the trustees was to meet the cost of maintaining the patient, including medical and other expenses. HMRC maintained that such recurrent payments were paid for an income purpose and were therefore income in the hands of the beneficiary and thus liable to income tax and they raised assessments accordingly. In disagreeing with this stance the court distinguished its ruling from the precedent set in the *Brodie case*. In *Stevenson v Wishart*, the payments were deemed to be wholly of a capital nature and, apart from their recurrence, there was nothing to indicate that the payments were to be seen as income. It was suggested at the time that the case was only of limited application although experience does not seem to have borne this suggestion out. The decision in this case appears to indicate that where trustees are not specifically required to augment income out of trust capital, regular payments of capital to a beneficiary from a discretionary trust or an accumulation and maintenance trust should present no income tax problems, provided they have powers of advancement and exercise their discretion in making any such payments.

15.17   When considering interest in possession trusts it should be borne in mind that under such trusts there is an individual or individuals who are entitled to the income produced by the trust. If the trustees select a single premium bond as their investment, this is a non-income producing asset and thus any trustees

---

1   [1933] 17 TC 432.
2   [1987] STC 266.

contemplating this course of action should ensure that the trust confers powers on the trustees to make advancements of capital to the person or persons with the interest in possession.

For interest in possession trusts, however, the possibility of an attack by HMRC using the *Brodie* decision remains if regular capital payments are made to the life tenant of the trust. If a single premium bond is contemplated as a trustee investment in these circumstances it is recommended that the trustees take irregular withdrawals of income at irregular intervals in order to reduce the chances of such an attack.

The final point to consider is the tax treatment of the bond when it is encashed. Prior to 18 March 1998 where a policy was held in trust, any gains arising on the occurrence of a chargeable event were assessed on the creator of the trust. Thus, if the chargeable event occurred in a tax year following the death of the creator, provided there was no one beneficiary who was absolutely entitled to the trust fund at that time, there would be no charge to higher rate tax, as there would not be anybody living on whom it would be possible to raise an assessment[1] – this was referred to as 'the dead settlor' rule. This created some useful estate planning opportunities. Any bond that was effected by trustees of a trust created under a will could obviously benefit from this legislation. During lifetime, to take advantage of the dead settlor rule, an investor (normally the older spouse) could effect a joint lives last survivor single premium bond, of which he had sole ownership. The bond had to be subject to a trust to take advantage of this rule (although the trust could have been created during lifetime or under the terms of the investor's will).

The aim of the arrangement was to avoid any liability to higher rate tax by encashing the bond in a tax year following the death of the creator of the trust. This obviously relied on the sole owner actually being the first of the lives assured to die. In order to be certain that any such liability was minimised, it was often preferable to split the investment, so that the investors each effected a joint lives last survivor single premium bond and put it in trust (either during lifetime, or in the terms of their wills).

Another way of taking advantage of this rule was for the investor to purchase a capital redemption bond. Under this type of policy, the death of the investor (who would have been the creator of the trust) is not a chargeable event, and so, provided the 'term' is long enough, use could always be made of the 'dead settlor rule'. It was preferable for a trust of a capital redemption bond to remain 'flexible' for 80 years (to be consistent with a perpetuity period, see Chapter 9, Section 6) thereby retaining flexibility for a longer period than in the standard specimen trust forms (see below) provided by life offices which commonly provide for the flexibility to cease two years after the death of the investor.

These rules still apply in situations where the creator of the trust died before 18 March 1998 and the policy was already in force at that date provided that the policy is not enhanced in any way after that date. In all other situations new rules contained in what was a revised section 547(1) of ICTA 1988, and is now sections 465 and 467 of ITTOIA 2005, apply. These new rules also state that when

---

1   ITTOIA 2005, s 465.

a chargeable event occurs in respect of a bond written subject to a trust the tax charge will still be based on the income of the settlor of the trust provided he is alive and resident in the UK. However, if the settlor is dead or non-UK resident, any chargeable event occurring in a tax year after the death of the settlor would be assessed on the trustees. The gain would be chargeable on the trustees at the rate of 40% in respect of an offshore bond but if the policy was effected with a UK life office, the trustees would get credit for savings rate tax deemed to have been paid within the fund and thus would only have to pay tax at 20% on the gain.

It may be possible to avoid this charge if the bond, or segments thereof, were to be assigned by the trustees to the beneficiaries assuming that they have attained the age of 18. Such an assignment would not trigger a chargeable event and any gain arising on a chargeable event after the assignment would then be assessed on the beneficiaries.

3   Miscellaneous uses

15.18   Life assurance can help in minimising the effect of IHT by providing a medium for taking advantage of the annual exemption. For example, where an estate is to pass to children and consists mainly of readily realisable assets, bank or building society deposits, the individual might use capital to pay premiums, within the limits of the available exemptions, for a life policy written under trust. The policy proceeds would provide a tax-free 'legacy' on the life assured's death and, moreover, the IHT liability on the estate would be reduced by the withdrawal of capital.

Similarly, if an individual wishes to make a lifetime transfer of cash (ie income) to his children, he may make use of the annual exemption to build up a tax-free lump sum by paying premiums towards an endowment assurance written in trust for the children's benefit.

Furthermore, in some instances, IHT will be payable as a consequence of the donor dying within seven years of making a gift. This applies to gifts which are not fully exempt but which are either PETs or CLTs. Upon a donor dying within the seven-year period, a tax liability may arise in respect of the gift. The tax liability decreases over the seven years (after the third year) due to taper relief which could, if appropriate, be planned for by a seven-year decreasing term assurance.

It would not be appropriate to use a seven-year decreasing term assurance where, at the date of the particular PET or CLT, there are no relevant previous transfers and the amount of the PET or CLT falls within the nil rate band. The nil rate band is applied first of all against lifetime transfers and so in the event of the PET or CLT proving chargeable, it could be covered by the nil rate band and no IHT would be payable. The appropriate policy in this instance may be a seven-year level term assurance, in trust for the residuary beneficiaries of the investor's estate in order to cover the increased amount of IHT which would be payable by the personal representatives as a result of the nil rate band being used (in whole or in part) by lifetime transfers of value, thereby reducing the amount of the IHT-free estate upon death.

SECTION 2   DECLARING TRUSTS OF POLICIES

15.19   The proceeds of a whole life policy effected by a person on his own life and for his own benefit will be aggregated with his estate on his death and chargeable to IHT. For estate planning purposes, therefore, it is better to assign the policy or declare a trust of it in order to remove the value of the policy at the time of the gift (and any sum assured which becomes payable) from his estate. Further advantages are that the sums assured will be paid to the trustees (the policyholders) upon proof of death of the life assured and proof of their title to the policy, without having to wait until a grant of representation is obtained.

In the case of an endowment assurance, it may be desirable for the policy to remain for the assured's own benefit if he survives, where, for example, it is to provide for retirement. HMRC have confirmed that the retention by the settlor of a reversionary interest under an interest in possession trust effected before 22 March 2006 is not considered to constitute a gift with reservation of benefit[1].

SECTION 3   LIFE OFFICE SPECIMEN TRUST FORMS

15.20   Many life offices (and financial advisers) have specimen trust forms which a proposer or policyholder may use to place a policy in trust. In all cases, these trust forms are provided as specimens. Due to the nature of trusts and of the relevant surrounding personal circumstances of the investor, it is strongly advisable that the investor takes independent legal advice to ensure that the particular specimen trust form meets his requirements in the particular case and does not conflict with any existing arrangements.

Commonly, life offices have two categories of trust form, a trust request form and a declaration of trust form. These are designed to be used in two different sets of circumstances. The trust request form is designed for use by the investor at the time of proposing for a policy (or any time *before* the date of assurance), whilst the declaration of trust is designed for use at any time *after* the date of assurance. It is important that these forms are used correctly.

If an investor wishes a policy to be written in trust from the outset[2], the trust request must be submitted to the life office before the date of assurance, and preferably at the same time as the proposal form is submitted. In this way, the policy is placed in trust as a matter of contract between the investor and the life office. A common form of wording in the trust request form is as follows:

> 'I hereby declare that I make the proposal dated [   ] on the terms that the policy of assurance effected and issued as a result of that proposal on my life should be issued to me as trustee and all moneys payable and benefits under the policy (the Trust Fund) shall be subject to the following trusts: . . .'

---

1   Inland Revenue letter, 18 May 1987.
2   Note that this is particularly important for trusts for business assurance purposes, in order to avoid with certainty the possibility of a charge to capital gains tax. See further Chapter 17, Section 1A.

If the trust request form is not received by the life office before the date of assurance, there is some doubt as to whether, legally, a valid trust will be created (ie whether the trust will be completely constituted). If the trust is not completely constituted, it cannot be enforced, the settlor could revoke the trust and there could potentially be problems as between any competing beneficiaries or potential beneficiaries of the investor's estate.

The standard trust forms should also contain suitable clauses giving the trustees power to surrender, mortgage, charge or otherwise deal with the policy, together with wide powers of investment, power to delegate investment decisions, power for the investments to be held by nominees, an extended power to advance capital to a beneficiary up to the full amount of his or her vested or prospective share, and clauses providing for the remuneration of corporate or professional trustees and for the appointment of new trustees.

A standard trust form for a Scottish trust should also contain express powers of delegation, as the common law and the Scottish statutes do not allow any form of delegation.

A   Power of appointment interest in possession trust

15.21   The most popular type of trust for life policies has traditionally been the power of appointment trust which gives an interest in possession to named or identified beneficiaries. However, this is likely to change following the changes to the IHT treatment of trusts from 22 March 2006 as set out in Chapter 14, Section 6B. From that date, all new interest in possession trusts will be treated for IHT purposes as discretionary trusts and will be potentially liable to the ten-yearly and periodic charges.

The power of appointment trust is usually in two parts, giving an immediate interest in possession to named or identified beneficiaries, known as the default beneficiaries, with an overriding power in the hands of the trustees to change the beneficial interest, either revocably or irrevocably, to any of a class of 'potential beneficiaries' listed on the trust form. For trusts created prior to 22 March 2006 this gave all the advantages of placing a policy in trust already referred to (eg proceeds free of IHT), whilst retaining the ability to change the beneficiaries and being able to cater for unforeseen circumstances at the time the trust was created, eg by way of changes in the needs or structure of the investor's family and dependants.

The specimen trust forms will often provide a choice for the investor as to whether he wishes the default beneficiaries to hold their interest *in equal shares absolutely* or *absolutely*. Subject to the trustees' power to appoint the beneficial interest to another, *in equal shares absolutely* means that on the death of a beneficiary, his beneficial interest would pass according to his will (or the Intestacy Rules), whilst *absolutely* (without more) could mean that his beneficial interest passes to the remaining beneficiaries.

Life office trust forms are often drafted in such a way that the power of appointment exists until two years after the date of the death of the settlor. This is to be consistent with the IHTA provisions[1] relating to the variation of disposi-

---

1   IHTA 1984, ss 53, 142.

tions comprised in the settlor's estate and the reverter to settlor or settlor's spouse exemption within two years of death (see Chapter 14). Therefore, unless the trustees make an irrevocable appointment, the power of appointment does not cease until the expiry of that period.

15.22   It has already been noted that life policies are non-income producing assets. The beneficiaries are given an interest in possession in these standard trust forms by the use of a deeming provision. This, in essence, has the effect of giving the default beneficiaries a *right* to have the present enjoyment of the income. It is immaterial that these particular assets are non-income producing, as the test is met — that if there was income, the default beneficiaries would have a right to it (see Chapter 14, Section 6B).

Prior to 22 March 2006 this trust was very popular, due to its flexibility, but it should not have been used if the investor felt that the power of appointment would be frequently exercised. As explained in Chapter 14, where a beneficiary has an interest in possession, he is treated for IHT purposes as owning the under-lying capital. Therefore, when the power of appointment is exercised, this con-stitutes a PET, a transfer of value from the beneficiary who was entitled before the exercise of the power, to the new beneficiary. Thus the former beneficiary would have to survive seven years in order for there to be no possibility of an IHT charge. If such a PET proved chargeable, the primary liability to pay the charge would fall on the trustees[1].

It was therefore important for an investor to think carefully about whom he wished to benefit and the terms on which he wished them to receive the benefits. Where the purposes of the trust fail and there is no indication as to where the policy moneys should be paid upon such a failure, the policy moneys will form part of the estate of the grantee and therefore be liable to IHT.

If the power of appointment is exercised after 5 April 2006 under a pre-22 March 2006 trust, and the trust remains in existence, this will have the effect of turning the trust into a 'relevant property' trust and thus causing it to be poten-tially liable to the ten-yearly and exit charges (see Chapter 14, Section 6B).

15.23   A common mistake is to create (not always intentionally) a life interest in a bond. The intention may be to provide, for example, the spouse or registered civil partner, with 'income' during her lifetime, and for the remainder to pass to the children upon her death. As a bond is non-income producing, and a life tenant is entitled only to income, a trust drafted in this way will not normally achieve its objectives. The trust should be drafted carefully to ensure that the trustees have power to make capital withdrawals and to advance capital to a life tenant.

It is important, however, if a trust policy is to fulfil the purpose for which it is effected, that the provisions of the trust should clearly and correctly set out the grantee's intentions regarding the persons he wishes to benefit and the nature of their interests. The following section considers the various dispositions of the policy benefits most frequently required by proposers, draft forms of trust wording for incorporating those dispositions in the trust policy, and discusses the

---

1   IHTA 1984, s 201.

tax and legal implications of doing so although some of these wordings are now of historical interest only owing to the fact that all new policies effected on or after 22 March 2006, unless written subject to absolute or bare trusts, will be treated as discretionary trusts in which no individual will have an interest in possession and all benefits will be payable at the trustees' discretion.

Before considering these draft trust wordings, it is necessary to mention a number of preliminary matters.

If not exempt as normal expenditure out of income, or by use of the £3,000 annual exemption, the premiums paid towards trust policies (if the trust is an interest in possession or accumulation and maintenance trust created before 22 March 2006)[1] will be lifetime transfers for IHT purposes and may be treated as PETs. In order for such transfers to be PETs, the property transferred must become settled property[2]. This presents no problems in relation to the first premium paid, but will obviously not become *settled* where a premium is paid by an investor on a life policy *already* held on trust. The second or subsequent premiums therefore will only be PETs to the extent that the value of the estate of the beneficiary(ies) is increased. This means that only the part of the second or subsequent premiums which actually increases the market value of the policy will be a PET. The investor could ensure that these payments constitute PETs by making gifts of cash to the trustees who would then pay the premiums, rather than paying the premiums to the life office directly. For policies effected on or after 22 March 2006, if an absolute trust is used, the position will be as set out above. If this is not the case, any premiums in excess of the annual exemptions will be chargeable lifetime transfers.

15.24   Although a policy is written under trust, it will not automatically constitute a settlement for IHT purposes (and in most cases, in trusts with an absolute adult beneficiary it will not, as this will not satisfy the definition of a settlement for IHT purposes)[3]. This is important because if there is no settlement then the legal personal representatives are primarily accountable for the tax on the death of a beneficiary whereas, if there is a settlement, the trustees are primarily accountable to the extent of the property which they hold.

The wordings given here may be used for policies issued under the Married Women's Property Act 1882 (where the beneficiaries are those included in the Act), or for policies issued in trust outside the Act. The comments are, however, restricted to the positions in England and Wales. Special mention is then made in relation to the position in Scotland.

The IHT effect on the various trust wordings which follow may be better understood if the nature of the beneficiary's interest is first considered. The following comments are of general application to any fixed trust. The position would be different if the trust was a flexible power of appointment trust created pre-22 March 2006. Generally, an adult beneficiary with a vested or contingent interest in the policy trust will have an interest in possession. This is because

---

1   Within the terms of IHTA 1984, s 71; see Chapter 14, Sections 6B and 6D.
2   IHTA 1984, s 3A(3).
3   IHTA 1984, s 43.

section 31(1)(ii) of the Trustee Act 1925 operates, subject to any prior interests, to entitle a beneficiary to the intermediate income arising from his interest once he has attained the age of 18 — unless there is a contrary intention shown in the trust instrument (eg, where a direction is made for income to be accumulated or for it to be paid somewhere else, such as to a charity) or if section 31 is expressly excluded. The income from a minor's interest in a settlement must be accumulated during his minority in so far as it is not used for his maintenance, education or benefit.

Where the beneficiary under the trust is a minor, one of three situations may exist:

(1) The beneficiary may have an interest in possession. This will be the case where, for example, there is a deeming provision which gives the minor immediate entitlement to any income.

(2) The beneficiary may not have an interest in possession but the trust is one which is protected as an accumulation and maintenance settlement within section 71 of the IHTA 1984 (ie broadly a settlement in which no interest in possession subsists but where one or more persons will become entitled to an interest in possession on or before attaining age 25). Thus, the policy trust would be exempt from the lifetime, exit and principal (ten-yearly) tax charges normally applying to settlements without an interest in possession (see Chapter 14, Section 6C). (Note that the income tax consequences of creating an accumulation and maintenance settlement for parental settlors should be considered carefully. If capital or income is generated in excess of £100 it is all treated as the settlor's income[1]. Clearly this taxation consequence will not arise where a life policy is subject to an accumulation and maintenance trust as it is a non-income producing asset).

(3) The beneficiary may not have an interest in possession and the trust is *not* within the provisions of section 71 of the IHTA 1984 so that the policy trust is subject to the original chargeable transfer, the principal (ten-yearly) charge and the exit charges to IHT.

B Interests of children

15.25 The interests of children may be made contingent on attaining a specified age, or on surviving the grantee, or may be limited in such other manner as the settlor desires. Before drafting any trust of a policy which is to be for the benefit of children it is important to determine:

(1) Whether the children are to be named, so that any further children born will be excluded.

(2) Whether, if not named, the class of children is to be limited to the children of the existing marriage or to the legitimate children of the life assured. (A

---

1 ITTOIA 2005, s 629.

provision for children without further description will include any illegitimate, legitimated or adopted children of the grantee and the children of any marriage.)

(3) Whether any child's interest is to continue for the benefit of his or her estate:

(a) if he or she predeceases the grantee, or dies before the event upon which the sum assured becomes payable;

(b) if he or she dies before attaining the specified age.

C Interests of spouse or registered civil partner

15.26 Where an own life policy is effected by a husband or wife for the benefit of the other *named* spouse, or by one civil partner for the benefit of the other, which is not conditional upon the named spouse/civil partner surviving the grantee, that spouse/civil partner takes an immediate vested interest in the trust of the policy, which on death before the grantee will pass to his or her personal representatives[1] and is unaffected by the grantee remarrying.

If there is no named spouse/civil partner and the trust wording refers to eg '*my wife*' or '*my wife immediately before my death*' and the wife dies before the husband (who does not remarry), the general view is that the policy moneys would form part of the estate of the husband for IHT purposes[2]. This is so, even if the wife's interest is unconditional upon surviving the husband. If the husband had remarried, and the second wife was alive at the death of the husband, she would be entitled to the policy moneys[3], unless there is an indication to the contrary in the trust instrument[4]. Similarly, if the trust is expressed to be for the benefit of eg '*my widow*', the second wife would be entitled to benefit[5].

Where the trust is declared to be for the benefit of a spouse and children, their interest is presumed to be a joint tenancy, unless there appears to be a contrary intention[6].

To avoid repetition in the following comments, no detailed reference is made to the intestacy or succession rules nor to the valuation of a beneficiary's interest in a policy, as both have been dealt with earlier. Similarly, the question of the exemptions available to free a transfer from an IHT charge has already been considered in Chapter 14, Section 4.

---

1 *Cousins v Sun Life Assurance Society* [1933] Ch 126, CA.
2 *Re Collier* [1930] 2 Ch 37.
3 *Re Browne's Policy, Browne v Browne* [1903] 1 Ch 188.
4 *Re Griffith's Policy* [1903] 1 Ch 739.
5 *Re Parker's Policies* [1906] 1 Ch 526.
6 *Re Seyton, Seyton v Satterthwaite* (1887) 34 Ch D 511; *Re Davies' Policy Trusts* [1892] 1 Ch 90; *Re Browne's Policy, Browne v Browne* [1903] 1 Ch 188.

SECTION 4   POLICY TRUST WORDINGS

15.27   Trust wordings can cater for virtually any scenario desired by the settlor. Some common provisions include:

(1)   making the beneficial interest in the capital contingent upon attaining a specified age;

(2)   making the beneficial interest contingent upon living at the time the policy moneys becomes payable; and

(3)   a per stirpes clause.

Examples of appropriate trust wordings for the above are as follows:

(1)   *Upon trust for [my son] A absolutely upon attaining the age of [21].*

(2)   *Upon trust for [my son] A absolutely provided that if he should not be living at the occurrence of the event upon which the policy moneys become payable then for [my daughter] B absolutely.*

(3)   *Upon trust for [the Beneficiaries] provided that if any of the Beneficiaries shall die before the occurrence of the event upon which the policy moneys become payable leaving children then such children living on the occurrence of the said event shall take by substitution and if more than one then in equal shares the share which their deceased parent would have taken had he or she been living on the occurrence of the said event.*

The trust wordings and their IHT impact are considered in more detail in the following scenarios where the policy is effected in trust for:

(1)   named person absolutely;

(2)   named persons in equal shares absolutely (their interests to pass to their estates if they predecease the settlor);

(3)   such of the grantee's children as survive him or if none survive then for the last to die;

(4)   A failing whom B (neither being the grantee);

(5)   a person should he survive the grantee otherwise for the grantee;

(6)   a person if living at the death of the grantee before maturity of an endowment policy, otherwise for the grantee;

(7)   such of A, B, C, and D (none of whom are the grantee) as the grantee shall appoint and failing appointment for D absolutely;

(8)   the survivor if any (of husband and wife on a joint lives first death policy), failing whom, the children.

The inheritance tax position of trusts will depend on whether they were effected on or after 22 March 2006 or before that date. If the trust is an absolute trust, in both cases the trust property should be outside the 'relevant property' regime as described in Chapter 14, Section 6C (subject to the comments below about minor beneficiaries). If the trust is a settlement which confers an interest in possession then if effected prior to 22 March it should be outside the relevant property regime but if effected on or after that date it would fall within that regime.

A Policy effected in trust for named person absolutely

15.28 Draft wording: *'Upon trust for [my son] A absolutely.'*

If A is over 18 then the policy trust does not constitute a settlement for IHT (as it does not satisfy the definition of a settlement)[1]. If A is a minor then, at the time of writing, HMRC's view is that a settlement has been created and the trust property is thus within the 'relevant property' regime as described in Chapter 14, Section 6C. HMRC concedes that this view is not shared by others and that it has not yet reached a definitive decision on this point. On the death of the grantee, no IHT charge arises unless the grantee was beneficially entitled to the policy at his death, eg if A had predeceased him and the policy had devolved upon the grantee under the will or upon the intestacy of A.

If A predeceased the life assured, on his death, the value of the policy at that time would not form part of his estate. If HMRC subsequently take the point that an absolute trust for a minor is not settled property, there would be a transfer of value on A's death of the open market value[2] of his interest in the policy at that time, which would form part of his taxable estate on death. A's interest in the policy would pass in accordance with his will or the intestacy rules.

B Policy effected in trust for named persons in equal shares absolutely (their interests to pass to their estates if they predecease the settlor)

15.29 Draft wording: *'Upon trust for [my son] A and [my daughter] B in equal shares absolutely.'*

Similar principles as in **15.28** apply in determining whether the policy trust is a settlement or not for IHT, and in deciding whether a tax charge arises on the death of the grantee. In itself, this wording creates a tenancy in common which means that if A and/or B predecease(s) the life assured then his or her interest in the policy will pass in accordance with their will(s) or the intestacy provisions and, assuming it is an interest in possession trust, a transfer of value occurs of the deceased beneficiary's half-share in the value of the policy at that time.

This form of wording is used, for example, where the grantee wishes to benefit his existing children and there will be no further children (or separate provision is to be made for them). There could be a disadvantage with this wording in that, on the death of a minor beneficiary, his interest in the policy trust passes to the parents, not to the surviving beneficiary. Thus the wording is, perhaps, not

1 IHTA 1984, s 43.
2 IHTA 1984, ss 160 and 167(2)(a).

wholly suitable for a policy to provide the children with funds to cover the IHT on other assets passing to them under the grantee's will for, in the event of a minor beneficiary's death before the life assured, the parents must transfer to the surviving child (eg by assignment) the interest in the policy which passes to them on the minor beneficiary's death. On the other hand, this form of wording does mean that if a beneficiary who predeceased the life assured is married and has a family then they, and not the surviving beneficiary, could take his interest in the policy. However, this could be covered expressly by a per stirpes clause.

C   Policy effected in trust for such of the grantee's children (unnamed) as survive him or if none survive then for the last to die

15.30   Draft wording: *'Upon trust for such of my children whenever born [of my marriage to X] as shall be living on the occurrence of the event upon which the policy moneys become payable and if more than one then equally between them Provided that if none of my said children shall be living on the occurrence of the said event then in trust for the last of them to die.'*

In view of the changes to the taxation of trusts created by the Finance Act 2006 the concept of the accumulation and maintenance trust for new trusts created on or after 22 March 2006 no longer exists. This wording and comments that follow are therefore included for historical interest only.

This form of trust wording constitutes a settlement for IHT. Furthermore, unless one or more of the children is aged 18 or over, it is a settlement in which, unless the trust instrument expressly provides for it by a deeming provision, there is no interest in possession. However, provided section 31 of the Trustee Act 1925 has not been excluded (either expressly, or by necessary implication) then, as each child attains the age of 18 he or she will become entitled to the income from his or her presumptive share in the settled fund and will, accordingly, then have an interest in possession in a corresponding share of the settlement[1]. Thus, the policy trust constitutes an 'accumulation and maintenance' settlement within section 71 of the IHTA 1984 because one or more of the beneficiaries will become entitled to an interest in possession on or before attaining a specified age (in this case 18) not exceeding 25[2]. It is therefore protected from the harsher IHT treatment for settlements in which there is no interest in possession.

There will be no IHT charge on the death of the grantee unless all the beneficiaries have predeceased him and he has acquired an interest through the will or intestacy of the last of them to die.

If an *adult* beneficiary predeceases the life assured then a transfer of value occurs because the beneficiary's interest in possession is terminated. IHT will be charged on the proportion of the value of the policy represented by the deceased beneficiary's presumptive share in the settled fund at the time of his death. As a

---

1   *Re Jones Will Trusts, Soames v A-G* [1946] 2 All ER 281.
2   See Statutory Concession F8.

consequence of his death, the presumptive shares of the remaining beneficiaries in the settled policy are increased. If a *minor* beneficiary predeceases the life assured then, as the beneficiary has no interest in possession, there will be no transfer of value on his death and no IHT will be chargeable. This will be so even if there is an adult beneficiary in existence whose presumptive share is increased as a result of the death of the minor. The death of the *last surviving* beneficiary will give rise to a transfer of value whether the beneficiary is an adult or a minor at the time.

On the birth of a child to the grantee each existing beneficiary will suffer a reduction in his or her presumptive share, and this will constitute a transfer of value by an adult beneficiary who has an interest in possession which is thereby reduced.

This form of wording (which should be used only if there is at least one child in existence or en ventre sa mere) is suitable where the grantee wishes to benefit by means of life assurance children, including those born after the commencement of the policy, who survive him. The wording is useful, therefore, for policies effected to provide funds for those children who benefit under the grantee's will, to cover the IHT liability.

D Policy effected in trust for A failing whom B (neither being the grantee)

15.31 Draft wording: *'Upon trust for [my son] A Provided that if he shall not be living on the occurrence of the event upon which the policy moneys become payable then in trust for [my daughter] B absolutely.'*

This form of trust wording also constitutes a settlement for IHT and, if A is a minor, the same matters must be considered as stated above (in particular to see if there is a deeming provision) to determine if there is an interest in possession. Again, if there is no deeming provision (so there is not an interest in possession during the beneficiary's minority), unless section 31 of the Trustee Act 1925 has been excluded, the policy trust will fall within the accumulation and maintenance provisions.

The death of the grantee will not be a transfer of value unless he was beneficially entitled to the policy at the date of his death (see the discussion at **15.28**).

On the death of A, during the lifetime of the life assured, B will become entitled absolutely. If A is an adult, the termination of his interest in possession will be a transfer of value and IHT will be chargeable on the open market value[1] of the policy at that time.

B's death before A and the life assured will not give rise to a transfer of value as B has only a reversionary interest, which is 'excluded property'[2]. B's death after A but before the life assured's gives rise to a transfer of the open market value of the policy at that time.

---

1   IHTA 1984, ss 160, 167(2)(a).
2   IHTA 1984, s 48.

This form of wording is principally employed where the grantee wishes to benefit, for example, his children, but with a 'long stop' provision in favour of another (in order to prevent it reverting to himself).

E   Policy effected in trust for a person should he survive the grantee otherwise for the grantee

15.32   Draft wording: *'Upon trust for [my son] A Provided that if A shall not be living on the occurrence of the event upon which the policy moneys become payable for me absolutely.'*

As stated earlier, such a provision, where a gift is made into trust, and the settlor retains a reversionary interest under the trust does not constitute a gift with reservation of benefit[1].

F   Endowment policy effected in trust for a person if living at the death of the grantee before maturity, otherwise for the grantee

15.33   Draft wording: *'Upon trust for [my son] A Provided that if I am living at the time the policy moneys become payable or if A shall not be living at my death before the time the policy moneys become payable then in trust for me absolutely.'*

The comments in relation to **15.32** apply equally hereto[2].

G   Policy effected in trust for such of A, B, C and D (none of whom are the grantee) as the grantee shall appoint and failing appointment for D absolutely

15.34   Draft wording: *'Upon the following trusts:*

(i)   *for such of A, B, C and D and in such shares (or wholly to one) as I may by deed or deeds revocable or irrevocable or by will or codicil appoint;*

(ii)   *subject to and in default of any appointment and insofar as any appointment shall not extend or shall fail for any reason then in trust for D absolutely.'*

This is a 'flexible', power of appointment trust and constitutes a settlement for IHT purposes. For trusts effected on or after 22 March, see **15.37**. For trusts

---

1   Inland Revenue letter, 18 May 1987.
2   See also Inland Revenue letter from the Life Insurance Council of the Association of British Insurers to members of the LIC after seeking clarification from the Inland Revenue, 21 November 1986.

effected before that date, if D is an adult then, unless section 31 of the Trustee Act 1925 is excluded (expressly or impliedly), it is a settlement with an interest in possession because D has a vested defeasible interest and is entitled to the intermediate income arising from the settled property. On the other hand, if D is a minor then, unless there is a deeming provision, there is no interest in possession; moreover, the settlement would not be protected by section 71 of the IHTA 1984 as an accumulation and maintenance settlement, because it cannot be said that a beneficiary will become entitled to an interest in possession on or before attaining a specified age not exceeding 25 (eg an appointment may be made away from D before he was 18 in favour of someone already over 25). It is not sufficient that the power of appointment is not exercised, the terms of the trust must be restricted so they cannot be exercised to prevent at least one beneficiary becoming so entitled.

In practice, most trusts providing for this arrangement contain an income direction, directing that D would be entitled to the intermediate income, thus making it an interest in possession trust. If not, unless D is an adult the policy trust would face the potentially harsher IHT treatment of trusts without interests in possession. (See further, Chapter 14, Section 6C.)

15.35 Assuming this to be the case, if D is an adult then his death, or an appointment away from him, will give rise to a transfer of the value of the policy at that time by D. On the death of A, B or C, before an appointment has been made in their favour, there will be no transfer of value, as they had no interest in possession in the settled policy. On the death of the grantee there will be no transfer of value unless at his death he was beneficially entitled to the policy (eg if it had devolved upon him under the will or intestacy of a beneficiary in whose favour an irrevocable appointment had been made).

The exercise of the power of appointment will give rise to a transfer of value every time an appointment is made to someone who immediately prior to the appointment had no interest in possession. (Thus, in this example, an irrevocable or revocable appointment in favour of A is a transfer of value, but an appointment in favour of D is not[1].)

If an appointment of the whole beneficial interest is made by the grantee in his will then a transfer of value based on the *policy proceeds* occurs, the rate of tax being determined by reference to the cumulative transfers of the person having the beneficial interest prior to the appointment. For this reason, careful consideration should be given before making an appointment by will.

Despite the problems of possible IHT charges on the exercise of the power of appointment, this form of policy trust prior to 22 March 2006 was often favoured by the grantee who wished to have some flexibility in his choice of ultimate beneficiary, without suffering the potentially higher tax charges of a discretionary trust.

1   IHTA 1984, s 53(2).

H   Joint lives first death policy (jointly owned by husband and wife) effected in trust for the survivor (if any), failing whom, the children

15.36   Draft wording: *'Upon trust for [the children] as shall be living 28 days after the occurrence of the event upon which the policy moneys become payable. Provided that if none of [the children] shall be living 28 days after the occurrence of the said event then for the last of them to die. Provided always if the survivor of us shall be alive on the said event then in trust for the survivor of us absolutely.'*

This type of wording is not thought in itself to constitute a gift with reservation of benefit for the same reasoning as expressed at **15.32**, namely that the retention of a reversionary interest under the trust is not, in itself, considered to constitute a gift with reservation of benefit.

I   The position from 22 March 2006

15.37   Power of appointment interest in possession trusts created before 22 March 2006 will continue to be outside the scope of the regime for 'relevant property' trusts (ie the ten-yearly and exit charges) assuming no appointments are made away from the persons who were default beneficiaries as at 22 March 2006. However, if trustees make appointments away to new beneficiaries before 6 April 2006, those new beneficiaries will be treated as though they were the beneficiaries in existence at 22 March 2006 and the existing IHT treatment will continue. If appointments are made after 6 April 2008 and the trust continues, if the appointment away is as a result of the death of the original beneficiary, the value of his or her interest in the trust property will form part of their estate as now, but the trust will then become a 'relevant property' trust. If the appointment was made whilst the original beneficiary was still alive, this would constitute a chargeable lifetime transfer by him. Again, the trust would then become a 'relevant property' trust.

Accumulation and maintenance trusts created before 22 March 2006 will continue to be outside the scope of the regime for 'relevant property' trusts only until 6 April 2008 at which point they will become 'relevant property' settlements and the first principal charge will be at the next ten-yearly anniversary from the creation of the settlement (although this will be proportioned as the trust had not contained 'relevant property' for the whole of the ten-year period). The only way of avoiding this is either if the trust provides for the beneficiaries to become absolutely entitled to the trust property at the age of 18 or if the trust could be amended before 6 April 2008 to provide for this to happen.

All trusts created on or after 22 March 2006 which would, in the old regime, have been interest in possession trusts or accumulation and maintenance trusts will now be treated for inheritance tax purposes as though they were 'relevant property' (ie discretionary) trusts. Thus, gifts into such trusts to the extent that they are in excess of the available exemptions will be chargeable lifetime transfers and the trustees may be liable for the ten-yearly and exit charges in addition, depending on the value of the trust property.

J   Scottish trust policies

15.38   The rules relating to property rights in Scotland are different from those under English law, as too are the principles of vesting (ie those rules which govern the moment at which the interest in trust property can be said to be acquired). Section 31 of the Trustee Act 1925 does not apply in Scotland, nor is there an equivalent provision in any Scottish statute. Moreover, in the absence of an express direction to the contrary, the general presumption under Scottish law is that any intermediate income arising will not be paid to a beneficiary under a settlement (unless he has an absolute interest), but will be accumulated and form part of the capital.

As a consequence of these differences in trust law, many policy trust wordings which could have been used safely under English law to create settlements with an interest in possession, or accumulation and maintenance settlements within section 71 of the IHTA 1984 would be treated in Scotland as creating settlements without interests in possession and not protected by the section. Such policy trusts would, as a result, be subject to initial, principal (ten-yearly) and exit charges.

It was important, therefore, prior to 22 March 2006, to take care when drafting policy trust wordings for policy trusts subject to Scottish law, so that interests in possession were created at the outset or, alternatively, in the case of trusts for minors, that they were brought within the protection of section 71 as accumulation and maintenance settlements. This was, perhaps, best done by express directions that beneficiaries who were to have interests in possession were given the right to the income arising from the settled property. There should have been clear statements as to when the right to income was to commence, the duration of that right, and what was to happen to the income on the death of a beneficiary under a settlement in which there were successive interests (eg A failing whom B). If an accumulation and maintenance settlement was to be created, then there should have been explicit directions as to when interests were to vest and as to entitlements to income arising thereafter, with clear provisions, for the use or accumulation, of income arising beforehand.

In that way, with care in drafting the appropriate amendments and additions, the policy trust wordings used in England could also have been employed in establishing policy trusts under Scottish law, resulting in similar IHT treatment.

As a result of the changes to the IHT treatment of trusts contained in the Finance Act 2006 and effective from 22 March 2006, the comments contained above are now of only historic interest due to the fact that from that date, all new trusts (except absolute or bare trusts or trusts for the benefit of disabled persons) will effectively be treated as though they were discretionary trusts.

CHAPTER 16

The tax framework for Registered Pension Schemes

SUMMARY

SECTION I   INTRODUCTION

16.1   Registered Pension Schemes involving insurance policies can take various forms, as explained in Chapter 14, Section 9. This chapter looks at the tax framework which governs the tax reliefs available to these schemes. The entire tax framework of private pension provision was radically changed with effect from 6 April 2006 (commonly referred to as A-Day). The previous jumble of different tax regimes and rules has been replaced with a single universal set of rules.

Within the context of this publication, the authors have sought to give only a general view of the new rules from 6 April 2006. The changes are, however, fundamental, complex and deep-rooted and it is stressed that reference should be made to HMRC's 'Registered Pension Schemes Manual' to obtain a more detailed view. This manual is available on the internet, and can be found at: www.hmrc.gov.uk/manuals/rpsmmanual/index.htm

SECTION 2   BACKGROUND

16.2   It has been government policy for many years to provide tax privileges to pension schemes. The aim is to encourage saving (by individuals and/or their employers) for the purpose of providing an income in old age, to reduce dependency on the state. HMRC has the task of controlling those tax privileges. This control is implemented by a framework of prescribed requirements that pension schemes must adhere to if their tax privileged status is to be maintained. Since the provisions introduced by the Finance Act 1970, these requirements have been imposed in two ways – directly through detailed legislation, and indirectly through decisions taken by HMRC under their discretionary powers which are provided by legislation.

Many different types of pension schemes have developed over the years, either as a result of legislation to reflect government policy or because of fresh ideas within the pensions industry. Each development has resulted in a different raft of HMRC requirements to fit the circumstances. This layering approach resulted in a profusion of different rules for different types of pension arrangements.

Prior to 6 April 2006, the legislation governing tax-approved pension arrangements was contained in Part XIV of the Income and Corporation Taxes Act 1988. Because of the way the legislation had been developed and modified over many years (starting with the Finance Act 1970), a number of different regimes for tax-approved pension arrangements had emerged. Each regime had its own complex rules limiting the amount an individual could contribute to a pension scheme and the benefits a scheme could pay out.

16.3   The following table provides a summary of the way the tax privileges were controlled for the different types of pension arrangements before 6 April 2006.

The pensions tax framework before 6 April 2006	
Type of pension arrangement	Method of controlling the tax privileges
Employer-sponsored Occupational Pension Schemes (OPS) in their various forms, ie: • Defined Benefit OPS • Money Purchase OPS on a group 'defined contribution' basis • Money Purchase OPS on an individual 'mutually determined' basis (eg Executive Pension Plans and Small Self-Administered Scheme)	These schemes had to be approved by HMRC under the provisions of Chapter I of Part XIV of ICTA 1988. Chapter I laid down some basic rules, but mainly it gave HMRC discretionary powers, and hence flexibility, to specify the details. The level of tax relief was controlled by: Limiting the maximum benefits that could be provided, by reference to earnings at the time of retirement and length of service. The criteria for those limits had been varied over the years – ie the pre-87, 87–89 and post-89 regimes. Limiting the way the maximum benefits could be funded in advance.

Type of pension arrangement	Method of controlling the tax privileges
'Left scheme' policies in their various forms, ie: • section 32 buy-out policies • assigned policies • trustees buy-out policies • (secured on an OPS winding-up)	These policies derived from Chapter I schemes and were regulated by the same rules.
Provider-sponsored Free-Standing AVC Schemes	These schemes had to be approved by HMRC under the provisions of Chapter I.
Provider-sponsored Personal Pension Schemes (PPS) in their various forms, ie: • Fully insured PP Scheme • Self-Invested PP Schemes	These schemes had to be approved by HMRC under the provisions of Chapter IV of Part XIV of ICTA 1988. Chapter IV defined everything in detail (and left little to HMRC's discretion). The level of tax relief was controlled by: Limiting the maximum contribution that could be paid each tax year.
Provider-sponsored Stakeholder Pension Schemes (SHPS)	These schemes are just a special form of Personal Pension Schemes and were subject to the same HMRC requirements.
Retirement Annuity policies	These policies were approved by HMRC under the provisions of Chapter III of Part XIV of ICTA 1988. Chapter III defined everything in detail (and left little to HMRC's discretion). The level of tax relief was controlled by: Limiting the maximum contribution that could be paid each tax year. (The limits were different to those for PP Schemes.)

Following a lengthy period of consultation and development, which started in 2002, the government has swept away all the existing pensions tax legislation and introduced a single set of rules which came into force on 6 April 2006. The new rules are laid down wholly in legislation – principally Part 4 of the Finance Act 2004. In particular, it should be noted that HMRC no longer has any discretionary powers – hence there can be no variations.

Because the new pensions tax legislation lays down a single set of rules, it does not need to distinguish between the different types of pension arrangements. The legislation uses the general term 'registered pension scheme'. This means a pension scheme that has been registered with HMRC as being a scheme that meets all the requirements of Part 4 of the Finance Act 2004. But it must be borne in mind that simply because every pension arrangement is called a 'registered pension scheme' for the purposes of the tax legislation, there are still many different types of 'registered pension schemes', each with their own characteristics. It does not matter whether the arrangement is a multi-member scheme (such as an occupational pension scheme) or a single contract (such as a Retirement Annuity), each will be classified as a 'registered pension scheme'.

16.4   The following table provides a summary of the way things have changed from 6 April 2006.

The new pensions tax framework from 6 April 2006	
Type of pension arrangement	Regulatory controls
Employer-sponsored OPSs in their various forms	The benefits under all these types of pension arrangements are covered by a single set of tax rules.
'Left scheme' policies in their various forms	The tax privileges are controlled by:
Provider-sponsored Free-Standing AVC Schemes	Monitoring the amount of input each tax year into pension arrangements for the individual against a maximum value which is defined in legislation – the 'annual allowance'. The input for an individual will be made up of all contributions to money purchase arrangements, and/or the increase in the capital value of benefits accruing under any Defined Benefit OPS. The annual allowance has been set at £215,000 for the tax year 2006/07.
Provider-sponsored PPSs in their various forms	
Provider-sponsored SHPSs	
Retirement Annuity policies	
	Monitoring the total capital value of an individual's pension benefits from all arrangements against a maximum value which is defined in legislation – the 'standard lifetime allowance'. If the total capital value exceeds the standard lifetime allowance, a special tax charge (the 'lifetime allowance charge') will be levied on the excess. The standard lifetime allowance has been set at £1.5m for the tax year 2006/07. There are transitional arrangements for individuals where the capital value of their benefits accrued before A-Day already exceeds, or are likely to exceed, that maximum value.

SECTION 3   CONTRIBUTIONS AND TAX RELIEF

16.5   There is no limit on the amount of contributions that can be paid to a registered pension scheme. But there is a limit on the amount that will be eligible for tax relief. (In addition, if the annual allowance limit is breached a tax charge will arise on the member – see **16.6**.)

Tax relief on member contributions is limited to 100% of the earnings in the particular tax year (subject to the annual allowance). For a member with low earnings, or no earnings, a contribution can be made up to £3,600 and be eligible for tax relief.

Tax relief on member contributions will normally be given on the 'relief at source' basis – ie each contribution will be treated as though it was paid net of basic rate tax. The scheme administrator will then claim the tax direct from HMRC to apply to the pension arrangement. The member will claim any higher rate relief through the tax return.

For occupational pension schemes only, it is possible to operate the 'net pay' method. Here member contributions are deducted from salary before tax is applied, and the gross contribution paid to the scheme. This gives immediate tax relief at the highest rate.

Contributions by a member's employer are always gross.

The question of whether an employer's contribution will be allowable as a deduction from the taxable profits of the business will depend on whether the contributions can be considered as being paid 'wholly and exclusively for the purposes of the trade' as described in section 74(1)(a) of the Income and Corporation Taxes Act 1988. This will be a matter for the Tax Office dealing with the employer's affairs to decide. Where contributions are allowed as a deduction, companies will obtain corporation tax relief and partnerships/sole-traders will obtain income tax relief.

Allowance as a deduction will not normally be a problem where the contribution is for an ordinary employee. But a contribution may not be allowed where it is for a controlling director, or for a person connected with a controlling director (such as the director's spouse or registered civil partner). HMRC has indicated that a contribution will not be allowed if there is a non-trade purpose. An example given is where the level of the remuneration package, including the pension scheme contribution, is excessive for the value of the work undertaken by that individual for the employer.

Where the remuneration package paid in respect of a director, who is also a controlling shareholder, or in respect of an employee who is a close relative or friend of the business proprietor or controlling director, is comparable with that paid to unconnected employees, employer contributions will normally be accepted as being paid wholly and exclusively for the purposes of the trade. When there are no employees whose duties are generally comparable with the proprietor or relative, an assessment will be made by the Tax Office of whether the amount is a genuine payment for services rendered in the business. Evidence that the amount may not be a genuine business expense may be that it exceeds a reasonable rate of remuneration on a commercial basis.

SECTION 4   THE ANNUAL ALLOWANCE

16.6   The annual allowance imposes an upper limit on the amount of tax privilege that is available during a tax year.

Where the total contributions paid in a tax year to a money purchase arrangement, plus the increase in the value of any benefits under a defined benefits arrangement, exceeds the annual allowance, a tax charge will arise. This tax charge is known as the 'annual allowance charge', and is payable by the individual. The rate is 40% of the excess over the annual allowance.

Monitoring against the annual allowance, and the imposition of any charge, is dealt with through the self-assessment tax return.

The annual allowance has been set at the following levels:

- £215,000 for the tax year 2006/07

- £225,000 for the tax year 2007/08

- £235,000 for the tax year 2008/09

- £245,000 for the tax year 2009/10

- £255,000 for the tax year 2010/11

The following is an example of how the annual allowance works.

An individual has earnings of £150,000 in the tax year 2007/08, and makes contributions to a money purchase arrangement of £100,000. In addition, the employer also makes contributions of £200,000.

The individual will receive tax relief on the £100,000 contributions.

However, the individual will have to report on the self-assessment tax return that the total input for the 2007/08 tax year has been £300,000. This will lead to a tax charge of 40% x (300,000 - 225,000) = £30,000.

(Note that it makes no difference whether or not the employer's contribution has been allowed as a deduction under the 'wholly and exclusively' rule.)

SECTION 5   THE LIFETIME ALLOWANCE

16.7   There is no limit on the amount of the benefits that may be provided for an individual under registered pension schemes. But if the value of the benefits being paid under a particular scheme, when accumulated with benefits previously paid under that or any other scheme, exceeds a ceiling called the 'lifetime allowance', a tax charge will arise. This tax charge is known as the 'lifetime allowance charge'.

This charge is 25% of the excess where the excess benefits are taken in pension form, and 55% where the excess benefits are taken as cash.

The standard lifetime allowance has been set at the following levels:

- £1.50m for the tax year 2006/07

- £1.60m for the tax year 2007/08

- £1.65m for the tax year 2008/09

- £1.75m for the tax year 2009/10

- £1.80m for the tax year 2010/11

The standard lifetime allowance will be reviewed every 5 years thereafter.

The legislation specifies the various occasions when an individual will use up part of their lifetime allowance. These occasions are referred to as 'benefit crystallisation events' (BCEs). A BCE arises when benefits under a registered pension scheme become payable, such as when a pension commences or on death.

The way benefits are valued for the purpose of monitoring against the lifetime allowance is as follows:

- Under a money purchase scheme, the accumulated fund value is used.

- Under a defined benefit scheme, the value is determined as 20 times the pension. If part of the pension is commuted for a lump sum, the value is the lump sum plus 20 times the balance pension.

16.8   The following is an example of how the lifetime allowance works.

An individual takes benefits under a defined benefits occupational pension scheme in the tax year 2007/08. The benefits comprise a tax-free lump sum of £300,000 and a pension of £45,000. This benefits package has the following value for monitoring against the lifetime allowance: £300,000 + 20 × 45,000 = £1,200,000.

Hence at this stage the lifetime allowance has not been exceeded. The individual is treated as using up 75% of the lifetime allowance – ie (1,200,000 / 1,600,000) × 100.

In the tax year 2010/11 the individual takes benefits under a personal pension scheme. The fund stands at £500,000. The individual has already used up 75% of the lifetime allowance, so the available portion of the lifetime allowance in 2010/11 is 25% × £1,800,000 = £450,000. Hence there is an excess of £500,000 – £450,000 = £50,000. The individual takes the benefits in the following form:

- A tax-free lump sum of 25% × £450,000 = £112,500.

- A pension secured by the balance of £450,000 – £112,500 = £337,500.

- A lump sum from the excess. There will be a lifetime allowance charge of 55% × £50,000 = £27,500. The scheme administrator will withhold this tax and account for it to HMRC. The individual will receive the balance of £22,500.

The introduction of the lifetime allowance charge could have had a retrospective effect by catching large pension benefits that had already accrued before 6 April 2006. The government accepted that it would be unfair to penalise individuals who had accrued large benefits quite legitimately in accordance with the rules that existed before 6 April 2006. So, special provisions have been introduced to enable those individuals to protect the value of their pre-6 April 2006 benefits against the lifetime allowance charge that could otherwise arise. (But it should be noted that the government has still effectively placed a cap on the benefits that might have been expected under the old rules as accrual has been stopped at 5 April 2006.)

There are two types of protection – primary protection and enhanced protection. To take advantage of this facility, individuals must register for protection with HMRC before 6 April 2009. It is possible to register for either type of protection or for both.

The way primary protection works is that the total value of the individual's pension benefits is determined as at 5 April 2006. That is compared to the value of the maximum benefits that would have been approvable by HMRC under the pre-6 April 2006 rules. The lower of the two values is then compared to the standard lifetime allowance. If it is higher than the standard lifetime allowance, the individual can register for primary protection. The higher value will then form the individual's 'personal lifetime allowance' going forward. The personal lifetime allowance will increase each tax year in line with the rate of increase in the standard lifetime allowance. The individual can accrue further benefits from 6 April 2006, but any excess over the personal lifetime allowance will be subject to the lifetime allowance charge.

Enhanced protection works in a different way. The total value of the individual's benefits has to be determined as at 5 April 2006. If that exceeds the value of the maximum benefits that would have been approvable by HMRC under the pre-6 April 2006 rules, the individual has to give up the rights to the excess. The individual will not then incur any lifetime allowance charge in the future, no matter how much the fund grows. But, there must be no benefit accrual from 6 April 2006. Any sort of accrual will result in the loss of enhanced protection.

SECTION 6   RETIREMENT BENEFITS

16.9   The legislation allows registered pension schemes to provide benefits in various forms. It should be noted, however, that the forms of benefits available under a particular registered pension scheme will depend on what is allowed by the rules governing the scheme.

The term 'retirement benefits' is still commonly used. But the concept of 'retirement' in the sense of being in full-time employment one day then ceasing all employment the next is becoming increasingly blurred. It is being gradually replaced by the concept of 'phased retirement', which allows a gradual transition from full-time employment, into part-time employment, and then eventually full retirement. Indeed, the legislation has been deliberately constructed to ensure that the rules on benefit provision from tax-approved pension arrangements can support phased retirement.

The rules of any registered pension scheme (occupational as well as personal) can allow some or all of the benefits to come into payment at any time from the 50th birthday up to the day before the 75th birthday, irrespective of the individual's employment status. (From 6 April 2010, the minimum age at which benefits can commence will be increased to the 55th birthday.)

This is a radical change from the legislation that applied before 6 April 2006 which generally prevented benefits under an employer's occupational pension scheme from coming into payment before the individual had actually left the employment.

Not all employers will take advantage of the flexibility for the phased provision of benefits as it could increase the costs of the administration of their occupational pension scheme. But the opportunity is there for those employers who can see advantages in retaining access to the expertise of their experienced staff, whilst at the same time allowing them to move gradually into retirement.

Benefits can be drawn before the 50th/55th birthday in the event of incapacity or ill-health.

Where, exceptionally, the value of the benefits takes the individual over the lifetime allowance, the excess benefits must be dealt with separately, and the appropriate lifetime allowance charge paid. The remainder of this section is written in the context of benefits that come within the lifetime allowance.

The rules of a registered pension scheme can allow the members to take part of their benefits in the form of a tax-free lump sum. The lump sum must not exceed 25% of the value of the benefit package coming into payment at that time (except where the member has a protected lump sum entitlement deriving from benefits accrued before 6 April 2006). This lump sum is referred to as a 'pension commencement lump sum'. It cannot be paid before the date on which the pension is treated as commencing, and it must be paid within three months of that date.

In the case of benefits under a money purchase arrangement, the maximum pension commencement lump sum is simply 25% of the fund available to secure benefits.

In the case of a defined benefit arrangement, the maximum pension commencement lump sum is more difficult to determine. The maximum lump sum is 25% of the value of the benefit package. The value of the benefit package is made up of the lump sum plus 20 times the reduced pension that is left after commuting part of the full pension for the lump sum. A formula has to be applied which works out how much of the full pension has to be commuted to produce the requisite lump sum, using the scheme's own commutation factors.

The pension income can be provided in various ways, depending on the type of pension arrangement:

- on the 'secured pension' basis (by means of a 'scheme pension' or 'lifetime annuity') – which may include a guaranteed period of up to ten years and/or a reversionary annuity payable to a dependant (widow(er), civil partner or other individual financially dependent on the member);

- whilst the member is under age 75, on the 'unsecured pension' basis; or

- when the member reaches age 75, on the 'alternatively secured pension' basis.

Generally, whatever the basis, the pension will be taxed under the PAYE system. The only exception is where the pension arises under a registered pension scheme in the form of a retirement annuity contract. Here tax at the basic rate is deducted from the pension. Pensions under retirement annuity contracts are due to come onto the PAYE system with effect from 6 April 2007.

SECTION 7   DEATH BENEFITS

16.10   The benefits under registered pension schemes can take various forms. It should be noted, however, that the forms of benefits available under a particular registered pension scheme will depend on what is allowed by the rules governing the scheme.

Benefits can be provided for a 'dependant'. This term is defined in the legislation and covers:

- the member's wife, husband, civil partner, or any other individual who is financially dependent on the member;

- a child of the member who has not reached the age of 23 (please note any income withdrawals would cease on the child's 23rd birthday);

- a child of the member who has reached age 23 and is dependent on the member because of physical or mental impairment; or

- any other individual who is dependent on the member because of physical or mental impairment.

Where, exceptionally, the value of the benefits takes the individual over the lifetime allowance, the excess benefits must be dealt with separately, and the appropriate lifetime allowance charge paid. The remainder of this section is written in the context of benefits that come within the lifetime allowance.

A   On the member's death before drawing retirement benefits

16.11   Benefits can be provided in the following forms:

- a lump sum (which could derive from the retirement fund and/or a separately insured lump sum death benefit);

- a pension to a dependant – which can be provided in various ways depending on the type of arrangement:

  — on the 'secured pension' basis (by means of a 'scheme pension' or 'lifetime annuity');

  — where the dependant is under age 75, on the 'unsecured pension' basis; or

  — where the dependant is aged 75 or over, on the 'alternatively secured pension' basis.

There is no tax charge on the lump sum within the pensions tax framework. But in some cases the lump sum could be treated as forming part of the estate for inheritance tax purposes (see Chapter 14, Section 9).

Generally, a pension to a dependant will be taxed under the PAYE system. The only exception is where the pension arises under a registered pension scheme in the form of a retirement annuity contract. Here tax at the basic rate is deducted from the pension. Pensions under retirement annuity contracts are due to come onto the PAYE system with effect from 6 April 2007.

B   On the member's death whilst drawing a pension before the 75th birthday

16.12   Benefits can be provided in the following forms:

- where the member's pension was being paid on the 'secured pension' basis (ie by means of a 'scheme pension' or 'lifetime annuity'):

  - continuation of pension payments for any remaining guaranteed period;

  - payment of a lump sum associated with the pension (under 'pension protection' or 'annuity protection'); and/or

  - commencement of any associated pension to a dependant.

- where the member's pension was being paid on the 'unsecured pension' basis, the remaining fund would be disposed of by:

  - payment of a lump sum; or

  - provision of a pension for a dependant on the 'secured pension' basis (by means of a 'scheme pension' or 'lifetime annuity'), or on the 'unsecured pension' basis where the dependant is under age 75, or on the 'alternatively secured pension' basis where the dependant is aged 75 or over.

Any lump sum payment out of the scheme will be subject to a 35% tax charge. The scheme administrator is responsible for deducting the tax and accounting for it to HMRC. In addition, in some cases the lump sum could be treated as forming part of the estate for inheritance tax purposes (see Chapter 14, Section 9).

Generally, a pension to a dependant will be taxed under the PAYE system. The only exception is where the pension arises under a registered pension scheme in the form of a retirement annuity contract. Here tax at the basic rate is deducted from the pension. Pensions under retirement annuity contracts are due to come onto the PAYE system with effect from 6 April 2007.

C   On the member's death whilst drawing a pension on or after the 75th birthday

16.13   Benefits can be provided in the following forms:

- where the member's pension was being paid on the 'secured pension' basis (ie by means of a 'scheme pension' or 'lifetime annuity'):

  - continuation of pension payments for any remaining guaranteed period; and/or

  - commencement of any associated pension to a dependant.

- where the member's pension was being paid on the 'alternatively secured pension' basis, the remaining fund would be disposed of as follows:

(i)   If there is a dependant, the fund must be used to provide a pension for that dependant. The pension could be on the 'secured pension' basis (by means of a 'scheme pension' or 'lifetime annuity'), or on the 'unsecured pension' basis where the dependant is under age 75, or on the 'alternatively secured pension' basis where the dependant is aged 75 or over.

(ii)   If there is no surviving dependant, the fund can be paid as a lump sum to a charity, or charities. This would normally be in accordance with directions given by the member to the scheme administrator.

(iii)   If there is no surviving dependant, the fund could also be disposed of as an unauthorised payment (ie paid out of the scheme to a recipient other than a charity, or transferred to another arrangement within the scheme for the benefit of another individual), subject to the consequent tax charges.

Generally, a pension to a dependant will be taxed under the PAYE system. The only exception is where the pension arises under a registered pension scheme in the form of a retirement annuity contract. Here tax at the basic rate is deducted from the pension. Pensions under retirement annuity contracts are due to come onto the PAYE system with effect from 6 April 2007.

The position with regard to inheritance tax is quite complex in this situation. Details are given in Chapter 14, Section 9.

D   On a dependant's death whilst drawing a pension before the 75th birthday

16.14   Where the dependant's pension was being paid on the 'secured pension' basis (by means of a 'scheme pension' or 'lifetime annuity'), no further benefit would arise.

Where the dependant's pension was being paid on the 'unsecured pension' basis, the remaining fund would be disposed of by payment of a lump sum.

The lump sum payment out of the scheme will be subject to a 35% tax charge. The scheme administrator is responsible for deducting the tax and accounting for it to HMRC. In addition, in some cases the lump sum could be treated as forming part of the dependant's estate for inheritance tax purposes (see Chapter 14, Section 9).

The position with regard to inheritance tax is quite complex in this situation. Details are given in Chapter 14, Section 9.

A particularly penal tax charge arises in the following circumstances:

- a dependant dies whilst taking pension on the 'unsecured pension' basis;

- the fund derived from the fund of a member who had died whilst taking pension on the 'alternatively secured pension' basis.

Here the lump sum paid out of the scheme would be subject to the 35% tax charge in the normal way. But firstly it could be subject to an inheritance tax charge based on the original member's estate. So, potentially the fund could be hit with a 40% IHT charge, and then a further 35% tax charge – making a total tax charge of 61%. The scheme administrator is responsible for deducting the inheritance tax charge, as well as the 35% tax charge, and accounting for both to HMRC.

E   On a dependant's death whilst drawing a pension on or after the 75th birthday

16.15   Where the dependant's pension was being paid on the 'secured pension' basis (by means of a 'scheme pension' or 'lifetime annuity'), no further benefit would arise.

Where the dependant's pension was being paid on the 'alternatively secured pension' basis, the remaining fund would be disposed of as follows:

(i)   if, exceptionally, there is another surviving dependant of the member, the fund must be used to provide a pension for that dependant. The pension could be on the 'secured pension' basis (by means of a 'scheme pension' or 'lifetime annuity'), or on the 'unsecured pension' basis where the dependant is under age 75, or on the 'alternatively secured pension' basis where the dependant is aged 75 or over; or

(ii)   if there is no other surviving dependant, the fund can be paid as a lump sum to a charity, or charities. (This would normally be in accordance with directions given by the member to the scheme administrator.)

(iii)   If there is no other surviving dependant, the fund could also be disposed of as an unauthorised payment (ie paid out of the scheme to a recipient other than a charity, or transferred to another arrangement within the scheme for the benefit of another individual), subject to the consequent tax charges.

The position with regard to inheritance tax is quite complex in this situation. Details are given in Chapter 14, Section 9.

SECTION 8   UNAUTHORISED PAYMENTS

16.16   If a scheme makes a payment to a member that is not authorised by the legislation, various tax charges will arise. Examples of unauthorised payments would be:

●   a lump sum is paid to the member on retirement which is in excess of the permitted maximum;

●   a lump sum is paid to the member on retirement more than three months after the pension commenced;

●   the member receives retirement benefits before the minimum permissible age;

- the scheme sells an asset to the member for less than it is worth;

- on the member's death whilst taking pension on the 'alternatively secured pension' basis, where there is no dependant, the remaining fund is paid out of the scheme to a recipient other than a charity, or transferred to another arrangement within the scheme for the benefit of another individual.

Whenever an unauthorised member payment is made, the following tax charges will arise:

(a)   an unauthorised payments charge of 40% of the unauthorised payment;

(b)   if the unauthorised payment is 25% or more of the total value of the rights under the arrangement, an unauthorised payments surcharge of 15% of the unauthorised payment.

The member is liable for these tax charges and accounts for them through the self-assessment tax return. They are free-standing tax charges which means that any losses a taxpayer may have cannot be set against the charges.

In addition, the scheme could be liable to a scheme sanction charge of 15% of the unauthorised payment (or higher if the member has not paid the other charges). The scheme can withhold this charge from the payment made to the member.

Overall, there is potential for a tax charge of 70%.

SECTION 9   RECYCLING TAX-FREE LUMP SUMS

16.17   The process of recycling involves drawing the benefits from an existing pension fund, then using the tax-free lump sum (pension commencement lump sum) as a direct or indirect means of paying additional contributions to a registered pension scheme on which tax relief will be generated. Higher rate relief could be used to pay further contributions. Benefits would then be drawn from the further pension fund created, and the tax-free lump sum used to repeat the cycle. So, effectively, the same money is going round in a circle, and picking up extra tax relief on the way.

Not surprisingly, the government considers the recycling concept to be an abuse of the tax reliefs made available to encourage saving for retirement.

The recycling concept is not new. It had always been possible under the pre-6 April 2006 legislation governing personal pensions and retirement annuities. However, the advantage to be gained under that legislation was fairly minimal because of the restrictions placed on the amounts that could be paid as contributions which were eligible for tax relief (ie based on a percentage of earnings, starting at 17.5%, and with the earnings being capped for personal pensions). Those restrictions were removed with effect from 6 April 2006. Individuals can now get tax relief on contributions up to 100% of their uncapped earnings (subject to the annual allowance). So, whilst the government did not think it was worth doing anything about recycling under the pre-6 April 2006 legislation, the tax advantage to be gained by recycling is now too great to be ignored.

The new legislation counters recycling by deeming an unauthorised payment to have been made when a tax-free lump sum is recycled. An unauthorised payment will trigger the various tax charges outlined above.

The recycling rule will be triggered if:

- the recycling was pre-planned;

- the amount of the lump sum, aggregated with any other lump sums taken in the previous 12-month period, exceeds 1% of the standard lifetime allowance (ie £15,000 for the 2006/07 tax year); and

- as a consequence of the lump sum being taken, the amount of contributions paid into a registered pension scheme is significantly greater than it otherwise would have been. The measure here is that the cumulative amount of the additional contributions exceeds 30% of the lump sum received.

The recycling rule is only intended to catch the relatively small number of larger potential recyclers. The government feels that the legislation strikes a balance between deterring recycling activity, catching the more blatant and artificial cases, and leaving unaffected those smaller pensions savers and those undertaking normal retirement planning.

However, the mere existence of the recycling rule could have a widespread effect on administration. Scheme administrators might feel that they need to make the appropriate warning noises to all cases. Whilst a member might only have a small fund under the particular scheme, the scheme administrator will have no way of knowing what funds are available under other schemes, nor what the individual's intentions might be.

SECTION 10 INVESTMENTS

A General

16.18 The legislation that existed before 6 April 2006 imposed specific restrictions on the investments that could be held by schemes such as small self-administered schemes and self-invested personal pension schemes, where the members were able to direct the way the funds were invested. Those restrictions have been removed in the new legislation from 6 April 2006, and there is now a single set of investment rules for tax purposes applying to all types of registered pension schemes. However, as explained later, certain investments held by certain types of registered pension schemes will attract tax charges.

Schemes will still be subject to any relevant restrictions arising from DWP legislation, or other general restrictions outside tax law. The scheme trustees have a duty under general trust law to act prudently, conscientiously and honestly when making decisions in respect of the scheme. Trustees must always act in the best interests of the scheme members.

The tax legislation does not impose any restrictions on the investments that may be made by registered pension schemes. Instead, everything is regulated by the imposition of unauthorised payment tax charges if certain conditions are breached. The conditions which may be breached are:

- Any loan made by a scheme to an employer who is connected with the member will give rise to a tax charge on the member. But a registered pension scheme in the form of an occupational pension scheme can make a loan to the sponsoring employer without incurring any tax charges providing the loan does not exceed 50% of the fund value and it is done on specified terms.

- Any loan to a scheme member will give rise to a tax charge.

- Schemes can borrow funds for any purpose – for example, to assist with the purchase of an asset, or to meet a short-term liquidity problem. But the borrowing must not exceed 50% of the fund value (less any amounts previously borrowed), otherwise tax charges will arise.

- There is a limit on the amount which a registered pension scheme in the form of an occupational pension scheme can invest in the shares of the sponsoring employer, without giving rise to tax charges. The market value of the shares must be less than 5% of the fund value.

- Certain types of registered pension schemes are categorised as 'investment-regulated pension schemes'. Under these schemes tax charges will arise when the scheme holds assets, either directly or indirectly, that are classed as 'taxable property' (see **16.20**).

B   Tax exemptions

16.19   The following tax exemptions apply to registered pension schemes:

(a)   income derived from investments or deposits held for the purposes of a registered pension scheme is exempt from income tax (section 186 of the Finance Act 2004);

(b)   underwriting commissions applied for the purposes of a registered pension scheme are exempt from income tax if they would otherwise be chargeable to tax under Case VI of Schedule D (section 186(1)(b));

(c)   income from futures contracts and options contracts are deemed to all be from investments as is any income derived from transactions relating to futures contracts or options contracts (section 186(3));

(d)   profits or gains arising from transactions in certificates of deposit are exempt from income tax (section 56 of the Income and Corporation Taxes Act 1988);

(e)   profits from sale and repurchase agreements (repos) and 'manufactured payments' are exempt from income tax (SI 1995/3036);

(f)   a gain arising from the disposal of investments (including (c) above) held for the purposes of the scheme is exempt from capital gains tax (section 271 of the Taxation of Capital Gains Act 1992).

The exemptions above do not apply to income derived from investments or deposits held as a member of a property investment limited liability partnership.

There is nothing to prevent a registered pension scheme entering into trading activities. But as income derived from trading is not investment income or income from deposits, the tax exemptions (including those relating to capital gains on assets used by a scheme for trading purposes) do not apply. So, a registered pension scheme would be liable to pay tax on any income derived from a trading activity.

C   Investment-regulated pension schemes

16.20   Because the legislation does not impose any restrictions on the investments that may be made by registered pension schemes, there is potential for schemes to invest in assets which may provide the opportunity for private use by the members. The government is keen to prevent tax-advantaged pension funds being used in that way, So, the legislation contains special provisions for certain types of registered pension schemes (referred to as 'investment-regulated pension schemes') which remove the tax advantages where the investments may create an opportunity for private use.

The term 'investment-regulated pension scheme' is used in the legislation to describe a registered pension scheme where the member, or a person related to the member, can self-direct the investments held by the scheme.

A registered pension scheme that is not an occupational pension scheme will be classified as an 'investment-regulated pension scheme' where a member (or person related to the member) is able (whether directly or indirectly) to direct, influence or advise on the manner of investments held for the purposes of the member's arrangement under the scheme. This encompasses registered pension schemes in the form of self-invested personal pension schemes, and fully insured personal pension schemes where a personal managed fund facility is made available.

A registered pension scheme that is an occupational pension scheme will be classified as an 'investment-regulated pension scheme' where the scheme has fewer than 50 members and has at least one member who meets the 'self-direction' condition, or the scheme has 50 or more members and has at least 10% of members who meet the 'self-direction' condition. The 'self-direction' condition is met if the member (or person related to the member) is able (whether directly or indirectly) to direct, influence or advise on the manner of investments held for the purposes of the scheme. This will encompass registered pension schemes in the form of small self-administered pension schemes and possibly some large self-administered pension schemes.

Whenever an 'investment-regulated pension scheme' holds assets, either directly or indirectly, that are classed as 'taxable property' there will be tax charges.

'Taxable property' consists of residential property and most types of 'tangible moveable' property.

657

Residential property can be in the UK or elsewhere and is:

- a building or structure that is used or suitable to be used as a dwelling;

- any related land that is wholly or partly the garden for the building or structure;

- any related land that is wholly or partly grounds for the residential property and which is used or intended for use for a purpose connected with the enjoyment of the building;

- any building or structure on any such related land;

- ground rents (long leaseholds) held in respect of residential property;

- hotel or similar accommodation where ownership is conferred via time-share rights.

Tangible movable property comprises things that can be touched or moved such as art, antiques, jewellery, fine wine, boats, classic cars, stamp collections, rare books.

16.21 It is important to note that the legislation refers to 'taxable property' that is held 'directly or indirectly'. The reference to 'indirectly' ensures that 'taxable property' held by companies and other vehicles owned by pension schemes is also caught. That acts as a deterrent to the pension scheme owning, for example:

- 100% of the shares in a company that owns a flat in a desirable holiday resort which could be used by a member;

- 100% of the shares in a trading company that deals with, for example, fine wines or antiques, that could be available for the private use of a member.

Unfortunately, the scope of this part of the legislation also catches investments in companies involved in trading activities for which there is no possibility of private use. This could have the effect of stopping schemes holding unquoted company shares, which has traditionally been a popular form of investment for small self-administered schemes.

Where an 'investment-regulated pension scheme' holds an interest in 'taxable property', whether directly or indirectly, the value of the interest will be treated as an unauthorised payment, and the following tax charges will arise. The value of the interest would be 100% of the value of the property if held directly by the scheme. If held indirectly, the value would be based on a percentage, to take into account the fact that only a part of the interest in the taxable property is held by the investment-regulated pension scheme.

- The member will be subject to the unauthorised payments charge at 40% of the value placed on the interest.

- If certain limits are exceeded, the member will also be subject to the unauthorised payments surcharge at 15% of the value placed on the interest.

- The scheme administrator will be subject to the scheme sanction charge, normally at 15% of the value placed on the interest.

- Income or deemed income received in relation to the 'taxable property' will be subject to the scheme sanction charge at 40% of the value placed on the income.

- Any capital gain on the disposal of the 'taxable property' will be subject to the scheme sanction charge at 40% of the value placed on the capital gain.

CHAPTER 17

Life assurance for special purposes

SUMMARY

Section 1   Business assurance   **17.1**

Section 2   Key man policies   **17.25**

Section 3   Policies for children   **17.30**

Section 4   Long-term care   **17.44**

Section 5   Miscellaneous   **17.56**

This chapter considers some taxation, legal and practical aspects of contracts issued by life assurance companies or long-term insurance contracts, effected for a number of special purposes, which could not appropriately be dealt with, or are referred to only briefly, elsewhere in this book.

SECTION I   BUSINESS ASSURANCE

17.1   It is important for the members of professional partnerships and small companies to give consideration to the consequences of the death of a partner, director or shareholder. Under English law, aside from a limited liability partnership, created in accordance with the Limited Liability Partnerships Act 2000 effective from 6 April 2001, a partnership is not recognised as a legal entity (although it is in Scotland). Unless there is a partnership agreement which provides otherwise, a partnership will automatically dissolve on the death of a partner[1] and any capital belonging to the deceased partner will form part of his estate for inheritance tax (IHT) purposes. The loss of this capital may cause financial and practical difficulties for the surviving partners and it may also leave the deceased partner's spouse with a business interest for which he or she may have little use or wish to hold.

Similar considerations apply in the case of private companies, with a relatively small number of people owning the company as shareholders and running it as

---

1   Partnership Act 1890, s 33.

directors. A company is recognised as a distinct legal entity so it will not dissolve upon the death of a director or shareholder, but the deceased director/share-holder's shares may pass in accordance with his will or the intestacy rules, to someone with no interest in the company.

In both types of organisation, therefore, it is normally far better for all parties if there is a pre-planned arrangement to cater for the parties' aims, needs and desires as appropriate. A vital part of partnership planning is to have a written partnership agreement, setting out what is to occur upon death or retirement. It must be noted, however, that if the relevant part of the partnership agreement contains what amounts to a binding buy and sell agreement, the business interest will not be treated as 'relevant business property' for IHT business property relief purposes[1].

A vital part of the planning for either organisation is the means of funding the purchase of the deceased's business interest. Similar considerations apply to both types of organisation, and reference will generally be made below to partnerships, with specific comments in relation to private companies where it is appropriate. The main aims of business assurance planning are:

(1)   to provide cash in the right hands at the right time;

(2)   to avoid liability to capital gains tax (CGT);

(3)   to avoid liability to IHT;

(4)   to ensure an equitable division of the cost of funding the planning; and

(5)   to ensure the arrangements are flexible enough to cater for changes in the organisation's constitution.

Life assurance can assist in providing sufficient funds in the right hands at the right time.

A   Method of effecting the policies

17.2   There are a number of ways of trying to attain the above aims. The following text refers to partners but the same issues will generally apply to share-holding directors in private companies.

I   Own life policies cross-assigned

17.3   At one time this was a popular method of arranging partners' policies. Each partner takes out a policy on his own life for the amount required, pays the premium himself and assigns the policy in favour of his partners.

The main disadvantages of this arrangement are that it may become an admin-istrative burden (requiring a fresh assignment each time there is a change in the constitution of the organisation) and the fact that any gain under the policy (ie the

1   IHTA 1984, s 113; see Chapter 14.

profit element) could be subject to CGT[1]. (The reasoning for such a charge is fully explained at **17.8**.) For these reasons, this method is not, in general, to be recommended.

2 Life of another policy

17.4 Each partner effects, as grantee, a policy on the lives of each of his other partners, with a sum assured in each case to provide for his interest in the particular partner's business interest. As each policy would be the property of the grantee, who pays the premium, there would be no element of gift, and no IHT liability on receipt of the policy moneys, which would be received by the grantee, at the death of the other partner(s) to enable him to purchase the interest. The policies owned by a deceased partner (on the lives of the surviving partners) would be part of the deceased partner's estate for IHT purposes – the value being the market value, or premiums paid, if greater, at the date of death.

One disadvantage of this method is that if there is a wide disparity of ages it may be difficult for a young partner to afford the premiums required under policies on the lives of older partners. In addition, if there are several partners, it will result in many policies being effected and it will be inflexible in situations where new partners join a firm or existing partners leave.

3 Joint lives (first death) policies

17.5 Under this arrangement, the partners effect one policy on all their lives for the capital sum required on the death of any one of them, and each partner pays an appropriate proportion of the premium. On the first death the proceeds are payable to the surviving partner or partners. The benefit payable is the same whichever partner dies first and the arrangement is not suitable, therefore, where the partners' interests in the business are unequal. Furthermore, changes in the organisation's constitution cannot easily be accommodated; and a new policy would be required each time a partner dies. For these reasons, this arrangement is virtually never used, except for a two-person partnership, where the partners have equal business interests. In such a partnership, an assurance on this basis may be the most suitable. The premium is usually less than the combined premiums would be under two single life assurances for the same combined sum assured. Provided the premiums are split on an actuarial basis, there should be no IHT liability on death.

Following the changes to the taxation of trusts from 22 March 2006 as described in Chapter 14, all trusts effected on or after that date will be treated as discretionary trusts (unless they are absolute or bare trusts or trusts for disabled persons). However, it is felt that provided that any arrangements entered into are part of normal commercial arrangements and there is no intention to confer a gratuitous benefit, premiums under such trusts should not be treated as gifts at the outset.

1 Taxation of Chargeable Gains Act (TCGA) 1992, s 210.

4 Automatic accrual and own life policies

17.6   Another method, sometimes recommended for its apparent simplicity, where the business interests are equal, is that known as automatic accrual. This involves a special provision in the partnership agreement concerning the retirement or death of a partner, viz that the retired or deceased partner's interest in the goodwill and his capital account, subject sometimes to an upper limit, passes automatically to the remaining or surviving partners on his death or retirement. Coupled with this, each partner effects a whole life policy on his own life, to compensate his estate for the value of his interest passing to the co-partners. However, if automatic accrual is to operate on retirement where there is a fixed retirement age, an endowment policy might be more appropriate than a whole life policy.

The policy proceeds, if written under trust, would normally be free of IHT subject to the comments contained in Chapter 14, unless the trust used was of the absolute variety. There are no difficulties with changes in the partnership as each partner has his own policy and no one else has an interest in that policy.

5 Individual trust policies for other partners/directors

(a) The position for policies already in force as at 22 March 2006

17.7   Traditionally, this has been the most popular way of writing business assurance. Each partner effects only one policy on his own life written subject to an interest in possession trust for the others in whatever interests they hold in the business at a stated point at some time after the life assured's death.

An example of a typical trust wording on this basis is as follows:

> 'UPON trust for the benefit of such of the person or persons (other than myself) who seven days after the occurrence of the event upon which the policy money becomes payable ('the Event') shall be partners in the firm known as [XYZ] or its successors in business ('the Firm') provided that such persons were partners in the Firm immediately before the Event and in the like shares in which they are then entitled to share in the profits of the business of the Firm as if I had retired from the Firm on the happening of the Event
>
> Provided always that if I should cease to be a partner in the Firm otherwise than by reason of my death then for the benefit of myself absolutely
>
> I direct that the trusts hereof shall carry any intermediate income and the right to such income shall be vested in the partners in the Firm (other than myself) in existence at the time such income arises and he or they shall be entitled to receive such income in the same proportions as they would be entitled to the trust property from which such income arises as if it was seven days after my death and the said partners had satisfied any and all contingencies set out above.'

This form of wording is flexible in catering for changes in the partnership as new partners are automatically included and outgoing ones automatically excluded, although incoming partners will need to effect a policy on their own lives under a similar trust in order to retain the commerciality of the arrangement (see below). It should of course be borne in mind that any new policies effected on or after 22 March 2006 which are written subject to similar interest in possession trusts will be within the 'relevant property' trust regime as set out in Chapter 14, Section 6C.

17.8   This form of wording, determining who the beneficiaries are and giving them their rights seven days after the death of the life assured, creates a continuing settlement for CGT purposes. This is important to avoid a charge to CGT under section 210 of TCGA 1992, upon a disposal of rights under a policy. A disposal of rights is defined as the payment of the sum assured, the transfer of investments or other assets to the owner of a policy, or the surrender of a policy[1]. Section 60 of TCGA 1992 is also relevant. It states that where the trust is a bare trust (where the beneficiaries are absolutely entitled as against the trustees) the acts of the trustees are to be treated as if they were the acts of the beneficiaries. Thus, under a bare trust wording which provides that the beneficiaries are those person(s) who are partners in the firm known as [XYZ] *immediately before the event* upon which the policy moneys become payable, the beneficiaries are absolutely entitled as against the trustees at the time of the disposal and will be treated as effecting the disposal themselves.

Section 210 provides that a disposal under a life assurance policy is exempt from CGT *unless*:

(1)   the person making the disposal is not the original beneficial owner; *and*

(2)   he acquired the rights for a consideration in money or money's worth.

There is no definition of 'original beneficial owner' in TCGA 1992, or any other statute, nor has it been significantly considered judicially. In the authors' view, it is likely to mean the persons who have the interest in possession in the policy from the outset.

In relation to the right to income, the above wording provides that the partners from time to time be deemed to have satisfied the contingency and thereby, or by the operation of section 31 of the Trustee Act 1925, the partners for the time being will have an interest in possession in the trust. Section 31(1)(ii) provides that if an adult has a contingent interest in a trust, the income and any accretion thereto shall be paid to him until he either attains a vested interest or dies or until failure of his interest. The partner beneficiaries have a contingent interest, in that their interest is liable to fail, eg if they cease to be partners. Their interests are not vested because the contingency which is required may determine at any moment, ie by ceasing to be a partner, therefore section 31 applies, giving the partner beneficiaries an interest in possession.

Thus, where the original beneficial ownership has changed (eg where there are incoming partners since the time of writing the policy in trust), the first requirement to bring the proceeds into charge (ie (1) above) is met. It is hard to envisage a business assurance situation where the second requirement (ie (2) above) will not be met, as one partner will effect an own life assurance policy in trust in

---

1   TCGA 1992, s 210.

consideration for the other partners doing the same thing, such mutuality amounting to a consideration in money or money's worth. The arrangement must, by its very nature, be a commercial one (see (a) and (b), below). For the reasons stated above, it is important to ensure that the trust is a continuing one for CGT purposes. This is the reason for the suggestion above that the trust vests seven days after the death of the life assured.

17.9 Under the Capital Transfer Tax regime, the trusts used were often flexible, power of appointment trusts (see Chapter 15). The use of the flexible trust is not viable, however, under the IHT regime, as, due to the potential lack of commerciality (see below) it could fall within the gift with reservation of benefit (GWR) provisions of section 102 of the Finance Act 1986[1] and thus the policy proceeds would be treated as being in the estate of the person declaring the flexible trust.

The GWR provisions apply where, on or after 18 March 1986, an individual disposes of property by way of *gift* and, inter alia, the property and any benefit to him by contract or otherwise'[2] is not enjoyed to the entire exclusion or virtually to the entire exclusion of the donor. The inclusion of each partner as a beneficiary or potential beneficiary under the other partners' trusts may amount to 'a benefit to him by contract or otherwise', which may bring the arrangement within the GWR provisions, with the result that the policy would continue to form part of the estate for IHT purposes.

Further, where the beneficiaries and potential beneficiaries include individuals other than the partners (eg, where a partner's spouse and children are included), the arrangement would not appear to be commercial. It would contain an element of bounty and would constitute a gift, bringing the arrangement within the GWR provisions.

Sometimes, flexible power of appointment trusts are used, with the beneficiaries being limited to the partners for the time being, or limited to specified partners, rather than all the partners at a particular time. There is a considerable risk of such trusts not being viewed as 'commercial' as the power of appointment may be exercised to give a greater share of the trust fund to a particular partner than his share of the business actually warrants. There is thus, potentially, an element of gift and such a trust wording may bring the GWR provisions into operation.

17.10 To avoid the application of the GWR provisions, therefore, it is necessary to ensure that the arrangement is fully commercial, without any element of gift. HMRC have said that what is 'commercial' will depend on the individual facts of each case.

(I) COMMERCIALITY OF THE TRUST ARRANGEMENT

17.11 The policies must be effected subject to reciprocal trusts by each partner in trust for all the other partners (excluding himself). HMRC have confirmed that

---

1 See Chapter 14.
2 FA 1986, s 102(1)(b).

it is acceptable, however, for the benefits to revert back to the settlor if he ceases to be a partner for any reason such as the business ceasing to exist or the individual partner leaving the firm or retiring.

(II)   COMMERCIALITY OF THE PREMIUMS

17.12   HMRC have confirmed that arrangements can be 'commercial' even if, for example, the partners are of different ages and as a result one partner will appear to be spending more for the benefit of his partners than the other partners are spending for him, or if two partners have respectively a 20% and 80% share of the business and the 80% partner writes a larger policy in trust for the 20% partner than that partner writes for him[1]. However, if there is a disparity in the amounts of the premiums paid by each partner, it could be argued that the arrangement is not commercial. Consideration should therefore be given to equalising the premiums between the parties. This could be achieved by, for example, each person's policy being limited to the amount of cover available for the cheapest premium (probably for the youngest) and by the parties topping-up the cover required by 'life of another' policies to provide for the required deficiency in the cover resulting from the equalisation. This method does have disadvantages in that, for example, younger partners would have to pay higher premiums on the lives of senior partners and, unless it is a small partnership, with relatively few changes, the number of policies required can become high and can become an administrative burden. This method is the most appropriate for company directors, but partners may use a method which is simpler and where equalisation of the premiums is not necessary.

Under this method, the premiums could become the first charge on the profits of the partnership, charged to the relevant partners' capital accounts. In this way, the arrangement will be treated as commercial, and the GWR provisions should not apply.

A further method of trying to ensure that the arrangements are commercial with regard to the premium payments for directors of companies is the undertaking and cost adjustment method.

17.13   A company is likely to consist of owners of different ages owning unequal shares in the company. For example, the policy effected by an elderly major shareholder director will probably have the highest sum assured and premiums. Yet, conversely, because of his age, he has the lowest expectation of benefiting from the arrangement. The owners, could therefore, equalise the cost of the arrangement to endeavour to exclude any element of bounty. Therefore, suitable cost adjustments between the owners ensures that each owner contributes to the total cost in proportion to the extent he expects to benefit from the arrangement. A suitable formula for calculating the necessary 'should pay premiums' for a number of owners is illustrated below. The formula can be extended to cater

---

1   See letter dated 6 April 1987 from the Life Insurance Council (LIC) to members of the LIC following clarification from the Inland Revenue Circular No LIC 60/87.

for any number of owners and assumes the surviving owners will purchase the deceased's shares rateably according to their existing shares in the company.

$$\text{A's should pay premium} = \frac{\text{A's share of business X B's premium}}{(\text{Total value of business} - \text{B's share})} + \frac{\text{A's share of business X C's premium}}{(\text{Total value of business} - \text{C's share})}$$

$$\text{B's should pay premium} = \frac{\text{B's share of business X A's premium}}{(\text{Total value of business} - \text{A's share})} + \frac{\text{B's share of business X C's premium}}{(\text{Total value of business} - \text{C's share})}$$

$$\text{C's should pay premium} = \frac{\text{C's share of business X A's premium}}{(\text{Total value of business} - \text{A's share})} + \frac{\text{C's share of business X B's premium}}{(\text{Total value of business} - \text{B's share})}$$

To endeavour to show the arrangement has been set up on a commercial basis, in other words there is no element of bounty in favour of any of the owners, an undertaking should be completed. In simple terms, the undertaking states the owners have effected and will keep in force the policies as part of a business arrangement. It also details the necessary 'should pay premiums' which should remove any element of bounty.

In addition to effecting the trust policy, each partner should address a letter or memorandum to his co-partners, which clearly states that he is undertaking to effect a policy on his own life in trust for them *in consideration* for them doing the same and that the arrangement is a business transaction between them and is *not intended to confer any gratuitous benefit* on his co-partners. A new, incoming partner should execute a similar letter or memorandum when completing his proposal.

A specimen undertaking to be addressed by each partner to the other partners is as follows:

> 'TO: [all of the partners] in [XYZ]
>
> I hereby undertake to effect a [ ] policy on my life in trust for you and to maintain the said policy in full force by payment of the premiums when due, in full consideration of you each severally undertaking to effect a policy on your own life in trust for me proportionate to my share of the business and to maintain the said policy in full force by payment of the premiums when due. I hereby declare that the above mentioned life assurance arrangements are made between us at arm's length we having arranged for any appropriate financial adjustments to be made, and the said arrangements are not intended to confer any gratuitous benefit on any person.
>
> Signed..............................
>
> Dated..............................'

The introduction of a new member into the partnership would, unless the new partner entered into mutual commercial arrangements, before 22 March 2006 have caused a PET to be made, as there would be, in effect, a transfer from the existing partners to the new partner, of a slice of their interests in possession under the existing trust policies. This would normally be measured by reference to a proportion (depending on the number of partners) of the total premiums paid up to the time of introducing the new partner or the market value of the policy if higher[1].

1   IHTA 1984, ss 160, 167.

The death of the life assured under a policy written in trust in the way described above should not give rise to any IHT liability. The death of a partner/beneficiary could, however, be a transfer of value as there is a termination of the deceased's interest in possession, which would increase the value of the survivors' estates[1]. The value of the transfer would not be based on the sum assured, but only on the deceased beneficiary's share in the value of the trust interest at the time of his death, which would normally be calculated by reference to the open market value of the policy[2]. However, in the majority of cases, it is hoped that the arrangement would be 'commercial' (see above) and so any transfer of value would fall within the section 10 exemption, of no intention to confer any gratuitous benefit on anyone, and thus, there would be no charge to IHT.

(III)   APPOINTMENT OF ADDITIONAL TRUSTEES

17.14   If the trust is declared using a letter of request, forming part of the contract between the proposer and the life office, so that the trust is constituted from the outset (fully explained in Chapter 15, Section 3), the assured will be sole trustee of the policy from the outset. It is recommended that other persons (eg other partners) should be appointed as additional trustees by a separate deed of appointment, once the policy has been effected, so that they can act as trustees immediately on the death of the life assured.

(IV)   DECLARING TRUSTS OF EXISTING POLICIES FOR BUSINESS ASSURANCE PURPOSES

17.15   Careful consideration should be given to the possible CGT ramifications of using existing policies to declare trusts for the surviving partners on the basis expressed above, rather than effecting the contracts in trust from the outset. The relevant sections in this regard are sections 210 and 60 of TCGA 1992 (referred to at **17.8**). It will be recalled that section 210 states that disposals under life assurance contracts are exempt from CGT unless the person making the disposal is not the original beneficial owner and acquired his rights or interest for a consideration in money or money's worth.

Where a contract is effected free from trust, the original beneficial owner is clearly the grantee of the policy. If a bare trust of the contract is subsequently declared, there is obviously a change in the beneficial ownership to the beneficiaries. The relevant question is then, whether the beneficiaries acquired their rights or interest under the policy for a consideration in money or money's worth. If so and they then make a disposal, eg a claim on the policy, then a chargeable gain may accrue. In the example above, the policy moneys would be paid on death to the trustees. If the trust is a bare trust, section 60 will treat the disposal as being effected by the beneficiaries – the surviving partners (who will not be the original beneficial owners). The surviving partners would have acquired their interests for consideration, by way of the mutual declaration of trust of policies on commercial terms. Thus, there could be a charge to CGT, on

---

1   IHTA 1984, s 3A(2)(b).
2   IHTA 1984, ss 50, 160, 167(2)(a).

any gains to the extent that the amount received on the disposal exceeded the allowable expenditure (in effect, the premiums) plus indexation up to 5 April 1998 and taper relief thereafter.

It may be possible to avoid such a charge at the time of the disposal by ensuring that the person making the disposal has not acquired his rights for consideration, ie by drafting the trust to ensure that the trustees will be effecting the disposal, and by drafting the trust to ensure that section 60 will not apply, ie so that there is not a bare trust at the time of the disposal. It is not entirely certain, however, that section 210 may be avoided when declaring trusts of existing policies. HMRC has not given any guidance on this point.

Since 6 April 2005, there may also be a problem for business assurance policies in respect of pre-owned assets tax. As far as this is concerned, the authors can do no better than quote verbatim from the HMRC Guidance Notes on Pre-owned Assets Tax as follows:

> 'In some cases, policies are taken out on each partner's life solely for the purposes of providing funds to enable their fellow partners to purchase his/her share from the partner's beneficiaries on their death. The partner is not a potential beneficiary of his/her "own" policy. In such circumstances, a charge to tax under Schedule 15 paragraph 8 Finance Act 2004 will not arise.
>
> However, in many cases, the partner retains a benefit for themselves, for example, they can cash in the policy during their lifetime for their own benefit. In such cases, even if the arrangement is on commercial terms so that it is not a gift with reservation for inheritance tax, the trust is a settlement for inheritance tax purposes and a charge to tax under paragraph 8 will arise.
>
> The valuation of a partner's, or settlor's, interest in a policy for the purposes of paragraph 8 of Schedule 15 should be his share of its open market value as at 6 April each year. That valuation will be relevant for determining the amount of charge for that year of assessment.
>
> Where the policies are term assurances, in the vast majority of cases the policyholder will be in normal health, and therefore it is likely that the chargeable amount, as calculated under paragraph 9 of Schedule 15, will have little marketable value and will fall below the de minimis exemption in paragraph 13. Therefore, a policyholder in normal health at the valuation date may assume that he will survive beyond the term of the assurance, and complete his tax return accordingly. However, in circumstances where the policyholder has been advised that their state of health is such that it casts doubt on their survival to the end of the term of assurance (ie there becomes a realistic prospect of the policy paying out and therefore having a material market value), then consideration should be given to obtaining actuarial advice about the value of the policy.'

It has to be said that there is some doubt within the industry as to whether HMRC's views in this area are correct but, at the time of writing, the views expressed above remain the official HMRC line.

(b) New policies effected on or after 22 March 2006

17.16 If a new policy is written subject to an interest in possession trust as described above on or after 22 March 2006 then the trust will fall within the relevant property regime for IHT purposes. As far as the premiums are concerned, again if the arrangements are treated as commercial transactions by HMRC then payment of premiums would not involve any gifts – the points made at **17.12** and **17.13** continue to be relevant.

The trust will also potentially be liable to the ten-yearly and exit charges but HMRC have confirmed that they will be looking at the market value of the policy at each ten-yearly anniversary rather than the premiums paid and so this may not be a significant issue unless the sum assured under the policy is substantial or the life assured is in ill-health at the ten-yearly anniversary.

Even for very large sums assured, any problems at the ten-yearly anniversary can be largely avoided by the settlor effecting several policies on different days. This would have the effect of giving each policy its own nil rate band and thus dramatically reducing the chances of any future ten-yearly charge.

It is envisaged that many settlors would still wish to include themselves as potential beneficiaries under these arrangements so that, should circumstances change, the benefits can revert back to them. Again, provided the arrangements are viewed as commercial, this should not have any implications from a gift with reservation point of view.

(l) TYPES OF ASSURANCE

17.17 To cover the situation on death, unit-linked whole life assurances are suitable. If the intention is to buy out a partner's interest upon his retirement, endowment assurances, written to the anticipated date of retirement, should also be considered, although equalisation of premiums is not generally possible under these contracts.

When discussing planning for the death of a partner, consideration may also be given to the inclusion of critical illness cover. If a partner contracts a critical illness and wishes to retire early from the business, the remaining partners may therefore have the necessary funds to purchase his share of the business. However, including critical illness cover can lead to possible problems and these should be fully considered at the outset:

- The partner suffering the critical illness may not wish to sell at that time; he may wish to return to work, for example, after a mild heart attack.

- A partner disposing of a business interest following a critical illness claim must give consideration to the taxation consequences. The sale to the remaining partners will be treated as a disposal for CGT purposes and therefore a liability to tax may arise. It should be noted that in some cases CGT retirement relief and/or taper relief may be available. On subsequent death, the cash that had been received from the sale of the interest in the business could be liable to IHT in full. However, if the partner retained his business interest until death, his estate should be entitled to business property relief for IHT purposes as described in Chapter 14.

The first potential problem can be resolved by the partners having a properly drawn up agreement that includes a single option clause to cover critical illness benefits. In simple terms, the single option clause states that in the event of a critical illness claim, the partner suffering the critical illness will have the option to sell his interest in the business to the remaining partners. The other partners cannot, however, force the partner with the critical illness to sell his share. If the option is exercised it is binding on the remaining partners. Using this type of agreement enables the partner suffering the critical illness to carefully consider his future working circumstances and personal taxation position before deciding to sell his business interest.

It must, however, be emphasised that this action does not overcome the taxation problems outlined above.

The situation may arise whereby a critical illness claim arises but the partner does not wish to exercise his option to sell his interest in the business to the remaining partners. In these circumstances a claim will still be made and the proceeds paid to the trustees. The trustees should reinvest the policy proceeds for the benefit of the other partners until such time as the partner suffering the critical illness dies. At that time the trustees can irrevocably appoint the trust proceeds to the surviving partners, who can then exercise their option to purchase the deceased partner's interest in the business.

If critical illness cover is included in an arrangement, the terms of any option agreement should be such that the critical illness benefit will be 100% of the sum assured. This would ensure that the remaining partners will have the necessary funds to fully purchase the critically ill partner's interest in the business.

In view of these potential problems, it may be more appropriate for each partner to have separate critical illness cover, if required, aside from any 'business assurance' arrangement.

6 Pension term assurance written in trust

17.18 As an alternative to the above arrangements, it was possible for each partner to effect a pension term assurance and obtain income tax relief at their marginal rate on the contributions. Each partner would effect such a policy in trust for the other partners to ensure that they would be able to purchase the deceased's interest in the event of his death before a predetermined date, eg retirement age.

The premiums payable under such arrangements would need to be set off against the individual's annual allowance (see Chapter 16, Section 4). Furthermore, should lump sum benefits become payable as a result of the individual's death, these will also count against his or her lifetime allowance (see Chapter 16, Section 5). Thus, where the sums assured are substantial, this may make pension term assurance unattractive to some individuals.

The pre-Budget report of 6 December 2006 announced the Government's intention to abolish tax relief for stand alone pension term assurance policies. Policies effected before 6 December 2006 are unaffected. At the time of writing, HMRC has issued a statement indicating that pension term assurance policies applied for but not issued before that date will continue to benefit from tax relief provided the following conditions are met:

- The application for the policy must have been fully completed on or before 6 December 2006 and submitted to the insurance company and receipt recorded by the insurance company by midnight on 13 December 2006.

- The sum assured issued is no greater than that applied for on or before 6 December 2006.

- The insurer must process the business by no later than 5 April 2007.

7 Company effecting life of another policies

17.19 A final alternative arrangement is for the company to effect life of another policies on the lives of the relevant shareholders.

Until 1981, it was not possible for a private limited company to purchase its own shares. However, provisions were introduced in the Companies Act 1981 to allow this. The introduction of these provisions enables company share purchase to be used as the basis of a share protection arrangement. The company effects policies on the lives of each of its shareholders with a sum assured to cover the value of each shareholding. On death, the policy proceeds are paid to the company and this gives it the necessary funds to purchase the deceased's shares and cancel them. This process effectively increases the proportionate sharehold-ing of the remaining shareholders. Whilst this type of arrangement achieves the same effect as the surviving owners purchasing a deceased shareholder's shares the following points must also be considered:

- The policies are effected by the company and therefore all policies, whether qualifying or non-qualifying, are potentially subject to corporation tax on any chargeable gain. This is unlikely to be viewed as a problem with pro-tection policies with very low cash values as, in practice, chargeable gains should not arise. However, it will be a disadvantage if savings policies are being used to provide funds on retirement as well as death.

- The company's Articles of Association must authorise the company to pur-chase its own shares. For companies incorporated prior to 1982 it is unlikely that this power will be included in the company's Articles and therefore these would have to be changed. A change in the company's Articles to permit purchase by the company may increase the value of the shareholding.

- A further important requirement is that before a company can effect a pur-chase of its own shares, the directors must give a statutory declaration of solvency (ie that the company will still be solvent after the purchase) backed by a favourable report from the company's auditors.

- It is usual for the option agreement to be one-way only, ie the company should have the option to purchase. If the deceased's personal representa-tives had the option to sell to the company and they elect to enforce the option, the directors may not be able to provide the necessary statutory dec-laration and thus the company would not be able to buy the shares.

- Assuming the company is able to legally purchase its own shares (and there are various conditions to satisfy under the Companies Act 2006), HMRC require certain conditions to be satisfied if the purchase is to be treated as a capital transaction and not a distribution in the hands of the shareholder. To achieve this, legal advice in the matter should be sought by the company.

• It should be borne in mind that the proceeds of a life assurance policy effected by the company to facilitate the purchase of the shares of a shareholder director will increase the value of the company. The deceased's personal representatives may wish this to be taken into account when selling the shares to the company and this could result in the policy moneys being insufficient to actually purchase the shares. A further factor to be taken into account, however, is that the death of the shareholder director has probably deprived the company of one of its principal assets and also, any loans he may have made to the company will have to be repaid. This may have a balancing effect of reducing the value of the company.

The complexity of the company share purchase arrangement means it is a method of share protection assurance which should not be considered without the assistance of legal advisers, as it needs to comply with both Company and Revenue law.

B   The agreement

17.20   The arrangements described above may ensure that sufficient funds are in the hands of the surviving partners to enable them to purchase the deceased's interest in the business. This in itself, however, is not sufficient, as, for example, the deceased's spouse may not wish to sell, or the personal representatives may decide to take an interest in the running of the business. It is therefore highly desirable to have an agreement in place. The agreement may take several forms.

I   Automatic accrual

17.21   This has already been mentioned (see **17.6**).

2   Buy and sell agreement

17.22   This agreement may be contained in the partnership agreement or in the Articles of Association, or may be entered into separately. It binds the surviving partners to buy a deceased partner's share from the personal representatives and equally binds the personal representatives to sell the share to the surviving partners. Where this is enforceable (ie binding from the outset), it is HMRC's view that it amounts to a binding contract for sale[1] and business property relief for IHT purposes as described in Chapter 14 will not be available.

3   Double option agreement

17.23   This is by far the most common type of agreement, as it does not prejudice the availability of business property relief. Such an agreement would provide that:

---

1   See Statement of Practice SP 12/80 (13 October 1980) and Press Release Memorandum TR 557 (19 September 1984) Institute of Chartered Accountants of England and Wales.

(1)   on the death of a partner, the surviving partners have the option to buy his interest from his personal representatives within a fixed time period of his death; and

(2)   the personal representatives have the option to require the surviving partners to purchase the deceased's interest, also within a fixed period (not necessarily of the same time length).

If either of the parties exercise their option, the agreement would then become binding on the other party. As it is not a binding agreement from the outset, it does not fall within section 113 of IHTA 1984 and business property relief should be available on all 'relevant business property'.

Care should be taken to ensure that the double option agreement is worded to mirror the terms of the trust. For example, taking the wording of the trust example above, the double option agreement should give the options from a time period beginning seven days after the death of a partner. If the agreement does not mirror the trust and if, for example, there was a new partner in between the dates of death and seven days after death, this could result in the new partners being able to exercise the option even though they are not beneficiaries under the trust and so would not have the funds to purchase the deceased's share. Similarly, the personal representatives could bind the new partners, even though they have no funds. An example of a double option agreement is given in Appendix 11.

C   Premiums paid by the organisation

17.24   The organisation may of course wish to pay the premiums in respect of the arrangements described above. In relation to a company, it is straightforward to consider its paying the premiums as a 'paying agent' on behalf of the director/shareholders, out of post tax and National Insurance income. It would normally be the case that the premiums would have been equalised and the value of the premium payment in respect of each director/shareholder would then be debited from the director's post-tax salary. If the premiums are not paid in this way, they will be treated as additional remuneration of the directors and will be added to their taxable income, giving rise to additional tax and National Insurance charges. As a partnership is not a legal entity, any payment out of the partnership account in respect of premiums will have to be debited from the post-tax profits of the partners. It can be seen that there are no significant taxation advantages for the business paying the premiums, although there may be advantages from an administrative and certainty point of view.

SECTION 2   KEY MAN POLICIES

17.25   In many companies it is often the case that a few employees (both male and female) are most important or valuable to the business. There are many reasons why this might occur, eg:

(1) they may have a special knowledge or skill;

(2) they may be expert salesmen; or

(3) they may control a project.

Each in his own way makes a major contribution to his company's profit and profitability and in consequence each may be considered a key member of personnel. The death of such a person might result in a serious setback to the company's prosperity and progress. There may be no ready successor and the period of readjustment required after death might lead to a loss of confidence, a reversal in company fortunes and, in the worst instances, the collapse of the company.

For these reasons companies often consider it a wise precaution to assure the life of a key director or employee so that in the event of premature death the proceeds of the policy will be available to offset the financial strain of the loss.

Although it is possible that a key man will continue to be of essential importance until retirement, it is even more likely that within a much shorter time a replacement will have to be trained, or the key man's role in the company may have changed. For many reasons, therefore, the vital period for a key man may extend over five to ten years. This being so, temporary assurance should provide adequate cover.

Although an employer may have an insurable interest in the life of his employee (see Chapter 1) it is sometimes difficult to determine the extent of that interest in respect of a policy on the life of a key man. In practice, a good estimate may be made if consideration is given to certain factors such as the following:

(1) How much would it cost to find and train a suitable replacement if the key man were to die?

(2) How much company profit can be traced to the key man, ie how much would be lost in turnover and profitability if the key man were to die? (This is usually easiest to answer in the case of a salesman.)

(3) How much investment would be wasted if the key man died? (He might, for example, be responsible for the development of a specialised department.)

(4) What is the key man's salary? Cover will amount to some convenient multiple of this figure, perhaps, in most cases between five and ten times. This formula is based on the broad assumption that a salary tends to reflect an individual's contribution to the organisation. This might be a better approach where it is impossible to measure the loss accurately.

A   Taxation

I   Corporation tax

(a) Premium payments

17.26   The circumstances in which premiums in respect of key man policies may be treated as an allowable business expense deductible against profits for corporation tax purposes were clearly laid down by the then Chancellor of the Exchequer, Sir John Anderson, in answer to a question in the House of Commons on 27 July 1944[1]. He stated that the general practice in dealing with insurances by employers on the lives of employees is to treat the premiums as admissible deductions, and any sums received under a policy as trading receipts, if:

(1)   the sole relationship is that of employer and employee;

(2)   the insurance is intended to meet loss of profits resulting from the loss of services of the employee; and

(3)   it is an annual or short-term [temporary] insurance.

The sum assured must also be reasonable (considering the matters raised above). HMRC appears to hold the view that most employees can be effectively replaced within five years and so the sum assured should not reflect loss of profits for more than that time.

The general rules as to allowable deductions are to be found in section 74 of ICTA 1988, which provide that the expense must have been incurred wholly and exclusively for business purposes and it must be a revenue, not a capital, expense.

If the key man has a significant proprietary interest in the company (the rule of thumb at the time of writing is broadly 5%, although each case will be looked at on its own merits), HMRC may not allow relief as it could be argued that the policy has been effected for the life assured's own advantage and has thus not been incurred wholly and exclusively for business purposes.

Where a parent company effects the policy and pays the premium for a key man of a subsidiary company, this is not an allowable expense as the payment has not been incurred wholly and exclusively for the parent company's own business[2].

(b)   Policy proceeds

17.27   If premiums are allowed as an expense deductible against profits for corporation tax purposes, the policy proceeds will be taxed as a trading receipt (ie income) of the company and will be brought into the computation of profits in the year in which the proceeds are payable. This may result in an abnormally high tax charge, for example, where a company usually pays corporation tax at the small companies' rate, but the proceeds cause the company to have to pay at the full rate. The policy could be arranged so that the proceeds are due in instalments, so as not to cause the profits to exceed the small companies' rate[3]. However, if the death of the key man results, as expected, in a fall in a company's profits, such taxation of the proceeds may not be severe.

1   402 HC Official Rep (6th series) col 890 (27 July 1944).
2   *Samuel Dracup & Sons Ltd v Dakin* (1957) 37 TC 377. See also FRP5/A6.
3   With effect from 1 April 1994, the small companies' rate can be claimed by UK resident companies whose profits are below £300,000: ICTA 1988, s 13.

However, each case is considered on its own merits and in order to avoid, so far as is possible, any future dispute the company should explain the purpose of the policy to its local Inspector of Taxes and establish the tax position in advance. It should be noted, however, that in certain circumstances an advance clearing given by a local Inspector of Taxes may be subsequently withdrawn by HMRC[1].

2   Inheritance tax

17.28   Payment of the sum assured to the company in the event of a key man's death will not, in itself, be liable to IHT.

If, however, the key man is himself a major shareholder of the company, HMRC could argue that the payment of the sum assured has inflated the value of his shareholding for the purposes of IHT, although a counter argument could be that the death of the key man has deprived the company of one of its principal assets and may thus have a balancing effect of reducing the value of the company. Furthermore, it is possible that the payment of the sum assured may create a large cash balance in the company which is in excess of future business requirements. If this is the case, such excess cash may be treated as an excepted asset for IHT purposes and, as such, will not attract business property relief, see Chapter 14, Section 4D). It may be prudent, therefore, to arrange for the policy proceeds to be paid as a series of instalments which should minimise any possible increase in the value of the shares (and may also minimise the company's corporation tax liability, see above).

B   Type of policy

17.29   Taking into account considerations such as the view that a key man should be replaced within about five years and the taxation position, temporary assurances are the most usual types of policy to be recommended, which would normally expire at the key man's expected retirement age. In certain situations, however, a whole life or endowment policy may be more appropriate.

The policy could be assigned to the employee when he leaves service prior to retirement or at retirement if the policy is a whole life, endowment or continuing term policy.

The assignment is likely to be treated as an assignment for money or money's worth being in recognition of past service given by the employee. This would give rise to a chargeable event with the usual tax implications. The gain would be based on the difference between the market value (ie usually the surrender value) of the policy at the time of assignment and the premiums paid. For term assurance policies this is likely to be nil unless the life assured is in serious ill-health. There is an argument that as past consideration is no consideration, the assignment would not even constitute a chargeable event. This may well be the case but, in the absence of any known case or view being expressed by HMRC, the safer view

1   See *Matrix Securities Ltd v IRC* [1994] STC 272.

may be to assume that the assignment is for consideration. It is reiterated, though, that with term assurance this is unlikely to be a significant problem.

However, an assignment of a qualifying policy which remains qualifying at the time of assignment and has run for ten years or three-quarters of its term if less at the time of assignment would not give rise to a chargeable event regardless of the money's worth point.

The value of the payment, ie the surrender value, is likely to be a deductible expense for the company and will therefore counterbalance any tax charge on the chargeable gain if it arises in the same tax year.

The surrender value of the policy at assignment would be assessed on the employee under Schedule E as a reward for past service. It would be usual for a payment made as a reward for services to be treated as an emolument. If the payment can be seen to be a termination payment not an emolument then it should be taxable under section 148 of ICTA 1988, and it could be that the first £30,000 will be tax free.

If actual consideration is given, which seems likely, then following the assignment (a disposal of rights within section 210 of TCGA 1992) the policy would be a chargeable asset within section 210 TCGA 1992. In these circumstances any subsequent full or part encashment under the policy will be treated as a disposal or part disposal for capital gains tax purposes if the policy is a qualifying policy. Taper relief and the annual gains exemption (£8,500 for 2005/06) should help to ensure that any chargeable capital gains are exempt or minimised.

With a non-qualifying policy, death, maturity and full or partial encashment after the assignment will give rise to a chargeable event with the tax charge falling on the employee, or his legal personal representatives, in the event of death. Where income tax and capital gains tax are both relevant, as here, the income tax charge takes precedence. Credit for any chargeable gains that may be subject to income tax is given against any capital gain. In practice, this means that a capital gains tax liability is unlikely to occur. If subsequent to assignment the individual transfers the policy into a trust (say for the benefit of his family), the policy will be outside any potential capital gains tax charge since the new owners (trustees) will not have acquired it for consideration.

If the policy remains in the ownership of the individual until his death, no capital gains tax charge will arise since no disposal will occur on death by virtue of section 62 of TCGA 1992.

Similarly, if the individual (assignee) subsequently assigns his interest gratuitously into trust, the 'chain' will have been broken and there will be no capital gains tax on subsequent death.

The above comments have all concerned the situation where a key man dies, but the position where such a person contracts a critical illness should also be considered and the company should certainly consider the inclusion of critical illness cover to cater for this situation.

The effect of the Finance Act 1989 is that policies owned by companies and taken out after 13 March 1989 or policies effected before that date which are materially varied after that date are treated as non-qualifying policies (see Chapter 13). Thus, most payments will give rise to a chargeable event, and if a chargeable gain arises, it will be treated as income of the company and be subject to corporation tax.

SECTION 3   POLICIES FOR CHILDREN

A   School fees

17.30   The cost of privately educating children needs, at the very least, careful financial consideration, and ideally, careful financial planning. School fees have increased enormously over the last few years. Although inflation is relatively low at the time of writing, its possible influence must be borne in mind. The cost of funding higher education has also risen in real terms, as the higher education grant has now been abolished and has been completely replaced by the student loan scheme.

Parents or other relatives can make advance provision for the payment of private school fees and the earlier any scheme is started the better the results will be. Provision can be made out of income, by investment of a capital sum, by borrowing (as a last resort) or a combination of these. The choice of provision is invariably determined by practical personal considerations, but consideration should be given to the following:

(1)   the number of children for whom funding is required;

(2)   the extent of the child's education which it is desired to fund privately;

(3)   the imminence of the requirement to pay school fees;

(4)   the likely cost of the fees;

(5)   the likely extent and cost of sundry and miscellaneous expenses, eg uniforms, books, sports equipment, school trips;

(6)   the available funds, of an income and capital nature with which it will be possible to pay the school fees, or to plan for them at as early a stage as possible;

(7)   who may be providing the funds;

(8)   whether the choice of school may change;

(9)   the most tax-efficient method of providing the funding.

When deciding on the most appropriate type of investment vehicle, consideration should be afforded to the following:

(1)   the safety of the investment, both in terms of the investment strategy (ie risk averse or not) and any available minimum guarantees;

(2)   the flexibility of the investment, including the penalties for terminating the plan or changing the school attended;

(3)   the relevant tax positions.

Provision for school fees can be made by individuals utilising banks, building societies, national savings certificates, or any other investment vehicle. The following discussion considers some of the mainly life assurance related options, and their taxation consequences.

1   Endowment assurance

17.31   One method of funding fees from income would be to consider endowment assurance policies (with-profit or unit-linked) for terms of at least ten years. The proceeds from such policies can be taken tax free after ten years, or, if sooner, three-quarters of the policy term, and are therefore suitable plans in situations where the fees are required at some time in the future. One option would be to invest in a series of endowment assurances, the maturity dates of which are designed to coincide with the dates at which fees will need to be paid.

Endowment assurances will provide a sum assured in the event of the premature death of the life assured, and so there is certainty that funds will be available for the payment of fees.

2   Individual Savings Accounts (ISAs)

17.32   In a non-life insurance context, the use of Individual Savings Accounts (ISAs) as a tax efficient investment vehicle has been possible since 6 April 1999. Under current legislation, there is no liability to income tax or CGT on investments within an ISA although where ISA investments are held in shares, dividend tax credits cannot be reclaimed since 5 April 2004. The proceeds from an ISA are tax free and they may be effected on a lump sum or a regular saving basis. The maximum contribution in any tax year is £7,000 so husband and wife could invest up to £14,000 per tax year. The annual investment may be split into three components: a cash component (bank and building society accounts and designated national savings products), life assurance and stocks and shares. Not more than £3,000 can be invested in cash and not more than £1,000 in life assurance. The whole amount may be invested in stocks and shares if the saver wishes.

3   Single premium bonds

17.33   It is often the case that grandparents, for example, wish to invest money for the benefit of their grandchildren. A popular choice of investment is the single premium bond, with a desire to have the grandchildren as the lives assured. In this scenario, there is no automatic and very rarely any insurable interest as between the grandparents and the grandchildren. Some life offices will contract on this basis if the bond is effected in absolute trust for the grandchild whose life is assured. This is in order to ensure that the 'mischief' which the insurable interest provision in the Life Assurance Act 1774 was designed to prevent is not possible, ie that whatever occurs, the entire beneficial interest in the policy will lie with the life assured.

One angle that is becoming increasingly popular is for parents or grandparents to utilise offshore bonds in planning for university fees. The settlors effect the policies in trust for the benefit of the children/grandchildren and then the policies are assigned to the beneficiaries to assist with university funding as and when they attain the age of 18. Any gains under the policies can thus be set off against the personal allowances and starting rate bands of the beneficiaries.

4 Other possibilities

17.34 These could include unit trust or investment trust savings schemes under which a tax efficient 'income' may be taken each year by making encashments of units or shares within the annual exemption for CGT purposes. Furthermore, there will be some individuals with existing Personal Equity Plans (PEPs) or Tax Exempt Special Savings Accounts (TESSAs) and these investments can still be used as a tax efficient way of funding school fees. National Savings products such as Children's Bonus Bonds could also be considered.

5 Deferred annuities

17.35 A parent may purchase a deferred annuity, to commence when the fees are required. It is also possible to purchase a deferred annuity with regular premiums, paid until the end of the child's school life. At the time of writing, it should be noted that the rates offered on deferred annuities are not thought to be particularly attractive and thus this method of funding might not be so appropriate.

(a) Income tax

17.36 For tax purposes, such annuities are treated as part capital and part income and are actuarially apportioned at inception[1]. The capital element is exempt from income tax, whilst the income element will normally be subject to deduction of the basic rate of income tax applicable to savings income (20% for the tax year 2006/07) at source.

(b) IHT

17.37 If the annuity ends on the death of the purchaser, there will be no IHT liability. If there is a guaranteed element, or a return of capital upon death, its value will form part of the deceased's estate for IHT purposes.

6 Borrowing

17.38 As a last resort, parents may have to borrow to fund the school fees. Life assurance policies may play a part in this method, for example, by a loan back facility on the surrender value of a policy or as collateral security under a property-based scheme. A loan on a policy should mean that the life office continues to receive the regular premiums and interest payments on the loan, actuarial calculations are not upset and the policyholder need not surrender his contract[2]. If the policyholder dies, the loan is repaid from the proceeds of the policy, thus, in many cases, providing a surplus which will normally be paid to the

1   ICTA 1988, s 656(1).
2   But see ITTOIA 2005, s 501 and Chapter 13.

policyholder's estate (which will therefore be potentially liable to IHT), and which will be available to fund school fees.

B   Children's policies

1   Contractual capacity and insurable interest

17.39   The contractual capacity of children was discussed in Chapter 1. Essentially, under English law, life assurance contracts with minors are likely to be treated as voidable, whilst under Scottish law, although contractual capacity applies from the age of 16, in some circumstances, contracts may be repudiated up to the age of 18. Because of the difficulties of contractual capacity and the general lack of need for children to have life cover, the volume of 'children's policies' has never been significant.

A further consideration is that of insurable interest. In England, there is no automatic insurable interest between parent and child (unlike Scotland) thus parents cannot effect a contract on the lives of their children and vice versa, unless insurable interest can be established in some other way.

2   Taxation of children

17.40   For tax purposes, children are not treated any differently to adults.

3   Parental settlements

17.41   Section 660B of ICTA 1988 contains an exception to the general rule that a child's income is taxed on the child. It provides that where any income from a parental settlement, subject to a de minimis provision of £100 per year, is paid to or for the benefit of a minor and unmarried child, of the settlor, during the life of the settlor it will be treated for income tax purposes, as the income of the settlor parent for the particular tax year.

Prior to 9 March 1999, this anti-avoidance provision could be avoided by the use of an irrevocable bare trust, in which the income was not distributed. Thus, so long as any income arising was not applied for the benefit of the child, it was treated as the child's income, and not that of the parents. It was, however, necessary to take care as if any accumulated income was applied for the benefit of a child of the settlor, it too was treated as the income of the settlor for income tax purposes[1]. The effect of this provision could not be avoided by making distributions out of capital. If such a distribution was made at a time when there was accumulated income within the trust, the amount of the distribution, to the extent that there was accumulated income, was taxed as income of the settlor[2].

From 9 March 1999, such trust arrangements ceased to be effective, and all income arising is now taxed as that of the parent, subject to the £100 limit. This

1   ICTA 1988, s 664.
2   See *Postlethwaite v IRC* (1963) 41 TC 224.

change does not apply to trusts in force as at 9 March 1999 unless the trust fund is added subsequent to that date.

In this sense, a life assurance policy may be an ideal investment, as it is non-income producing, so there is no income upon which the settlor may be taxed.

4   Child's policy

17.42   Irrespective of the difficulties occasioned by the general position in relation to contractual capacity of children, some life offices, Friendly Societies and Industrial Provident Societies are in a position where, due to a specific Act of Parliament, they are able to issue policies on the life of a child and obtain a valid legal discharge from the child. Some other life offices have devised a policy which has many different product names but which, for convenience, may be described as a child's policy.

These are designed to provide either a cash sum for the child at, say, age 18, 21 or 25 or, alternatively, to enable the child, on the attainment of the selected age, to effect a whole life or endowment assurance on his or her own life at a low rate of premium, irrespective of the state of health, residence or occupation of the child at that time.

The policy will normally be a regular premium endowment assurance (on a with-profit or unit-linked basis) effected by the parent on his or her own life for the selected term and put in trust for the child.

5   Friendly Societies

17.43   Most friendly societies offer a scheme whereby a lump sum can be used to purchase a 'baby bond', which will usually cover investment for a period of at least ten years through a guaranteed income bond, a temporary annuity or insurance bond. The bond can only be taken out for someone under 18 and there are maximum limits of contributions to such policies, which are currently £25 per month or £270 per annum. The advantage of Friendly Society investments is that their investments accumulate tax free.

SECTION 4   LONG-TERM CARE

17.44   With an aging population, care of the elderly is becoming an increasingly important issue. It is outside the scope of this book to go into great detail regarding legislative provision for those in need of health care, but a brief overview is given below together with details of possible insurance-based methods of assisting with the problem.

A   NHS-funded care

17.45   The NHS has responsibility to pay all the costs of a person's care when they meet the 'eligibility criteria'. These criteria vary between different Primary

Care Trusts (PCTs) although in theory there should be some similarities as all eligibility criteria have to comply with the National Health Service (NHS) national guidance. However, in practice there are wide differences throughout the country both in the criteria themselves and their interpretation. Eligibility for fully-funded continuing care will be determined by factors such as whether or not the patient's condition has stabilised and how complex their needs are. Reference is also made to whether the patient has a primary need for nursing care in which case the NHS pays or whether their primary need is for personal [or social care] in which case the patient has to pay.

The boundaries between these distinctions are grey and subjective yet they carry an enormous financial consequence.

If the patient meets the criteria then this is all paid for by the NHS if not then the most that can be hoped for by way of contribution is a payment under the rules governing Free Nursing Care. Here too the amount received will depend upon an assessment of the 'nursing' needs of the older person as set out below:

Low band	£40 per week	Minimal nursing input
Medium band	£83 per week	People with multiple care needs
High band	£133 per week	People with high needs for registered nursing care

B   Local authority-funded care

17.46   Local authorities have a statutory obligation under section 47 of the National Health Service and Community Care Act 1990 (which took effect from 1 April 1993) to both assess a person's care needs and then to go on to meet those needs. However, they are also required under the National Assistance Act 1948 to require the applicant for care to contribute to the cost of that care if they have over a certain level of assets.

Furthermore, from 10 April 2006 if they have more than £21,000 in means-testable assets then they will have to use all of this excess before the local authority will contribute. For assets between £21,000 and £12,750 the individual will be deemed to have £1 of 'tariff income' for every £250 of capital. See Example below.

The applicant has to contribute all their income apart from a Personal Expense Allowance of £19.60 per week (from 10 April 2006) towards the cost of care.

Example

Mrs Smith has assets valued at £18,500. She has income of £165 per week.

Her care fees are £390 per week. Her tariff income will be £23 per week (£18,500 – £12,750 = £5,750 divided by £250 = £23).

Her total assessable income is therefore £165 + £23 = £188 less Personal Expenses Allowance of £19.60 = £168.40.

The Local Authority contribution for care costs will therefore be £390 – £168.40 = £221.60.

C   Assessment of applicant's resources

17.47   Local authorities must use National Guidance in making these assessments. These are contained in the Charging For Residential Accommodation Guide [CRAG].

1   Income

17.48   The income taken fully into account includes:

- Most Social Security benefits.

- Trust Income.

- Income from letting (or subletting part of a property which is not part of the living accommodation).

- Attendance Allowance.

Some income is fully disregarded and this includes Council Tax benefit.

Some income may be partly disregarded, eg 50% of an occupational or personal pension if the partner or spouse relies on that income to continue living at home.

2   Capital

17.49   The capital test includes potentially taking into account the value of the home (see below). Other items include buildings, land, building society and bank accounts, cash, stocks and shares, National Savings Certificates. (This list is not exhaustive).

Items that are disregarded include surrender value of any life insurance policy.

For some time there was discussion as to whether the definition of life assurance for the purpose of the local authority means test included an investment bond. Indeed, some local authorities had sought to take investment bonds into account as assessable assets despite the fact that, strictly speaking, most investment bonds (other than capital redemption policies) are policies of life assurance.

The October 2003 version of CRAG makes it clear that such practice is not acceptable and has always been an unlawful practice. Any capital assessments which took account of such assets should be brought to the attention of the relevant local authority with a view to obtaining a refund of homecare fees incorrectly paid as a result.

It is useful to specifically quote some of the statements from CRAG on this point.

Paragraph 6.002A of CRAG states:

> 'The treatment of investment bonds in the financial assessment for residential accommodation is complex because, in part, of the differing products that are on offer. For this reason councils should seek the advice of their legal departments when they arise. However it is possible to offer some general advice and councils are referred to the Social Security Commissioners decision R (IS) 7/98.'

Paragraph 6.002B of CRAG states:

> 'Councils are advised that if an investment bond is written as one or more life insurance policies that contain cashing-in rights by way of options for total or partial surrender, then the value of those rights has to be disregarded as a capital asset in the financial assessment for residential accommodation. . . In contrast, the surrender value of an investment bond without life assurance is taken into account.'

Paragraph 6.002C of CRAG states:

> 'Income from investment bonds, with or without life assurance, is taken into account in the financial assessment for residential accommodation. Actual payments of capital by periodic instalments from investment bonds, with or without life insurance, are treated as income and taken into account provided that such payments are outstanding on the first day that the resident becomes liable to pay for his accommodation and the aggregate of the outstanding instalment, and any other capital sum not disregarded, exceed £16,000.'

17.50   Of course, the 'deliberate deprivation' rules as set out at **17.52** also need to be taken into account when considering the use of investment bonds. In addition to the surrender value of life assurance policies, the following are also disregarded:

- Payments in kind from charities.
- Social funds payments.
- Reversionary interests.

Further to this, some assets are disregarded for 26 weeks or longer, eg capital received from the sale of the former home where the capital is to be used by the resident to buy another home.

A resident may be treated as possessing a capital asset even where he does not actually possess it. The test is whether or not the capital would be available to him if he applied for it.

Married couples will be assessed individually. The value of jointly held assets will be divided equally amongst all the owners irrespective of how much each has individually contributed. The jointly held assets of married couples will be halved to determine the value of each one's share.

If, however, the assets of a married couple are held in the name of one of the parties alone, the full value of this asset will be attributed to that party in determining their liability to contribute to any long-term care costs. (The Guidelines do not take into account the other spouse's potential inheritance claims, nor indeed the possibility of the assets being shared if the parties divorce.)

3   The family home

17.51   The local authority cannot enforce the provisions of the National Health Service and Community Care Act 1990 and sell an applicant's home if he goes into care and his partner is still living in the property. Certain other situations may also prevent the local authority forcing a sale. These are:

(1) A child under sixteen resident in the property (and whom the applicant is liable to maintain).

(2) A relative is living in the property who is either:

    (a) elderly (defined as 60 years or over); or

    (b) incapacitated (defined as being eligible to claim one of the range of social security disability related benefits).

Note, since 9 April 2001, the value of the applicant's home will be disregarded for 12 weeks from the date that the applicant enters a residential setting for care. This means that if, but for the value of the home, the applicant would have been eligible for local authority funding, then the local authority will contribute towards the cost of their care during this period.

D   Deliberate deprivation

17.52   Local authorities are empowered to take effective action against residents who *deliberately* attempt to avoid paying charges. The burden of proof in these cases is on the local authority who have to establish that the motivation of the donor was to diminish their assets in order to preclude payment due to the local authority.

Local authorities only have to prove that deliberate deprivation was a significant motive for the transfer of assets, not the only motive.

The 'Charging for Residential Accommodation Guide' (CRAG) does not specify what constitutes deliberate deprivation, however, they do indicate policy.

A guideline which is frequently used is that it would not be reasonable for a local authority to infer that the motivation for the passing of a lifetime gift was deliberate deprivation if 'the gift was made at a time and in circumstances in which the donor was in good health and did not anticipate care'.

Various decisions in the courts have emphasized that there is no time limit which constrains the right of local authorities to 'look back' at disposals of assets in terms of the donor's motivation. This is a very difficult area and practice varies from authority to authority which can make any planning process very problematic.

Generally speaking, it is accepted that when planned well ahead, there is nothing wrong with conversion of non-disregarded assets, such as cash/shares, into a disregarded form such as a non-qualifying life policy. This, of course, must always be subject to the personal circumstances and any investment objectives of the individual concerned. The emphasis must also be on the words 'planning' and 'well ahead', as a last minute avoidance measure, such as transferring assets into a life assurance bond shortly before making an application for assistance, is likely to be caught by the provisions dealing with deliberate deprivation. This is also specifically dealt with by the new CRAG.

Paragraph 6.061 of CRAG states that a deprivation of capital may occur if:

'capital has been used to purchase an investment bond with life insurance. Councils will wish to give consideration, in respect of each case, to whether deprivation of assets has occurred, ie did the individual place his capital in such an investment bond so that it would be disregarded for the purpose of the Assessment of Resources Regulations.'

It is important that in considering whether deprivation has occurred, the most important aspect is the motive or the intention of the investor. It may therefore be all the more important that good financial planning reasons are given for investment bond purchases and recorded in suitability letters.

The local authority may in certain circumstances have the power to place a legal charge over a person's share of a property even though the presence of one of the above categories prevents the immediate enforcement of the sale.

The effect of this legal charge would be that on the eventual sale of the property the local authority would be able to reclaim the money spent on that person's care.

In its capacity as a creditor the local authority would technically be able to use any of the enforcement procedures available through the courts (subject, of course, to any restrictions within the National Health Service and Community Care Act 1990 itself. This currently restricts local authorities to taking action within three years).

E   Use of insurance products in the long-term care market

17.53   There are basically two options when considering the use of insurance products in conjunction with long-term care planning, pre-funded plans and immediate needs annuities.

I   Pre-funded plans

17.54   Claims under these plans are based upon failing a specific number of activities of daily living, which are generally, washing, dressing, feeding, continence, mobility and transferring. Payment can also be triggered by mental impairment such as Alzheimer's disease or dementia. These plans pay out whether the care is delivered in a care home or in the client's own home. Advance funding will help the client to overcome the problem of potentially needing long-term care at some stage in the future.

2   Immediate needs annuities

17.55   This product is designed to make regular monthly payments for an individual's care for the rest of their life in return for a single premium. In order to take a policy out the care recipient needs to be failing an activity of daily living or suffering a cognitive impairment and will typically, though not necessarily, be in receipt of formal care either at home or in a care home. The payments can be made totally free of tax providing they are paid directly to a registered care provider, whether that be a care home or care agency. Some companies offer the option to have the benefits paid directly to the policyholder, although in these circumstances the payments will be taxed at source in the same way as a purchase life annuity and could give rise to further taxation for higher rate taxpayers. However, any tax liability is, of course, based only on the interest element of the payments and not on that part which is considered to be a return of capital. The life expectancies involved with these cases are generally short so the payments tend to include only a small amount of interest.

Another option that is available is the ability to have the payments increase by an amount of indexation each year – either RPI or a fixed amount. A more important option for many is the option to protect a proportion of the premium against early death. None of the provider companies offer 100% protection although, obviously, a stand-alone whole of life policy could be effected. The availability of this option may be limited or the cost of it may be prohibitive bearing in mind the age and state of health of the client.

SECTION 5   MISCELLANEOUS

A   Family income policies

17.56   Policies called family income policies or something similar usually provide on death within a specified period (normally 20 years commencing at the issue of the policy) fixed monthly or quarterly sums payable until the expiry of that period.

The policy is basically a temporary decreasing assurance payable by instalments. The instalments, although termed income, are in the nature of capital, and, under long-standing HMRC practice, are not subject to income tax.

It would be normal to write such a policy subject to trust in order to prevent the benefits forming part of the deceased's estate on his or her death.

B   Home income plans

17.57   Home income plans became very popular in the mid to late 1980s. In a situation where, invariably elderly persons, owned a property in which they had considerable equity, and wanted more income, they could effect a Home Income Plan to provide them with income, and enable them to retain their home. A reversion scheme was offered, although this was not very popular, as it involved selling the reversionary interest in the property. The more popular scheme was a mortgage scheme. Under this scheme, the property was mortgaged on an interest-only basis and an annuity or a single premium bond purchased to repay the interest and to provide 'income' for the mortgagors. The capital would be repaid on subsequent sale of the property, usually on the death of the homeowner.

The taxation treatment of purchased life annuities and single premium bonds have been discussed elsewhere[1].

---

1   See Chapter 13.

From 9 March 1999 interest relief on loans to purchase life annuities has no longer been available. However, borrowers with existing qualifying loans at that date will continue to benefit up to a £30,000 limit for the remaining period of the loan. Furthermore, existing Home Income Plan owners will be able to remortgage or move home without losing the relief. Despite the lack of availability of relief on the loan, it appears that there is still a demand for this type of product and that lenders are still prepared to lend on this basis.

C   Structured settlements

17.58   Structured settlements have an unusual tax history because they existed for some time before the introduction of any rules dealing with their tax treatment. There was a substantial delay between the implementation of the first structured settlement in the late 1980s (*Kelly and another v Dawes* Times Law Reports 27 September 1990) and the introduction of legislation in the Finance Act 1995.

Following the recommendations of the Law Commission on the tax treatment of structured settlements, the taxation of structured settlements was considerably simplified in 1995 and 1996. However, it may be relevant, by way of background, to outline the previous tax treatment, particularly as it had a considerable bearing on the development of structures in the UK.

In a structured settlement three parties would be involved: the general (liability) insurer, the life office and the plaintiff (the injured party). As far as the general insurer was concerned, the insurer would normally treat the premium for the annuity as reinsurance of the liability to make the payments and such treatment would be approved by the ABI and DTI for regulatory purposes (model agreements have already been agreed by the ABI with HMRC). The reinsurance premium would be a trading expense for tax purposes. Although the general insurer would have been liable to tax on the receipt of the annuity, it would also be able to deduct an amount equal to the cost of the instalment payment and therefore the two payments would be tax neutral. The general insurer therefore suffered no tax costs.

17.59   As far as the life office underwriting the annuity was concerned, an argument would generally be put forward that since the payment was not pure income profit in the hands of the payee (general insurer) then there was no need for the life office to deduct tax on paying the annuity to the general insurer. Even where it was argued that the annuity should have been paid net, the general insurer could reclaim the tax at the end of the financial year, although this clearly would have created a cash flow problem for the general insurer. Also it would only allow for a tax reclaim where the general insurer had a tax liability in the first place. As far as the payment to the plaintiff was concerned, although strictly any payment should have been made from the life assurer to the defendant's insurers and then to the plaintiff, in order to reduce administration the general insurer would normally arrange for the life office to act as his paying agent although a problem could arise where the general insurer and the life assurer were both separate departments of the same company on the basis that it is impossible for a person to contract with himself. In short, the administration of structured settlements provided a considerable burden on both insurance companies.

The payments received by the plaintiff were not subject to tax on the basis they were capital payments.

In 1995 the government acted to remove tax on annuities received for injury damages. The Finance Act 1995 inserted additional section 329A in the Taxes Act 1988 headed 'Annuities purchased for certain persons'. This was replaced by sections 329AA 'Personal injury damages in the form of periodical payments' and 329AB 'Compensation for personal injury under statutory or other schemes' ICTA 1988 (now incorporated into sections 731–734 ITTIOA 2005) which provide that in a case where an agreement is made settling a claim or action for damages for personal injury and on agreement the damages are to consist wholly or partly of periodical payments and the person entitled to the payments is to receive them as the annuitant under one or more annuities purchased for him by the person against whom the claim was brought, or that person's insurer, such agreement would be a qualifying agreement and where payments are made under such a qualifying agreement then they will not be treated as the annuitant's income for any purposes of income tax and will be paid without deduction of tax.

17.60 In 1996 the scope of the exemption was widened to include damages in the form of regular payments awarded by the court (now section 731 of ITTIOA 2005). While the 1995 changes allowed for damages in the form of an annuity payable to the victim to be exempted from tax if the annuity was purchased by the person responsible for the injury or that person's insurers, where a personal injury claim was settled by an agreement there was a need to extend the same treatment to situations in which a third party may step in to discharge the damages, for instance the Motor Insurers' Bureau in the case of a claim against an uninsured driver. The Damages Act 1996 affirms the power of a court to award, by way of consent order, damages for personal injury not as a lump sum but as regular amounts over the life of the victim of the injury. Such payments will also be exempt from tax. The exemptions also apply where the damages are handled by trustees which will be necessary in some cases of injury or a child plaintiff (the trustees holding absolutely for the plaintiff during his lifetime).

Where an annuity continues after the death of the injured party the HMRC make it clear that 'the exemption from tax is personal to the victim of the injury and does not continue beyond his death. An annuity purchased as part of a structured settlement will often be payable for a guaranteed period even if the victim should die prematurely. Payments made after the death of the victim are chargeable to tax in the normal way and can be expected to represent a purchased life annuity with an exempt capital element'.

It should also be noted that the Criminal Injuries Compensation Act 1995 similarly provided that a structured settlement of compensation payable by the Criminal Injuries Compensation Board should receive the same taxation treatment, ie such payments are also exempt from tax.

In conclusion, at present all the periodic payments made in respect of personal injuries are exempt from tax.

APPENDIX 1

Life Assurance Act 1774

(14 Geo 3 c 48)

An Act for regulating Insurances upon Lives, and for prohibiting all such insurances, except in cases where the persons insuring shall have an interest in the life or death of the persons insured

WHEREAS it hath been found by experience, that the making insurances on lives or other events wherein the assured shall have no interest, hath introduced a mischievous kind of gaming:

1. No insurance to be made on lives, etc, by persons having no interest. From and after the passing of this Act no insurance shall be made by any person or persons, bodies politick or corporate, on the life or lives of any person or persons, or on any other event or events whatsoever, wherein the person or persons for whose use, benefit, or on whose account such policy or policies shall be made, shall have no interest, or by way of gaming or wagering; and that every assurance made contrary to the true intent and meaning hereof shall be null and void to all intents and purpose whatsoever.

2. No policies on lives without inserting the names of persons interested etc. And . . . it shall not be lawful to make any policy or policies on the life or lives of any person or persons, or other event or events, without inserting in such policy or policies the person or persons name or names interested therein, or for whose use, benefit, or on whose account such policy is so made or underwrote.

3. How much may be recovered where the insured hath interest in lives. And . . . in all cases where the insured hath interest in such life or lives, event or events, no greater sum shall be recovered or received from the insurer or insurers than the amount or value of the interest of the insured in such life or lives, or other event or events.

4. Not to extend to insurances on ships, goods etc. Provided, always, that nothing herein contained shall extend or be construed to extend to insurances bona fide made by any person or persons, on ships, goods, or merchandises; but

693

every such insurance shall be as valid and effectual in the law as if this Act had not been made.

NOTE

Words omitted in sections 2 and 3 were repealed by the Statute Law Revision Act 1888.

APPENDIX 2

The Policies of Assurance Act 1867

(30 & 31 Vict c 144)

An Act to enable Assignees of Policies of Life Assurance to sue thereon in their own names, 20th August 1867.

1. Assignees of life policies empowered to sue. Any person or corporation now being or hereafter becoming entitled, by assignment or other derivative title, to a policy of life assurance, and possessing at the time of action brought the right in equity to receive and the right to give an effectual discharge to the assurance company liable under such policy for monies thereby assured or secured, shall be at liberty to sue at law in the name of such person or corporation to recover such monies.

2. Defence or reply on equitable grounds. In any action on a policy of life assurance, a defence on equitable grounds, or a reply to such defence on similar grounds, may be respectively pleaded and relied upon in the same manner and to the same extent as in any other personal action.

3. Notice of assignment. No assignment made after the passing of this Act of a policy of life assurance shall confer on the assignee therein named, his executors, administrators, or assigns, any right to sue for the amount of such policy, or the monies assured or secured thereby, until a written notice of the date and purport of such assignment shall have been given to the assurance company liable under such policy at their principal place of business, then at some one of such principal places of business, either in England or Scotland or Ireland, and the date on which such notice shall be received shall regulate the priority of all claims under any assignment; and a payment bona fide made in respect of any policy by any assurance company before the date on which such notice shall have been received shall be as valid against the assignee giving such notice as if this Act had not been passed.

4. Principal place of business to be specified on policies. Every assurance company shall, on every policy issued by them after the thirtieth day of September, one thousand eight hundred and sixty-seven, specify their principal place or principal places of business at which notices of assignment may be given in pursuance of this Act.

5. Mode of assignment. Any such assignment may be made either by endorsement on the policy or by a separate Instrument in the words or to the effect set forth in the schedule hereto, such endorsement or separate Instrument being duly stamped.

6. Receipt of notice of assignment. Every assurance company to whom notice shall have been duly given of the assignment of any policy under which they are liable shall, upon the request in writing of any person by whom any such notice was given or signed, or of his executors or administrators, and upon payment in each case of a fee not exceeding [25p] deliver an acknowledgment in writing, under the hand of the manager, secretary, treasurer, or other principal officer of the assurance company of their receipt of such notice; and every such written acknowledgment, if signed by a person being de jure or de facto the manager, secretary, treasurer, or other principal officer of the assurance company whose acknowledgment the same purports to be, shall be conclusive evidence as against such assurance company of their having duly received the notice to which such acknowledgment relates.

7. Interpretation. In the construction and for the purposes of this Act the expression 'policy of life assurance,' or 'policy' shall mean any instrument by which the payment of monies, by or out of the funds of an assurance company, on the happening of any contingency depending on the duration of human life, is assured or secured; and the expression 'assurance company' shall mean and include every corporation, association, society, or company now or hereafter carrying on the business of assuring lives or survivorships, either alone or in conjunction with any other object or objects.

8. Saving of Contracts under 16 & 17 Vict c 45 or 27 & 28 Vict c 43, and of engagement by friendly societies. Provided always, That this Act shall not apply to any policy of assurance granted or to be granted or to any contract for a payment on death entered into or to be entered into in pursuance of the provisions of the Government Annuities Act 1853 and the Government Annuities Act 1864, or either of those Acts, or to any engagement for Payment on Death by any Friendly Society.

NOTE

Government Annuities Act 1853; Government Annuities Act 1864. These Acts were repealed with savings by the Government Annuities Act 1929, s 66, Sch 2, Pt II. See now Part II of that Act.

9. Short title. For all Purposes this Act may be cited as 'The Policies of Assurance Act 1867'.

Schedule

I *A.B. of, &c.*, in consideration of, &c., do hereby assign unto *C.D.* of, &c., his Executors, Administrators, and Assigns, the [within] Policy of Assurance granted, &c., [here describe the Policy]. In witness, &c.

Association of British Insurers statement of long-term insurance practice

The following Statement of normal insurance practice applies to policies of long-term insurance effected in the UK in a private capacity by individuals resident in the UK. Nothing in this statement should be interpreted as conflicting with or overriding the rules of LAUTRO in respect of long-term insurance policies which are treated as investments for the purposes of the Financial Services Act 1986.

1   Proposal forms

(a)   If the proposal form calls for the disclosure of material facts a statement should be included in the declaration, or prominently displayed elsewhere on the form or in the document of which it forms part:

    (i)   drawing attention to the consequences of failure to disclose all material facts and explaining that these are facts that an insurer would regard as likely to influence the assessment and acceptance of a proposal;

    (ii)   warning that if the signatory is in any doubt about whether certain facts are material, these facts should be disclosed.

(b)   Neither the proposal nor the policy shall contain any provision converting the statements as to past or present fact in the proposal form into warranties except where the warranty relates to a statement of fact concerning the life to be assured under a life of another policy. Insurers, may, however, require specific warranties about matters which are material to the risk.

(c)   Those matters which insurers have commonly found to be material should be the subject to clear questions in proposal forms.

(d)   Insurers should avoid asking questions which would require knowledge beyond that which the signatory could reasonably be expected to possess.

(e)   The proposal form or a supporting document should include a statement that a copy of the policy form or of the policy conditions is available on request.

(f) The proposal form or a supporting document should include a statement that a copy of the completed proposal form is available on request.

2 Policies and accompanying documents

(a) Insurers will continue to develop clearer and more explicit proposal forms and policy documents whilst bearing in mind the legal nature of insurance contracts.

(b) Life assurance policies or accompanying documents should indicate:

(i) the circumstances in which interest would accrue after the assurance has matured; and

(ii) whether or not there are rights to surrender values in the contract and, if so, what those rights are.

(Note: The appropriate sales literature should endeavour to impress on proposers that a whole life or endowment assurance is intended to be a long-term contract and that surrender values, especially in the early years, are frequently less than the total premiums paid.)

3 Claims

(a) An insurer will not unreasonably reject a claim. In particular, an insurer will not reject a claim or invalidate a policy on grounds of non-disclosure or misrepresentation of a fact unless:

(i) it is a material fact;

(ii) it is a fact within the knowledge of the proposer; and

(iii) it is a fact which the proposer could reasonably be expected to disclose.

(It should be noted that fraud or deception will, and reckless or negligent non-disclosure or misrepresentation of a material fact may, constitute grounds for rejection of a claim.)

(b) Except where fraud is involved, an insurer will not reject a claim or invalidate a policy on grounds of a breach of warranty unless the circumstances of the claim are connected with the breach and unless:

(i) the warranty relates to a statement of fact concerning the life to be assured under a life of another policy and that statement would have constituted grounds for rejection of a claim by the insurer under 3(a) above if it had been made by the life to be assured under an own life policy; or

(ii) the warranty was created in relation to specific matters material to the risk and it was drawn to the proposer's attention at or before the making of the contract.

(c)   Under any conditions regarding a time limit for notification of a claim, the claimant will not be asked to do more than report a claim and subsequent developments as soon as reasonably possible.

(d)   Payment of claims will be made without avoidable delay once the insured event has been proved and the entitlement of the claimant to receive payment has been established.

(e)   When the payment of a claim is delayed more than two months, the insurer will pay interest on the cash sum due, or make an equivalent adjustment to the sum, unless the amount of such interest would be trivial. The two-month period will run from the date of the happening of the insured event (ie death or maturity) or, in the case of a unit-linked policy, from the date on which the unit linking ceased, if later. Interest will be calculated at a relevant market rate from the end of the two-month period until the actual date of payment.

4   Disputes

The provisions of the statement shall be taken into account in arbitration and any other referral procedures which may apply in the event of disputes between policyholders and insurers relating to matters dealt with in the statement.

5   Commencement

Any changes to insurance documents will be made as and when they need to be reprinted, but the statement will apply in the meantime.

Note regarding industrial assurance policyholders

Policies effected by industrial assurance policyholders are included amongst the policies to which the above Statement of Long-Term Insurance Practice applies. Those policyholders also enjoy the additional protection conferred upon them by the Industrial Assurance Acts 1923 to 1969 and Regulations issued thereunder. These Acts give the Industrial Assurance Commissioner wide powers to cover inter alia the following aspects:

(a)   Completion of proposal forms.

(b)   Issue and maintenance of Premium Receipt Books.

(c)   Notification in Premium Receipt Books of certain statutory rights of a policyholder including rights to:

   (i)   an arrears notice before forfeiture,

   (ii)   free policies and surrender values for certain categories of policies,

   (iii) relief from forfeiture of benefit under a policy on health grounds unless the proposer has made an untrue statement of knowledge and belief as to the assured's health,

(iv) reference to the Commissioner as arbitrator in disputes between the policyholder and the company or society.

The offices transacting industry assurance business have further agreed that any premium (or deposit) paid on completion of the proposal form will be returned to the proposer if, on issue, the policy document is rejected by him or her.

Specimen 'Power of Appointment' or 'Flexible' or Discretionary Trust (without an interest in possession for Inheritance Tax purposes)

NOTE: This document is provided as a specimen for the consideration of the parties and their legal advisers. Whilst every care has been taken in the preparation of this document, no responsibility can be accepted for the legal and/or taxation consequences of its use. The parties must consider their own personal circumstances in this respect.

TRUST DETAILS (Please use Block Capitals)

Section A – Settlor

Full Name of first settlor   Full name of second settlor *(if any)*

Section B – Policy

New Policies   / /200   **Existing Policies**
  Date of Proposal   Policy Number

  Type of Policy   Date of policy   / /200

Life/lives assured (1) .... (2) ....

701

Section C – Intended Beneficiaries

Full names *(this box must not be left blank)*	Share
	100%

Section D – Potential Beneficiaries

Any of the following persons:

(i)   any child or descendant of the Settlor whenever born

(ii)   any spouse/Civil Partner or former spouse/Civil Partner of the Settlor (except where such person is also a Settlor)

(iii) any spouse/Civil Partner or former spouse/Civil Partner of any child or descendant of the Settlor whenever born

(iv) any person or charity (other than the Settlor) nominated in writing by the Settlor to the Trustees to be a Potential Beneficiary

(v)   any person (other than the Settlor) who has an interest in the estate of the Settlor by will or codicil, under the intestacy rules, by right of survivorship or otherwise

(vi) any Intended Beneficiary

(vii) any of the following named persons

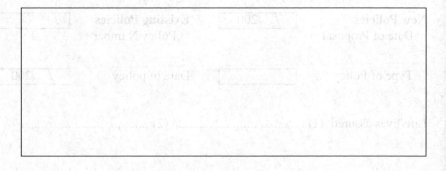

PROVIDED ALWAYS THAT THE SETTLOR MAY NOT BE A BENEFI-CIARY IN ANY CAPACITY WHATSOEVER

Section E —Additional Trustees

Full name of first Additional Trustee	
First Additional Trustee's address	
Full name of second Additional Trustee	
Second Additional Trustee's address	
Full name of third Additional Trustee	
Third Additional Trustee's address	

THIS TRUST is made on   200   **BETWEEN** the Settlor and the Trustees

NOW THIS DEED WITNESSES as follows:

1   IN this Trust the following definitions apply:

Expression	Meaning
'Accumulation Period'	The period of 21 years beginning with the date of this Trust
'Additional Trustees'	The persons mentioned in Section E
'Beneficiary'	Any Potential Beneficiary or any Intended Beneficiary but not the Settlor
'Civil Partner'	A person who is a registered civil partner in accordance with the Civil Partnership Act 2004
'Intended Beneficiaries'	The persons mentioned in Section C
'Policy'	The policy or policies mentioned in Section B
'Potential Beneficiaries'	The persons mentioned in Section D
	'Settlor' The person mentioned in Section A or where there are two settlors then 'Settlor' shall where appropriate mean either or both of them

'Trust Fund'	The Policy and all property representing it and any income thereof
'Trust Period'	The period of 80 years beginning with the date of this Trust
'Trustees'	The Settlor and the Additional Trustees or the trustees for the time being

2   (1) In the case of a new Policy the Settlor

        (a) appoints the Additional Trustees to act with him as trustees of this Trust

        (b) directs that the Policy shall be issued to the Trustees to be held by them on the terms of this Trust and declares that he holds all rights and obligations under the Policy on behalf of the Trustees

or

    (2) In the case of an existing Policy the Settlor

        (a) assigns the Policy to the Trustees

        (b) directs the Trustees to hold the Policy on the terms of this Trust and

3   (1) (a) THE Trustees shall hold the Trust Fund for such of the Potential Beneficiaries on such terms and in such shares and for such interests (including creating any further trusts) as they may by deed or deeds revocable or irrevocable appoint in writing at any time or times during the Trust Period

        (b) No exercise of this power of appointment shall invalidate any prior payment or application of all or any part of the Trust Fund

    (2) Subject to any appointment the Trustees may accumulate the whole or part of the Trust income during the Accumulation Period. That income shall be added to the Trust Fund. The Trustees shall but only whilst the said power of appointment subsists apply the remainder of the income to or for the benefit of such one or more of any persons named or specified in Section D above in such shares (or wholly to one) as the Trustees may in their absolute discretion think fit.

4   THE Trustees shall have the following further powers:

    (1) A Trustee who is or may be a Beneficiary may exercise the power of appointment under the Trust for his own benefit provided he is not a sole Trustee.

    (2) The Trustees may deal with the Policy as if they were beneficial owners.

    (3) The Trustees may

        (a) apply or invest the Trust Fund as if they were the absolute beneficial owners whether or not such application or investment produces income

(b)   vary such applications or investment

(c)   effect any life policy

(d)   make loans with or without security and/or with or without interest.

(e)   borrow with or without the security of the Policy or other trust assets.

5   Any trustee (other than the Settlor) being a solicitor or other person engaged in any profession or business shall be entitled to charge and be paid all normal professional or other charges for business done and all time spent by him or his firm or company in the execution or exercise of the trusts and powers whether in the ordinary course of his profession or business or not and although not of a nature requiring the employment of a solicitor or other professional person.

6   (1)   The Settlor (or where the Settlor is more than one person the settlors jointly or the survivor of them) shall have the power to appoint trustees and may by deed remove or replace Trustees.

      (2)   UPON the death of the Settlor the power of appointing a new or additional Trustee shall vest in the trustees.

      (3)   The Trustees may remove or replace a Trustee who cannot be found provided that:

            (a)   Reasonable efforts have been made to find the Trustee being removed; and

            (b)   The removal is made by deed executed by all the other Trustees.

      (4)   In relation to any persons dealing in good faith with the Settlor or Trustees or any other persons claiming through them a deed removing a trustee will be conclusive evidence that the trustee was properly removed.

7   No power conferred on the Trustees shall be exercised and no provisions of this Trust shall operate so as to allow any part of the Trust Fund to become in any way payable to or applicable for the benefit of the Settlor.

8   (1)   The receipt of any parent or guardian of any minor Beneficiary shall be sufficient discharge to the Trustees for any moneys payable to such Beneficiary.

      (2)   If the company liable to pay the benefits from any policy does so in accordance with the instructions of those appearing to it to be the Trustees this will (in the absence of actual fraud of the company) be a full discharge for the company. The Trustees not the company are responsible for passing benefits on to beneficiaries.

9   Notwithstanding the trusts declared by this Trust and the provisions of the Policy the power to exercise any option in the Policy rests solely with the Settlor unless the exercise of the Option gives rise to payment of any benefit in part or in full under the Policy when the agreement of all Trustees is also required to exercise the Option.

10   This Trust is governed by English Law.

IN WITNESS WHEREOF the parties hereto have executed this Deed the day and year first before written

SIGNED and **DELIVERED** as a Deed by the said

Print name of Settlor

Signature of Settlor

IN THE PRESENCE OF:

Full name of Witness

Signature of Witness

Address and occupation of Witness

SIGNED and **DELIVERED** as a Deed by the said

Print name of second Settlor/
Additional Trustee

Signature of second settlor/
Additional Trustee*

* delete as appropriate

IN THE PRESENCE OF:

Full name of Witness

Signature of Witness

Address and occupation of Witness

SIGNED and **DELIVERED** as a Deed by the said

Print name of Additional Trustee

Signature of Additional Trustee

IN THE PRESENCE OF:

Full name of Witness

Signature of Witness

Address and occupation of Witness

SIGNED and **DELIVERED** as a Deed by the said

Print name of Additional Trustee

Signature of Additional Trustee

IN THE PRESENCE OF:

Full name of Witness

Signature of Witness

Address and occupation of Witness

APPENDIX 5

Statutory Declaration

Type of policy:

Policy Number:

Insurance Company:

Grantee:

(hereinafter called 'the Policy')

I the undersigned of

do solemnly and sincerely declare:

1. That I am legally entitled to the Policy and to the moneys assured thereby, and to give an effectual discharge for the same by virtue of [having myself effected the Policy . . .].

2. That the Policy was to the best of my knowledge and belief last in my possession in . . . 19 . . .; that it has since been lost, mislaid or destroyed; and that I have made diligent search for it but without success.

3. That the Policy has not, to the best of my knowledge and belief been pledged, assigned or otherwise parted with for value or otherwise to any person or persons whomsoever who has or could have any right, title or claim thereto as against or paramount to my title and I have not received notice of and am not aware of any such claim.

And I make this solemn declaration conscientiously believing the same to be true and by virtue of the provisions of the Statutory Declarations Act 1835.
Declared this   day

of...at

before me

A Commissioner for Oaths

Specimen Deed of Indemnity

THIS DEED OF INDEMNITY is made the   day of   19

in relation to a policy of assurance, details of which are set out in the Schedule hereto

(hereinafter called **'the Policy'**)

BY

(hereinafter called the **'Policyholder'**)

WHEREAS

(i) The original policy documents relating to the Policy have been lost or destroyed.

(ii) No dealings have taken place with the Policy by way of assignment, charge or deposit. Nor has any other form of encumbrance or interest in the Policy been created by me to my knowledge.

THIS DEED HEREBY WITNESSETH

In consideration of [the Company] agreeing to issue a duplicate policy document(s) for the Policy, the Policyholder undertakes [jointly and severally]* to indemnify [the Company] and any of its officers against any and all losses, claims, demands (and any expense thereof) which may be made by or against [the Company] or its officers in consequence whether directly or indirectly, of [the Company] agreeing to issue the said documents including but not limited to anything arising from or in connection with payment being made under the Policy without the production of the said original policy documents or any interest created thereunder.

Schedule

Type of Policy:

Policy Number:

Insurance Company:

Grantee:

SIGNED AND DELIVERED as a Deed by ....

in the presence of: ....

NAME: ....

ADDRESS: ....

                                             ....

OCCUPATION: ....

SIGNED: ....

Payment into Court by Life Assurance Company (CPR 1998, Practice Direction 37, paras 7 and 8)

7.1 A company wishing to make a payment into court under the Life Assurance Companies (Payment into Court) Act 1896 ('the 1896 Act') must file a witness statement or an affidavit setting out –

(1) a short description of the policy under which money is payable;

(2) a statement of the persons entitled under the policy, including their names and addresses so far as known to the company;

(3) a short statement of –

(a) the notices received by the company making any claim to the money assured, or withdrawing any such claim;

(b) the dates of receipt of such notices; and

(c) the names and addresses of the persons by whom they were given;

(4) a statement that, in the opinion of the board of directors of the company, no sufficient discharge can be obtained for the money which is payable, other than by paying it into court under the 1896 Act;

(5) a statement that the company agrees to comply with any order or direction the court may make –

(a) to pay any further sum into court; or

(b) to pay any costs;

(6) an undertaking by the company immediately to send to the Accountant General at the Court Funds Office any notice of claim received by the company after the witness statement or affidavit has been filed, together with a letter referring to the Court Funds Office reference number; and

(7) the company's address for service.

7.2   The witness statement or affidavit must be filed at –

(1)   Chancery Chambers at the Royal Courts of Justice, or

(2)   a Chancery district registry of the High Court.

7.3   The company must not deduct from the money payable by it under the policy any costs of the payment into court, except for any court fee.

7.4   If the company is a party to any proceedings issued in relation to the policy or the money assured by it, it may not make a payment into court under the 1896 Act without the permission of the court in those proceedings.

7.5   If a company pays money into court under the 1896 Act, unless the court orders otherwise it must immediately serve notice of the payment on every person who is entitled under the policy or has made a claim to the money assured.

APPLICATION FOR PAYMENT OUT OF MONEY PAID INTO COURT BY LIFE ASSURANCE COMPANY

8.1   Any application for the payment out of money which has been paid into court under the 1896 Act must be made in accordance with paragraph 4.2 of this practice direction.

8.2   The application must be served on –

(1)   every person stated in the written evidence of the company which made the payment to be entitled to or to have an interest in the money;

(2)   any other person who has given notice of a claim to the money; and

(3)   the company which made the payment, if an application is being made for costs against it, but not otherwise.

Deed of Assignment

THIS DEED OF ASSIGNMENT is made the   day of   19

BETWEEN

(1)

(2)

(hereinafter called the Assignor(s)) of the one part and

(hereinafter called the Assignee(s)) of the other part

WITNESSES as follows:—

The Assignors as Settlors hereby give and assign to the Assignee(s) ALL THAT Policy of Assurance with

on the life/lives of

effected on

numbered

and all moneys assured by or to become payable under the said Policy and the full benefit thereof

TO HOLD unto the Assignee(s) absolutely

It is hereby certified that this instrument falls within Category L in the Schedule to the Stamp Duty (Exempt Instruments) Regulations 1987

IN WITNESS whereof the parties hereto have hereunto set their hands the date first above written

Notice of Assignment

To: [the Company]

I hereby give you notice that by a deed dated   19   and made between [A   of] (hereinafter called 'the Assignor') of the one part and [B   of] (hereinafter called 'the Assignee') of the other part, the Assignor assigned unto the Assignee all that policy issued by your company on the life of   numbered   and dated   19   and all sums assured or thereby payable or to become payable thereunder.

And I request you to deliver to me a written acknowledgement of the receipt of this notice.

Dated   19   Signed

Acknowledgement by Company

The [Company] hereby acknowledges the receipt of the notice of which this is a photocopy/the notice dated

Signed (for and on behalf of the Company)

NOTE

It is desirable for the Company to add a memorandum that in acknowledging the receipt of the notice, it is in no way admitting the title of the assignee, and that production of the original document will be required before payment is made.

APPENDIX 10

Inheritance Tax and Pensions

A. SP10/86 IHT: death benefits under superannuation arrangements (9 July 1986)

The Board of Inland Revenue have confirmed that their existing practice of not charging capital transfer tax on death benefits that are payable from tax-approved occupational pension and retirement annuity schemes under discretionary trusts, will also apply to inheritance tax.

The practice will extend to tax under the gifts with reservation rules as well as to tax under the ordinary inheritance tax rules.

B. Notes on approval under Chapter IV, Part XIV, ICTA 1988 issued by the Inland Revenue Superannuation Funds Office on the authority of the Board of Inland Revenue (personal pension schemes)

Any lump sum may be paid to the member's legal personal representatives, or a beneficiary nominated by the member, or distributed at the discretion of the scheme administrator; it is not necessary to limit nomination or distribution to dependants. The money may continue to be held under the rules of the scheme for a period not exceeding two years if this is necessary for the scheme administrator to determine who is to benefit and interest may accrue as part of the benefit. It should be paid over to the recipients (or a trust fund for their benefit) promptly once they have been selected, or transferred to a separate account outside the scheme if they have not been selected after two years.

C. Extracts from a letter from the Inland Revenue, Capital Taxes Office to the Association of British Insurers, dated 5th June 1991

RETIREMENT ANNUITIES UNDER TRUST — SECTION 3(3) INHERITANCE TAX ACT 1984

1. We do understand the concern which has been expressed by the pensions industry about the application of section 3(3) to retirement benefits. Our conclusion is that while a section 3(3) claim may be appropriate in particular limited circumstances genuine pension arrangements should not be affected. Our purpose in this letter is:

717

(a)   to clarify the basis for the claim and the very limited circumstances in which we might raise one;

(b)   to reassure you that your fears of wider repercussions are misplaced; and so

(c)   to remove uncertainty as far as possible about what our approach will be.

2. The annex deals point by point with the technical arguments advanced in your Memorandum.

The scope for a Section 3(3) claim

3. It is worth emphasising that, in practice, we expect to see very few cases where a claim would even be considered. First, the vast majority of policyholders exercise their right to take an annuity during their lifetime or survive to the age beyond which deferment cannot be made. All these cases fall outside the scope of the potential claim.

4. Second, the field is further restricted in practice to those policyholders whose chargeable estate exceeds the inheritance tax threshold. If no tax is actually payable we would obviously not pursue a claim.

5. Third, we would generally expect any claims that do arise to be limited to retirement annuity contracts or personal pension schemes. Only exceptionally would claims involve occupational pension schemes.

6. Fourth, there is no question of a claim being raised in cases of *genuine* pensions arrangements, ie where it is clear that the policyholder's primary intention is to provide for his or her own retirement benefits.

7. We would consider raising a claim in such cases as remain only where there was prima facie evidence that the policyholder's intention in failing to take up retirement benefits was to *increase the estate of somebody else* (the beneficiaries of the death benefit) rather than benefit himself or herself.

8. To this end, we would look closely at pensions arrangements where the policyholder became aware that he or she was suffering from a terminal illness or was in such poor health that his or her life was uninsurable and *at or after that time* the policyholder:

—   took out a new policy and assigned the death benefit on trust;

—   assigned on trust the death benefit of an existing policy; or

—   paid further contributions to a single premium policy or enhanced contributions to a regular premium policy where the death benefit had been previously assigned on trust.

9. In these circumstances it would be difficult to argue that the actions of the policyholder were intended to make provision for his or her own retirement given the prospect of an early death. Even then we would not pursue the claim where the death benefit was paid to the policyholder's spouse and/or dependants.

10. Our firm view is that this approach will give rise to only a small number of section 3(3) claims; the overwhelming majority of pensions arrangements will be unaffected.

11. I hope you find this explanation both helpful and reassuring.

[The Annex is not repeated here]

D.   Statement of Practice E3 September 1975

E3. Superannuation schemes

1. This statement clarifies the IHT liability of benefits payable under pension schemes.

2. No liability to IHT arises in respect of benefits payable on a person's death under a normal pension scheme except in the circumstances explained immediately below. Nor does a charge to IHT arise on payments made by the trustees of a superannuation scheme within IHTA 1984, s 151 (formerly FA 1975, Schedule 5, para 16) in direct exercise of a discretion to pay a lump sum death benefit to any one or more of a member's dependants. It is not considered that pending the exercise of the discretion the benefit should normally be regarded as property comprised in a settlement so as to bring it within the scope of IHTA 1984, Part III (formerly FA 1975, Schedule 5). The protection of IHTA 1984, s 151 would not of course extend further if the trustees themselves then settled the property so paid.

3. Benefits are liable to IHT if:

(a)   they form part of the freely disposable property passing under the will or intestacy of a deceased person. This applies only if the executors or administrators have a legally enforceable claim to the benefits: (if they were payable to them only at the discretion of the trustees of the pension fund or some similar persons they are not liable to IHT); or

(b)   the deceased had the power, immediately before the death, to nominate or appoint the benefits to any person including his dependants.

4. In these cases the benefits should be included in the personal representatives' account (schedule of the deceased's assets) which has to be completed when applying for a grant of probate or letters of administration. The IHT (if any) which is assessed on the personal representatives' account has to be paid before the grant can be obtained.

5. [the remainder of the statement of practice is not relevant for these purposes]

E.   Practice Notes IR12 (in relation to occupational schemes)

The lump sum may be paid to the employee's legal personal representatives or a nominated beneficiary, or distributed at the discretion of trustees/*administrator*; it is not necessary to limit nomination or distribution to *dependants*. The money may continue to be held under the rules of the pension scheme for a period not exceeding two years if this is necessary for the trustees/*administrator* to determine who is to benefit, and interest may be credited provided the lump sum thus payable (excluding refunded contributions and interest thereon) does not exceed the limit in whichever is appropriate of paragraphs 11.2 and 11.3. The money should be paid over promptly to the beneficiaries (or to a trust for their benefit) once they have been selected, or transferred to an account outside the scheme if they have not been selected after two years.

Draft 'Double Option' Agreement

DRAFT: FOR APPROVAL OF LEGAL ADVISERS

'DOUBLE OPTION' AGREEMENT

N.B.   THIS DOCUMENT SHOULD NOT BE SIGNED. IT IS A SUGGESTED VERSION ONLY. YOUR LEGAL ADVISER SHOULD BE CONSULTED.

THIS AGREEMENT is made the   day of   19

BETWEEN

(1)   (Director)/(Partner)

(2)   (Director)/(Partner)

(3)   (Director)/(Partner)

etc.

WHEREAS:—

1.   The parties hereto are shareholders and directors/partners in the Company/Firm known as (Name of Company)(Name of Partnership)

2.   The parties hereto desire that 7 days after the death of any party hereto his personal representatives shall have the option to sell and the surviving parties hereto shall have the option to purchase the deceased party's shares on the terms hereinafter appearing

WHEREBY IT IS AGREED as follows:—

1.   In consideration of the provisions of Clause 2 hereof 7 days after the death of any party hereto the surviving parties shall have the option to purchase the deceased's shares interest in the said Company/Firm from the deceased's personal representatives such option to be exercised by notice in writing served within three months from the date upon which a grant of representation is issued and on the exercise of such option the deceased's personal representatives shall sell the shares to the survivors on the terms hereinafter appearing

2.   In consideration of the provisions of Clause 1 hereof 7 days after the death of any party hereto the deceased's personal representatives shall have the option to sell the deceased's shares interest in the said Company/Firm to the surviving parties such option to be exercised by notice in writing served within six months from the date upon which a grant of representation is issued and on the exercise of such option the surviving parties shall purchase the shares from the deceased's personal representatives on the terms hereinafter appearing

3.   The price shall be such price as may be determined as the fair value thereof by the Company's/Firm's Auditor in accordance with the Company's Articles of Association/Firm's Partnership Agreement

4.   If either option is exercised then the surviving parties hereto shall purchase the deceased's shares interest in the following proportions: equally/rateably according to their existing shareholdings

5.   This Agreement shall:

(a)   bind the personal representatives of all the parties hereto

(b)   cease to bind any party hereto when he shall have ceased to be a shareholder of more than (nominal amount:) shares

(c)   cease to have effect on the winding up/dissolution of the Company/ Firm

(d)   take effect only in compliance with and subject to the Articles of Association of the Company/Partnership Agreement of the Firm which shall take precedence over the terms hereof should there be any conflict between the two

AS WITNESS etc.

Index

[all references are to paragraph number]

A

'A man and his own life'
insurable interest, and, 2.9

ABI
statement of long-term insurance practice,
Appendix 3

Acceptance
e-commerce contracts, and, 1.42
formation of contracts, and, 1.5–1.9

Accumulation and maintenance trusts
introduction, 14.62
post-21 March 2006, 14.63
pre-22 March 2006, 14.64

Accumulations
generally, 11.99
reform proposals, 11.100

Actuaries
with-profits funds, and, 6.33

Administration
corporate insolvency, and, 12.31

Administrative receivership
corporate insolvency, and, 12.30

Administrators
distribution of estate
England and Wales, in, 9.56–9.59
introduction, 9.55
Northern Ireland, in, 9.64
Scotland, in, 9.60–9.63
generally, 9.37

Adoption
distribution of estate, and, 9.66

Advancement
care of children trusts, and, 11.27

Advertising Standards Authority (ASA)
financial promotion, and, 5.29–5.30

'Advised'-'non-advised' sale
ICOB, and, 5.106

Advising and selling
ICOB, and
commission, 4.57
fees disclosure, 4.58
Gap rules, 4.61
prohibitions, 4.60
status disclosure, 4.58
suitability, 4.59

Agents
acting for whom, 4.67
authority, 4.65
duties, 4.64
general principles, 4.63–4.70
introduction, 4.62
knowledge, 4.68–4.70
nature, 4.63
notice of assignment, and, 10.23

Agents – *contd*
overview, 4.2
payment, 4.66

Aggregation
reassurance, and, 8.11

Agreement
discharge of contract, and, 9.2

Agricultural property relief
inheritance tax, and, 14.34–14.36

Aliens
capacity to contract, and, 1.18

Alternatively secured pensions
and see Registered pension schemes
generally, 14.78
'left scheme' policies, 14.108
retirement annuities, 14.90

Annual allowance
registered pension schemes, and, 16.6

Annual exemption
inheritance tax, and, 14.26

Annual report
with-profits funds, and, 6.17

Annuities
capital element, with, 13.70
capital gains tax, and, 13.74
income tax, and
capital element, with, 13.70
deduction of tax, 13.65
foreign residents, 13.69
payment without deduction, 13.66–13.69
purchased life annuities, 13.70
UK residents, 13.67–13.68
inheritance tax, and
joint lives, 14.74
single life, 14.73
long-term care, and, 17.55
payment with deduction of tax, 13.65
payment without deduction of tax
foreign residents, 13.69
introduction, 13.66
UK residents, 13.67–13.68
proposal form, and, 1.29
purchased life annuities, 13.70

Anti-money laundering
introduction, 5.97
JMLSG Guidance Notes, 5.101
Money Laundering Sourcebook, 5.100
obligations, 5.99
relevant legislation, 5.98
SYSC Handbook, 5.100

Appeals
FSMA, and, 3.13

Appendices
reassurance, and, 8.10

733

Sanctions
FSMA, and, 3.46
Schedule
policy document, and, 1.58
reassurance, and, 8.10
Schemes of arrangement
corporate insolvency, and, 12.32
School fees
borrowing, 17.37
deferred annuities
income tax, 17.36
inheritance tax, 17.37
introduction, 17.35
endowment assurance, 17.31
individual savings accounts, 17.32
introduction, 17.30
investment trust savings schemes, 17.34
single premium bonds, 17.33
unit trust savings schemes, 17.34
Scotland
distribution of estate, and, 9.60–9.63
equitable assignment, and, 10.6
grants of probate, and
confirmation dative, 9.49
confirmation nominate, 9.49
introduction, 9.49
resealing, 9.50
interest in possession settlements, with, 14.48
MWPA 1982 trusts, and, 12.54
trusts, and, 11.16
trusts of life policies, and, 15.38
Secured debts
bankruptcy, and, 12.8
Segments
policy document, and, 1.59
Set-off
bankruptcy, and, 12.9
Settlements
accumulation and maintenance trusts
introduction, 14.62
post-21 March 2006, 14.63
pre-22 March 2006, 14.64
charging provisions
introduction, 14.49
liability, 14.53
primary beneficiaries, 14.51
quick succession relief, 14.54
rate of tax, 14.53
remaindermen, 14.52
settlor, 14.50
definition, 14.45
interest in possession, with
charging provisions, 14.49–14.52
introduction, 14.46–14.47
liability, 14.53
quick succession relief, 14.54
rate of tax, 14.53
Scotland, in, 14.48
introduction, 14.44
no introduction interest in possession, with
creation, 14.56
exit charge, 14.58–14.61
introduction, 14.55

Settlements – *contd*
no introduction interest in possession, with –
contd
principal charge, 14.57
ten-yearly charge, 14.59
pre-27 March 1974, and, 14.60
Shortfall
cancellation, and, 5.95
Single event
reassurance, and, 8.12
Single-premium bonds
school fees, and, 17.33
Sinking fund policies
gains on policies chargeable to tax, and,
13.48
Small gifts
inheritance tax, and, 14.27
Small self-administered schemes
and see Registered pension schemes
generally, 14.77
Smoothing
with-profits funds, and, 6.7
Social security benefits
generally, 9.70
Solemn form probate
grants of representation, and, 9.44
Special Conditions
reassurance, and, 8.10
Spes successionis
insurable interest, and, 2.8
Spouse exemption
inheritance tax, and, 14.24
Stakeholder pension schemes
and see Registered pension schemes
death after deferring drawing benefits,
14.93
death before vesting date, 14.91–14.92
death in annuity guaranteed period, 14.94
death whilst taking income on alternatively
secured pension, 14.96
death whilst taking income on unsecured
pension, 14.95
dependant's death whilst in receipt of pension,
14.97
introduction, 14.77
Stakeholder products
COB, and, 4.47
Stamp duty
assignment of policy, and, 10.42, 11.103
land, on, 11.101
life policies, on, 11.102
policy document, and, 1.66
trusts of life policies, on, 11.104
State benefits
generally, 9.70
Statement of long-term insurance practice
text, Appendix 3
Status disclosure
ICOB, and, 4.58
Statutory power of sale
mortgage of life policy, and, 10.66–10.67
Statutory receipt
mortgage of life policy, and, 10.72